ALSO BY WILLIAM LEE MILLER

The First Liberty: Religion and the American Republic

The Business of May Next: James Madison and the Founding

*Arguing About Slavery: John Quincy Adams and the
Great Battle in the United States Congress*

Lincoln's Virtues

Lincoln's Virtues

AN ETHICAL BIOGRAPHY

WILLIAM LEE MILLER

ALFRED A. KNOPF   NEW YORK

2007

Grateful acknowledgment is made to the following for permission to reprint previously
published material:
Abraham Lincoln Association: Excerpts from *Collected Works of Abraham Lincoln* by Roy
P. Basler, editor, and Marion Delores Pratt and Lloyd A. Dunlap, asst. editors. Reprinted
courtesy of the Abraham Lincoln Association. *Houghton Mifflin Company:* Excerpt from
Abraham Lincoln by Albert J. Beveridge, copyright © 1928 by Catherine Beveridge. All
rights reserved. Reprinted by permission of Houghton Mifflin Company. *University of
Illinois Press:* Excerpts from *Herndon's Informants,* edited by Douglas L. Wilson and
Rodney O. Davis. Reprinted courtesy of University of Illinois Press.

Library of Congress information available upon request

Printed in the United States in 2008
ISBN: 978-0-307-29140-0

9 8 7 6 5 4 3 2 1

Frontispiece: photograph of Abraham Lincoln,
courtesy of Meserve-Kunhardt Collection, Mt. Kisco, New York

For
Emiko,
Ethan,
Dylan,
Sibylle,
Sophia,
Cassandra,
and
Benedict

CONTENTS

Preface: The Moral Preparation of a Great Politician   xi

Chapter One: Who *Is* This Fellow? He Is Smarter
    Than He Looks   3
  1. A Startling Disparity   3
  2. Moral Reasoning   13
  3. Disregarding Legends   15
  4. Destiny Obscure?   16

Chapter Two: Noble Rage   26
  1. Young Lincoln's Great Rejections   26
  2. The Lifeline of Print   44

Chapter Three: He Will Be Good—But God Knows When   54
  1. Poor Man, Free Man, Free Moral Agent   54
  2. He Studied with No One   57
  3. Tom Lincoln and His Boy   59
  4. The Awkward Age of Goodness   62
  5. A Name That Fills All the Nation and Is Not Unknown Even
    in Foreign Lands   67

Chapter Four: I Want in All Cases to Do Right   71
  1. Humor in His Composition   71
  2. Not a Rebel, Not a Revolutionary   74
  3. The Gem of His Character   76

4. Be Emulous to Excel 79

5. Something More Than Common 82

6. No More Scoffing 83

7. A Poetry in His Nature 86

8. Self-Improver 90

Chapter Five: Was This Man a Politician? 92

1. Worthy of Their Esteem 92

2. A Political Career 95

3. A Free People Divide into Parties 99

4. The Party of National Improvement 106

Chapter Six: Rising Public Man 116

1. Why This Vote? 116

2. Don't Shoot Editors 129

3. Hail, Fall of Fury! 140

4. They Are as We Would Be 147

5. The Three Whigs from the Seventh, or, Honorable
   Maneuvering 153

Chapter Seven: Another President, Another War 164

1. Spotty Lincoln 164

2. Politically Suicidal Nonprinciple? 171

3. Letters Home 183

4. Speech Notes 186

Chapter Eight: Politics and Morals 192

1. The Congressman as Moralist (and Political Operative) ... 192

2. The Congressman as Political Operative (and Moralist) ... 209

3. The Same Hatred of Slavery 212

4. Shall These Things Be? 216

5. The Vocation of a Politician 221

Chapter Nine: Thunderstruck in Illinois 231

1. The Senate Acts and Lincoln Decides 231

2. Fugitives, the Law, and the Principle 234

3. No Man Is Good Enough to Govern Another Man 240

4. Lincoln Reads Douglas's Opponents 243

5. A Self-Evident Lie? 245

6. Lincoln's Rise 247

Chapter Ten: I Shall Try to Show That It Is Wrong — 252
  1. Monstrous Injustice — 252
  2. Just What We Would Be in Their Situation — 255
  3. "Sacred" Self-Government? — 256
  4. Men Are Not Angels but They Have a Sense of Justice — 263
  5. The Spirit of '76 — 267
  6. What Was He Doing? — 269

Chapter Eleven: Our Duty as We Understand It — 273
  1. If Slavery Is Not Wrong, Nothing Is Wrong — 273
  2. How to Make a Strong Moral Argument Without
    Being Moralistic — 286

Chapter Twelve: The Worthy Work of Party-Building — 298
  1. A Point Merely Personal to Myself — 298
  2. Following His Own Advice — 316

Chapter Thirteen: Not So Much Greater Than the Rest of Us — 325

Chapter Fourteen: Lincoln's Defense of Our Common Humanity — 340
  1. Douglas's Assault on Lincoln's Egalitarianism — 340
  2. The Modern Assault on Lincoln's "White Supremacy":
    Some Considerations — 353
  3. On Lincoln's Moral Composition — 363
  4. Lincoln Attacks the Imbruting of Black America — 368

Chapter Fifteen: Such an Impression — 375
  1. Mental Culture in New York — 375
  2. The Hugeness of Slavery — 384
  3. How Did This Man Ever Become President? — 391
  4. The Candidate of Moral Argument — 397
  5. Lincoln for President — 401

Chapter Sixteen: The Man with the Blue Umbrella — 406
  1. A Very Poor Hater — 406
  2. The Great Reaper Case — 410
  3. The President Appoints a Secretary of War — 418

Chapter Seventeen: Let Grass Grow Where It May — 427
  1. Once a Friend and Still Not an Enemy — 427
  2. Here I Stand — 433
  3. The Union Is Unbroken — 442

Appendix 1: Reflections on Two War Presidents   457

Appendix 2: The Election of 1860 "Thrown Into the House"   465

Notes and Sources   469
Acknowledgments   493
Index   497

PREFACE:
THE MORAL PREPARATION
OF A GREAT POLITICIAN

It is a curious truth—is it not?—that an unschooled nineteenth-century American politician named Abraham Lincoln, from the raw frontier villages of Illinois and Indiana, has turned out to be among the most revered of the human beings who have ever walked this earth. Curious—and perhaps a little moving, if you think about it. Except for religious figures, he has had few superiors on the short list of the most admired, and the even shorter list of the most loved, of humankind. Among his countrymen, I believe, he has—given the vicissitudes of Jefferson's reputation and a certain loss of popular attachment to George Washington—no equal. There he stands: tall, homely, ready to make a self-deprecating joke, stretching higher than the greatest of his countrymen, an unlikely figure among the mighty of the earth.

To be sure, historical circumstances—the Civil War, the ending of slavery, and his dramatic death—made essential contributions to the size and shape of Lincoln's reputation. He probably would not have become nearly so imposing a figure had he lived on for decades after the war, and he certainly would not have if he had lived and served in peacetime. Lord Charnwood, the Englishman who wrote an early biography of Lincoln, made a remark about Lincoln's Second Inaugural Address that might almost be extended to his life. Charnwood wrote, about that greatest of Lincoln's speeches, "Here is one of the few speeches ever delivered by a great man at the crisis of his fate on the sort of occasion which a tragedian telling his story would have devised for him." One might also say something like that of the whole sweep of Lincoln's life: his lowly origins; his ascent; the eloquent and fitting profundity of his speaking; the neatness of his presidency, coinciding exactly with the war; the passage by Congress of the climactic Thirteenth Amendment a brief time before his death, and, above all, the timing, and the manner, of his assassination. As is rarely true in "history"—which is to say, real life—the tragic tidiness of Lincoln's story is almost exactly as a dramatist might have imagined it.

But neither the dramatic design of his career nor the historical weight of the matters with which he came in the end to deal would by itself have worked so powerfully upon the imagination of his countrymen and -women and the world had he not revealed himself in and through them to be an unusually worthy human being, in ways that did not necessarily describe other "great" persons of history.

This book is a biographical exploration of those worthy qualities, as they developed in his preparation—his unintended preparation—for the office of president, for the role of war leader, and for the great deeds of emancipation. The story of his rise to power has been told many times; it is told here, selectively, for its moral meaning.

Lincoln's overwhelming popular prestige and unassailable legendary standing—often beyond the reach, as historians sometimes complain, of mere fact—is mostly, for the purposes of this book, not an impediment, but an advantage. But there are a couple of ways in which the legend and the myth may interfere. First, and fundamentally, they may undercut the project by stipulating the answers already before we begin. And second, they may camouflage by his presumed near-sainthood the true nature of Lincoln's career.

Legend and myth present Abraham Lincoln as a poor and humble rail-splitter from the backwoods of the American West, unschooled, without family or social place, a common man down to his toenails, who then, altogether through his own efforts, rose to become the tip-top figure in the whole nation, the very president himself. He was the myth made real, rising from an actual Kentucky cabin made of actual Kentucky logs all the way to the actual White House in Washington.

And in the legend and myth there is more: While in the White House he did mighty deeds. He freed the slaves and he won the war and he saved the Union and he reconciled a nation and he brought a new birth of freedom. He wrote sentences that would live forever in the national memory. He brooded over the sins of the nation and counseled charity and avoidance of malice. And then he died a martyr for his mighty deeds, and went on to lasting fame and universal approbation, and was turned into a national monument.

And in the legend and myth there is still more: While accomplishing that vertiginous rise and doing those mighty deeds and achieving that martyrdom and monumental fame, he remained a humble, generous person.

I do not mean altogether to mock or debunk this mythic picture; on the contrary, on the whole, I accept it, and would defend its main features, more than would some others. But I do suggest that it may have, ironically, a perversely damaging effect on our understanding of Lincoln as a real human being in a real world. If his instant and constant wonderfulness is stipulated in advance, taken for granted from the outset, and woven into the national memory as a universally accepted fact, then his actual moral achievements are discounted. Exaggerated preliminary expectations that he was a spectacularly virtuous man may diminish our appreciation of the ways in which he may actually have become one.

Something like exasperation with this perversely distorting ritual celebration, this apotheosis after his dramatic martyrdom, drove his law partner William Herndon, who was a great admirer but who felt he knew Lincoln as myth-makers did not, to undertake his interviews and his lectures and his complicated efforts to produce a book. And something like a parallel exasperation, I think, has fueled the work of most of Lincoln's Northern detractors.

Southern detractors, although they may also be exasperated by the enormous, once invincible power of the Lincoln myth—Garry Wills amusingly refers to a couple of modern critics of Lincoln on the Right as "suicidal conservatives"—do not characteristically reflect the element of disillusionment, since they were not illusioned in the first place. They were and are simply in straightforward and fundamental disagreement with what Lincoln did, said, and stood for. But in the rest of the country, geographically and ideologically, the expectations aroused by the myth give a sharper edge to the disillusioned criticism.

I think this is particularly true of the recent attack on Lincoln as a "white supremacist" and even—anachronistically using our modern word—a "racist." There he stands in American national memory, the Great Emancipator, with capital letters. There was his picture on the wall, in the old days, of thousands of African-American homes. There were those touching stories of the devotion of the first generation of freed slaves to "Father Abraham." There was that (originally) affecting Emancipation Monument, "Freedom's Memorial," erected in Lincoln Park in Washington, initiated by the savings of a former slave, an aging washerwoman, built with the pennies of thousands of freed slaves. There was in Benjamin Quarles's 1962 book *Lincoln and the Negro* that moving summary: "It is a matter of historical record that they [the "colored Americans"] loved him first and loved him longest."

But now we find—maybe not longest. Years pass. The emotional appropriation of the meaning and the difficulty of the battle over slavery fades; racial equality moves to the center of the national moral drama. A new generation, black and white, looks at Lincoln with new eyes. And when one looks with new eyes at that Emancipation Monument, with Lincoln standing tall and the freed slave kneeling in front of him, perhaps in supplication, it may now be offensive rather than moving. The apotheosis invites iconoclasm. Because he is, or was, grandly celebrated as the Great Emancipator, in disillusionment some now find him to be a Reluctant Emancipator, or not an Emancipator at all.

And with the immense outpouring of writing about Lincoln seeming to have filled every spot in the department of praise and celebration, what is left? In the musical chairs of literary effort the only places left open, it would seem, are those of skepticism and attack—those that not only show Lincoln warts and all, but find some new warts.

I don't intend to find any new warts, but I do want to acknowledge those that are there, in the young man making his way in a realm of life defined by power, interest, collective action, and the limits of the possible.

Among the omissions in the folklore figure is the central fact about his career. Where, in what realm of life, did this backwoods poor boy accomplish the remarkable ascent that the myth celebrates? What talent made it possible? How was he able to come to be the nation's leader, and then to do those great deeds that won his fame? Was it not by—"politics"? Was he not—a "politician"?

Young people in American schools, with Lincoln's picture on the schoolroom wall (at least in the North), listening to teachers and reading textbooks that take for granted his superlative worth, are not encouraged to perceive that this revered figure was in the same line of work as the fatuous candidate for city council they were forced to listen to, squirming, in assembly hall.

But if Abraham Lincoln was not a politician, then words have no meaning.

If he is to become to some degree a moral exemplar, then it will be of a different sort from those who withdraw into a commune, a sanctuary, or a library, or those who preach a pure moral message or write a lasting moral treatise or organize a single-minded moral movement. He will be engaged in collective undertakings—political parties, legislative bodies, governments—in which his decision and action must take account of the decisions, actions, and convictions of others. He will be engaged in collective undertakings that, whatever they embodied of value, also entailed seeking and exercising power. He will realize a moral ideal only in the fragments and distortions possible in a particular time and place.

I have called this book an "ethical biography." An ethical biography presupposes the freedom of the subject, within some limits, to choose different courses of action. It assumes that he can, by a sequence of choices, shape abiding patterns of conduct—virtues. It presupposes that out of his margin of freedom, with whatever the given conditions of his life may be, he can over time mold a structure of conduct, a certain character.

An ethical biography takes for granted that a human being, a rational moral agent, can make appraisals of the alternative courses—one's own and others'—as better and worse, as serving something good or not, sometimes as evil. It assumes that human beings can have a meaningful exchange of views about those appraisals and the ground upon which they rest.

An ethical biography—at any rate, this one—also assumes that history does not roll on through the centuries independently of human reason and will and decision and action. Of course there are mammoth "forces" and huge constraints. We citizens of Abraham Lincoln's country probably do overestimate the role of free human agency in the great movements of history. Nevertheless, it did matter, even before he became president, that Abraham Lincoln decided in the summer of 1854 that he would challenge Stephen Douglas over the Kansas-Nebraska Act, and that in 1859–60 he would accept an invitation to speak in New York, and that in 1861 as president-elect he would oppose any compromise on expanding slavery and insist on the preservation of the Union.

I take these assumptions for granted for the purpose of this book, aware that the picture of a human being as a rational moral agent has a certain old-fashioned ring, and has been under intellectual attack for perhaps a century and a half.

Abraham Lincoln turns out to have been a man who thought more, and expressed himself more often, on right and wrong, on the better and the worse, in human conduct, than one might have anticipated. To be sure, the popular figure of Honest Abe is seen through the mists of legend to have been loaded with homely virtues and homely moral instruction as well; but one discovers that the actual, much more complex human being, when one reads him in bulk, also did a good deal of quite explicit moral thinking, and wrote it down on paper.

In the case of this particular man's life, an ethical biography must attend also to the moral component in public policy and social philosophy, because he was an actor in great public events.

Whether it would be fruitful for any other person I cannot say, but I came to feel in the doing of it that an ethical biography of this man is altogether fitting and proper.

The place and moment and lineage of his birth, and the events of his time, were given, beyond all choosing, as for any man or woman; but within those limits there were many choosings. There was, alongside the elements of necessity, the reality of freedom, and therefore of moral choice. It is the purpose of this book to examine some of the shaping moral choices made by Abraham Lincoln as he rose to power, and perhaps simultaneously to suggest something about moral life in the American democracy for which he would become such an eloquent spokesman, so worthy an exemplar, and so potent a symbol.

Lincoln's Virtues

CHAPTER ONE

Who *Is* This Fellow? He Is Smarter Than He Looks

1. A STARTLING DISPARITY

In the summer of 1830 the great preacher, evangelist, and politician Peter Cartwright, renowned throughout central Illinois, made a stop in a cornfield in Macon County while campaigning for the state legislature. Cartwright, "a tremendous cultural force in central Illinois" in those years, was "dressed as became his station" as a presiding elder in the Methodist Church. In the audience there was a "shambling and shabbily dressed" youth, only a few months beyond his twenty-first birthday and only a few months a resident of the state of Illinois and Macon County. This young man was working as a hired hand breaking prairie on a nearby farm, while still residing at his father's home, not yet having struck out on his own. To the amazement of the great preacher, the unlikely youngster presumed to engage him in argument, and made points that were remarkably intelligent. "The Great Methodist," it was later to be written, "was equally astonished at the close reasoning and the uncouth figure of Mr. Brown's extraordinary hired hand."

Throughout the life of that extraordinary hired hand whose name was Abraham Lincoln, there would be a recurrent pattern: an initial impression of the boy or the lad or the man, derived from externals and superficialities, would then be overthrown by the shock of recognition of his intellectual power.

Someone will have assumed, from some surface indication, that this fellow is a perhaps entertaining and distinctive but still, intellectually

3

considered, an unremarkable specimen of the American common man in the settlements on the western frontier. And then they will be— astonished.

They will have made their initial assumption, first, from his physical appearance, for which those who have described him, sometimes including Lincoln himself, have used, among others, the words "ungainly," "stooped," "lanky," "long-armed," and "homely." David Turnham, his older friend, said of him in Indiana: "Abe was a long tall raw boned boy— odd and gawky." His good friend Joshua Speed remembered him having been in Springfield "a long, gawky, ugly, shapeless, man." Anna Gentry used this word "gawky" also: "Abe was a long—thin—leggy—gawky boy." The words "tall" and "long" appear often in the descriptions of him, and "raw" and "rawboned" and "bony": "His hands were large and bony," said Robert Wilson, who knew Lincoln in the state legislature. Wilson also said that his arms were longer than those of any man he had ever seen. "When standing straight, and letting his arms fall down his Sides, the points of his fingers would touch a point lower on his legs by nearly three inches than was usual with other persons." Also, said Wilson and others, his feet were unusually big. All these, note, were people who *liked* and *admired* Lincoln—everyone I have quoted so far. One can imagine what those who were hostile, in 1860–65, would say of his appearance.

And what of those who did not know him and were seeing him for the first time? His homeliness was of a particular western type that was not associated with high intelligence. Those just encountering Lincoln would have assumed his intellectual ordinariness also from his dress, which in his youth was the makeshift costume of a poor boy, but which even in his better-financed adulthood seems often to have been inadequate, featuring in particular the failure of his pants to reach his shoe tops. Nathaniel Grigsby drew a picture that many others confirmed about his dress in Indiana: "Between the shoe and Sock & his britches—made of buckskin there was bare & naked 6 or more inches of Abe Lincoln shin bone." In New Salem his sartorial inadequacies continued. Abner Y. Ellis, a merchant in the little village to which the young man moved after the encounter in the cornfield, said of him: "Frequently he had but one Suspender— no vest or Coat." Colman Smoot, a successful farmer who became justice of the peace in New Salem and who would loan Lincoln the money to buy a suit when he managed to be elected to the legislature, would paint a picture of Lincoln's dress much like that from many others: "His Pantaloons were very Short Causing him to look very awkward." And buying that suit, and later suits, and rising in position and solvency apparently did not altogether solve the problem. Jonathan Birch, a young Illinois lawyer who heard and saw Lincoln during the great debates of 1858, told Jesse Weik: "It is well-known that he was more or less careless of his personal attire, and that he usually wore in his great canvass with Douglas a linen cast, generally without any vest, a hat much the worse for wear, and carried with him a faded cotton umbrella which became almost as famous in the canvass as Lincoln himself."

Lincoln's appearance was not his only misleading attribute. Those who knew him as a boy might assume in him a lack of notable sharpness from his heredity, particularly his paternity: Could anything much be expected of the son of Thomas Lincoln? (This particular puzzle has generated a stream of genealogical speculation.)

Once he moved out into the slightly larger world of an Illinois village, where there would be a surprising sprinkling of college graduates, his intellectual limitations might have been inferred from his evident lack of formal education. Although in the one-room school in Indiana he was regarded as a "wizzard" at spelling, in more exacting settings the educated would notice that he often doubled consonants that were not supposed to be doubled, and throughout his life he made that error particularly calculated to set English teachers' teeth on edge, writing "it's" for the possessive of "it."

As he moved into the ever larger worlds of Springfield and statewide politics and law practice, many would underestimate him because he so plainly came out of the backwoods. And on his arrival on the national scene, all of those clues would be compounded by the Hoosier accent and the farmyard figures of speech and the vocabulary and imagery that are not the refined product of a cultured world.

At every stage along life's way, he might have been discounted by the company he kept and the friends and supporters he had won—by the Clary Grove Boys and their continuing equivalent. Can one be intellectually gifted whose companion is that whiskey-drinking, ballad-singing lowbrow Ward Lamon?

And not only throughout his life but on out into his posthumous fame and glory his penetrating mental activity would be obscured by his reputation as a teller of jokes, by the great thread of humor that ran through his life and his being. One can't tell jokes and stories like those, and collapse in convulsions of laughter, and have humor as an essential constant part of one's being, if one is an intellectually serious person. So when he comes before you, expect at best some entertaining, if a little coarse, jokes and stories.

But then he will speak—and some hearers will, to borrow a phrase that John Keats used in another connection, look at each other in wild surmise.

Abraham the boy in Kentucky for his first seven years, although we don't know much about him, does not appear to have been a precocious child or any kind of a natural genius. But the time would come when he would recognize that he was markedly superior in intellectual ability to those around him—to his father, on whom the events of life forced implicit comparisons; to his fellow students in the subscription schools, the "blab" schools that he attended for those five brief stints, and to the teachers of those schools, whom he was reported before long to have surpassed; and to the other adults in the little settlements in which he found himself. "He was always at the head of his class"; "He progress rapedly in all of his studies," Nathaniel Grigsby told Herndon about their school days in Indiana. Anna Gentry, who as Anna Roby had gone to school with Lincoln (she later married Allan Gentry, with whom Lincoln would make his first raft trip to New Orleans), would in later years warmly remember young Lincoln explaining to her the movements of the heavenly bodies. "He often . . . commented or talked to me about what he read—seemed to read it out of the book as he went along—did so with others—he was the learned boy among us unlearned folks—he took great pains to explain—could do it so simply."

Among the adults in Pigeon Creek, "Colonel" William Jones clearly was struck by the unexpected abilities of this interesting teenager who worked in his store—this "learned boy among us unlearned folks," to whom he loaned his copies of the *Louisville Journal* and the *National Intelligencer,* and whom he went to the trouble of persuading to support Clay, not Jackson.

Douglas Wilson has described Lincoln's impact when in 1831 he first appeared in New Salem, the little settlement on the Sangamon River. He was ungainly, he was penniless, he was uneducated, he was poorly and eccentrically dressed, and he was notably unhandsome. Those who met him at first assumed him to be another ordinary backwoods Hoosier lad.

But then they were startled to encounter an intelligence they had not suspected. Wilson quotes Caleb Carman, a shoemaker in New Salem, as one example: "When i first [met] him i thought him a Green horn. His appearance was very od, but after all this bad Appearance i Soon found

[him] to be a very intelligent young man . . . after half hours Conversation with him I found him no Green Horn." Denton Offutt, the perhaps rather scatterbrained entrepreneur who hired Lincoln to take a second raft trip to New Orleans and then to work in his store and then to manage his mill, extravagantly admired Lincoln not only because of his stunning universal knowledge (as it seemed to Offutt) but also because of his inventiveness and his physical strength. In fact it was Offutt's bragging about the latter (Nicolay and Hay quote a wonderful observation about Offutt by one of his fellow citizens, that he "talked too much with his mouth") that led to Lincoln's famous wrestling match with Jack Armstrong of the Clary Grove Boys, which match, in turn, led to Lincoln's popularity with that group.

When he first got up to make political speeches, hearers expecting humorous stories would be startled, as Cartwright had been, by a cogent discourse. Judge Stephen T. Logan, who would be young Lincoln's second law partner, first heard him speak in 1832 when he was running for the legislature. "He was a very tall, gawky, and rough-looking fellow then," Logan was later to remember, "his pantaloons didn't meet his shoes by six inches. But after he began speaking I became very much interested in him. He made a very sensible speech."

Lincoln's first law partner, John T. Stuart, a key figure in launching both Lincoln's political and his legal career, must have had some similar experience when he encountered the popular young captain of A Company in the Thirty-first Regiment of the Illinois Militia in the Black Hawk War. Stuart, who had been to Centre College in Danville, Kentucky, and was already established as a lawyer in Springfield, was himself a major in that militia. He was impressed enough with this rough young fellow to make him both his political protégé and his law partner.

When, in November 1834, Lincoln made the trip to Vandalia to take his seat as a state legislator, he was twenty-five years old, just three and a half years away from having been, by his own famous description, a "strange, penniless, friendless, uneducated, boy working on a flatboat for ten dollars a month." He was appearing for the first time on the great stage of public affairs. Just four years later he would be his party's nominee for speaker of the house. Robert Wilson, his fellow Whig legislator and member of the Long Nine,* said of him:

---

* The Long Nine was a jocular name for the nine Sangamon County legislators, all of them tall, who sought to bring the capital to Springfield.

He was, on the stump, and in the Halls of Legislation a ready Debater, manifesting extraordinary ability in his peculiar manner of presenting his subject. He did not follow the beaten track of other Speakers, and Thinkers, but appeared to comprehend the whole situation of the Subject, and take hold of its first principles. . . . his memory was a great Store house in which was Stored away all the facts, acquired by reading but principally by observation; and intercourse with men Woman and children, in their Social, and business relations; learning and weighing the motives that prompt each act in life. Supplying him with an inexhaustible fund of facts, from which he would draw conclusions, and illustrating every Subject however complicated with anecdotes drawn from all classes of Society, accomplishing the double purpose, of not only proving his Subject by the anecdote, that no one ever forgets, after hearing Mr Lincoln tell a Story, either the argument of the Story, the Story itself, or the author.

When the prairie politician would make a brief appearance on the national political scene, as the lone Whig congressman from Illinois, representing the Seventh District in the Thirtieth Congress in 1847–49, the speech his fellow congressmen probably would have remembered was an entirely humorous partisan production mocking the pretensions to military glory of the 1848 Democratic candidate for president, Lewis Cass. The lanky and amusing westerner strode up and down the aisles of the House comparing to Cass's his own military glory, when he bravely attacked wild onions and engaged in bloody battles with mosquitoes. The young Whig congressman got laughs, but the speech probably did not increase his reputation for gravitas. (It is usually difficult to sustain a reputation both as a humorist and as a "serious" thinker; that has something to do, in general, with the comparative underemphasis on Lincoln as thinker.) But as we will see on a later page, an observer did note that this congressman spent his time in an unusual way. He did not do all the other things congressmen did; he spent his hours in the Library of Congress. For all his folksiness and joking, he was a bookworm.

When he came back into politics in 1854 after a partial interruption, and focused exclusively on the extension of slavery, and retooled intellectually, he made a new reputation as the intellectual, moral, and rhetorical leader of the forces in the state of Illinois opposed to the spread of slavery. He had already been known as something of a leader in the Eighth Judicial Circuit and the Seventh Congressional District in particular. But now he surprised even those who had known and supported him with speeches of a new depth and power: at the state fair in Springfield, and other places, including Peoria, in the fall of 1854; in Bloomington in the spring of 1856, at the founding of the Republican Party in Illinois, his famous "lost speech," which so inspired and overwhelmed the audience that no one got it down on paper; in his speech responding to the Dred Scott case in Springfield in the summer of 1857; in his "house divided" speech accepting the party designation as their "first and only choice" for the Senate in 1858. His Illinois supporters would not be surprised by his ability to trade blow for blow with the great national figure Stephen Douglas; but as the news reports, and then the book reprinting the debates, would reach a national audience, there would be exclamations of wonder and surprise in other places both because of the quality of Lincoln's argument and because he fought the Democrats' national champion to a virtual draw.

Then as the presidential election of 1860 approached there would be a moment of discovery for the intelligentsia of New York City, when this new figure from the West would be invited to speak in Henry Ward Beecher's church in Brooklyn, and the speech, as history would forever record, would be shifted to Cooper Union.

No doubt the snobberies of the East, of the Great City, of the college-bred, and of the social elite all colored the superficial first impression of this uneducated and, despite his efforts, rather ill-dressed small-town western politician as he was introduced by the distinguished editor and poet William Cullen Bryant and rose to address the fifteen hundred members of the New York audience, by far the most "distinguished" he had ever addressed. It is probable that these prejudices were reinforced as he unfurled himself to his great height and began, with his Hoosier accent, "Mr. *Cheerman . . .*" and proceeded to pronounce words differently than they were pronounced either in New York or in Boston. But gradually it was borne in upon the audience, as the speaker worked his way through the utter thoroughness and painstaking clarity of his argument against Douglas about what the "fathers" held about the power of Congress to restrict slavery in the territories, that they were listening to quite a remarkable production from quite a remarkable mind. The New York intelligentsia and literati who came to hear this raw, unlettered westerner were indeed impressed by the sheer *research,* and the clarity of the organization and the presentation of that research, by this man they had now heard of but whom they scarcely knew.

But meticulous research clearly presented was not the only merit of the speech. After that foundation, Lincoln took up the issues of the day, addressing first with rare eloquence and clarity "the Southern people" (although of course, as he said, the South wasn't listening) and then his fellow Republicans. He said careful, wise words about John Brown's foolish raid—wiser, indeed, than many of the eastern intelligentsia had been. He was as conciliatory as principle allowed, without any note of condemnation, to the South. And he rose to a moving moral appeal to his fellow Republicans at the end.

One who was there described his own initial transformed response as follows: "When Lincoln rose to speak, I was greatly disappointed. He was tall, tall—oh, how tall! and so angular and awkward that I had, for an instant, a feeling of pity for so ungainly a man." But then as Lincoln developed his speech, this member of the audience, in a rather pure epitome of the point we are making, said of him: "[H]is face lighted up as with an inward fire; the whole man was transfigured. I forgot his clothes, his personal appearance, and his individual peculiarities. Presently, forgetting myself, I was on my feet like the rest, yelling like a wild Indian, cheering this wonderful man."

After Lincoln's nomination in Chicago a group of party eminences took the train to Springfield to give him the formal notification of what he already knew: that he was the nominee. Most had never met, or even seen, this man, and almost all had supported other candidates, and many were laboring under feelings of deep disappointment about the convention's choice.

In the small parlor at Eighth and Jackson these dignitaries, mostly from the great eastern cities, presented this unknown westerner with the letter formally notifying him of his nomination. The chairman, George Ashmun of Massachusetts, made a brief, formal speech. The lanky stranger then lifted his head and made a short, dignified reply, thanking them, hinting at an awareness of the size of his responsibility, promising to write a formal acceptance, and expressing a wish to shake each of them by the hand. After they left the house, the surprised governor of an eastern state remarked: "Why, sir, they told me he was a rough diamond; nothing could have been in better taste than that speech." And the dignitaries, conferring, said to each other: Perhaps we have not done so badly after all.

A. K. McClure, a senator and important Pennsylvania Republican, came to see the president-elect in Springfield in January of 1861 on the contentious matter of fellow Pennsylvanian Simon Cameron joining Lincoln's cabinet. McClure had never met or seen Lincoln before. He would tell the story years later:

> I went directly from the depot to Lincoln's House and rang the bell, which was answered by Lincoln himself opening the door. I doubt whether I wholly concealed my disappointment at meeting him. Tall, gaunt, ungainly, ill clad, with a homeliness of manner that was unique in itself, I confess that my heart sank within me as I remembered that this was the man chosen by a great nation to be its ruler in the gravest period of its history. I remember his dress as if it were yesterday— snuff-colored and slouchy pantaloons; open black vest, held by a few brass buttons; straight or evening dress-coat, with tightly fitting sleeves to exaggerate his long, bony arms, and all supplemented by an awkwardness that was uncommon among men of intelligence. Such was the picture I met in the person of Abraham Lincoln. We sat down in his plainly furnished parlor, and were uninterrupted during the nearly four hours that I remained with him, and little by little, as his earnestness, sincerity, and candor were developed in conversation, I forgot all the grotesque qualities which so confounded me when I first greeted him. Before half an hour had passed I learned not only to respect, but, indeed, to reverence the man.

As this ungainly westerner then was nominated, and elected, and inaugurated, rising abruptly to national visibility, the secret of his intellectual power, discovered now by some, was newly obscured to the larger audience by the much denser smoke screen of national mass politics, with all its partisan distortions and simplifications from both sides. To detractors and opponents, his dress, his accent, his manners, his geographical origins, his abysmal lack of education, his jokes, all the manifestations of his commonness, underscored by their loathing for what the Republicans stood for, told them plainly that such a fellow—this long-armed gorilla, as Democrat Edwin Stanton quite ungraciously put it—was certainly not going to produce any work of the mind or pen that would have any distinction. If you are an orthographic snob, you probably do not expect history's greatest inaugural address to be produced by a man who thinks the word is spelled "inaugeral."

But the smoke screen may have been thicker still as it came from admirers and supporters. Most of those attributes of commonness and humility that detractors deprecated, were precisely what supporters celebrated, because they had political value. At the state Republican convention in Decatur before the national convention in Chicago in the spring of 1860, friends, including John Hanks, had had the bright idea of bringing into the hall what they alleged to be an actual rail split by Lincoln in his first year in Illinois, and he became to all the world and forever after the Rail-splitter.

His jokes began to circulate, as he became a national figure, and he gained a reputation as a humorist, a teller of tall tales, a skilled practitioner of the wonderfully leveling force and pretension-puncturing power of humor. His kindheartedness became known, and legends grew around it as around these other emerging Lincolnian characteristics. The power and clarity of his mind were obscured to the broader public by the more politically usable and publicly accessible externals of his persona.

Reporters covering his inauguration as President of the United States would pen observations like the following: "He was arrayed in a full suit of regulation black including a dress coat, an article he had probably never worn before in his life . . . a costume in which the owner looked, and was, exceedingly uncomfortable and awkward." But they would also end like this: " . . . as I heard his closing paragraph [of the Inaugural Address] I concluded that we have elected a President who was a great, strong man."

As the administration developed, those who worked closely with him discovered, often to their surprise, that, intellectually considered, this new president was *not* a common man. William Seward had been a major political figure for two decades (while Lincoln was nothing) and had been the favorite to win the Republican nomination that went instead, merely for reasons of "availability," as he might see it, to this novice from a swing state. He rather expected to be the key figure, the "prime minister," in the first Republican administration. He wrote an astonishingly presumptuous memorandum on April 1, 1861, effectively proposing to his new boss that he run things—only to be deftly and graciously put in his place. He was soon writing to his wife about Lincoln, saying, "He is the best of us"—the most quoted part—but also that "executive force and vigor are rare qualities." When he was asked by one who had just heard the Gettysburg Address whether he had had a hand in the president's speech, Seward replied that "no one but Abraham Lincoln could have made that address."

But the broad public did not fully understand what Seward, Stanton, and other cabinet members came to understand. The broad public was learning other things about Lincoln that obscured his distinctive powers of mind. That happened in his lifetime—and has continued out into the vast reach of his legend after his death. To his detractors, of whom there were many during his life, and still are a few, dissenting from his apotheosis after his death, he was (as for Edwin Stanton before his conversion) a "low, cunning clown" of utterly undistinguished origins, and/or a tyrant, a dictator. To the much larger body of his admirers, as his memory has worked its way through American history, he has been the Emancipator and the Savior of the Union, a Christ figure forgiving his enemies and dying for the Union and the slave; and he has been the amiable democratic western folk hero, splitting rails and telling jokes; and he has been Honest Abe, exemplar of the sturdiest moral virtues, joining or replacing George Washington in the national pantheon; and he has been the poor boy from a log cabin who raised himself by heroic exertions to great fame and glory, the self-made man. None of these feature at the center that this man was quite an extraordinary *thinker*, on moral-political subjects, with depth and power, whose clarity of mind and firmness of will and developed powers of expression reciprocally reinforced each other.

2. MORAL REASONING

To some extent we may say the particular ways this intelligent provincial used his good mind may have added to the misperception of him, as the United States moved on into the faster-paced world of modern industry and urban life. He did not indulge in wide-ranging speculation or sponge-like absorption or sparring disputation. The dominant mode of expression of his mind was not quickness, speedy analysis, rapid-fire response. He did not use his extraordinarily good memory to reproduce what he remembered with éclat. He did not characteristically do what Samuel Johnson tried to restrain himself from doing: "talking for victory"—scoring points on others, displaying what he knew, winning contests of knowledge. He did not aim to be, and never became, a learned man. The prime quality of his mind was not *speed*—which in the different world a century and more later would be thought to be almost the defining feature of intelligence. It also was not *breadth*—the embrace of the best that has been thought and said in the world of learned persons, which Thomas Jefferson aspired to—or the instant knowledge of the inner details of public affairs of the twentieth-century policy wonk. Lincoln's mind instead cut deeply, perhaps slowly or at least with effort and concentrated attention, into a relatively few subjects. It was *purposive*—personally, politically, morally.

Joshua Speed wrote a letter to Herndon giving this account of Lincoln's own appraisal of his own mind: "I once remarked to him that his mind was a wonder to me; that impressions were easily made upon it and never effaced. 'No,' said he, 'you are mistaken; I am slow to learn, and slow to forget that which I have learned. My mind is like a piece of steel—very hard to scratch anything on it, and almost impossible thereafter to rub it out.' "

Lincoln believed that he was not a good speaker spontaneously or extemporaneously; in the tests we have—for example, in the little speeches he made as president-elect on the way to Washington, or as president when the public called him to the balcony—he often is apologizing or explaining that he does not have any speech prepared, and did not want to make a speech without preparation. As a lawyer he had the reputation of being much better when he had time to prepare thoroughly than when he had to respond without much preparation.

Lincoln was not facile or glib, nor could he call up an immense range of knowledge. Faster-talking products of a later urban world would have interrupted him while he was pausing for his first semicolon. But those who would get to know the tall, gauche, strange, funny fellow from Illinois, and to read his carefully written papers, and to hear him when he could prepare and talk without interruption, and tell stories, would begin to discover in him remarkable qualities.

His was a mind inclined to plow down to first principles and to hold to them—not as a metaphysician does, abstracting from particulars and spinning great webs of speculation, linking abstraction to abstraction, but as a lawyer, a politician, a moralist does at his or her best: by tenaciously analyzing one's way through the particulars, seeking the nub of the matter. Lincoln would be good at finding the nub of the matter. He would become a thinker in particular about moral ideals as they intersect with politics.

And his qualities of mind meant not only that facts and ideas, once acquired, stayed with him, but that political and moral positions, once he worked them out, would not be lightly abandoned. Mary Todd Lincoln used the word "stubborn" about her husband's positions once he had taken them. It seems that Lincoln made a point of this. In one of the interviews Frederick Douglass had with President Lincoln—on August 10, 1863—Lincoln told Douglass that he objected to the public charge that Douglass had made that Lincoln was slow and vacillating. He did not make any objection to "slow"; but "vacillating" was another matter. "Mr. Douglass, I do not think the charge can be sustained; I think it cannot be shown that when I have once taken a position, I have ever retreated from it."

3. DISREGARDING LEGENDS

To some extent, this misperception of Lincoln would continue after he died and became a legend. But some writers on Lincoln, exposed to him, as Edmund Wilson would say, "in bulk," *would* come to see—in a way analogous to the episodes of discovery we have noted—that the more important fact about this man is not his jokes or his pants legs or his rustic origins, but his mind in its connection to his moral judgment, to his will, and to his powers of expression. One of those making such a discovery was Herbert Croly, the early-twentieth-century editor of the *New Republic,* whose book *The Promise of American Life* had a wide impact, including an effect on Theodore Roosevelt. In his excellent section on Lincoln, Croly wrote:

> His peculiar distinction does not consist in the fact that he was a "Man of the People" who passed from the condition of splitting rails to the condition of being President. No doubt he was in this respect as good a democrat as you please, and no doubt it was desirable that he should be this kind of a democrat. But many other Americans could be named who were also men of the people, and who passed from the most insignificant to the most honored positions in American Life. Lincoln's peculiar and permanent distinction as a democrat will depend rather upon the fact that his thoughts and his actions looked towards the realization of the highest and most edifying democratic ideal.

Croly emphasized the centrality of Lincoln's intellectual work to his historical accomplishment: "Lincoln's peculiar service to his countrymen before the war was that of seeing straighter and thinking harder than did his contemporaries . . . In 1858 there were plenty of men who had the courage, whereas there were very few who had Lincoln's disciplined intelligence and his just and penetrating insight."

Croly sets Lincoln's intellectual undertaking precisely in contrast to the characteristics of the American West with which one strand of folklore identifies him. He said the "average Western American of Lincoln's generation was fundamentally a man who subordinated his intelligence to certain dominant practical interests and purposes." He was not "a stupid or slow-witted man," this average westerner. On the contrary, his wits had been sharpened by the traffic of American politics and business, and his mind was shrewd, flexible, and alert. Croly goes on to picture this "average Western American" rather in the way that many foreign observers had seen Americans in general: as untheoretical or antitheoretical, *practically* minded. "He was wholly incapable either of disinterested or of concentrated intellectual exertion." Although this western pioneer world "developed a body of men with great resolution of purpose and with great ingenuity and fertility in adapting their insufficient means to the realization of their important business affairs . . . their almost exclusive preoccupation with practical tasks and their failure to grant their intelligence any room for independent exercise bent them into exceedingly warped and one-sided human beings."

I quote all of this because Croly is setting it up as a *contrast* to that product of the western frontier who is often presented as a pattern westerner, a pattern American, Abraham Lincoln: "Lincoln, on the contrary, much as he was a man of his own time and people, was precisely an example of high and disinterested intellectual culture." Lincoln as "an example of high and disinterested intellectual culture," in *contrast* to prevailing culture in the practically minded American West? That is not at all what the broad populace, and the usual celebrants of the Lincoln legend, see in him.

We might take as another example Edmund Wilson, writing in his *Patriotic Gore* about the inadequacy of Carl Sandburg's Lincoln when compared with the real thing:

> The amorphous and coarse-meshed Sandburg is incapable of doing justice to the tautness and the hard distinction that we find when, disregarding legends, we attack Lincoln's writings in bulk. These writings do not give the impression of a folksy and jocular countryman swapping yarns at the village store or making his way to the White House by uncertain and awkward steps or presiding like a father, with a tear in his eye, over the tragedy of the Civil War. . . . This is a Lincoln intent, self-controlled, strong in intellect, tenacious of purpose.

That intellectually strong Lincoln, tenacious and self-controlled, is discovered again and again by those who make their way behind the mythic façade.

4. DESTINY OBSCURE?

Lincoln's unexpected abilities would open doors for him. It is not to take anything away from the extraordinary exertions of young Lincoln to observe that once he had made his own remarkable initial self-shaping effort, he had then some good fortune and some help, and that that help reflected the particular characteristics of this new nation. We can see that if we make comparisons with poor persons elsewhere.

Lincoln famously told John L. Scripps of the *Chicago Tribune* that it would be a mistake to try to make anything of his early life. It was all contained, said Lincoln, in one single phrase, and that phrase could be found in Thomas Gray's "Elegy Written in a Country Churchyard": "the short and simple annals of the poor." The books about Lincoln almost a century and a half later that cite that exchange and that quotation from the "Elegy"—it is not easy to find a Lincoln book that does *not* repeat it— might be said to supply their own curious contradiction to it. The "annals" of this particular poor man would prove to be, when his life was completed and he was put to rest in his grave, to put it mildly, not short and not simple.

It is not surprising that Lincoln would know that poem; he liked poetry, particularly of certain kinds, and Gray's "Elegy" was, and is, one of the best-known poems in the English language.

The most familiar of its themes, a rueful awareness of our inescapable common mortality, which puts all our alleged accomplishments on this earth into the larger perspective ("The paths of glory lead but to the grave"), was the sort of poetic strain that Lincoln responded to. His favorite poem had a similar mood and theme: "Oh why should the spirit of mortal be proud?" One might apply to Gray's "Elegy Written in a Country Churchyard" the wisecrack attributed (probably falsely) to Lincoln when asked to appraise another production: For the Lincoln who likes this kind of poem, this is the kind of poem that Lincoln will like.

As it turned out, that poetic theme would apply with terrible aptness to Lincoln's own life. He found the path to glory, and it did indeed lead suddenly to the grave. "The inevitable hour" that waits at the end of all earthly glory would come for him with brutal abruptness in Ford's Theater at 10:13 P.M. on April 14, 1865, and in a last breath in a house across the street at 7:21 the next morning. The path of glory led but to an assassin's bullet.

The other main theme in Gray's poem, however, would be spectacularly inapplicable to Lincoln. Gray surmised, moodily contemplating the graves of these poor villagers, that some among those dead might have had great talent, which their poverty and obscurity suppressed: "Some heart once pregnant with celestial fire, / Hands, that the rod of empire might have sway'd" may be laid in this neglected spot. "Some mute inglorious Milton," "some village Hampden," "some Cromwell guiltless of his country's blood," all may have found the "genial current of the soul" frozen by their poverty. We may descend abruptly from all this poetry and put the point in our barbaric modern prose: These poor people were not able to realize their potential.

But that did not apply to Mr. Brown's extraordinary hired hand. The short and simple annals of the poor notwithstanding, he was not a flower born to blush unseen and waste his sweetness on the desert air, or a gem of purest ray serene stuck in the dark unfathomed caves of the ocean. Chill penury did not repress his noble rage, as Thomas Gray inferred that it had done for some unknown poor persons buried in that country churchyard. His noble rage led not to a "destiny obscure" but, in time, to his name being attached to, among a great many other things, a luxury automobile, a life-insurance company (now a "financial group"), a major highway, a great vehicular tunnel, and a gigantic replica of his face carved on a western mountain. That name that he wrote in his copybooks became the name of twenty-two counties and thirty-five cities and towns in the country of which he had once been such an obscure citizen. The day would come when "ambition" and "grandeur," far from mocking this poor man's "useful toil" or hearing his tale with "disdainful smile," would pay a king's ransom to sleep one night in his White House bedroom.

The short and simple annals of the poor! The annals of this particular originally poor man stretched already in 1939 to 3,958 volumes, and now stretch to vastly more, large and small, great and fatuous, including multiple varieties of multiple-volume biographies, filling shelves, filling libraries, more than has been written about a thousand kings and nobles and generals and heroes. Edmund Wilson wrote that more rubbish has been written about Lincoln than about any other American, with the possible exception of Edgar Allan Poe—but I doubt that Poe is remotely competitive.

The short and simple annals of the poor! Earnest students spend entire careers examining in minute detail the life, or one part of the life, or one part of a part of the life, of this erstwhile poor country villager. Persons in Indiana and Illinois who had the slightest knowledge of him (and some one suspects of not having had the slightest) would be quizzed and questioned and interviewed, their words pored over by swarms of writers for a century and a half and still counting. One writer would construct a complete harem of girls in Indiana who were said, sometimes by themselves, to have been courted by the young Lincoln—or at least spoken to on one occasion. Writers would paint his picture in dozens of colors, from Robespierre to Christ. Scholars would correct each other about this feature and that feature of his life, and then a new wave of scholars correct the correctors: his mother was illegitimate—no, she wasn't; his ancestors were altogether undistinguished—no, they weren't; his father was a shiftless vagrant—no, he was a respected property owner, carpenter, participant in civic affairs; Thomas Lincoln took his family from Kentucky to Indiana because of slavery—no, he didn't; his family lived for a whole year in the half-faced camp when they moved to Indiana—no, they didn't; Abraham was a believing Christian—no, he wasn't—yes, he was—no, he wasn't— at least, he became one in the White House—maybe; he swore as a young man on a trip to New Orleans that, given a chance, he would hit slavery hard—no, he didn't; Ann Rutledge was his one true love—no, she wasn't (was there such a person as Ann Rutledge?)—yes, she did exist and he did love her; Mary Todd was a tigress and their marriage was a misery— no, no, Mary has been misunderstood, a worthy woman with severe troubles, and with enemies, and theirs was a happy marriage; his part- ner Herndon is reckless with the truth and can't be trusted—well, maybe he can.

The short and simple annals of the poor! David Herbert Donald, at an earlier stage of his career, named in a magazine article one of his favorites among the immense proliferation of Lincoln books, *Lincoln on the Coming of the Caterpillar Tractor* (not Lincoln *on* the Caterpillar Tractor, but Lin- coln on the *Coming* of the Caterpillar Tractor). One might add these fur- ther contributions: *Abraham Lincoln as a Potential Lion,* which started as a talk to the Lions Club of Millerburg, Pennsylvania; *Lincoln the Comforter Together with a Story of Lincoln's First Pet; Lincoln the Athlete and Other Stories;* and *Abe's First Fish,* a play. There are treatments of Lincoln from head, literally, to toe—or, anyway, foot. (There is a book that tells the story of one Dr. Kahler measuring Lincoln for a pair of shoes, together with a diagram of Lincoln's feet. Also a book about Lincoln's chiropodist.) There are, of course, books connecting Lincoln to political parties, across the spectrum, not only to the Republican Party but to Communists (a book by the party's American general secretary), Socialists (*Little Sermons on Socialism by Abraham Lincoln*—culled and commented on by the *Chicago Daily Socialist*), and Democrats (including *Abraham Lincoln, the New Dealer of His Day,* which in addition to the topic indicated by its title performs the further service of measuring Lincoln by the postulates of Kipling's "If.") There are books not only for and against Lincoln's connec- tion to Christianity, but to other religions as well; *Lincoln and the Jewish Spirit* shows that Lincoln's principles come from Jerusalem. A writer man- aged somehow to stretch out to book length the story of *The Man Who*

Married Lincoln's Parents. There are books with the wonderful old, endlessly rolling titles that hark back to the disputatious pamphlets of the seventeenth century: *Abraham Lincoln The Friend of Man His Life Was Another Drop in That Vat Where Human Lives, Like Grapes in Gods' Vintages, Yield the Wine That Strengthens the Spirit of Truth and Justice in the World* (with a title like that, who needs a book?). Among biographies there is a 1905 tour de force called *The Life of Abraham Lincoln for Young People, told in words of one syllable.*

Perhaps you had not considered this point: both the name "Abraham" and the name "Lincoln" have *seven* letters. The author of *The Mystic Number Seven in the Life of Abraham 7 Lincoln 7,* who in another stage of his career showed that Bacon wrote Shakespeare, in this book demonstrates that the number seven and multiples of seven appear too often in Lincoln's life to be considered merely a coincidence, and also helpfully prints on his last page the text of Wordsworth's poem "We Are Seven."

The life of the sometime poor boy Abraham Lincoln proved to be different, in the end, from that of the unfulfilled unknowns in the country churchyard in the little village of Stoke Poges in Buckinghamshire in England, over which brooded Thomas Gray, as the curfew sounded the knell of parting day. Pigeon Creek in Spencer County, Indiana, was surely a good deal poorer, and a good deal more remote, than Stoke Poges, which is close to Eton, the site of a famous educational institution, and only twenty-four miles from London, the immensely sophisticated capital of the English-speaking world. The newly formed village of New Salem, on the Sangamon River in Illinois, although it had more to it than Pigeon Creek, still was said to have had at its peak only about twenty-five families and would also have been poorer and much more remote and certainly much newer than this village in England with its little church built in the fourteenth century. New Salem was not five centuries old, but about three *years* old, when this poor boy arrived there, and it did not have any church building at all. And it fizzled out ten years later.

One primary reason this "strange, penniless, friendless, uneducated boy working on a flatboat for ten dollars a month" was able to make his way from his poor and obscure beginnings to world-class greatness and fame had to do with the great purposive effort of his self-education. Gray, musing on these thwarted ones in the churchyard, says that

> *Knowledge to their eyes her ample page,*
> *Rich with the spoils of time, did ne'er unroll:*

And so we are to infer that these rude forefathers had been sitting there placidly waiting for "knowledge" on its own motion to unroll her ample page before their eyes? Young Lincoln did not do that; he, on the contrary, reached out himself and did the unrolling by his own effort.

He was not going to be content to keep "the noiseless tenor" of his way, in the "cool sequester'd vale of life." The cool sequestered vale of a farmer's life was exactly what he wanted to get away from. He was not going to stay complacently a long way from the madding crowd's ignoble strife; he was going to head right toward it by running for the state legislature, a madding crowd if you ever saw one, almost before he got his saddlebags unpacked. If the state legislature of a rapidly growing state on the American frontier is not the "ignoble strife" of a "madding crowd," I don't know what would be.

But the contrast between Lincoln's life and that of the churchyard poor in the English village is not the result solely of Lincoln's greater natural ability. Suppose Thomas Gray, ruminating on those graves, posited someone with native ability fully equal to Lincoln's: would that person, in that village, have developed comparably intense thirst for personal distinction? It is to be doubted. We need clues from the world around us to develop our ambitions; Lincoln's world was telling him, as theirs was not, that for all his poverty and lack of formal education he could be something more than was defined by the conditions of his birth.

And if that English poor person developed an ambition equal to Lincoln's, would she, or he, have been able to realize it? Would doors open, possibilities appear, sponsors offer a hand? It is to be doubted. For Lincoln, they did.

For all the poverty and obscurity and unpromising character of his origins, Lincoln was in some other ways fortunate. He was not born in Albania or Ecuador, not to mention the shores of the Niger River in the African Sahel, the remote mountains of Montenegro, or the outer reaches of Mongolia—or the slave cabins of Alabama. Or as a Winnebago or a Sioux in the territory that would become Minnesota. Or, in any class or place whatever, as a woman. He was born a white male citizen of a budding new power among the nations of the earth, a repository across the water of the liberal idealism of Europe, of which rising nation he himself would one day give incomparable definition. And that meant, as no one emphasized more than he, that the path was open to him to rise, and that his rising could come to the attention of his fellows and the world.

A scholar proposed the word "yeoman" to describe his father, Thomas

Lincoln—but then took it back. It is not quite right for anyone in American society, especially in the newly forming West of the early nineteenth century. The word "yeoman" implies a position in a stratified society; a son of a yeoman does not start making political speeches at age twenty-one, after only six months' residence in a town, or propose to become—at age twenty-three, with no rank, no family connection, no wealth, no education, and only two years residence, a real nobody—one of the community's lawmakers; nor, on volunteering for service in the armed forces, does he find himself *elected* captain by his fellows. One has the distinct impression that officers in His Majesty's army were not chosen by election, and that they were not sons of poor country farmers.

A yeoman may be an honorable role, but it is a class-defined one; to our American ears, it sounds as though it would entail a certain amount of forelock-pulling before one's "betters." Who were Abraham Lincoln's "betters" during those fourteen years when he was growing up in the Indiana woods, or in those days in New Salem when he was starting out on his own? I think the answer is, essentially, nobody. Not "betters" in the sharply defined sense one might find in England and in many other places— perhaps most—on the globe. The Lincoln log cabins in Sinking Spring and Knob Creek in Kentucky were similar to ninety percent of the cabins in the area. Most others in Pigeon Creek lived essentially as Thomas Lincoln's family did. About twenty other such cabins made up the settlement of Pigeon Creek. One could name a man with more money than others— James Gentry, for whom Gentryville was named—but despite his name he was not "gentry" in the sense that Englishmen once used that word: the class *above* the "yeomanry" in rural England. That he would send young Abraham with his own son Allan on the raft down the rivers on the first trip to New Orleans would suggest that there was little sense of social class; I am not sure that members of the English gentry would be riding rafts down rivers, with or without poor boys as companions. In rural Indiana neither Mr. Gentry nor anyone else was categorically "better" than Abraham, requiring unquestioning deference.

And beyond the comparative classlessness of Pigeon Creek in Indiana and New Salem in Illinois there was the ethos of the new country, particularly in the West. The "culture" of this new nineteenth-century United States would encourage as expansive a view of what each individual could do and could make of himself, as diminished an understanding of social ties and ranks and limitations, as one was likely to find anywhere in the world's distinctive civilizations. What this lanky, awkward youngster dressed in homespun could become, in the view of the nation, was not limited to carrying on the role of his father or fitting into the constricted life of the frontier settlements to which his father took him. He was not necessarily confined to the poverty and obscurity of his father's world. He could be, by his own effort, something more.

That expansive view of the "freedom" of the individual human being to make himself and to make his world, and of human beings in general to master nature and to escape any alleged necessities of history, was encouraged by each aspect of the new country's life.

Young Lincoln accomplished his stunning ascent primarily though his extraordinary efforts, as we might say, but he might not have undertaken those efforts, or persisted in them, if the ethos of the new country had not encouraged his ambition. The young Frenchman Tocqueville was describing the "individualism" of American democracy just at the time Lincoln was exhibiting one form of it in Indiana and Illinois. The institutions of the New World, such as they were, encouraged the picture of individuals with possibilities not bound by social ties and limits.

The villagers in that cemetery of an Anglican parish would have been baptized as infants by their parents' decision, taken for granted into the faith of the established church with ties to a hierarchy embracing in theory the whole nation, and reaching in theory back through the centuries of Christian history to the Apostles. When members joined the Pigeon Creek Baptist Church, one by one, they were not linking themselves to any hierarchy, or any nation-state, or any long parade of apostles. On the contrary, they were a gathering of converted individuals into a body separated from "the world," especially as represented by the state—by the engines of the collective and of coercion. And far from being linked to all those bishops, their vision of Christian history jumped from New Testament times all the way (we might say) to their own gathering beside Pigeon Creek, regarding most of the intervening Christian history as a giant mistake.

Could some mute inglorious Milton in that English village, if he dropped poetry and turned to the law, by reading Blackstone all by himself, gain admittance to the bar and become a "solicitor" or a "barrister" or a member of the "Inns of Court"? It is to be doubted. Lincoln not only became a lawyer and eventually argued important cases before the supreme court of his state—but before he was done was appointing members of his nation's highest tribunal.

Young Lincoln not only could sell his labor in a long list of undertakings in his twenties in New Salem; he could also, with no money, nevertheless secure just with his note half-ownership of one of the three general stores in town. One has the impression that such a possibility was not open to a poor man in Stoke Poges.

Once Lincoln is on his own, in his early twenties, intellectually self-confident as well as amiable, personable, humorous—it is striking how rapidly his life opens out and heads upward. How easily the doors open for him. How few barriers there appear to be. How readily he finds sponsors, and supporters—including persons in the upper ranks of New Salem and Springfield, insofar as New Salem had any upper ranks. The entrepreneur Denton Offutt not only hires this able, affable young man to make another raft trip to New Orleans, but engages him to manage his store, and then expands his role to management of the gristmill and sawmill. The Clary Grove Boys, after his wrestling match with Jack Armstrong, befriend and support him. He is invited to join New Salem's growing men's debating society. Justice of the Peace Bowling Green allows him—encourages him— to participate in the workings of the local court. Although he has only been in New Salem a few months, elder statesmen propose that he run for the state legislature. When he volunteers for the state militia to fight in the Black Hawk War, and is elected captain, John T. Stuart, a major in his battalion, an already established Springfield lawyer with a good education and social connections, befriends him. Although he does not win a seat in the legislature that first try—his only defeat ever in a popular vote—New Salem gives him, as a total novice and a newcomer at twenty-three years of age, 277 out of 300 votes. A store owner sells him half-interest in a general store—for no money whatever (Lincoln does not have any) but only his note. Mentor Graham the schoolmaster befriends and helps him. When the store fails, friends get him appointed postmaster—even though he is a Clay man and Jackson is president. His friends also persuade John Calhoun, an ardent Democrat, to appoint Lincoln his deputy surveyor. When the sheriff takes possession of his horse and surveying tools and auctions them off to help pay for the store debt, an admirer buys them and gives them back to Lincoln. In his second try for the state legislature he not only wins but comes in second in a field of thirteen (with the top four chosen). Encountering lawyers, and encouraged by Stuart, he borrows and reads Blackstone and in 1837 is licensed as a lawyer. He is reelected to the legislature and his fellow Whigs make him their leader, and he is a leader also of the Sangamon "Long Nine" who bring the capital to Springfield.

When he moves to Springfield in 1837, though he has no money, Joshua

Speed offers him room in his place. William Butler, clerk of the county court, generously offers to board him. Simeon Francis, publisher of the *Sangamon Journal,* offers to print whatever he writes. John T. Stuart takes him on as his law partner and introduces him to Springfield society.

When he begins to court Mary Todd, he encounters the first hint of a barrier of social class anywhere that I have discerned in young Lincoln's story, and it is slight. Ninian W. Edwards, the Kentucky aristocrat to whom Mary Todd's sister is married, at whose house Abraham and Mary mostly meet, with his wife has initial reservations about Mary going with this uneducated newcomer of no family. So does Robert Todd, Mary's aristocratic father, back home in Lexington. But these people are "aristocrats" only by the standards of the nineteenth-century American heartland; they would not count for much in the great landed gentry in England. Their mild initial resistances were overcome, and soon the only complication in the Lincoln-Todd romance was provided by the couple themselves.

At thirty years of age, this onetime uncouth farmhand in an Illinois cornfield has become a leader of his party in the state legislature, and the partner of a leading lawyer in the state capital, and is soon to begin courting the well-educated daughter of a leading family of Kentucky.

He has made his way upward so quickly and strikingly that now he has to answer hints from those who knew him back in New Salem that because of his ties to the Edwards-Todd clan and to Stuart's Springfield law office he is the candidate of the aristocratic element! It is in shocked (and politically sensitive) response to such hints that Lincoln writes in a letter the clause all of us Lincoln writers now quote, sometimes three or four times in a book, as in this one, about his having been a "strange, penniless, friendless, uneducated boy working on a flatboat for ten dollars a month." The context slightly qualifies this much-quoted self-description—not that it wasn't, in most of its factual element, true (But was he "friendless"? Not long. Was he "strange"? In what way?), but it was colored by his effort to show himself to have been as far as possible from anything aristocratic.

I cite all these boosts and helps and open doors and befriendings, not to take away from Lincoln's remarkable self-shaping, but to indicate that when he reached a certain point in his self-education, given his intelligence and his humorous amiability, the social environment of the American nation, particularly in the West, would cooperate in his achievement.

Such were the reasons—to quote the "Elegy" just one last time—that this particular poor village youth did not prove to be, in the end, "to Fortune and to Fame unknown."

CHAPTER TWO

Noble Rage

1. YOUNG LINCOLN'S GREAT REJECTIONS

Young Lincoln, growing up in "unpromising" Kentucky, Indiana, and Illinois settings, would accomplish a remarkable work of independent self-definition. One side would be a rare sequence of self-initiated projects in reading, study, and self-education. The other side would be a striking series of rejections and disengagements from what others around him did and thought and believed.

These refusals, rejections, and disengagements—choices, great ones and small ones, "moral" ones and personal ones—make quite a striking list, when you line them up.

He did not hunt. He lived, as a boy and a young man, in Kentucky, particularly in the Indiana woods, and for a year with his family in Illinois, in settings in which most males hunted. These settings abounded with birds and animals, and with men with guns shooting those birds and animals. Families like his would live for some periods mostly on the game they could shoot.

Dennis Hanks described what Abraham's father did in Indiana as he had done in Kentucky: "Like most Pioneers [Thomas Lincoln] delighted in having a good hunt. The Deer, the Turkeys the Bear the wild cats and occasionally a big Panther afforded him no small amusement and pleasure—and was a great Source of Subsistence as the wild Turkeys and Deer were very abundant . . . Thomas Lincoln could with propriety be classed with the 'Hunters of Kentucky' he seldom failed of success."

But his son Abraham would not be classified with the Hunters of Kentucky, or of Indiana, or of Illinois either. He himself recalled, in the autobiography that he would write, in the third person, for John L. Scripps and other editors in June of 1860: "A few days before the completion of his eighth year, in the absence of his father, a flock of wild turkeys approached the new log-cabin, and A[braham], with a rifle gun, standing inside, shot through a crack, and killed one of them. He has never since pulled a trigger on any larger game."

One turkey when he was eight, and that was it.

I don't think he fished much, either, even though his family lived successively near Nolin Creek, Knob Creek, Pigeon Creek, and the Sangamon River, and American boys as romanticized, particularly in the West, are supposed to come equipped with a fishing rod. We read that in New Salem there was an intriguing fellow named Jack Kelso, who was said by another resident to be "one of those peculiar, impractical geniuses—well educated, a lover of nature, with the soul of a poet," who became, understandably, a great friend of the intellectually aspiring and rather free-spirited bachelor and flatboatman Abraham Lincoln. One who knew them said that "Kelso loved Shakespear and fishing above all other thing. Abe loved Shakespear but not fishing—still Kelso would draw Abe; they used to sit on the bank of the river and quote Shakespear—criticize one another."

There is a picture: two young American males, sitting on a riverbank in the great American West. One of them holds a fishing rod and is quoting Shakespeare. But the other, who is also quoting Shakespeare and will become the greatest of American heroes from the West, is not holding a fishing rod.

He was kind to animals, and insisted that others be kind to animals. There was no Animal Rights League in Spencer County, Indiana, in 1816–1830, and boys then, as now, could be cruel. Abraham, by contrast, not only behaved "kindly" toward them, but came to their rescue and campaigned in their behalf. His stepsister Matilda Johnston Moore said he once preached a youthful sermon defending the right-to-life of ants.

Anecdotes about his rescuing animals and birds abound in the memories of people who knew him, extend beyond his boyhood into his adult life, and include terrapin turtles, wandering kittens, a pet dog that fell behind on the 1829 trek to Illinois, two little birds the wind had blown from their nest, a little squealing pig that was being eaten by its mother, and a hog mired in the mud. In some cases—the dog left behind, the birds blown from their nest—Lincoln's insistence on going out of his way to save creatures in distress would go against the expectations of the human creatures around him.

As to the hog, Mary Owens Vineyard told Herndon that Lincoln once related a story to her of how he was "crossing a prairie one day, and saw before him a hog mired down, to use his own language; he was rather fixed up and he resolved that he would pass on without looking towards the shoat, after he had gone by, he said, the feeling was eresistable and he had to look back, and the poor thing seemed to say so wistfully—*There now! my last hope is gone*—that he deliberately got down and relieved it from its difficulty." Lincoln surely must have been one of the few men among all of the pioneers of the Great Plains who could not resist the wistful appeal in the eyes of a mired-down hog.

When the boys in your neighborhood put hot coals on the backs of turtles to entertain themselves by watching the turtles' reaction, there are several courses of action open to you. As a good fellow, you can go along with the fun. As one who does feel the turtle's pain, but is intimidated, you can keep your objections to yourself. As one who has more important business elsewhere, you could ignore the whole matter. As a budding representative of the relativisms of the century to come, you could shrug your shoulders and say: "They like to put hot coals on turtles, I don't like to put hot coals on turtles—preferences differ. Who is to choose? Don't be judgmental."

Or you can do what the ten-year-old Abraham Lincoln did: You can tell your companions that what they are doing is wrong. You may "chide" them, and say that it hurts the turtle, and that they should not do what they are doing. And you may even, as young Lincoln did, draw out the larger moral principle, and write a composition—cruelty to animals is wrong—and argue publicly on its behalf in your one-room school.

His father's most distinctive skill was as a carpenter. He helped build the Pigeon Creek Church; he assisted Joseph Crawford in building his house; he built a wagon for James Gentry. Louis Warren found decorative mantels in Elizabethtown, Kentucky, and eight corner cupboards, with inlaid decoration, still extant in Indiana when he wrote in 1959, all said to have been done by Thomas Lincoln. And Warren understandably infers that that had to mean that his only living son, a big and strong boy for his age, for the first years in Indiana (before Dennis Hanks came) the only other male in the group, had to have helped his father in his carpentry: splitting logs, whipsawing lumber, making the pegs that held logs together, daubing clay between the logs.

But whatever Abraham did, the activity itself did not take. There is no sign that he ever gave the slightest consideration to taking up carpentry on his own, even as an avocation, let alone a vocation.

Most important, the Lincolns, like virtually all their scattered neighbors in Kentucky, Indiana, and Illinois, were farmers. Each of Thomas Lincoln's places in Kentucky was a farm: first 238 acres on Mill Creek; then in 1809 the 300-acre farm called Sinking Spring Farm (named after its cave-originating bubbling spring) on Nolin Creek, where Abraham was born; then, because Sinking Spring land proved poor, the smaller but more fertile tract of land on Knob Creek, when Abraham was two. In Indiana and again in Illinois the Lincoln party broke ground and hacked a farm out of the woods. They grew some corn to take to the mill on his acreage in Kentucky, and did so again in the Indiana woods. By 1824 Thomas Lincoln and Dennis Hanks, according to the latter, had about ten acres of corn, five of wheat, two of oats, and one acre of meadow, along with some livestock. Abraham perforce had to join in the family farmwork, and in addition, owing his labor to his father until he was twenty-one, was loaned out by his father for work on neighbors' farms.

But for all that, young Lincoln never took to farming, never liked farmwork. John Hanks would remember that "farming, grubbing, hoeing, making fences" had no attraction for Abraham. And in presenting himself later he distinctly kept farming at arm's length. In the short autobiography that he wrote for Jesse Fell in 1860 he said, with a kind of noncommittal matter-of-factness: "I was raised to farm work, which I continued till I was twenty-two." And—it is implied by the ensuing silence—he then promptly, when on his own, stopped.

In a letter to his friend Joshua Speed, on April 2, 1842, Lincoln, before he turns to the serious matter of Speed's new marriage, rather brusquely thrusts aside the other topic that Speed has written about, his undertaking on a farm: "As to your farm matter, I have no sympathy with you. I have no farm, nor ever expect to have; and, consequently, have not studied the subject enough to be much interested with it. I can only say that I am glad you are satisfied and pleased with it."

More striking still, when he became a politician, and might have wrung some political benefit from his own indisputably authentic farm connections to an electorate composed in large part of farmers, Lincoln went out of his way to avoid any such identification.

On September 30, 1859, as a rising politician beginning to have large ambitions indeed, he was asked to address the Wisconsin State Agricultural Society—the state fair, in other words—in Milwaukee. What an opportunity! Most politicians, throughout American history, however meager their participation in farming, would seize such an opportunity to extract every last drop of advantage from the faintest connection with plows and furrows and wheat and corn and cows and pigs. Lincoln, instead, makes no reference at all to his own farming and makes it clear that he is not a farmer. "I suppose it is not expected of me to impart to you much specific information on Agriculture. You have no reason to believe, and do not believe, that I possess it—if that were what you seek in this address, any one of your own number, or class, would be more able to furnish it."

In other words: I am definitely *not* one of your number or class.

Lincoln had already long since voted with his feet. We may certainly interpret Lincoln's departure from under his father's roof, in the new farm in Macon County, Illinois, in the spring of 1831, as a departure forever from farming. Mark E. Neely Jr., in his tightly written short book *The Last Best Hope of Earth,* puts the point with characteristic succinctness: "Lincoln fought his entire political life for industrialization and there was not a pastoral bone in his body."

More broadly, we may say that young Abraham clearly rejected, for himself, the life of manual labor by which he was surrounded, and which when he was young was imposed upon him by necessity and by his father.

Spencer County, Indiana, when the family arrived there in 1816, was "woods, woods, woods, woods." Abraham, seven years old when they arrived, big for his age, had an ax put in his hand and, as he said, rarely put it down from then until he was twenty-one. And one could make quite a list of the kinds of physical labor he did, in both Indiana and Illinois while he was still with his family and in his first years on his own. But when he had a choice, he read books and newspapers.

As a result of his disinclination to manual labor, and his desire to read, he was sometimes thought to be lazy. Even Dennis Hanks said that Abraham "was lazy—a very lazy man. He was always reading, scribbling, writing, ciphering, writing Poetry, etc." (Notice the implied definition of what it is to be "lazy.") Hanks's son-in-law said that "Lincoln was not industrious as a worker on the farm or at any kind of manual labor. . . . He only showed industry in the attainment of knowledge."

This man was not, spiritually speaking, a rail-splitter.

In the rough male world of these frontier western places physical combat was a regular feature, not only for enjoyment, and as a serious method of what would not have been called in that setting "conflict resolution," but also as a test of one's "manhood." Douglas Wilson wrote about the world in which young Lincoln grew up: "Attaining manhood entailed more than reaching a certain age; in practice it meant proving oneself physically in contests with other boys and eventually with other men." Fortunately for young Lincoln, he grew to be enormously strong, and became able to do more than hold his own in wrestling and fighting. A man with a different makeup from Lincoln's might have taken advantage of that and become a bully, or at least swaggered about and issued challenges. It is striking in Lincoln's case, however, that he did not do that. He seems to have been drawn into each of the famous fights in which he is reported to have been engaged not by his own initiative but by someone else:

• In 1828 (perhaps; the date is in doubt) in Indiana, when he was nineteen, he joined William Grigsby in a fight in order (apparently; the reports are confused) to rescue his stepbrother, John D. Johnston.

• In 1831, newly arrived in New Salem, his most famous fight, his wrestling match with Jack Armstrong of the Clary Grove Boys, apparently came about because his employer Denton Offutt bragged about his new employee's great strength, and bet five dollars that Lincoln could defeat Armstrong.

• In the spring of 1832, as a volunteer in the militia in the Black Hawk War, he was not only elected captain but put forward as the company's champion in wrestling matches with the leading wrestlers of other companies, and usually—perhaps all but one time—was victorious, upholding his company's honor.

These frontier places were full of both formal contests and informal outbreaks of violence. But Lincoln, strong as he was and victorious in most encounters, nevertheless was not belligerent or combative, did not like fights or "confrontation," and was generally speaking a peacemaker. Russell Godbey, a Menard County man who employed Lincoln to resurvey his land, said: "When a fight was on hand Abe used to Say to me 'Lets go and Stop it—tell a joke—a Story—Say Something humorous and End the fight in a good laugh.'" Isaac Cogdal, a farmer and stonemason friend of Lincoln's, said: "Salem was a great place for fighting and Lincoln was called peacemaker." John Rowan "Row" Herndon, co-owner of the store Lincoln bought there, wrote to his cousin William about Lincoln in New Salem that he "never Quareled or fought But always was the Pease maker . . ." and in a later letter that "if there was any fighting about to Commence he would try to stop [it]."

Liquor in quantity accompanied all the corn-shuckings and log-rollings and hog-billings and quilting bees that provided the social life on the frontier. And drinking was by no means confined to these festive occasions. "Incredible quantities of whisky were consumed," wrote Albert Beveridge, who assembled a collection of quotations from participants' memories and visitors' observations that make the point convincing indeed: "No difference if grain was scarce or dear, or times hard, or the people poor, they would make and drink whiskey. The custom was for every man to drink it, on all occasions that offered; and the women would take it, sweetened and reduced to Toddy. In 1819 alone, three licenses were granted to retail liquor in Boonville, Warrick County [adjacent to Spencer County], although that town had a population of fewer than one hundred." One kept a bottle and offered a friendly drink to a visitor. Of course this meant that Abraham's abstention would be noticed and remembered. Apparently it was noticed already in his Hoosier youth; among the many, many quotations attesting to his abstinence is this interesting item from his stepmother: "He never drank whiskey or other strong drink—was temperate in all things—too much so, I thought sometimes."

That the adult Lincoln did not drink runs regularly through the recollections of him; a few recalled that he took an occasional dram, but most reported that he never drank at all: "I never knew him to drink a drop of liquor—or get drunk"; "He never drank liquor of any kind"; and "One could with safety wager any sum that no man in Springfield ever saw Lincoln take a drink." In the late nineteenth century, while persons who had known Lincoln were still alive, a reward of fifty dollars was offered, apparently with no winners, for any evidence that he ever took a drink of an intoxicant. A reporter interviewed several of the older citizens and elicited this vivid picture from Springfield's oldest merchant, E. R. Thayer, who declared positively (as did everyone else interviewed) that Lincoln never drank intoxicants:

> When Harrison defeated Van Buren, there was a great frolic in Springfield. I do not believe there has ever been such a jollification since then. The center of the celebration was a high saloon, and there champagne flowed like water. It was a favorite trick to knock off the head of the bottle by striking it on the stove. Lincoln was present and made a great deal of sport with his speeches, witty sayings, and stories. He even played leap-frog, but he did not drink a thing.

In a world of much smoking and chewing and spitting, by most men and many women, as the title of one of the 3,958 books about him already published by 1939 put it, *Lincoln Never Smoked a Cigarette.* Notice the word "even" in this quotation by Abner Y. Ellis: "He [Lincoln] did not in those days even smoke or chew Tobacco." He appears not to have done *even* that in later days either.

There are reports by several who knew him that, among folk from whom we might expect a rich vein of strong language, he did not use profanity. Abraham's stepmother, Sarah, said that he did not use profanity. Row Herndon wrote in answer to his cousin William's inquiry in May of 1865 that Lincoln "Never used Bad Langag."

He did not gamble. Henry McHenry, of the Clary Grove Boys, told Herndon: "During all this time—during all these years—I never knew Mr Lincoln to run a horse race—it then being Common, if not universal over the whole County. I never knew him to . . . gamble or play Cards." James Short, one of young Lincoln's best friends in New Salem, who proved this friendship by buying Lincoln's surveying equipment when it was being sold at auction and then returning it to him, testified to three of our points at once: "He never played cards, nor drank, nor hunted." William Greene made another all-purpose response to a Herndon interrogatory: "Mr Lincoln while he lived in New Salem was entirely *free* from the vices mentioned in your 3rd Interrogatory viz running after Women Drinking whiskey or playing Cards for Money." Caleb Carman: "never gambled—probably never attended horse races—I never saw him at one." One who knew him many years later when he was a congressman noticed that he did not bet, did not gamble.

But now let us list a rejection of a different sort—a rejection of one set of moral rejecters, as it were. It is not the point of this list to present Lincoln as a perfect model of the older individualistic conventional morality, consisting largely of prohibitions. It is rather the point to present him as one who made his own independent judgments, which sometimes coincided, and sometimes did not, with a widely held aspect of conventional personal morality. These personal abstentions by Lincoln—not smoking, chewing, swearing, or gambling, and particularly not drinking—of course would meet with favor in the circles of aggressive benevolence and moral improvement that were just then in Lincoln's youth pouring forth from the evangelical Protestant churches, making their first distinctive trip across the American cultural landscape. They would keep on making trips in later American history, often using Lincoln, after he had become a maximum hero, as an example.

But Lincoln's scruples and choices did not take quite the shape that the forces of aggressive benevolence took. His view was not simple or absolutistic or officious or intrusive. His sense of proportion is suggested by the anecdotes about his amiably humorous response to violations by others. This comes from his days as president:

> "[William Pitt] Fessenden, enraged over an issue of patronage, exploded to Lincoln, losing control of himself in abusive profanity. Lincoln waited until his rage was spent and then asked softly, 'You are an Episcopalian, aren't you, Senator?' 'Yes, sir,' said his opponent stiffly, 'I belong to that church.' 'I thought so,' said Lincoln. 'You Episcopalians all swear alike. Seward is an Episcopalian. But Stanton is a Presbyterian. You ought to hear him swear.'"

The temperance movement would be spawned by the same wave of religious revivals that brought into being the new, more insistent form of abolitionism, and it would be a considerable presence in the social life and politics of Illinois by the time young Lincoln went into politics. But although Lincoln was personally abstemious, he did not join in the thoroughgoing evangelistic and moralistic teetotalism and the use of the law to prohibit alcohol that marked that movement. Several of the Springfield residents who testified to his refraining from drink said also that he was "liberal" with respect to drinking by others.

Lincoln told a story about himself that showed a self-mockery not notably present in the temperance folks. The story appears in different versions from different hearers; this one from Herndon himself is the fullest and best version. It seems that as Lincoln set out from a tavern in Springfield, early in the morning, on his way to Washington in the spring of 1849,

the only other passenger in the stage for a good portion of the distance was a Kentuckian, on his way home from Missouri. The latter, painfully impressed no doubt with Lincoln's gravity and melancholy, undertook to relieve the general monotony of the ride by offering him a chew of tobacco. With a plain "No, sir, thank you; I never chew," Lincoln declined, and a long period of silence followed. Later in the day the stranger, pulling from his pocket a leather-covered case, offered Lincoln a cigar, which he also politely declined on the ground that he never smoked. Finally, as they neared the station where horses were to be changed, the Kentuckian, pouring a cup of brandy from a flask which had lain concealed in his satchel, offered it to Lincoln with the remark, "Well, stranger, seeing you don't smoke or chew, perhaps you'll take a little of this French brandy. It's a prime article and a good appetizer besides." His tall and uncommunicative companion declined this last and best evidence of Kentucky hospitality on the same ground as the tobacco. When they separated that afternoon, the Kentuckian, transferring to another stage, bound for Louisville, shook Lincoln warmly by the hand. "See here, stranger," he said, goodhumoredly, "you're a clever, but strange companion. I may never see you again, and I don't want to offend you, but I want to say this: my experience has taught me that a man who has no vices has damned few virtues. Good-day."

Lincoln enjoyed telling this story on himself. Generally speaking, the forces of aggressive benevolence and personal "morality" did not tell self-mocking stories like that.

The western United States—and Illinois in Lincoln's day was part of the West—had a particularly strong version of the common prejudice among white Americans against Native Americans (then, of course, called "Indians"). The period of Lincoln's youth would be the time of the worst of the broken promises and mistreatments of the indigenous population by the continent's newcomers—the Trail of Tears, the Seminole War, the Indian fighting of Andrew Jackson.

Abraham Lincoln had in addition to the general attitude around him a personal and family reason for bitterness toward Indians. His paternal grandfather, also named Abraham, had been killed by Indians, as the famous grandson himself would tell it, "not in battle, but by stealth, when he was laboring to open a farm in the forest" in Kentucky. That event was an important cause of the poverty of Thomas Lincoln, who "was but six years of age" when his father was killed, and hence a cause also of the poverty of his son Abraham, because by the then prevailing law of primogeniture all of his father's property passed to the older brother. As a result of this episode, it was said, Abraham's uncle Mordecai was a fierce Indian-hater all his life.

But Abraham did not share in this ubiquitous western prejudice. He would show his disengagement from it most notably many years later than the time we are now considering, when as president of the United States he declined to allow the mass execution of 303 Sioux, strongly urged upon him by inflamed associates and fellow Republicans after raids and killings in the upper Middle West. He personally went through the records one by one and reduced the number to be hanged from 303 all the way down to 38 whom he found to have committed genuine atrocities.

His rejection of "malice" in that case was anticipated by an episode in his younger days, during the Black Hawk War.

If an old Indian stumbles into the camp of the militia company of which you are captain in the midst of an Indian war, and he shows an official paper from one of your government's officials stating that he is "a good and true man," but your men don't believe it, and call him "a damned spy," and say, "We have come out to fight the Indians and by God we intend to do so," and propose to shoot him—there are a number of ways you can choose to respond. You can let them do it because you agree with them; one can't be too careful about spies, or, you may think, about Indians. Or you can let them shoot the fellow even though you don't agree with them because you want to retain your popularity with the men. You were elected captain, after all, in a popular contest when this rough bunch first gathered, and you were elected unanimously, and you would say later in life that that election pleased you more than any other victory in your life—so don't disturb your popularity, don't defy them and disappoint them. You could put it to a vote, letting the majority decide, and they would outvote you and shoot him, but you would have kept yourself morally pure by voting against it.

Or you could do as the twenty-three-year-old Lincoln did: You could put yourself "between the Indian and the outraged man" and tell them, "Men, this must not be done. He must not be shot and killed by us." You might argue, as Lincoln did, "We must not shed his blood. It must not be on our shirts." You would mean that there is some sort of moral universe and some sort of accounting or judgment. You would mean that to take this innocent fellow who trusted you, trusted that this paper from an official in your white man's world would protect him, this fellow who was all alone and no threat to anyone, and then to shoot him and kill him, would be a violation of something fundamental in the universe—something "registered in heaven," as the mature Lincoln would put it in another connection.

But then, when some of the men would call you "cowardly" because you were not "savage" enough for an Indian fighter, you could now subside and acquiesce, outnumbered and overborne by the men's contemptuous misunderstanding. Or you could, as young Lincoln did, defy the men again, and say: "If any man thinks I am a coward let him test it"—proposing to fight not only on behalf of the Indian but in demonstration of your own courage. And when the men protest that you have the advantage in strength and size, you could say, as young Lincoln did, "Choose your weapons then," and put to rest any notion that you were a coward, and save the Indian's life.

Abraham Lincoln's family and friends were supporters of Andrew Jackson ("So was his father—so were we all," said Dennis Hanks). His new friends in Illinois the Clary Grove Boys were supporters of Andrew Jackson. Abraham Lincoln's age and social location and geography and family and friends and purported populistic inclinations could have been expected to make *him* a supporter of Andrew Jackson.

Jackson was the hero and representative of common men, farmers and mechanics and clerks in stores and deputy surveyors and rail-splitters and uneducated boys working on flatboats for ten dollars a month. Jackson was the candidate of the new West, of lands just being settled and becoming states, like Indiana, and towns just formed on a western river, like New Salem, Illinois. Jackson was the opponent of the "monster bank" on Market Street in Philadelphia that ground the faces of the poor farmer and workingman. Jacksonian democracy was the great movement of young Lincoln's generation.

And young Lincoln's politics? He supported Jackson's opponent Henry Clay.

The Democratic Party was the party of Thomas Jefferson, the party of the people against Federalist aristocrats and Hamiltonian bankers and merchants, the party of the West and South against New England and the North, the party of the farmer and the rural interest against the cities. Most of Lincoln's family and friends supported the Democratic Party in general, as well as Jackson in particular. Beveridge says that "all the Lincolns continued to be Democrats, none of them voting for Lincoln in 1860"—also the Hanks family, except for John. Illinois would be dominated by the Democratic Party all the way through Lincoln's youth and political career up to the coming of the Republican Party. For success in Illinois politics, it helped to be a Democrat—no Whig was ever elected to statewide office.

And Lincoln? Lincoln became a Whig.

Among the four major political parties in American history, it was the Whig Party that was most dominated by Protestants and by descendants of the early immigrations from England. It was therefore the primary original political home, before the formation (mostly out of Whig sources) of a party distinctly devoted to nativism, of those who might be inclined to oppose the new immigrants, and in particular Catholic immigrants. The Irish coming to this country in numbers in the 1830s, in larger numbers in the 1840s, in larger numbers still after 1848, eyeing all the Protestant clergymen and businessmen and temperance advocates in the Whig Party, headed straight for the Democratic Party. There was a considerable Irish presence in Illinois, to work on the railroad. (Wherever there were railroads, there were Irish.) Many of those with whom Lincoln was associated were inclined toward nativism, including even his wife, who had quarrels with, and stereotypes of, Irish maids, and who, had she had the vote, might have voted in 1856 not for John C. Frémont, the Republican, but for Millard Fillmore, the candidate of the American Party (which is to say the "Know-Nothing" party, the nativists).

But Lincoln never exhibited any trace of nativism, and specifically condemned it in a letter to Speed on August 24, 1855, often quoted:

> I am not a Know-Nothing. That is certain. How could I be? How can any one who abhors the oppression of negroes, be in favor of degrading classes of white people? Our progress in degeneracy appears to me to be pretty rapid. As a nation, we began by declaring that *"all men are created equal."* We now practically read it "all men are created equal, *except negroes."* When the Know-Nothings get control, it will read "all men are created equal, except negroes, *and foreigners, and catholics."* When it comes to this I should prefer emigrating to some country where they make no pretence of loving liberty—to Russia, for instance, where despotism can be taken pure, and without the base alloy of hypocracy.

Young Lincoln, according to his testimony when he was grown, was already and always opposed to slavery, as was by no means true of all those around him in southern Indiana and central Illinois.

To be sure, we should not read back into his youth, as the myth has tended to do, a central determination, even as a young man, to "hit that thing hard." Opposing slavery, we may surmise, was not at the center of young Lincoln's purposes; it was over on the periphery, visible out of the corner of his eye. On the other hand, we do not want to go too far in the other direction, and dismiss his stipulated lifelong opposition as unimportant. He had always been opposed to slavery and—according to his adult memory, at least—could not remember a time when he had not. In a letter to Kentucky newspaperman Albert Hodges on April 4, 1864, President Lincoln famously wrote that he was "naturally" antislavery, and that if slavery is not wrong, nothing is wrong. And even though both Indiana and Illinois were nominally free states in the time of Lincoln's youth, they had been settled first, in the southern and central parts, largely by immigrants from Kentucky and other slave states who did not necessarily leave behind their support for, or tacit acquiescence in, the institution they had lived with. And in fact there were still slaves in Illinois, folded into the free state by the permission of the 1818 constitution, written by many who were themselves slaveholders. For a man looking back at himself as a youth, to discover clear-cut opposition to slavery in himself all the way back as far as he can remember, in those environments, is a point of some significance.

Young Lincoln was always, as far as we know, cordial and welcoming in his treatment of individual African-Americans whom he met. This was true all the way from Billy the Barber, whom he met in New Salem, out of money and out of luck, and helped out in the fall of 1831, to Frederick Douglass, the distinguished writer and lecturer, whom he went out of his way to welcome to the White House and the reception after his second inauguration as president of the United States.

That was certainly not the pattern for most white persons in the world in which he lived, as repeated votes to exclude blacks, and many other signs, would indicate. After his family left slave state Kentucky when he was seven, until they moved to Illinois when he was twenty-one, young Lincoln lived his adolescent years in an almost entirely white world; there were only five Negroes in all of Spencer County in 1820. We can certainly infer that there was, in this community mostly of immigrants from slave states, a thick, pervasive racial prejudice. But although Lincoln is known to have told jokes that involved "darkies" and "colored fellows," and doubtless used the ubiquitous n-word, there is no evidence that he joined in the more intentionally demeaning anti-Negro acts and attitudes common in his world.

One day in the fall of 1831 (so the story goes) Abraham Lincoln, just twenty-two years old and newly out in the world on his own, wearing a red flannel shirt and carrying an ax (the story continues), was returning to New Salem from a day's work in the woods when he encountered a black man, a little older than himself, with whom he fell into conversation. This black man, a Haitian named William de Fleurville, had been making his way, after many adventures, to Springfield, but had run out of funds. Young Lincoln learned that the man was trained as a barber. He took him to the Rutledge Tavern in New Salem, his boardinghouse, and told his fellow lodgers about Fleurville's plight and trade and drummed up enough haircutting and beard-trimming to make Billy the Barber solvent and send him happily on his way the next morning to Springfield. Billy the Barber opened a barbershop in Springfield—actually, *the* barbershop—and after Lincoln moved to Springfield in 1837 he went to Billy's shop for the rest of his Springfield life, and served as Billy's lawyer and friend. Lincoln as president sent Billy messages by way of his friend A. G. Henry and Governor Richard Yates; Billy when Lincoln was president sent him on New Year's Day 1864 a sympathetic and encouraging letter which expressed among other things the hope that the year would see him elected to a second term.

Frederick Douglass, after his three or more meetings with President Lincoln, made statements that are often quoted—for example, "I was never more quickly or more completely put at ease in the presence of a great man than that of Abraham Lincoln." Another such statement—most often quoted now—praising Lincoln for always treating him, Douglass, as completely as an equal, includes a clause not often underlined: that such a response is particularly remarkable in one who came from *a state with black laws*. Douglass knew what Lincoln's background meant.

Lincoln would not be sentimental about the traditional one-room schoolhouse where he received his very limited formal education. Hundreds of great persons have said about some teacher in their youth what James Madison said of Donald Robinson, the learned Anglican clergyman to whom his father sent him for instruction: "All that I am and have become, I owe to that man." What Lincoln said, rather, about the five subscription-school teachers who got their names forever in history books by having him briefly in their log cabin schools was that "there were some schools, so-called, but no qualification was ever required of a teacher, beyond 'readin', writin', and cipherin' to the rule of three.'" (The dropping of the g's—the lapse into dialect—is Lincoln's own.)

In the later and longer of the two short summaries of his life Lincoln would give the names of these teachers—the two in Kentucky, the three in Indiana (getting one name incomplete and slightly wrong)—but not a word more. David Herbert Donald, after granting that Lincoln's "censure [of these schools] was largely deserved," generously added that "a school system that produced Abraham Lincoln could not have been wholly without merit." "Produced"? Would Lincoln himself have agreed that he was "produced" by those schools? Louis Warren, a scholar who would be generous to a fault to the Lincoln family and Abraham's youthful experience, even suggests that having five different teachers at five different times and places might have had advantages. Abraham Lincoln, however, states or implies no such views; he wrote this scornful sentence, often quoted, about the whole scene: "If a straggler supposed to understand Latin, happened to sojourn in the neighborhood, he was looked upon as a wizzard."

A romanticized picture of his country's frontier schools would sentimentally suggest that although the teachers might not have had the best training, or the school the best books or equipment or method, nevertheless the *aspiration* would be high. Lincoln would say to the contrary about Pigeon Creek that there was "absolutely nothing to excite ambition for education." That is a comment not only about the schools but about the entire social scene: *absolutely* nothing to excite (even the) *ambition* for education.

Did the itinerant preachers who would travel to Spencer County to preach their fiery sermons plant something in the bright young boy? Abraham Lincoln's life corresponded almost exactly to a period that is called the Second Great Awakening, and was lived in the sections that were most affected by that wave of religious revivals—the border states and the West—and was lived as well in familial association with the burgeoning new Protestant denominations, the free churches, the churches of the common man—the Baptists and Methodists—that grew most rapidly in that setting. Thomas and Nancy had been married by a Methodist minister, and in Kentucky they belonged to the Separate Baptists. On June 7, 1823, Thomas joined the Pigeon Creek Baptist Church in Spencer County, Indiana. Sarah Johnston Lincoln was taken into the church with Thomas, and his daughter Sarah joined that church on April 4, 1826.

But his son Abraham never did join.

As a Baptist church, Pigeon Creek was a church that one was gathered into by individual adult decision. Baptists believed in *adult* baptism, not infant baptism, though "adult" in that setting could mean as young as twelve, or even younger. Abraham was fourteen years old when his father was enrolled, seventeen when Sarah was, twenty-one when they left Indiana—long since old enough to have professed his faith and been baptized and taken into the church.

He did not join in Pigeon Creek; he did not join a church in New Salem (where there was not yet a building); and he would not join a church in Springfield—or in Washington.

Abraham, when he was about fifteen (as his stepsister Matilda Johnston Moore would remember it), would "call the Children and friends around him," "take down the Bible, read a verse—give out a hymn—and we would sing"; "he would preach and we would do the Crying." He would "get up on a stump and repeat almost word for word the sermon he had heard the Sunday before."

Whatever one may want to argue about Lincoln's connection to Christianity in his later life, the surface facts of his youth seem rather plain: he was not sitting there in the pew absorbing what he heard with heartfelt agreement.

There he is, in New Salem, twenty-two years old, on his own for the first time, able now to express freely whatever is in him. And what he expresses is an attitude of skepticism toward religion. He reads Tom Paine's *Age of Reason* and another "freethinking" book of the time, Constantin de Volney's *The Ruins: A Survey of the Revolutions of Empires.* He liked and memorized and recited poems of Robert Burns that puncture the pretensions of religious folk. And he wrote a composition of his own about religious matters sufficiently shocking for friends to burn it. His religious skepticism would hurt him when he went into politics.

In a society of hunters, Lincoln did not hunt; where many males shot rifles, Lincoln did not shoot; among fishermen, Lincoln did not fish; among many who were cruel to animals, Lincoln was kind; surrounded by farmers, Lincoln fled from farming; with a father who was a carpenter, Lincoln did not take up carpentry; in a frontier village preoccupied with physical tasks, Lincoln avoided manual labor; in a world in which men smoked and chewed, Lincoln never used tobacco; in a rough, profane world, Lincoln did not swear; in a social world in which fighting was a regular male activity, Lincoln became a peacemaker; in a hard-drinking society, Lincoln did not drink; when a temperance movement condemned all drinking, Lincoln the nondrinker did not join it; in an environment soaked with hostility to Indians, Lincoln resisted it; in a time and a place in which the great mass of common men in the West supported Andrew Jackson, Lincoln supported Henry Clay; surrounded by Democrats, Lincoln became a Whig; in a political party with a strong nativist undercurrent, Lincoln rejected that prejudice; in a southern-flavored setting soft on slavery, Lincoln always opposed it; in a white world with strong racial antipathies, Lincoln was generous to blacks; in an environment indifferent to education, Lincoln cared about it intensely; in a family active in a church, young

Lincoln abstained; when evangelical Christianity permeated the western frontier, Lincoln raised questions—and gave different answers than his neighbors.

2. THE LIFELINE OF PRINT

Young Lincoln did not, if he could avoid it, hunt, fish, swear, fight, farm, perform manual tasks, gamble, despise Indians as many around him did, vote as his neighbors did, join the church as his family did, believe what his neighbors did; what he did do, when he could, was to read. The other side to young Lincoln's remarkable shaping of himself—the positive side, as it were—was his stunning work of self-education.

That positive work was accompanied by a surprising educational self-deprecation. Asked for a thumbnail biography for a directory of congressmen, he took one of the six short lines to say with stunning succinctness: "Education defective."

In the first autobiographical piece, the "little sketch" (only two-and-a-half handwritten pages) he composed in the first person at the request of his Bloomington supporter Jesse Fell in December of 1859, Lincoln spent more than a quarter of its total on his education and its defects; I count thirteen out of fifty-seven lines. That is more than he spent on his four-term state legislative career (nine lines) or his congressional term (one line), or his becoming a lawyer (two lines). He does not mention his work as a Whig politician, or his debates the previous year with Senator Douglas that were his main claim to fame. He does not say, as many politicians would, that he had been a postmaster, a surveyor, an expert on river transportation, the owner of a small business and a merchant, an inventor, a raftsman, a mill manager, a town clerk, a presidential elector, or a lecturer. He does mention having been "raised to farm work," but that is the way he puts it, and that dismissive phrase is all he says. He does not mention his religion, his wife, his three (living) sons, or anything about his law practice. But he does tell the world about the deficiencies of his education.

In his longest self-description, nine or ten pages, provided for John L. Scripps of the *Chicago Tribune* and other editors six months later, Lincoln did treat other topics, but the limitation of his education is still a major point. It was in this production (writing about himself in the third person) that he made the oft-quoted estimate that "the aggregate of all his schooling" did not amount to one year. And then he explained, "He was never in a college or academy as a student; and never inside a college or accademy

building till since he had a law-license. What he has in the way of education, he has picked up. . . . He regrets his lack of education, and does what
he can to supply the want."

If you had been in that position, a rising fifty-year-old political leader
striving to be nominated by your party for president of the United States,
would you have chosen to go back across the years of your adult success to
emphasize, even to seem to apologize for, the limitations of your early educational background? Would Lyndon Baines Johnson go out of his way to
explain the defects of San Marcos State Teachers College as compared to
Harvard, or Harry S. Truman go into the limitations of a Kansas City
night-school education in the law, or Jimmy Carter explain the narrowness
of the Naval Academy, or Ronald Reagan apologize for Eureka College?

In Lincoln's earlier piece, in the first person, there is similar educational self-deprecation. "Of course when I came of age I did not know
much. Still somehow, I could read, write, and cipher to the rule of three;
but that was all. I have not been to school since. The little advance I now
have upon this store of education, I have picked up from time to time
under the pressure of necessity." "Still somehow, I could read." "From
time to time under the pressure of necessity" he "picked up" a little. It is
modest—but is it really modest?

In the late 1850s Lincoln, now an established politician and lawyer
about to turn fifty, would try his hand at the popular and sometimes
(although not for him) lucrative mid-nineteenth-century undertaking of
preparing and delivering lectures to self-improving audiences on topics of
general interest. The one lecture he actually gave in a few Illinois towns
had as its subject "Discoveries and Inventions." It has not been judged to
have been a success, either by Herndon (who said it was "commonplace")
or by Lincoln's friends (Herndon said it met with their "disapproval") or
apparently by the audiences (in one place it was necessary to cancel
because so few came) or by later scholars generally (Randall says that disparagement of this effort has been the stock comment) or by biographers
in later years (who have generally dismissed this effort if they mention it at
all) or even, it seems, by Lincoln himself, who dropped the project.

Nevertheless, it is of interest to us now, looking back at this young
man's formidable self-education, because he came to devote a major
portion of the lecture to speech, to writing, and to printing. An earlier version that has survived, perhaps only in part, which he delivered before
the Young Men's Association in Bloomington on April 6, 1858, was a
boring enough, encyclopedia-derived and Bible-illustrated treatment of

"improvements" in spinning and weaving and harvesting and water power and steam power and the like. The second version, which he delivered in a college setting in Jacksonville on February 11, 1859, and later in Decatur and Springfield, was rewritten and given a tighter structure and a new emphasis. Now he would shift from the technical and mechanical marvels the audience might expect to hear discussed, to the great invention of human speech, and then of writing, and then of the printing press. The point he makes about print is its democratizing effect: "At length printing came. It gave ten thousand copies of any written matter, quite as cheaply as ten were given before; and consequently a thousand minds were brought into the fields where there was but one before."

Surely one might say that he is himself one of those thousand minds of obscure rank in a remote place who were now "brought into the fields" by the production of vastly increased numbers of books—enough copies of the King James Version of the Bible so that there could be a copy even in the bookless Lincoln cabins in Kentucky; enough copies of John Bunyan's *Pilgrim's Progress* so that this American boy in the Indiana woods could, while his horse was resting at the end of a row, commune with the mind of a pious Puritan tinker writing in jail a century and a half earlier; enough copies of *Robinson Crusoe* that the illiterate widow Sarah Bush Johnston could bring a copy with her to her new household, where her remarkable stepson could read it and join Crusoe on his island.

And Lincoln the lecturer in 1859 would make a further point that we rhapsodists of print do not always make: that humble person whom the efficient genius of print has brought within the circle of shared life and thought across time and space may also acquire, from his solitary communing with the writers of other times and places, a new confidence in his own powers.

> It is very probable—almost certain—that the great mass of men . . . were utterly unconscious, that their conditions, or their minds were capable of improvement. They not only looked upon the educated few as superior beings; but they supposed themselves to be naturally incapable of rising to equality. To immancipate the mind from this false and under estimate of itself, is the great task which printing came into the world to perform.

And surely one of those in the great mass of men whose minds were "immancipated" from a "false and under estimate" of itself by printing was this lecturer himself, when he was a boy. (It would be important, just a couple of years after he gave his lecture, that he add to his knowledge how to spell the word "emancipation.")

Surely the 1859 lecturer himself had been, when a boy, a supreme example of his point that by much reading of printed books, by joining in a conversation across the years and across the ocean with minds of distinction, he could acquire confidence in his own powers. I can, if I apply myself, understand what this writer from another time is saying; I can remember it, I can respond. Lincoln developed a confidence in his own powers of understanding and of judgment that would be a key to all his accomplishments.

He developed confidence in himself, that he could take up a subject, read the books about it, and acquire a mastery of it sufficient to his purpose—as he would do repeatedly throughout his life. And he developed a confidence with respect to others, that he need not defer to those with more formal learning.

Young Lincoln's reading could not have been easy. Although Mrs. Johnston's arrival as his stepmother when he was ten meant a marked improvement for the Thomas Lincoln family, and especially for Abraham, she brought her three children with her, and that made for crowded living quarters. The 1820 census for Spencer County, Indiana, lists eight persons in the one-room Lincoln cabin: Thomas, forty-two; Mrs. Sarah Johnston Lincoln, thirty-two; Dennis Hanks, twenty-one; Sarah Lincoln, thirteen; Elizabeth Johnston, thirteen; Abraham Lincoln, "male under sixteen" (actually eleven); Matilda Johnston, nine; and John D. Johnston, ten. In 1823 John Hanks, the half-brother of Dennis, the man destined thirty-six years later to carry a rail into the Illinois state Republican convention in Decatur claiming it had been split by Abraham Lincoln, joined the group in that one-room eighteen-by-twenty-foot cabin—nine people. The Indiana cabin when fully built had a loft that Abraham reached by climbing pegs in the wall, but it was not a place for solitary reading.

An impediment to his reading and thinking and self-education more important even than the severe limitations of space and privacy must have been the severe limitation of time and, presumably, energy. The Tom Lincoln family had to hack its living out of the woods by physical labor. Abe was the only son, big and strong for his age—before cousin Dennis Hanks arrived, the only male in the household other than his father. "Farming, grubbing, hoeing, making fences"; assisting his father's carpentry, building cabins, splitting logs, whipsawing lumber, daubing clay between the logs. In addition to all the labor that was required to feed and house the Lincoln family itself, as neighbor Nathaniel Grigsby would put it: "Thomas Lincoln the father of Abraham was a man of limited means so that it became necessary for Abraham to work from home."

Green Taylor, the young son of James Taylor, a farmer and ferry operator, said "Abe Lincoln . . . worked for my father for 6 or 9 Months worked on the farm—run the ferry for my father from the Ky shore to the Indiana shore . . . he plowed—ferried, ground Corn on the hand mill—grated Corn . . . Abe helped to kill hogs . . ."

Elizabeth Crawford, who moved with her husband from Kentucky and became a near neighbor to the Lincolns, wrote of young Abe: "He use to work in the Shop with his father and he us to makes rails make fence clear ground work in the firleds cut rok and any other kind of work done on A farm."

It does not sound as though there would be much time for reading books.

Lincoln read the books that were available, and that he could borrow, often going to some trouble (as in the legend) to borrow them. And read whenever he could. The legend has him reading, as in a well-known painting, by firelight; his stepmother explicitly contradicted that, telling Herndon he went to bed at night and read by daylight in the morning.

Candlelight notwithstanding, it would be quite a study to go through the available record to identify all the places, times, and postures in which those who had known Abraham in Indiana and in New Salem remembered him reading a book: reading while the horse rests at the end of a row, reading while walking on the street, reading under a tree, reading while others went to dances, reading with his legs up as high as his head, reading between customers in the post office, reading stretched at length on the counter of the store. In Lord Charnwood's classic biography an employer says: "I found him . . . cocked on a haystack with a book."

Others who knew him said: "He read setting lying down & walking in the streets he was allways reading."

"His favorite way of reading when at home was lying down on the floor."

"He would turn a Chair down on the floor and put a pillow on it and lie thare for hours and read."

"He was fond of . . . reading especially in warm weather by Laying down & putting his Feet a gainst a wall or if in the woods up a Tree."

"He was a constant and I my Say Stubborn reader."

Just what did he read? We may propose a theory of benign deprivation: print made books available, but remoteness meant there would not be too many. Perhaps it also meant that on the whole they would be better books. Although print has certain intrinsic superiorities over later means of communication, in the skills that it requires and the reasoning and reflecting and imagining that it encourages and the repeated reference and leisurely absorption that it permits—it is easily the best medium for ideas—still there is plenty of trash in print, too. But perhaps not much of it made its way to cabins on the Indiana frontier. One may speculate that a book had to have some kind of importance to make its way to Sinking Spring, Knob Creek, or Little Pigeon Creek—to be printed in enough copies for that to happen, and to be valued by families without high literacy.

Both the paucity of books and his own intellectual bent led Lincoln to repeated reading of a relatively small number of books. He did not skim across the top of a thousand books but immersed himself in a dozen or two. Although *Pilgrim's Progress* and Aesop's *Fables* and *The Arabian Nights* have a large imaginative component, he did not read novels, or read purely for distraction.

The first on the list of books that made its way to the cabins in which young Lincoln lived would, of course, have been the Christian Bible in its King James translation. It would have been one of the few books available to him as he learned to read. Legend has it that his mother, though she couldn't write, could read well enough to read the Bible to her bright son even back in Kentucky.

His stepmother and Dennis Hanks would say, in interviews after his death, that the teenage Lincoln they knew did not read the Bible as much as was by then asserted, but one may sense that they were correcting the overwhelming pious appropriation of the martyred Lincoln as he turned into a mythic figure with a religious aura. One cannot read much from Lincoln's own hand without becoming aware of his knowledge of the Bible. Whatever we make of young Lincoln's contrariness with respect to the doctrines and beliefs of churchgoers in the villages in which he lived, there cannot be much doubt that he read and reread and came to know a good deal of the Bible.

And he read it in the great seventeenth-century English translation that itself became a part of the literary heritage of the English-speaking peoples. It is commonly observed that the language and style of that translation—

made in a high period of English literature and language, just after Queen Elizabeth, while Shakespeare was still alive—would be evident influences on Lincoln's own style. When he wanted to state the prosaic "eighty-seven years" in language with a kind of sober elevation, he would echo the biblical form and say "fourscore and seven years." Whereas his speeches as a Whig and a Republican politician are marked, at their best, by the style of a logician, a good lawyer, a reader of Euclid—by clarity and logic and intellectual force (at their worst by bombastic extravagance)—his speeches as president are suffused with echoes and flavorings of the King James translation.

He *knew* the specific content of the Bible, and would regularly quote and paraphrase and make reference to it. In those days, many more quotations and episodes from the Bible were common currency, known more or less to everyone whether one read the Bible or not, as part of a common culture, than would be the case today. But Lincoln made many specific quotations of, and references to, the Bible that went well beyond those that would be most familiar. In the greatest speech of his life, the Second Inaugural, he would make use of three biblical quotations: "Judge not that ye be not judged" would be well known, but Psalm 19 would be slightly less so, and the "woes" from the eighteenth chapter of Matthew would not be part of the common stock at all. William I. Wolf, writing in 1959 in his book now called *Lincoln's Religion,* said that "Lincoln's knowledge of the Bible far exceeded the content-grasp of most present-day clergymen."

Next to the Bible, there was Shakespeare. One might almost say that if one has the King James Version of the Bible and the plays of Shakespeare, and reads them repeatedly and memorizes great parts of them, one is well connected to the core of the English-speaking civilization, even if one has no other book. They furnished common reference points for the society, even for people who did not have a religious attachment to the Bible and had never seen a play of Shakespeare's performed.

Perhaps Lincoln was not able to read complete plays of Shakespeare until he got to New Salem, where there were more people with books than there had been in Pigeon Creek, but the collections that he did have in his earliest days of reading would include some passages. A pedagogical book that fell into his hands, William Scott's *Lessons in Elocution,* published in Plymouth, Massachusetts, in 1825 ("in the forty-ninth year of the independence of the United States of America"), contained, in its "Selection of Pieces in Prose and Verse for the Improvement of Youth in Reading and Speaking," a number of passages from Shakespeare's plays, including

Henry V's stirring exhortation to his army before the battle of Agincourt. At least when he got to New Salem, if not before, he was able to read entire plays of Shakespeare, and reread them, and talk about them with Jack Kelso, and find his favorite plays to be *Macbeth* and *King Lear,* along with *Hamlet* and *Richard III.*

Scott's *Lessons in Elocution* included, in addition to the selections from Shakespeare and some instructions about how to make gestures to convey particular emotions that now seem rather comical, an extensive selection of readings that don't seem comical at all. There are selections, necessarily short, divided into "Lessons in Reading" and "Lessons in Speaking" (subparts: "Eloquence of the Pulpit"; "Eloquence of the Senate"; "Eloquence of the Bar"; "Dramatic Pieces") that span much of English literature up to that time. There were passages from Hume, Gibbon, *The Spectator,* Pope, Samuel Johnson, Lord Chesterfield—a considerable dose of eighteenth-century England—and, reaching a little further back in time in English literature, John Dryden and John Milton; and there were a few Greek and Roman classical writers, Homer, Virgil, Livy. And, of course, Shakespeare. One imagines young Lincoln sitting (or standing or walking or lying on the floor or the store counter) with this book in his hand, absorbing an acquaintance with the literary art, the "eloquence" and the moral teaching of Western civilization. One could certainly do worse than this book.

And young Lincoln got hold of books about his own country. He read William Grimshaw's *History of the United States,* published in Philadelphia, destined to run through fifteen editions, which was not bashful about affirming the greatness of its subject. Young Lincoln probably borrowed from David Turnham a book called the *Revised Statutes of Indiana,* which may not sound like a book an energetic youngster would seek out and read and reread, but Lincoln did. It contained, in addition to the technical legal materials one would expect, "the Declaration, the Constitution, the first twelve amendments, the Virginia Act of Cession of the Northwest Territory, the Ordinance of 1787, the act admitting Indiana [which had come about at just the time when Thomas Lincoln and his family crossed the Ohio River from Kentucky into the new state], and the first state constitution." We all know that Lincoln read the famous Parson Weems *Life of George Washington;* he also read the biography of Washington by David Ramsay and a life of Ben Franklin.

In Indiana, and again in New Salem, the books he read he borrowed from neighbors. In the larger town of Springfield, still borrowing from neighbors, he also made extensive use of the state library. In his late thirties, when he served his two years in Congress, Lincoln stayed in a lodging house—Mrs. Sprigg's—that was directly across the street from the Library of Congress. Douglas Wilson has unearthed the picture of his activities that we have referred to earlier:

> In Washington Mr. Lincoln had been a puzzle, and a subject of amusement to his fellows. He did not drink, or use tobacco, or bet, or swear. It would seem that he must be a very rigid churchman. But no, he did not belong to any church; and soon he became reckoned an "unbeliever." How did he occupy his spare time? He was mousing around the books of the old Congressional Library . . . "Bah!" said his fellow Congressmen, "He is a book-worm!"

Lincoln's life would be punctuated by intense projects in self-education and research, starting with his "picking up" "somehow" reading and writing. Surely it is a little unusual for a twenty-three-year-old man, now on his own and making his way in the world, to go to some trouble to borrow a textbook on grammar—walking six miles to borrow it—and then on his own (asking for some assistance) to teach himself that rudimentary subject. Lincoln himself, in his longer autobiographical piece, included two of the more striking of his grown-up personal educational projects. (Again: If you were fifty-one years old, a possible candidate for president, writing a short summary of your life, would you include such long-ago undertakings in self-education?) The first of these was his studying grammar: "After he was twenty-three, and separated from his father [!], he studied English grammar, imperfectly of course, but so as to speak and write as well as he now does"—imperfectly of course.

The second of his remarkable projects in adult self-education—this one perhaps still more impressive—further along in life and reported now to the world by himself, was this: "He studied and nearly mastered the six books of Euclid, since he was a member of Congress." "Nearly mastered": I hear in his reporting on his educational background a gentle drip of self-deprecation, mixed with a dash of pride.

Lincoln left out of his account his teaching himself surveying in order to take a job as a deputy surveyor. He had to learn the practical application of the principles of trigonometry, and got two books on the subject and on surveying, and learned enough to do the job.

Most important, he studied the law. He borrowed books from John T. Stuart, read and studied Blackstone, taught himself to be a lawyer. In New

Salem, according to the answer that Robert Rutledge, Ann Rutledge's younger brother, gave to Herndon's question about Lincoln's studies:

> He studied first Kirkhams Grammar and the Arithmetic, then Natural philosophy, Astronomy & Chemistry, then Surveying, and Law, In the mean time read history & other books, the news papers of the day, in fact any and all books from which he could derive information or knowledge . . . Would alternately, entertain and amuse the company by witicisms jokes &c, and study his lesson. He never appeared to be a hard student as he seamed to Master his studies with little effort, until he commenced the study of Law, in that he became wholly engrossed.
>
> I think he never avoided men until he commenced the study of Law, further than to read & study at late hours after the business of the day was disposed of . . .

It is not every president who would get books on military science from the Library of Congress, studying the subject in order to deal with the generals. Lincoln would develop rare powers of concentration, and he would use them all his life. He developed a confidence that he could dig in books for what he wanted, and would do so repeatedly in the years ahead. And that confidence in his powers of understanding what was written on the page seems to have encouraged a broader self-confidence, in his judgment and his critical powers—let us call it a moral self-confidence.

CHAPTER THREE

He Will Be Good—
But God Knows When

1. POOR MAN, FREE MAN, FREE MORAL AGENT

Abraham Lincoln was not born, after all, on Mount Rushmore. He did not come into the world as a certified hero with his memorial already built on the Mall and his face already stamped on the penny. He came into the world as you and I did, as a bare and gurgling bundle of possibilities. He was, as you and I were, free, within some limits, to make of himself what he would.

The limiting conditions of young Lincoln's life were, as we know, quite severe. His admiring ten-volume biographers would one day write, with a pardonable exaggeration, that he was born "in the midst of the most unpromising circumstances that ever witnessed the advent of a hero into this world."

Not just his birth cabin but the first four places where this boy lived all had one room and a dirt floor: the Sinking Spring place on Nolin Creek in Hardin County, Kentucky, where he was born; the Knob Creek place ten miles northeast of Sinking Spring, to which Thomas Lincoln moved his family when Abraham was two, and which would be the first place Abraham would remember; certainly the "half-faced" camp—the contraption of poles, trees, brush, and leaves, with one side open, that Thomas Lincoln put up when his family first arrived in the Hoosier woods in 1816, when Abraham was seven (one might say that, from that point, for this future president, a log cabin would be a move *up*)—and, in its first days, the cabin that Thomas then built there at Pigeon Creek in Indiana.

If this is correct, then the residence of Abraham Lincoln, the future president of this quite advanced country, did not have a wooden floor until some time after his stepmother, Sarah Bush Johnston Lincoln, arrived at the end of 1819, when he was almost eleven, and pressed her new husband to fix the place.

But for all the crudeness of the log cabins and the lack of schooling and the smallness and remoteness of his frontier homes, this youngster did have some distinct advantages.

First of all, he was a male child. Two years before Abraham's birth his parents had had, in addition to a boy baby who died, another child, who lived—a girl to whom they gave the oft-repeated biblical name Sarah. Her short life would be much more constricted than his.

Young Abraham, moreover, would be free of the even greater impediments of race and slavery. He would one day be "free, white, and twenty-one." When they made a count in 1811, he was one of the 1,627 white persons in Hardin County, Kentucky, not one of the 1,007 black slaves.

And although his own beginnings were poor and remote, the nation in which they took place was not. He had been born in February of 1809 in the western part—the new and growing section—of an audacious new country, a spilling-over of the idealism and enterprise of Europe, that had just three decades before his birth claimed for itself a distinctive world role. His nation had been born in the Enlightenment springtime of the modern world, and he was born in the early stage of its development. The story of that rising nation would fire his youthful imagination. When Lincoln was born, its president was still, then in his last month in office, Thomas Jefferson, whose words would have a particular resonance with this boy. Jefferson had called this new land an "Empire of Liberty."

And for the able white boy Abraham Lincoln, though not for others, it was such an empire.

Young Lincoln was "free" in the political and external senses whose opposites are slavery or prison or tyranny or exclusion.

But for the purposes of an ethical inquiry there is a deeper sense in which he was also free—the sense in which all who are human are free. This is the freedom that philosophers and sophomores debate, and that our moral thinking presupposes—that ultimate freedom in which the opposite is necessity or determinism. His fate was not already somehow ordained when he was born. What he would become was not fixed by his birth in the Kentucky backwoods, or by the string of dirt-floor cabins, or by his father's shortcomings, or by his mother's early death, or by his family's economic scramble, or by the feebleness of the local schools, or by any psychological or social necessity. Whatever the influence of these and other conditions of his life may have been, he was nevertheless free in the ultimate sense that even slaves and prisoners and oppressed women and victims of despotisms can be free: free still to make choices of better and worse, however constrained; free still in the sense that all our praise and blame and moral judgment implies—that the person judged had some choice.

We know that young Lincoln himself, when he grew up and read some books and carried on arguments, would hold for a time to a kind of fatalism, a "doctrine of necessity," that denied this ultimate human freedom; but we may be permitted to say, since he was not gifted with omniscience, that he was on this point wrong. We might say that his own life, which would be shot through with choices that made a difference, would disprove his own youthful theory.

Out of their margin of freedom, whatever it may be, human beings make choices. The choices that have an impact for good or ill, that are in accord (or not) with some standard of worthy human conduct, receive our praise or our censure—they are "moral" choices. Lincoln made that long list of choices we assembled in the previous chapter, many of which we may say were moral choices, although some were just "preferences," matters of personal taste. And as his life unfolded, he would make many more, some of them of huge consequence.

Beyond the particular dilemmas and quandaries and initiatives of choice, day by day, decision by decision, there is the cumulative effect, and the shaping by some interplay with the world around him, of characteristic patterns of conduct. One of the most influential pieces of writing (or lecturing) on these matters early in the history of the "Western" civilization of which this young lad out in the Indiana woods will be such a peculiar offshoot made "habit" the center of the discussion of ethics. Although the word "character" will have multiple meanings shifting with time, there will be—still is—a use of it as a positive word for a person's abiding moral structure. We will shortly see Lincoln himself refer to a particular moral trait as the "gem" of his "character." Older ways of talking about these matters—not altogether vanished—spoke of "virtue" in general, and of lists of "virtues," that is, of abiding moral traits.

2. HE STUDIED WITH NO ONE

When we ask, about young Lincoln, what the influences were, among the human beings and institutions around him as he was growing up, that shaped his moral understanding, his "character" and his "virtue," we have a hard time naming anyone or anything of transcendent importance.

From what he would write, and not write, and from the reports of others, we infer that this young Hoosier had fewer face-to-face original powerful moral influences than most human beings do, and that he shaped himself, by his conscious choice, more than most human beings do. As remarkable even as Abraham Lincoln's much-celebrated intellectual self-development may have been his closely related moral self-development, as we might put it: his shaping of his moral composition. That does appear to have been, like his famous self-teaching, to an unusual degree his own work. He appears to have been in this regard also (to use this slightly musty phrase) something of a self-made man. "He studied with no one," he wrote of himself in the third person, in the longer of his autobiographical sketches, about his reading of the law; he might have written it about his education in general, including his moral education.

To be sure, no man is an island, and we may overstate our sense that he was something like a self-made moral man. But the immediate face-to-face influences that play upon this particular boy and young man surely do appear to have been skimpier than usual. It is striking, when one examines what Lincoln himself would write as an adult, that he does not look back in piety and gratitude to any mentors and examples from those days of his youth—not his father, not really his mother or stepmother, not the school, not the church, not any adults in Pigeon Creek or New Salem.

There was no adult in his household who would take the bright and curious boy by the hand and seat him beside her on the sofa (there was no sofa, either) and read to him, as Abigail Adams did for John Quincy, from Rollins's *Ancient History,* or teach him, as Abigail Adams also did for John Quincy, a noble patriotic poem that the son would remember all his life and be able to quote from memory, missing only one word, when he was seventy. The poetry that Abraham Lincoln could quote from memory in his adult life—of which there would be a good deal—he would have memorized altogether by himself.

In these unimaginable days up here in what Abigail Adams would have called futurity, when this Indiana lad would have become impossibly famous and celebrated and the most written-about of all his countrymen, the eager swarm of researchers and writers would be hard-pressed to learn anything solid about his mother. Both the Lincolns and the Hankses, unfortunately for researchers, kept using the same first names over and over; it is reported, to the bafflement of researchers and the amusement of a later reader, that "Abraham Lincoln's mother was one of at least eight Nancy Hankses born during the 1780s." The particular Nancy Hanks who gave birth to the particular Abraham Lincoln, however, would be consistently reported by the persons who knew her to have been amiable and of good character, with unusual intelligence, and the one from whom her remarkable son inherited more of his "disposition and mental qualities" than he got from his father. But she died when young Abraham was just nine years old; she was illiterate or nearly so; and in the documents that we have, her remarkable son wrote almost nothing about her.

His stepmother, Sarah Bush Johnston Lincoln, came into the boy's life when he was ten, after the terrible period in which his mother had died of "the milk sick" and then Thomas and Dennis Hanks* and Abraham had lived in the squalor of the dirt-floor cabin with sister Sarah, age twelve, doing what cooking was done. The stepmother who took over and cleaned things up is celebrated in the Lincoln legend as a kind of reverse of the stepmothers of children's stories. What she brought to young Abraham was not only a household remade but some appreciation of this stepson's qualities. Lincoln scholar Mark E. Neely Jr. has written: "No one in all the vast Lincoln literature has an unkind word to say about her. She apparently came to like Abraham better than her own progeny, and he apparently came to like her better than his own father." And to compound this curious criss-crossing of relationships, Thomas Lincoln seems to have come to like his stepson, John D. Johnston, better than he did his own son.

One of the best of all the interviews that William Herndon would obtain, when he set out to gather material after his great partner's assassination, was his meeting with the widow Sarah Bush Johnston Lincoln on September 8, 1865, at her farm eight miles south of Charleston, Illinois. It started out poorly, and Herndon did not think he would get much; then, as the seventy-five-year-old woman's mind warmed up, she gave him one comment after another that illuminated the life of her great stepson.

---

* Dennis Hanks's relationship to Lincoln was a complicated one; he was, according to Douglas Wilson and Rodney Davis in their *Herndon's Informants* (p. 981), "President Lincoln's cousin-once-removed, foster brother, and step-brother-in-law."

Part of what she effectively conveyed, and Herndon got in his notes, was the great love she felt for this boy and man—that they felt for each other. At one point she has to stop and wipe her eyes; her reaction to Lincoln becoming president was not pride and reflected glory but regret, because she sensed that something bad would happen.

She saw that she and he were on the same wavelength: "His mind & mine—what little I had—seemed to run together—move in the same channel." She gave one of the best of the many pictures of her stepson as a diligent reader and careful student with an excellent memory, studying and studying and studying, all on his own, until he got something straight. Although she was herself illiterate, she clearly encouraged this unusual new son. Still, Abraham's stepmother was, by her own modest admission, not equipped to be a mentor to this unusual boy. Her contribution seems to have been her recognition that he *was* unusual, and the emotional sustenance she gave him. She would be enormously important to the young boy, but more as one who provided support for the boy's own course than as one offering guidance in charting it.

If the face-to-face human surroundings of Lincoln's youth were as severely limited as he said and implied they were, where did young Lincoln's ideas of worthy life purposes come from? The first answer is the same as the answer about his education in general: he taught himself. He "picked up" (the phrase he uses twice) whatever education he had, "from time to time," "somehow." But we might give another answer, or the same answer in another way: the printing press. He was not really alone, because of all those voices that spoke to him, all the figures and ideals he read about, on the printed page.

3. TOM LINCOLN AND HIS BOY

The picture of Thomas Lincoln would vary somewhat as scholars corrected each other across the generations, as scholars do: revisions, and then revisions of the revisions. Some early biographers, rooted in the East, knowing and celebrating Lincoln as the great martyred president, would treat the illiterate or semiliterate farmer-hunter back there in the western woods with disdain, as a shiftless vagrant. Perhaps in addition to whatever there was of snobbery there was also the hidden impetus that making the father a bum lent added distinction to the son's rise from so low a beginning.

Later scholars would repair, somewhat, Thomas Lincoln's reputation. I think we can now say that Thomas Lincoln was not "shiftless" or a "vagrant" and certainly not "poor white trash," as some early biographies with geographical prejudices or ideological purposes suggested. Thomas Lincoln was not Pap Finn. He did not abandon his family or abuse them. He did not deserve to have every mention of his name accompanied by some derogatory comment, as is the case in Albert Beveridge's influential biography. He did take the initiative to bring his family through two long and complicated moves, the second involving an entourage of thirteen people. He did take the initiative to return to Kentucky to find a woman he had known, Sarah Johnston, to be a wife and mother to his children. One has sympathy for him when, in the fall of 1818, he has to make a long series of pine coffins for folk who have died of the milk sick, including his wife's cousins the Sparrows and finally his wife herself, Abraham's mother. Herndon's interviews with folk who knew Thomas Lincoln present a more favorable picture than some biographies do, although perhaps not with respect to the same traits: Thomas Lincoln was said to be, in addition to being physically strong and a talented storyteller, "good-humored," "lively and cheerful," a man of "moral habits." Nancy's cousin John Hanks made a comment that seems to sum up Thomas Lincoln: "Happiness was the end of life for him."

But he had a son for whom happiness was not the end of life—not "happiness" in Tom Lincoln's sense. That was his problem and his fate. What happened to poor Tom Lincoln was that, somehow, he had the bad luck to have this impossibly bright and strong-willed son. Had that not happened, his deficiencies, such as they may have been, would not have been spread across the pages of a thousand books for all the world to read. He appears to have been a limited man, not a bad man. But clearly there was a mismatch between father and son.

Abraham Lincoln, discovering intellectual abilities in himself and discovering books, came to value education, intellectual development, exceedingly highly—and it is difficult for any of us to value something highly, and strive for it mightily, and not then to be disdainful of those, perhaps especially those who are close to us, who seem not to value it at all.

The critic of Thomas Lincoln who is most convincing, partly by what he does not say and do, is Abraham, his son. He may have been unfair to his father, as ambitious and able sons sometimes are to not very talented and not very successful fathers, but his lack of filial piety is striking. If you are looking for some fault in Abraham Lincoln to offset his too consistent goodness, I suppose you might name his insufficient obedience to the commandment to honor his father.

In both autobiographical sketches Abraham noted his father's lack of education—and that was almost all that he said of him. In the shorter sketch he wrote: "My father, at the death of his father, was but six years of age; and he grew up, litterally without education." He then repeated that phrase about his father, word for word with the same misspelling, "and grew litterally without education," in the longer autobiographical piece he wrote about six months later. In both autobiographical pieces there may be a slight touch of sympathy with the early plight of his father, who "by the early death of his father, and the narrow circumstances of his mother," suddenly became "even in childhood . . . a wandering laboring boy." (But does the word "even" imply that Tom was still a wandering laboring boy when he was grown and the father of Abraham?)

By contrast, Abraham's devotion, so far as we know, to his "angel mother" and, as we certainly do know, to his stepmother was warm and strong. One may infer that there was a certain family drama playing itself out there in the Indiana woods, centering around this boy's insistence on reading and on making something of himself beyond what he saw in his family and the village, and his limited father's inability to comprehend that.

There is another, adult chapter to the story of his relationship to his father. For the twenty years after he left home, as he was rising in the world, Abraham would only very rarely go to see his father, who had moved to Coles County. Abraham's wife, Mary Todd, would never meet her father-in-law, and their sons would never meet their grandfather Lincoln.

Recent scholars have made a point of the adult Abraham's cool treatment of the old man. The most damning evidence in these scholars' eyes is the forty-one-year-old Abraham's response to requests by his stepbrother John Johnston that he come to see his father in what would prove to be Thomas's last illness in January 1851. John Y. Simon pungently summarizes the criticism of Lincoln's performance on this occasion: "Lincoln did not immediately answer two letters from Johnston about the impending death of his father; he offered two weak excuses for not visiting the dying man and wondered whether a visit 'would not be more painful than pleasant'; and he urged his father to call upon God, 'who will not turn away from him in any extremity' rather than his son, who did turn away." Lincoln's most recent and most excellent biographer, David Herbert

Donald, produced two devastating sentences about Abraham's appraisal of his father. At the end of a section on the relationship of father and son, Donald wrote: "In all of his published writings, and, indeed, even in reports of hundreds of stories and conversations, he had not one favorable word to say about his father." And as the last sentence of the chapter on Abraham's boyhood Donald wrote: "He did not yet know who he was, or where he was heading, but was sure he did not want to be another Thomas Lincoln."

4. THE AWKWARD AGE OF GOODNESS

The twentieth-century American playwright and novelist Thornton Wilder took a sentence from one of his own novels, *The Woman of Andros*, and used it as an epigraph for another of his novels, called *Heaven's My Destination*. This second novel is the affectionately told comic story of a middle-western Protestant American good boy—the sort of fellow who will write in the margins of an encyclopedia article about Napoleon, "I am a great man, too, but for *good*." The epigraph quoted from the other book—Wilder quoting himself—is this: "Of all the forms of genius, goodness has the longest awkward age."

Abraham Lincoln was in most ways quite different from Wilder's rather innocent and bumbling fictional hero, who keeps getting into scrapes because he doesn't recognize or measure the evil in the world or the distorting egotism in himself. Young Lincoln did not have either of those problems. Lincoln would prove to be a good man, but he was not a *naive* good man. Yet he was like Wilder's character, and he does illustrate that epigraph, at least in this: that his goodness, his moral worth, though it would prove to be extraordinary and in the end triumphant, would be for a certain time a work in progress.

We know that this gangling, ill-clad Indiana teenager would be generous, kind, sensitive to suffering, honest to the point that would one day be famous. His stepmother, Sarah Bush Johnston Lincoln, in that Herndon interview, gave one of the most impressive of the testimonies to young Abraham's conduct: "I can say what scarcely one woman—a mother—can say in a thousand and it is this—Abe never gave me a cross word or look and never refused in fact, or even in appearance, to do anything I requested him. I never gave him a cross word in all my life. He was kind to everybody and to everything . . ." We have seen that he had the moral backbone to chide his schoolmates when he was ten for cruelty to terrapins, to stop his company when he was twenty-three from killing an old Indian. We know that students of his life have found his reputation as "Honest Abe" largely deserved. And this young man had in him, we will find, not only particular admirable qualities, but also a more general defining intention to make his life accord with a moral ideal. So he was in some original, essential way a good boy.

But now let us notice another cluster of characteristics, also admirable—but at the same time morally precarious.

He acquired, from the implicit comparison with his father, his teachers, his peers, the illiterate adults in those Pigeon Creek cabins, a powerful awareness of his clear-cut intellectual superiority. There was no one in the schools he attended, including the schoolmaster, who was his match. As we have not found a moral mentor in his immediate world, so I believe we will not find anyone whom he will have to acknowledge as his intellectual equal or superior. Although as an adult he would go out of his way to deprecate his education, and to give off sounds of modesty or humility, was he in truth so humble about his intellectual powers?

Students of Lincoln may remember, with respect to the role of his mother, that he is reported once to have said, "All that I am or ever hope to be I owe to her." But what he meant, one judges from the context, was not her teaching or her moral instruction or even primarily her example but her *genes,* and that by a kind of default. As Herndon tells the story, he and Lincoln were riding in a buggy one day, perhaps in 1850, on their way to the courthouse in Menard County, to try a case that dealt with inherited characteristics. Lincoln, who was usually shut-mouthed about such topics, told Herndon that his mother had been the "bastard" child of a Virginia gentleman. Interpreters generally have been distracted by the issue of Nancy Hanks's legitimacy. But there is another significance to Lincoln's comments to Herndon. To be sure, the comment about his debt to his mother does mean that he found worthy qualities in her (and by implication not in his father). But, given the subject at hand, we may infer that Lincoln also was trying to explain where his own intellectual abilities came from. In the version of the story that Herndon put into his biography Lincoln even specifies the abilities he has observed in himself: "his power of analysis, his logic, his mental activity, and all the qualities that distinguished him from the other members and descendants of the Hanks family." He could have added, as is attested by many others, his remarkable memory. He discovers in himself intellectual abilities that are not evident in his relatives among the Hankses or in Tom Lincoln.

Or, apparently, in anyone else in Pigeon Creek. He does not find, as an intelligent youngster might in a more elaborated environment, other persons whose abilities would temper his intellectual self-confidence. His sense of his powers, no matter how many times he uses the word "humble" about himself, becomes quite impressive. There will be little glimpses throughout his career of his solid intellectual self-confidence at least, and sometimes a little more than confidence. William Greene, Lincoln's helper in Denton Offutt's store and lifelong friend, told Herndon in 1860 that after studying and learning grammar in just three weeks, Lincoln had said to him, cockily, "Bill, if that is what they call a science I'll subdue another."

We may read back into his youth the beginning of a quality that John Hay would observe all the way up in his presidency, and describe in a quotation that is often cited: "[Lincoln's] intellectual self-confidence was galling to vastly better educated men, learned men, like Sumner and Chase: It would be absurd to call him a modest man. No great man is ever modest. It was his intellectual arrogance and unconscious assumption of superiority that men like Chase and Sumner could never forgive."

In addition to discovering his mental powers and acquiring a powerful confidence in them, the young Lincoln was also developing his strength of will—his resolution, the gem of his character indeed. Among its other roles, that strong will would hold him to the tasks of developing those intellectual abilities. Not every person in young Lincoln's situation, no matter how smart, would have had the strength of purpose to carry out that remarkable series of self-initiated projects of self-education that started with virtually teaching himself to read and then proceeding to read "everything he could get his hands on" throughout a wide radius from Pigeon Creek.*

Out of the potent stew of these ingredients there was brewed within him an intense drive to make his name mean something in the world—a "thirst for distinction." Lincoln is consistently said to have been "ambitious." There is, in fact, a quotation from Herndon that has become a cliché, about

* At some point the Lincoln legend would get carried away and claim that young Abe had read every book he could find in a circuit of fifty miles. Lincoln scholar, and knowledgeable Hoosier, Louis Warren knew too much about the actual territory, and also about what fifty miles meant when the only transportation was by horse, to let that pass. He wrote in evident contradiction that within a fifty-mile circuit from Pigeon Creek "were the Indiana towns of Boonville, Corydon, Evansville, New Harmony, Princeton, Rockport, Troy, and Vincennes, and across the Ohio in Kentucky, still within fifty miles, were Brandenburg, Cal-

Lincoln's ambition being "a little engine that knew no rest." When you read a steady diet of Lincoln interpretations and you see on the page the word "ambition," you say to yourself, Here comes that engine again, and sure enough, the quotation from Herndon comes chugging along soon thereafter.

But there are many different expressions of "ambition," many meanings of the word, and a wide variation in its moral significance, from virtue to vice, from praiseworthy energy, persistence, resolution, and discipline, over to blameworthy selfishness, main-chance seeking, hostile rivalry, corner-cutting, self-promotion, killing Duncan while he sleeps in your own house as your guest (at your wife's prompting) in order that you may succeed to his throne. What we mean by the word "ambition" is morally ambiguous.

At issue in that ambiguity are not only the methods we allow ourselves to use to achieve the glory we seek, but also the larger ends, beyond ourselves, that our glory may serve or damage: whether one with "ambition sufficient to push it to the utmost stretch" (as a twenty-eight-year-old Illinois lecturer will put it) seeks glory by "emancipating slaves or enslaving free men."

Lincoln's intense desire that he leave a scar upon the earth with his name attached would be one source of his greatness. But it would also be— Lincoln being human—a root of deeds that may not be so worthy of praise. It would not have been, in the early years, quite clear what the result of his yearning for distinction would be.

We are dealing now with a range of moral life more complex than the attributes listed in the Boy Scout oath, or Benjamin Franklin's amusing chart of virtues he wanted to check off one by one. Here we have characteristics lined with moral ambiguity, or with mixed and divergent possibility. Had Lincoln been simply an honest, kindly, modest, "humble" person (he kept saying he was humble, but was he?) who always told the truth and took great trouble to return your pennies and helped you home when you were drunk in the snow, but who out of his humility never put himself forward or sought preference or argued against you or tried to organize to get votes to beat you—then he would have been another solid, worthy, but unremembered citizen of the American West. And the moral loss to the world would have been immense.

---

houn, Cloverport, Hardinsburg, Hartford, Hawesville, Henderson, and Owensboro" (Warren, *Lincoln's Youth: Indiana Years*, p. 164).

But at the same time, that eager seeking of personal distinction and display of his powers was the source of a little fringe of mildly unworthy, "un-Lincolnian" episodes surrounding Lincoln's worthy life in its early stages. Out of the cocky exuberance of his verbal facility and satirical inclination, he wrote and said things that wounded. Recent scholars have been patiently exhuming examples.

One early example is well known and did not need any exhuming. In Indiana when he was barely out of his teens Lincoln wrote a pseudo-scriptural satire, mocking and getting even with the neighboring clan of Grigsbys,* that he called "The Chronicles of Reuben"; those who have tried to read it have called this production "scurrilous" (David Herbert Donald); "rude and coarse" (Herndon); "some bawdy doggerel" (Richard Luthin); and "out of [the] local Indiana context . . . so topical as to be neither funny nor comprehensible" (Robert Bray). Later, as a young lawyer, he would write wounding anonymous articles, and as a young politician on the stump, make wounding speeches, including a famous "skinning" of an opponent.

He would show that overreaching yearning for distinction in rather a different way when as a young professional making addresses to Springfield audiences he would, rounding into the home stretch, indulge in the most overwrought prose, and on one occasion pictured himself as the brave, last, lonely defender of freedom. When the still rather young Lincoln would first appear on the national political stage, as a new congressman, the lone Whig congressman from Illinois, in the Thirtieth Congress in December of 1847, he would try too hard, too fast, to make his name ring from the rafters. His attack on President Polk's justification for the Mexican War would be surprisingly personal and sarcastic.

This thirst for personal distinction was by no means absent when, in 1854, he would rise to a new moral level and challenge the great senator Stephen Douglas on the spread of slavery. Mixed with his genuine moral revulsion at the prospect of the spread and legitimation of slavery surely there was also an ingredient of opportunism: this time his old rival Douglas had overreached and become vulnerable. Lincoln's admirer William Herndon even spoke of Douglas's "downfall"—a potential downfall at the hands of Herndon's ambitious law partner.

Why did this Great Emancipator not oppose the Fugitive Slave Law of

---

* His sister, Sarah, had married a Grigsby, and Lincoln appears to have blamed them for some neglect in her early death.

1850? Why in those debates with Douglas did he explicitly disavow any intent to bring about the social and political equality of the races? Why did he never protest the harsh black codes of Illinois, in force all the years he lived there? Why did he specifically say he did not support Negro suffrage in Illinois? The answer to such questions surely includes not only that he did not want to damage his party's prospects in Illinois, but also that he did not want to destroy his own political future. He wanted to be congressman; he badly wanted to be senator; and although he did not start perceiving the possibility of being president until late in the day, the time would come when he would admit about that ambition, too, that "the taste is in my mouth a little."

5. A NAME THAT FILLS ALL THE NATION AND IS NOT UNKNOWN EVEN IN FOREIGN LANDS

It is certainly not unusual for exceptionally able persons when young to dream of magnificent world-encircling personal triumphs that will make their names ring down the ages.

Young Lincoln would write his own name in the firm clear hand the world will come to know. He writes his name, let us guess, as a million youngsters have done, over and over, partly as practice in penmanship and signature-signing, partly as reinforcement of his identity, partly in the self-indulgent fancy that that name will someday ring bells. He writes his name in his copybook, with some familiar schoolbook doggerel of the sort that pupils in all ages seem to pass on from one generation to the next:

> *Abraham Lincoln*
> *his hand and pen*
> *He will be good*
> *But God knows when*

We may surmise that there would be hovering over this repeated name-writing the fantasy that that name would somehow echo around the world. If one so easily outstrips one's fellow scholars, even those older than oneself, and outstrips Andrew Crawford, the teacher, in the little school in Pigeon Creek—why not then also in Boonville, Corydon, Evansville, New Harmony, Princeton, Rockport, Troy, and Vincennes, and across the Ohio in Brandenburg, Calhoun, Cloverport, Hardinsburg . . . Why not even in the vast world beyond?

Think of the context of comparison of his learning to write, when he was a young Indiana teenager. His angel mother, wonderful though she may have been in other ways, had signed her name with an X. His step-mother, wonderful though she certainly was in other ways, could not sign her name, either.

After Abraham wrote, in the longer of his autobiographical sketches, that his father grew up without any education, he would add this sentence: "He never did more in the way of writing than to bunglingly sign his own name."

In the first place, why add that sentence? He has already said his father was completely uneducated.

In the second place, why add that devastating adverb "bunglingly"? From a writer's point of view that word is quite effective. It certainly evokes the picture—if that is the picture you want to evoke. But why evoke that picture? Is there not in that word "bunglingly" more than the hint of a sneer?

Maybe not: you insist that Abraham Lincoln does *not* sneer. The fact that he came up with that word, however, does suggest a picture. There is the unusually bright and exceedingly diligent and ambitious young son, who would virtually teach himself to read and to write, who would practice his penmanship until he had a clear hand and while still a teenager could write documents for illiterate adults, and who would practice and practice, writing and writing, along with much else, his own name. And there is the father, while the son watched, trying to get his wavering hand to form the unfamiliar magic markings that make the letters that made his name. Bunglingly.

Young Lincoln, whose sturdy signature even in his youth is not bungling, imagines his name being known far beyond the world of Tom Lincoln.

An able youngster's private imaginings often do take the form of the hope that all the world will have cause to remember his name—and the fear that it won't, that his name will be, as another ambitious young man, John Keats, would put it, "writ on water." Keats had fears that he would "cease to be" before his pen had "gleaned his teeming brain." Young Lincoln feared that he would cease to be before he brought off any great public accomplishment that would make his name known, in the way that those names in the books he was reading were then known. In his despondent state over his dealings with Mary Todd in March of 1841 he told Joshua Speed that he was willing to die—except for this one deterrent, that "he had done nothing to make any human being remember that he had lived."

This incident was vivid enough for Lincoln as president to recall it to Speed when he signed the Emancipation Proclamation: now he had done something to make the world remember his name. It was vivid enough for Speed, then, to tell Herndon in 1866 that Lincoln had had the desire "to connect his name with the events transpiring in his day & generation" and hoped that he would "so impress himself upon [those events] as to link his name with something that would redound to the interest of his fellow man. . . ."

After his enlargement of his purpose in 1854, even though the stakes were higher and the conflict fiercer, Lincoln would become not less but more disciplined in his generosity and would begin to tie his ambition to a larger end. Nevertheless, at some moment in the middle of the 1850s, he would produce, as we will see, one last little clear-cut evidence of his own share in the egotism of humankind: a private jotting enviously comparing his own unknown failing self to the splendid success of Stephen Douglas, whose name "fills the nation and is not unknown even in foreign lands."

But why should it be expected that one's name should "fill the nation"? Where is the necessity (beforehand, as it were) that Abraham Lincoln's name, or Stephen Douglas's name, or John Keats's name, should be written not on water but on stone, to be read "to the last generation," as Lincoln might say? The names of the great bulk of mankind, presumably including some with as great ability, and even as great merit, as Lincoln (or Douglas or Keats), while usually not exactly written on water— remembered in some circle of kinship and acquaintance—cannot, by the sheer finitude of human memory and the capriciousness of history, be known to the great world public. The knowledge and memory of humankind is necessarily severely limited. "History" and fate are volatile and fickle. The race is not to the swift, nor the battle to the strong, neither yet bread to the wise, nor yet riches to men of understanding, but time and chance happeneth to them all.

And, as that poem that Abraham Lincoln clipped from a newspaper and kept quoting would put it: "Oh why should the spirit of mortal be proud?"

We know what would happen to this particular mortal with his pride. That name he had written in his copybook would become known to an extent beyond his gaudiest youthful imagining, far beyond that of Douglas, not only in his own country but "even in foreign lands."

But by the time Lincoln's name would become so widely known, his personal ambition would have been swallowed up in the events for his nation "of highest consequence," as Roger Williams used to say. And Lincoln's moral capacities would rise to match the profound seriousness of the events with which it fell to him to deal.

It certainly could have been otherwise. Edgar Lee Masters, the Illinois poet of the next century, who would in some dyspeptic moment write a surprisingly crabbed and hostile book about Lincoln, would, in his better moments, creating his Spoon River characters, have one of them warn against "the man who rises to power from one suspender." Lincoln could have been like that—an arrogant and disdainful man to be warned against, because he rose to power from a one-room dirt-floor cabin. I made my way upward, without any help—so why can't you? And Lord Acton notoriously said that power tends to corrupt. Lincoln could have been an epitome of that famous warning, for in that unimaginable day in the long future he would not only be the top executive of his nation but a war president, who would hold in his hand power far beyond that of any previous president.

Put those two together and you could have had a moral monster: an ambitious man, arrogant because he had made his way, as others had not, from darkest obscurity to the supreme position, and ruthless because on reaching that position he could exercise the war power of an increasingly mighty nation in a terrible civil war. He could have become, as indeed he was to be called at the last awful moment when he was shot, a "tyrant."

CHAPTER FOUR

I Want in All Cases to Do Right

1. HUMOR IN HIS COMPOSITION

You might think that in the rough-and-tumble of newly formed settlements in pioneer America, a young lad who read books while he plowed and read books while he tended store and even read books while he was walking on the street, and who would not hunt and would not drink and would not gamble or swear, and who didn't like farming or manual labor, and who told you not to put hot coals on the backs of turtles, would be something less than popular, in fact a miserable and lonely outcast. But young Abraham Lincoln definitely was not that at all—indeed, the opposite.

Among the reasons Lincoln was not only accepted but well liked were two that we may infer he inherited from his father, and perhaps should have been more grateful for than he appears to have been: first, his physical strength and athletic ability, and second, his storytelling, joking, and amiability.

If Lincoln had been a hundred-pound weakling he would probably have been in trouble in the externalized masculine worlds in which he spent his youth, and if he had also been a physical coward then life surely would have been quite different than it was, both then and later. But, like his father, he was physically strong. Thomas Lincoln, shorter and stockier than his son ("square built"), was "a larger man of great muscular power," "a stout athletic man, 5 feet 10 inches high and weighed when in the prime of life 196 lbs," who easily won the only fight he is known to have had "without receiving a scratch"; "a strong brave man." His son, Abraham—although, as we have said, a peacemaker and not one to seek confrontation—nevertheless in the fights and wrestling matches in which he was engaged acquitted himself well.

Although Abraham was not a fighter, he could lick you if you did fight; "I think it safe to say he was never thrown in a wrestle," said one of Herndon's witnesses. He could perform other feats of strength and excel at other physical contests. When he was a captain in the militia it was said, "The genial Captain jumped, ran, boxed, and wrestled better than any man in the expedition." Albert Beveridge, reading through the stories of Lincoln's physical feats, wrote that "Lincoln had great physical strength, so great that tales of his performances are well-nigh unbelievable"; Abraham's sinking an ax in a tree deeper than anyone else, and lifting huge loads, were among the tales. In his adult career this physical superiority would only rarely come into play—as when he would impress Union soldiers by holding an ax extended straight out at arm's length, which none of the much younger soldiers could do. In his youth, however, that capacity must have been of great importance to his acceptance and reputation and to his self-confidence.

Again—had Mr. Lincoln been shy, reserved, dull, and laconic, his place in Pigeon Creek and New Salem would have been quite different than it was. But once again we infer that he had a gift—his storytelling, inherited in some part from his father, which helped to give him popularity. The descriptions of Thomas by those who knew him repeatedly emphasize this trait or activity: Dennis Hanks even told Herndon that "Thomas Lincoln the father of Abraham could beat his son telling a story—cracking a joke." The testimonies to Abraham's talents in that line stretch out on all sides, and were already in place when he was young. Telling stories was only part of it; he was also "sociable," "companionable," "amiable," "gregarious"; he "liked lively, jovial company, where there was plenty of fun and no drunkenness." "Abe was a cheerful boy—a witty boy—was humorous always." "He made fun and cracked his jokes making all happy but the jokes were few and at no mans expense." "He was the most entertaining person I ever knew." "The more I became acquainted with him the more humorous I found him to be." "The open frank manner of Mr. Lincoln in his youthful days coupled with a flow of good humor and great witticism, always made him a welcome member of any group." Beveridge wrote, about the Indiana years: "It cannot be too often stated that cheerful friendliness was the most striking feature of his personality—so striking, that it is noted with emphasis in all accounts given by acquaintances and observers of Abraham Lincoln in those days."

We may surmise that Abraham surpassed his father in the continuing flow of wit and humor that goes beyond joke telling and requires a humorous imagination. Abraham Lincoln, young and old, was more than a teller of jokes, although he certainly was that. He had also a droll and witty ingredient in his daily interaction with his fellow human beings and in his reactions to the events of the day that gave flavor to his whole personality.

There are persons who learn to tell memorized jokes as social strategy, who are nevertheless not humorous to their core. Although Lincoln would insist he was only a retail dealer in the anecdotes he told, it is easy enough to see from the record we have that that metaphor does not cover the subject. However many jokes he remembered and retold from someone else's telling, he was certainly the manufacturer and wholesale dealer in the colorfully amusing remarks and imaginative figures that are sprinkled throughout his letters and speeches and the reports of his conversation. "When he first came among us his wit and humor boiled over," said James Matheny of his coming to Springfield. "There was a good deal of humor in his composition," said Dr. Jason Duncan of New Salem. That is the point I want to underscore: the "humor in his composition."

And as to his telling set-piece jokes, he was the retail dealer who would know just the right story to make his point, which is certainly a creative act in its own right. Somebody else may have first told the story of Paddy, the Irish teetotaler who never took a drop of liquor but who wouldn't mind if somebody else put a little of the critter into his drink, "unbeknownst to meself," but it was Lincoln who—at least twice—made perfectly apt use of that story in high politics. Somebody else invented the joke-book story of the spectacularly misplaced neutrality of the wife who came out of the frontier cabin to see her husband fighting a bear and shouted, in grandly impartial encouragement, "Go it, husband! Go it, bear!" but it was Lincoln who would tell that story in contexts with a perfect application. Whether it was his or not, Lincoln joyfully told the story of the undaring young soldier going off to war, whose sweetheart made him a sash to wear into battle bearing the brave motto "Liberty or Death"; the cautious soldier boy asked whether it might be amended to read "Liberty or Badly Wounded."* Lincoln not only remembered and told a great storehouse of anecdotes and jokes and stories; he told them with great storytelling talent. As Joshua Speed would tell Herndon (as Herndon already knew), "His world-wide reputation for telling anecdotes—and telling them so well—was in my judgment necessary to his existence."

* A variant—perhaps a better version—had it "Liberty or Hurt Pretty Bad."

Jason Duncan said of Lincoln's humorous exchanges with Justice of the Peace Bowling Green in New Salem not only that young Lincoln had a fund of anecdotes, and that "the occasion of his rehearsal [of these anecdotes] was always timely," but also that "many were the laconic remarks made by the gentlemen [Green and Lincoln] to the amusement of any neighbor or friend who might happen to be present." There is a scene: the poor and ill-dressed youth of twenty-two carrying on a joshing exchange with the justice of the peace, to everyone's amusement. The young man who has these talents and characteristics at the core of his being is not going to be rejected but rather affirmed and sought out.

Abner Y. Ellis asked, and then answered, our question: "Salem in those days was a hard place for a temperate young man like Mr. Lincoln, and I have often wondered how he could be so extremely popular and not drink and carouse with them." Ellis continued: "He used to run footraces and jump with the boys and also play ball.... He was great at telling stories and anecdotes and I think that was one great reason of his being so popular...." In addition, his distinction of mind and of will were esteemed already by the young company of Pigeon Creek and New Salem. When one reads through the interviews and letters that Herndon gathered after his partner's death—for example, from his stepsister Matilda Johnston, from Anna Gentry, from Nathaniel Grigsby—one comes to see young Lincoln as already much respected, and in fact a leader.

We have noted that the motley collection of young volunteers from the frontier state in the spring of 1832 elected Lincoln as their captain. And the testimonies about him are strong: "All the men in the Company—as well as the Regiment to which he & they belonged loved him well—almost worshipped him" (Henry McHenry); "His Men idolized him" (William Greene). Benjamin Irwin gave this report: "Wm Miller who Belonged to another Company says that Lincolns Company was the hardest set of men he ever saw and no man but Lincoln Could do anything with them and that Lincoln was their Idol and there was not a Man but what was obedient to every word he spoke and would fight his death for Lincoln."

All of this in spite of his opposing them, offering to fight them if they disagreed, in the matter of the old Indian.

2. NOT A REBEL, NOT A REVOLUTIONARY

You might think that however fully a young man may have been accepted and liked by those around him, if he disengaged from as many activities and attitudes as Lincoln did he would be, in his own mind and heart, a thoroughgoing opponent of his social world. But Lincoln was not that at all, either; he lived in and affirmed the world in which he found himself.

He was not a "rebel." He was not "alienated" from the world in which he found himself. He was not engaged in a clenched-fist "protest" against it. He was not a "revolutionary" intending to overthrow it. He was not a lonely "prophet," like Amos, issuing a sweeping condemnation of it. He was not even (more in keeping with early-nineteenth-century American possibilities than these terms from other times and places) a "reformer" wanting to reform it. His disengagements, it seems to me, were particular and personal, not systematic and ideological. He was not making any general judgments against the world he was living in. He was not condemning, as the young German revolutionary Karl Marx would do in his manifesto while Lincoln was in Congress, the "idiocy of rural life"; he was simply saying that he himself did not want to farm. He was not making any of these disengagements as part of a group or movement. (The Whig Party was no movement of protest.) He was not part of a self-conscious "happy few," congratulating itself on its moral superiority to the mass of lesser beings. He was not withdrawing to a pond, a monastery, a commune, or a revolutionary cell in order to keep himself pure from the contaminations of the world or to preserve the flame of radical ideas. What these rejections or disengagements that I have grouped together show, as it seems to me, is that he came to know, and to trust, and to act upon, the judgments of his own mind. This was a developing young thinker, appraising life pretty much on his own, who in his first two major public addresses, given when he was twenty-eight and thirty-two, would appeal, with extraordinary emphasis, to "reason, cold, calculating, unimpassioned reason," and to "mind, all conquering mind."

He did not construct or adopt any general theory condemning the world in which he found himself. He was not an ideologue. Or, if he was, he was devoted to an "American" idealism by which his world was imbued, and not any opponent or alternative. He was subjecting each aspect of his life and experience—independently, one might say—to the criticism of moral reasoning (or, sometimes, just personal preference). Lincoln was engaged not in the overthrowing of society—far from it—but in the criticism and appraisal of particulars within a society, on the basis of its own professed principles.

Or its own professed principles taken more seriously than most people took them.

3. THE GEM OF HIS CHARACTER

He certainly does appear to have taken seriously the ostensible principles of his world about courtship and marriage. Perhaps in this domain
he did lack self-confidence.

Let us guess that his appearing to be, in Indiana, "not very fond of
girls" (his stepmother), or one who "didn't love the Company of girls"
(Dennis Hanks), or one who "did not go much with the girls" (Anna
Gentry) was the result of a compound of shyness and that lack of self-
confidence with his conscientiousness. Anna Gentry said he thought them
"too frivalous"—or perhaps that was in part a rationalization. He was an
awkward teenager, a boy who had lost his mother when he was nine, who
had abruptly shot up in height in his early teens, who had already the long
arms, coarse black hair, and swarthy complexion that would cause more
than one hostile critic, looking in his later political years for a stinging epithet, to call him a "gorilla." Lincoln's looks, as we have seen, regularly provoked the adjective "gawky," and throughout his life he would describe
himself as homely.

Let us guess that young Lincoln was shy, and lacking confidence in his
appeal to girls and in what we today would describe by the unfortunate
term "social skills." There are reports that his stepbrother, John Johnston, was one of those who upstaged and outshone him in that department. John Y. Simon makes what seems to me the plausible inference that
young Lincoln's apparent lack of interest in girls may simply have been his
"making the best of circumstances." Usually articulate, he had trouble talking in the company of eligible women, and made rather a point of becoming friends, as he moved out on his own in New Salem, with older, married
women—a domain of safety.

When he lived in New Salem as a bachelor in his early twenties, by the
testimony of his companions, he did not, as Henry McHenry put it, "fool
nor seduce Women." Or as William Greene put it, in response to a Herndon interrogatory: "Mr Lincoln while he lived in New Salem was entirely
free from the vices mentioned in your 3rd Interrogatory viz . . . running
after Women."

As to his life after he moved to Springfield, David Davis, the future
judge and Lincoln political operative, specifically testified to Lincoln's
conscientious restraint: "Lincoln was a Man of strong passion for
women—his Conscience Kept him from seduction—this saved many—
many a woman." Herndon quoted with relish that statement from Davis

and added his own confirmation, again with dramatic emphasis on Lincoln's passion on the one side and principled restraint on the other: "Lincoln had terribly strong passions for women, could hardly keep his hands off of them. And yet he had honor and a strong will, and these enabled him to put out the fires of his terrible passions. . . . I have seen Lincoln tempted, and I have seen him reject the approach of woman."

Lincoln's actual "courting" seems to have been rather a botch. We do not really know much about his romance with Ann Rutledge and so we can attribute to that connection all the perfection we want to. But in his romantic dealings that we do know more about, there was clumsiness mixed with conscientiousness. In his dealings with Mary Owens he famously showed himself to be "deficient in those little links which make up the great chain of a woman's happiness." Lincoln's maladroit dealings do seem to include, along with the other elements, a considerable effort to conduct himself in a worthy manner toward her, as toward women in general. In one of the climactic letters to her, dated August 16, 1837, Lincoln said explicitly: "I want in all cases to do right, and most particularly so, in all cases with women. I want, at this particular time, more than any thing else, to do right with you."

It is not clear that Lincoln *did* "do right," exactly. Certainly it was not commendable of him, after she had rejected him, to comment adversely on Mary Owens's weight while recounting the episode in a letter to an older woman confidante. "A fair match for Falstaff"—not a gallant remark.

When one reads in Douglas Wilson's carefully wrought, illuminating book *Honor's Voice*, on "the Transformation of Abraham Lincoln," about his difficult decision to marry Mary Todd, as he and she believed he had promised to do, one is impressed by Lincoln's own explicitly exacting moral standards for himself. As Wilson presents Lincoln's quandary, it is a contest between his *resolution*—his ability to stay the course once a decision was made (the decision in this case being *not* to marry Mary Todd)—and his *honor* (his being bound by his promise to marry her, as she expected).

He had decided, after encountering and perhaps even falling in love with the beautiful eighteen-year-old Matilda Edwards,* that he did not

---

* The Edwardses are almost as difficult to keep straight as the Hankses. There was a territorial governor named Ninian Edwards. He had a brother, Cyrus Edwards, a Whig politician from Alton, and a son also named Ninian—Ninian W.—who married Elizabeth Todd and thus become Mary Todd's brother-in-law. Matilda Edwards was the "strikingly beautiful eighteen-year-old daughter" of Cyrus Edwards, and was thus Ninian W. Edwards's cousin. Cyrus as well as Ninian W. will figure in the story later. (Douglas Wilson has carefully worked out the Lincoln–Matilda Edwards story in *Honor's Voice*.)

love Mary, and did not want to marry her, and had therefore resolved that he wouldn't, so this alternative came under the moral heading of resolution, and that was no minor matter to this young man shaping himself. He refers in a letter to Joshua Speed to an already formulated central virtue—the "gem" of his character: "[B]efore I resolve to do the one thing or the other, I must regain my confidence in my own ability to keep my resolves when they are made. In that ability, you know, I once prided myself as the only, or at least the chief, gem of my character; that gem I lost—how, and when, you too well know. I have not yet regained it; and until I do, I can not trust myself in any matter of much importance."

This "gem of my character," a self-conscious central moral attribute, has already, apparently, been discussed with Speed. And Lincoln's resolution—his "ability to keep my resolves when they are made"—will, indeed, prove to be one of his central virtues, up in that unimaginable day when he becomes president of the United States; he will manage to make the difficult combination of resolution with charity in a quite distinctive way. Now, however, as a young man stewing about his engagement, he does suggest that long awkward age of goodness, perhaps with the word "awkward" underlined.

Many bridegrooms, either in nineteenth-century Illinois or in the contemporary world, are beset on the eve of their marriages by an attack of the doubts—but do they characteristically cast them in such exclusively *moral* categories as Lincoln did? He manages, as I interpret the way Wilson tells the story, to get *both* sides of his dilemma cast in the highest and strictest moral terms.

No doubt the qualms of many marriage eves feature, along with more mundane and self-oriented considerations, some such moral ingredient—about high duty, solemn promises, strict obligations—but one would think that, even back then, in most cases there would also be a "consequentialist" element, as the moralists now call it, a utilitarian or calculating element that asks how this marriage will turn out. And one would expect that this calculating would include an altruistic but hedonistic element: Will this conduce to her happiness? And then one would think it would include, to get down to brass tacks, a selfish consideration: Is this going to make *me* happy?

But young Lincoln, this unusually scrupulous fellow, is apparently a long way from all that. He managed—as Wilson presents it—to get not just one but *both* sides of his dilemma cast in terms of sheer Kantian duty, or something very like it: the potential betrayal of a character-defining virtue on the one side; a solemn promise, by which he is honor-bound, on the other. The "gem of his character," his resolution, on the one side; his "honor," his promise to Mary, on the other.

As to his later life, Herndon did insist that Lincoln, "a man of terribly strong passions," was nevertheless "true as steel to his wife during his whole married life."

4. BE EMULOUS TO EXCEL

Young Lincoln, self-confident with books and argument if not with girls, could find in those pedagogical books that were available to him an explicit and unembarrassed didactic purpose, and not only with reference to "elocution" and style and "reading" but also with respect to the conduct of life.

One section in that William Scott collection of "elocution" readings is explicitly labeled "moral lessons" and, in the old-fashioned way, includes fables that teach improving principles of hard work, sacrifice, and the like. Many of the literary selections are chosen, evidently, for their service in moral improvement—but from writers of distinction, which may rescue them from banality.

Some of the readings have a particular resonance when one thinks of young Lincoln reading them. One of the "select sentences" might be a text for the present chapter: "Men commonly owe their virtue or their vice, to education as much as to nature." The following "select sentence" might almost be the text for the address Lincoln would give to the Temperance Society when he was thirty-two: "It is idle as well as absurd to impose our opinions upon others. The same ground of conviction operates differently on the same man in different circumstances, and on different men in the same circumstances." Lincoln would learn a moral realism, like that reflected in the sentence, that would qualify any simple moralism.

Some of the readings might seem to describe exactly what Lincoln was doing, stealing every minute he could from the plow, the store, the post office in order to read:

If your own endeavors are deficient, it is in vain that you have tutors, books, and all the external apparatus of literary pursuits. You must love learning, if you would possess it. In order to love it, you must feel its delights; in order to feel its delights, you must apply it, however irksome at first, closely, constantly, and for a considerable time. If you have resolution enough to do this, you cannot but love learning; for the

mind always loves that to which it has been so long, steadily, and voluntarily attached. Habits are formed, which render what was at first
disagreeable, not only pleasant, but necessary.

This one—from the great teacher of rhetoric Hugh Blair—may be even
more directly applicable to young Lincoln, working away with his books:

> Redeeming your time from such dangerous waste, seek to fill it with
> employments which you may review with satisfaction. The acquisition
> of knowledge is one of the most honourable occupations of youth. The
> desire of it discovers a liberal mind, and is connected with many
> accomplishments and many virtues. But though your train of life
> should not lead you to study, the course of education always furnishes
> proper employments to a well disposed mind.

And these further words from Blair might be taken to describe Lincoln's
own drive:

> Whatever you pursue, be emulous to excel. Generous ambition and
> sensibility to praise, are, especially at your age, among the marks of
> virtue. Think not that any affluence of fortune, or any elevation of
> rank, exempts you from the duties of application and industry. Indus-
> try is the law of our being; it is the demand of nature, of reason, and of
> God. Remember, always, that the years which now pass over your
> heads, leave permanent memorial behind them.

When Lincoln himself, as a moderately successful middle-aged man—a
congressman, a lawyer, a politician—would have occasion to write a letter
(dated Christmas Eve, 1848) of moral admonition to his rather feckless
stepbrother, John D. Johnston, his letter deploring "idleness" and procras-
tination and not settling down would sound a good deal like some of the
"moral lessons" from the books he read in his youth.

Roy Basler, the Lincoln scholar who was the primary editor of Lincoln's collected works, made a statement about the relationship of young
Lincoln's reading to the learning of "elocution and grammar" that I
believe could almost be duplicated with respect to the study of ethics, if we
make certain allowances: "A careful examination of the books on elocution
and grammar which Lincoln studied both in and out of school will not
impress anyone with Lincoln's poverty of opportunity for the study of

grammar and rhetoric. It is safe to say that few children today learn as much through twelve years of formal schooling in these two subjects as one finds in several textbooks which Lincoln is supposed to have studied."

To be sure, young Lincoln did not, as far as we know, read any formal text in ethics,* as he did in those other two subjects; but formal texts are much less complete, as sources of the substance to be learned, in the domain of norms for conduct—ethics—than in the more self-contained, rule-bound world, particularly, of grammar. If we mean not just the formal ethical theory but the more elusive underlying reality of moral practice that the theorists theorize about, then—insofar as it can be taught and learned from books—young Lincoln probably was better taught in this area, too, than many children today with twelve years or more of formal schooling.

Basler shifts from the phrase "elocution and grammar" to the phrase "grammar and rhetoric." "Rhetoric," to those who put together the readers Lincoln read, was not trivial, as the word has come to suggest today ("mere rhetoric"), but was a substantial intellectual inquiry. And it was not a merely *technical* inquiry, a how-to field, separated from the worthiness of the message communicated. Rhetoric as a classical field had a closer connection to ethics than a modern mind might imagine. So it was not an anomaly for these editors putting together readers in "elocution" and "rhetoric" that would be perused by a young Indiana reader to include explicit and implicit treatments of moral life.

Often our "moral" formation is affected more by readings and teachings that open up to us the range and depth and ultimate seriousness of life than by specific intentional efforts to teach rules of conduct. Lincoln would read Shakespeare throughout his life, very much including his time as president of the United States. As president, according to his son Robert, he carried constantly with him a volume of Shakespeare's plays.

Although Lincoln apparently did read, at some time in his youth, that ubiquitous American classic *The Autobiography of Benjamin Franklin,* with its checklist of discrete virtues and vices—temperance today, check that off, then work on honesty tomorrow—Lincoln never refers to it. His moral universe was less that of Franklin than that of Shakespeare.

Scholars and readers and playgoers across the centuries have searched, mostly in vain, to discover the playwright's own moral positions behind the universe of richly imagined characters and events. What Shakespeare

---

* I will make an argument in a later chapter that he may have read as an adult Francis Wayland's *Elements of Moral Science.*

does is not to inculcate any specific program for living, but profoundly to deepen and enlarge one's understanding and vision of life.

Lincoln benefited from a benign deprivation in another way, in addition to the convenient paucity of books and "media" mentioned in an earlier chapter. He was also benignly deprived in the timing of his self-education. The intellectual world, at least as it reached out feebly to Spencer County, Indiana, had not yet felt the full philosophical and methodological impact of that strain of modern science, or philosophy allegedly derived from modern science, that insists that "fact" be sharply disconnected from "value" all across the realms of thought, often leaving "values" as a shadowy vapor. He also was separated, by geography or time, from the unmasking subversive thinkers on the Continent in the nineteenth century—Marx, Feuerbach, Nietzsche, not to mention Freud and multiple others in the twentieth—from all the strands of thought that would tend to undermine or overthrow or deny the notion of each human being as a rational moral agent. The books that Lincoln read had confidence, still, in reason and in responsibility. If any sounded a contrasting note, it would not be that of the undercuttings and reducings that were to come, but that of romanticism. Lincoln a few years later would read Lord Byron, and there certainly is a flavor of romanticism, along with that cold, calculating reason, in Lincoln.

5. SOMETHING MORE THAN COMMON

Not only in the books he read but in the society around him young Lincoln found two great bodies of opinion with ethical implications. He would respond to both with an unusually high level of seriousness. One was the idealism of the new American republic. The other was the religion drawn from the Bible there in the cabin, and promulgated by the Pigeon Creek Baptist Church and by the various gatherings of sects in New Salem.

The books about the United States that Lincoln had available were not by any means loftily objective or strictly factual. We know, and will be reminded, that he read Parson Weems's distinctly uncritical biography of George Washington. William Grimshaw's *History of the United States* furnished not just a report but a celebration of the new nation, culminating in the last paragraph in an exhortation of which the young Indiana reader would one day furnish an echo: "Let us not only declare by words, but demonstrate by our actions that 'all men are created equal; that they are endowed by their creator, with the same [sic] inalienable rights; that among these are life, liberty, and the pursuit of happiness.'" The United States was not simply one nation alongside other nations, but the bearer of universally applicable ideals for the governing of peoples.

In addition to these American books, filling a young man with large ideas, there were the newspapers he began to read in William Jones's store in Gentryville and kept on reading all his life. In the lively press of the new republic he learned about its ideals in action. He read about Henry Clay, who would become Lincoln's beau ideal in politics. Clay presented himself as a poor, orphaned, uneducated youngster, the "Millboy of the Slashes," who became a "self-made" man—Speaker of the House, eventually four times candidate for president. The new country evidently offered opportunity, with no impenetrable barriers, to poor boys in Hanover County, Virginia—or in Pigeon Creek, Indiana. At about the time the Lincolns and their party made their way from Indiana to Illinois, the Lincoln boy, about the time he became twenty-one, read in the papers the great exchange between Daniel Webster and Robert Hayne in the United States Senate, with Webster's great peroration "Liberty and Union, one and inseparable, now and forever."

6. NO MORE SCOFFING

Lincoln would have occasion to say something about the Bible at least twice in later life when he was presented with a Bible as a gift—a rather special circumstance with its own requirements. On the first occasion, Joshua Speed's mother made him such a present after he visited her Kentucky home in 1841; he said in a letter to Speed that he intended to read it regularly. And he picked up and joined in her assertion that it is the best cure for the "Blues"—but then he added, significantly, "could one but take it according to the truth."

There would be no such reservation when as president in 1864 he was presented by "the loyal colored people of Baltimore" with "a very elegant copy of the Great Book of God," as he called it in his thank-you letter. In that instance he made some sweeping statements that might be discounted slightly because the situation demanded politeness and gratitude; but still, they certainly are unequivocal: "[The Bible] is the best gift God has given to man"; "All the good that the Savior gave to the world was communicated through this book"; "All the things most desirable for man's welfare, here and hereafter, are to be found portrayed in it." Even in such large affirmations, and even with the category "the Savior" included, one may still detect a subtle margin of distance from a personal testimony of faith or a creedal affirmation.

Most relevant to an ethical inquiry, Lincoln said, "But for [the Bible] we could not know right from wrong." Tom Paine did not believe that assertion, nor did Thomas Jefferson—or the young Abraham Lincoln. One central project of the eighteenth-century Enlightenment had been to separate morality from religion, to ground morality in a universal reason, not in a special revelation. We can say that Lincoln had changed his mind. Or we can say, with Samuel Johnson, that truth is not a requirement in lapidary utterance. One could scarcely ask the president—even "Honest Abe"—to make carefully discriminated and qualified statements in response to such a gift.

In any case, Lincoln as an adult not only affirmed the central *moral* importance of the Bible to his own understanding, but showed its moral importance in practice. But he did so as a man in conversation with the Bible, making up his own mind.

The towns in which Lincoln grew up were saturated, not by one institutional Christian presence, but by varieties of the free-church, Bible-based evangelical Protestantism that spun out of the left wing of the Reformation in England. They expanded and divided and redivided into denominations that contended with each other in jumping-up-and-down camp meetings and fiery revivals on the western frontier. A raw new little town like New Salem—with no more than three hundred residents—was not going to be dominated by just one taken-for-granted village church that almost all attended or stayed away from; there would be, instead, different sorts of Baptists—hard-shell and otherwise—and Methodists, and Cumberland Presbyterians, and "Campbellites" (the Disciples of Christ—a wholly new entry in the American West), and varieties of preachers with followings, all disagreeing and contending with one another.

And there would be another party to the dispute, particularly among the young men who read books and liked to talk and argue, the freethinkers who read Tom Paine's *Age of Reason* and would explain to you how unbelievable Bible stories were and how outrageous Christian doctrines. Abraham Lincoln, coming to New Salem in 1831 at the age of twenty-two, for the first time permanently on his own out from under his father's roof, enjoying his newly discovered intellectual powers, joined this group, reading, debating, arguing, even putting shocking ideas on paper.

Although the great theme of the Enlightenment criticism of orthodox Christianity was to find its claims incredible by the test of reason's use of evidence and proof, a great accompanying theme was to find its performance and its belief immoral by the test of reason's conception of the good, the just, the humane. The "moral" criticism of Christianity, one might suggest, was more prominent in the practical English-speaking world than in the cloudland of the Continent; in any case it was certainly a prime element in the work of Tom Paine, that Englishman turned into a citizen of the world who had his biggest impact in the newly minted country the United States. To be sure, Paine did what other deist critics did, attack the whole idea of "revelation" and expose the contradictions and impossibilities of Bible stories. But through all of Paine's simple-minded, passionate book there is a fierce indignation at the allegedly immoral consequences of Christian belief and practices: "What is it the Bible teaches us? Rapine, cruelty, murder."

Douglas Wilson, who has recently and carefully assembled the evidence of young Lincoln's religious skepticism in New Salem, emphasizes also Lincoln's appreciation of a poem of Robert Burns's ("Holy Willie's Prayer") that satirizes a smug Scottish Presbyterian confident of his own "election," excusing his own sins because he was of the "elect" but ferocious against the sins of others who allegedly were not. James Matheny, the Springfield clerk and lawyer who would be groomsman to Lincoln at his wedding in 1841, told Herndon—a bit extravagantly, no doubt—that this poem of Burns's "was Lincoln's religion."

Lincoln carried some, at least, of his religious skepticism to Springfield when he moved there in 1837. The question is whether he carried it with him, privately, all his life.

Of course the topic of Lincoln's religious views is caught in a great tug-of-war of interpretation because of the immense value he represents in the wars of culture. Believers would start right away, after Lincoln was shot and killed on Good Friday of 1865, to construct an interpretation of Lincoln as a believing Christian; and nonbelievers, led by Herndon, would start right away contesting it.

For our purposes—studying Lincoln's ethics in theory and in practice—we may be able to come in under the radar and avoid the heavy bombardment on his ultimate religious views. I am not persuaded that he ever changed his original youthful decision, which was, on the basis of reason, not to accept the central Christian creedal affirmations. But on the other hand, it does seem clear that he changed markedly in other respects from the Tom Paine–quoting "infidel" in New Salem who wrote such a shocking attack on Christian doctrine that it had to be burned.

His change is to some extent described by his own hand, in the handbill he circulated in 1846, in the campaign for the congressional seat against Peter Cartwright, answering charges that he was "an open scoffer at Christianity." He concedes that he is not a member of any Christian church, and that "in early life" he was inclined to believe, and in private to argue for, the "Doctrine of Necessity." But, he says, he has not done any such arguing "for more than five years" (he does not exactly say he has left off the private *belief*), and he adds that he has "always understood the same opinion to be held by several of the Christian denominations." Lincoln as a thirty-seven-year-old candidate for political office, running against the area's best-known evangelist, under attack for "infidelity," now carefully insists not only that *he* does not do any more scoffing, but that he could not himself support for office anyone whom he knew to be "an open enemy of, and scoffer at, religion." The reason he could not, as candidate Lincoln states it with prudent circumspection in this campaign-time handbill, has not to do with the truth of the matter but with public morals and sensitivities. "Leaving the higher matter of eternal consequences between him and his maker," Lincoln says—what a candidate *really* believes is between him and God—"I still do not think any man has the right thus to insult the feelings, and injure the morals, of the community in which he may live."

Some who knew the young Lincoln, and some writers drawing upon them, conclude that the older Lincoln, the political candidate, at the very least practiced discretion in presenting his religious views—or avoiding that presentation. And he may have gone further and "played a sharp game" on the religious folk of Springfield and beyond by presenting himself (presumably falsely, to critics) as full of regret that he could not bring himself to an affirmation of Christian faith, and as a continual candidate for conversion. In this interpretation his reading of William Paley, the distinguished eighteenth-century English Christian apologist, and of *The Christian's Defense* by Springfield Presbyterian pastor James Smith, and of a few other such books, was a charade.

7. A POETRY IN HIS NATURE

I don't think it was a charade, a "sharp game," exactly. Was not Lincoln, in addition to being a politician, also a book-reading self-educator? Surely it is *not* true that this continually thoughtful and self-examining man took on board a bundle of beliefs in his youth and carried them with him undisturbed throughout his life. We can discern, from Lincoln's own hand—

without resort to the contending testimony of writers and scholars—a developing interpretation of the great drama of human life that is much more profound than that of Tom Paine. The dimensions of his understanding became larger than that of an unsubtle pamphleteering attack on conventional belief like Paine's. Mary Lincoln made a good statement to Herndon after her husband's death about his religion. He was not a "technical Christian," she said, but "he was a religious man always," and he had a "kind of poetry in his nature." One would not say this last about Paine. Paine not only would never have written anything approaching Lincoln's Second Inaugural; he would not have produced the adumbrations and approaches to it that appeared increasingly in Lincoln's life leading up to it.

In his developing double relationship to Christianity—his continuing private rejection doctrinally speaking, but his increasing selective appropriation, morally speaking—we may discern a high moral element in both directions.

First, there was a "universalism" (that is, an inclusive embrace of all humankind) both in his rejecting and in his borrowing from Christianity. Douglas Wilson, drawing on Herndon interviews, sees Lincoln's rejection of eternal punishment as one of Lincoln's more persistent negations. "Though Lincoln was increasingly unwilling to discuss his religious views in later years," wrote Wilson, "the apparent injustice of eternal damnation was one theological topic that he was said by friends to have addressed early and late." Isaac Cogdal, who knew Lincoln across the years, told Herndon in 1865–66, "He did not believe in Hell—Eternal punishment as Christians say—his idea was punishment as Educational. He was a Universalist tap root & all. . . ." Cogdal claimed to have talked about such matters with Lincoln "often and often" all the way from 1834 to 1859, and Herndon, perhaps in hearty agreement with what Cogdal was telling him, added in parentheses to his notes on the conversation, "This is correct. Herndon." "[Lincoln] could not believe that [God] created a world and that the result of it would be eternal damnation . . . ," said Cogdal.

We may infer a moral criticism of the starkest form of this doctrine. What sort of a God would that be, who would in his omniscience and foreknowledge create all those souls whose destiny was to roast forever in the flames of hell? A large swatch of the evangelical Protestantism that flourished in the American South and West had a "Reformed" (a "Calvinist") theological background, and one of the blunter theological assertions to flow from the concept of predestination in that unsubtle environment was the doctrine of *double* predestination—that is to say, not only has God selected from before all time and predestined for salvation those who are among the *elect,* but he has selected specifically also those who will be *damned.* We may surely infer that much of Lincoln's rejection of all this rested in its moral absurdity. It might be seen to be absurd in its picture of God and, as in "Holy Willie's Prayer," morally absurd in its effect on smug believers as well.

Lincoln did, however, not reject but drew upon familiar biblical stories and affirmations when they affirmed rather than denied a universalism, an inclusion of the whole human family. After 1854 the center of his activity became a vigorous defense of human equality (a quite abstract but nonetheless essential, ultimate equality, strongly affirmed). In that defense he used, at least as illustration and reinforcement, references to the Bible and Christian teachings—to the injunction to Adam (and therefore to all human beings) to earn his bread by the sweat of his own brow (and therefore *not* to get bread by the sweat of someone else's brow, as in slavery).

Because Jefferson when composing, and the Continental Congress when proclaiming, the Declaration of Independence had included in the key summary of philosophical premises in the second paragraph the phrase "that all men are created equal, and Endowed by their Creator with certain inalienable rights," and because the Declaration had by Lincoln's time gone through the shifts from being a revolutionary document to being almost forgotten to being partisan to being accepted as normative for the nation, and because Lincoln, picking up what others had done, would make the Declaration the constant reference point of his argument for equality, so then the Creator and a universal original creation of all human beings would become a major theme.

As Jefferson had written it, the Declaration's affirmation was deistic rather than biblical—the reference was to "nature and nature's God" rather than to God the Father of Jesus Christ or the God of Abraham, Isaac, and Jacob—but those distinctions had faded sufficiently for Lincoln and many others to meld Jefferson's phrases with Christian belief to buttress and ground their argument. In his six-year encounter with Senator Stephen Douglas, as we will see, he would make unusually clear the link he asserted between God as creator and the American belief in equality. And Douglas would join the issue. It often helps us to understand what the terms of argument really were in some past or remote setting to see what an opponent accuses a protagonist of affirming. Stephen Douglas, with heavy sarcasm, would charge that Lincoln "holds that the negro was born his equal and yours, and that he was endowed with equality by the Almighty, and that no human law can deprive him of these rights, which were guaranteed to him by the Supreme Ruler of the Universe."

A second relationship of Christian belief to Lincolnian belief is complicated in a different way. Lincoln is said by many to have been "fatalistic," and Herndon presented him as arguing in behalf of "determinism," and Lincoln, as we have seen, said he had defended the "doctrine of necessity," and sometimes this package is ascribed to his having been imbued with in his youth in the Baptist church, and continuing to hold in mind the after-effects of, a belief in "predestination." But if one homes in on these terms, they break apart. A universe rolling on with relentless uncaring necessity through an endless sequence of precise causes producing unchangeable effects is one thing; a spooky universe in which Fate plays out the ineluctable consequences of ancient curses and unspeakable deeds is another; a Calvinist universe in which providence actively intervenes to mark the fall of every sparrow and to order the fall of every raindrop is quite another. Not to skate too long on the thin ice of all these philosophical and theological questions, let us try to sort out the important elements of all this to Lincoln, the practical-moral thinker and actor. First, although he made those arguments for "necessity," they do not appear to have had any practical effect on his own or other persons' moral responsibility. Second, he does seem to have had a profound sense of the unfolding of events quite beyond his own power, perhaps beyond the control of any human agents. Third, he does seem either to have held all along or to have come to during the terrible pressures of the war—perhaps more strongly after his son Willie's death in 1862—a belief in the God that Bible-believers believe in. The key questions behind this nest of issues about necessity-determinism-providence and what-causes-what are whether the whole process is *meaningful,* whether it is *purposive,* and whether such purpose is *benign.* One certainly can hold deterministic outlooks that see the empty universe as a tale told by an idiot, or as a heartless impersonal clanging along of material causes of material effects. Lincoln as the author of the Second Inaugural surely held nothing like that, and perhaps a younger Lincoln did not, either.

But if he held, or came to hold, a belief in the biblical God, this continually moral thinker held it in a deeper way, a critical way, that rejected the political effects of many God believers, the jihads, the crusades, the certainties that God is on our side. He became a profound critic of all that.

If one holds that "charity," as the King James Version called it, is the core at least of Christian ethics if not of the Christian religion itself, and that "forgiveness" is its highest form, then Lincoln would increasingly as his life went on be appropriating and expressing, in practice and sometimes theory as well, that Christian virtue. As a youth and a young man he was often kind and generous, but sometimes cutting as well. In his temperance address when he was thirty-two he would include explicit religious references, and a sympathetic realism, that might be interpreted as a better reading of the religious ethic than was expressed by the believers who heard him. When as a congressman, as we will see, he would argue against President Polk's action at the outset of the Mexican War, he would invoke—in correspondence with a Baptist preacher at any rate—the Golden Rule, fully quoted from Matthew, as applied to nations. As his role expanded in the 1850s, the egotism and anonymous attacks and cutting satire dropped off, and he would begin to show himself to be unusually respectful and magnanimous. He would explicitly, and more than once, disavow "malice." As president he would display charity in many ways, and sometimes give expression to it in religious themes. He would show magnanimity to rivals and critics, mercy to the accused, patience with insolent generals, eloquent sympathy to the bereaved, generosity to associates and subordinates, nonvindictiveness to enemies. He would explicitly disavow planting thorns, malicious dealing, holding grudges. As war leader, he would write to his secretary of war that the government "can properly have no motive of revenge, no purpose to punish merely for punishment's sake." After four years of the terrible scourge of fratricidal war, begun in response to his own election, he would in his greatest speech recommend binding up the nation's wounds "with malice toward none, with charity for all."

8. SELF-IMPROVER

Lincoln writers often say that Lincoln "grew." That word is used in particular about his presumably changing racial attitudes in the last years of his life, but it has been applied much more widely—indeed, to his life as a whole. I agree that what the word is intended to describe did in fact happen, but in order to make a point I want to put aside the word—the metaphor.

That Lincoln "grew" is a cliché, and is vague, and—if the metaphor is taken literally—is misleading. Plants and animals and human beings grow without effort or thought; suddenly in one's middle teens one shoots up to six foot four. Every acorn grows into an oak; every human being "grows" bigger with the years. But Lincoln's important changes did not unfold through the working-out of a pattern of nature; they came by his own intent, through thinking, and might otherwise not have happened. Although it is another cliché to say that men "grow" in the presidency, James Buchanan did not "grow"; Andrew Johnson did not "grow."

This Lincoln was a *learner.* He was in particular a *moral* learner. If the term "self-improvement" did not now have such banal associations, we might use that term for Lincoln's own serious lifetime undertaking.

He learned what it took for his ambition to serve his virtue: it took subordination to a worthy end, and self-restraining generosity in seeking it. The story of his life, morally considered, would be the increasing development, by his own conscious effort, of his original worthiness, so that it would come to correspond to the increasing vastness of the political field within which he would act.

CHAPTER FIVE

Was This Man a Politician?

1. WORTHY OF THEIR ESTEEM

Abraham Lincoln was not a rail-splitter who wanted to keep on splitting rails, a backwoodsman who wanted to stay in the backwoods, a raftsman who fell in love with the river, a farmer who wanted to stay on the farm, a penniless boy who expected to stay penniless, and certainly not an uneducated boy who expected to stay uneducated. He was not a small-town lad who loved the small town and wanted to stay there; as he left his home and the farm as soon as he could, so he left the village of New Salem to make his way to the new capital of the state.

The choice of a line of work—for those human beings who have a choice—can be one of the foremost "moral" choices one makes: a decision, perhaps, not only about one's own preferences and abilities, but also about what it is worthwhile to spend one's life doing. Young Lincoln, significantly, chose to be a politician.

He could have become a farmer like his father, but he fled from that alternative as fast as his long legs would take him.

He made those two famous raft trips on the river, which might have roused in him aspirations like those that moved Samuel Clemens, and are given classic expression in *Life on the Mississippi*. In his first presentation of himself as a political candidate in the *Sangamon Journal* in 1832, he claimed he had "given as particular attention to the stage of the water in the Sangamon River," for the previous twelve months, as any other person in the country. But he soon left the romance of the river behind, except as it figured as subject to "improvement" in his political career.

That time he spent as co-owner with young William Berry of a disastrous store—and earlier as a clerk in Samuel Hill's store, and earlier still as an employee of Denton Offutt in interstate commerce by way of the rivers—might have sparked in him an entrepreneurial glow. Here was this raw new developing society on the frontier with people pouring in daily, looking for ways to make a fortune. An energetic young man like Lincoln might have profited. He certainly saw the possibilities of an economically developing Illinois; helping it to develop economically would be the core of his activity in the General Assembly. But that was the role he chose—not to join in the moneymaking himself, but to encourage it by legislation as a politician, as a legislator. All his own participation in capitalistic ventures did for him was to leave him with a huge "national debt" of $1,100 that it took years to repay, and an issue (whether or not liquor was sold in his store) that Stephen Douglas would exploit against him in their debates.

Lincoln would impress the whole town of New Salem with his ingenuity in getting Offutt's stranded vessel over the mill dam by boring a hole and draining water from it. Most of Lincoln's admirers in later years do not know that he is the only president of the United States to hold a patent: In 1848 he invented an apparatus that used "adjustable buoyant chambers" to lift steamers over sandbars. Why not a career as an inventor?

Lincoln was all his life a reader of, and some of his life a writer for, newspapers. So why didn't he become a journalist? The coming of the steam press, the telegraph, the wire services, and the new and more popular penny press, in the early years of his adult lifetime, all were beautifully timed to give Abraham Lincoln a fine career, like other young Americans from small towns in the backwoods who love words and reading and writing and who also love public affairs, as a newspaperman.

Or he could have started out as an ink-stained wretch, as so many American writers have done, and then moved into creative writing. It is commonly said that Lincoln is almost unique among American presidents in that one could imagine him, in another life, as a writer.

Why didn't this astonishingly bookish boy—bookish against all odds—become a teacher? Or, hearing those preachers at the Pigeon Creek Baptist Church, why did he not decide to preach and evangelize and moralize and look down on politicians?*

---

* James G. Randall, explaining that Lincoln was no Leonardo da Vinci, nor as many-sided as Thomas Jefferson, nevertheless produced two impressive lists of roles and activities in Lincoln's youth, some of which might have been developed into a line of work. "In the period before his career took shape," wrote Randall, "he had been ferry boy, flatboatman, mill manager, small town clerk, and merchant, day laborer at odd jobs, and

While still in Indiana, he did begin to find his secondary occupation. He drew up legal documents for his neighbors, and he started reading some law books clear back in his late teens. When he came out of the Black Hawk War and consciously considered vocational alternatives, the law was high on the list—but he said he thought his education was deficient. Later, after he had been elected to the state legislature (perhaps after seeing some lawyers), he decided that was not so much an impediment after all and started to study law in earnest.

But by then he had found what was to be his true vocation. As we have said, Lincoln clearly was a young man who wanted to distinguish himself, and politics was a way to do that. But it was also a way to do something worthwhile. Lincoln succinctly put these mingled motives together in his rather touching first effort at political self-presentation. Coming before the people of Sangamon County on March 9, 1832, he said: "I have no other [ambition] so great as that of being truly esteemed of my fellow men, by rendering myself worthy of their esteem." One renders oneself worthy of esteem—and realizes an ambition to make one's name known—by being and doing something worthy, and Lincoln proposed to do that in and through politics. He ran that first time, in 1832, just back from attacking the wild onions in the Black Hawk War, and he did not win; he finished eighth among the thirteen candidates for the four seats from Sangamon County. But it is significant that with respect to this activity, he did not quit. He ran again two years later, and won, and never stopped running thereafter.

Being a politician entailed activities that Lincoln was good at: making speeches, writing, being the center of attention, persuading people by his logical and rhetorical powers, being an advocate. It gave expression to that interest in public affairs that made him read newspapers and talk with Colonel Jones even as a Hoosier lad and that appeared in his early admiration for Henry Clay. But there was something more than that: his romantic attachment to his country, and to his country's system of governing itself. In that first political statement when he was twenty-three he said he was making his views known not only because it was the custom to do so but

---

postmaster." As his career as politician and lawyer was taking shape he was also, wrote Randall, "an inventor, a surveyor fond of geometry, something of a specialist in Western river transportation (no mean subject), an athlete, a soldier (for a brief period, including enlistments, in the Black Hawk War, 1832), a lecturer (briefly), a newspaper owner (again briefly), and an orator" (*Lincoln the President,* vol. 1 [New York: Da Capo, 1997], pp. 40–41 [originally New York: Dodd, Mead, 1945]).

also because it accorded with "the principle of true republicanism." The principle of true republicanism requires some citizens to become politicians, and in that honorable activity to attempt to render themselves worthy of their fellow citizens' esteem.

2. A POLITICAL CAREER

Lincoln ran for the Illinois House of Representatives, the lower house in that state's General Assembly, six times: the first time in 1832 (when he was barely twenty-three years old) and then in 1834, 1836, 1838, 1840, and in the special case of 1854, and he won election every time except the first. (In 1854 he was elected, but for political reasons he promptly resigned.) He served four two-year terms as an active Whig legislator in the state capital (Vandalia, and then Springfield; Lincoln the politician helped to get the capital moved). Although still quite young, he rose rapidly to become minority leader, and was twice the Whig party's nominee for Speaker of the Illinois House.

He twice sought the Whig Party nomination for the seat in the United States House of Representatives from the Seventh Congressional District in Illinois, in 1843 and 1845; he was nominated and elected in 1846, and served in Washington in the Thirtieth Congress in 1847–49.

He twice sought election (by the state legislature, then the constitutional method) to the United States Senate, in 1855 and 1858. In the former year he was the leading candidate on the first ballot in the legislature, but finally threw his diminishing support to fellow anti-Nebraska candidate Lyman Trumbull to prevent the election of a Democrat. In 1858 he was uniquely designated by the Republican state convention as the Republican choice for the Senate, and engaged in the famous debates throughout the state with the Democratic incumbent, Stephen Douglas.

In an extraordinary display of convention nominating politics, he secured the 1860 nomination of his party—against strong rivals—for president of the United States, and was elected to that office. He managed—against strong opposition, even within his own party—to be reelected in 1864.

He was an active *party* politician. He was not one who disdained the contention between parties, or the organized effort to obtain power that the party represented. He was a loyal, active, and regular Whig as long as there was a Whig Party—longer than some others—and then became a loyal, active, and partisan Republican, and a chief organizer of that new party in Illinois. He was a loyal and active partisan politician in his support of candidates, in his positions on the issues, and in his organizational activity.

He supported candidates of his party at every level, and actively campaigned for many, including every presidential nominee of his party (except himself) in his adult lifetime. In 1836, the first presidential year of its existence, the Whig Party put forward only a series of regional candidates; young Lincoln let voters know that, like other Whigs in Illinois and other western and border states, he supported one of them, Hugh L. White of Tennessee. He actively campaigned, with extensive speech-making, for every national presidential candidate the Whig Party ever put forward for the office of President of the United States. He campaigned, on the stump and in letters, for William Henry Harrison in 1840; for Henry Clay in 1844; for Zachary Taylor in 1848 (in Maryland and Massachusetts as well as Illinois); and for Winfield Scott in 1852. He served as a presidential elector of his party in 1840, 1844, 1852, and 1856.

In 1848 as a young congressman he worked actively with others to secure the nomination for Zachary Taylor; he went to the national convention in Philadelphia as a Taylor supporter; he argued for Taylor on the House floor; when the first session of the Thirtieth Congress—his congress—adjourned, he stayed in Washington to work in the Taylor campaign; and he made speeches for the candidate in the East before returning to Illinois.

In 1856 he campaigned for John C. Frémont, the nominee of his new party, the Republican Party, with more than fifty speeches.

In 1860 and 1864 he did not actively campaign for his party's presidential nominee for the only time in his adult lifetime, because he was himself that nominee, and the custom then was that one did not campaign for oneself.

He was a good party politician not only in campaigning for the party's nominees but also in defending the party's positions on issues. He believed, as did Whigs generally, in governmental action to support commercial development, particularly in the West. In his earliest appeal to voters he presented himself, with what would become a Whig theme, as a proponent of "the public utility of internal improvements"—good roads, the clearing of navigable streams (particularly the Sangamon River), railroads, and canals. He introduced, and fought for, Whig proposals in the Illinois General Assembly for a major program of internal improvements for the state. He defended, as Whigs did, the national bank that Jackson and the Democrats attacked. He favored, in its Whig form, a "sound currency." He did not fear, as Democrats tended to do, the industrializing of the nation; instead, as Whigs did, he did what he could to favor it. He strongly favored, as Whigs like Daniel Webster did, the Union, the nation as a whole, and as Whigs like Joseph Storey did, the broad construction of the Constitution, against the Democratic inclination to favor states' rights, localism, and strict construction. He held, as Whigs did, that public lands should be used and sold for public purposes; he defended, as Whigs did, the protective tariff.

As a Republican after 1855, he would play a key role not just in defending but in defining the position of the new party: in focusing rigorously on opposition to the extension of slavery, and in dismissing or subordinating other issues.

He was an active party politician, and so, in a necessarily more restricted way, was the woman he married. Mary Todd of Lexington, Kentucky, was unusual among women of her day and her class for her strong political interests. She was a fervent Whig who had met Henry Clay himself, a friend of her father's, when she was a little girl, and she read newspapers and followed public affairs and talked politics all her life. Most of the beaux she had were politicians—Stephen Douglas himself was one of them—and politics was a central theme in the courtship of Mary Todd by the gangling and awkward and slightly uncouth young state legislator Abraham Lincoln. (When he met her, he was in his third term as one of the state representatives from Sangamon County.) As politics was a theme of their early courtship, so politics helped to bring them back together after a famous breakup. In their marriage, in Illinois and in the White House, Mary Todd was an active and knowledgeable participant in politics—as much as social convention permitted, and sometimes a little more. Her expectation of her husband's political success—including, according to a number of witnesses, an early prediction that he would be president—was a not unimportant theme in their marriage. She too could count and calculate votes—filling notebooks with the names and inclinations of Illinois legislators when he had a chance to become senator. She followed editorial opinions for him, and interpreted him in letters to her well-connected friends.

It may have been she who pasted into a notebook the newspaper clippings of her husband's debates with her onetime suitor Stephen Douglas, out of which Lincoln later had a book made. When her husband received the presidential nomination, the national press on visiting Springfield was surprised to find a candidate's wife with unusual political knowledge. In the White House she had political friendships of her own, notably with Senator Charles Sumner, in a way that has been rare for first ladies.

Lincoln was a politician not only in the interests that he shared with the woman he married, and in repeatedly running for office himself, and in supporting every party candidate, and in holding the party's positions on issues; he was also a proponent of, and a participant in, partisan political activity—organizing, calculating, negotiating, planning particular appeals, putting together particular units of power. In a word, he engaged throughout his life, certainly including the presidency, in "politicking."

When he put down on paper a "plan" for the performance of Whigs in the important election of 1840, he did so not as an amateur or a newcomer or a follower or a disapproving outsider but rather as one who already had practical political experience and who applied his mind to the organizational problem. He was then barely into his thirties. "Appoint one person in each county as county captain, and take his pledge to perform promptly all the duties . . ." And then he spells out those duties, in a way that will be familiar to political workers across the centuries. "1st. To procure from the poll-books a separate list for each Precinct of all the names of all those persons who voted the Whig ticket in August." It is mostly a matter of *names,* and linking names to responsibilities. "2nd. To appoint one person in each Precinct as Precinct Captain" and get a pledge from *him,* and "3rd. To deliver to each Precinct the list of names as above." And each precinct captain is "to divide the list of names delivered him by the county captain, into sections of ten," and to appoint a section captain, and give him the list of names.

And now one is down to that face-to-face level in a neighborhood to which all politics eventually comes: the first duty of that section captain is "to see each man of his Section face to face, and to secure his pledge that he will for no consideration (impossibilities excepted) stay from the polls on the first Monday in November and that he will record his vote as early on the day as possible." (Party workers in precincts, then and now, like to have their loyal voters vote as early as possible, to clear the lists for concentrated effort on the others as the hours grow short at the end of the day.)

And then "add to his Section the name of every person in his vicinity who did not vote with us in August, but who will vote with us in the fall."

Why is the great Abraham Lincoln doing this sort of thing? In the first place, he did not know he was slated to be great. In the second, he was good at it and enjoyed it. And in the third, hovering over this lowly practical activity there were not only some possible personal and collective fulfillments but some large social ideals as well.

Illustrations of Lincoln as a functioning practical politician spread themselves across the pages of his collected papers, from almost the beginning to almost the end, especially in his letters, a large portion of which are devoted to quite particular partisan political operations. Several of the episodes one may cite in evidence of the younger Lincoln's use of his "power to hurt" by sarcasm and pungent attack occur in the midst of—and are partly excused by—partisan combat. What came to be called the "skinning of Thomas" is one example. Lincoln was fully capable of strongly supporting a candidate (Zachary Taylor in 1848) just because he thought he could *win* against a candidate who he was sure would have been a better president (Henry Clay). He could recommend to Herndon getting the "wild boys about town" to sing and holler in a campaign. He could even in his campaign for the Senate against Douglas in 1858 hint to the chairman of the State Republican Committee, Norman Judd (in a letter written on October 20, 1858), of steps to be taken to counter the "fraudulent votes" of "celtic gentlemen with black carpet sacks in their hands"—Irish railroad workers—whom, he surmised, the Democrats were moving about to vote where needed in doubtful districts. What steps? Just a "bare suggestion." Perhaps a "true man, of the 'detective' class," could be "introduced among them in disguise," to "control their votes." How? Lincoln does not specify. Mark E. Neely Jr. commented severely: "Suborning votes by private detectives was election fraud by any standard."

3. A FREE PEOPLE DIVIDE INTO PARTIES

To some extent the party young Lincoln joined inherited the disdain for "parties" that, for all their realism otherwise, older eminences, including Founders, exhibited. John Quincy Adams was in a sense one of the founders of the Whig Party, but at the same time was, like his father, disinclined to identify himself as a party man. Daniel Webster was one of the most eminent Whigs—next only to Henry Clay—but at the same time, similarly reluctant to be identified completely with a party.

One might say that at least at first the Whigs were a political party that was not sure that it should be a political party—that *anybody* should be "political" in that partisan way. That is what *Jacksonians* did, and the Whig Party was born in opposition to Andrew Jackson and the Jacksonian Democrats.

But Abraham Lincoln would be one of the Whigs who would lead the party *away* from this early inclination. One may illustrate with reference to two points: *conventions* and *patronage*.

The Jacksonians chose their nominees in party conventions and, having chosen them, insisted on party regularity in their support—they thus increased their strength and effectiveness by prior arrangement and concert of effort. The Whigs in the Illinois Senate said in 1835 that not only "every man who is eligible for the office of president has an undeniable right to become a candidate for the same . . . without the intervention of caucuses and convention" but also that "we disapprove of the convention system attempted to be forced upon the American people by the Van Buren party [i.e., the Democrats]." Lincoln himself in that year, 1835, early in the life of both the Whig Party and his political career, voted for a similar Whig motion in the House, denouncing the Democratic "scheme" of conventions as something that "ought not to be tolerated in republican government."*

But Lincoln's opposition to conventions did not last long. The Democrats rolled on to victory in 1836 both in Illinois and in the nation. Their convention-nominated national party candidate for president, Martin Van Buren, won out over the several sectional candidates put forward by an uncoordinated Whig Party. Lincoln and other younger Whigs learned the lesson. A year later he was writing that he regretted to hear that any Whigs "should any longer be against conventions," and, indeed, he went on to become one of the primary Whig advocates of the convention system.

Some moralistic older Whigs objected to the Jacksonians using hoopla in campaigns, making unabashed appeals to class and region, and exploiting a military hero's popularity for electoral gain. Younger Whigs, of whom Abraham Lincoln in Illinois was a particular leader, came to recommend and to use all of those "Jacksonian" "political" methods, sometimes defensively justifying doing so by saying that Whigs *must* do so to counter the Democrats. Abraham Lincoln, before his days as a Whig were over, would have campaigned, in the space of just four presidential elections

---

* A leader in organizing the first Democratic convention in Vandalia was Stephen Douglas.

(1840–1852), for not one or two but *three* generals, whose popularity grew from military exploits, and in the case of one of them—Zachary Taylor in 1848—was an early and ardent supporter, before his nomination, exactly because he could *win*.

Older Whigs objected to the Jackson Democrats' practice of the "spoils system"—"rotation in office," as it was sometimes euphemistically called. But the realistic Whig Lincoln would become fully aware of the importance, for party organization, of rewarding the faithful. He tried to persuade the new Whig Taylor administration to do more in that line and finally sought a particular patronage appointment himself—partly because that job, in its turn, controlled other jobs that would be useful in shaping the Whig Party in Illinois.

When he became president, he would be the leader of a new party that had never held national office before, and that swarmed with eager office-seekers. President-elect Lincoln out in Springfield, and then newly inaugurated President Lincoln in Washington, would spend all too much of his day coping with Republicans who aspired to office. Of the result, let us simply quote a summary: "Lincoln initiated the most sweeping removal of federal officeholders in the country's history up to that time. Of 1,520 presidential officeholders, 1,195 were removed; and since most Southern offices were left unfilled, that was almost a complete overturn. He appointed Republicans to almost all of the jobs. Lincoln's administration, the President explained frankly in 1862, 'distributed to its party friends as nearly all the civil patronage as any administration ever did.'"

I don't mean to overstate the point; young Lincoln the Whig politician, and the middle-aged Lincoln the Republican politician, were always committed to what they thought to be worthy public purposes as the guiding reason both for participating in general in the political contest in which a free people "in times of peace and quiet" engage, and also for participating in it on the side that they did. Lincoln certainly was not doing it just to gain power and position, without regard to real conviction about public policy. I will argue later in these pages that he was to become, to an unusual degree, a politician of moral argument. But that is not to say that he was to any degree a reluctant politician.

On this point, I think one may disagree with the great Lincoln biographer and scholar James G. Randall, the central figure in Lincoln scholarship in the middle of the twentieth century, who showed an amusing disinclination to identify his hero as a "politician."

Discussing what he regarded as the distasteful "political merry-go-round" in Illinois, the Lincoln biographer had with great reluctance to concede that Lincoln was a part of it: "It was of course with parties and politicians that Lincoln had to work," Randall wrote, implying ("had to work") that Lincoln was holding his nose as he did so. "It cannot be denied that Lincoln was a party man; he had to be if he wanted a political career. He worked by and through party organization; he engaged in party maneuvers; it was as a party candidate that he obtained elective office." All this Randall, obviously holding *his* nose, had to concede. Of course a corrective counterclaim is coming. "But it is also worth noting," he went on to say, "that he saw the evils of party politics and that worst party excesses never had his approval." That depends upon what one includes in "worst party excesses." Lincoln did not engage in coercion, intimidation, or vote fraud, although that letter to Judd about the "true man, of the 'detective' class" controlling the votes of the "celtic gentlemen" may come pretty close to the line. But he certainly did organize, calculate party advantage, support candidates who could win; believe in, and enjoy, party activity. To attempt to vindicate his contrary point Randall jumped all the way forward (he had been discussing Lincoln in the politics of Illinois of the 1830s and 1840s) to a quotation from Lincoln in June of 1863 as the embattled president leading the Union in a war for its existence, saying (of course he would say—any politician in the situation would say) that he would prefer to meet on a level one step higher than any party platform. It is significant that Randall had to reach so far, to such a different situation, to get the quotation criticizing party politics that he wanted.

In another chapter, in a discussion of Lincoln as orator, speaker, rhetor, Randall wrote: "Though it cramped his soul to operate within the limitations of a party, and though as a candidate he was to be everyone's game, he appreciated the meaning of statesmanship." And: "He was made of better stuff than that of politicians reaching out for the spoils of office." Well, in the first place, Lincoln himself certainly *was* a politician reaching out for office, including if you will some "spoils" of office. But then as to "better stuff": He proved to be an unusually worthy man, better stuff indeed than other politicians, but also better stuff than most nonpoliticians and antipoliticians as well.

At the end of a section of his biography arguing that among the great Founders Lincoln was much closer to Jefferson than to Hamilton, and that Lincoln had almost no affinity with Hamilton (a claim that itself might be challenged with respect to Lincoln the Whig), Randall concluded with a quotation from Lincoln saying that Jefferson "was, is, and perhaps will continue to be, the most distinguished politician of our history." Professor Randall felt it necessary—comically, to my reading—to explain carefully in a footnote that "Lincoln was using the word 'politician' here in the sense of a man concerned with political affairs."

One disagreement a reader may have with this view has to do with Lincoln's feelings about being a politician—whether it "cramped his soul." I say no. Where is the evidence that it did? On the contrary, to my reading, Lincoln's letters and activities show him realizing he was good at this, enjoying it, and recognizing that he was carrying on party activity in the service of not only his own possible rise and that of his party but also of worthy social purposes.

One can exhume a quotation in which he seemed to be joining in the stereotyped disparaging of politicians as such. But was he really? When he was a twenty-seven-year-old Whig state legislator and was defending the state bank from a proposed inquiry by governmental officials (in a speech in the House on January 11, 1837), he made a half-joshing comment about "politicians" that is sometimes quoted seriously: "a set of men, who have interests aside from the interests of the people, and who, to say the most of them, are, as a mass, at least one long step removed from being honest men." But there was a joking and self-deprecating flavor to his statement; he said immediately: "I say this with the greater freedom because, being a politician myself, none can regard it as personal." The more common disdainers of politicians usually do not stoop to including *themselves* in the disdained category. And Lincoln's actions would speak louder than these words.

And there are many more significant words on the subject from him. He would, for example, observe in his eulogy for the public figure he first and most admired, Henry Clay, who was unmistakably a lifelong politician, that "a free people, in times of peace and quiet—when pressed by no common danger—naturally divide into parties. At such times the man who is of neither party is not—cannot be—of any consequence. Mr. Clay, therefore, was of a party." That observation would be loaded with significant implications: Not only would he take for granted ("neither party") a two-party system; he would also take for granted the dividing up ("naturally") of a people who are free, in normal times, into such contending organized units. And he would assert—quite an extraordinary and exaggerated claim—that one could be "of consequence" only by participating in that party contest.

Surely we can say that young Lincoln believed that the most successful central feature of this young republic was exactly the "political" system at its core—"the principles of true republicanism." The Founders whom young Lincoln, along with most of his fellow citizens, were now turning into demigods had been, we may say without much stretching of the word, politicians. And if you say they were founders of a state, and "statesmen," rather than "politicians," then we say the new state that they founded was distinctive exactly in that it had "politics" at its foundation rather than authority, tradition, blood, soil, myth, or command. Being founded upon and governed by "the people," instead of a king or nobles or priests or warriors or dictators or commissars, means politics—politics in the form of free elections between and among groups of people competing freely for governmental power.

The "people," as the American Founders saw and the French revolutionaries did not, are not one tidy unity, with one great single "will"; the "people" are divided and in conflict in many ways. Usually. It is significant that Lincoln said that, except in great emergencies, the people divide into parties. We may add, also into an enormous spread of actual and potential groups, with a great variety not only of interests but of values. The American Founder James Madison saw this and expressed it better than it had been expressed. Human beings differ, and keep on differing, and their differences are exaggerated and strengthened in groups. These differences include differing *interests,* of which differing economic interests may be the strongest and most durable, but differences over ideas as well, and differences in other regards—some of them, as Madison remarked to his philosophical friend Thomas Jefferson, rather trivial. To be governed by "the people"—for the people to govern themselves—means an endless adjusting and readjusting of these differences, in the controlling of the shared instruments of self-rule.

Abraham Lincoln had absorbed all this in his reading and in his American environment. Like the American Founders, he was neither an anarchist nor a pacifist; he did believe in the necessity and possibility of government. One element—not the only one—defining government is coercion: the imposition of some will on the community. Part of the genius of a free republic is that the people impose that "coercion" on themselves, through their representatives; they are ruled by themselves through the "gentle coercion of the magistracy," in Madison's phrase. Lincoln will have occasion in the winter of 1860-61, in matters of highest consequence, to think through and write out his argument on these matters: majority rule and the rights of those who disagree; "anarchy" and "coercion." On some

February days in 1861 he and William Seward, these two politicians in this republic, sitting together in the Willard Hotel in Washington, will work out a statement of ultimate governing authority under the Constitution of this free republic, finally arriving at this complicated but adequate formulation: "A majority held in restraint by constitutional checks and limitations and always changing easily with deliberate changes of popular opinions and sentiments is the only true sovereign of the people." This is government not only of and for the people, but also by the people: through a continuous process of mutually deliberating power-seeking and power-yielding collaboration—through politics.

Lincoln would be presented, by himself and American myth, as the very archetype of the poor boy who would rise to high position. How did he rise? He did not take his patented invention, add new ones, and have them produced for a market and make a fortune like Cyrus McCormick. He did not decide that he could manage a river-traffic business better than Denton Offutt, and exploit the growing western economy to obtain money and power. He did not, with his talent as a writer and storyteller, send funny pieces to journals, like Mark Twain, and move East and become a famous writer. He did not use his ability as a speaker and tree-stump preacher to become, like Charles Finney, a famous touring evangelist. He did not, like his friend David Davis, buy property in burgeoning Illinois as he went around the judicial circuit and become a rich judge. The way Abraham Lincoln rose in the world was by making political speeches, becoming a good political organizer, and being voted into a series of political offices.

The significance of Lincoln being a lifelong politician, for an appraisal of the conduct of his life, is that he acted within fairly narrow limits of the possible; that the opinion of the great public was one of those limits; that he was not a lone-wolf moral hero but participated with others in collaborative efforts—parties, legislatures, governments; that calculation and compromise were therefore of the essence in his decision and action; that the great object of his and others' joint efforts was to accomplish society-wide goods through the instrument of government. It would perhaps be a little grand to say of the twenty-three-year-old who ran for the Illinois state legislature on a program of improving navigation on the Sangamon River, that he "put his hand to the wheel of history." And yet that turned out to be what he did.

4. THE PARTY OF NATIONAL IMPROVEMENT

Young Lincoln not only made the morally significant decision to be a politician; he also made the morally significant decision to be a Whig. What social good did this aspiring young politician in Illinois mean to promote when he chose the Whig Party?

One seeks votes not only to achieve power for oneself and one's party companions, but in more cases than stereotyped derogation would grant, also to serve some conception of the common good. Of course the competing parties represent competing "interests." But they also represent, both through and beyond those interests, competing notions of social goods.

The Whig Party has vanished into the mists, and Lincoln has gone on to become first a Republican and then a national monument, so for the general public the significance of this first long partisan attachment has been obscured. But his becoming a Whig meant something. He would be a loyal Whig as long as there was a Whig Party. He was a Whig for more than twenty years; he would be a Republican for fewer than ten.

Three nonideological reasons for Lincoln's Whiggery: because Colonel Jones influenced him; because he admired Henry Clay; and because he distinguished his life purposes from those around him.

Three ideological reasons: his agreeing with the Whig program of economic development; his sharing in the aspiring, improving, intellectualizing, even moralizing element in Whig culture; and his vibrating in tune with Whig nationalism and devotion to the Union.

Abraham Lincoln was a boy of fifteen in the Hoosier backwoods, learning fast, in 1824 when Andrew Jackson was cheated out of the presidency (as the Jacksonians saw it) by the "corrupt bargain" between John Quincy Adams and Henry Clay that made Adams president and Clay secretary of state. Perhaps fifteen was too early even for Abraham Lincoln to have independent political convictions; apparently at that stage he shared in the support for Jackson by which he was surrounded in Pigeon Creek. But four years later, in 1828, when he was nineteen, he may already have been changing; that was the year the Jacksonians had their revenge, elected their hero, and spilled whiskey on the White House rugs in celebration of the onset of Jacksonian democracy. Maybe Abe, even as a teenager, was not celebrating. Four years later, in 1832, when he was twenty-three, and now living on his own in New Salem, Illinois, he definitely had anti-Jackson, pro-Clay convictions.

Back in Indiana, Colonel Jones let the young Abraham, while he worked in Jones's store in Gentryville, read the *Louisville Journal* and the *Missouri Republican,* both of which were strongly anti-Jackson and pro-Clay papers. Dennis Hanks would say years later that it was Colonel Jones who made Abe a Whig. Hanks also said that Abe liked Henry Clay's *speeches.* Lincoln, this young man of words, liked the articulate Clay rather than the inarticulate man of action, Andrew Jackson. Clay, moreover, was young, a charmer, and from Kentucky.

Henry Clay also stood for something. Youthful attachments to personalities, shaped in the enthusiasm of a moment, can be reversed by later enthusiasms. Love so wrought can be unwrought so. Hillary Rodham did not remain a Goldwater girl; Ronald Reagan did not continue to be a New Deal Democrat. But Abraham Lincoln would *remain* a Whig when youthful rebellion was no longer meaningful, when later voices had supplanted the voice of Colonel Jones, and when the vicissitudes of politics would lead him to oppose Henry Clay within the party.

Becoming a supporter of Henry Clay, and then in the winter of 1833–34, when the opponents of Jackson began to use the word, a Whig, was one of the important choices he made as a young man.

Lincoln, the loyal party man, had a particular scorn for politicians in Illinois who switched from the Whigs to the more dominant Democrats. John T. Stuart told Herndon that from 1830 to 1837 the tendency in Illinois was for every man of ambition to turn Democrat. He listed as examples Thomas Ford, the governor who wrote a sour book about Illinois politics that is much quoted by historians; his brother-in-law George Forquer, a Sangamon County leader, with whom Lincoln had a famous exchange in which Lincoln mocked Forquer for changing parties; and Peter Cartwright, the evangelist and politician, whom Lincoln at twenty-one had so startled in that Macon County cornfield, and at thirty-seven would defeat in the 1846 race for Congress. There was a fear on the part of the dominant Democrats that some who moved to Illinois from New England and the Northeast (a secondary influx, after the earlier immigration from Kentucky, Tennessee, Virginia) would, given their regional roots, be Whigs; but when they arrived in Illinois, the ambitious among them often turned out conveniently to decide they were Democrats.

It would appear that the popular young Lincoln himself was encouraged by the Sangamon County Democracy to come over to their side; both his fabled job as postmaster and his perhaps more significant job as deputy surveyor were political appointments controlled by Democrats. Technically, Lincoln was appointed postmaster by President Jackson himself; Lincoln, instead of segueing quietly into the party that had thus favored him, insisted on maintaining his identity as a Clay man, and joked that he was appointed by the Democrats because it was too minor a job for them to care. When he ran for the state legislature in 1834 a number of his friends and admirers in New Salem who were Jackson-supporting Democrats nevertheless proposed to vote for him, and he won with significant Democratic support. But again, already in these youthful dealings, he was careful to make his partisan allegiance clear: He was a Clay man, a Whig.

It does seem that once young Abraham Lincoln had learned the political complexion of Illinois, if he had been altogether opportunistic in his political ambition, he could have discovered in himself, with that ideological dexterity that a cynical public attributes to politicians, an affinity with the dominant and rising party, the Democrats. He was never going to achieve that highest of his ambitions, being a United States senator, as a Whig; no Whig would ever be elected senator, or to any statewide office, in Illinois. The Whigs would never carry Illinois for their presidential candidate, even in 1840 and 1848, when they won nationally and Lincoln had high hopes for Illinois. During Lincoln's four terms in the Illinois House of Representatives he rose to be Whig floor leader and *nominee* for Speaker—but he was never elected Speaker, because the Whigs were always in the minority. When he served his one term in Congress in 1847–49, he was the *only* Whig among Illinois's seven congressmen.

One of the main reasons that Stephen Douglas's career was so much more successful than Lincoln's was that Douglas had chosen his political party more wisely for the purposes of advancement in politics in the state in which they both pursued their careers. By superficial criteria it made more sense for Douglas to be a Whig than for Lincoln to be one: Douglas was the son of a doctor in the arch–New England state of Vermont, and educated in a preparatory school there; Lincoln, as we know, was a contrast on all points. One might almost say that Lincoln and Douglas each by original identity belonged in the other's party.

Lincoln's ambition was qualified by a prior partisan commitment, which in turn rested on social-moral convictions.

Because the demography and philosophy of the parties in America's two-party system are loose, rough, inexact, overlapping with each other, and subject to change, with many internal contradictions within each party, some may conclude that these major parties have no moral core. But that complexity does not mean that adherence to one party rather than the other had no moral meaning. Proportions and tendencies can matter a great deal.

The core of a Whig program, expressed in the "American System" of Henry Clay, was government action, very much including federal government action, in aid of economic development. That included governmentally aided "internal improvements." The Whig Party was the party that was somewhat more committed (again, it is a matter of degree and proportion) to *developing* the new nation—to *industrial* development. On the whole, the Whigs did not share the Jeffersonian preference for the rural life and for farming, or the Jeffersonian abhorrence of the growth of cities.

Abraham Lincoln, certainly a poor laborer in the West when he made his partisan decision, did not join in the Democrats' populistic hostility to, or states' rights or strict construction restriction on, national governmental action. Instead he seems to have shared almost from the start the contrasting moral vision of Henry Clay (and to a large extent of President John Quincy Adams before Clay) of a developed, improved, prosperous new nation, with vast undeveloped land and manifold other resources, and a burgeoning, educated population, less constrained than Europe by a settled, feudal past, ready to become affluent and powerful, brought to its higher state of development by deliberate, collective action—by governmental policies. Young Lincoln is said to have dreamed of becoming "the DeWitt Clinton of Illinois"—the prairie equivalent of the celebrated governor of New York who was given credit for developing the much-celebrated Erie Canal.*

Lincoln's prime commitment to governmentally aided economic development was evident in his first political statement—when he presented himself as a candidate to be one of the representatives from Sangamon County in the state legislature in 1832, when he was only twenty-three, and had lived in New Salem, on his own, for only eight months. "To the People of Sangamon County" was his first formal expression in writing of his

---

* G. S. Boritt, in an influential book called *Lincoln and the Economics of the American Dream* (Memphis: Memphis State University Press, 1978), showed Lincoln's Whig economic convictions running through his whole life's politics. Boritt found the moral underpinning of Lincoln's attachment to this system in its link in the opportunity a prospering American economy is alleged to provide for every man, specifically for the poor man, to make his way by industry to a better life—to "rise." And certainly that was a repeated theme in Lincoln's own speeches, often using himself as an example.

political views. As "a candidate for the honorable office of one of your representatives in the next General Assembly of this state," the young Lincoln wrote, in accordance not only with established custom but with "the principles of true republicanism," he would make known his "sentiments with regard to local affairs."

And what is the first of these sentiments, in the first of Abraham Lincoln's self-presentations as a public figure? His support for "internal improvements." In fact, he composed a little essay on the proven public utility of these improvements—that is, of better means of transportation like good roads and navigable streams. It is amusing to note that he conceded—Lincoln as speaker, debater, and lawyer would be a great conceder—that there was now appearing on the scene an internal improvement even better than the developed roads, rivers, and canals that he was himself advocating—namely, the "rail road." "No other improvement can equal [it] in utility," wrote the young philosopher, because it will provide "a never failing source of communication, between places of business remotely situated from each other."* "Upon the rail road," wrote the very young candidate Lincoln, "the regular progress of commercial intercourse is not interrupted by either high or low water or freezing weather . . ." But "however high our imaginations may be heated at thoughts of it"—this rail road of the future—we are forced to "shrink from our pleasing anticipations" by "a heart appalling shock" at the cost. Therefore, "the improvement of the Sangamon River is an object much better suited to our infant resources." Abraham Lincoln was just the man to tell you how to do that, which he would do, in detail—unusually impressive detail for a local campaign document.

Sangamon County needs "some more easy means of communication." And there's the river. But whatever the river's natural advantages may be, it will never be useful to any great extent "without being improved by art." Art means deliberate human intervention. And in context (running for the legislative seat) it means: deliberate intervention by collective action, by government. Lincoln in this document, as in his strong support for "internal improvements" throughout his legislative career, would take for granted that these projects must be public, undertaken by government. Government in a developing nation must supply what economists of a later age would call the "social overhead capital" for a developing nation.

* Because the telegraph, first used in 1844, had not quite yet, in 1832, separated "communication" from "transportation," so the two had not yet quite been separated verbally and conceptually, and one used the word "communication" when we now would say "transportation."

What young Lincoln stood for when he first came before the public as a candidate for office was not an end to the abomination of human slavery, or an appeal for the spread of democracy, or a proclamation of the ideal of equality, or a proposal for a more perfect union, but rather the clearing of the Sangamon River in central Illinois so that it would be navigable by vessels of from twenty-five to thirty tons as high as the mouth of the South Fork.

He ran rather well in that first race, for a young newcomer, but—as previously noted—he finished eighth in a field of thirteen candidates, of whom only the first four were elected. When he ran again two years later and won, he had visions going far beyond the driftwood in one river. This time, in 1834, he finished second and thus was chosen to one of the four Sangamon County seats, and he spent the whopping sum of sixty dollars (borrowed) buying a new tailor-made suit, and he proceeded to the state capitol in Vandalia at twenty-five to begin his lifelong career of, as we say now when we want to be lofty about it, "public service."

Mark E. Neely Jr. gently chided Lincoln scholars in later centuries for their lack of interest in Lincoln's early efforts in support of economic development. They have been discomfited by Lincoln's early career, "occupied as it was," Neely went on to say, "with canal companies, bank stock subscribers, and builders of toll bridges." His consorting with people like that was (now quoting Neely again) "not an alliance of convenience, necessary to promote his serious career in pursuit of liberty and equality and Union: the developers' program *was* his serious career, his life-work until the 1850's . . ."

Perhaps we may qualify this pithy summary to say that Lincoln's serious career was *not* exactly that of the developer; his serious career was as *legislator*, as a *politician* supporting, among other things but at the top of the list, development. As a legislator—a distinct career in itself. Lincoln may have had some direct dealings with builders of toll bridges and bank stock subscribers; but he *certainly* had dealings—daily and intense each winter during the session—with his fellow legislators, and with his party comrades and the voting public in the other months. He was not a developer; he was a politician and a legislator.

He was a supporter of a thriving capitalist economy, and an advocate of energetic positive government action to assist in its thriving, because he believed that would serve the ordinary person making his way from poor beginnings to a better material situation, as he himself would do.

. . .

The Whigs had different cultural emphases than the Democrats. When you read Daniel Walker Howe's *The Political Culture of the American Whigs* you find yourself picking up from page after page two words: "improvement" and "industry," both used in more than one application. Economic improvement, certainly, but not superior to, or divorced from, a broader cultural improvement, or even—it was an age and place not embarrassed to say it—moral improvement. Also self-improvement. But not "self-improvement" in formulas and in isolation, and not as narrow and shallow as some of the vast later American cult of "self-improvement" would be. Social improvement—the self and society joined. Intellectual improvement, educational improvement, even—perhaps especially—moral improvement.

The Whigs in general were less expansionist than the Jackson Democrats, and some Whigs put the point this way: Rather than *quantitative* development by the spreading of the American population over ever more territory, let us continue the *qualitative* development of the young society where it is. The Whig Party was a combination of elements unlike that of either of the later parties. It was the party of commerce, industry, and the economic elite; businessmen and bankers were usually Whigs. But it was also the party, as we have said, of positive government (the Jacksonians would say, because government action aided business and commerce—to the detriment of the farmer and the poor man). And it was also, somewhat more than the Democrats, the party of *reform:* The Whig Party included Horace Mann, the great originator of public schools; Joshua Giddings, the leading opponent of slavery in Congress (and almost all other opponents of slavery in Congress, who were few); Lyman Beecher, the leading clergyman, from whose influence (and family) would come a host of reforms. It would also be, somewhat more than the Democrats, the party of artists and intellectuals, of leading lawyers and judges. Lincoln had in him, the extravagant endings to his early speeches reveal, and as his later life would certainly reveal, a powerful moral idealism: a yearning, a purpose, to move toward something more worthy—in and for himself, certainly, but by no means only that. Something more worthy generally—morally better, as we might say. But he was not the sort of moral idealist who regards the material base of life as beneath the dignity of a moralist's attention.

The Whig Party had been born in conflict with one whom they regarded as an overbearing president, a "tyrant," "King Andrew" Jackson, with his "usurpations." And there was doctrine in the English Whig past and the classical sources upon which they drew that centered "republicanism" in legislatures, with the menace found in tyrants, Caesars, kings, and courts. The American Whigs inherited some of that, so that even though they were, as compared to the least-government Jacksonian Democrats, the party of positive government, they were *not* the party of positive *executive* government. (The parties in this different time put together the elements of politics and morals in different ways from later days; one cannot make one-to-one analogies between their parties and ours.) When in 1837 this Illinois Whig would give that first major public address, the much-examined Lyceum speech, a central theme would be a very Whiggish warning against a Caesar.

It would prove most significant, as Lincoln's career turned out, that the Whig party was also the party of nationalism and of the Union.

In January of 1830—early in Andrew Jackson's first term as president— there took place on the floor of the United States Senate the most famous debate in its history. It featured what would be the most celebrated of all American speeches until it was supplanted by greater addresses given one day by Lincoln himself—Daniel Webster's famous reply to a supporter of John C. Calhoun, Robert Hayne. Webster's great theme was the Union, the Nation. More than that: the Unified Nation as the bearer of a great destiny and a moral ideal, these last represented by the word "liberty." The Union and liberty were intertwined, inseparable; liberty was not superior or prior to, or more fundamental than, the Union, but inextricably bound up in it. As Webster's famous ringing peroration concluded: "Liberty *and* Union, now and forever, one and inseparable."

When one pictures young Lincoln, at some moment near his twenty-first birthday, reading this peroration of Webster's speech, one might notice Webster's anticipation of the loss of national meaning if the Union should be "broken and dishonored fragments"; "discordant, dissevered, discordant, belligerent"; "a land rent with civil feuds, or drenched, it may be, in fraternal blood." Thirty years later Lincoln would sit at a table in Springfield, hidden away from visitors, writing the speech that would be the first he would give to the whole body of Americans as president-elect of the United States, and he would ask that three documents—only three— be brought to him as resources. One of them was Webster's reply to Hayne.

The argument was made by some Democrats and Calhoun supporters that the states had preceded and created the Union, that they granted to the federal Union only limited and specified powers, retaining all others themselves, and even that a state had a right on its own motion to secede from the Union, or at least to "nullify" particular federal actions. Two years after the Webster-Hayne debate there would come the Nullification Crisis, in which Clay and Webster (and presumably young Lincoln, by then living on his own in New Salem) would *support* President Jackson—whom they otherwise opposed—in his blunt rejection of the South Carolinians' claim of a right to "nullify" a federal law. Another of the three items Lincoln would use, in the secession winter of 1860–61, in composing his First Inaugural Address, was President Jackson's message in 1832 against South Carolina's attempt at nullification.

Here was this unusual new country that had been put together out of pre-existing, formally separate colonial entities. *E Pluribus Unum.* How *unum* were they, or was it? How "united" were the states, when the young Hoosier in Pigeon Creek started thinking about which side he was on? The perennial and universal pulling and tugging between the center and the periphery, the whole and the parts, which occurs in every human society, in this huge and variegated new country took the form of a struggle over the respective powers, and beyond that the respective moral meanings, of the Union on the one side and of the states on the other. Young Lincoln as a Clay man instead of a Jackson man, and an admirer of Daniel Webster, would have been on the national side, the Unionist side, of that question.

The full measure of this young man's high and aspiring romantic attachment to an entity larger than himself was deposited, not within the boundaries of Indiana or Illinois, but in the *Union,* in the *nation* that our fathers brought forth upon this continent.

It was that union, moreover—and not any lesser entity, not any mere state—that was the bearer of moral principles of universal value. Daniel Webster had said that liberty and Union were inseparable; the one did not precede the second, nor was it to be realized outside it. When in 1852 it fell to the more mature Lincoln to give that eulogy for the greatest of Whigs, Henry Clay, he would say that "he [Clay] loved his country partly because it was his own country, but mostly because it was a free country." And so, then, it might be said of the young Whig (and the older Republican) Abraham Lincoln. He saw this Union as the bearer of universal values—as conceived in liberty and, he significantly added, dedicated to the proposition that all men are created equal. He believed that on its fate turned a great world issue: whether any nation so conceived and so dedicated could long endure.

. . .

For that small minority of writers about Lincoln who are detractors, on the Left or on the Right, it may serve their debunking purpose to hold that indeed Abraham Lincoln was, through and through, a lifelong career *politician.* But other Lincoln students, who share the celebration of Lincoln on the one side and the cultural disdain for politicians on the other, may find themselves, as they learn more and more about the actual details of his life, with a problem.

One way they may solve it is to chop Lincoln in two: They may present him as a mere politician up to March 4, 1861, but then imply that he abruptly changed into The Greatest Man in the World. Or the transforming moment can be moved back to 1854, when the Kansas-Nebraska Act provoked him to make opposition to slavery his central purpose, and so saw him suddenly lifted up from having been an ordinary politician, dealing with legislative committees and party calculations, with rivers and harbors and quorum calls and appeals to the German vote, to become instead a transcendent moral hero dealing with liberty, equality, and union.

But although, to be sure, Lincoln changed, as we all do, and kept learning, as some do—I believe Lincoln learned a great deal—I suggest, nevertheless, that there was on this point no radical discontinuity in his life. Having the awareness and doing the deeds that are encompassed by the term "politician" would be essential to his achievement. In fact, some of his most impressive political accomplishments came toward the end of his life: getting himself renominated in 1864 and, with the help of Sherman's armies and the soldiers' vote, reelected, and then, in the last months of his life, persuading enough Democrats in the Thirty-ninth Congress to support the Thirteenth Amendment, ending slavery, so that it passed in Congress and was on its way to ratification.

There would never come a time when Abraham Lincoln abandoned the role of politician, or rose above it to some allegedly higher moral realm. What he did instead as a lifelong politician was to realize that role's fullest moral possibilities.

CHAPTER SIX

Rising Public Man

1. WHY THIS VOTE?

Vandalia, Illinois. The temporary state capital, a river-bluff town with perhaps eight hundred residents, perhaps one hundred buildings, perhaps six taverns or inns, and certainly one jail.

The morning of January 20, 1837. More than eighty white males, not one of whom had been born in this frontier state, seated at long tables, three to a table, in the west end of a not-yet-finished two-story building with the plaster still wet—hastily built in the effort to try to keep the capital in Vandalia. The House of Representatives of the new state of Illinois.

HOUSE SPEAKER: The question now comes on the adoption of the joint committee resolutions on the subject of domestic slavery, as amended.

The Illinois General Assembly had been asked by the governor to respond to passionate appeals from the legislatures of Virginia, Kentucky, Alabama, and Mississippi to their northern counterparts to do something, *please,* to stamp out the new menace of abolitionism that had arisen in the early 1830s. The slave-state resolutions were full of words like "insurrection" and "incendiary" and "peril"—in fact, "imminent" peril. Kentucky's legislature said that the abolitionists' pamphlets with their "disgusting" woodcuts were inciting "insubordination, perhaps insurrection," among slaves. Their actions were "calculated to deluge our country in blood," is the way Alabama put it. Alabama said to the sister legislatures in the North, "We have believed and still believe that when you are fully apprised of the evils which this unholy band of cowardly assassins was bringing upon us," you will take action. What action? Mississippi urged the northern lawmakers to "suppress by penal laws those who are plotting . . . to undermine, disturb or abolish our institutions of domestic slavery."

So a joint committee of the two branches of the Illinois legislature considered these heartfelt appeals. Illinois was then a sparsely populated frontier state, almost all of whose residents were newcomers, most of them from slave states. Immediately after statehood, Illinois had enacted a harsh black code, and had only narrowly defeated a serious effort to restore legalized slavery in the state. Slavery lingered as a de facto presence. In 1831, just six years before this vote, this same state legislature had passed a law effectively excluding free black persons from settling in the state by requiring a $1,000 bond (a prohibitive sum) to guarantee good behavior while in the state. The people of Illinois had overwhelming racial prejudices, a powerful repugnance for the new abolitionists, and not a little sympathy with slavery itself.

So, not surprisingly, the joint committee's statement expressed "a deep regard and affection for our brethren of the South," and an assurance "that upon any proper occasion they would fly to their assistance." And it adopted many of the slave-state pejoratives in condemning the abolitionists. The committee resolved "that the purposes of the abolitionists are highly reprehensible, and that their ends, even if peaceably attained, would be productive of the most deleterious consequences for every portion of the Union."

"Your committee cannot conceive," the report said, "how any true friend of the black man can hope to benefit him through the instrumentality of abolition societies."

And so now on this January morning the question came to the House of the proposed acceptance of this joint committee report.

Mr. Hardin and Mr. Walker of Morgan County asked for the yeas and nays: a recorded vote.

SPEAKER: The Clerk will call the roll.

Mr. Able?—Aye.
Mr. Aldrick?—Aye.
Mr. Ball?—Aye.
Mr. Barnett?—Aye.
Mr. Bentley?—Aye.
Mr. Carpenter?—Aye.

Mr. Cloud?—Aye.

The ayes continue through Cartwright, Craig, Crain, Cullom, Davidson, Davis.

Mr. Dawson? (John Dawson, at forty-five, was the oldest of the Long Nine.)—Aye.

Mr. Douglass? (Yes, it is Stephen Douglas, disguised under two *s*'s, one of which he will later drop: delegate from Morgan County, twenty-six years old.)—Aye.

Mr. Dubois? (Jesse Dubois—at twenty-four back in 1834, the youngest delegate—a friend of Lincoln, and a future state official. When, twenty-four years later, the train bearing President-elect Lincoln will leave Springfield on the first leg of the journey to Washington, one of those on board will be Jesse Dubois.)—Aye.

Mr. Edmonston?—Aye.

Mr. Edwards? (This is indeed Ninian W. Edwards, the future brother-in-law of Abraham Lincoln, a handsome and wealthy Kentucky aristocrat.)—Aye.

Mr. Elkin? (W. F. Elkin, another of the Long Nine, was at forty-four second to Dawson in age.)—Aye.

Mr. English?—Aye.

Mr. Enloe? (Benjamin Enloe of Johnson County, who wanted to continue as warden of the state penitentiary at Alton, was not supported by Lincoln or most others of the Long Nine in that quest, but votes for Springfield nonetheless.)—Aye.

Mr. French?—Aye.

Mr. Galbreath?—Aye.

Mr. Hardin? (John J. Hardin would be a leading Whig politician, and later a successful rival to Lincoln for the Seventh District seat in Congress.)—Aye.

Mr. Harris?—Aye.

Mr. Hinshaw?—Aye.

Mr. Hogan? (The Reverend John Hogan of Alton, "Honest John," a former Methodist circuit rider, a friend of Lincoln's who when Alton no longer had a chance to be chosen as the capital would vote for Springfield.)—Aye.

Mr. Huey?—Aye.

Mr. Hunt?—Aye.

Mr. Lagrow?—Aye.

Mr. Lane?—Aye.

Mr. Leary?—Aye.

Mr. Lincoln?—Nay.

When in a legislative body the steady drone of expected votes is interrupted by an unexpected vote, there may be a suppressed stir, a rustle of surprise, veiled glances, an exchange of significantly raised eyebrows. The twenty-eight-year-old Lincoln, now in his second term as representative from Sangamon, was the first voice to vote no.

As the vote went on, the ayes continued overwhelmingly to predominate. These included, as was to be expected, James Ralston of Adams County and the future Civil War general John McClernand, both leading Democrats, the chairmen respectively of the joint committee and of the House committee on revisions; and James Shields, another emerging Democratic leader.*

But there would now be a sprinkling of occasional "nays"—five more, including two others of the Long Nine, Andrew McCormick and Dan Stone—before the roll call ended.

The vote is seventy-seven in the affirmative, six in the negative, the ayes have it, the motion is carried.

The clerk will inform the senate, and ask their concurrence.

With the senate's *unanimous* concurrence (which meant that there were only six votes in *both* houses against the motion), Illinois would officially respond to the slave-state appeals with an expression of its abhorrence of abolitionism and its sympathy with slaveholders under abolitionists' assault.

But the vote in the house had not been quite unanimous.

Why did young Lincoln vote no?

Did this vote in any way serve his political ambitions? Did it advance his interests? Not in the immediate situation in the General Assembly, and not back home with the voters, either. And not in any future role in Illinois politics that he could then have foreseen.

---

* Readers of Lincoln biographies will remember Shields as the short, fiery, vain Irishman whom Mary Todd and her friend Julia Jayne mocked in a journalistic effort for which Lincoln then, perhaps out of gallantry, took the blame, so that Shields and Lincoln almost ended up fighting a duel with broadswords in 1842.

There would have been no pressure to vote as he did—rather the opposite.

He voted no on a proposal on which his colleagues, associates, and friends were overwhelmingly—better than twelve to one—voting yes.

Four of his six house colleagues in the Long Nine voted yes.

By inference from the unanimous senate vote, both of his Long Nine colleagues in that body (thus, six of the nine) voted yes.

Almost all of the fellow delegates whose votes he and the Sangamon Nine needed in their effort to win the capital for Springfield voted yes.

His elders, his mentors voted yes. If John T. Stuart had been there, we can surely infer from his subsequent politics, he would have voted yes.

His present and future opponents—Douglas(s), Shields, Hardin— certainly voted yes.

There surely would not have been any party pressure to vote as he did. He certainly did not vote with the bulk of the Whigs.

And what of the voters back home, and of his political prospects? He was going to (and did) face the voters again. All of the political risk would have been in voting no, and perhaps appearing to have been soft on abolitionism.

One cannot help but conclude that he voted no on the merits.

After the vote on the domestic slavery resolutions this January morning the House proceeded to other business, mingling big matters and small matters in the way legislatures do: "an act to encourage the killing of wolves"; a remonstrance against relocating part of a state road from Springfield to Lewistown; an amendment to an act incorporating the Alton Marine and Fire Insurance Co. But the two big matters that occupied this 1836–37 session soon returned to the table and, after much politics, were brought to conclusion.

One of these was a costly new undertaking for the developing frontier state, providing for the building of a far-reaching system of railroads, canals, and navigable rivers. This was one of the most memorable sessions of the Illinois House. There was campaigning to be done with one's colleagues for a railroad spur here, and canal there, a river widening in one's district. There were lobbyists with their proposals surrounding the legislators. If you had told the legislature, in the excitement of their debate on that great project, that historians in a later century would pay less attention to that legislation than they would to that going-nowhere resolution about abolition, they would have had a hard time believing you. And among those who would have been surprised would have been the lanky young Whig leader from Sangamon County. Lincoln was one of the most enthusiastic supporters of the internal improvement system, wheeling and dealing to get it done.

The other major item on the agenda of that session of the Illinois General Assembly in which Lincoln and his fellow tall legislators from Sangamon had a particular interest was the selection of a permanent site for the state capital. Vandalia was an expressly temporary choice, its tenure as capital due to last only until 1840, although it had aspirations to continue. But there were other candidates, and the strong argument that the increase in population to the north indicated the need for a capital located nearer the center of the state than Vandalia. Lincoln was wheeling and dealing on that matter too.

The Internal Improvements Act was passed on January 31, with much rejoicing in Vandalia; the relocation of the state capital to Springfield was passed on February 28, with much rejoicing in Springfield but not in Vandalia.

And then on March 3, just before the house's March 6 adjournment, two of the legislators made a little reprise, on paper only, of that abolition matter. Lincoln and his Long Nine colleague Dan Stone did "spread upon the record" (as legislative bodies often grandly put it) their reasons for voting as they had done on the antiabolitionist resolutions passed six weeks earlier.

Stone had been a member of the original joint committee—but then in the end voted against the passage of the final product. He was a man originally from Vermont, part of the New England influx that was now beginning to dilute the heavy flow into Illinois from slave states. He was a graduate of Middlebury, a lawyer who had already had a political career in Ohio; he would be appointed a judge in the summer following this episode, and so would not face the electorate again.

Stone joined his tall colleague as they (so we may picture them) conferred in some room at the Vandalia Inn or the National Hotel about a written explanation for the record of the vote they had cast six busy weeks before.

Why did they do this?

. . .

"Protest" is their word for what they produced, but their statement does not have the unequivocal clenched-fist character that militants in other situations would associate with the word. It has instead a certain on-the-one-hand, on-the-other-hand quality. An early biographer of Stephen Douglas remarked that it "makes a statement, and then, as though afraid of it, backs off like a crab."

Here's what Lincoln and Stone said in their "protest." I will separate the paragraphs and number the three key "they believe" sections for convenience of later reference.

> Resolutions upon the subject of domestic slavery having passed both branches of the General Assembly at its present session, the undersigned hereby protest against the passage of the same.
>
> [1] They believe that the institution of slavery is founded on both injustice and bad policy; but that the promulgation of abolition doctrines tends rather to increase than to abate its evils.
>
> [2] They believe that the Congress of the United States has no power, under the constitution, to interfere with the institution of slavery in the different States.
>
> [3] They believe that the Congress of the United States has the power, under the constitution, to abolish slavery in the District of Columbia; but that that power ought not to be exercised unless at the request of the people of said District.
>
> The difference between these opinions and those contained in the said resolutions, is their reason for entering this protest.
>
> *Dan Stone*
> *A. Lincoln*
> Representatives from the county of Sangamon

"The undersigned"; "hereby"; "the passage of the same"; "the people of said District"; "said resolutions": These men were obviously lawyers (Stone for some years, Lincoln just since the previous September). One can almost hear the "whereas" before the first sentence.

By putting their "protest" in this form, these "Representatives from the county of Sangamon" played a trick on the troops of biographers and researchers who would in later decades be swarming over every moment in Lincoln's life. They did not make clear exactly what their "protest" was. They did not do what one might expect protesting legislators who voted no in a very small minority to do—to make a ringing, or at least a clear, statement of their objection: the assembly has said *x*, but we on the contrary say *y*. Instead, they composed three carefully written sentences beginning with "They believe," two of which are compound sentences containing two contrasting assertions connected by the conjunction "but," and then asserted, laconically, that the difference between these multiple and complex carefully controlled statements and the resolutions the assembly passed is the reason for the negative vote. They leave it to the reader to discern just what that difference is.

So what is the difference from what the assembly said? Start with the second, the middle point in the three Lincoln/Stone points, the simplest one, about slavery in the slave states. The original joint committee report rather awkwardly had said:

> Resolved, that the right of property in slaves is [made?] sacred to the slave holding States by the Federal Constitution, and that they cannot be deprived of that right without their consent.

Lincoln and Stone say:

> They believe that the Congress of the United States has no power, under the Constitution, to interfere with the institution of slavery in the different States.

Lincoln and Stone drop the claim that something is "sacred" and drop any reference to a right to property. The focus and subject shifts from the *states*, with their allegedly "sacred" alleged "right," to *Congress*. What the Constitution is said to do shifts from a heightened moral guarantee of a sacred right to a more strictly legal limitation of congressional power.

Now to the two compound sentences. On the first point, the assembly simply said "that we highly disapprove of the formation of abolition societies, and of the doctrines promulgated by them," without committing themselves one way or the other about slavery. But not Lincoln and Stone. They say, in effect, "We join in criticizing abolitionists, but let us keep things straight by saying *first* that we find slavery to be immoral: 'the institution of slavery is founded on both injustice and bad policy.' After which we then criticize the abolitionists."

But they don't criticize them in the sweeping and many-sided way the committee did. The joint committee, and therefore presumably the Illinois General Assembly by its overwhelming majority, included a pungent collection of evils of many kinds the abolitionists were supposed to have caused:

- forging new irons for the black man;
- adding an hundred fold to the rigors of slavery;
- scattering the fire brands of discord and disunion;
- arousing the turbulent passions of the monster mob;
- threatening the violation of the sacred rights of private property;
- producing, even if their ends were to be peaceably attained, the most deleterious consequences for every portion of the Union.

None of this, or anything like it, appears in the "protest." Lincoln and Stone criticize the abolitionists instead specifically and only for the single reason that abolition "tends rather to increase than to abate [slavery's] evils." They say "*tends* to increase"—not a sweeping assertion of a long list of evils actually produced, but a discriminate judgment of a tendency. And the tendency emphasizes again the *evils* of slavery. The new abolitionism may be the wrong way to fight those evils.

And their preliminary statement—unmatched by the house—that slavery is unjust surely is a major point of difference. Albert Beveridge rather minimized the importance of Lincoln and Stone's statement that slavery is unjust: "The only real difference between his [Lincoln's] views and those of the majority of the House was moral—the 'injustice' of slavery." Why does he say "only," as though that were not important? It is a key fact about Lincoln's whole career that he was *always* clear that slavery was a great moral wrong, and he always said so—beginning here (in his public life) as a young state legislator. That is the kernel in the whole event: that Lincoln and Stone did, and the assembly did not, say plainly that slavery is unjust. Lincoln's doing so at this early stage, when he is twenty-eight (he had a birthday on February 12, between the vote and the protest), adumbrates what he will do in the 1850s: to keep clearly and explicitly stating the relevant general moral principle, even though its implications cannot at the time be fully realized, even though practical men would say, What is the point of such general moral statements where there is no immediate practical application?

Only after having stated thus the moral foundation, the injustice of slavery, do young Lincoln and his older colleague Stone join in criticizing the abolitionist movement; they do so, as stated above, in a much calmer, more discriminate, and limited way than the sweeping and florid many-sided condemnation by the joint committee.

Beveridge, it seems to me, also gets this wrong. In an undue eagerness to keep Lincoln radically separated from anything that smacks of abolitionism, he remarks (I don't know on what possible evidence) that "as to Abolitionists, no member disapproved of them more strongly than he [Lincoln]."

Now, it is presumably true that Lincoln disapproved of the abolitionists—but can one actually say that *no* member of this radically racist, southern-derived legislature disapproved *more*? Not Usher Linder, who eight months later in the same year—incredibly, while serving as attorney general of the state—would in a demagogic speech and parliamentary action help to rouse the mob in Alton that would kill the abolitionist editor Elijah Lovejoy? And then propose to prosecute, not the members of that mob, but those who had tried to defend Lovejoy?

Or—not the members who wrote that joint committee report, with its sweeping, many-sided condemnation of abolitionists? There is nothing approaching that hostile fervor in any existing writing of Lincoln. When he would give his first important public speech to a general audience the next January—the much-examined Lyceum Address—although he condemned mob violence, he certainly did not blame the recent incidents of mob violence, as did many members of the legislature (as in effect the joint committee had done before the fact with its reference to the "monster mobs") on the abolitionists. Although Lincoln in that speech would be cautious and indirect, he condemned not the abolitionists but (along with others) the mobs that persecuted abolitionists—including, not by name but by clear implication and one oblique reference, the mob that killed Elijah Lovejoy.

The third of the careful sentences by the Sangamon pair, about the District, has not drawn much attention from writers in later decades, because slavery-in-the-District was a particular, if detailed, preoccupation of the moment, which would be overborne by mighty events in the 1850s and the war. When slavery in the District was finally ended in 1862, it was done by a Congress from which the southern states had withdrawn, passing a law that would be signed by President Lincoln in the midst of a great war for so much higher stakes that the action would be overshadowed. But in 1837 it mattered what you said about the possibility of ending slavery in the District of Columbia. It was the epitome of one's view of the *Union,* and both the first of the incremental steps toward someday ending slavery and the symbolic battleground, before the territories acquired from Mexico took over this role, of the nation's future with respect to slavery.

While the gag-rule conflict over the capacity of Congress to end slavery in the District tied up the House in Washington—argument about it raged in Washington—out in Illinois the joint committee proposed this resolution:

> Resolved, That the General Government cannot abolish slavery in the District of Columbia, against the consent of the citizens of said District, without a manifest breach of good faith.

Once again, this Illinois resolution, severe though it may sound to the ears of another time, fell short of the harshest position of the defenders of slavery—John C. Calhoun, James Henry Hammond, Waddy Thompson, Henry Wise—in Washington. They held that it was *unconstitutional* for the "General Government" to propose to abolish slavery in the District— indeed, even to discuss, even to mention, the topic—and they were scathing in denunciation of those who indulged in mild timidities like merely saying that it would be "a manifest breach of good faith." I infer from the record in the *House Journal* that this third resolution provoked dispute and efforts at amendment, as the other two had not done, and that the discussion in the Illinois House echoed to some degree the battle in the United States House. In Illinois there were repeated efforts to move a "division of the question" specifically so that the third resolution could be considered, and there were motions to amend it from opposite directions.

These contrasting efforts at amendment were offered by two members from Sangamon who would before long be brothers-in-law. The amendment offered by Ninian W. Edwards would have had the resolution say not only that efforts to end slavery there were "unwise" but also that they were "unconstitutional." It received only six votes. In the last days of the 1838–39 session Edwards tried again, proposing a resolution stating that efforts to abolish slavery in the District of Columbia were "inexpedient, unwise, and unconstitutional." The last of these words was the root of the controversy. Lincoln's friend Jesse Dubois moved to strike the word "unconstitutional," which the house voted to do, and then passed Edwards's denatured resolution.

The contrasting proposal, back in the previous session in 1837, was offered by a man who would soon be a frequent visitor in Edwards's home.* Lincoln moved to insert, at a relevant point, the phrase "unless the people of said District petition for same"—thus not only implying that Congress had the constitutional power to end slavery in the District but also hinting, more positively than anything the assembly would pass, that it might be possible someday under these specific conditions actually to do so. His amendment was, without a recorded vote, "not agreed to."

Then came the vote on the whole proposal, supporting it 77–6, with Lincoln one of the six, and six weeks later, his and Stone's explanation of their vote.

The sentence on the District in the original joint committee proposal, to repeat, had said:

Resolved, That the General Government cannot abolish slavery in the District of Columbia, against the consent of the citizens of said District, without a manifest breach of good faith.

Lincoln and Stone in their "protest" turn it around, first emphasizing the positive power, not what cannot be done but what can be:

They believe that the Congress of the United States has the power, under the Constitution, to abolish slavery in the District of Columbia; but that that power ought not to be exercised unless at the request of the people of said District.

In the U.S. House of Representatives, where the issue was just then in that year forced upon the body by the abolition petitions and the gag rule, the flat, explicit positive statement in the first clause would have been very bold.

Twelve years later, when he would himself be a United States congressman, Lincoln would take the initiative to devise a bill—aborted, of course—that would have provided for the ending of slavery in "said District."

Biographers and historians emphasize the long delay between the vote, Friday, January 20, and the Lincoln/Stone "protest," Friday, March 3, and note also that the written protest was spread upon the record just

---

* It was in just this year that Edwards's wife's half-sister Mary Todd came to visit for the first time and met Abraham Lincoln. Edwards, to Lincoln's chagrin, would become a Democrat in 1852 and would support Douglas in 1858 and 1860.

at the end of the session, too late for discussion. Some infer that this postponement had the purpose of keeping Lincoln and Stone's controversial opinions on the hot but abstract issue of abolitionism from interfering with their work on the quite concrete issue of getting Springfield named the capital—accomplished on February 28. That does seem plausible. But putting all the emphasis on that point may have obscured another, perhaps more striking point—that they issued any written "protest" at all.

Why did they do it? Legislators do not often do that—six weeks after a vote has been taken, now to write out one's position and put it in the record. Legislators vote and go on to the next thing. The other four who voted no—not to mention the seventy-seven who voted yes—did not feel it necessary to explain, in writing, for the house record, *their* vote. But Lincoln and Stone did.

Douglas Wilson suggests that the primary motive may have been to make clear that their "no" vote did *not* signify that they were sympathetic to abolitionism. That may have been one subordinate motive, but if you look at their statement you see that that cannot have been the whole story, can it? If making clear that they agreed in denouncing abolitionists had been their entire or their primary purpose, they could have written a much simpler and more straightforward statement of that single point. And they would not have gone out of their way to say that slavery was unjust and bad policy. As their "protest" is complex, so their reason for writing it must have been complex.

It is tempting to make it simple. When writing about Lincoln in a later century, after his transcendent reputation has been established in the minds of both reader and writer, one may be inclined to say: Young Lincoln at age twenty-eight bravely stepped forward in the Illinois Assembly and condemned slavery. But that is not quite what happened. He condemned slavery, but he did not step forward; he was faced with the necessity to vote on resolutions that arose on the initiative of others. And condemning slavery is not all he did.

Or one may want to say that the assembly adopted "proslavery resolutions" that Lincoln then opposed—but they were not exactly proslavery resolutions. Some of the members surely would have said, if pushed to it, that they, too, disapproved of slavery; the long joint committee report, written partly from the point of view of the colonization movement, included phrases that, although in the context of condemning abolition or of saying nothing could be done about it, nevertheless implied that slavery was wrong—"the unfortunate condition of our fellow men, whose lots are cast in the thraldom in a land of liberty and peace," for example.

Well, then, one might say that at least Lincoln's statement was explicitly and clearly *anti*slavery, and I think that is correct as far as it goes. But we do have to go on to say that he also made explicit his disapproval of abolitionism and his recognition that Congress could not touch slavery in the states and should not do so in the District unless the people there petitioned for it.

I suggest a purpose at a different level: that Lincoln and Stone wanted to put down on paper a cool, rational, succinct summary statement on this complex, irrational, passion-filled topic. Stone, one may infer, sat through the overheated discussions in the joint committee (to judge by its product) with, presumably, mounting frustration (to judge by the fact that he tried on the house floor to move a division of the question—separating for consideration part by part—resolutions proposed by a committee of which he had himself originally been a member, and even more by the fact that in the end he voted no.) Lincoln was the young lawyer/politician who, ten months later, in the midst of the fierce excitements of the furor over abolitionism and mob action will give a public lecture counseling "cold, calculating, unimpassioned reason."

I infer that we can interpret their purpose in that way from the characteristics of their "protest": its name notwithstanding, it is a page of carefully formulated lawyers' prose, of moral reasoning—or, rather, of moral conclusion reflecting unstated moral reasoning—in a political context. It was a work not of sweeping moral stand-taking, but of discriminate judgments. Their statement was several notches less critical of abolition than was the assembly's and clearly stated, as the assembly did not, that Congress could constitutionally end slavery.

And they stated explicitly what the resolutions did not state at all (and some members would not agree to, and many more would not want to state explicitly in this time and context), the fundamental moral statement that Abraham Lincoln would keep clear and make explicit throughout his career from beginning to end: that slavery is unjust.

2. DON'T SHOOT EDITORS

Ten months later Lincoln had occasion to condemn, obliquely but pointedly, the action of the mobs that were attacking abolitionists.

This happened in Springfield. A month after he and Stone put that

protest in the record, and the portentous 1837 internal improvements session of the Illinois General Assembly came to an end, he rode into the new
capital-city-to-be with all his belongings in his saddlebags. He now would
make Springfield, the new capital and a growing center with a population
of fifteen hundred, his home.

He was a bachelor still. The sad romance with Ann Rutledge was a
short time back in his New Salem past; his rather inept courting of Mary
Owens, and his tumultuous courtship with Mary Todd, were just ahead.
With John T. Stuart's encouragement, he had read Blackstone's *Commen-
taries* and other books of the law, been admitted to the bar, and now joined
Stuart as partner in his law firm.

One of his new activities, as not only a politician but also a rising young
professional man, was to give lectures. He gave his first on January 27,
1838, just eight months after moving to Springfield, to an organization
called the Young Men's Lyceum.

Lyceums were a typical expression of the self-improving, culturally
uplifting voluntary associations of nineteenth-century Protestant America.
The members of lyceums would take turns lecturing to each other and
debating with each other on the kinds of topics one would expect of a
nineteenth-century debating/lecturing society. (Some of their topics could
still be debated and lectured about in the twenty-first century: "Ought
capital punishment to be abolished?" was the first question for both of the
two Springfield lyceums.)

An older lyceum sometimes heard nonpolitical addresses—on the
properties of water, on the philosophy of vision, on the heart, circulation,
nutrition, and longevity—while the newer group that Lincoln joined stuck
mostly to politics and civic life.

So there is Lincoln at twenty-eight, newly arrived in town, an earnest
self-improver, signed up to give a lecture in January to this lyceum. It was a
chance to display to a different audience from the legislature or the stump
his powers of intellect and oratory.

Of course he wrote out carefully all that he would say, as he would do
with major speeches all his life. His topic was a slightly pompous one of
the sort lecturers often did choose: "The Perpetuation of Our Political
Institutions." Perhaps his choice of that subject was stimulated by a general discussion at the lyceum on the previous December 13 on the question: "Do the signs of the present times indicate the downfall of this
government?"

The signs of the time prominently included "outrages committed by mobs," as Lincoln would call them, and chief among these (he did not say explicitly) were outrages committed by mobs against abolitionists. And one such outrage (he also did not quite say explicitly) had happened right there in Illinois, not seventy miles away, in Alton, and not twelve weeks before Lincoln gave his address. This was the killing of the abolitionist minister and editor Elijah Lovejoy.

When Lovejoy and his press had been driven out of Saint Louis, he moved across the river to Alton. A welcoming mob in Alton promptly upon his arriving threw his press into the Mississippi. When he promised not to discuss abolition, the good citizens of Alton, indignant at the action of the mob, bought him a new one. When he did not keep his promise, another mob performed the same service for *that* press. When indignant abolitionists nationwide raised funds to buy yet another press, and pleas on the part of responsible Alton citizens could not stop Lovejoy from printing yet more inflammatory editorials, still another press joined the others in a curious collection on the river bottom off Alton, Illinois. The one that joined its fellows when Lovejoy was shot and killed by rioters' muskets was his fourth press. All of this was accompanied by the most intense public discussion, uproar, and conflict, not only in Alton but, particularly after Lovejoy's killing, across the nation.

So young Lincoln, seated at a table somewhere in his new hometown (in John T. Stuart's law office? in the room above the store he shared with his new friend Joshua Speed?) wrote out by hand what he was going to say to that lyceum about mob violence.

At least, that is what he wrote about for the first half of the address. But then he rather abruptly veered off onto another theme, another danger to our institutions (so he said): the possibility that some new, ambitious demagogue will overturn them—and in the twentieth century, interpreters looking back would seize upon that theme with psychologizing glee, and apply it one way and another to Lincoln himself, and thereby almost displace attention to his original theme, the danger of mob violence. One may wish that Lincoln had stayed with his first theme throughout: The danger of mob violence was real; the danger of a nation-threatening demagogue, Whig opinions of Andrew Jackson notwithstanding, was not.

What Lincoln did or did not do about the Lovejoy killing has been criticized by the biographer of his days as a state legislator, Paul Simon, because Lincoln did not stand forth immediately to specify and condemn the recent and nearby and shocking killing of Lovejoy.

But I suggest that he *did* condemn it. He strongly condemned the general phenomenon of which the Lovejoy killing was an example; he linked it to analogous mob actions, more distant than Alton, which his Springfield audience might more readily join in deploring; he analyzed step by step why the general phenomenon of which these were examples—the mobocratic spirit—was a danger to all, and to the nation itself.

And he did make it specific, with a single surgical strike. He did not place his argument at so general a level as to leave his audience oblivious to its local application. At one point in the address he deftly made quite clear—unmistakably clear—that the killing of Lovejoy was an example of the danger he was deploring.

To appraise what Lincoln did and did not do one must re-create imaginatively the nationwide passionate hostility to the abolitionists—not in the South only, but in the North—rising higher in just these months; the wide and deep racial prejudice in Illinois, together with a good deal of sympathy with slavery, particularly in southern Illinois; and then this shocking event in Alton, the "Alton riots."

Although of course there were condemnations of the Alton mob across the North, and statements in defense of freedom of the press, even in Boston there were strong countercurrents. At the big abolitionists' protest meeting in Faneuil Hall on December 8, 1837, the attorney general of Massachusetts rose on the floor to defend the Alton mob, saying that the spirit of their throwing Lovejoy's presses into the Mississippi resembled that of the colonials who threw British tea into the ocean. He said of Lovejoy that he "died as the fool dieth." If that could be said by the attorney general of Massachusetts speaking in Boston, what then would attitudes be in south-central Illinois?

We have already noted the performance of Illinois's own attorney general, Usher Linder, a recent colleague of Lincoln's in the house, whose career would intersect Lincoln's in many ways: that his speech in Alton may have *encouraged* the mob, and that he proposed to prosecute not the mob that killed Lovejoy but Lovejoy's defenders!* One may confidently guess that in the midst of widespread and vigorous popular detestation of all abolitionists, and particularly of Lovejoy, that respectable opinion in southern and central Illinois, while "of course" deploring the killing and the action of the mob, would also fairly quickly arrive at a more passionate counterstatement beginning with "but"—suggesting at the very least that

* In the end, significantly, nobody was prosecuted for killing Lovejoy.

Lovejoy had done much to bring on his fate, that he "died as the fool dieth," and even perhaps hinting, good riddance.

Given that setting, perhaps the more notable feature of Lincoln's address is not that he did not devote it exclusively to a full, explicit, and particular condemnation of the mob killing of Lovejoy, but rather:

1. that in that time and place he chose even to address a topic like mob violence (how about another instructive lecture on the properties of water or the philosophy of vision?);

2. that he did make unmistakable (if brief and inferential) reference to the Lovejoy killing; and

3. that he did not at all say or imply that Lovejoy and the abolitionists bore any part of the blame.

With respect to this last point, can you not imagine what many were saying, at least in private, about the killing of that scoundrel abolitionist Lovejoy? That of course it was too bad, but really—it was his own fault. He asked for it.

And in such a climate can you not imagine what an ambitious politician might say in public? The speech writes itself: One grants, with a long face, that to be sure the mob attack on, and killing of, Lovejoy was unfortunate indeed. But then one feels obliged to add, at the same time, that Lovejoy's persistent incendiary writings and the extremely provocative actions of the abolitionists created a climate in which such events occur. So one must reject "extremism" on both sides.

Lincoln did *not* do that. There is in Lincoln's address no suggestion that the abolitionists (like Lovejoy) provoked the mobs or that they might be said to have brought their fate on themselves. There is no criticism of them at all.

Lincoln's General Assembly colleagues, in that 77–6 vote the previous January, had bluntly blamed the abolitionists for bringing on the actions of the "monster mob." Lincoln, by contrast, devoted himself exclusively to condemning mob violence against individuals like Lovejoy.

But he did it deftly. His rhetorical strategy was first to enlarge, surround, and generalize. No external threat can destroy American institutions, only an internal one—like the "outrages committed by mobs." They occurred, he is careful to say, "from New England to Louisiana": "they are neither peculiar to the eternal snows of the former, or the burning suns of the latter . . . neither are they confined to the slaveholding or the nonslaveholding states. Alike, they spring up among the pleasure hunting masters of Southern slaves, and the order loving citizens of the land of steady habits."* He did not say—I suggest he did not need to say—"and here in Illinois as well."

But he did not stop with generalities. He drew from his avid newspaper reading two recent specific examples, one from Saint Louis and one from Mississippi—both, if you want to say so, a comfortably greater distance from Springfield than was Alton. In the spring of 1836 a young mulatto named Frank McIntosh, newly free, according to Lincoln—a seaman on a steamboat that docked in Saint Louis—left the boat to call on a girl, nervously aware that he was in a slave state, where free Negroes were sometimes seized and sold into slavery. He was accosted by police. He resisted, stabbed and killed an officer and wounded another, and tried to escape. He was quickly caught. Let Lincoln tell what happened in this "horror-striking scene": McIntosh was "seized in the street, dragged to the suburbs of the city, chained to a tree and actually burned to death; and all within a single hour from the time he had become a freeman, attending to his own business and at peace with the world." What Lincoln does *not* say—although presumably at least some of his hearers would know—was that the chief exposer of this horror-striking deed, who deplored it vigorously in public, had been Elijah Lovejoy. He had then still been publishing his paper in St. Louis; he had strongly attacked the mob that killed McIntosh, and then he had criticized a judge who told the grand jury they could not indict if the lynching had been done by "congregated thousands" whose names were not available. What Lovejoy printed about the McIntosh case caused a mob to attack his paper—this episode, in fact, was what drove him to move to Alton. A year and a half later, by specifying the evil deed in the McIntosh case, Lincoln was silently circling the Lovejoy case as well.

His other concrete example, much more recent, had occurred after the killing of Lovejoy and had to do with mobs in Mississippi. It began with the lynching in Vicksburg of three white men, professional gamblers, and then went on, to quote Lincoln again: "Next, negroes, suspected of conspiring to raise an insurrection, were caught up and hanged in all parts of the State: then, white men, supposed to be leagued with the negroes; and finally, strangers, from neighboring States, going thither on business, were, in many instances, subjected to the same fate." That the killing of the "white men, suspected to be leagued with the negroes" and the "strangers,

---

* "Land of steady habits" was a well-worn characterization of Connecticut.

from neighboring states" was part of the nationwide attack on abolitionists
Lincoln does not explicitly say, circling that topic too. He ended his passage on the Mississippi lynchings with a figure eerily anticipatory of the
bitter image in the twentieth-century song and novel "Strange Fruit"
(lynched bodies dangling like fruit from southern trees).* Lincoln, a century before that song and novel, condemned "this process of hanging, from
gamblers to Negroes, from Negroes to white citizens, and from these to
strangers; till, dead men were seen literally dangling from the boughs of
trees upon every road side; and in numbers almost sufficient, to rival the
native Spanish moss of the country, as a drapery of the forest."

As Lincoln almost did not specifically refer to Alton and Lovejoy, but
hovered over them through the whole speech, so he also almost did not
mention abolitionists, while hovering over that topic, too. But as with
Lovejoy, so with abolition: there was one moment when that specific current application of his general point was made unmistakable.

Unfortunately, the way Lincoln made his argument against mob attacks
on abolitionists is all too vulnerable to civil-libertarian objection, so that
the point he was making may be deflected for a modern reader. He
attempted to make a succinct, tight argument:

> In any case that arises, as for instance, in the promulgation of aboli-
> tionism, one of two positions is necessarily true; that is, the thing is
> right within itself, and therefore deserves the protection of all law and
> all good citizens; or, it is wrong, and therefore proper to be prohibited
> by legal enactments; and in neither case, is the interposition of mob
> law, either necessary, justifiable, or excusable.

That worthy conclusion is what he wants to say, both on this point and
throughout the speech, but his way of getting there is obviously objectionable. His second hypothesis provokes in the reader a double take: If it is
"wrong," then abolition has no right to freedom of speech? For that matter,
is it because it is "right" that it deserves "the protection of all law and all

---

* "Strange Fruit," a song composed by a white New York City high school teacher in the
1930s, really *was* a "protest" against lynchings in the South ("Black bodies swinging in the
Southern breeze, / Strange fruit hanging from the poplar trees.") Billie Holiday sang the
song in public first in 1939, and many times thereafter, often creating an uproar. A Georgia
white woman named Lillian Smith took the phrase as the title for the novel *Strange Fruit*
(1944) about a tragic interracial love affair, and it, too, produced an uproar. It is a little startling to find this twenty-nine-year-old border-state white man anticipating this bitter
metaphor in 1838.

good citizens"? One would have thought that whether it was "right" or "wrong" or whatever mixture of the two, it would—independently of that—like all other schools of thought and speech, deserve that protection. Rightness and wrongness in somebody's eyes, in this new republic, has nothing to do with the fundamental liberty to speak. Lincoln in this paragraph, as indeed throughout the speech, is trying to find the way to argue for the civil liberty of a very unpopular movement, but here he picked an unfortunate way of doing it.

What he wanted to say—what he *did* say, at the start of that very paragraph—was that "there is no grievance that is a fit object of redress by mob law." (Implicit: not even your grievance against obnoxious abolitionists like Lovejoy.)

Perhaps one cannot fault his rhetorical strategy in general—given the climate of opinion. The politically difficult cases of civil liberty always involve—do they not?—by definition the liberties of persons who are disliked, rejected, loathed, and also often feared. In the following century there would be Communists, putative Communists, and "Reds"; anarchists; Jehovah's Witnesses; flag burners; gay rights advocates; neo-Nazis. In the previous century, sympathizers with the French Revolution, radical opponents of the Federalist administrations—the editors and others who provoked the Alien and Sedition Acts. In all centuries there would be the opponents of various wars and the question raisers about settled moral practices. They come from the Left and from the Right—from all sides. Anyone who has any strong conviction is liable to the temptation to want to suppress those who print newspapers, make speeches, organize, vociferously object to that conviction. That is why the fight for civil liberty is never completely won.

In the heated atmosphere of antiabolitionist 1830s Illinois Lincoln did *not* use the rhetorical strategies one might use elsewhere. Except for a little spark of sympathy for McIntosh in his "horror-striking" end, Lincoln did not try to arouse in his audience any sympathy or identification with the victims. What he says about them, in fact, is hardboiled and dismissive and perhaps even chilling:

> Abstractly considered, the hanging of the gamblers at Vicksburg, was of but little consequence. They constitute a portion of population, that is worse than useless in any community; and their death, if no pernicious example be set by it, is never matter of reasonable regret with any one. If they were annually swept, from the stage of existence, by the plague or small pox, honest men would, perhaps, be much profited,

by the operation. Similar too, is the correct reasoning, in regard to the burning of the negro at St. Louis. He had forfeited his life, by the perpetration of an outrageous murder, upon one of the most worthy and respectable citizens of the city; and had he not died as he did, he must have died by the sentence of the law, in a very short time afterwards.

His hearers could extend the point to Lovejoy: the issue was not whether you had sympathy with *him* or not (Lincoln knew that his hearers mostly did not, any more than with the gamblers or McIntosh), but rather what happens as a result of the mobocratic spirit.

He did not argue, as would a twentieth-century member of the American Civil Liberties Union, perhaps paraphrasing Voltaire (I hate what you say but defend your right to say it), on the grounds of universal principle and abstract human right, as embodied in American founding documents. Although intellectually and morally sound, that position is difficult to make rhetorically effective in a heated, angry, fearful situation.*

Lincoln also did not make, except possibly indirectly, the sometimes more effective argument on behalf of civil liberty that links *your* freedom with the threat to this other person's: next time, once the protections are breached, it may be *your* freedom of belief and speech that are suppressed. Presumably not many in his audience worried about having their presses thrown in the river.

What he did argue was that the spirit that carried out these deeds was a threat to our treasured institutions: those institutions are endangered (implicit: not by the abolitionists but) by the mobs. He went carefully through the steps of the argument:

> When men take it in their heads today, to hang gamblers, or burn murderers, they should recollect, that, in the confusion usually attending such transactions, they will be as likely to hang or burn some one, who is neither a gambler nor a murder as one who is . . .
>
> [T]he innocent, those who have ever set their faces against violations of law in every shape, alike with the guilty, fall victims to the ravages of mob law;

* To those misguided souls who might raise issues of free speech and free press, the Kentucky legislature's appeal to northern legislatures had exclaimed: "What grosser prostitution of freedom of the press could be conceived than the effort of the abolitionists to stir up a portion of the population . . . of eleven states to rebellion and bloodshed!"

and thus it goes on, step by step, till all the walls erected for the defense of the persons and property of individuals, are trodden down, and disregarded.

But all this even, is not the full extent of the evil. By such examples, by instances of the perpetrators of such acts, going unpunished, the lawless in spirit, are encouraged to become lawless in practice . . .

Having ever regarded Government as their deadliest bane, they make a jubilee of the suspension of its operations . . .

While, on the other hand, good men, men who love tranquility, who desire to abide by the laws . . . seeing their property destroyed; their families insulted, and their lives endangered; their persons injured; and seeing nothing in prospect that forebodes a change for the better; become tired of, and disgusted with, a Government that offers them no protection . . .

[T]hus, then, by the operation of this mobocratic spirit . . . the strongest bulwark of any Government, and particularly of those constituted like ours, may effectually be broken down and destroyed—I mean the attachment of the People.

That government of, by, and for the people required as its constant foundation the attachment of the people would be a conviction of Lincoln throughout his career.

It is in the context of this full argument about how mobs undermine the people's attachment to government that Lincoln, with a delicate but unmistakable touch, included the events in Alton among the evils that will have that pernicious effect:

[If] the vicious portion of the population shall be permitted to gather in the bands of hundreds and thousands, and burn churches, ravage and rob provision stores, throw printing presses into rivers, shoot editors, and hang and burn obnoxious persons at pleasure and with impunity, depend on it, this government cannot last.

"Throw printing presses into rivers"? No one in Illinois in January of 1838 could be in any doubt what that referred to. (For that matter, no newspaper reader in the country could be.) "Shoot editors"—that nails it down. *Don't* shoot editors—because such actions, step by step, undercut our institutions.

So the young Lincoln showed, without ever directly saying so, that the mobocratic spirit that murdered Lovejoy is a prime danger to our government, our institutions.

Remembering the context, one may interpret Lincoln's Lyceum Address as an implicit response to the battle over the new abolitionism, a continuation and expansion of the "no" vote he cast exactly a year earlier, and of the carefully crafted "protest" he and Stone entered in the house record in March. Whereas the assembly's joint committee report and resolutions had been, as we have seen, concentratedly, sweepingly antiabolitionist, blaming that movement for a wide range of ills, including the behavior of the "monster mob," Lincoln's criticism is aimed—mostly implicitly, mostly obliquely—not at the abolitionists at all, but at the irrational and extralegal efforts to suppress them that culminated in the killing of Lovejoy.

"The question recurs," said Lincoln, "'How shall we fortify against it [this mob spirit]?'" By law and by reason.

Lincoln's climactic exhortations to obey the law and to be guided by reason, not passion, were stated with the kind of sweeping extravagance that he often fell into when young, especially as he swung into the last paragraphs of his speeches. The Lyceum Address has been described as the most conservative address Lincoln ever gave, because he exhorted his hearers to "swear by the blood of the Revolution never to violate in the least particular the laws of the country, and"—more striking still— "never to tolerate their violation by others." He did not simply recommend obedience to the law; he put in insistent "never"s and "every"s and a "swear[ing] by the blood of the Revolution." He exhorted his hearers to make the law—in a phrase often to be quoted in the Lincoln books—"the political religion of the nation." We should all "sacrifice unceasingly"— whatever that may mean—"upon its altars."

He was speaking in the context of, and on the topic of, an extraordinary outbreak of mob violence—a widespread, half-condoned violation of law, of the sort that the nation would see again, on the subjects of slavery and race, both in his lifetime and later. In that setting it is understandable that his exhortation to obey the law might become heightened, sweeping, insistent.

The same is true of his rather paradoxically passionate appeal for reason in place of passion. Although he says that we Americans now need, in place of the passions of the nation's beginning, "cold, calculating, unimpassioned reason," his own climactic invocation of reason was anything but cold or calculating or unimpassioned.

3. HAIL FALL OF FURY!

The extravagance of Lincoln's wind-up of the lyceum lecture would be matched by similar passages in others of his youthful addresses. A lecture he gave to a Temperance Society rally on Washington's birthday in 1842, four years after the Lyceum Address, although wise in its core, would also have passages marked by oratorical overkill. I think these passages, overdone to the point of being comic, nevertheless show a level of yearning, of intention, of aspiration, that once he has learned discipline and economy in its expression will have great power. But not yet in these speeches.

Full-throated rodomontade was almost expected in these nineteenth-century speech fests. Lincoln, a reader of Daniel Webster and other princes of the purple platform, a homegrown lecturer in a tradition that also featured traveling stars, took these opportunities to give his Springfield audiences their money's worth.

As we have said, in the lyceum lecture, after treating the theme of mob violence, Lincoln rather suddenly veered off to another alleged danger to American institutions, that of an ambitious genius who might become a demagogue. The founding generation was provided, said Lincoln, with "celebrity and fame, and distinction" (clearly that was a significant criterion for this lecturer), but now the "field of glory is harvested, and the crop is already appropriated." Just "supporting and maintaining an edifice that has been erected by others" won't be enough for "some man possessed of the loftiest genius, coupled with ambition sufficient to push it to its utmost stretch." Merely being a congressman, a governor, or even a president(!) in this already established edifice will not satisfy "such as belong . . . to the family of the lion, or the tribe of the eagle." "What! Think you these places would satisfy an Alexander, a Caesar, or a Napoleon? Never! Towering genius disdains a beaten path." This lion or eagle will seek distinction by building something up, it may be, or, if not, by tearing something down; by "freeing slaves or enslaving freemen"—apparently a "towering genius" of the "tribe of the eagle" is not going to care which.

Lincoln was obviously trying hard to make a striking speech, and if he did not succeed in Springfield in 1838 he certainly would succeed in twentieth-century interpretation. The distinguished literary critic Edmund Wilson would flatly claim "that Lincoln has projected himself into the role against which he is warning them." Harry Jaffa, in the most intellectually serious of treatments of Lincoln's youthful addresses, responded to Wilson that Lincoln was implicitly identifying with an *opponent* of this demagogue. Various candidates for the demagogue other than Lincoln have been proposed—Andrew Jackson, Aaron Burr, Stephen Douglas. The striking point to me is not exactly the identity of a possible demagogue but the extraordinary picture this young man has in his mind of the power and reach of ambition.

Lincoln ended his lyceum speech with an embarrassingly grandiloquent reference to George Washington that has been garbled in form as it has been passed down to us. He would end his Temperance Address four years later with a longer and even more unrestrained apostrophe to Washington, with the excuse this time that he was speaking to the Washington Society on Washington's birthday:

> This is the one hundred and tenth anniversary of the birthday of Washington. We are met to celebrate this day. Washington is the mightiest name of earth—long since mightiest in the cause of civil liberty; still mightiest in moral reformation. On that name, an eulogy is expected. It cannot be. To add brightness to the sun, or glory to the name of Washington, is alike impossible. Let none attempt it. In solemn awe pronounce the name, and in its naked deathless splendor, leave it shining on.

As to the Temperance Address, Harry Jaffa went so far as to suggest that in the overblown parts Lincoln was carrying on a silent, subtle satire. In the beginning and in the end of that address Lincoln, Jaffa argued, was deliberately *caricaturing* the style of the temperance reformers: "Lincoln's exaggerated style, in the most rhetorical parts of his speech, is a rhetorical device to show how purely rhetorical are the sentiments therein expressed!" Jaffa continues: "Humorless critics, who have failed to perceive the difference between the sober accents that are Lincoln's own and the high style of his mimicry, have called the speech an immature work. We can not readily recall a more precocious example of literary skill."

I would like to believe that; but, at the risk of being called a humorless critic, I can't. *Deliberately*—without any clear signal—mimicking the reformers? Implicitly satirizing them? To an audience of temperance advocates in a Presbyterian church in Springfield, Illinois, in 1842? Subtly appealing to his audience on two levels? I don't believe it. Why, if this is so, is the same sort of thing equally present in the Lyceum Address and other speeches in the same time period? One can imagine Artemus Ward, one of the newspaper humorists Lincoln admired, who later on would have an act that he took on the road that burlesqued these lecturings, doing a dead-pan satire of the kind of thing that Lincoln did in the endings of these addresses. And one can also imagine Lincoln—at least the mature Lincoln—enjoying *that* satire, directed against himself.

As each lecture rises into its peroration, the orator pulls out all the stops in unqualified celebration of George Washington, the Founders, the Revolution, the Law, and—perhaps a rather surprising entry—Reason. Reason! Capitalized and exclamation-pointed.

The young orator wants to recommend that Reason subordinate and control our appetites and our passions, persuading us to submit in toto to the law, and to accomplish a still grander revolution than the merely political one of '76. In the lyceum speech: "Passion has helped; but can do no more. It will in future be our enemy. Reason, cold, calculating, unimpassioned reason, must furnish all the materials for our future defense." In the Temperance Address: "Happy day, when, all passions subdued, all matters subjected, mind, all conquering mind, shall live and move the monarch of the world. Glorious Consummation! Hail fall of Fury! Reign of Reason, all hail!" It cannot have been easy actually to deliver a line like "Hail fall of Fury!" to an audience of small-town lecture-goers, ex-drunkards, and church folk in a frontier village.

There is another, much-less-examined speech that provides a yet gaudier example of Lincoln's rodomontade, this time featuring himself. This speech came just in between those two addresses, in December of 1839, in the early stages of one of the most vigorously contested presidential elections of early American national history, the Harrison–Van Buren "Tippecanoe and Tyler too" contest of 1840.

Illinois state legislators of the two parties debated the great issue of a national bank in the house during their sessions in the daytime, and then they spilled the debate over into some sessions open to the public in the evening. One of the leading debaters on the Democratic side was Stephen A. Douglas. And on the other side, the leading Whig on the house finance committee, the last and summing-up debater for the Whigs, was the delegate from Sangamon County, A. Lincoln.

Being the cleanup debater was no doubt an honor, but it turned out to be awkward with respect to the timing: Lincoln's speech fell on the day after Christmas. For that reason, and perhaps because the Springfield public had by that time heard all it wanted to hear on the subject of banking, his audience was small. As he rose, with his long and carefully written speech, he felt disappointed, as all speakers feel disappointed when the turnout to hear them is embarrassingly sparse. But not all speakers make their disappointment known to the crowd (or rather to the little scattering of people before them). Lincoln did. He spoke some initial words on that topic that came to be preserved in the *Sangamon Journal,* and passed on in the pamphlet the Whigs used in the campaign, and from there passed on to the great collections of his speeches that scholars pore over to this day. (Was he saying to himself, with a little pout, "Douglas drew a lot more people than this"?)

> FELLOW CITIZENS: It is peculiarly embarrassing to me to attempt a continuance of the discussion, on this evening, which has been conducted in this Hall on several preceding ones. It is so, because on each of those evenings, there was a much fuller attendance than now, without any reason for its being so, except the greater interest the community feel in the Speakers who addressed them then, than they do in him who is to do so now. I am, indeed, apprehensive, that the few who have attended, have done so, more to spare me of mortification, than in the hope of being interested in any thing I may be able to say. This circumstance casts a damp upon my spirits, which I am sure I shall be unable to overcome during the evening.

Many speakers have felt that way; few have said so with Lincoln's astonishing candor.

Dampened or not, Lincoln proceeded with a long argument that the Whig/Federalist national bank had been and would be superior to the Jackson/Van Buren alternative. And then, once again as he approached the finish line, Lincoln rather suddenly, in the second sentence here, shifted into overdrive:

> Mr. Lamborn [a Democratic opponent] refers to the late elections in the States, and from their results, confidently predicts, that every State in the Union will vote for Mr. Van Buren [the Democratic incumbent whom the Whig Harrison opposed] at the next Presidential election. Address *that* argument to *cowards* and to *knaves;* with the *free* and the *brave* it will effect nothing. It *may* be true, if it *must,* let it. Many free countries have lost their liberty; and *ours may* lose hers; but if she shall, be it my proudest plume, not that I was the *last* to desert, but that I *never* deserted her.

Why do we jump suddenly from a debate about banking and assertions about the coming election all the way to the loss of liberty? And why does this one young western state legislator abruptly cast himself as the last man on the bridge—or not just as the last man, but as the one who *never* deserted? "My proudest plume"? "I *never* deserted her"? The emphatic italics, of course, are his. Lincoln was a man of a romantic era, including its florid and individualistic qualities; one hears in this grandiloquent speech ending an anticipation of something like Cyrano, posturing around the stage with dramatic claims about his unsullied plume.

Lincoln went on to condemn the Van Buren (Jackson) Democratic administration then in Washington with the metaphor of a "volcano":

> I know that the great volcano at Washington, aroused and directed by the evil spirit that reigns there, is belching forth the lava of political corruption in a current broad and deep, which is sweeping with frightful velocity over the whole length and breadth of the land, bidding fair to leave unscathed no green spot or living thing, while on its bosom are riding like demons on the waves of Hell, the imps of that evil spirit, and fiendishly taunting all those who dare resist its destroying course, with the hopelessness of their effort; and knowing this, I cannot deny that all may be swept away.

Is this not a little disproportionate, not to say goofy?

This next passage, totally extracted from its context, would be quoted by Bishop Matthew Simpson at the funeral for Lincoln himself at the Oak Ridge Cemetery in Springfield in 1865, implying in that context of course that the subject to which Lincoln was vowing steadfast faith was opposition to slavery. This is Lincoln speaking in this 1839 speech, to be quoted by Bishop Simpson over his bier in 1865:

> Broken by it, I, too, may be; bow to it I never will. The probability that we may fall in the struggle ought not to deter us from the support of a cause we believe to be just; it shall not deter me.

G. S. Boritt begins his excellent book on Lincoln's economics with Bishop Simpson's use of this quotation, and then wryly remarks: "Bishop Simpson quoted Lincoln accurately. He had unearthed a long lost speech that would be soon lost again. But he did make one error. Lincoln's speech had said nothing about slavery. Its subject was banking."

And there were in Lincoln's speech still more of these passages. David Herbert Donald, quoting the passage that follows that "Broken by it" para-

graph, makes a similar little joke in a paragraph about young Lincoln's
style; what follows next appears, Donald wryly observed, "in the unlikely
context of defending the national bank":

> If ever I feel the soul within me elevate and expand to those dimen-
> sions not wholly unworthy of its Almighty Architect, it is when I con-
> template the cause of my country, deserted by all the world beside, and
> I standing up boldly and alone and hurling defiance at her victorious
> oppressors. Here, without contemplating consequences, before High
> Heaven and in the face of the world, I swear eternal fidelity to the just
> cause, as I deem it, of the land of my life, my liberty and my love.

One might suggest a very mild semi-demi-defense of Lincoln against
the jokes of Boritt and Donald: that at this point in the speech, with
that volcano passage, he had enlarged the subject beyond banking to the
possibility of a Van Buren–Democratic victory in general. But even so,
did the threat of such a victory require all the high drama of Lincoln hurl-
ing defiance and standing boldly alone before High Heaven? "Without contemplating consequences" (a phrase one might underline here to
serve as a contrast to the more mature "consequentialist" Lincoln of later
years)?

And he still was not finished. Here's the way he ended this speech:

> And who, that thinks with me, will not fearlessly adopt the oath that I
> take. Let none faulter,* who thinks he is right, and we may succeed.
> But, if after all, we shall fail, be it so. We still shall have the proud con-
> solation of saying to our consciences, and to the departed shade of our
> country's freedom, that the cause approved of our judgment, and
> adored of our hearts, in disaster, in chains, in torture, in death, we
> NEVER faultered in defending.

One theme in this melodramatic nineteenth-century political oratory
seems to have been a kind of morbid relish of anticipated defeat—the more
utter, the better—so that one could then dramatize one's own heroic stead-
fastness in midst of total ruin. In point of prosaic fact, the Van Buren
Democrats not only did not sweep with frightful velocity over the whole

---

* Lincoln apparently felt that because, as he knew, the word "fault" had a *u* in it, it was
only just that the word "falter," which sounds so much like it, should be given a *u* also.

length and breadth of the land, leaving unscathed no green spot or living thing, but on the contrary, *lost* the election. Lincoln's candidate, William Henry Harrison, *won*. And in any case, even if Van Buren had won another term, whatever else one might have thought about his administration and its position on banking, one would not realistically have expected it to have dealt with its opponents by disaster, chains, torture, and death.

Obviously we are a long way in these speech endings from the Gettysburg Address and the Second Inaugural. And yet at the same time, with their manifest faults, these extravagant perorations may tell something about the young orator. They tell something about the objects of his devotion—his nation, its founders, the law, the use of reason, his devotion to liberty—and about the depth of feeling that he attached to them. The fact that in his overreaching he fails comically to convey those feelings does not necessarily mean that they were not real. As time would tell, he did indeed hold, and he would indeed come to be able to express, a high vision of, and a deep devotion to, the moral meaning of his nation. At this point he was working on it.

As it is said that writers of great prose often start as writers of bad poetry (Lincoln did indeed himself write some poetry, and appreciated and kept quoting poems by others, good and bad, with strong romantic feeling), so it may be said that this writer of great short speeches started by writing bad long ones. Partly bad—the endings particularly.

There is a passage in Carl Becker's little book *The Declaration of Independence* on something missing in Jefferson's style that compares a tortured piece of the rejected passage on slavery from the draft of the Declaration with the great penultimate passage in Lincoln's Second Inaugural that begins, "Fondly do we hope—fervently do we pray—that this mighty scourge of war may speedily pass away," and ends, "the judgments of the Lord are true and righteous altogether." Becker says about this passage from Lincoln that "there is a quality of deep feeling . . . an indefinable something which is profoundly moving; and this something, which informs and enriches much of Lincoln's writing, is rarely, almost never, present in the writing of Jefferson . . . This something, which Jefferson lacked but which Lincoln possessed in full measure, may perhaps for want of a better term be called a profoundly emotional apprehension of experience."

Lincoln in 1838 and 1839 and 1842 was trying to impress his audiences with his powers but also trying to find the way to express that profoundly emotional apprehension of experience.

4. THEY ARE AS WE WOULD BE

Along with the oratorical fireworks in these early speeches of Lincoln, there were also passages that in their moral reasoning would anticipate the mature Lincoln—particularly in the Temperance Address.

When Lincoln gave this speech, on February 22, 1842, he was a young Whig politician and lawyer, thirty-three years old, just about to retire from his career in the state legislature and to resume his courtship of Mary Todd. Before the year was over he would have married her.

He had been invited to give the address by the newly formed branch of a leading national temperance organization named—rather incongruously as it may seem to us now—for George Washington. The local branch planned a "rally" to be held on the 110th anniversary of Washington's birth and invited this rising local politician to give the address. The meeting was held in the Second Presbyterian Church.

The battle with "demon rum" was another expression of that zeal for reform to which Lincoln would have a complex relationship. Abolitionism is the one item from that nest of movements born out of the wave of revivals called the Second Awakening that gets attention now, but temperance was almost equally prominent in its own time.

Lincoln's younger law partner and eventual biographer, "Billy" Herndon, both was given to binges and was a temperance advocate. In their eighteen-year association Lincoln was often embarrassed by Herndon's drinking but apparently never nagged him. He mentioned the subject to Herndon only once, as he was leaving to be president, and then did so with a light touch. Otherwise Lincoln "never chided, never censured, never criticized my conduct," according to Herndon.

In the early 1840s Lincoln the nondrinker did give several speeches to temperance groups. He was a young man aspiring to distinction, and this was a topic of the day. What he did in this Temperance Address in 1842, however, surely differed from the usual temperance lecture, and has significance going beyond the topic.

His rhetorical device was to praise this new movement, in sharp contrast to the old. The new method was for former "drunkards" themselves to band together, to sign a pledge, and to bring comradely persuasion to bear on those still caught in the snares of "drink"—in a way an anticipation of Alcoholics Anonymous. But Lincoln spent much less of his speech praising the new method and much more of it criticizing the old.

His remarks reveal a wisdom about human nature that does not always mark—as he said—efforts toward the moral remaking of the world and of humankind. "Too much denunciation against dram sellers and dram-drinkers was indulged in," he said. "[I]t is not much in the nature of man to be driven to anything; still less to be driven about that which is exclusively his own business; and least of all, where such driving is to be submitted to, at the expense of pecuniary interest or burning appetite." (Lincoln would later indicate a sharp sense of the role of "pecuniary interest" in the slavery controversy.) It did not work well, said the younger Lincoln, when the saloon keeper and drinker were told "not in the accents of entreaty and persuasion, diffidently addressed by erring man to an erring brother, but in thundering tones of anathema and denunciation, with which the lordly Judge often groups together all the crimes of the felon's life, and thrusts them in his face just ere he passes sentence of death upon him, that *they* were the authors of all the vice and misery and crime in the land. . . ." Lincoln then rolled on through a thundering sequence of his own, and finished:

> It is not wonderful that they were slow, *very slow,* to acknowledge the truth of such denunciations, and to join the ranks of their denouncers, in a hue and cry against themselves.
>
> To have expected them [the roundly denounced dram-sellers and dram-drinkers] to do otherwise than they did—to have expected them not to meet denunciation with denunciation, crimination with crimination, and anathema with anathema, was to expect a reversal of human nature, which is God's decree, and can never be reversed.*

Young Lincoln went on to recommend to these ardent temperance advocates the device of a sincere friend's sweet *persuasion,* in place of moral denunciation, and then he returned to a colorful and psychologically acute criticism of the *older* style of temperance crusading:

> On the contrary, assume to dictate to his judgment, or to command his action, or to mark him as one to be shunned and despised, and he will

---

* This is one of at least four times when the pre-presidential Lincoln refers to a fixed human nature—but not always with the more usual "realistic" application. (See Chapter 10.)

retreat within himself, close all the avenues to his head and his heart; and tho' your cause be naked truth itself, transformed to the heaviest lance, harder than steel, and sharper than steel can be made, and tho' you throw it with more than Herculean force and precision, you shall no more be able to pierce him, than to penetrate the hard shell of a tortoise with a rye straw.

(There's the young writer at work, trying to think up a sufficiently dramatic impossibility: to penetrate a tortoise shell with a straw.)

"Such is man," said Lincoln, "and so *must* be understood by those who would lead him, even to his own best interest."

Reading this speech of Lincoln, with its wisdom about human makeup in contests over moral conduct, of course one hears anticipation of the debate over slavery, already then strongly joined but not yet by Abraham Lincoln, and echoes and anticipations of dozens of other moral crusades, before and after down to the present, crisscrossing this giant moral project, the United States of America.

Lincoln's first point was that moralistic denunciation was "impolitic"— unstrategic, impractical, ineffective, because of the human resistance he described. His second main point was that it was also *unjust*. He described, again with colorful detail, how thoroughly the imbibing of "intoxicating drink" was woven into the society in which all of them lived, how accepted, how expected, and well regarded. "The universal *sense* of mankind, on any subject, is an argument, or at least an *influence* not easily overcome." That was another point he would make again, in the context of the later controversy.

The moral realism that marks the whole speech included a reminder of the limitations on the human capacity to act on behalf of remote and unknown persons at some great distance from oneself, including distance in time: "What an ignorance of human nature does it exhibit," exclaimed the young politician/lecturer, "to ask or expect a whole community to rise up and labor for the *temporal* happiness of *others* after *themselves* shall be consigned to the dust . . . Great distance, in either time or space, has a wonderful power to lull and render quiescent the human mind. Pleasures to be enjoyed, or pains to be endured, *after* we shall be dead and gone, are but little regarded, even in our *own* cases, and much less in the cases of others."

It was on this point—the impotence of promises and threats of results a great way off—that Lincoln told his one joke. "Paddy," who stole a shovel, was told that he would pay for it at Judgment Day. "By the powers," Lincoln's Paddy responds, "if ye'll credit me so long, I'll take another!"

His moral realism included an acute awareness of the influence on all of us of the opinions of those by whom we are surrounded. Lincoln always had that. It would be a big part of his condemnation of Stephen Douglas in the 1850s for his "don't care" attitude on slavery that he was warping the public mind. For his formal lecture on this occasion he thought up a homely example: "[W]hat compensation will [a man] accept to go to church some Sunday and sit during the sermon with his wife's bonnet upon his head? Not a trifle, I'll venture. And why not? There would be nothing irreligious in it; nothing immoral; nothing uncomfortable. Then why not? Is it not because there would be something egregiously unfashionable in it? Then it is the influence of *fashion;* and what is the influence of fashion, but the influence that *other* people's actions have on our own actions, the strong inclination each of us feels to do as we see all our neighbors do?"

In his most significant deviation from the general inclination of the American moralistic culture, he explicitly rejected any claim of superiority on the part of nondrinkers (like himself) and of temperance advocates over those who were then called "drunkards." He rejected the "error" into which "the old reformers" fell, "the position that all habitual drunkards were utterly incorrigible and therefore must be turned adrift, and damned without remedy. . . ." That radical rejection, separating the drunkard from the rest of us is "repugnant," "uncharitable," "feelingless." But more: Lincoln explicitly said that those (like himself and some of his listeners) who "have never fallen victims" to drink "have been spared more from absence of appetite, than from any mental or moral superiority over those who have."

Abstainers not morally superior to drinkers? *That* was a doctrine that cut sharply against one of the deepest inclinations of a moralizing movement, perhaps anywhere and inherently, but certainly in America throughout its history and particularly in the movements of the nineteenth century. When Lincoln would make his arguments against the expansion of slavery because it was a moral wrong, the sharpest single difference between his position and that of the main body of abolitionists would be that whereas they repeatedly condemned slaveholders for their reprehensible individual wrongdoing, Lincoln did not do that, and explicitly disavowed any such sharp moral contrast, with respect either to himself personally, or to his region, or to those who shared his moral condemnation of slavery.

Lincoln would insist from the start—in his first, key speech at the Illinois State Fair in October 1854, and regularly thereafter—that "they [the Southern people] are just as we would be in their situation." He would go on to state explicitly the reversals that a changed situation would make, not only for the Southern people but also for his Northern listeners: "If slavery did not now exist amongst them, they would not introduce it." And now the parallel in the North: "If it did now exist amongst us, we should not instantly give it up. This I believe of the masses North and South"—although he conceded individual exceptions both ways.

"They are just what we would be in their situation" is a very hard doctrine for human beings generally, especially for those in the grip of some excellence, and in particular moral excellence. When we strive for some great good, or oppose some great evil, it is extremely difficult not to spill out some of the goodness onto ourselves and the evil onto our opponents, creating a deep *personal* moral gulf. It is very difficult, in other words, professing or striving for something righteous, to avoid self-righteousness and moralistic condemnation. Abstainers (like myself) are on the one side; drunkards are way over on the other. Abolitionists (like myself) are high up; slaveholders, over there, are way down—they are separated by an absolute moral gulf. The moral crusades of American history, taking form especially just in the period of Lincoln's life, have been, down to the present day, particularly prone to self-righteousness and moralism—not, of course, that any other time and people are free of them.

The evangelical Protestant culture of that time was especially so inclined. A person could become someone new—be born again—in a moment, by a change of will or heart. This radical individualism was linked to a moral melodrama starring the proponents by its exaggerated picture of the range and freedom and the simplicity of changes in the individual heart and will. If this picture of human life be so, then praise and blame both abound: My goodness is the product of my own decision; your badness is the result of yours. Drunkards and slaveholders (and, in other settings, and for various branches of this ethos, abortionists, homosexuals, generals of armies, prostitutes, poor people, Communists, welfare mothers) are categorically bad people, doing something wicked by their own free decision. They are subject, as Lincoln said, to "denunciation," "crimination," "anathema." By plain implication, if not explicit statement, there stand on the other side of a great moral divide those who do the denouncing and the crimination, who are by their own free decision *not* drunkards or slaveholders or wielders of military power or participants in other (alleged) evils, who are therefore good and righteous people, to be praised.

The passage in his speech in which he disavowed any "mental or moral" superiority of nondrinkers (like himself) to drinkers had been preceded and introduced by a paragraph that—Herndon would report—also, and more particularly, offended churchgoers in his audience. This Washington Society, it seems, encouraged the signing of a personal *pledge* not to drink excessively. Lincoln urged *everyone,* including those not touched by drink, to join in the effort, to sign the pledge and join the society so that excessive drinking might become as unfashionable, as much discouraged by the weight of opinion, as a man's wearing his wife's bonnet in church.

And then he cited a morally snobbish objection some might have: "But, say some, we are no drunkards, and we shall not acknowledge ourselves such by joining a reformed drunkards society, whatever our influence might be."

Lincoln, who throughout his life showed himself one who, while not explicitly himself identifying with Christian belief, nevertheless got the nub of it better than many Christians did, answered this moral snobbery thus:

> Surely no Christian will adhere to this objection. If they believe, as they profess [he says "they," not "we"], that Omnipotence condescended to take on himself the form of sinful man, and, as such, to die an ignominious death for their sakes, surely they will not refuse submission to the infinitely lesser condescension for the temporal, and perhaps eternal salvation of a large, erring, and unfortunate class of their own fellow creatures.

Lincoln then proceeded to a statement that was rather bold, particularly before this audience. He said that the "condescension" (of sober churchgoers signing a pledge used mostly by drunkards) would not be very great, because, first, we nondrunks do not deserve any particular credit, and second, drinkers just may be our superiors!

> Indeed, I believe, that if we take habitual drunkards as a class, their heads and hearts will bear an advantageous comparison with those of any other class. There seems ever to have been a proneness in the brilliant, and the warm-blooded, to fall into this vice. The demon of

intemperance ever seems to have delighted in sucking the blood of genius and of generosity.

What? *What?* What is that young politician saying up there in front of the crowd of temperance advocates in the Second Presbyterian Church? Not only that we nondrinkers don't get any moral credit for superiority— but that (can this be?) drunkards are not only *like* the rest of us but *better?* More brilliant, more warm-blooded, more generous? Can it be that he is saying *that?*

This passage—and the proposal that they all sign the pledge—apparently did not go down very well with the churchgoers who were his main audience. "The truth was," wrote Herndon, "the society was composed mainly of the roughs and drunkards of the town, who had evinced a desire to reform," who were in many cases "too fresh from the gutter to be taken at once into the society of such people as worshipped at the church where the speech was delivered." Benevolent work to "rescue the fallen," Herndon wrote—in the different atmosphere of the time he wrote his book, nearly a half-century later—was not common back then in the 1840s. The worshippers of that earlier day objected to Lincoln's speech. Herndon stood at the door of the church as they filed out. "Many of them were open in their expressions of their displeasure," Herndon reported. One man said, "It's a shame that he should be permitted to abuse us so in the house of the Lord."

When Lincoln later ran for Congress against the evangelist Peter Cartwright in 1846, the memory of this speech, Herndon reported, hurt him with some churchgoers.

5. THE THREE WHIGS FROM THE SEVENTH, OR, HONORABLE MANEUVERING

That run for Congress would not come easily. Lincoln would be a successful state legislator for three terms, but would not run again in 1842. He aimed higher. But it took some doing just to get the nomination of his party for the seat in the United States Congress.

Although Illinois was in general a Democratic state, the Seventh Congressional District, which included Springfield and Sangamon County, was the one strong Whig district in the state. It was represented when the decade of the forties began by Lincoln's mentor and law partner and fellow Whig, John T. Stuart, who spent so much time on his political duties that he left much of the legal work to Lincoln.

But Lincoln wanted to spend his time on politics, too. He was in his thirties; after the tumult of their courtship he had married Mary Todd in November of 1842, and they had their first child, Robert Todd, in 1843. Robert Todd's father, Mary Todd's husband, a short time earlier an uneducated, ill-dressed, backwoods odd-jobs bachelor, had been transformed into a settled family man, a practicing lawyer riding the circuit, and, above all, a persevering politician.

I believe one can say of his effort to become a congressman that it plainly exhibited his "thirst for distinction," but that it showed also some anticipations of the scrupulosity that would restrain and guide it.

The three leading Whigs in the Seventh Congressional District conducted a little do-si-do around that office. John J. Hardin and Edward D. Baker did not know that their rival would one day belong to the ages and so did not step aside for him.

When you read his letters from this period you see Lincoln striving to conduct this intricate little dance among friends in such a way as eventually to *win*, but also to be, throughout, fair.

Edward D. Baker, English-born and a talented orator, had an office next to Lincoln in a Springfield building and was enough of a friend—at a later stage of the congressional contest—for the Lincolns to name their second son—"Eddie," born in 1846—for him. That did not mean, however, that Lincoln was going to let Baker have the Whig nomination, and therefore probably the seat in Congress, that was coming open back in 1843, when John T. Stuart would give it up.

In the jockeying for that valuable nomination, Lincoln explicitly requested support with a kind of diffident persistence: "If there are any Whigs in Tazwell [County] who would as soon I should represent them as any other person, I would be glad they would not cast me aside until they see and hear further what turn [events may] take."

Lincoln is careful to be respectful of those he asks for assistance as well as of his opponents: "Do not suppose, Esq., that in addressing this letter to you, I assume that you will be for me against all other Whigs; I only mean, that I know you to be my personal friend, a good Whig, and an honorable man, to whom I may, without fear, communicate a fact which I wish my particular friends (if I have any) to know."

That interposed "if I have any" is typical of a kind of modesty, perhaps pseudo-modesty, that marks Lincoln's efforts. In another letter he would say, "If there are any who would be my friends in such an enterprise . . ." But the fact that he keeps writing such appeals for support shows also his desire and persistence. "If you should hear any one say that Lincoln don't want to go to Congress," he wrote ungrammatically to another possible supporter, "I wish you as a personal friend of mine would tell him you have reason to believe he is mistaken. The truth is, I would like to go very much."

But Baker beat out Lincoln already at the Sangamon County level before they went up to the district convention.

In part at least, Lincoln attributed his defeat to two whispered personal attacks, about which he might have been more indignant, both in general and toward Baker, than he was.

Incredibly, one negative rumor put Lincoln down as a candidate of "pride, wealth, and arristocratic family distinction," as Lincoln with his misspelling put it, presumably because of his marriage into the Todd-Edwards clan and perhaps also because he had been taken in as a partner by prominent Springfield lawyers, first Stuart and then Stephen Logan. It was in response to this astonishing charge that Lincoln produced the repeatedly quoted sentence about his having been a short time earlier "a strange, uneducated, penniless boy . . ."

The other whispered attack had to do with Lincoln's religion, or lack of it. Baker was a Campbellite (the Disciples of Christ, the church came to be called), and, wrote Lincoln, presumably Baker "got all that church," with a few exceptions. Mary Todd Lincoln had some relatives who were Presbyterians and some others who were Episcopalians, and Lincoln's opponents could use each of these attachments against him. But the larger charge had to do with Lincoln himself: "[i]t was every where contended that no Christian ought to go for me, because I belonged to no church, was suspected of being a deist, and had talked about fighting a duel." Lincoln realistically judges that these "influences" did cost him votes—"levied a tax of a considerable per cent upon my strength throughout the religious community"—but he nevertheless does not condemn anybody for them. Certainly not Baker: "With all these things Baker, of course, had nothing to do"—which is not what every defeated candidate in that situation says, with or without evidence. Lincoln did not blame anyone else for these "influences," either—"Nor do I complain of them"—and he specifically rejects any notion that there was an unfair collaboration, a conspiracy: "[t]hough [these influences] were very strong, it would be grossly untrue and unjust to charge that they acted upon them in a body or even very nearly so."

As all too many candidates for office know, the mischief of personal attacks in intraparty fighting includes their being given legitimacy for use later by the opposing party in the general election—as indeed would be the case three years later, when both of these charges would be used against Lincoln by Democrats.

Not everybody who has lost out for an office he "wanted very much" as a result of "very strong" "influences" like this—whispered personal attacks—would refuse to blame anybody for them, insist there was no concerted effort, specifically absolve his opponent—and three years later name a son for him. Usually in such a situation most of us need somebody to be mad at.

After choosing Baker over Lincoln as the county's candidate for the nomination, the Sangamon County convention chose Lincoln himself to be one of the eight delegates to carry that message to the district convention. Lincoln wrote to Speed that he was a good deal like "a fellow who is made a groomsman to the man what cut him out, and is marrying his own dear gal."

Having lost out at his own county's convention, Lincoln rejected any hanky-panky to snatch the nomination at the district level by trying to get the votes of other counties. If some unlikely event threw Baker out of the race, he would *then* be at liberty to accept the nomination if he could get it—but he felt himself "bound not to hinder [Baker] in any way from getting the nomination . . . I should despise myself were I to attempt it."

When the rumor reached him that Baker himself was trying to get delegates from other counties to throw over their instructions to vote for another candidate and to vote for him, Baker, Lincoln sprang to the defense of his opponent's integrity and flatly denied that it could be so: "Surely Baker would not do the like." And again: "I repeat, such an attempt on Baker's part cannot be true." Lincoln, the proponent not only of the convention system but of the moral obligations of the convention system, indignantly repudiated violating the instructions on his own behalf: "I should feel myself strongly dishonoured by it."

Then at the district convention in Pekin itself, when Baker and John J. Hardin at first ended in a tie, "many counties were instructed for Lincoln" and Lincoln "could have beaten both candidates." But according to an account by a local Whig, when Lincoln was asked if he would become a candidate, he said no—"that he would rather Cut his arm off, rather than become a Candidate under the circumstances."

So after all this the Pekin district convention just barely chose, over Baker, the third in this Whig triumvirate, John J. Hardin from Jacksonville over in Morgan County, to be the Whig nominee. Lincoln and Hardin had been state legislators together, and Hardin had been one of those who intervened to prevent a near-duel with Shields that had been an embarrassing event in Lincoln's career.

And then the honorable delegate from Sangamon County did still another honorable thing—honorable and/or shrewd, depending upon how one interprets it.

Having been sent as a delegate to support Baker (the groom who had beat him out for his own dear gal), he proposed to the Pekin convention a resolution, which passed, recommending that Whigs of the Seventh District support Baker in the *next* congressional election. Of course that meant that Lincoln himself would be closed out of the opportunity not only this time, when Hardin was nominated, but also the next, when, by his own resolution, Baker would be the nominee.

But one can say that it also had the effect of foreclosing Hardin from running for reelection, and perhaps by implication and analogy Baker as well, so that the Seventh District Whigs could then at last nominate . . . the other leading district Whig, the one who had conducted himself honorably through all these dealings. To be sure, there was no guarantee that all that would come about.

As Lincoln seeking to be a congressman in the forties by conducting himself honorably at one stage may have predisposed his fellow party members to support him at the next, so he would do the same, as we shall see, seeking to be a senator in the fifties. In the second case, as not in the first, there would be at issue not only party morality but also a great matter of public policy.

Hardin feared that, given this history, the Whigs of Sangamon County might not support him "cordially" in the general election, but Lincoln assured him that he could dismiss all such fears. "We have already resolved to make a particular effort to give you the very largest majority possible in our county"—to the point even of betting Morgan County (Hardin's home county) that Sangamon would give Hardin twice the majority that Morgan would, "on pain of losing a barbecue." "I got up the proposal," Lincoln wrote to Hardin. Hardin was handily elected to Congress.

One year later Baker would indeed be nominated, as prearranged, to be his successor. Lincoln would campaign vigorously in Baker's behalf, and also for the Whig nominee for president in the 1844 election, Henry Clay. Clay lost to the Democrat Polk, but the Whig Baker was elected congressman from Illinois's Seventh District.

And who would then be Baker's successor? When the time came,

Abraham Lincoln checked, just to be sure, with Baker, who assured him that "the track for the next congressional race was clear [for Lincoln] so far as he was concerned." But Hardin, who had acquired a taste for it, did not think he was foreclosed from now coming back into the fray to seek another term. Lincoln's ambitious and skillful politics, and his magnanimity, would both be given another trial by the contest (should there ever have been a contest?) with Hardin. He had more to complain of with Hardin than he had had with Baker, but although he argued his case vigorously, he did not reproach Hardin.

His sole argument, he said many times, was that "turn about is fair play"; he scrupulously avoided attacks on Hardin, and told his supporters to avoid them. "Let nothing be said against Hardin . . . nothing deserves to be said against him. Let the pith of the whole argument be 'turn about is fair play.'" "That Hardin is talented, energetic, usually generous and magnanimous, I have, before this, affirmed to you, and do not now deny. You know that my only argument is that 'turn about is fair play.' This he, practically, at least denies."

Supporters of Hardin proposed in a newspaper that Lincoln be nominated for governor—a phony honor indeed, because no Whig had ever been elected governor, and the futile run for that office would have removed Lincoln from the contest over the valuable nomination for congressman. Lincoln for his part did not want a newspaper close to him to return the favor: he did not want it to be suspected that "I was attempting to juggle Hardin out of a nomination for congress by juggleing him into one for Governor."

More seriously, Hardin tried to change the way Whig nominees were chosen in the Seventh District. The Pekin convention had recommended the continued use of the convention system to nominate future congressional candidates, and as we have noted Lincoln was, among Whigs, a strong advocate of that convention system. But there was a residual antiparty spirit in Whig culture that associated too much organizing with Democrats; any person who wanted to should simply put his name forward, and voters should then choose which person they preferred, without any party intervening. That seemed to many old Whigs more moral, more republican, more upright—and less Jacksonian—than joining to agree to support a convention nominee, even if he was not one's own first choice.

Lincoln made his most thorough argument against such views and in favor of the prior concert of party conventions in a campaign circular he had written (nominally with two others) back on March 4, 1843. He would refer to that argument in a letter on March 7—a letter in which he said, "I am sorry to hear that any of the whigs of your county, or indeed of any county, should longer be against conventions." In that circular, "you will find a brief argument in favour of conventions; and although I wrote it myself, I will say to you, that it is conclusive upon this point—that it can not be reasonably answered." His argument in the circular was fully illustrated from recent elections, displaying Lincoln's detailed knowledge of Illinois and of national politics. The point, he had written, was not to argue "whether the system is right in itself" but to show that "while our opponents use it, it is madness in us not to defend ourselves with it." When Whigs have failed to observe the requirements of the convention system, the common enemy had "chucklingly" borne off the spoils.* In union is strength. A house divided against itself cannot stand. "If two friends aspire to the same office, it is certain both cannot succeed. Would it not, then, be much less painful to have the question decided by mutual friends some time before, than to snarl and quarrel till the day of election, and then both be beaten by the common enemy?"

Lincoln had abided by the moral requirements of party regularity and conventions even when they operated against his personal interest, and friends would have been willing to violate them—as we have seen in this tale of the Three Whigs. So—when now suddenly Hardin proposed to abandon the convention method when it would surely operate in Lincoln's interest (and against Hardin's)—one might excuse Lincoln for being indignant.

In two letters responding to Hardin he was not overtly indignant, but he was brisk and forthright and thorough. He bluntly said he did not wish to join in Hardin's proposal; he was entirely satisfied with the convention system—under which, Lincoln pointed out, both Hardin and Baker had been successively chosen and elected to Congress. As to Hardin's ridiculous proposal that candidates not only simply offer themselves individually (as had been done under the old, preorganizational, antipolitical Whig way) but confine their activities, and their friends' activities, to their own counties, he said, with impressive patience: "[I]t seems to me that on reflection you will see, the fact of your having been in congress, had . . . so

---

* Would any other Whig in 1840s Illinois have invented that adverb "chucklingly"? Seeing that word, one would suspect that Lincoln had written this circular even if he had not himself later said so.

spread your name in the district, as to give you a decided advantage in such a stipulation."

Hardin, as an ex-congressman known throughout the district, would have an insurmountable advantage by the method he proposed, with no convention, and in addition each candidate agreeing to stay within his own county. It was a transparent effort to serve Hardin's own interests ostensibly in the name of avoiding intraparty conflict. On this last point Lincoln wryly noted that he appreciated Hardin's desire to keep down excitement, and would himself promise to "keep cool."

"I am satisfied with the old system, under which such good men have triumphed [like you, friend Hardin], and . . . I desire no departure from its principles." If there should be a departure, though, by the way, how about making a more accurate and more just apportionment of delegate votes to the counties? Lincoln goes into specifics to show the malapportionment, and observes "the advantage of it" is "all manifestly in your favor"—and yet somehow Hardin while redoing things had taken no notice of this matter in which the old system most needs adjustment. "I have always been in the habit of acceding to almost any proposal that a friend would make; and I am truly sorry I cannot in this." As a last fillip Lincoln observed that friends in different places had been seeking the convention for their towns and would not "feel much complimented" if Hardin and Lincoln should make a bargain that it should sit nowhere.

Hardin's response to Lincoln's rejection of his proposal was such as to provoke a long letter from Lincoln, on February 7, 1846, that came right up to the border of indignation. Lincoln had to set apart a day when he had time to write it. His letter is one long vigorous repudiation of all of Hardin's complaints. Hardin had used the terms "management," "manoevering," and "combination" "quite freely" as pejoratives to characterize Lincoln's activities. Lincoln denied any impropriety in what he had done, and said, near the end, "Feeling, as I do, the utter injustice of these imputations, it is somewhat difficult to be patient under them." He concludes: "I believe you do not mean to be unjust, or ungenerous; and I, therefore am slow to believe that you will not yet think *better* and think *differently* of this matter."

Enough Whig leaders told Hardin that they did indeed believe that it was now Lincoln's turn to persuade Hardin to withdraw his candidacy. On May 1, 1846, Abraham Lincoln was (finally) chosen, by a convention of Whigs meeting in Petersburg, as the Whig nominee for Congress from the Seventh District of Illinois.

. . .

Isaac Arnold, who would much later be a Republican congressman from Illinois and a biographer of Lincoln, observed in that biography that "few congressional districts in the republic . . . have been represented by such a succession of distinguished men" as the Seventh District in this period— Arnold adds Stuart to the three rotating Whigs. Arnold also observed (writing in 1884) that only Stuart was still alive; that the three Whig rivals in our little story had all died by violence: "Hardin was shot on the field of Buena Vista [in the Mexican War]. Baker received a volley of bullets as he was leading his troops at Balls Bluff [early in the Civil War]. And Lincoln was assassinated."

Ten days after the Whigs of the Seventh Congressional District in Illinois nominated Abraham Lincoln, President James K. Polk sent a war message to Congress and Congress declared war on Mexico.

In Illinois, as in other western and southwestern states, it was, at the start at least, a popular war. Soon after the declaration of war, still in May of 1846, there came word of two dramatic triumphs by the army under General Zachary Taylor, at Palo Alto and Resaca de la Palma on the Rio Grande. The parades, cheering, and celebrations were bipartisan, or non-partisan, widespread. In Illinois, as in other western places, volunteers flocked to the recruiting stations. It resembled another summer of patriotic and idealistic volunteerism, 1861. The volunteers included, significantly, both John J. Hardin and Edward D. Baker. Hardin, as noted, would be killed during Taylor's great victory at Buena Vista. His body would be brought back to Illinois to be buried with military honors. The constitutional convention meeting at the capitol at that time adjourned in respect. Congressman Baker would organize a unit in the Illinois volunteers, be wounded, return to Washington to deliver in uniform on the House floor an ornate speech urging support for the volunteers, would then resign his seat as congressman in December of 1846, return to battle, and be wounded again at the battle of Cerro Gordo in April of 1847.

And meanwhile, what had that third Whig, now the congressional candidate, been doing? He spoke, along with Governor Thomas Ford and other political leaders, at a mass meeting to encourage volunteering on May 30, 1846, in Springfield, but otherwise was silent about the war. Critics of the speeches Congressman Lincoln would make when he got to

Washington would sometimes ask: Why did he not say any of that back in Illinois, when the war was going on? Lincoln would give this answer, such as it may be: "When the war began, it was my opinion that all those who, because of knowing too *little*, or because of knowing too *much*, could not conscientiously approve of the conduct of the President, in the beginning of it, should, nevertheless, as good citizens and patriots, remain silent on that point, at least till the war should be ended."

The war was not an issue in his campaign against the Democratic nominee, the evangelist-politician Peter Cartwright. Then as now campaigns would often concentrate on personal matters that had little to do with the great issues of national policy. Lincoln had to fend off the reprise of those charges that had been floated in the first Whig scramble for the nomination: that he was an aristocrat and that he was a scoffer at religious belief. He issued that careful statement saying that he did not scoff anymore, or approve of scoffing.

He defeated Cartwright in the August 1846 election by a comfortable margin, 6,340 to 4,829.

As congressman-elect he had that long wait produced by the nation's original constitutional arrangement, before the lame duck amendment of 1933: Elected August 3, 1846, he would not take his seat until December 6, 1847.

He was elected while the Polk administration was working its will in the Democratic Twenty-ninth Congress in Washington, to be a member of the next Congress, the Thirtieth, in which the Whigs now would have a majority in the House. During the twenty months that Lincoln was the Whig nominee, and then congressman-elect, the Mexican War would be fought.

When, on September 17, 1847, while Congressman-elect Lincoln was still in Springfield, the American army under General Scott captured Mexico City, the fighting was effectively over. But the war was not over, because no treaty had been signed. The peace treaty in this instance was of great importance, because the Americans insisted on an "indemnity"— i.e., territory. So the war was still formally unfinished and the issues it raised still in the air when the Lincolns came to Washington.

On the trip to take his seat Lincoln, with Mary and the boys, visited her hometown, Lexington, Kentucky, and while they were there the great Henry Clay himself gave a speech of national importance in Lexington, which Lincoln almost certainly attended. In that speech Clay said that the Mexican War was a war of aggression that had been unjustly initiated by

President Polk's order to General Taylor to advance into what was (at best) disputed territory.

Arriving in Washington, the Lincolns soon found lodgings at the boardinghouse of Mrs. Anna Sprigg, a widow, whose place had often had a certain concentration of antislavery Whigs. Her lodging house had been the home of congressmen who joined John Quincy Adams back in the early days of the gag-rule fight, and it had been and still was the lodging of Joshua Giddings of Ohio, who was not only the leading congressional opponent of slavery but also a thoroughgoing opponent of Mr. Polk's war.*

The Lincoln boys, rather undisciplined, had the run of Mrs. Sprigg's house. Mary Todd Lincoln, one of the few wives to have accompanied her husband, tended to keep to her room, and with her eager new congressman husband absorbed in his work, went back to Lexington with the boys after four months.

Lincoln fared poorly in the lottery for seats, drawing number 191 in the rear of the chamber. On December 6, 1847, he was sworn into office as a member of the United States House of Representatives—his first official participation in the work of the federal government, indeed his only participation except as its chief executive—and his first appearance on the national stage.

---

* On May 31, 1861, the new president of the United States would send a note to his secretary of the interior, Caleb B. Smith, asking him to do whatever favor it was (we do not know) that was asked by Mrs. Anna G. Sprigg, "a most worthy and deserving lady."

CHAPTER SEVEN

Another President, Another War

1. SPOTTY LINCOLN

A congressional session began, then as now, with an address by the president. In those days, however, it was not delivered in person but read to the Congress by clerks. As his first official act, new congressman Lincoln listened to a clerk read the message of President Polk.

Polk's message, like the four that Lincoln would one day send, like the annual presentations and State of the Union addresses of other presidents, would eventually go around the circle of departments and issues, like Santa Claus on Christmas morning, with a little something for each. But Polk's message relegated all that to the last pages. After introductory pieties the great bulk was his justification in detail, page after page, of every one of the actions of the United States, and the Polk administration, in the war with Mexico.

The most salient quality of this long presentation was its relentless self-righteousness. Its *total* defensiveness. Polk and America were *always* and in *every* regard in the right; Mexico was always and in every way in the wrong. Doubly wrong: Mexico was not just the aggressor who started the war; Mexico was also wrong in every point leading up to that beginning, and has been wrong at every point since. And Mexico is now further wrong in not agreeing swiftly to her own dismemberment—to the "liberal" and "generous" terms that we now are offering.

Mexico's wickedness had long preceded the blood-shedding "invasion." There was her "wanton violation of the rights of person and property of our [American] citizens; her repeated acts of bad faith through a long series of years, and her disregard of solemn treaties stipulating indemnity to our injured citizens . . ." It was not enough for Polk to find in these Mexican misdeeds "ample cause of war on our part"; no, they constituted "not only" that ample cause "but were of such an aggregated character as would have justified war before the whole world in resorting to this extreme remedy." In other words, we were already doubly justified in initiating the use of force even before and without Mexico's blood-shedding "invasion."

But we "forbore for years to assert our clear rights by force." Polk's treatment of the role of the United States is one long stream of self-praise and self-sympathy for our forbearance, our restraint, our great reluctance to use force, and now the great liberality of our proposed terms of settlement (which amounted only to taking a major fraction of the country, although Polk hinted that if Mexico persisted in her "wholly inadmissible," "unreasonable" counterproposal, the United States just might swallow the whole).

New congressman Lincoln resolved to take a leading part in the Whig response to this remarkable message. Both his actions and his letters to Herndon indicate that Lincoln was distinctly eager to make his mark, and to do so quickly. One might think that he would wait—as thousands of Phineas Finns, coming shyly for the first time into a parliament, have done. There you would be, getting shakily up on your legs, with all of those practiced legislators and confident orators turning now to look curiously at you, this new fellow. There would be these two hundred pairs of eyes watching and of ears listening as you made your maiden effort. Joshua Giddings, the great legislator from the Western Reserve of Ohio, now Lincoln's senior messmate and an imposing figure—the "Lion of Ashtabula"—had not been such a lion ten years earlier, when he first spoke. "I expected to be greatly embarrassed and to have my voice tremble," he would write in his journal, and was pleased that it did not. But newcomer Lincoln does not seem to have suffered such freshman qualms.

He did try his voice on a minor postal matter, this sometime postman from New Salem, and wrote to Herndon on January 8, 1848, that he was not much more nervous as he rose to speak before his two hundred colleagues in Washington than he had been before appearing in court back in Illinois. He displayed a revealing jocular bravado: "As you are all so anxious for me to distinguish myself, I have concluded to do so, before long."

Perhaps he was only half-joking; apparently he *did* try to distinguish himself, fast, by his speeches. But he did not succeed.

The congressman voiced his first major utterance on December 22, after just ten legislative days, most of them filled with opening routine. The excuse for this earliness would be that he was responding, as part of a general Whig response, to that presidential message. But still—a newly minted first-time congressman ten days into his legislative career, aggressively challenging the president of the United States?

Lincoln's speech dealt, of course, with the war. It included his notorious "Spot Resolutions," demanding to know by a series of prosecutorial interrogatories on just what "spot" it was, on American soil, that American blood had been spilled—with the obvious implication that it had *not* been American soil.

The preamble to his resolution is often omitted, but his pointed recitation of Polk's insistent repetition across the changing phases of the war may be the most effective part of Lincoln's little presentation. Lincoln, typically having done some research and dug out previous claims by Polk, quoted them one after another. Polk's belligerent self-justification had not begun with the current message:

> [T]he President of the United States, in his message of May 11th, 1846, has declared that "The Mexican Government not only refused to receive him [the envoy of the U.S.] or listen to his propositions, but, after a long continued series of menaces, have at last invaded *our* territory, and shed the blood of our fellow *citizens* on *our own soil.*"

Then in his annual message of the following December, after seven months of war, the president, Lincoln noted, was still going back to the origins and was even more insistent and defensive:

> And again, in his message of December 8, 1846, [Polk said] that "We had ample cause of war against Mexico, long before the breaking out of hostilities. But even then we forbore to take redress into our own hands, until Mexico herself became the aggressor by invading *our soil* in hostile array, and shedding the blood of our *citizens.*"

And in the message to this Congress now beginning, after twenty months of war, Polk is still and once again insisting in an unpersuasively self-sympathizing way on American forbearance and Mexican aggression in the war's beginning:

And yet again, in his message of December 7, 1847, [the president said] that "The Mexican Government refused even to hear the terms of adjustment which he" (our minister of peace) "was authorized to propose; and finally, under wholly unjustifiable pretexts, involved the two countries in war, by invading the territory of the State of Texas, striking the first blow, and shedding the blood of our *citizens* on *our own soil.*"

So Polk had not just avowed but had repeatedly and argumentatively insisted upon the claim about "our soil" and "our blood" and Mexico altogether without provocation striking the first blow.

Unfortunately, the device that Lincoln then used to make his opposing point was not effective. He proposed a resolution asking the president to inform the House whether this, that, and the other historical or contemporary condition "was, or was not," "did, or did not," "is, or is not" such and such. The word "spot" is reiterated in the first three of the eight interrogatories, the phrase "blood . . . was shed" in the first and two more. It was not a successful device either rhetorically or intellectually. It was insistent in tone, too much a lawyer's contrivance, and its manner interfered with its matter. Lincoln had a point to make, that the place where that first skirmish happened was Mexican soil, in the midst of a Mexican settlement, or that the territory was at best disputed. But the point was upstaged by his device. (To be sure, the point was not original with Lincoln; Whig and other opponents had been arguing against Polk's statements about the war's beginning for twenty months.)

Lincoln's resolutions were ignored in Washington—but not in Illinois. Opponents gleefully attacked him; a few friends disagreed with him; Herndon was bothered. The word "spot" would become a derisive weapon against "Spotty" Lincoln, not only in that moment but later.

Then on January 3 Lincoln voted along with most Whigs in favor of an amendment offered by George Ashmun, a Massachusetts Whig, to a resolution of thanks to General Taylor. One may infer that the Whigs who opposed Polk's initiation of the war were tired of being trapped into apparently supporting the war when they voted for resolutions like this one. Of course they were grateful to General Zachary Taylor and wanted to honor him—but not to imply by doing so unequivocal support for Polk's war. So Ashmun proposed to add to the resolution of thanks the phrase "in a war unnecessarily and unconstitutionally begun by the president . . ." And Ashmun's amendment carried the House by a vote of eighty-five to eighty-one (only to be killed in the Democratic Senate).

Lincoln voted for the Ashmun amendment, as did most Whigs, including other Whigs from the West. This amendment was not a particular assertion by Lincoln himself but a widely shared Whig position—enough so to carry a majority of the House.

And then on January 12 the new Whig from Illinois was on his legs again to make a speech—this one longer, more carefully worked out, his first major speech on the national stage.

Again, his point was to challenge President Polk on the single issue, the legitimacy of the beginning of the war. He claimed to be explaining his vote on the Ashmun amendment. He presented a closely reasoned argument, with distinctions and metaphors, pursuing his disagreement (the disagreement of many) with the president about the boundary between Texas and Mexico at the time of the war's beginning.

This speech, too, provoked Democratic denunciation and some Whig wariness back in Illinois—but almost no response in Washington. He had not made his mark, after all. President Polk, against whom Lincoln's utterances were directed in a most personal way, who recorded in his journal detailed accounts of all the daily doings and who would mention many congressmen, never once referred to Congressman Lincoln.

If one permits oneself a reservation or two about the Mexican War, one might be sympathetic to the general position taken by Congressman Lincoln (along with the main body of Whigs). It is possible to hold, on the facts of the initial boundary dispute, a position at odds with the defenders of Polk and the war, and in sympathy with the position Congressman Lincoln took. In fact one (untypical) scholar would write, in 1967:

> There is no doubt now, as there was none then, that the established boundary ran through the uninhabited region between the Nueces and the Rio Grande. During the Mexican War, in a discussion of the origins of the War in the House of Representatives, Abraham Lincoln showed that Polk's argument on the matter was the "sheerest deception." He ridiculed the President's implication that since the territory of Texas and the United States extended beyond the Nueces it therefore extended to the Rio Grande. He observed that after all "it is *possible* to cross one river and go *beyond* it without going *all the way* to the next, that jurisdiction may be exercised *between* two rivers without covering *all* the country between them."

This scholar then made this striking assertion: "Lincoln's analysis of the several aspects of the boundary question, and his appraisal of President Polk's responsibility for the initiation of the War in that address in the House, is superior to the treatment in any histories of the Mexican War now available." Lincoln did better, in this perhaps slightly idiosyncratic scholarly opinion, than professional historians had done, up to 1967—that is, *American* historians. Mexican historians, one gathers, would be a different story.

I suggest, though, that there were defects in Lincoln's speeches on the war, not in the position he (and most Whigs) took, or in the "principle" or lack of it which it represented, or in its partisan character—charges that, as we will see, were to be made against them—but in their extravagant personal tone and insistent narrowness. A large part of the mature Lincoln's genius will be the depth and care and courtesy with which he expresses the political moralities of the actual situation. In this case he does not do that.

One does not have the sense that Lincoln drew back and thought deeply and wrote carefully about the complex of moral/political issues involved—as he would do in the summer of 1854, getting ready to speak on the extension of slavery, and again in the winter of 1859–60, getting ready to speak in New York City, and again in the following winter preparing an inaugural address. Instead, as a newcomer eager to make his mark, he rushed into the fray with a belligerent challenge to the president.

The December 22 speech consisted entirely of the famous Spot Resolutions, which insisted, in a hectoring manner, that the President indicate the precise spot on American soil on which American blood had been spilled.

The January 22 speech dealt at greater length with the same point, and became in places surprisingly personal against Polk, and even, in a few lines, nasty in a way not characteristic of Lincoln. Perhaps in his congressional days he did not yet have his full moral maturity. Or perhaps, like most human beings, he had different levels of moral maturity in him simultaneously, and at different ages.

Lincoln's January 22 speech made with relentless lawyer's thoroughness the argument that the Rio Grande was not accepted as the boundary of Texas (hence of the United States) at the time of the commencing of the war, and therefore that Polk's order to General Taylor to move to the Rio

Grande was a provocative act. Whatever one may hold on that central matter, the tone of Lincoln's speech is more prosecutorial than one would expect: a young, new congressman bluntly interrogating the president, invoking George Washington and "the Almighty" and peremptorily and personally insisting upon answers:

> Let him answer, fully, fairly, and candidly. Let him answer with facts, and not with arguments. Let him remember he sits where Washington sat, and so remembering, let him answer, as Washington would answer. As a nation should not, and the Almighty will not, be evaded, so let him attempt no evasion—no equivocation. If the president cannot or will not give the desired answers ... then I shall be fully convinced, of what I more than suspect already, that he is deeply conscious of being in the wrong—that he feels the blood of this war, like the blood of Abel, is crying to Heaven against him.

Polk deeply conscious of being in the wrong? Polk mired in guilt for the blood spilled? That seems unlikely in the extreme with this externally minded, morally unimaginative president, and in any case is both too personal and too speculative an attack. It is a dubious charge to have made, even if there were some basis for it, which there doesn't appear to have been.

There are similar objections to the further charge that the utterly unglamorous Polk hoped to cover that guilt with the glamour of military glory, about which the ambitious young writer squeezes out two metaphors:

> That originally having some strong motive—what, I will not stop now to give my opinion concerning—to involve the two countries in a war, and trusting to escape scrutiny, by fixing the public gaze upon the exceeding brightness of military glory—that attractive rainbow, that rises in showers of blood—that serpent's eye, that charms to destroy— he [Polk] plunged into it, and has swept, on and on, till, disappointed in his calculation of the ease with which Mexico might be subdued, he now finds himself, he knows not where.

Actually, Polk knew better than most presidents do where he was. The question is whether he should have been there.

Lincoln ended this patronizing paragraph with a particularly unworthy charge:

How like the half insane mumbling of a fever-dream is the whole war part of his late message!

If you read Polk's long, dreary, defensive speech you may have strong objections to it, but it will not seem like "the half insane mumbling of a fever-dream." Lincoln's attacks remind one of the overblown quality of the endings of his youthful lectures and addresses, but now with the added ingredient of being nastily personal. (He will be good—but God knows when.)

Lincoln also said of the president:

His mind, tasked beyond it's power, is running hither and thither, like some tortured creature, on a burning surface, finding no position, on which it can settle down, and be at ease.

And this thirty-eight-year-old, brand-new congressman ended this long attack on the president—ended this speech—with more of the same:

As I have before said, he knows not where he is. He is a bewildered, confounded, and miserably perplexed man. God grant he may be able to show, there is not something about his conscience, more painful than all his mental perplexity!

I think we see in these passages something of the qualities of the young Lincoln in his use of his power to hurt (not that he laid a glove on Polk), his skinnings, his sarcasm and personal invective. Lincoln's attack not only was objectionably personal; it was also the *wrong* personal attack. Polk was not "bewildered," "confounded," or "perplexed." He was, rather, a man with tunnel vision. Here is a quotation from a twentieth-century biographer of Polk: "Literal-minded and unimaginative, he had so little feeling for the moral dimensions of questions like slavery and expansionist aggression that he could not understand how other men were affected by them." That does not sound like a perplexed man with fever dreams and blood guilt.

2. POLITICALLY SUICIDAL NONPRINCIPLE?

Congressman Lincoln's role in the debate over the Mexican War would be subjected to a different and more severe criticism than the one I have voiced—not just about his tone and his psychologizing of Polk but on the merits. With these criticisms I want to disagree, in particular because they are sometimes cast in moral terms.

The most potent critic would be, not surprisingly, Senator Stephen A. Douglas.

In the very first of the famous 1858 debates, in Ottawa, Illinois, Douglas would include personal reminiscences, apparently amiable but with barbs, about his friendly rival with whose career by that time his own had intersected for nearly twenty-five years. "Mr. Lincoln served with me in the legislature in 1836," Douglas said, "when we both retired [not true: Lincoln did not retire until 1841] and he subsided, or became submerged, and was lost sight of as a public man for some years." Perhaps Lincoln was lost sight of as he continued to toil in the state legislature by so lofty a person as Douglas, who rose rapidly to statewide office, to the United States House of Representatives, and to the United States Senate.

"In 1846," Douglas went on, being careful to link Lincoln's reemergence to abolitionism, "when Wilmot introduced his celebrated proviso, and the abolition tornado swept over the country, Lincoln turned up again as a member of Congress from the Sangamon district." (In fact the "abolition tornado" had nothing to do with Lincoln's trip to Congress.) "I was then in the Senate of the United States," said His Loftiness Senator Douglas, noticing this submerged acquaintance from Springfield on his lower level, now coming back into his line of sight, "and [I] was glad to welcome my old friend and companion." And what does he say then, in total summary about the congressional career of his old friend and companion? "Whilst in Congress, he distinguished himself by his opposition to the Mexican War, taking the side of the common enemy against his own country [voice from audience: "That's true"] and when he returned home he found the indignation of the people followed him everywhere, and he was again submerged or obliged to retire into private life, forgotten by his former friends [voice from the crowd: "And will be again"]."

Lincoln answered Douglas in Ottawa with respect to the heavy charge that he had taken the side of the country's enemy, with the argument he had made and repeated, in some exasperation, to Herndon ten years earlier: when the Democrats' efforts "to get me to vote that the war had been righteously begun by the president, I would not do it. But whenever they asked for any money . . . or anything to pay the soldiers there, during all that time, I gave the same votes that Judge Douglas did."

Through the rest of the Lincoln/Douglas debates the exchange on this matter had that same shape, with Douglas insisting, later with joking references to "spots," that Lincoln had opposed his country's side in the war

(Lincoln, said Douglas, thought the war was not commenced on the right *spot*) and Lincoln insisting on his (and the Whigs') distinction between voting for supplies, which they would do, and affirming the righteousness of the war's beginning, which they would not do. The issue of the effect on Lincoln at home in the aftermath—whether "the indignation of the people followed him everywhere," and he was "submerged," "forgotten," "obliged to retire"—was not taken up again in the debates.

It gained a new life, however, and a memorable tag line, more than thirty years after the war, more than twenty years after the debates, from a quite different source: the irrepressible Herndon, finally bringing out his life of Lincoln in 1889. And through the mist of memory Herndon recalled his arguing with Lincoln about his position on the war: "I earnestly desired to prevent him from committing what I believed to be political suicide." Lincoln's vote and speeches on the war, wrote Old Man Herndon, "sealed Lincoln's doom as a congressman" and cost the Whigs the district.

Other writers about Lincoln in the nineteenth century made no such interpretation, but in the twentieth century it was picked up by Albert Beveridge and fed into the bloodstream of Lincoln literature. The reader will not be surprised that Beveridge would take this negative line about Lincoln and the Mexican War. Beveridge was an unabashed expansionist who would dislike a person who opposed wars and opposed expansion, even if his name was Abraham Lincoln.

From Douglas, Herndon, and Beveridge the political-suicide theme entered into shelves of Lincoln books. It was then to be stated in its most sizzling form in a book by mid-twentieth-century scholar Donald Riddle.

> Without conscientious principle, and activated only by political motive, Lincoln for the first time in his life was completely mistaken in his estimate of a political situation. Within two weeks he had committed three costly blunders [Riddle means the two speeches and the vote on the Ashmun amendment] ...
>
> It must be repeated that if Lincoln had based his position on principle, and had maintained it as a matter of conscience, he would have been justified in following his course even though it entailed the loss of political friends or resulted in the loss of his Congressional seat to the Democrats. But he had no such motivation.

Thus we see that in full bloom, in the most fully developed negative view, Congressman Lincoln on the war was seen to be wrong, partisan, unprincipled, and politically stupid, all at once.

When I lay it out like that, I think one can see that there may be a certain tension among the points. One can be principled though wrong, which is the way we see our most honorable opponents to be (and which it is important to preserve as a possibility if democracy is to work well); and, even more, one can be unpopular though principled—indeed, unpopular *because* principled. This last possibility, also important to democracy's functioning, is, in fact, something of a stereotyped model of political morality in popular understanding. Leaders make an unsubtle appeal to it when they say, dismissively, "That would be the *popular* thing to do," and then add piously, "but I must do what is *right*."

When in the following century a young senator from Massachusetts who would later be president would be laid up in a hospital in western Massachusetts and would look for something to occupy his time (and that of his assistant Theodore Sorensen) and also for something to promote his political prospects, as writing a book is said to do, he would decide to respond to a remark by the distinguished columnist Walter Lippmann on the paucity of upright politicians, to produce a book of historical examples in contradiction to that claim. The form of the politician's uprightness is the same in each chapter: John Adams defending British soldiers in the Boston Massacre case in defiance of Boston opinion; his son, John Quincy, supporting Jefferson in defiance of the Massachusetts Federalists who sent him to the Senate; Senator George W. Norris of Nebraska (how did the total easterner John F. Kennedy happen onto this Nebraskan? Ted Sorensen's father had been Norris's close adviser) supporting New Deal measures in defiance of anti-Roosevelt opinion in his home state; Edward Ross of Kansas going against his party and home-state opinion to vote against the conviction of Andrew Johnson under impeachment in 1868. All of them bravely took a position they believed in—in spite of the opinion in their home base. Well, then—what about Congressman Lincoln?

The critics of Congressman Lincoln somehow discerned that Lincoln did not really believe in the position he took, but adopted it solely as an opportunistic effort to attain party advantage. One of the bad things Lincoln is alleged by the strongest critic, Donald Riddle, to have done in Washington was to have fallen "under the influence of the Eastern and Southern party," and to have come to look at the issue in a "national scope" (which, the reader may perceive after a double take, the critic was *condemning* him for doing). Lincoln "lost contact with the situation in Illinois."

To this charge one may respond: Maybe so, to some degree—but is that a major transgression? Although Lincoln did send and receive a string of letters and other mailings to and from Illinois, and although he did use his frank to send home copies of more speeches than almost any other congressman, nevertheless, being in this new environment probably did affect this continuing lifelong learner. One may surmise that the still fairly young and fairly provincial, but quite intelligent and conscientious, new congressman, in a national setting for the first time in his life, might indeed have been stimulated by his new association with national leaders like Alexander Stephens of Georgia, who gave a speech that impressed him a great deal; and Joshua Giddings, his messmate; and John Palfrey, the Harvard professor, Unitarian minister, and opponent of slavery; and George Ashmun of Massachusetts, who introduced the key resolution against Polk on the war and twelve years later would preside at the convention at which Lincoln would be nominated; and maybe even, briefly, the towering figure of John Quincy Adams himself.* But is Lincoln to be criticized for that? Surely part of the moral meaning of representative government is that the representatives from all the parts of a vast nation coming together in a great mosaic not only represent the interests and visions of their respective localities but also then learn from each other, affect each other, reason together, diminish their respective provincialisms, and shape something nearer to the common good.

We might, just to furnish a contrast to the critics of Congressman Lincoln on the war, formulate this contrary interpretation: As a bright and conscientious man now coming onto the national scene for the first time, he heard Clay in Lexington, read the *Intelligencer* in Washington, talked to Giddings in Mrs. Sprigg's mess, heard other Whigs' arguments, read the president's message defending his war policy quite carefully and critically (clearly he did this), and concluded in his mind and conscience that his latent belief or suspicion back in Illinois throughout the twenty months of the war was correct, that Polk had initiated the war, and that it was a war of conquest.

That this was a genuine conviction we may surely discern particularly from his earnest private letters, as we will see in a moment. He took the floor to challenge the president with an awareness of the bellicosity and

---

* Adams collapsed on the House floor in late February of 1848 and died, still in the Capitol, three days later, just three months after Lincoln had taken his seat, so there probably was not much association between these two giants of American history, if indeed any at all. Lincoln was appointed to be one of the geographically representative honorary pallbearers at Adams's funeral.

eagle-screaming expansionism of his home district and state, bluntly expressed by the state's senior senator, Stephen A. Douglas. He must therefore have known that it would cost him politically. If all this be true, might we not begin to discern in Lincoln's speeches (for all their excess) the faint suggestion of the beginnings of a hint of something like a Profile in Courage?

The critics, to be sure, would protest strongly, saying among other things that Lincoln did not have the requisite solitariness. He was not standing alone in his conscientious defiance in the way that Courageous Profiles are supposed to do, but instead had a great deal of company as just one spokesman for the majority of his party. And some would say if he were going to do so eastern and un-Illinoisian a thing as opposing the war, then he should have gone all the way to do so in the "principled" and "consistent" (though of course mistaken) way that it was done by Adams, Giddings, and the so-called "Immortal Fourteen," who refused even to vote for supplies. But can we imagine what the results would have been, had this Illinois congressman taken that position? It was bad enough just with his condemning Polk's *commencing* the war; what would it have been if he had refused in addition to support supplies for the men who were fighting it?

Only a handful of congressmen had the effrontery, or the courage, or the right constituency, to oppose Polk all the way on the war. All who did—the "Immortal Fourteen"—came from safely antislavery and anti-expansionist Whig districts in the Northeast: five, including Adams and Ashmun, from Massachusetts: five, including Giddings, from the Western Reserve—the Connecticut Reserve—in Northern Ohio; one each from Rhode Island, New York, Pennsylvania, and Maine. None came from a district even beginning to be as far west as the Seventh District in Illinois. It tells one something further about the real politics of that time that some other Whigs may *not* have voted in that "principled," "consistent" way exactly because they did not want to be identified with the perfectionist, quasi-abolitionist "Immortal Fourteen."

Lincoln was already chided, given just what he did do, by the comparison between his role and that of others from his district. Many Sangamon County men, including Whigs, had fought, and some had died, in the war. Lincoln's Whig predecessors, and a sometime Democratic opponent, had covered themselves with glory. John Hardin, who had won the seat when Lincoln first sought it, had rushed to enlist and—as we have said—had been killed at Buena Vista. Edward Baker, who had won the seat the second time Lincoln sought it, had put on a particularly dramatic display, returning from the front in full uniform while still a member of the House, asking in a thrilling speech for support for troops; he then resigned his seat, returned to the front, and became a hero in the battle at Cerro Gordo. James Shields, the Democrat with whom Lincoln had often sparred in state government, whose U.S. Senate seat he would strive to attain, and with whom he once almost fought an actual duel, had fallen with grapeshot through his lungs.

And what had our present Seventh District congressman been doing (an opponent might ask) while these fellow political leaders of both parties covered themselves with glory on the field of battle? That congressman had introduced resolutions demanding to know about spots; he had voted for a Whig resolution that the war had been "unnecessarily and unconstitutionally begun"; and he had made a speech ascribing "half insane mumbling of a fever-dream" to the Commander-in-Chief. If in order to be "principled," he would also have refused to vote for supplies to these men facing gunfire in battle, that would surely have been altogether too sharp a profile of altogether too much "courage," and "political suicide" indeed.

Lincoln did not commit political suicide. He took, along with the majority of his party, the discriminate position already explained. Refusing to support Polk's justification of the war was unpopular in Illinois, but it was not fatal. Recent scholarship has heavily qualified, if not obliterated, in the following ways, the Douglas-Herndon-Beveridge view that Lincoln's actions on the war were a disaster for Whigs in the district:

1. Lincoln did take the position taken also by the majority of the Whigs in the House—eighty-five of them, a victorious majority—on the Ashmun resolution. That majority included Whigs from the most comparable western state, neighboring Indiana. (Lincoln, as we know, was the only Whig from Illinois.) So if he did something politically stupid, he did so in a large company.

2. "The indignation of the people" did not "follow him everywhere"; although the indignation of *Democrats* followed him a certain distance and was still there for Douglas to resurrect ten years later (voice from the crowd: "That's true!"). He was called Benedict Arnold and mocked as "Spotty" Lincoln and condemned in some public meetings, but the condemnations that Beveridge and Riddle spread across pages come almost entirely from Democrats, from Democratic papers, from gatherings initiated by Democrats. Mark Neely reports that "Whig newspapers defended

him, and no editor broke ranks." It does seem also to have been true—David Herbert Donald reports—that Lincoln was troubled by "the faintness of the praise" his speech received in the Whig papers, and by the sprinkling of Whigs like Herndon himself and his old friend Dr. A. G. Henry, who objected to Lincoln's position either on its merits or for reasons of political strategy or both. But what this adds up to is that Lincoln had been in the position that any party politician will sometimes find himself in—to have supported a position held by the bulk of one's party that is not popular in one's own district.

3. Lincoln, however, was not "obliged to retire into private life" because of his alleged unpopularity for having opposed the war. The primary, perhaps the sole, reason for his not running again—as Lincoln himself would say in the little autobiography he would write in 1860—was the "turn about is fair play" theme that he himself had initiated back in 1843: Hardin and Baker had their turns; Lincoln had his turn; now there was someone else—his old law partner Stephen Logan—who wanted a shot at it.

It may also be that with his large ambitions he had come to be slightly disillusioned with the role of a congressman. He needed to resume his law practice to support his family. And perhaps there was not any possible role then in sight for an Illinois Whig that fit his own expectations. Lincoln himself would write, "His profession had almost superseded politics in his mind." However these elements are sorted, his unpopularity because of his war stand was not the key to them.

4. Logan's loss of the congressional seat did not spring, at least not primarily, from the position on the war of his Whig predecessor Lincoln. Logan lost by only 106 votes out of 18,000 cast. Logan's Democratic opponent, Thomas Harris, was a popular hero of the Battle of Cerro Gordo, and gained because of his military glory. It was a presidential year, and even though the congressional election took place in August 1848, before the November presidential election, the excitement of the latter may have generated greater interest in the former in Democratic Illinois. Most important, Logan was a spectacularly inept campaigner. Lincoln would remark of a later campaign that Logan was "worse beaten than any other man since elections were invented." Neely remarks that Logan "was a notoriously poor campaigner fully capable of losing the district on his own."

5. Lincoln was not "forgotten by his former friends" or in such bad odor with Illinois Whigs as to be driven away from politics; on the contrary, he remained, although a lawyer in private practice, a leading Whig—

a Whig elector, and campaign speaker, in 1852, and the man selected to give eulogies both for Taylor in 1850 and for Clay in 1852. The most impressive of the several indications of this was that they still wanted him to campaign in Illinois in the presidential election in November after Logan had been defeated in August. If Lincoln had been cast into outer darkness, "submerged" and "forgotten by his former friends," as Douglas suggested, those friends (including Herndon) would not have complained to him that he ought to come home from his campaigning in the East to help out in Illinois.

But of course Douglas, Herndon, and Beveridge and others do not criticize Congressman Lincoln simply on grounds of his allegedly poor political tactics; they also think he was wrong—and that his wrongness led to, or was itself, his political suicide. The key to these fierce attacks on Lincoln's speeches on the Mexican War, in both centuries, is a wholehearted support of President Polk and of the American role in that war. Lincoln was wrong (and partisan and unprincipled and submerged and forgotten) because he opposed that war, with all its glorious results, as they are seen to be by his critics.

Sometimes the attack on Congressman Lincoln's position on the war deals with his motive, explicitly in moral terms. That attack furnishes, therefore, material for our examination of Lincoln as just possibly a virtuous politician, in its explicit insistence that Lincoln was not, in this phase of his life at least, anything of the sort.

Professor Riddle produced repeated statements like this: Lincoln's position on the war was "without conscientious principle, and activated only by political motive." About the Spot Resolutions Riddle wrote: "If Lincoln had opposed the administration's war policy from conscientious motives his opponents ought to have respected an attitude based upon principle. But the Spot Resolutions give no indication of being based upon principle, nor of appealing to principle. They seem to have been a shrewd, clever, and opportunistic means of discrediting the President."

It is not just the Spot Resolutions that lack principle and spring from no conscientious motives, according to Professor Riddle; the same is true of Lincoln's other acts on this subject: "This work has asserted that Lincoln, in his Spot Resolutions, his vote for the Ashmun amendment, and his Mexican War speech was not acting upon principle, but was taking partisan advantage of the war issue."

Professor Riddle's position represents in particularly blunt and explicit form a common outlook in these discussions of the rights and wrongs, the principles and the nonprinciples, of politics, and is therefore a convenient foil with which to disagree. To be morally praiseworthy, for him, a political act must be founded on a "principle" that is uncomplex, unvarying, explicit, and suprapartisan.

This position would say (did say, in effect) if you were going to oppose the war, do it completely, the way it was done by the "Immortal Fourteen" who voted against the Polk bill even when it provided supplies for the troops already engaged in battle. Riddle says that the antiwar position of John Quincy Adams was "certainly defensible." He adds "nor should a just estimate scorn"—interesting words—"the position of Joshua R. Giddings; it was mistaken, but it was based"—as Lincoln's in his view was not—"upon principle and was consistent."

This last word, "consistent" (by which he meant that these men voted against supplies as well as against Polk's justification of war), is of the essence of the first—to act upon "principle" is to be "consistent." I believe one can detect here a quite common attitude in popular American political moralizing: To be principled, conscientious, "moral," "right," one must take a position that is unqualified, apodictic, and "pure." To be principled is to be simple. To be principled is to be (as the word often is) "absolute": to act on only the one absolutely overriding moral claim, which shuts out everything else and rolls on to the most extreme expression. The contrary view is expressed in a dictum of Oliver Wendell Holmes that Reinhold Niebuhr liked: "It is not the man of Principle I admire but the man of principles"—plural. Such a man confronts moral problems as they exist in real life—relating one principle to another, one moral consideration to another.

Lincoln, and the large group of Whigs, had more than one moral claim: the dubiety of the war's beginning, on the one hand, and, on the other, the validity of claims by the men and the nation in battle now that it had in fact begun. In my view, they were not the less "moral" because their moral reasoning was more complicated.

The backhanded endorsement of Adams, Giddings, and the fourteen— that, though "mistaken," they were at least "consistent" and therefore "principled"—while having only "scorn" for Lincoln and the main body of Whigs, reflects a fairly common outlook, in the complexities of politics. The most extreme representatives of a position I reject, so "pure" as to be outside the present political possibilities, and therefore no threat at all to my position, I can praise in a patronizing way, for their admirable, though mistaken, moral purity, while those who hold more complex and politically realistic positions, nearer to, and therefore a threat to, my own, I denounce for their unprincipled partisanship.

It is also a requirement for this politics of "principle," that morally praiseworthy positions must be stated in explicitly "moral" terms. Riddle said of Lincoln's Spot Resolutions that they "give no indication of being based upon principle, nor of appealing to principle. They seem to have been a shrewd, clever, and opportunistic means of discrediting the President." I suggest in response that they were almost the reverse of this. They were not "shrewd," and they were not "clever" (or perhaps they were, as the English say, too clever by half). Why they were any more "opportunistic" than any other action, very much including Polk's, is not clear. Were they not grounded in a moral conviction that it is wrong to attack one's peaceful neighbor, that it should be a "principle" that one should not be the aggressor, that one should not fudge and falsify the facts of a war's beginning in an attempt to justify oneself?

Lincoln in his maturity would often use explicit moral language, particularly with respect to slavery. But he would do so in a carefully formulated and thoughtful way that avoided the perils of self-righteousness and of moralizing oversimplification. He was to be an unmoralistic moralist. It is not necessary always to slap on these labels—"moral," "right," "principle"—in an oversimplifying way in order to make a serious argument about what ought to be done. Often the too-simple use of explicit moral terms is an impediment, rather than a help, to moral understanding, because it heightens the emotional stakes while oversimplifying.

Another requirement of "principle," in this common view, is that it must not coincide with partisan objectives; it must not be "partisan"; it must not be "political." Polk in his diary would refer dismissively to the Whigs acting "on party grounds" in a way that by implication does not apply to his own party, the Democrats: "[I]f the Whigs on party grounds acted with him [Democratic Senator Benton, not persuaded by Polk's war message] the bill might be defeated"; "The Whigs in the Senate will oppose it [his war bill] on party grounds." And Riddle would write the Whig congressman from Illinois that "his Mexican War speech was not acting upon principle, but was taking partisan advantage of the war issue"; he was "the politician following party policy because he believed that to do so would be of advantage to the party."

My response to the charge that Lincoln's antiwar arguments were partisan is to say, yes, in some part they were. Lincoln did indeed calculate at first that the war issue might be the only way to beat the Democrats in 1848. And he did, indeed, then calculate that the way for Whigs to beat them was to turn the war issue around by nominating the war hero Zachary Taylor. But these calculations of party advantage were not the sole reason; nor, I think, can one determine from his private letters the ultimate reason for opposing the Polk interpretation of the beginning of the war. It was not the case that Lincoln had no genuine opinion about the war's beginning, but adopted the view he expressed altogether to further Whig interests and damage Polk—still less that he held a secret opinion *contrary* to the one he expressed. As is often the case, the opinion he would have come to in any event, and the bulk of Whig opinion and perceived interest, coincided and affected each other in his mind. So I infer.

Political parties can be, and often are, the practically effective organizing of clusters not only of interests but also of values—of moral visions. Actually, they almost always are both at once: a combination of interests, a combination of values or visions. Abraham Lincoln came to be a Whig, as a great many persons have come to consider themselves supporters of other parties, out of convictions about social ideas—"moral," we may say, in a large sense. Although those social-moral ideas may be affected by one's social location, and one's economic and occupational and regional interests—among others—still, that does not ordinarily altogether vitiate, though it may qualify and complicate, the moral vision.

But now let me stop short of the most thoroughgoing defense of Lincoln on the war. There are those who go too far in the opposite direction from Douglas-Beveridge-Riddle. "[I]n the 1840s," it is said, "[Lincoln] was as thoroughly principled in his opposition to the Mexican War as he was in the 1860s in opposition to slavery." Or again it is said that Lincoln's position on the Mexican War was the first time that "economics took a back seat" and he took "an exclusively moral stance," and again that "it should be clear that Lincoln's opposition to the Mexican War had as firm an ethical foundation as did his antislavery beliefs." I think those interpretations overdo it. One should not put Congressman Lincoln's speeches on Polk and the war on the same plane with Republican leader Lincoln's speeches and actions on slavery, or those of President Lincoln. The mature Lincoln not only would hold a worthy position on slavery but would also draw back and think deeply and examine the implications prudentially and present his arguments with care and rhetorical power in their political context. He would be a leader in shaping a new party and keeping it focused on the moral core in its prudential application. Those may sound like different points from the question of whether the two were equally "moral" or "principled." But public leadership on such great questions is not just a yes/no quiz. Congressman Lincoln did not think deeply and express all the considerations respectfully and carefully on the Mexican War. He rushed in, and overdid the attack on Polk personally.

3. LETTERS HOME

When Lincoln spoke, the war was effectively over, and the events he criticized were twenty months into the past. The issue now was the peace and the indemnity, which indeed would be resolved not long after he spoke. He would keep on expressing—working out—his view throughout that spring in letters home, even after the peace treaty was signed and public attention was moving on to other matters.

He was better in those letters defending his speeches than in the speeches themselves—in letters he wrote to Herndon, and in a letter to a Baptist minister who was a constituent.

In the first letter, on February 1, Lincoln was responding to Herndon's fear that his vote for the Ashmun amendment would mean that they would disagree about the war. Lincoln first insisted that had Herndon been in Lincoln's place, he would have voted as Lincoln did, and second, that he could not have "skulked" (avoided) the issue: resolutions introduced "before I made any move . . . make the direct question of the justice of war, so that no man can be silent if he would . . ." And on that unskulkable question of the justice of the war, Lincoln explained again that he and many other Whigs made the key distinction between voting for supplies to the fighting armies, which they did, and voting support for Polk's justification of war, which they did not do.

To Herndon's claim that Whigs fighting in the war must thereby support its justice, and that to denounce the war must be to denounce the brave men fighting in it, Lincoln listed individual Whigs, including Edward Baker, who had fought in the war but agreed with the Ashmun amendment.

At the end of that first letter Lincoln wrote that when Herndon would see the pamphlet of his January speech, he might be "scared anew." But "after you get over your scare," Lincoln said, "read it over again. . . ."

Herndon presumably did read it, and whether or not he got over his scare, he then wrote again, apparently arguing that it was the constitutional prerogative of a president to begin wars by a kind of preemptive invasion when in the president's sole judgment it was necessary. Lincoln responded on February 15 that even the Polk people had not gone quite as far as that: "Their only positions are first, that the soil was ours where hostilities commenced, and second, that whether it was rightfully ours or not, Congress had annexed it, and the President, for that reason was bound to defend it, both of which are as clearly proved to be false in fact, as you can prove that your house is not mine."

The treaty of peace was signed in Mexico on February 2, and was received in the Senate on February 22, after which the public debate about the war more or less evaporated. The Senate ratified the treaty on March 10, and it was then promulgated in ceremonies on July 4. Although the treaty ceded to the United States an immense region, including what are now California, Nevada, Utah, New Mexico (mostly), Arizona (mostly), and parts of Colorado and Wyoming, the insatiable appetite of Polk and other expansionists had grown in the months since the president had given his negotiator in Mexico City, Nicholas Trist, his instructions. Some now entertained, as noted above, the taking of all of Mexico and Central America, down to the Isthmus of Panama. Polk had fired Trist, but the message did not get to Mexico City in time for the envoy to know he was fired, so that Trist completed his negotiation and brought the treaty he had negotiated home, and the expansionists had to be satisfied with a mere 619,000 square miles.

Although the war was now over, there was further mention of it in connection with the coming presidential campaign, and the candidacy on the Whig ticket of the war's first great hero, Zachary Taylor. So, on June 22, Lincoln was writing Herndon again about the war, in the course of a letter about the coming presidential campaign. Lincoln was exasperated ("now this makes me a little impatient") by Herndon's request for war speeches he had already sent him, and also by Herndon's apparent continued failure to understand the Whig (and his) position on the war. So, a little testily, he explained it again: "You ask how Congress came to declare that war existed by the act of Mexico. Is it possible you don't understand that yet? You have at least twenty speeches in your possession that fully explain it. I will, however, try it once more." Grinding his teeth, as we may say figuratively, he explained it yet once more, and finished by asking: "Is there any difficulty in understanding this?"

.   .   .

Meanwhile Lincoln had had occasion to express his views in another private letter. A paper including an oration celebrating the battle of Buena Vista, given by a prominent Baptist minister in his district named John M. Peck, had been sent to him, he assumed by the Reverend Mr. Peck himself. In that oration Lincoln read what he would call "a laboured justification of the administration on the origin of the Mexican War," which, Lincoln wrote to Mr. Peck, "disappoints me." It concluded that "in view of all the facts . . . the government of the United States committed no aggression in Mexico." Lincoln wrote a response to Mr. Peck respectfully disagreeing— Lincoln was much more respectful of Peck than he had been of Polk. If you deny these facts, said Lincoln, "I think I can furnish proof." If you admit them, then what law "human or divine" would hold that there was "no aggression"? Reverse roles, Mr. Peck. If some nation committed such acts "against the humblest of our people," would you then hold that they are too small for notice? Lincoln then asks of the Reverend Mr. Peck: Is the Golden Rule obsolete?

Lincoln had occasion to return to the subject yet another time, a month later, on July 17, in the speech on the House floor promoting General Taylor's candidacy for president. The treaty ending the war had, as noted above, been ratified back in March, so the issues of the war were no longer alive. They returned in retrospect, though, in the argument about Taylor's candidacy as a Whig: "[A]s you democrats say we Whigs have always opposed the war, you think it must be very awkward and embarrassing for us to go for General Taylor." But it is not, Lincoln explains, and in the course of his explanation wrote his clearest short sentence condemning "marching an army into the midst of a peaceful Mexican settlement."

There are only hints of Lincoln's appraisal of American expansionism, but there *are* hints. In September of 1848, after the war was over and he was campaigning in (significantly) Massachusetts on behalf of the Whig ticket, he gave a speech in Worcester that was reported thoroughly in the *Boston Advertiser*. In that speech there was one brief passage affirming those who, for moral reasons, "did not believe in enlarging our field, but in keeping our fences where they are." He was silent—he made no sweeping statements about America's God-given destiny to take over this, that, and the other territory.

In 1860, then, when he would be a candidate for the Republican nomination for president, the autobiographical pages he wrote for Scripps and the others would give a succinct, clearly stated summary of points he had made in that earlier time.

I believe it would be possible to construct the elements of a Lincoln speech on the Mexican War from materials he wrote later that would be better than the speech, or speeches, that he *did* give—not a speech, but some notes toward a speech.

4. SPEECH NOTES

Notes toward the speech that Lincoln might have given on the American Role in the Commencement of the War with Mexico:

It is a fact, that the United States Army, in marching to the Rio Grande, marched into a peaceful Mexican settlement, and frightened the inhabitants away from their homes and their growing crops. . . .

It is a fact, that Fort Brown, opposite Matamoras, was built by that army, within a Mexican cotton-field, on which, at the time the army reached it, a young cotton crop was growing and which crop was wholly destroyed, and the field itself greatly, and permanently injured, by ditches, embankments, and the like. . . .

It is a fact, that when the Mexicans captured Capt. Thornton and his command [the Americans whose blood was spilled], they found and captured them within another Mexican field.

(Letter to the Reverend John M. Peck, May 24, 1848)

The President had sent Genl Taylor into an inhabited part of the country belonging to Mexico, and not to the US and thereby had provoked the first act of hostility—in fact the commencement of the war . . .

(Autobiographical sketch, June 1860)

That soil was not ours, and Congress did not annex or attempt to annex it.

(Letter to WHH, February 15, 1848)

[T]he country bordering on the East bank of the Rio Grande, was inhabited by native Mexicans, born there under the Mexican government; and had never submitted to, nor been conquered by Texas, or the US nor transferred to either by treaty . . . although Texas claimed the Rio Grande as her boundary, Mexico had never recognized it, the people on the ground had never recognized it, and neither Texas nor the US had ever enforced it . . . [T]here was a broad desert between that, and the country over which Texas had actual control . . . [T]he country where hostilities commenced, having once belonged to Mexico, must remain so, until it was somehow legally transferred, which had never been done.

(Autobiographical sketch, June 1860)

[The most the president could truthfully say] would be about as follows: "I say, the soil was ours, on which the first blood was shed; there are those who say it was not."

(Speech on the House floor, January 12, 1848)

The marching of an army into the midst of a peaceful Mexican settlement, frightening the inhabitants away, leaving their growing crops, and other property to destruction, to you may appear a perfectly amiable, peaceful, unprovoking procedure; but it does not appear so to us.

(Speech on the House floor, July 27, 1848)

[O]ur "citizens," whose blood was shed [were] at that time, armed officers and soldiers, sent into that settlement, by the military order of the President through the Secretary of War. . . .

[T]he military force of the United States, including those "citizens" [was] sent into that settlement, after General Taylor had, more than once, intimated to the War Department that, in his opinion, no such movement was necessary to the defense or protection of Texas.

(Spot Resolutions in the House, December 22, 1847)

[T]he act of sending an armed force among the Mexicans was *unnecessary* inasmuch as Mexico was in no way molesting, or menacing the US or the people thereof, and . . . it was *unconstitutional,* because the power of levying war is vested in Congress, and not in the President.

(Autobiographical sketch, June 1860)

Allow the President to invade a neighboring nation, whenever he shall deem it necessary to repel an invasion, and you allow him to do so, whenever he may choose to say he deems it necessary for such purpose—and you allow him to make war at pleasure. . . .

Kings had always been involving and impoverishing their people in wars. . . .

This, our Convention understood to be the most oppressive of all Kingly oppressions; and they resolved to so frame the Constitution that no one man should hold the power to bringing this oppression upon us.

(Letter to WHH, February 15, 1848)

You say "Paredes [Mariano Paredes y Arrillaga, a hard-line Mexican leader] came into power the last of December 1845, and from that moment, all hopes of avoiding war by negotiation vanished." A little further on . . . you say, "All this transpired three months before Gen Taylor marched across the desert of the Nueces." [Y]ou evidently intend to have it inferred that Gen Taylor was sent across the desert, in consequence of the destruction all hope of peace, in the overthrow of Herara [José Joaquín Herrera, a more moderate Mexican leader] by Paredes . . . the material fact you have excluded is that Gen Taylor was ordered to cross the desert . . . before the news of Herara's fall reached Washington—before the administration, which gave the order, had any knowledge that Herara had fallen.

(Letter to the Reverend John M. Peck, May 24, 1848)

The news reached Washington of the commencement of hostilities on the Rio Grande, and of the great peril of Gen. Taylor's army. Every body, whig and democrat, was for sending them aid, in men and money. It was necessary to pass a bill for this. . . .

The [Democrats] had a majority in both Houses, and they brought in a bill with a preamble, saying—Whereas war exists by the act of Mexico, therefore we send Gen. Taylor men and money. The whigs moved to strike out the preamble, so that they could vote to send the men and money, without saying any thing about how the war commenced; but, being in the minority they were voted down, and the preamble was retained. . . .

Then, on the passage of the bill, the question came upon them, "shall we vote for preamble and bill both together, or against both together." They could not vote against sending help to Gen. Taylor, and therefore they voted for both together.

(Letter to WHH, June 22, 1848)

I have always intended, and still intend, to vote supplies. . . . The [Democrats] are untiring in their effort to make the impression that all who vote supplies, or take part in the war, do, of necessity, approve the Presidents conduct in the beginning of it; but the whigs have, from the beginning, made and kept the distinction between the two. In the very first act, nearly all the whigs voted against the preamble declaring that war existed by the act of Mexico, and yet nearly all of them voted for the supplies. . . .

That vote [for Ashmun's resolution] affirms that the war was unconstitutionally and unnecessarily commenced by the President; and I will stake my life, that if you had been in my place you would have voted just as I did. Would you have voted what you felt you knew to be a lie? . . . Would you have gone out of the House—skulked the vote? . . . Richardson's resolutions [upholding Polk on the war] introduced before I made any move . . . make the direct question of the justice of war, so that no man can be silent if he would.

(Letter to WHH, February 1, 1848)

If to say "the war was unnecessarily and unconstitutionally commenced by the President" be opposing the war, then the whigs have very generally opposed it. Whenever they have spoken at all, they have said this; and they have said it on what has appeared good reason to them. . . .

But if, when the war had begun, and had become the cause of the country, the giving of our money and our blood, in common with yours, was support of the war, then it is not true that we have always opposed the war. With few individual exceptions, you have constantly had our votes here for all the necessary supplies. And, more than this, you have had the services, the blood, and the lives of our political brethren in every trial, and on every field.

(Speech on the House floor, July 27, 1848)

As to the whig men who have participated in the war, so far as they have spoken in my hearing, they do not hesitate to denounce, as unjust, the Presidents conduct in the beginning of the war. . . .

(Letter to WHH, February 1, 1848)

[T]he distinction between the cause of the President in beginning the war, and the cause of the country after it was begun, is a distinction which you [Democrats] can not perceive. To you the President, and the country, seems to be all one. You are interested to see no distinction between them; and I venture to suggest that possibly your interest blinds you a little. We see the distinction, as we think, clearly enough;

and our friends who have fought in the war have no difficulty in seeing it also.

(Speech on the House floor, July 27, 1848)

At one time, [the president's message claimed] the national honor, the security of the future, the prevention of foreign interference, and even, the good of Mexico herself, as among the objects of the war; at another [it tells us] that "to reject indemnity, by refusing to accept a cession of territory, would be to abandon all our just demands, and to wage the war, bearing all its expenses, without a purpose or definite object." So then, the national honor, security of the future, and everything but territorial indemnity, may be considered the no-purposes, and indefinite objects, of the war! . . .

But, having it now settled that the territorial indemnity is the only object, we are urged to seize, by legislation here, all that he was content to take, a few months ago, and the whole province of lower California to boot, and to still carry on the war—to take all we are fighting for, and still fight on.

(Speech on the House floor, July 12, 1848)

[A]ll real Whigs, friends of good honest government . . . wished to keep up the character of this Union . . . did not believe in enlarging our field, but in keeping our fences where they are and cultivating our present possession, making it a garden, improving the morals and education of the people; devoting the administration to this purpose.

(Speech in Worcester, Massachusetts, September 12, 1848)

I still think the defensive line policy the best to terminate it. In a final treaty of peace, we shall probably be under a sort of necessity of taking some territory, but it is my desire that shall not acquire any extending so far South, as to enlarge and aggravate the distracting question of slavery.

(Fragment: "What General Taylor Ought to Say," March 1848)

If you admit that they are facts [the United States army marching by presidential order into a peaceful Mexican settlement] then I shall be obliged for a reference to any law of language, law of states, law of nations, law of morals, law of religion—any law human or divine, in which an authority can be found for saying those facts constitute "no aggression." . . .

Possibly you consider those acts too small for notice. Would you venture to so consider them, had they been committed by any nation on earth, against the humblest of our people? I know you would not. Then I ask, is the precept "Whatsoever ye would that men should do to you, do ye even so to them" obsolete?—of no force?—of no application?

(Letter to the Reverend John M. Peck, May 24, 1848)

Fourteen years later, when he sat where Polk had once sat, and interpreted his own war, Lincoln would depict the moral role of the nation he led differently than President Polk had done. He would not stoke the fires of national self-righteousness. His interpretation of America's role in the world, in the vastly different context of civil war, would stand as something of a corrective to blatant national egotism and self-deception. President Lincoln would not insist, as President Polk had insisted, that the other side in his war was altogether and absolutely to blame for the war's beginning and for its continuance—even though some might say President Lincoln would have had far more justification for doing so than had President Polk. Lincoln would not reiterate the South's guilt; he would recommend amnesty toward the Confederate leaders and generosity to the Southern people; he would say that neither side wanted war, and would describe its beginning impersonally: "And the war came."

President Lincoln, with the strongest of motives to do so, would not claim that God has marked out a superior role for the United States, or for his side in the war. In the Second Inaugural he would say that "the Almighty has His purposes," meaning exactly that those purposes were larger than those of either side, including his own.*

---

* For further discussion of the issues raised in this chapter, the reader should consult Appendix One, "Reflections on Two War Presidents."

CHAPTER EIGHT

Politics and Morals

1. THE CONGRESSMAN AS MORALIST (AND POLITICAL OPERATIVE)

Even the younger Abraham Lincoln seems to have been more reflective about moral ideas than most politicians, or practical persons of any kind. Is it just Lincoln's posthumous reputation, and the preoccupation of this book, that makes it seem so? Even in the comparatively dry period of his stint as congressman there are more passages of moral reasoning than one might expect. To be sure, they were altogether interwoven into his political objectives; does that make them merely window dressing? I don't think so. He was developing, on the run, an ethic of responsibility, of prudence, of realism, like that of many serious politicians—but more explicit and, eventually, profound (and beginning in 1854 it will be reshaped by an overriding moral purpose, and in the winter of 1860–61 it will be given its no-compromise boundaries).

Back on October 3, 1845, before he managed to become a congressman, he had occasion in answering a letter from an abolitionist in Ohio named Williamson Durley to discuss whether one could ever do "evil" in order to do good.

The background was this. In the 1830s, while Lincoln was a young state legislator, as we have noted, there arose a new and more insistent abolitionist movement. Toward the end of the thirties the movement split, with one part getting involved in politics and the other maintaining "purity." Although both major parties, the Whigs and the Democrats, tried to avoid the subject of slavery and abominated the abolitionists, the Whigs had a very small—growing—minority of leaders who were explicitly anti-slavery; one of them was Joshua Giddings of Ohio, Lincoln's messmate at Mrs. Sprigg's on Capitol Hill. The Whigs were on the whole, in their dominant northern branch, slightly less anti-antislavery than the southern-dominated Democrats. All of the handful of about a dozen congressmen (in Congresses of well over two hundred members) who were consistent opponents of slavery in the 1830s and early 1840s were Whigs.

But such close distinctions were not significant for the abolitionists. Engaged in a great moral undertaking, they were not interested in making subtle discriminate judgments. They had formed their own abolition party, called the Liberty Party, and had run their candidate, James G. Birney, for president in the election of 1840, the year of "Tippecanoe and Tyler Too," in which the Whig, William Henry Harrison, defeated the incumbent Democrat, Martin Van Buren. Birney on the Liberty Party ticket in that year did not hurt anybody; he received all of 7,069 votes nationwide.

But the presidential election of 1844 would be a different story. This was the election in which Texas and expansionism dominated all, and Polk knocked aside Van Buren in the Democratic primary and then—this really hurt from Lincoln's point of view—narrowly defeated Henry Clay himself in the general election. These major-party candidates in 1844 were both slaveholders, but Clay opposed slavery (in the qualified way of the colonizers' movement, but that was significantly more than Polk did), and Clay was less of an expansionist, and less eager to annex Texas, than was Polk—points that were important to abolitionists. But the Liberty Party nevertheless put Birney forward as a candidate again, and this time he received a nationwide vote of 62,263. The popular majority of Polk over Clay nationwide was only 38,792. To be sure, we do not elect presidents by popular vote, but by the electoral college; and to be sure, small numbers here and there that would change the result can be discovered every time an election is close. Nevertheless, it was the quite plausible belief among Whigs that the Liberty Party took enough votes from Clay to give New York State's big bloc of electoral votes to Polk, and that large bloc of votes made Polk, instead of Clay, president. Polk defeated Clay in New York State 237,588 votes to 232,482—a margin of just over five thousand votes. Birney received 15,812 votes in New York.

And so, eleven months after that fateful election, Clay's strong supporter the Illinois Whig Abraham Lincoln is answering a letter from Williamson Durley in Ohio:

Friend Durley:

Until I saw you, I was not aware of your being what is generally
called an abolitionist, or, as you call yourself, a Liberty-man; though I
well knew there were many such in your county. I was glad to hear you
say that you intend to attempt to bring about, at the next election . . . a
union of Whigs proper, and such of the liberty men as are Whigs in
principle on all questions save only that of slavery.

Having commended Durley for his responsible politics in this future case,
Lincoln then went on to chastise him and his ilk for their conduct in the
past case, the presidential election of 1844:

If the Whig abolitionists of New York had voted with us last fall,
Mr. Clay would now be president, Whig principles in the ascendant,
and Texas not annexed; whereas by the division [the splitting off of
Whig-inclined Liberty Party voters in New York], all that either had at
stake in the contest, was lost. And, indeed, it was extremely probable,
beforehand, that such would be the result.

Although in many cases it is difficult to know what the effects of one's
actions may be, in this case, with only a little practical wisdom one could
have known the probable results of the election, and what those results
would mean for policy.

Mr. Lincoln, the lay moralist, proceeded to give this argument against
the Liberty Party's individualistic perfectionism:

As I always understood, the Liberty-men deprecated the annexation of
Texas extremely and, this being so, why they should refuse to cast
their votes as to prevent it, even to me, seemed wonderful ["wonderful" here meaning strange, odd, weird, provoking wonder].

The great issue in the election was the annexation of Texas, which abolitionists strongly opposed, because Texas would be a new slave state—
possibly even, because of its size, more than one, perhaps as many as five
new slave states, overturning the power balance in the Senate and throughout the American government. Moreover, as we have said, because Mexico
had formally abolished slavery throughout its realm, including Texas, in
1829, annexing Texas to the United States would move it backwards from
freedom to slavery. If you brought yourself to be just minimally informed
about the candidates and parties, you would have known what the results

with respect to Texas would probably be of electing one or the other candidate and party. So, that the "Liberty-men" voted as they did seemed "wonderful" to Lincoln.

> What was their process of reasoning, I can only judge from what a single one of them told me. It was this: "We are not to do evil that good may come."

What the Liberty-man meant by "evil" in this case was to cast one's vote for a slaveholder, Clay. That outlook, and that particular phrase—"We are not to do 'evil' that good may come"—was, and still is, quite common in the oversimplified moral outlook that the Abraham Lincolns of this world reject.

There would come in the next century a widely read essay—an address, originally—by the great German social thinker Max Weber, which would be translated under the title "Politics as a Vocation." Toward the end, after discussing other topics, Weber would take up "ethics and politics," and would provide a term to describe the ethic by which Abraham Lincoln would in the main conduct himself, an "ethic of responsibility." A politician who followed Weber's ethic of responsibility would reject the alternative perfectionist ethic which says that "from good comes only good; but from evil only evil follows"; the responsible politician says, to the contrary, that often the reverse is true. Indeed, "anyone who fails to see this [that good alone does not always follow from good, or evil alone from 'evil'] is . . . a political infant." Those advocates of an abstractly "pure" ethic, like the Liberty men Lincoln was arguing against, and like a pacifist/syndicalist colleague Weber was disputing, hold that one must do what seems intrinsically and absolutely "Right," and "leave the results to God." A responsible politician, by contrast, must himself attend to "the foreseeable results of his action." Durley, you could have seen, if you had just looked, what the results of voting for Birney instead of Clay would be.

Lincoln himself was far from being a political infant, and his life would be such that he might in some later instances, in the midst of the appalling choices of a tremendous civil war, have to argue in the way Weber would do—that is, to defend some fearfully harmful action ("evil," if you will) as necessary to serve some larger good: to shorten the war; to save the Union. But in the present case he did not respond as Weber would do; he did not write that it is part of the tragedy inextricably interwoven into all high politics that one must sometimes do (or allow) "evil" at one level to achieve a good, or prevent a greater evil, at another. He was not going to regard voting for Henry Clay as an "evil." For the purpose of this exchange he accepted Durley's general proposition, but denied its application in the present case: this wasn't, or wouldn't have been, an "evil," to give one's support to Clay and the Whigs.

How does one judge it not to be an "evil"? By the "fruits"—the results, the "consequences."

> This general proposition is doubtless correct; but did it apply? If by your votes you could have prevented the extension, &c. of slavery, would it not have been good and not evil so to have used your votes, even though it involved casting of them for a slaveholder? By the fruit the tree is to be known. An evil tree can not bring forth good fruit. If the fruit of electing Mr. Clay would have been to prevent the extension of slavery, could the act of electing him have been evil?

In other words, Clay's personal situation, that he was a slaveholder, was not the pivot upon which this moral decision should turn; that pivot was, rather, the effect upon government policy, the outcome in American history: What good in the world will be brought about (or impeded) by your act?

After an intervening paragraph, in which he explains why he was not as much opposed to the annexation of Texas as the Liberty people were—the part of this letter that is most often quoted rather than the part I am quoting—Lincoln concluded:

> I understand the Liberty men to have viewed annexation as a much greater evil than I ever did; and I would like to convince you if I could, that they could have prevented it, without violation of principle, if they had chosen.

I read that to say: there are principles that determine action decisively, but absent those, the moral case should be determined by the consequences, the results, the fruits.

Lincoln was here arguing against one familiar attitude prevalent perhaps especially in American culture—more, indeed, than in Weber's Germany—as it encounters the complexities of politics. It appears even at the comparatively simple level of casting ballots for candidates who are not as pure in some regards as one would like them to be. Lincoln says: Look at the fruits. Look at what can be expected to happen in the real world as a result of one and another election outcome. Do not decide on the basis of a single objectionable feature of the personal situation of the individual you are considering voting for. That is insufficiently attentive to the relevant consequence, and it also may be suspected of having in it (as in much American experience in moralizing politics, or moralizing avoidance of politics, it has had) a certain self-indulgent convenience. No need to know facts, analyze complexities, estimate probabilities. (What are the Whigs like, on the whole? The Democrats? The proportions? The supporters of each, with respect to Texas, war with Mexico, slavery? How does the electoral college work, and what are the possible balances?) Instead, one feature of the rejected candidate is taken to determine it all: He is a slaveholder. The followers of an ethics of responsibility say that doing what is good and right in politics entails use of observation and intellect; the followers of an ethics of abstract purity tend to say it doesn't. Slavery is bad; Clay is a slaveholder; voting for Clay would therefore be evil. Easy.

The outlook Lincoln criticizes may be self-indulgent in another way: in reflecting an inappropriate attention to one's own "purity" or rectitude rather than to effects in the world. I have kept myself pure by never voting for a slaveholder . . . and never mind the outcome of the election, or the effect upon the nation. That is someone else's problem, or God's problem. But Polk, another slaveholder, and a slaveholder who had never expressed his disapproval of slavery as Clay had done, was elected president. New York was lost by Clay to Polk; Polk, another and "worse" slaveholder, was thereby elected; Texas was annexed; there was war with Mexico; the cause of slavery was advanced. With even the smallest dose of discriminate judgment Durley and his fellow Liberty men would have voted for Henry Clay and made a large historical difference—a better outcome, by the Liberty men's own moral criteria.

Lincoln himself came to Congress in 1847, as we have seen, at the end of Mr. Polk's war, and had his vociferous say on that war. But that was not quite his only topic in Congress. Among the few others was the old Whig standby, rivers and harbors.

Polk had vetoed one internal-improvements bill while Lincoln was congressman-elect, and the first national meeting that Lincoln, then thirty-seven years old, ever attended was one held in the burgeoning metropolis of Chicago (population sixteen thousand) to protest Polk's action. Now, with Lincoln in Congress in June of 1848, Polk vetoed another one, and the new Illinois congressman took the floor in the committee of the whole to respond to Polk's arguments—rejecting, as a Whig, Polk's claim, as a Democrat, that the Constitution did not allow such projects. Lincoln said that Polk's argument that such projects unequally favored some places at the expense of others applied also to state-funded improvement and therefore would result in nothing. The sum of Polk's message is, said Lincoln: "Do nothing at all, lest you do something wrong." One is reminded of the satirical description of a certain kind of conservative whose guiding principle is: *Nothing* should be done for the first time.

As Lincoln argued for a more active general government, so he argued also the interdependence of the national community. Polk's message held, said Lincoln,

> that the burdens of improvements would be general, while their benefits would be local and partial, involving an obnoxious inequality. That there is some degree of truth in this position, I shall not deny. No commercial object of government patronage can be so exclusively general, as to not be of some peculiar local advantage; but, on the other hand, nothing is so local, as to not be of some general advantage.

The navy, although of general advantage, is more of an advantage to seaports than to inland places, and the development of the Mississippi to the thirteen states on her borders than to the seventeen others: "[T]here is something of local advantage in the most general objects."

But—says Lincoln—"the converse is also true. Nothing is so local as not to be of some general benefit": for example, the Illinois-Michigan canal. Lincoln's conclusion:

> [I]f this argument of "inequality" is sufficient any where—it is sufficient every where; and puts an end to improvements altogether. I hope and believe, that if both the nation and the state would, in good faith . . . do what they could in the way of improvements, what of inequality might be produced in one place, might be compensated in another, and that the sum of the whole might not be very unequal.

Some "inequality" may remain nevertheless. Lincoln the reflective young congressman then formulated a generalization:

> The true rule, in determining to embrace, or reject any thing, is not whether it have any evil in it; but whether it have more of evil, than of

good. There are few things wholly evil, or wholly good. Almost every thing, especially of governmental policy, is an inseparable compound of the two; so that our best judgment of the preponderance between them is continually demanded.

We can, and we must, continually make such judgments on the preponderance of good over "evil," which in the real world come mixed in varying proportions. There is a moralizing impulse that wants to present the world as constantly and clearly divided between a Right and a Wrong: plain, clear, sharply divided. But many reflective moralists, and most serious politicians, including Abraham Lincoln, perceive rather that good and evil come mixed and that the moral life most of the time (not quite all of the time) consists of making discriminate judgments, judgments at the margins, discernments of less and more—or as Abraham Lincoln put it, "our best judgment of the preponderance between them."

Congressman Lincoln in 1848 did not, however, spend most of his energy on ad hoc moral philosophizing, or on arguments about legislation, either; what he mostly did was to promote a presidential candidacy. He had come to Congress just as yet another presidential election year—1848—was starting, and although he had written Durley that he should have supported Clay in 1844, in 1848 Lincoln himself did not support Clay. On the contrary, he worked hard for the candidate who defeated Clay in the contest for the Whig nomination for president, the emptiest of empty candidates, the Mexican War general who had never voted and did not know where he stood on any public issue: Zachary Taylor.

There is no doubt which of the two men who came to be the leading candidates for the Whig nomination in 1848 Lincoln in his heart, and in the abstract, preferred. There was no comparison. As it would happen, Lincoln would be called upon to give eulogies for both men, for President Taylor when he died in office in 1850 and for Henry Clay in 1852. The contrast between the two eulogies would be stark. Henry Clay had been his favorite politician above all others, a man who stood for everything Lincoln stood for—internal improvements, the bank, the tariff, a commerce-enhancing, West-developing "American system," and a certain kind of cautious sections-sensitive opposition to slavery. But there was more to it than just Clay's positions on issues, his "American System." Clay was also a marvelous orator and a great political leader, "charismatic," as we have learned to say, one of those Harrys of the West around whom a certain romance had been woven. Zachary Taylor was not a political leader at all, not a speaker at all, not a legislator at all, and stood for nothing. He was just, as the term then was, "available."

Why did Lincoln support him—work hard for him? The reader of course knows the answer: Taylor could win; Clay could not. Or so Lincoln and many others believed. Lincoln wrote, with striking candor, about his candidate: "Our only chance is Taylor. I go for him, not because I think he would make a better president than Clay, but because I think he would make a better one than Polk, or Cass, or Buchanan [all Democrats] or any other such creatures, one of whom is sure to be elected if he is not." In another of his many candid political letters of the time he said it still more bluntly: "Mr. Clay's chance for an election, is just no chance at all . . . We can elect nobody but General Taylor."

Congressman Lincoln made a realistic judgment about which candidate could lead the party to victory. Presidential candidacies are not, he and his defenders might say, awards for long years of service, or choices of the abstractly best person, not even of the abstractly best president. They are embattled choices in a concrete political situation. For the realistic-responsible-prudential politician, as for William James's pragmatist, every difference makes a difference, and 1848 was different from 1844.

What happened between those two elections? The Mexican War. The Whigs were not in a good position with respect to the war. Henry Clay was not in a good position with respect to the war. Lincoln himself was not in a good position with respect to the war. But there now was a chief hero of that war, General Zachary Taylor—a possible president? After victories in Mexico Taylor had had differences with President Polk over the conduct of the war, had asked to be relieved of his command, and returned home to Louisiana. So he was at odds with the Democrat in the White House. A possible Whig president? Congressman Lincoln, an energetic Taylor supporter (even though Clay had entered the race), fairly chortled at the political sagacity of his party, being accused of being opposed to the war, nominating as its standard bearer a hero of that war. "Taylor's nomination takes the locos"—Whig epithet for Democrats—"on the blind side," Lincoln wrote to Billy Herndon on June 12, 1848: "It turns the war thunder against them."

Congressman Lincoln became a member of a group of seven Whig congressmen, most of them freshmen, who were called the "Young Indians" and who committed themselves together, early, to work for the nomination of General Taylor. One of the Young Indians was a congressman from

Georgia whom Lincoln came to like and admire, Alexander Stephens, whom we shall meet again.

One of the reasons to choose Taylor over Clay was that Clay had lost favor with the big Whig plantation owners, slaveholders, in the South. These slaveholding Southern Whigs felt that the great section-transcending, balancing-everybody compromiser Henry Clay had by now leaned too far to the Northern antislavery side. It did not help that Clay's most visible backer was Horace Greeley and his *New York Tribune.* And Zachary Taylor was a Louisiana plantation owner with two hundred slaves. Lincoln was one of only two Northern congressmen in the seven "Young Indians"; the other five, including Stephens, were Southerners. So Clay, this time, in contrast to his past career, could not draw upon Southern support to get the nomination. Although William Seward and Thurlow Weed of New York were key backers of Taylor, nevertheless Taylor's victory in the convention was regarded, by others and by themselves, as a victory for Southern Whigs.

Congressman Lincoln went from Washington to the Whig convention in Philadelphia in early June of 1848 to work for Taylor's nomination, and at the convention apparently had fierce arguments with supporters of Clay. He had, indeed, already worked to prevent the sending of Clay delegates from Illinois and to encourage the sending of Taylor supporters.

Taylor led already on the first ballot at the Whig convention in Philadelphia, 111 votes to Clay's 97, with General Winfield Scott and Daniel Webster trailing; Taylor won on the fourth ballot. Clay was bitter, and his followers, including some in Illinois, angry. The realist supporters of the he-can-win victor in these nomination battles always argue (and Lincoln, in effect, argued in 1848) that the supporters of the defeated candidate will, perhaps after a period of licking wounds and maybe bitterness, come around and join in supporting the party's nominee: they have, say the realists (and Lincoln said in effect in 1848), nowhere to go. And usually that proves to be true. But not always. The defeated can go fishing, stay home, sulk. Henry Clay never did give any speeches for Taylor until, very reluctantly, at the very end of the campaign, he spoke in support of the ticket generally.

It was uphill work for Lincoln and the others to defend that illiterate frontier colonel whose entire fame rested upon his role in the Mexican War. Abraham Lincoln had occasion to stump for Taylor, starting in the halls of Congress itself. In July, after both nominees had been chosen, Congress pretty much gave up legislating and turned to political speeches. On July 27 the Illinois Whig held forth, striding up and down the aisles, getting many laughs with his attack on the Democratic nominee, the governor of Michigan Territory, Lewis Cass.

Lincoln held that neither Clay nor any other possible nominee could be elected—except Taylor. So Taylor meant a Whig victory; that proved to be accurate. But what did a Whig victory mean? If the Whigs were also able to carry Congress, it meant that a Whig Congress could pass Whig measures.

But the old Whig issues of the tariff, the bank, internal improvements, and public lands were losing altitude. To some extent the Polk administration had undone them. More important, in 1849 an economic boom commenced, accompanied by the California gold rush and the building of railroads, that lasted into the 1850s and made abundant private capital available to do what Whigs had proposed for the federal government to do. Other issues now arose. This was the period of the greatest prominence of both the temperance movement and of the anti-Catholic, anti-foreigner nativist movement. And most prominent of all now, in the aftermath of the Mexican War, was the issue of slavery in the territories.

The primary vehicle for its emergence now was the Wilmot Proviso— the provision, first introduced in the House by Pennsylvania Democrat David Wilmot, that slavery be excluded from whatever territory was acquired as a result of the Mexican War. Lincoln later claimed hyperbolically to have voted forty times for the Wilmot Proviso. In his congressional speech for Taylor and against Cass he had cited quotations purporting to show Lewis Cass's changes of position on the issue—and milked the changes for humorous effects. The upshot, however, was that Cass and the Democratic platform and party in 1848 were against the proviso, and in favor of a policy of nonintervention or popular sovereignty that left open the possibility that slavery might be permitted in the new territory.

And so where in 1848 did Lincoln's candidate stand? Said Lincoln on the House floor:

> I admit I do not certainly know what he [Taylor] would do on the Wilmot Proviso. I am a Northern man, or rather, a Western free state man, with a constituency I believe to be, and with personal feelings I know to be, against the extension of slavery. As such, and with what information I have, I hope and believe, Gen. Taylor, if elected, would not veto the Proviso. But I do not know it.

He admits that Taylor might veto the proviso. But Lincoln would still urge a vote for him, in a raw judgment of the lesser of two evils:

Yet, if I knew he would, I still would vote for him. I should do so, because, in my judgment, his election alone, can defeat Gen. Cass; and because, should slavery thereby go to the territory we now have, just so much will certainly happen by the election of Cass; and, in addition, a course of policy, leading to new wars, new acquisitions of territory and still further extensions of slavery. One of the two is to be President; which is preferable?

Once more this responsible realist is insisting that the actual alternatives be faced, and the probable consequences of each alternative be measured, and a decision made on a realistic basis: which (of the two results, one of which will certainly come) is preferable?

But not every conscientious politician, on every occasion, makes his or her decision on that basis. When Abraham Lincoln, a minor player, and his more important colleagues managed to get General Zachary Taylor nominated for president by the Whigs on June 9, 1848, in Philadelphia, a couple of the members of the delegation from Massachusetts declined to join in the usual festivities of phony unanimity and refused to support the candidate. Why? Not only because Taylor was a slaveholder on a large scale and the candidate of Southern Whigs, but also because neither he nor the party platform had endorsed the Wilmot Proviso—the litmus test on the extension of slavery.

Massachusetts was a very different state from frontier Illinois, and for many in the former the time had come to stop making those lesser-of-evils choices offered by the major parties and defended by party spokesmen like that one Whig congressman from Illinois.

The Democrats, from whom there was not much hope on slavery questions anyway, had already in May made their nomination, Lewis Cass— "General" Cass, with the pseudo–war record that Lincoln ridiculed—who favored "popular sovereignty" and would veto the Wilmot Proviso. So: General Cass or General Taylor? Lincoln had given his answer: Taylor and the Whigs are still preferable. But some citizens in Massachusetts had come to a different view. That view would be well expressed by an emerging leader from Boston named Charles Sumner—young, articulate, full of righteousness, and very learned, sprinkling his orations with classical references. At a great mass gathering in Worcester on June 28 Sumner said:

I hear the old saw that "we must take the least of two evils". . . It is admitted, then, that Cass and Taylor are evils. For myself, if two evils are presented to me, I will take neither.

Sumner conceded that on many issues one should compromise:

There are occasions of political difference, I admit, when it may become expedient to vote for a candidate who does not completely represent our sentiments. There are matters legitimately within the range of expediency and compromise. The Tariff and the Currency are of this character. If a candidate differs from me on these more or less, I may yet vote for him.

But there are other matters—like slavery—to which that compromising and expediential approach does not apply:

But the question before the country is of another character. This will not admit of compromise. It is not within the domain of expediency. To be wrong on this is to be wholly wrong. It is not merely expedient for us to defend Freedom when assailed, but our duty so to do, unreservedly, and careless of consequences . . .

Here again is that carelessness of consequences that makes one who follows an ethic of responsibility wary.

As there were antislavery ("Conscience") Whigs like Sumner who could not abide Taylor, so there were some antislavery Democrats upset with Cass and the Democratic party's position on the issue of slavery. These Democrats, especially in New York, had a grudge against the Southern members of their own party who had maneuvered to prevent the nomination of ex-president Martin Van Buren back in 1844 and who seemed to dominate the party.

The faction that felt this most strongly—the "Barnburners"—had already withdrawn from the New York Democratic party and had had a convention of their own in Utica, nominating Martin Van Buren as their candidate for president, before the Conscience Whigs had gathered in Worcester. Sumner in Worcester praised Van Buren and the Barnburners for showing the way and indicated the "true line of duty":

The lovers of Freedom, from both parties . . . must unite, and by a new combination . . . oppose both candidates [i.e., the Whig Taylor and the

Democrat Cass]. This will be the FREEDOM POWER whose single object will be to resist the SLAVE POWER.

And that is what happened: The disaffected antislavery Whigs and disaffected antislavery Democrats would join with the old Liberty Party and form a new party, the Free-Soil Party. To the charge that this party would surely fail, Sumner had already given his answer back in his thrilling moralistic and perfectionist speech at the June convention of Conscience Whigs in Worcester:

> But it is said that we shall throw away our votes, and that our opposition will fail. Fail, sir! No honest, earnest effort in a good cause can fail. It may not be crowned with the applause of men ... But it is not lost; it helps ... to animate all with devotion to duty, which in the end conquers all.

"Duty" in the end conquers all? Sumner had thrilling examples of what he meant:

> Fail! Did the martyrs fail when with their precious blood they sowed the seeds of the church? Did the discomfited champions of Freedom fail who have left those names in history that can never die? Did the three hundred Spartans fail when in the narrow pass they did not fear to brave the innumerable Persian hosts, whose very arrows darkened the sun? Overborne by number, crushed to earth, they left an example far greater than any victory. And this is the least we can do. Our example will be the mainspring of triumph hereafter. It will not be the first time in history that the hosts of slavery have outnumbered the champions of Freedom. But where is it written that slavery finally prevailed?

Three months after Sumner's speech in Worcester, after the Free-Soil Party had been formed and after it had entered its nominee (ex-president Martin Van Buren) in the list alongside Taylor and Cass, there came to that same city, which was much agitated by continuing disputes between old-line Whigs and these new Free-Soilers, another figure of future importance, the lone-star Whig from Illinois. He took a contrasting view to that of Sumner of the political choices of the day, and of the underlying moral outlook as well.

The congressman from Illinois's Seventh District was not as interested as Sumner was in spilling precious blood for a distant future triumph, or in making a name that history can never let die, or in being crushed like the dead Spartans at Thermopylae, thereby furnishing an example greater than any victory. What this congressman sought was, exactly, victory. Not victory morally speaking, but victory politically speaking. Not victory in some distant commemoration, but victory next November. Not victory for duty, or for honest, earnest effort, but victory for the Whig Party. (The time would come, as we shall see, when Lincoln would himself take a no-compromise position, a firm chain-of-steel stand on his duty. But it will be in a different context from Sumner's.)

Years later, looking back, Sumner would say that the Worcester convention to which he had spoken was the beginning not only of the Free-Soil Party but (therefore) also the true beginning of a new party that would enter American politics six years later—the Republican Party. There were, no doubt, many future Republicans in Worcester in the summer of 1848, most of them with Sumner at the Free-Soil convention in June. But there was also this one other future Republican who came there a little later exactly to argue against them.

When Congress had adjourned on August 14, Lincoln had stayed on in Washington (alone; Mary and the boys were in Lexington) as a kind of volunteer to what today we might call the Taylor-Fillmore Committee—the Whig election committee.

And then he took a trip to New England—Mary and the boys joining him now—and ventured into the heart of Whig defections to the Free-Soilers. He went, on the day before the Whig state convention was to be held there, to Worcester—the very city in which that thrilling Free-Soil convention had been held in late June. He had been making, in his New England appearances, essentially the same anti-Cass, pro-Taylor speech he had made in the House in July. But now he added a new insert directed at Van Buren and the Free-Soilers and at arguments like those advanced by Charles Sumner in the same city a few weeks before.

Once more he would take up the claim of duty, and argue in behalf of an ethic of consequences: By casting your votes for Van Buren, who cannot win, you will help elect Cass, who is the worst candidate on the principles, and therefore you will not help but hurt the cause of Free Soil. "In declaring that they [the Free-Soilers] would 'do their duty and leave the consequences to God' [they] merely gave an excuse for taking a course that they were not able to maintain by a full and fair argument."

Here Lincoln was dealing with another version of the familiar moral-political theme that recurs, across time and across cultures, that we have encountered before in his letter to Durley. "We are not to do evil that good may come"—the phrase that he cited in arguing against Durley—is one such formulation; "Do your duty and leave the consequences to God" is another, cited now in argument with ex-Whig Free-Soilers in Massachusetts. "The Christian does rightly and leaves the results with the Lord" is the way a version of the theme appears in Max Weber's essay. A classical formulation that was often cited, usually in Latin, by learned politicians— for example, by John Quincy Adams in a dramatic moment on the House floor—was "Do Justice though the Heavens fall." A responsible politician like Lincoln might respond, half-jokingly: Do as much justice as you can— *without* having the Heavens fall. The heavens falling sounds like a rather serious consequence indeed, one that ought to be given at least a little consideration. On whom are the heavens going to fall, by the way? I hope not on my constituents, but I hope not on anyone else's, either. Are you sure this "justice" is so clear and overwhelming as all that?

All of these quotations assume the clarity and unambiguous application of the governing moral terms ("evil," "duty," "rightly," "justice") and find it categorically determinative. They altogether reject moral conclusions derived from calculation of the presumed results of one's action. They make it a point of moral pride to ignore consequences. Do not be swayed by someone's measure of the (apparent) consequences to do what is "evil" (in Durley's case) or (in this Massachusetts Free-Soil case) to do what is other than your "duty." Don't do evil that (allegedly) good (consequences) may (allegedly) come; do your duty and leave the (presumed) consequences to God.

And so how did the prairie politician, who was not all that interested in reading Billy Herndon's copy of Immanuel Kant, deal with this theme in Massachusetts politics in 1848? He said: Let us attend a little more closely to what we label "evil," in the first case, and "duty," in the second. In both cases the lone-star Whig moralist from Illinois took up into the definition of these morally weighted words a rational consideration of alternative consequences. "Evil"? Casting one's vote for a candidate who is, among many other more immediately relevant characteristics, a slaveholder when such a vote actually helps the slaveholding side in the clearly foreseeable political outcome? "Duty"?

> To make this declaration did not show what their duty was. If it did we
> should have no use for judgment; we might as well be made without

intelligence, and when divine or human law does not clearly point out what is our duty, we have no means of finding out what it is [except] by using our most intelligent judgment of the consequences.

"Our most intelligent judgment of the consequences"—that is the way to discover our duty, not by assuming that duty to be self-defining, to be taken for granted as revealed.

If there were a divine law, or human law, for voting for Martin Van Buren, or if a fair examination of the consequences and first reasoning would show that voting for him would bring about the ends they pretended to wish then he [Lincoln] would give up the argument.

Mr. Lone Star was perhaps too severe in saying "the ends they pretended to wish"; he might have granted their sincerity on that point—the ends they *do* wish. But in any case Lincoln was denying that either of those two ethical methods had defined our duty for us in the way that the Free-Soilers claimed. God has not revealed that we should vote for Martin Van Buren and the Free-Soil Party. There is no clear moral law commanding that we do so. And Mr. Sumner and company have not done the careful examination of the alternative consequences, measured against first principles, that would tell us that it is our duty to vote that way. My moral reasoning examining those alternative consequences (says Lincoln) tells me that the better course—our "duty," if you will—even if measured solely by the "free-soil" moral test (Lincoln himself at the time had other tests as well), was to vote Whig.

But since there is no fixed [moral] law on the subject, and since the whole probable result of their action would be an assistance in electing General Cass, he must say they were behind the Whigs in the advocacy of the freedom of the soil.

But now we have to admit that Lincoln was not an unattached moral philosopher, examining with Olympian objectivity the great question of principles versus consequences in making moral choices; he was a thoroughly engaged Whig politician whose purpose in coming to Massachusetts was not to debate politics and morals but to persuade Whigs tempted to defect to the Free-Soil Party to stay with the Whigs. You will aid the free-soil cause better, said Lincoln, by voting Taylor and Whig, and thus preventing the election of Cass and the Democrats, who would open up the territories to slavery, than by voting for Van Buren, who cannot win.

Sumner would presumably reply to all of this that he found his duty not in the outcome of one election or even one administration but in the sowing of the seeds of a greater triumph, in the heavens today, and in the long reach of history tomorrow. Someday, if not in the election of 1848, Sumner might have said, There will come a great host who will fulfill what we have here begun, with a champion who will lead them to triumph indeed over the moral abomination of human slavery.

Sumner, a man well stocked with vanity, might secretly have imagined who would play that role, and would see him in the mirror. He would have been shocked beyond measure to have known, in the summer of 1848, who in fact that leader would be.

2. THE CONGRESSMAN AS POLITICAL OPERATIVE (AND MORALIST)

And what then happened? What were, in fact, the results—the "consequences"—of the American presidential election of 1848?

They were filled with an unusually large supply of ironies, and of outcomes that no one could have predicted. There were undeserved good results and undeserved bad results, for all sides—and particularly for the antislavery but Taylor-supporting Whigs like Lincoln of Illinois.

Taylor was in fact elected, with a comfortable margin in the Electoral College. He carried Massachusetts, so the Free-Soilers did not have the negative effect, in that key Whig state, that Lincoln had feared. And Taylor also carried New York—where the Free-Soilers (with New Yorker Democratic ex-president Van Buren at the head of the ticket) took votes (presumably) mostly from the Democrats. The Free-Soil vote in that state was considerably larger than the margin by which the Democrats lost it. So in these two key states the result in fact was the reverse of what Lincoln feared: the Free-Soil Party may have helped the Whigs instead of the Democrats (and thereby, by his rather forced reasoning, really did help the cause of free soil).

The Free-Soilers proved to be a much more serious third party than the Liberty Party had been; they had a vote exceeding the margin between the two major parties in eleven states. They elected thirteen members of the House of Representatives, which then had only 242 members. The two-party margin in the House was close enough that the Free-Soilers held the balance of power in the selection of a Speaker, and under the leadership of Joshua Giddings they carried on a long fight over the speakership, obtaining important concessions on committees as the price for their support in the end. They also had enough seats in the Ohio legislature to collaborate with Democrats to send to the Senate the solid antislavery leader Salmon P. Chase, a man whom Lincoln would one day come to know well. They elected enough members of the Massachusetts legislature so that after a protracted battle that body, again with a Free-Soil–Democratic coalition, on April 23, 1851, chose as senator none other than Sumner himself. As history would work out, there would prove to be more to be said on the Sumner–Free-Soil side of the argument (if your prime purpose was the restriction of slavery) than the Whig Lincoln in 1848 had been willing (or able, given his political circumstances) to grant.*

But now we come to the undeserved good results that came to antislavery Whigs like Lincoln. Zachary Taylor proved to be more resistant to the slaveholding interest, and to the extension of slavery, and more resolute (although inarticulate) in support of the Union, than they had any right (on the basis of what they knew in 1848) to expect. President Taylor's nonaction proved to be of a sort that would have allowed California and New Mexico to come into the Union as free states, without any balancing concession to the South. William Seward and Thurlow Weed of New York, shrewd and realistic antislavery politicians, came to be increasingly influential with Taylor. The Southern Whigs who had strongly supported Taylor's nomination—including Lincoln's congressional friends among the Young Indians—had a nasty surprise of their own, and had their own undeserved bad luck. They began to draw back, aghast at what they had done: they wanted no president who would allow two new free states.

Henry Clay, who might (by his own reckoning, at any rate) have been president instead of Taylor—and instead of Polk in 1844 and instead of Harrison in 1840—came back to the Senate for his last hurrah. He put together a compromise which Daniel Webster supported in a famous

* Although the Free-Soil Party itself did not develop into the national antislavery party, it planted seeds for the Republican Party to grow from in 1854–56. (See Eric Foner, *Free Soil, Free Labor, Free Men: The Ideology of the Republican Party Before the Civil War* [New York: Oxford University Press, 1970,] pp. 124–128.) And although Lincoln, with a career in Illinois as a Whig, could not have supported the Free-Soil Party, that others elsewhere differently situated did so might well be said to have been the better decision, if opposition to slavery is your overriding purpose. Lincoln's arguments against Durley did not apply to Free-Soil supporters.

speech and John C. Calhoun, in his last speech, opposed. Among the concessions to the South in this compromise there was included a much stricter Fugitive Slave Law, which was anathema to the antislavery forces. But the combination of elements in the compromise, and therefore the Fugitive Slave Law, was stalled by President Taylor's refusal to go along with the "Omnibus Bill" that represented the "compromise."

Now came, however, one of those intrusions of sheer accident, unpredictable, an act of fortune or of Providence that almost makes a mockery of human calculations—undeserved bad luck, one might say, for antislavery Whigs like Lincoln. Defenders of the political ethic of sheer duty—of doing what is intrinsically, immediately "right" and leaving the "consequences" to God—regularly include among their arguments that one cannot know all the consequences of one's actions, which are played out in all the changing vicissitudes of life and history, whereas one can know one's duty, which is clear, plain, immediate.*

The "undeserved" bad outcomes for antislavery Whigs that would follow upon their support of Taylor came in two doses, again colored with irony. First, after sixteen months in office, in the midst of the congressional debate over the Compromise of 1850, President Zachary Taylor ate or drank something he should not have while sitting in the hot sun of the Fourth of July and was dead within a week. So his surprising and unexpected opposition to the compromise was abruptly removed.

Second, Millard Fillmore, the upstate New Yorker who succeeded to the presidency, turned out to be much more acquiescent to the compromise—including the concessions to the slaveholding states, the first of which was a more severe Fugitive Slave Law—than might have been expected. He had been regarded as being at least mildly antislavery (more so, certainly, than the large-scale Louisiana slaveholder Zachary Taylor) but turned out to be more amenable to the concessions to the South in the Compromise than Taylor had been.

As a result, the complicated combination of measures called the Compromise of 1850 was enacted not in one package, but in a sequence, skill-

---

* "[R]eason is not sufficiently enlightened to discover the whole series of predetermining causes which will allow it to predict accurately the happy or unhappy consequences of human activities . . . But reason at all times shows us clearly enough what we have to do in order to remain in the paths of duty . . . [A]lthough politics in itself is a difficult art, no art is required to combine it with morality. For as soon as the two come into conflict, morality can cut through the knot which politics cannot untie" (Immanuel Kant, "Perpetual Peace: A Philosophical Sketch," in Hans Reiss, ed., *Kant's Political Writings* [Cambridge: Cambridge University Press, 1970], pp. 116, 125).

fully managed by the rising Democratic leader Stephen Douglas. Strong Northern opponents of its stricter Fugitive Slave Law protested on one wing, and strong Southern opponents of admitting California as a free state protested on the other, but the great center of opinion rejoiced and celebrated. It was widely claimed that the upsetting issue of slavery had been finally removed from American politics.

Had Lincoln's insistence that duty required "our most intelligent judgment of the consequences" been proven defective by the ironies and reversals and surprises of 1848 and afterward? Not necessarily, he might say. Of course there is a great deal we cannot predict. But still, he might say, there was finally nothing so "undeserved" in the chain of events. He had said Taylor could win, and Taylor did win; and he had said that Taylor would be better than the only real alternative, the Democrat Lewis Cass, and by Lincoln's lights Taylor had been better, and even Taylor/Fillmore was better, than Cass and the Democrats would have been. But those who supported the Free-Soil Party could make quite a strong argument, too, and not just on Sumner's vision of an effect in the long future but on the basis of the "most intelligent judgement of the consequences" exactly in 1848.

3. THE SAME HATRED OF SLAVERY

Meanwhile, what had been Congressman Lincoln's own adventures after his candidate won in November of 1848? While Taylor was president-elect but not yet president, Lincoln and the Thirtieth Congress had, under the peculiar old constitutional system, another session, a short second session from December 1848 until inauguration day, March 4, 1849. The first session of that Congress had been much affected by the coming presidential election; the second session would be much affected by anticipation of the new administration that election produced.

It was in these, his last moments in Congress—the last moments he would spend as a public official until he was sworn in as president—that Abraham Lincoln undertook his first initiative against slavery in American public life.

This lanky, humorous, midwestern Whig in seat number 191 was not a leader of the small but growing bloc of antislavery congressmen, as was his messmate Joshua Giddings. Given his situation, however, what Lincoln did do was perhaps more significant than what he did not do. He was a back bencher, and, as he would say later about this venture into the politics of slavery, "without influence." His constituency in the middle of Illinois was quite different, on the subject of slavery, from that of Giddings from the New England–flavored Western Reserve of Ohio, or that of the congressmen from Massachusetts. What Lincoln did, nevertheless, was on his own initiative to compose and to discuss with Giddings and to manage to read on the House floor a bill to end the scandal of slavery all around them there in the nation's capital.

In addition to not being able to claim constitutional protection, as could slavery in South Carolina, slavery in Washington, D.C., represented an appalling symbol. The District was the site of the capital for all Americans, for Illinois and Rhode Island and Vermont as much as for Virginia and North Carolina. Moreover, the Constitution, in making provision for such a site, had explicitly given to Congress the power to make laws of such a District "in all cases whatsoever." So there was no constitutional excuse. Citizens from Northern states, even those with some experience with slavery, like Mary Todd Lincoln, coming to enact the nation's business in the great capital of this free country would discover slaves, the slave trade, slave pens, coffles of slaves in manacles and leg irons marched through the streets, within sight of the Capitol itself. Foreign visitors could hardly avoid mocking the nation's moral pretension.

As the second session of the Thirtieth Congress began, the battle over Texas had ended, the treaty with Mexico had been signed, the fight over the Wilmot Proviso had stalled, a new Whig administration had been elected in November and was about to take office. The wounds of the battle with the Free-Soil defection were still fresh. Giddings, long a Whig, had gone over to the Free-Soil Party, and had earned the animosity of the regular Whig leadership. Lincoln, on the other hand, had remained a loyal Whig. Nevertheless Lincoln and Giddings, living and eating together in Mrs. Sprigg's mess, may have come to be, for the moment, almost collaborators.

Editorials in leading mainline local papers had indicated a certain openness to carefully graduated and compensated emancipation of slaves in the District. Giddings, on a Saturday in January in this new, short lameduck session, made a particularly powerful appeal in the House against "property in man" which reverberated beyond the usual antislavery circles. It is suggested that it may have reverberated specifically with Giddings's Illinois messmate. In any case, on the Monday following Giddings's speech, Lincoln came to Giddings's room and asked the great antislavery leader's opinion of a bill he was drafting.

. . .

Lincoln's proposed bill for the District included—as would all of President Lincoln's own proposals for ending slavery—the principle of *compensation*, a principle that Giddings in general would reject, but under the particular circumstances of the District in 1849 was willing to accept. Lincoln's proposed bill for the District in 1849 and President Lincoln's own proposals for ending slavery up to the Emancipation Proclamation also included the principle of gradual application. And his District proposal included the requirement that it be enacted by the voters of the District, as had the protest by Stone and Lincoln in 1837. Giddings, who ordinarily rejected these points, nevertheless went along with Lincoln's proposal in the discussions in Mrs. Sprigg's mess, and perhaps beyond that.

The Whig leadership of the House was not sympathetic to Lincoln's effort—which means he was almost collaborating with the Free-Soil renegade Giddings *against* the regular Whigs he had campaigned with in the fall. There was a heated and complicated floor battle over issues having to do with slavery in the District, in the midst of which Lincoln managed to squeeze the reading of his bill onto the floor and into the record under a five-minute limit, ostensibly just identifying an amendment. It now seems that he kept trying longer than had been thought, and made an effort again to present the bill, only to be stopped by the Speaker's ruling. His support melted away; the time ran out.

Lincoln went about this effort through compromise. The subject was already raised by the initiative of antislavery congressmen; Lincoln tried to work up a bill that was likely to be more widely accepted than theirs. He talked it out in Mrs. Sprigg's mess and got the support of Giddings and other antislavery congressmen, and then he—or, it appears from a new reading of Giddings's diary, he and Giddings together—visited William Seaton, the genial, socially prominent conservative Whig who was mayor of the city. Lincoln managed to get Seaton's endorsement of the bill under the impression, of which Lincoln did not undeceive him, that Giddings would oppose and possibly kill the bill, thus keeping Seaton's support from costing him politically with his fellow slaveholders. When Lincoln read his proposed bill onto the record, he claimed the support of "about fifteen of the leading citizens of the District," to whom he had shown his bill, and every one of them desired that "some proposition like this should pass." He tried to compose a compromise that would win support of citizens all the way from Giddings to Seaton; but Seaton, when Lincoln made it public, backpedaled under pressure.

Lincoln's proposal fell to earth in the crunch of the session and the politics of the time. But he made the attempt. He certainly did not need to take the trouble to work up and to introduce any bill to end slavery in the District—not for any reason back home in his conservative and racially prejudiced district, and not for any discernible reason for his own future either in Illinois or on the national stage. One cannot imagine that it would have furthered his ambition to be appointed to a high post in the incoming Taylor administration, for example, and certainly not in one day being elected senator from Illinois. So we may be permitted to infer that he went to the trouble to work it up and present it because he was indeed convinced that slavery in the capital of a nation conceived in liberty was a particularly egregious evil.

The next time Abraham Lincoln would deal with slavery in the District, he would not be, as he was then, "without influence."

Thirteen years and three months later, on April 16, 1862, it would be, as Nicolay and Hay remarked, the "strange fortune" of Abraham Lincoln, now President of the United States, to sign into law an act passed by a radically altered Civil War Congress that would at last wipe out the stain of slavery within sight of the Capitol on whose summit there waved the stars and stripes of freedom.

Nicolay and Hay remark on the continuity of Lincoln's principles; through upheavals of American history during which "there was scarcely a man on the continent who had not shifted his point of view . . . there was so little change in Mr. Lincoln." Here is the way these fully sympathetic and almost official biographers, in 1886, summarized Mr. Lincoln's positions on slavery across the years, up to 1862:

> The same hatred of slavery, the same sympathy with the slave, the same consideration for the slaveholder as the victim of a system he had inherited, the same sense of divided responsibility between the South and the North, the same desire to effect great reforms with as little individual damage and injury, as little disturbance of social conditions as possible, were equally evident when the raw pioneer signed the protest with Dan Stone at Vandalia, when the mature man moved the resolution of 1849 in the Capitol, and when the President gave the sanction of his bold signature to the act which swept away the slave shambles from the city of Washington.

4. SHALL THESE THINGS BE?

Lincoln's main work during the second session of the Thirtieth Congress and in the year 1849, however, had to do not with great issues of policy or philosophy, but with patronage.

Abraham Lincoln in 1848–49 was not a man with (to borrow from Sumner) "a name that history can never let die." He was a one-term congressman, just turning forty, whose career on the national scene, even as a minor player, was about to expire. One sign that history would be quite willing to let his name die was the difficulty he had extracting any patronage from the incoming, or newly installed, Taylor administration. He promoted a nonpolitical, supra-partisan war hero as the Whig candidate? He defended the Whig doctrine of a president who would exercise restraint of executive power? Alas, he got what he wished for. The nonpolitical president would not make the political appointments Lincoln wanted him to make.

Taylor's supra-partisan restraint meant that he was reluctant to turn Democrats out of office so that deserving Whigs could take their place, or give advertising just to Whig papers. The highest Whig officeholder in Illinois and a strong early backer of the president (For-Taylor-Before-Philadelphia) had to conclude, ruefully, in May: "Not one man recommended by me has yet been appointed to anything, little or big, except a few who had no opposition."

Originally he had hoped for a high office or two, a major appointment, for a deserving Illinois Whig. But as the weeks went by and the administration came into office and made actual appointments, the possibility shrank so that it seemed that the commissioner of the General Land Office was the highest post, and "the only crumb of patronage," any Illinois Whig could expect.

But that is the way it always is, is it not? Those hundreds and those thousands of volunteers and staff and campaign workers devote their eager days to the candidate, and of course to the program, and perhaps to the party, and do it because they believe in it, without any thought (well, with hardly any thought) about what victory might mean for themselves, nevertheless feel a certain sad emptiness when they find who it is, after all their work, who actually gets the jobs.

Lincoln himself could have had that good land-office job, if he had taken it right away, while he was still a congressman, and the new administration was not yet in office. At least he said he could have, in a letter written on his fortieth birthday to his friend David Davis, and again eight days later in a letter to Joshua Speed.

Why did Lincoln not accept the post back in February or March when he could have had it? Such a "second class" post, he wrote, "would not compensate me for being snarled at by others who want it."

He committed himself to try to get the appointment for Cyrus Edwards, who was prominent in the party, a former candidate for governor, and an uncle of his brother-in-law, Ninian W. Edwards. But Lincoln was now not the only Illinois Whig in national office. His old friend and predecessor in Congress, whom he had actually suggested for the cabinet, Edward D. Baker, home from the wars, had moved with his military glamour to another district (around Galena) and got himself elected to Congress. So now there was not a lone-star Whig from Illinois; there was, rather, the fading star Lincoln in the Thirtieth Congress, and the rising star Baker, already in Washington, anticipating being in the Thirty-first. And Baker did not like Edwards, and had a candidate of his own.

But then it appeared that northern Illinois Whigs had yet another candidate. This was a man named Justin Butterfield, who had a good deal to recommend him in addition to northern-ness. He was a distinguished attorney in Chicago, an older man, born in New Hampshire, a friend of Daniel Webster. He was a lifelong Whig, who had served for some years as district attorney, and he was now recommended by Henry Clay. So he had the recommendations of the two greatest names among living Whigs.*

Why did Lincoln oppose this man so fiercely? He certainly did so. There are two subjects in the story of his politics in the spring and early summer of 1849 on which he shows real passion: not his own personal prospects; rather, the outrage that Butterfield should get that appointment, and the sensitivity that Cyrus Edwards should believe that he, Lincoln, had betrayed him.

As to the Edwards matter, Albert Beveridge concluded from the evi-

---

* It would be Butterfield's fate to be largely remembered for one wisecrack, which is understandably quoted in many Lincoln biographies and other books. It seems that Butterfield had opposed the War of 1812 and had been badly damaged politically by doing so. So when he was asked whether he opposed the Mexican War, he responded, "Never again! I now support war, pestilence, and famine."

dence that "the very worst that can be said is that Lincoln did not push Edwards's application with much vigor because Baker was for [another candidate] and, unless one would withdraw, Illinois would lose the office." Lincoln was distressed that Edwards would think he had not done his best for him, and protested his innocence. The Lincoln of reality seems to match the Lincoln of myth in this regard: that he tried to be scrupulously honest and honorable in personal dealings, and cared a great deal about his reputation for being so.

As to Butterfield, any politician will understand the point. Butterfield had worked for Clay against Taylor. In a series of exasperated letters Lincoln acknowledged that Butterfield was a friend of his (in the way, we may observe, that the category of "friend" is rather loosely used in political affairs), and also that Butterfield was qualified—in another letter, "well qualified, and, I suppose, would be faithful in the office"—grudgingly conceded—"but of quite one hundred Illinoisans equally well qualified, I do not know one with less claims [sic] to it." (We are not talking about qualifications, or about "friendship"; we are talking about claims.)

Ex-congressman Lincoln summarized Butterfield's nonservice to the Whig Party in a way that should certainly put to rest any notion that the sainted Abraham Lincoln was above politics:

> In 1840 we fought a fierce and laborious battle in Illinois, many of us spending almost the entire year in the contest. The general victory came, and with it, the appointment of a set of drones, including this same Butterfield, who had never spent a dollar or lifted a finger in the fight. The place he got was that of District Attorney. The defection of Tyler came, and then B. played off and on, and kept the office till after Polk's election. Again, winter and spring before the last, when you and I were almost sweating blood to have Genl. Taylor nominated, this same man was ridiculing the idea, and going for Mr. Clay; and when Gen. T. was nominated, if he went out of the city of Chicago to aid in his election, it is more than I ever heard, or believe. Yet, when the election is secured, by other men's labor, and even against his effort, why, he is the first man on hand for the best office that our state lays any claim to.

And such an ungrateful appointment will have results; as the prudent realist will argue in a grander moment, when he is president, human beings—freed slaves fighting in the Union armies in that case—act from motives. And so it is with Whig workers in the present case: "Shall this thing be? Our Whigs will throw down their arms, and fight no more, if the fruit of their labor is thus disposed of."

The Whig Party workers in Illinois are not working for the party solely out of a selfless devotion to a lofty vision of what the Whig Party can do for the country; they do have, also, if truth be told, some other motives. They want jobs. Or, at least, they want fairness in the distribution of jobs.

We have called Lincoln's political ethic "responsible," which means he takes care to understand particular circumstances and consequences. To add the word "realistic" implies a wider point: to understand those inclinations of one's fellow human beings that do not necessarily accord with the most ideal conduct. Weber in the essay referred to would say that the responsible politician "takes account of precisely the average deficiencies of people . . . he does not even have the right to presuppose their goodness and perfection." The Lincoln we see in the spring of 1849, scrambling to get jobs in the Taylor administration for deserving Whigs, certainly is not presupposing anyone's goodness or perfection. To repeat: "Shall this thing be? Our Whigs will throw down their arms, and fight no more, if the fruit of their labor is thus disposed of." And then he goes on to say: "If there is one man in this state who desires B's appointment to any thing, I declare I have not heard of him."

In another letter he went so far as to say it were better that it go somewhere other than Illinois than to Butterfield.

Why? "In the great contest of '40 [Butterfield] was not seen or heard of; but when the victory came, three or four old drones, including him, got all the valuable offices, through what influence no one has yet been able to tell."

Butterfield, at Philadelphia now in '48, had "fought for Mr. Clay against Mr. Taylor to the bitter end." Why should the Taylor administration appoint someone like that? (Because sometimes it works that way. Henry Clay, as Lincoln well knows, is a very important Whig, even now in his old age, and he is about to come back to Washington as a United States senator again, for his last great performance on the national stage. Parties, like life, can be unfair. Sometimes supporters have to be squeezed, so that one can reconcile with one's erstwhile opponents.)

What was Lincoln's motivation in all this? Cynics would surely be wrong to say that like all politicians he was interested only, or truly, in his own advancement—getting high office for himself. Idealists would be almost equally wrong to say that he was motivated only or chiefly by a high vision of what the Whig administration could make of America: a nation prosperous with a thriving commerce, now newly about to stretch across the continent but still more committed to quality than quantity, to improvement in all its forms, moral as well as economic, offering to the poorest man an opportunity to rise as he had done, with slavery confined to its original states and on its way to extinction. Lincoln cared about all that, and it was latent within him and implicit in his support for the Whig Party, but it was not his chief immediate motivation. I think it is easy to answer the question: He was chiefly concerned that deserving Illinois Whigs receive good positions in the new administration.

When the dust had settled over the appointment battles it turned out that the chief appointment Illinois was going to get—the crumb that came to them—was that land-office job, and that the other contenders had canceled each other out and that Lincoln himself was the only possible alternative to Butterfield. On June 2 (Lincoln would later be precise about the date) Lincoln "determined, unconditionally," to be an applicant for the post he could have had for the asking in February. He now did so because he was "informed by a Telegraphic despach, that the questions had narrowed down to Mr. B. and myself." Better to take the job and put up with the snarling than to let Butterfield have it!

In fact, Lincoln went to the length of making a trip from Springfield back to Washington, which was not so lightly done in those days, to try to nail down the position now for himself. He did get an appointment with Secretary of the Interior Thomas Ewing,* but Ewing was already firmly committed to Butterfield.

In the letters that spewed from his pen he asked friends, if they thought it proper, please to plead his case to "old Zack."

Lincoln asked a federal judge named Nathaniel Pope to write, and here is what Pope wrote (Lincoln never saw this, of course; we recommenders like to keep our recommendations confidential, and in this case one can

---

* Ewing had been a leading Whig senator. When Lincoln wrote to him on April 26, 1849, he addressed him, as he had several times before, as Secretary of the Home Department. When he wrote to him fourteen days later, on May 10, 1899, he addressed him as Secretary of the Interior—the Department of Interior had come into being, and Ewing was its first secretary.

certainly see why). Judge Pope, asked by Lincoln to write for Lincoln (implicitly and necessarily, instead of Butterfield), wrote as follows:

> It is said that the respective friends of my most valued friends, Justin Butterfield and Abraham Lincoln Esquires, are presented to the President for the office of Commissioner of the Land Department. Allow me Sir to bear my testimony in favor of both. They are just such men as should be selected for the office. They are honest and capable. The appointment of either would, I think, give general satisfaction.

This was a friend?

And so what happened? Lincoln had argued for the better part of a year for a Whig president who would use restraint in the use of executive power, including giving much power to the heads of the cabinet departments. And, again, that is what he got. President Taylor turned the matter of the appointment of a commissioner of the land office over to the relevant cabinet member, Thomas Ewing.

And so the appointment went to: Justin Butterfield of Chicago.

When Lincoln returned from Washington to Springfield this second time in three months, from this futile effort, his brief career in national politics seemed to be concluded. The secretary of state offered him the consolation prize of an appointment as secretary to the governor of the territory of Oregon, and Lincoln promptly turned that down. (Hardly worth being snarled at for that job, and in any case he had already recommended someone for it.) Maybe the Taylor people were a little embarrassed, because now Ewing offered him the governorship of Oregon itself, but after brief conversation he turned that down, too, saying that his wife did not want to move. He went back to the practice of law, and—we might have written— was never heard of again.

5. THE VOCATION OF A POLITICIAN

On or about the Fourth of July, 1849, the former Whig congressman Abraham Lincoln was back in Springfield. For almost five years thereafter, through his early forties, he would be more or less on the sidelines. He was the father of a family of bouncing boys, with attendant happiness and sorrow. Robert, the earnest firstborn son who was destined to outlive them all, had been born in 1843. Eddie, born in 1846, died after an illness of fifty-two days in February of 1850. Willie, who would prove to be a particularly intelligent boy, "prematurely serious and studious," was born late in that same year. Tad, who with his liveliness and speech impediment—one day to be a "tricky little sprite" in the Executive Mansion—was born in 1853. The father of the family practiced law, with increasing eminence. In odd-numbered years he concentrated on the law to recoup the family fortunes after the even-numbered years, which in Illinois were the election years. Mary Todd Lincoln, abruptly reduced by her marriage from Kentucky aristocrat to middle-class lawyer's wife, coped with the management of their small house, disciplined the boys perhaps a little more than her lenient husband, had difficulties with Irish maids, yearned for eminence for her husband.

For the next five years he would either walk each day from his house at Eighth and Jackson to the offices of Lincoln and Herndon at Sixth and Adams or, for twelve weeks in the fall and twelve weeks in the spring, travel with Judge David Davis, Leonard Swett, Ward Lamon, and his other friends over the vast four-hundred-mile Eighth Judicial Circuit in central Illinois. They would argue with each other in court during the day, then swap stories and, except Lincoln, drink a pitcher of whiskey in the inns at night.

Lincoln's political motor was idling, but was not shut down. He was poised for the first great deeds of his life.

The mature Abraham Lincoln would exhibit, in an admirable way, a combination of the moral clarity and elevation of—what shall we say?—the prophet, with the "prudence," the "responsibility" of a worthy politician. The latter characteristics he had already acquired in his early forties. The moral clarity was to come.

I use the two words above in quotation marks instead of some variant of the overworked American word "pragmatism," because they imply a combination of practical wisdom with moral purpose, as "pragmatism" may not.

"Prudence" was once the name not only for a cardinal virtue but for the first of the cardinal virtues. Prudence as a virtue did not then exclude, as pragmatism tends to do, general moral ideals and larger moral patterns beyond the immediate situation. The term did not then mean, as it has shriveled to become in our modern vocabulary, a calculating, cautious self-regard: a prudent cat that does not step on a hot stove, a prudent driver who looks both ways before barreling out of the driveway, a prudent young person who prudently puts away some money in a prudential life insurance company. The classical virtue did share with this modern shrunken usage, and with the ubiquitous modern language of pragmatism, this quality: a careful attention to the particular situation in which one acts. And it shares with utilitarianism in all its varieties a careful weighing of probable consequences of one's action in that real world, as Lincoln told Durley he should have done. One does not act simply out of one's hopes, dreams, fantasies, or imaginings; one must look, and examine, and intelligently understand, the world out there, outside oneself, as it is in all its present particulars. A person imbued with the virtue of prudence must say to himself, or herself—to borrow from a source not available to Aristotle, Thomas Aquinas, and other interpreters of classical prudence, Jimmy Durante—"Dem's da conditions dat exist."

But the term did not originally imply that one should pay this scrupulous attention primarily or only because of the potential consequences for oneself, as our diminished usage now tends to do; nor did it disdain or ignore larger moral purposes and effects, as at least the popular use of the language of pragmatism tends to do, or reduce moral judgment to one future-oriented measurement, as utilitarianisms do. I am resuscitating this concept temporarily for my purpose here, just to indicate that there once was such a way of slicing moral understanding—and that it then could be applied to Lincoln. In the older usage—the one I suggest would have fit the maturing Lincoln—prudence was a virtue. That means it was a pattern or habit that should become ingrained. Prudence as a moral virtue made a bridge to the intellectual virtues, as they were called in the old schemes. That means it entailed a central role for cognition, for learning and knowing, in praiseworthy conduct. A prudent person in this older sense used his powers of observation and reasoning to take careful account of the real and concrete situation, the particular situation, not simply in order to protect his own skin, and not with the assumption that whatever "works" in that situation is what one ought to do, but in order continually to adapt the appropriate moral claims and purposes, also carefully considered, to the real world.

.   .   .

A brief passage—three sentences—in the Annual Message to Congress of the President of the United States in 1862 would state the point succinctly. It would also imply another aspect of responsible politics in a land the people rule: collaboration. President Lincoln would be making an eloquent plea, at the end of his message, for his plan to end slavery by compensated emancipation. The plea, appealing to his hearers—Congress, first of all— to join him in thinking anew that we "disenthrall ourselves" (including himself in the need to abandon the "dogmas of the quiet past") culminates in the memorable phrases about "the last best hope of the earth." I want now to call attention to sentences that just precede this graceful passage. He was asking Congress to join him. Here is what he said: "We can succeed only by concert. It is not 'can *any* of us *imagine* better?' but, 'can we *all* do better?'" Then he repeated the point: "Object whatsoever is possible, still the question recurs, 'can we do better?'"

One can always imagine some arrangement of life superior to the real one we encounter every day; our imagination has no limits. Wickedness, selfishness, laziness, malice, and stupidity, and all other vices and injustices, and perhaps death and taxes as well, can all be made to vanish in our imaginations. That evaluating of human conduct we call ethics has a critical aspect, and the criticism can be endless; and a visionary aspect, and the ideal worlds conjured in our minds can include all of the possible goods of human life, and the impossible ones, too, and need not notice that some are contradictory. In our imaginations we all can take this sorry world entire and remold it to our heart's desire. But in our actual living, the limits waved away in our imaginings are all there to face us every day. And if the goods and evils in question are social, then we are not, as in our imaginings, the sole and lonely actor; there are also these others occupying this planet with us, with their ideas of goods and evils, and their interests, diverging from ours. "Can we *all* do better?" "We can succeed only by concert." Often to the prudent and realistic politician following an ethic of responsibility, the ethical idealist seems simply to be indulging personal moral imaginings, without regard to how they connect with others or with the real situation: How can I be more right than my neighbor? But the social-moral problem is not how to refine and examine the superiority of your individual rightness, spending your night inside the Concord jail, but how to move the whole body politic these inches forward (or on rare occasions more than inches) toward something better. In your mind you can wipe slavery off the face of the earth. Your life may be situated so that you can seem to wash your hands of any connection with it. But meanwhile there remains the reality to be coped with by the slow boring of hard boards which is politics. "It is not," President Lincoln will one day say, "'can *any* of us *imagine* better?'"—of course we can—"but, 'can we *all* do better?'"

Responsibility, practical wisdom, and realism will remain shaping qualities for this politician even after the great alterations of his life that will come— his becoming a leading antislavery politician after 1854 and the chief executive in a civil war, with all of its terrible necessities, after 1861. But there are other dimensions to his, as to anyone's, moral life. Even for this responsible politician, who seeks to measure the results this way and that way, there will come moments that impose an imperative. And beyond deciding this case and that there are the developing qualities of the person—virtues, one would hope. And attending to "the fruits"—the consequences—does not answer the original question: By what standard are they judged?

As to imperatives: This is the form of conduct—when one is no longer sorting mixed goods and evils or calculating consequences, but standing where one must—that popular opinion may regard as the only aspect that really is "ethics." Principle. Duty. Doing what is right, "moral." Appeals of this sort are, from the point of view of an ethic of responsibility—of Lincoln, we might surmise—often premature and oversimple and self-indulgent. But that does not mean that they are never appropriate. It will be remembered that in Lincoln's own occasional flights of moral commentary there were provisos: Durley could have voted for Clay "without violation of principle"; we discover our duty by assessing consequences "when divine or human law" does not point it out; first principles and a fixed moral law might add to, or take precedence over, consequence weighing.

That essay of Max Weber's would seem to disparage an ethic of unconditional and peremptory absolutes and endorse exclusively an ethic of calculating responsibility. But then at the end of his essay (an address originally, in Munich in 1918), perhaps to the surprise of the reader, he describes the "immensely moving" occasion when the two ethics come together, and a mature man—no matter whether old or young in years— following an ethic of responsibility somewhere reaches the point where he says (as Weber's hearers would know, a quotation from Martin Luther): "Here I stand. I can do no other."

Lincoln, at his core a surpassingly dutiful man, would certainly come to such occasions. This book from one angle may be seen as the story of Lincoln's coming to that point. Weber's provision that the occasion involve a mature person, and that it represent not the overcoming of one by the other but the combining of those two kinds of ethics, suggests what is surely true in Lincoln's case: that the occasions on which he said his version of "Here I stand; I can do no other" were rare, profound, truly the end of the line beyond all calculating, deeply personal, still not detached from effects in the real world, and not undertaken for a self-indulgent display of rectitude. But there will be such occasions, all the more significant because they are rare and embedded in an ethic of responsibility.

There will come portentous moments, as we shall see, when the unfolding of events puts at risk the very essence of his bedrock commitments to the containment of slavery and the preservation of the Union. And on the latter point he will have taken an oath.

But all of this lay ahead, behind the veil of the future. In 1849–1854 Lincoln argued cases in Springfield and the Eighth Circuit about "malicious mischief" and fraud and "ejectment" and foreclosure and murder and bastardy and divorce and slander and adultery and "gaming" and desertion and manslaughter, and assumpsit and replevin and mandamus, and the trespass of cattle and the payment for arresting a horse thief and the infringement of a patent on a water wheel and the recovery of a debt of $40 with $54.80 accrued damages and all sorts of land disputes and particularly cases about the right of way of railroads.

In the two eulogies he was asked to give, for Zachary Taylor in 1850 and Henry Clay in 1852, assessing the whole careers of these eminent Whigs, he had occasion to touch on an older way of thinking about praiseworthy conduct, beyond a sequence of particular choices—the shaping of persisting patterns built into one's makeup. "Character." "Virtues."

Lincoln had to scratch a bit to find much to say about the virtues of Zachary Taylor. He was reduced to praising Taylor for his "sterling, but unobtrusive, qualities." "His rarest military trait," Lincoln the eulogist would say of General Taylor, was that he "was a combination of negatives—absence of excitement and absence of fear. He could not be flurried and he could not be scared . . . no man was so little disposed to have difficulty with his friends." He managed to praise him because, although he lived among men who often fought duels, he had never (as far as Lincoln could discover) fought one. Lincoln filled up two-thirds of his eulogy of Taylor with a detailed account of the general's military exploits in the Mexican War, including dramatic battlefield touches ("every eye is strained—it is—it is—the stars and stripes are still aloft!") that remind one of the overdone speech endings of his earlier years. Of Taylor as president Lincoln would say, "The Presidency, even to the most experienced of politicians, is no bed of roses [the eulogist himself will one day learn how true that is]; and General Taylor, like others, found thorns within it . . . I will not pretend to believe that all the wisdom or all the patriotism of the country died with Gen. Taylor." I guess not. One senses in the eulogy to Taylor that the eulogist himself is laboring under the necessity to exhibit one of the few virtues he can ascribe to his subject: "self-sacrificing, long-enduring devotion to his duty." He padded the ending by observing that this great man's death reminds us that we, too, must die, which then led him into—as the climax of his eulogy—the quotation of six whole stanzas of that melancholy poem he (alone) loved so well, "Oh why should the spirit of mortal be proud?" That material could have been used in a eulogy of any mortal being whatever.

But there is nevertheless in Lincoln's eulogy of Taylor one passage that does reveal something about the virtues of the eulogist. One way or another, it is significant what we select to praise in others. Lincoln said of Taylor: "[H]e pursued no man with revenge." Then he dramatized an incident involving "the gallant and now lamented Gen. Worth," who, when a colonel, had been so offended by a decision against him by his superior General Taylor as to leave the army in Mexico and to tender his resignation to army authorities in Washington. "It is said, that in his passionate feeling," reported Lincoln, "he hesitated not to speak harshly and disparagingly of Gen. Taylor," and that as a respected officer his word carried weight. An unexpected turn in the war then brought the prospect of what would be the Battle of Monterey, and Worth was now "deeply mortified" at being absent and seeing his laurels wither away. The government "both wisely and generously," Lincoln said, declined Worth's resignation and returned him to General Taylor's command.

"Then came Gen. Taylor's opportunity for revenge." But of course he did not take it. Instead of placing Worth so that "his name would scarcely be noted in the report," Taylor, feeling that "it was generous to allow him, then and there, to retrieve his secret loss," assigned him "what was, par excellence, the post of honor," and Worth went on to glory. The selecting of that story tells as much about the eulogist as about the eulogee— magnanimity would, in time, be one of Lincoln's prime virtues.

When it fell to Lincoln to eulogize Henry Clay, in Springfield in the summer of 1852, he had more to work with—a period of almost half a century during which Clay was "constantly the most loved, and most implicitly followed by friends, and most dreaded by opponents, of all living American politicians." "Jackson, Van Buren, Harrison, Polk, and Taylor, all rose after, and set long before him." Lincoln attributed Clay's "long enduring spell" to a cluster of virtues that, again, might in time have been assigned to the eulogist himself: excellent judgment, indomitable will, and a particular kind of eloquence. The eloquence was not that of fine types and figures but "rather of that deeply earnest and impassioned tone, and manner, which can proceed only from great sincerity and a thorough conviction in the speaker of the justice and importance of the cause."

And then Lincoln's central celebration of Clay was of his devotion to that cause. Once again it is significant what the eulogist chooses to eulogize: "Mr. Clay's predominant sentiment, from first to last, was a deep devotion to the cause of human liberty—a strong sympathy for the oppressed every where, and an ardent wish for their elevation."

"He [Clay] loved his country partly because it was his own country, but mostly because it was a free country." Lincoln praised "his ruling passion—a love of liberty and right, unselfishly, and for their own sakes." That might be a little too strong—even for so good a man as Lincoln would become—and partook of a funereal exaggeration in the case of Clay. But it puts in view the larger moral choice: In what cause do these "responsible" politicians labor?

An ethic of responsibility, of prudence, of realism, would differentiate a politician like Lincoln from the various utopians, perfectionists, moralizers, fanatics, and absolutists—in all directions. It would distinguish such a political person from those unpolitical ones who do not adapt their understanding of what they ought to do to "our most intelligent judgment of the consequences." It would distinguish him from Williamson Durley, with his vote for Birney, and Henry David Thoreau, with his proud insistence that he was not a member of any society he had not voluntarily joined. It would certainly distinguish him from those antislavery Northern intellectuals who would give secret support to the insane project of John Brown. To be sure, it would distinguish such a politician sharply also from those irresponsibles in quite another direction, the fire-eating Yanceys and Rhetts and Hammonds with their proud prickly uncompromising sense of Southern "honor," their haughty contempt for the mere clerks and mechanics and merchants of the North, their fantastic self-aggrandizing dream of a slave empire stretching southward. An ethic of responsibility, prudence, and realism would distinguish those who have a vocation for politics in a free republic, like Lincoln, from those who don't.

But what about Lincoln's fellow politicians of a different stripe? Could one not say that Stephen A. Douglas, whom Lincoln spent most of his pre-presidential career opposing, was "realistic" and "responsible" and maybe even—most of the time, anyway—"prudent"? His admirers find his career, particularly at the end, a most "responsible" effort to hold the Union together. What about even James K. Polk? Again, he was certainly "realistic"; perhaps "prudent." He adapted his purposes to the real world so effectively as to achieve in his short presidency almost exactly what he set out to achieve. Neither of these gentlemen could be accused of any utopianism or moralistic fanaticism. They certainly did adapt to the "average deficiencies of mankind"—maybe below-the-average.

For that matter, what about Lincoln's friend from congressional days Alexander Stephens of Georgia, now a key Democrat in the House? He will be "responsibly" arguing in behalf of the Union, against firebrands in his own state and party, right up to secession itself.

So now we have to ask a further moral question—what ends do these realistic politicians serve?

There will perhaps be some responsible, practically wise, realistic politicians on all sides across a great swath of policy until one gets to the outer fringes. And there will be irresponsible actors on each side and particularly every fringe. There were those who, although utopian, opposed slavery, and therefore had their faces toward Zion (as President Lincoln would one day put it). And there were those who, although quite realistic and by their lights responsible, were nevertheless facing in the opposite direction. And so the question arises: Which way is Zion?

When we responsibly ask "Can we all do better?"—what is the criterion of better? When we realistically ask "Which is preferable?"—what is the measure? Which of the "fruits" is good? Which "consequences" are worthy?

Lincoln's Zion had been the Whig vision, the Henry Clay vision, of Improvement and Industry promoted by action of the federal government, which, as Lincoln emphasized, particularly made possible the rise of poor men like himself by the work of their hands. There was a strong, even romantic, Daniel Webster nationalism in it. There had been, perhaps, a faint implicit universalism and even egalitarianism in it, in that this romanticized "Liberty" in America was supposed to break down ancient preferential barriers, and in that the economic opportunities through hard work were supposed to be open to everyone.

But—everyone? Although the handful of congressmen who were anti-slavery were Whigs, the bulk of the party was not; Whig plantation owners

in the South were not less fierce in support of slavery, nor less racist, than
their Democratic counterparts. That Whig vision of an economically, culturally, morally "improved" and developed nation, with the policies of a
national bank and roads that crossed state lines and canals and navigable
rivers, and public schools, and a tariff, represented "goods," desirable to
achieve. But now history pressed upon the nation a matter that cut deeper,
to a more fundamental level of justice and human right. On the issue of the
spread of slavery, and the inclusion of black persons in the nation's charter
of freedom and equality, Douglas and Polk and Stephens were not facing
toward Zion. The little band of antislavery agitators, impractical and unpolitical though they were, and sometimes self-righteous and imprudent and
perversely damaging to their own cause, nevertheless were facing toward
Zion.

Lincoln had always been opposed to slavery, but he had not been a
particular leader in antislavery politics, and certainly not in antislavery agitation. He had voted for the Wilmot Proviso, closing the Mexican cession
to slavery, but he had not made supporting it a litmus test, as the Free-Soil
folks like Sumner did. When the combination of bills called the Compromise of 1850 was put together, and a much more stringent Fugitive Slave
Law was part of it, the antislavery press and pulpit and platform erupted
against it. Abe Lincoln out in Illinois did not erupt.

But then there came in 1854 an event that would pull his antislavery
convictions to the center of his politics, and "arouse" the universalism
and egalitarianism, and the moral concept of the nation, that they rested
upon. Zion was now the human Equality affirmed in the Declaration of
Independence.

Lincoln would still be a calculator of possibilities. But possibilities
change with events and, in a republic, with a change in public attitudes.
Lincoln now became a political leader engaged with the deepest moral
fundamentals of the nation. He would come to combine with the realism of
the politician a new and unwavering moral clarity.

There he is in Springfield, reading the papers and the *Congressional
Globe*. And early in 1854 he is "aroused" by what he reads. The event that
called forth this reshaping of his politics was a truly ferocious struggle in
the United States Senate, and an extremely controversial new law that
came out of it over the repeal of the Missouri Compromise and the opening of new territory to slavery: Stephen Douglas's Nebraska Bill.

CHAPTER NINE

Thunderstruck in Illinois

1. THE SENATE ACTS AND LINCOLN DECIDES

At five in the morning of March 4, 1854, as the light of dawn peeped disapprovingly into the not-very-edifying spectacle in the World's Greatest Deliberative Body, the weary and half-drunken United States senators, after a seventeen-hour session, did what it had been known all along they would do. The Democrats had a large majority; the Democratic president, Franklin Pierce, had made the pending Nebraska bill an administration measure; they had help from Southern Whigs. Some senators had already staggered home, but enough remained to make the result 37–14 in favor of the bill.

The most dazzling explosion, in that final night of rhetorical fireworks, was the many-staged rocket from the bill's great sponsor, Senator Stephen Douglas of Illinois. He took the floor at eleven and issued an outburst of oratory that lasted until three in the morning. Everyone agreed it was a tremendous display, although they differed on just what made it tremendous. Length, certainly. Stamina, undoubtedly. A command of material, to be sure. "Tremendous in length, vigor, and ill-temper," the twentieth-century historian Allan Nevins would say. The appraisals of this Douglas performance vary widely from the moment he sat down in the early morning of March 4, 1854, to the present day. "The reports of his speech which will reach you," according to one report, called "A Night in the Senate," in the *New York Tribune*, "will convey but a faint idea of its violence and vulgarity." The *Tribune* correspondent said of Douglas: "His sneering tone and vulgar grimaces must be heard and seen rather than described. To Senator Seward he said in return to a courteous explanation, 'Ah, you can't

231

crawl behind that free nigger dodge.' He always uses the word 'nigger' and not 'negro' as it appears in his printed speeches."

The furious debate over this pending bill would continue through two months more in the House, but if we think of the semiretired politician Abraham Lincoln out in Springfield, Illinois, all through the early months of 1854, reading the debates in the closely printed columns of the *Congressional Globe*, we may think of him concentrating on the debates in the Senate. The Senate was where he wanted to be; one day he would say that he would rather be senator than president.

And there was another reason he would be particularly drawn to the Senate debates: the central role of Douglas. We might think of the speech that Lincoln was developing as he read those debates, which he then actually would deliver in the autumn of 1854, as his belated outsider's participation in the fierce debates on Douglas's Nebraska bill in the United States Senate the previous February and March.

In the House the leader of those who supported the bill was Lincoln's old friend from his congressional days Alexander Stephens of Georgia. Stephens forced and squeezed and pressed the bill "with whip and spur" through wild scenes, including drawn weapons, through March and April and May to its passage on May 22. Eight days later President Pierce signed it and the Kansas-Nebraska Act was the law of the land. Kansas and Nebraska were left to the vagaries of "popular sovereignty" in the decision about slavery, and the "sacred compact" in the Missouri Compromise was repealed.

By bringing about that repeal, Lincoln would say in his major speech in the fall, Stephen Douglas "took us by surprise—astounded us . . . We were thunderstruck and stunned." In the shorter of his two autobiographical sketches he would say: "I was losing interest in politics when the repeal of the Missouri Compromise aroused me again." He used the same verb in the longer sketch he produced a little later, this one in the third person: "In 1854, his profession had almost superseded the thought of politics in his mind, when the repeal of the Missouri Compromise aroused him as he had never been before."

"As he had never been before": so a moment now came, in the spring, summer, and fall of 1854, that was enormously important in the moral biography of this forty-five-year-old prairie politician. Of course he would change and learn and mature and develop—as what able person would not?—when, seven years later, he came to hold the highest office in the land in the time of its greatest trial. But there was also in his life this earlier moment of marked moral escalation, in 1854. He decided he would return to the political wars and take up the argument about that act and that repeal, and do it thoroughly, going down to first principles.

We tend to think of "moral" choices as those that life forces upon us—quandaries, perplexities, choices among goods and evils that we cannot evade—and we also tend to think of such choices as concentrated in a moment or a short period of time. The lifeboat is sinking and someone must be thrown out into the sea, so shall I throw out Albert Einstein or my own grandmother? That is the stuff of ethical "cases" in academies. But in life the larger part of our choice making does not have that shape. There are also those latent possibilities lying all around us all the time if we bestir ourselves. Lincoln in 1854 bestirred himself.

Although he would say that he at first reentered full-whistle politics that year simply to aid in the reelection of anti-Nebraska congressman Richard Yates, the evidence suggests that he had more than that in mind from the start. He had to know—indeed, he must also have intended—that making the case for a congressman opposed to Douglas, and the case against that Douglas act, in Douglas's home state meant, eventually, taking on the great statesman himself.

Lincoln was "aroused" in 1854—and he spoke out. But he thought and he studied before he spoke out.

In the midst of his law cases he thought and studied more than he had done before. His mind, and his pen, cut deeper. If you compare the speech he will give in the fall, listed in collections as "Peoria," October 16, 1854, with an effort a short time earlier—a spectacularly undistinguished partisan speech he had given, in two sessions, to the Winfield Scott Club in Springfield on August 14 and 26, 1852—you will see that something has happened. This speaker has lifted himself to a new intellectual and moral level with the 1854 speech.

Hostile newspapers said, in that summer, that he was "mousing about the libraries in the State House" and "nosing for weeks in the State Library, pumping his brain and his imagination for points and arguments." Part of this nosing and mousing was directed toward the immediate political situation: He read the Senate speeches by Douglas on the one side; Chase, Sumner, Seward on the other; the *Congressional Globe;* the newspapers. Another part of it was directed toward history: He carefully worked out the detailed story of the Missouri Compromise, and the course of events up to the present, that he would set forth, in a skillful summary, in the first part of his speech in the fall. But still another part of his summer's study was moral, philosophical, and rhetorical: He was thinking his way to first principles, clarifying his thought about American slavery, and carefully composing the sentences, the paragraphs, the illustrations, to make his points persuasive to an audience of ordinary white Americans on the frontier.

2. FUGITIVES, THE LAW, AND THE PRINCIPLE

Why now? Why had Lincoln's deepened antislavery politics not come about, as it had for a great many others, in response to the Fugitive Slave Law of 1850? The harsh provisions of this new law set off a firestorm among opponents of slavery in the North and East. But Lincoln played no role in the opposition to the law—in fact, he favored it, at least as part of the Compromise of 1850. And, after declining to join *that* antislavery campaign, why then did he speak out so strongly in the next antislavery campaign, against the Kansas-Nebraska Act in 1854?

One might make the argument that whereas the Kansas-Nebraska Act would deal only with legal and jurisdictional technicalities in a remote region of sagebrush, dirt, Indians, and almost no slaves, the Fugitive Slave Law dealt with hundreds, perhaps thousands, of live human beings, fleeing and fighting, sometimes bravely, for their freedom and their lives. It meant the fictional Eliza fleeing across the ice of the Ohio River. It meant the quite real Negro named Mitchum captured in Madison, Indiana, torn from his wife and children and "delivered up" to a "master" who claimed to have owned him nineteen years earlier. It almost certainly meant the unscrupulous capture of free Negroes who never had been slaves. Just now, in May of 1854, as the Nebraska bill was being passed and Lincoln was thinking out what he would say, it meant a brutal display of federal force in Boston. The armed forces were called out by President Pierce to effect the forcible return to slavery of one Anthony Burns. Burns had escaped to Boston and, after being captured, had been rescued from the courthouse by militant defenders of freedom, led by Theodore Parker. Burns, in shackles, and escorted by police, marshals, and eleven hundred soldiers, was marched through the streets of Boston to the ship that would return him to slavery, through the immense protesting crowds and signs ("The Funeral of Liberty") and flags flown upside down.

Thousands of Americans would be "aroused" "as never before" and "thunderstruck" by events like that, by that earlier act. Among them was the daughter of a leading clergyman, the wife of an Old Testament professor, who, reading the terrible stories about the recapture of slaves who had escaped to freedom, found coming into her mind and pen, as from the hand of God, a powerful story of slaves and their masters. She published it first in a series in an abolitionist journal, and then in January 1852 as a book called *Uncle Tom's Cabin*. It promptly became a publishing sensation that nothing else in American history has matched.

But none of that thunder struck Abraham Lincoln out in Springfield. Lincoln never mentioned Anthony Burns; never referred to—perhaps did not read—*Uncle Tom's Cabin;* and not only never opposed a Fugitive Slave Law but continually and explicitly (although reluctantly) granted that the slaveholders had a right to have such a law. His first argument was that there was an explicit constitutional provision for it. It was part of the original bond that created the Union and therefore was a "constitutional right."

Closely related to his argument from the Constitution was Lincoln's argument from the sheer logic of the institutional reality. Slavery was a great wrong, but it was an already present, constitutionally protected institution built into the lives and fortunes of a whole society in the original states. Therefore, as one had (very reluctantly) to acquiesce in the institution itself within those original slave-state boundaries (even the first-wave abolitionists had to grant that), so one had—also, to be sure, reluctantly—to acquiesce in a law for the return of fugitives. It "springs of necessity from the fact that the institution is amongst us" is the way he would put it in a letter to Seward on February 1, 1861. If you are going to have slavery, you have to return fugitive slaves.

He granted that right and that necessity, in spite of his own personal emotional resistance to the return of the fugitives, and his empathy both with the fugitives themselves and with those who sympathized with them. He was reported to have said in his first encounter with Douglas in the fall, in Bloomington, on September 12, 1854, "I own, if I were called upon by a Marshal, to assist in catching a fugitive, I should suggest to him that others could run a great deal faster than I could." He would say in his major speech at the state fair that "the legal obligation to catch and return ... runaway slaves" was "degrading" to the people of the free states, and was "a sort of dirty, disagreeable job, which I believe, as a general rule, the slave holders will not perform for one another." But he would concede that "when they [our brethren of the South] remind us of their constitutional rights [legislation for reclaiming their fugitives] I acknowledge them, not grudgingly but fully and fairly."

Having acquiesced (as was politically unavoidable) in the Fugitive Slave Law, he would use his having done so for debater's points. In his speech in the fall he used it as ballast to reassure his conservative Whig followers that it would be acceptable that one's opinions coincide, on discriminate occasions, with those of the much-detested abolitionists: "Stand with anybody that stands RIGHT, stand with him while he is right and PART with him when he goes wrong. Stand WITH the abolitionist in restoring the Missouri Compromise; and stand AGAINST him when he attempts to repeal the fugitive slave law."

Lincoln would carry this politically realistic acquiescence to a Fugitive Slave Law—to look ahead—all the way up to his becoming president. The first item in his First Inaugural Address, to the disgust of Frederick Douglass, would be that he would enforce a Fugitive Slave Law as "cheerfully" as any other. He would then be addressing for the first time the entire national audience, and trying to persuade the South of the new administration's irenic intention. He would say that he regarded the fugitive slave provision—which he actually read in toto—as standing on the same footing as all the other provisions of the Constitution which he on that day would take an oath to uphold. (President-elect Buchanan, four years earlier, had said that he would, and we all should, "cheerfully" abide by the forthcoming decision about the constitutionality of the Missouri Compromise—the Dred Scott case. Lots of announced presidential cheerfulness where there was nothing to be cheerful about.)

Because he believed in abiding by the law and the Constitution as he understood it, because there were obligations under the original agreement among the states, because the current objectionable law was the result of a bargain in which each side got something, because therefore it was, however distasteful, his *duty*, Lincoln did not oppose *a* Fugitive Slave Law. As an emerging political leader and shaper of opinion in 1854–1860, and as President of a war-torn nation in 1861–1865, he would always oppose slavery strongly—but *within* the law, *under* the Constitution, *affirming* the continuing bond of the Union. He did not refer, as William

Seward had done in a somewhat uncharacteristic moment in the Senate debate over the Fugitive Slave Law in 1850, to a "Higher Law." Lincoln explicitly disavowed any connection with Seward's phrase if it meant such a "Law" trumped the Constitution and positive law of the United States. He did not—of course he did not—disengage from the Union: he did not say "no Union with slave holders." And he certainly did not pitch the Constitution overboard, or burn it, because it, in some sense, recognized (without naming it) slavery. He certainly did not call it, as William Lloyd Garrison would do, "a Covenant with death and an agreement with hell." On the contrary: his whole project of fundamental moral opposition to slavery took place *within* the claims of Constitution, Union, Law.

When in an unimaginable future day he would serve as president of the United States, and when he would issue the Emancipation Proclamation, he would do so scrupulously as commander in chief of the armed forces, under the war powers of the president in the Constitution. The reason that the Emancipation Proclamation, when it finally came, would resemble the work of a "pettifogging lawyer" (as Karl Marx, serving as a newspaper correspondent, would write with a sneer), and have "all the moral grandeur of a bill of lading" (as the twentieth-century historian Richard Hofstadter would state in more than one book), was exactly that it was a closely justified *legal* document. It was exactly and deliberately of the same class of document as a "bill of lading" written by a "pettifogging lawyer"—a scrupulously particular, carefully justified *legal* document. This would be a narrowly justified executive action taken by the commander in chief of the armed services of the United States under the power granted to him only in wartime, doing something he absolutely could not have done in peacetime, or merely on the basis of his own opinion.

And when American slavery would finally be ended, it would be done altogether within the Constitution and the law, by the Thirteenth Amendment to the Constitution, recommended to the Republican Convention of 1864 by President Lincoln, finally passed by the Thirty-eighth Congress under the urging and through the political maneuvering of President Lincoln, joyfully signed by President Lincoln after Congress passed it (although Presidents don't need to sign amendments), ratified by three-fourths of the states after he was dead, and thus made a part of the Constitution, ending slavery forever—*constitutionally* ended, under the law, with the Union intact.

. . .

And now back to our contrast between these two antislavery occasions in the 1850s. The Kansas-Nebraska Act of 1854 was, for Lincoln, a different story altogether than the Fugitive Slave Law had been. It did not "spring of necessity from the fact that the institution is amongst us." There was no constitutional requirement. There was no original agreement. There was no duty to support it. There was no Union-protecting bargain, no peace-promoting compromise. On the contrary, this act was accompanied by the most blatant abrogation of the historic Union-protecting, peace-promoting bargain, the Missouri Compromise. It did not protect the Union; it endangered it. It did not preserve the peace; it threatened it. The Kansas-Nebraska Act was a new, aggressive departure by the supporters of slavery, altering the balance of power between the sections, between slavery and freedom. It broke *new* ground—it would add a huge spread of country open to slavery and, worse still, would alter the principle upon which the nation was based.

The terrible moral anomaly of American slavery had pushed its way into American politics before, but none of the earlier occasions, in Lincoln's view, entailed the alteration of the moral premise of the nation. The Missouri Compromise had not done so—the premise was still, as it had been for the Founders, that slavery was a wrong tolerated only by necessity. The Compromise of 1850, including the new Fugitive Slave Law, had not done so; it was a quid pro quo assuming the ancient compromises. The Wilmot Proviso, back in 1849, certainly would not have done so, from Lincoln's point of view; by barring slavery from any territory acquired from Mexico it would have been an *advancement* of the nation's original antislavery principles. It was, one might say, an act on the *offense* by the antislavery forces. But now, with the Kansas-Nebraska Act, there was a huge effort on offense by the slavery forces, pitching the rest of the nation back into the position of defending its moral essence. So it was for Lincoln.

The opening of territory to slavery was important, but not in Lincoln's view the core of the matter. That core was the radical alteration in the nation's moral postulates. The new act—its "avowed principle"—gave to slavery, Lincoln would say, a new position in the body politic. It "assumes there can be moral right in the enslaving of one man by another." The United States of America had never assumed that before—never assumed that it was right, however much it may have been necessary. But now, according to Lincoln, this act would obliterate the principled rejection of slavery—make the nation morally neutral as between slavery and freedom.

That was the arousing, astounding, thunderstriking event that brought

Lincoln back into politics and lifted him to a new level of public moral argument.

But now we must add the essential other reason Lincoln the politician took the lead opposing the Kansas-Nebraska Act in 1854 and had not opposed the fugitive slave provisions in 1850: opinion in Illinois.

He would later, as we will see, describe the effort to oppose the Fugitive Slave Law in Illinois as "hopeless." Illinois citizens, he would say, would regard such opposition as opposition to the Constitution itself, because the Constitution explicitly made provision for fugitives to be "delivered up."

He was no longer, if he had ever been, really proposing to be the lonely last leader who said of himself in an oratorical spasm in 1839 that his "proudest plume" was not that he was the *last* to desert Liberty, but that he NEVER deserted her. On the contrary, he was an ambitious and calculating Illinois politician who could see that there was no hope whatever in opposing the fugitive slave provision in racially conservative Illinois. The complicated Compromise of 1850, of which that provision was a part, which was supposed by both parties to have put an end to all this agitation about slavery, was overwhelmingly approved. Douglas, who had been instrumental in passing the bills that made up that compromise, was celebrated in his home state for having done so.

The Kansas-Nebraska Act was a different story altogether, in Illinois and nationwide. One strong objection was exactly that it upset the delicate sectional balance that the Compromise of 1850 had worked out, and the supposed putting behind us of agitation, and the peace and "finality" that supposedly had been achieved. Douglas was not on this issue a hero in Illinois, but was widely attacked. This act was vastly unpopular in the North. This time Douglas may have overreached. There was a wave of protest which spread, this time, into Douglas's (and Lincoln's) home state. The great advantage of being thunderstruck in 1854 instead of 1850 was that this time many of your fellow citizens—voters—were thunderstruck along with you.

You can say that the ambitious Lincoln saw that the reaction against this act presented a political opportunity to defeat Douglas and the Democrats, and to win power for Whigs and perhaps for himself, that had not been there before. And that he, opportunistically, seized the opening.

Or you can say that this conscientious and worthy mainstream politician, a lifelong opponent of slavery, saw in this act a threat to the moral premises of the nation, and a chance to contain slavery and put it more firmly on the road to extinction. And that he rose to the occasion.

And you would be right both times.

3. NO MAN IS GOOD ENOUGH TO GOVERN ANOTHER MAN

Why had Douglas done it?

The clearest motive would be his lifelong desire to see the nation expand, to see the West developed, to see the nation roll on to her continental destiny. He was the powerful chairman of the Senate Committee on Territories, with the admission of many states and territories already to his credit, and he badly wanted now to organize the northern part of the Louisiana Purchase, the "Nebraska" territory, in the nation's heartland. And another of his passions was the railroad: Unless Nebraska were organized, the new transcontinental railroad, binding the country, linking gold-rush California to the East, could not be built across the country's middle, but would probably take a southern route instead.

In 1852 the Democrats had swept to a huge victory against the fading Whigs and thought they had the votes to do what they wanted to do. Douglas's opponents charged (infuriating Douglas) that his Nebraska bill and the repeal were a bid for Southern support for the presidency next time around.

But Douglas's efforts to get Nebraska organized kept foundering on the slavery issue: proslavery senators wanted no new *free* territories and states. So Douglas tried to get that roadblock out of the way by including in his bill a principle that had been around in Democratic circles since the election of 1848, when candidate Lewis Cass had put forward the proposal that Congress keep its hands off ("nonintervention") and let the people of the territory decide whether it would be free or slave. This was now given the much more appealing label "popular sovereignty."

In the last throes of the politics over the bill it was (to quote Lincoln) "so modified as to make two territories instead of one; calling the Southern one Kansas." Douglas's amended bill meant, according to Lincoln "substantially, that the People who go and settle there may establish slavery, or exclude it, as they may see fit."

But if the people in their sovereign will decided that Nebraska (or Kansas) should be *slave* territory, would not that violate the "sacred compact" that for more than thirty years had kept peace (more or less) between the sections, the famous and celebrated Missouri Compromise? That sacred compact held, in return for permitting slavery south of the line and admitting Missouri, which extended north of the line, as a slave state, that there would never be in the Louisiana Purchase any further slave states north of the line 36°30′. The Missouri Compromise of 1821 had come, with the passage of the years, to be regarded as a "sacred" peace-preserving compact between the sections. The huge Nebraska territory was part of the Louisiana Purchase, covered by the compromise.

Douglas tried to argue that the Missouri Compromise had *already* been implicitly abrogated by the recent Compromise of 1850, which admitted New Mexico (a piece above the line) and Utah by allowing them to choose by "popular sovereignty." (Can that have been? Could the 1850 compromisers, without anyone noticing, have taken the *huge* step abrogating the "sacred" Missouri pact?) In any case, "implicitly" was not good enough for a cadre of proslavery senators, who put enormous pressure on Douglas. And then one of them—a Southern Whig, in fact—made a motion that there be an *explicit* statement that the Missouri Compromise was repealed, if they were to vote for the admission of new territories in the North.

Reluctantly Douglas, to get his bill through, agreed—predicting with spectacular accuracy "a hell of a storm."

Nicolay and Hay would write, in 1886, that "the storm of agitation which this measure aroused dwarfed all former ones in depth and intensity." A leading scholar of the following century, David Potter, would write in 1976 that the debate over the Nebraska bill from January to May of 1854 was "perhaps to this day America's fiercest congressional battle ... a struggle of unprecedented intensity."

I believe we may say of Douglas that his whole concentration and his great energies were devoted to topics *other* than slavery. His attitude toward black people was sneering disdain; his attitude toward slavery was that it was a huge nuisance, an immense impediment to what he wanted to accomplish. And he thought, or pretended to think, that the slavery issue had been put away in 1850. And he thought he and his party had the strength to do what he thought needed to be done. So he agreed to the explicit repeal of the Missouri Compromise.

Because he needed the support of the Pierce administration on this particularly sensitive point, he consulted with President Pierce (on a Sunday, against Pierce's principles), and it may even be that Pierce himself drafted the wording of the clause repealing the Missouri Compromise. In the event, it did not in fact include the inflammatory word "repeal"; it said instead, in an anticipation of President Nixon's press secretary Ron Ziegler during Watergate, 119 years later, that the compromise was now "inoperative."

And then came the fireworks in the Senate and the House, the signing of the bill into law, the furor in the country—and the decision to oppose the act on the part of an ex-congressman out in Illinois.

There are many indications that Lincoln, getting ready to make his argument, read the Senate debates closely. Although the House would have its own intensities—including, toward the end, the presence of weapons and the threat of bloodshed—it was the Senate that took the prize for vituperative extravagance. There were talented champions in that department on both sides: Douglas, of course, supporting his bill, with various Southern senators and conservative Democrats joining him and urging him on; and Sumner of Massachusetts and Chase of Ohio on the other, anti-Nebraska, antislavery side.

In Douglas's first long speech, on January 30, as he was winding down, he set forth a passage that we may picture Lincoln, out in the Lincoln-Herndon law office perhaps, reading with his glasses, marking now with his pen. Douglas was scornfully claiming that the "Abolitionists"

> would allow territorial governments to legislate upon the rights of inheritance, to legislate in regard to religion, education, and morals, to legislate in regard to the relations of husband and wife, of parent and child, of guardian and ward, upon everything pertaining to the dearest rights and interests of white men, but they are not willing to trust them to legislate in regard to a few miserable negroes. [The disdainful "few miserable negroes" was typical of Douglas throughout.] That is their single exception. They acknowledge that the people of the territories are capable of deciding for themselves concerning white men, but not in relation to negroes. The real gist of the matter is this: Does it require any higher degree of civilization, and intelligence, and learning, and sagacity, to legislate for negroes than for white men?

Douglas claimed in this passage to have stripped the whole controversy down to its essence, and in a perverse way maybe he did.

So there is Lincoln with his glasses on his nose, sitting at the long table in the law office (I am imagining—he did read it somewhere), shaking his head at the appalling moral obtuseness of this typical Douglas passage, figuring out how to explain its wrongheadedness and moral confusion to an audience of ordinary Illinois farmers, merchants, and politicians. When he would write it out for his speeches in the fall, he would put it this way:

> Judge Douglas frequently and with bitter irony and sarcasm, paraphrases our argument by saying "The white people of Nebraska are good enough to govern themselves, but they are not good enough to govern a few miserable negroes!!!"
>
> Well I doubt not that the people of Nebraska are, and will continue to be as good as the average of people elsewhere. I do not say the contrary. What I do say is that no man is good enough to govern another man, without that other's consent. I say this is the leading principle—the sheet anchor of American republicanism.

The point that Douglas had obscured Lincoln quietly, implicitly restores: The Negro is a human being.

4. LINCOLN READS DOUGLAS'S OPPONENTS

Sumner and Chase, whose speeches in the Senate Abraham Lincoln would be reading now out in Springfield, were Douglas's most vociferous opponents. They were men whom Lincoln would one day come to know well. They were unusually able, articulate, and intelligent men, and Sumner was one of the more learned men ever to serve in the Senate (as he was willing at any moment to demonstrate). We have already seen Sumner giving a thrilling speech to the Free-Soil gathering in Worcester.

And both Sumner and Chase, Douglas's sneers notwithstanding, were honorable men. They had taken initiatives for racial justice far ahead of most of their contemporaries, including Lincoln himself. Sumner as a lawyer had argued in a famous case in Massachusetts (the "Roberts" case, which he took without a fee) that the psychological and sociological effects made racially segregated schools inherently unequal, anticipating by more than a century the United States Supreme Court's decision in the school segregation cases in 1954. Chase had defended so many escaped slaves as to be given the informal title of "attorney for the runaways." And in the present case once again they did have (as they would relentlessly insist) Right on their side.

But although they certainly had their faces toward Zion, neither of them (perhaps Lincoln out in Springfield felt) showed much awareness that being "right" is not the only consideration in a complicated political situation. Neither of them displayed an iota of self-criticism, or much sympathetic understanding of their adversaries, or many scruples as to method, or the faintest glimmer of humor. " 'Did you ever see a joke in one of my speeches?' " [Sumner] sternly asked a young friend. 'No sir, I think I never did,' was the unhesitating reply. 'Of course you never did,' returned Sumner triumphantly. 'You might as well look for a joke in the book of Revelations.' "

Learning at the start of 1854 that Douglas had prepared another bill for the admission of the giant Nebraska territory, Sumner and Chase wrote out, in collaboration with four Free-Soil House members (one of them Joshua Giddings), a ferocious "appeal" whose subtitle told its subject: "Shall Slavery be Permitted in Nebraska?"

The Sumner-Chase appeal called the Douglas bill "a gross violation of a sacred pledge . . . a criminal betrayal of precious rights . . . an atrocious plot to convert [this territory] into a dreary region of despotism, inhabited by masters and slaves."

If we read through this vibrating, angry, accusatory, hortatory document, and we think of Abraham Lincoln poring over it out in Springfield, we are inclined to two conclusions: that he would have been stirred by, and in agreement with, much of its argument; but that he would have found uncongenial the tone of peremptory moral certitude in which it was couched. He had spoken that way when as a brash new congressman he attacked President Polk, but he was not going to present his arguments that way from now on. Lincoln would himself make many of the points the document made, in his clear, careful way, when his time came. But he would not join in the posture of disdainful moral superiority with which the document was suffused. It ended: "We will not despair, for the cause of human freedom"—in context meaning opposing the Nebraska bill—"is the cause of God."

Lincoln, when he would speak eight months later, would also use some strong negative adjectives and nouns to describe slavery and to describe the repeal of the Missouri Compromise. But he would do so with selectivity and restraint, and carefully in context. Lincoln's presentations would convey different relationships to the evil with which they were all involved. One can picture Lincoln reading this appeal, agreeing with much of it, even having his own conviction sharpened by it, and yet at the same time resolving that any speech he would give on the subject would differ in its posture, voice, and tone—indeed, in its implied underlying social-moral philosophy.

Douglas met the lofty righteousness of Sumner and Chase with a snarling, bullying contempt, much of it personal.

There was one other distinguished senatorial voice on the anti-Nebraska side, this one coming from the Whig side of the aisle in the sixty-two-member Senate chamber in the Capitol.* This voice was that of the leading Whig, former governor, now senator, William Seward of New York. He had not signed the appeal, and he waited until February 17 until he spoke. He claimed he did not make long speeches, but spoke—such was the atmosphere of the Senate—for almost three hours, making a particularly strong argument against Douglas's effort to claim that the Compromise of 1850 had already (without anyone noticing) "superseded" the Missouri Compromise. His speech also included a portentous picture of the emerging discord that anticipated both his own later reference to an irrepressible conflict and the opening passage, about a house divided, in a speech made by the Republican candidate for the Senate in Illinois in 1858.

We know that Lincoln read this speech by Seward. William Herndon wrote to Seward specifically to say that his law partner thought it was a splendid speech. Lincoln had once met Seward, when they had both been speaking in behalf of Zachary Taylor and the Whigs and against defections to the Free-Soil Party, in Boston in the fall of 1848. They had then heard each other's speeches, and shared a hotel room that night, and talked about opposing slavery. Lincoln is sometimes said to have ratcheted up his antislavery politics as a result of that encounter with Seward. Now, six years later, the ex-congressman from Illinois, whom Seward remembered only slightly as a pleasant enough fellow, sends him by way of his law partner congratulations on his splendid speech.

5. A SELF-EVIDENT LIE?

So Lincoln was reading along in the transcript of the Senate debates when he must have come across a colloquy on a topic that would soon

---

* Sumner and Chase, because of the deals between Free-Soil members and Democrats made in the state legislatures that chose them, were both seated on the Democratic side. Douglas would make scathing references to the way they had been chosen.

become overwhelmingly important to his own argument: the Declaration of Independence.

Up to this point in his life he had only rarely referred to the Declaration, and then mostly as an historical document rather than a current moral norm. In his Lyceum Address in 1838 he had made a parallel between the devotion the patriots of '76 had pledged to the Declaration and the devotion we now should pledge to the Constitution and the laws. He had begun his eulogy to Henry Clay in 1852 with a reference to "the people of a few feeble oppressed colonies of Great Britain, inhabiting a portion of the Atlantic coast," who had, on July 4, 1776, declared their independence—in other words, he had again referred to the Declaration in its historical context and function. Later in the eulogy, though, he condemned John C. Calhoun and some governors of South Carolina and a Virginia clergyman whom he quoted from a newspaper for their dismissive mockery of the Declaration's claim that all men are created equal, and said that "this sounds strangely in republican America." He was making the transition, by way of condemning those who denied its application, from treating the Declaration only in its historical context to using it as a moral norm for today—the same transition a considerable part of American public opinion was making.

Now he read in the Senate debates on the Nebraska bill an exchange between Benjamin Franklin Wade, the fiery colleague of Chase from Ohio (and eventually a leading radical Republican during the war), and a particularly strident Northern defender of the bill, Senator John Pettit of Indiana. Wade would make many of the points about the fundamental moral significance of the Declaration that, before the year was out, the Illinois Whig himself would be making. Wade would deplore, as Lincoln would, the deprecation of the Declaration by Nebraska bill supporters:

> Mr. President, the advocates of this bill in order to sustain it in principle, have rightly judged that the Declaration of Independence must also be superseded and rendered inoperative [Wade picks up that word from the bill itself]. I had supposed that the great principles touching upon the rights of human nature set forth in that immortal instrument, were universally acknowledged in this country. Judge my surprise when I heard them assailed, denounced, and repudiated, in the Senate of the United States as self-evident falsehoods. . . . The great declaration cost our forefathers too dear thus lightly to be thrown away by their children.

Pettit was the chief among those who would throw it away, and the one who had claimed, and kept on claiming, that the Declaration's statement that all men are created equal was false. We may picture Lincoln reading these exchanges, raising his eyebrows and reaching for his pencil. In his speech in the fall he would use that remark by Pettit to illustrate how far the nation has fallen when it adopts the Kansas-Nebraska Act and the repeal: "Nearly eighty years ago," he will say, "we began by declaring that all men are created equal, but now . . . we have run down to the other declaration, that for SOME men to enslave others is a 'sacred right of self-government.' These principles can not stand together. They are as opposite as God and Mammon, and whoever holds to the one, must despise the other. When Pettit, in connection with his support of the Nebraska bill, called the Declaration of Independence a 'self-evident lie,' he only did what consistency and candor require all other Nebraska men to do." Lincoln, reading the record in the Senate and the surrounding debate, found no exceptions: Defense of the Nebraska Act destroys the Spirit of '76. "Of forty odd Nebraska Senators who sat present and heard him [Pettit], no one rebuked him. Nor am I apprised that any Nebraska newspaper, in the whole nation, or any Nebraska orator, has ever yet rebuked him." If you support the Kansas-Nebraska Act, then you must agree that the egalitarianism of the Declaration is a "self-evident lie."

6. LINCOLN'S RISE

On August 9 Lincoln reentered active politics. He met Congressman Richard Yates on his return from Washington at the railroad station in Yates's hometown, Jacksonville, and urged him to announce his candidacy for reelection. Yates, who held the congressional seat Lincoln himself had once held, was a Whig colleague, now strongly anti-Nebraska, who would become one of the famous Republican war governors during the Civil War. Yates did run for reelection, with Lincoln's assistance all the way up to Election Day in November. Lincoln advised him to correct the impression that he was sympathetic to the Know-Nothings, defended him against the charge that he drank too much, joined him in joint debates, filled in for him in speaking engagements.

On September 4 the *Illinois Journal* announced, as part of the anti-Nebraska effort, that Lincoln himself was a candidate for his old post as a representative from Sangamon in the *state* general assembly—a candidacy that would later prove to be an embarrassment when Lincoln's sights would be set higher.

But meanwhile the statewide debate was being transformed by the return, in late August, to his home state of Mr. Kansas-Nebraska himself, Senator Stephen A. Douglas. Douglas faced immense and unaccustomed hostility in Chicago and northern Illinois; he was shouted down, finally, by an angry crowd after a two-hour effort to speak in Chicago on September 1. He campaigned defiantly for Democratic candidates and for his cause, first in strong "anti-Nebraska" centers in the northern part of the state. Then, on September 26, he came down to Bloomington to speak to a Democratic meeting—and the aroused, thunderstruck, and well-prepared Abraham Lincoln was there.

Lincoln proposed to the senator in Bloomington that they have a joint debate, but Douglas refused. Why should Douglas do that? So Lincoln joined Douglas's audience in the afternoon. Some in the crowd called for Lincoln to respond. He said he would not do so then, but would speak in the evening, and did, by candlelight—the first in a remarkable sequence of exchanges between these two men, almost entirely now on the subject of the expansion of American slavery.

Let us pause to say that the direct and persistent challenging of Douglas was an act of considerable moral courage on Lincoln's part. It is hard for us to recapture, now that it is Lincoln and not Douglas who is the Giant, what an act of intellectual self-confidence and risk-taking that was on the part of a mere private citizen and sometime local politician.

What was Lincoln, after all, compared to Douglas? Senator Douglas was one of the most powerful and famous men in the land, clearly of a stature larger than the president of the United States. Douglas himself had almost been nominated for president by the Democrats in 1852, at age thirty-nine, instead of the rather mediocre dark horse who finally had been nominated, and then elected, Franklin Pierce. There was little doubt that Douglas would one day soon be a nominee again. Meanwhile he was by all odds the leading politician in the dominant political party, the powerful chairman of the Senate committee on the territories, and the central figure in the making of policy on that immensely significant topic, and a major player across the board. He already had a list of major national accomplishments: a role second only to that of Lincoln's hero Henry Clay in achieving the complex series of acts called the Compromise of 1850; as chairman first of the House and now of the Senate Committee on Territories, and as a vigorous expansionist, a long string of states and territories he had shepherded into existence; and a major role in the legislation that built what Lincoln long ago had called the "rail roads." Douglas was the chief political sponsor of the Illinois Central Railroad, which was exactly the kind of "internal improvement" that Lincoln had entered politics to foster and had fought for when he was in the state legislature promoting "the system."

Douglas had subdued this Democratic president, Franklin Pierce, to his will, and would break sharply with the next one, James Buchanan. He now bestrode the narrow world like a colossus. And what, by comparison, was Abraham Lincoln? Approximately nothing. A one-term former congressman, now a private citizen.

Moreover, Douglas was no mild and polite opponent. He was a practiced, powerful debater, full of energy, articulate, sarcastic, scathing, formidable. From his years at the center of national policy he was full of information that no novice in the provinces could begin to match, and he could call it up in memory at will. All who watched politics had just seen him in February and March scorch and smash and skewer the distinguished national figures Chase, Sumner, and Seward, leaving them—in the view at least of his partisans—gasping, vanquished, and silenced. An historian who admired him, George Fort Milton, summarized the personal side of Douglas's triumph on the night of March 3–4 as follows: "[H]e had taken the measure of each of his three chief critics. He had forced Seward to admit that his whole contention was based upon a 'misapprehension,' Chase had been reduced to contemptible apology, Sumner's egotism had been pierced, his complacency shattered, his record exposed, and he sat stunned and speechless in his seat." If that is what this man could do to his opponents of the highest rank in the nation's capital, what might he do to some merely local adversary out in Springfield?

Even an historian of a later time who was not an admirer of Douglas, Allan Nevins, would write—choosing a most pertinent figure of speech— that Douglas "was doubtless the most formidable legislative pugilist in all our history." Not every amateur from the sweaty gyms of the state legislature would have the courage to enter the ring with this consummate heavyweight professional at the top of his game. Not every prairie lawyer, nor every one-term long-ago congressman, would have the nerve—the intellectual self-confidence—to step forward to challenge this man, and to persist in challenging him in debate after debate after debate.

And why should Lincoln do it? He had, after all, a good life now. He had made an enormous stride. He had risen from uneducated poverty and obscurity to a respectable middle-class life, had married into the Kentucky aristocracy, had a wife and three lively sons, had a growing and successful law practice and the respect of his neighbors. By his own admission he had let politics slide while he attended to his profession. Since his return from Congress he had spent more than four years absorbed in his law practice. So why now put himself forward? Why tangle with the immensely formidable Douglas, who had just mopped the Senate floor with some of the most distinguished of national leaders? Why?

One reason, surely, was his "thirst for distinction," his desire that his name be known, that he be "truly esteemed of his fellow men," by rendering himself "worthy of their esteem." Here was his chance. A related reason, surely, was that this time his longtime rival Stephen Douglas might be vulnerable. And Lincoln, after all, knew Douglas pretty well. He had been debating him one way or another since 1838. There may have been an element of personal rivalry as well as opportunism in what he did. But the depth and range and daring of his intervention went beyond anything that could be explained entirely by those motives.

I say that because of the extraordinary intellectual effort, and the reaching for first principles, that went into his three-hour autumn speech. Lincoln went well beyond anything needed to serve these immediate purposes. And the notes he wrote indicate fundamental moral thinking not required by narrow objectives. I suggest it is significant that he completely dropped all of the old Whig topics (the bank, internal improvements, the tariff) and paid no heed to the other whirling controversies of the moment (nativism, Mormon polygamy, temperance), some of which might have helped to promote the Whigs' prospects or his own or to damage Douglas and the Democrats. He would take up no other matters—not in the fall of 1854, and not for the next six years. He concentrated only on slavery. That suggests that he had, melding with his personal ambition, an overriding purpose of great intensity. I suggest that in addition to whatever there was of these lesser purposes he was stepping forward by his own initiative to join in the great argument about his country's future.

The most important of these 1854 encounters, and a major moment in Lincoln's life, would come on October 3 and 4 at the time of the Illinois State Fair in Springfield.

This manifestation of that great institution the midwestern state fair brought together not only the usual prize cows and prize pigs and prize jams and prize jellies and farmers and city dwellers, but also, as we might say, the usual prize politicians—the civic leaders of the state, happy to find a ready-made statewide audience. The state's outstanding senior senator, fresh from his triumph (if you thought it was a triumph) in Washington, had long been advertised as a major speaker on the first day of the fair. A bevy of anti-Nebraska leaders also was to be on hand. Douglas's presentation was supposed to have taken place outdoors in a grove, but it rained. The speech had to be moved into the Hall of Representatives in the State Capitol, with many hundreds turned away. At the end of Douglas's characteristically fiery presentation Lincoln, who had wedged in to hear him, announced that on the next day in the same place either Lyman Trumbull or he himself would respond to Douglas. The next morning handbills were scattered around the fairgrounds and the city announcing that at two o'clock Lincoln would speak in the hall. He had asked Douglas to be present and to reply, and Douglas was and did.

And so at two o'clock on the afternoon of October 4, 1854, Lincoln took the podium in the Hall of Representatives in the State Capitol in Springfield, with Senator Stephen Douglas sitting in front of him in a crowded room. With the memory of those Senate debates ringing in his ears, and a carefully written manuscript in his hand, Abraham Lincoln delivered the first great speech of his life.

CHAPTER TEN

I Shall Try to Show
That It Is Wrong

1. MONSTROUS INJUSTICE

Lincoln began carefully. He announced his topic—the repeal of the Missouri Compromise, and the propriety of its restoration—and then he gave some judicious introductory assurances. "I do not propose to question the patriotism, or to assail the motives of any man or class of men," he said, "but rather to confine myself to the naked merits of the question." On Lincoln's first response to Douglas back in Bloomington on September 24, the *Register* had noted, with a touch of surprise, that "Mr. Lincoln spoke of Judge Douglas in a less denunciatory manner than is the custom on such occasions"; and so it would be again here in Springfield. He certainly spoke in a "less denunciatory manner" than those speeches in the Senate. His speech would have neither the lofty presumption of superior righteousness of Sumner and Chase nor the snarling disdain and intellectual bullying of Douglas himself.

Lincoln, still getting started, was particularly careful to make another introductory limitation of his purpose, understandable under the political circumstances. He said: "I wish to make and to keep the distinction between the existing institution and the extension of it, so broad, and so clear, that no honest man can misunderstand me, and no dishonest one, successfully misrepresent me." He made the distinction, of course, because he did not want it concluded that he was proposing overthrowing slavery in the original slave states—an impossibly radical proposal. But, still, the *reasons* he opposed the *extension* of the existing institution all challenged its essence.

Lincoln started with the diligent history of the events surrounding slavery in the early Republic and of the Missouri Compromise that he had worked up in the library. He then illustrated the "high estimate" that had been placed on the Missouri Compromise with a quotation from Senator Douglas himself, and as recently as 1849. "Our distinguished Senator" had said that the compromise had been "canonized in the hearts of the American people" and was "a sacred thing which no ruthless hand would ever be reckless enough to disturb." Lincoln read a whole paragraph of Douglas's praise for the compromise, but he did not then milk it for all it was worth, as a vulgar political debater might have done. He did not say that now Douglas *himself* was the "ruthless hand" "reckless enough to disturb" this "sacred thing." Lincoln said instead that he did not read this extract "to involve Judge Douglas in an inconsistency. If he afterwards thought he had been wrong, it was right for him to change. I bring this forward merely to show the high estimate placed on the Missouri Compromise . . ." Of course, he had already read the whole paragraph of Douglas's praise for the compromise, and he himself introduced the category of "inconsistency" even as he disavowed charging it against Douglas.

He then described the Wilmot Proviso and the Compromise of 1850 and the events leading up to the repeal itself. Completing his succinct historical summary, he said: We now have before us "the chief material enabling us to correctly judge whether the repeal of the Missouri Compromise is right or wrong."

And so was it right or wrong? Having prepared the way slowly, painstakingly, he now drew back and fired all his guns with the first great paragraph, as we might put it, in his first great speech:

I think, and shall try to show, that it [that repeal] is wrong; wrong in its direct effect, letting slavery into Kansas and Nebraska—and wrong in its prospective principle, allowing it to spread to every other part of the wide world, where men can be found inclined to take it.

The repeal was, for Lincoln, far more than a change in policy with respect to a swatch of western territory; it was a change of *principle* for the nation as a whole, with respect to the institution of slavery. And the change of principle was morally objectionable, as Lincoln now stated unequivocally, in a succinct series of reasons:

This declared indifference, but as I must think, covert real zeal for the spread of slavery, I can not but hate. I hate it because of the monstrous injustice of slavery itself. I hate it because it deprives our republican example of its just influence in the world—enables the enemies of free institutions, with plausibility, to taunt us as hypocrites—causes the real friends of freedom to doubt our sincerity, and especially because it forces so many really good men amongst ourselves into an open war with the very fundamental principles of civil liberty—criticizing the Declaration of Independence, and insisting that there is no right principle of action but self-interest.

Repeal means "the spread of slavery." Slavery is a "monstrous injustice" that he "hates." In the "Protest" in the state legislature when he was twenty-eight, it was an "injustice"; now he says a "monstrous injustice." Not a mild word. Monstrous injustices, the distinction between the existing institution and its extension notwithstanding, are by definition to be resisted, opposed, and, when possible, eliminated.

Lincoln's first announced "hatred" is directed toward the "declared indifference" that masks, he claims, a "covert real zeal for the spread of slavery." That clause has been held to be the anticipatory nugget, the earnest, of his later "conspiracy" theme. But "conspiracy" would not be his word, or exactly his indictment. Instead it would be, as here: that there was indeed, in a powerful segment of the American nation, a "real zeal for the spread of slavery" (can anyone doubt that?), and that Douglas's indifference served as its implicitly collaborating preparation.

And then Lincoln does here for the first time what he will keep on doing from then on: he links the principle here implied about slavery to the moral meaning of America in the history of the world. If we not only have slavery as a fact in our free country but look with equanimity to its spread, and regard the spreading of slavery as the moral equivalent of the spread of freedom, then the republican movement around the world has reason to doubt us and the enemies of freedom have reason to laugh at our pretensions.

And then look at what happens at home: It undercuts our own moral self-understanding. "Good men" are forced to deny the nation's moral and egalitarian premises, and to found their politics on self-interest alone. I believe it should be underscored that in this key paragraph Lincoln points to a distorted political ethic as one abhorrent result of the Kansas-Nebraska Act's indifference to slavery: in order to defend it, men must twist their understanding of basic political principles—denying civil liberty and repudiating the egalitarianism of the Declaration of Independence. And they are led to adopt the cynical view that says there is nothing in politics but self-interest.

Lincoln specifically rejects (by a kind of billiard shot, if you will) the cynicism described by that last phrase. Like most politicians he had a healthy awareness of human selfishness, especially in collective life; but such an awareness is not the same as a systematic reduction of all action to that one motive. Although one can cite various references in Lincoln to selfishness and self-interest, Lincoln is actually more notable for his references to a natural sympathy, and a natural sense of justice in humankind. One of the objectionable results of the outlook underlying the Nebraska Act, he said, is its encouragement of a cynicism that warps and tries to deny that sense of justice.

2. JUST WHAT WE WOULD BE IN THEIR SITUATION

Immediately after this first great paragraph of moral testimony he did something that most opponents of slavery were not then doing: he went out of his way carefully and explicitly to assert that he had "no prejudice against the Southern people." This is the passage we noticed earlier in discussing his youthful Temperance Address. In a key assertion for his whole outlook he said, "They [the Southern people] are just what we would be in their situation. If slavery did not now exist amongst them, they would not introduce it. If it did now exist amongst us, we should not instantly give it up." He granted that this was *not* true of everybody. Doubtless there are individuals, he said, on both sides, who would not hold slaves under any circumstances; and others who would gladly introduce slavery anew, if it were out of existence. We know that some Southern men do free their slaves, go north, and become "tip-top abolitionists," while some northern ones go south and become most cruel slave masters. *But*—what he had said earlier was true of the masses, North and South. He put this giant evil in its huge social and institutional context, with realism about how large numbers of persons, in whatever geographical place, will respond to existing realities and proposed mammoth changes. These are bedrock Lincolnian principles: They are as we would be; we are as responsible as they.

Lincoln candidly said what not every Northern antislavery orator would say: "When Southern people tell us they are no more responsible for the origin of slavery than we, I acknowledge the fact." He frankly acknowledged the difficulty of overcoming a huge, deeply planted institutionalized evil. Moralizers—many abolitionists—often were glib. Not

Lincoln. He acknowledged not only shared responsibility, but shared bafflement. He continued: "When it is said that the institution exists; and that
it is very difficult to get rid of it, in any satisfactory way, I can understand
and appreciate the saying." Now Lincoln underlines his disinclination to
assess blame: "I surely will not blame them [the Southern people] for not
doing what I should not know how to do myself." Then he went overboard
in his assertion of his own bafflement: "If all earthly power were given me,
I should not know what to do, as to the existing situation." He followed
with one of the repugnant passages about what to do about "them" (slaves
and ex-slaves) that are embarrassing to his later admirers—an example of
the several instances in which Lincoln acquiesced in the racial prejudice
by which he was surrounded. But—as we shall suggest later when considering the argument over race—this and other such passages have some
mitigating elements in context. In this setting this passage is part of an
effort to understand, and to show he understands, the complexities of the
situation. It includes the assertion, in reference to white racial prejudice:
"A Universal feeling, whether well or ill-founded, cannot be safely disregarded." That does not mean one must endorse it. And he does, significantly, say "whether well or ill-founded," implying that it *might* be
ill-founded. Remember that he is talking to a deeply prejudiced white
audience, in an environment in which racial stereotypes are part of the
common culture.

His primary point in these passages is to indicate his understanding of
complexities. "It does seem to me," he concludes his paragraph of concessions and admissions to the South, "that systems of gradual emancipation
might be adopted; but for their tardiness in this, I will not undertake to
judge our brethren of the South." He does, however, call it "tardiness."

3. "SACRED" SELF-GOVERNMENT?

Lincoln spent the last half of his speech at state fair time in Springfield
answering one-two-three the arguments of those who defended repeal
(e.g., Stephen Douglas, sitting there in the audience). Nebraska could have
had territorial government without repeal—Minnesota and Iowa did. The
public never demanded repeal—where is any proof that they did? Nothing
in the history of the various recent contests—the Wilmot Proviso, the
admission of Utah and New Mexico—showed that the Missouri Compromise had been "superseded." Lincoln was presenting his version of
arguments on these points that Seward, Sumner, Chase had given in the
Senate.

. . .

But then with his response to the final argument for repeal he lifted the debate again to his distinctive level: This argument was that the repeal, with its avowed principle, is "intrinsically right." "I insist," Lincoln said, "that it is not."

The core of their claim of rightness is "the sacred right of self-government." Lincoln had already made a satirical theme out of that constant insistence on various sacrednesses. In his generally rather objective presentation of the history at the start of the speech, he rather abruptly veered into a satirical passage about the sudden discovery of a new sacredness that disallowed the exclusion of slavery from the territories. "In the pure fresh, free air of the revolution," he said, Jefferson's policy—the Founders' policy—of excluding slavery from the territories was put in place. "[T]hrough sixty-odd of the best years of the republic did that policy steadily work to its great and beneficent end." Then he broke into a satirical voice—you may even say sarcastic voice—that you may not associate with Abraham Lincoln. Here is Lincoln the satirist mocking the *new* and *sudden* discovery that, after all, *sacred* rights now disallow any such restrictions on slavery as the Founders had made:

> But *now* [after sixty-odd of the best years of the Republic] new light breaks upon us. Now congress declares this ought never to have been; and the like of it, must never be again. The sacred right of self government is grossly violated by it! We even find some men, who drew their first breath, and every other breath of their lives, under this very restriction, now live in dread of absolute suffocation, if they should be restricted in the "sacred right" of taking slaves to Nebraska. That *perfect* liberty they sigh for—the liberty of making slaves of other people—Jefferson never thought of; their own fathers never thought of; they never thought of themselves, a year ago. How fortunate for them, they did not sooner become sensible of their great misery! Oh, how difficult it is to treat with respect, such assaults upon all we have ever really held sacred.

Lincoln here in the last sentence is using the much overworked word "sacred" straightforwardly, in his own right, to contrast to all these sudden claims of sacredness that he satirizes. The use of that word to, in effect, defend slavery regularly pushed a button in Lincoln's mockery machine.

The most significant argument in the last part of his speech dealt with Douglas's so-called popular sovereignty, to which Lincoln regularly refers, with surely a little flavoring of satire, as we saw above, as "the sacred right of self government." And he is emphatically satirical about the "sacred" right to own slaves and take them as "property" anywhere you want to.

In a late part of the speech he would argue that the principle of the Kansas-Nebraska Act would justify revival of the slave trade. And he would reject the pro-Nebraska argument that taking slaves to the territory made no new slaves. His "sacredness" satirizing button has been pushed again.

> [I]f it is a sacred right for the people of Nebraska to take and hold slaves there, it is equally their sacred right to buy them where they can buy them cheapest; and that undoubtedly will be on the coast of Africa; provided you will consent to not hang them for going there to buy them. You must remove this restriction too, from the sacred right of self-government. I am aware that you say that taking slaves from the States to Nebraska does not make slaves of freemen; but the African slave-trader can say just as much. He does not catch free negroes and bring them here. He finds them already slaves in the hands of their black captors, and he honestly buys them at the rate of about a red cotton handkerchief a head. This is very cheap, and it is a great abridgement of the sacred right of self-government to hang men for engaging in this profitable trade!

Still later in his speech Lincoln would make an ingenious use of the point, regularly argued in antislavery circles, against the unfairness of the notorious three-fifths clause in the Constitution. In later centuries that clause would be slightly misunderstood, as being primarily a demeaning of black persons as worth only three-fifths of a white person. But the entire situation of slavery was utterly demeaning to black persons; the importance of that clause was that it enhanced the power of their white oppressors. That fraction was the portion of a state's slave population that was to be counted in assigning House seats to the state. Slaves would have been less badly served, therefore, if the number had been zero, and the slave state masters would have preferred—did indeed argue for—one to one, slaves to count every bit as much as white persons: a perverse "equality," if you will, because that would increase their own power by giving them more House seats, and more electoral votes for president.

"[I]n the control of the government—the management of partnership affairs—they [the slave states] greatly have the advantage of us," Lincoln would say. He then illustrated the point, as was often done in antislavery circles, by particular states and particular numbers: Maine and South Carolina have exactly the same number of senators (of course), of House members (because of the three-fifths clause), and of electoral votes in choosing a president (senators plus House members). Equal power. But Maine has more than twice as many white citizens as South Carolina; the "equality" is brought about by adding three-fifths of South Carolina's slave population. "The slaves do not vote; they are only counted and so used, as to swell the influence of white people's vote," said Lincoln. Equal power for the state with fewer than half the voters means that "each white man in South Carolina is more than the double of any man in Maine." And something approaching that doubleness runs all the way through the power relationship of slave states to free states. Lincoln brought the point home to his audience in Springfield: "[The South Carolinian] is more than double of any one of us in this crowd." As was often done in this antislavery attack on the three-fifths clause, Lincoln made or accepted a calculation of how many "extra" votes the clause gave to the slave states—and he gave it a quite recent and relevant application: "This principle, in the aggregate, gives the slave States, in the present congress, twenty additional representatives—being seven more than the whole majority by which they passed the Nebraska bill."

But what Lincoln is doing is not exactly what other antislavery protesters would do with this unfairness: to rail against it and to propose radical change to get rid of it. For example, in 1843 Charles Francis Adams had drafted, and the Massachusetts legislature had passed, and Charles Francis's father, John Quincy Adams, had introduced on the floor of Congress, a resolution proposing that the Constitution be amended to eliminate the three-fifths clause. But, of course, the fault that the amendment was directed against itself guaranteed that the amendment could not begin to be enacted.

Lincoln was not blowing against the wind in that way. What he did, rather, was, while taking for granted both the continued existence of the clause and its unfairness, to *apply it to the current debate.* The enhancing of slave-state power by the three-fifths clause is "manifestly unfair," he said, but it is already settled, and in the Constitution, and he did not propose to try to alter the Constitution. "I stand to it," he said alliteratively, "fairly, fully, and firmly."

But—here comes the current application—when it is proposed to add *new* territory, which might be free but also might be slave territory, in the second case threatening on the attainment of statehood to diminish still further his own citizenship (as that of all free state citizens), and when he is told that this possible dilution of his own comparative power is none of his business, he should leave it altogether to the people in the territories to decide whether to be slave or free, which means whether he shall or shall not be degraded further—then he does object.

> When I am told that I must leave it altogether to OTHER PEOPLE to say whether new partners are to be bred up and brought into the firm, on the same degrading terms against me, I respectfully demur. I insist, that whether I shall be a whole man, or only the half of one, in comparison with others, is a question in which I am somewhat concerned, and one which no other man can have a sacred right of deciding for me.

Lincoln's "sacredness" satire button has been pushed again. He now composed sentences in which the satirical touches mounted as he continued to the end of the paragraph:

> If I am wrong in this—if it really be a sacred right of self-government, in the man who shall go to Nebraska, to decide whether he will be the EQUAL of me or the DOUBLE of me, then after he shall have exercised that right, and thereby shall have reduced me to a still smaller fraction of a man than I already am, I should like for some gentleman deeply skilled in the mysteries of sacred rights, to provide himself with a microscope and peep about, and find out, if he can what has become of my sacred rights! They will surely be too small for detection with the naked eye.

What Lincoln is doing in this argument is showing the heavy importance of the Nebraska bill in the struggle over the relative power of the free and of the slave states, and their respective citizens, and therefore of the future of the nation.* And he insists that that question should not be left to the handful of settlers of a frontier state. Notice in this strong paragraph, concluding this argument, that he once again condemns acting only on self-interest.

---

* In 1861 the United States had been living under the Constitution for seventy-two years. During forty-nine of those years—or two-thirds of the time—the president had been a Southerner and a slaveholder. In Congress, twenty-three out of the thirty-six Speakers of

Finally, I insist, that if there is ANY THING which it is the duty of the WHOLE PEOPLE to never entrust to any hands but their own, that thing is the preservation and perpetuity, of their own liberties, and institutions. And if they shall think, as I do, that the extension of slavery endangers them, more than any, or all other causes, how recreant to themselves, if they submit the question, and with it, the fate of their country, to a mere hand-full of men, bent only on temporary self-interest. If this question of slavery extension were an insignificant one—one having no power to do harm—it might be shuffled aside in this way. But being, as it is, the great Behemoth of danger, shall the strong gripe of the nation be loosened upon him, to entrust him to the hands of such feeble keepers?

And how does he then end this whole long, key "self-government" section? With another little satirical reference to its alleged sacredness: "I have done with this mighty argument, of self-government. Go, sacred thing! Go in peace."

When he started out on that last point of his speech, that allegedly sacred right of self-government, Lincoln, the reader of the Senate debates, noted that there had been a certain diffidence about challenging Douglas on that particular republican-sounding theme. "It seems our distinguished Senator has found great difficulty in getting his antagonists, even in the Senate, to meet him fairly in argument." But Lincoln proposes now to be the (if it be so) fool who rushes in where such senatorial angels as Sumner, Chase, Seward, Wade, Fessenden, and Sam Houston had feared to tread.

The core of Lincoln's argument against Douglas's specious references to self-government and popular sovereignty can, I think, be stated quite simply: The Negro is a man—a fellow human being—and therefore like all others deserving of self-government. Lincoln argued:

But if the negro is a man, is it not to that extent, a total destruction of self-government, to say that he too shall not govern himself? When the white man governs himself that is self-government; but when he governs himself, and also governs another man, that is more than self-

---

the House and twenty-four of the thirty-six presidents pro tempore of the Senate down to 1861 were from the South. Before the war, twenty of the thirty-five Supreme Court justices had been from the South.

government—that is despotism. If the negro is a man, why then my ancient faith teaches me that "all men are created equal"; and that there can be no moral right in connection with one man's making a slave of another.

Lincoln then quoted the Declaration of Independence, down through the consent of the governed, and followed with this paragraph, astonishing in its time and place:

I have quoted so much at this time merely to show that according to our ancient faith, the just powers of governments are derived from the consent of the governed. Now the relation of masters and slaves is, *pro tanto* [just so far], a total violation of this principle. The master not only governs the slave without his consent; but he governs him by a set of rules altogether different from those which he prescribes for himself. Allow ALL the governed an equal voice in the government, and that, and that only is self government.

One would think that that last sentence could not avoid being taken as a fundamental philosophical repudiation not only of slavery, but of the restriction on the suffrage and political participation as well. It is Lincoln who put the word "ALL" in capital letters: Allow ALL persons an *equal* voice—my emphasis this time, but Lincoln's word—not just a voice, but an *equal* voice, and that *only* (my emphasis again, but Lincoln's word again) is the self-government that is the "ancient faith" on which this country is founded.

The unavoidable implication is that for there to be genuine self-government, the persons brought here from Africa, and their descendants, should have a voice equal to all others. Obviously that sentence rules out human slavery. It rules out a position like Douglas's that allows human slavery to expand if the "people" (meaning just those white males allowed to vote) vote for it. But it also would certainly seem to rule out racial (and sexual) restrictions on suffrage and on political participation. It is no wonder that Lincoln felt it necessary immediately to follow this paragraph with one of his disclaimers of any intent to establish "political and social equality between the whites and blacks." But the philosophical cat was out of the bag.

For all his caution about the racial prejudice of his audience, Lincoln would make repeated affirmations of a humane universalism and egalitarianism: "My faith in the proposition that each man should do precisely as he pleases with all which is exclusively his own, lies at the foundation of the sense of justice that is in me"; "[N]o man is good enough to govern another man *without that other's consent*"; "Allow ALL the governed an equal voice in the government, and that, and that only is self government."

4. MEN ARE NOT ANGELS BUT THEY HAVE A SENSE OF JUSTICE

Running through the remarks of this prairie political thinker was an explicit and implicit conception of the essential tendencies of his fellow human beings: a certain rough-and-ready conception of human nature, realistic but not cynical. His noncynicism is the more striking and distinctive element of his outlook.

He was, to be sure, realistic about human beings, in the way most politicians are. His first continuing career, after odd jobs, was as a member of the state legislature of a frontier state, dealing with canals and railroads and the fight over the location of the state capital—not an environment, one would surmise, that would encourage utopianism. As a practical politician and legislator, seeking votes from fellow citizens and fellow legislators, he could not help knowing the strength of human self-interest. He would have forced upon him the further fact that self-interest is much strengthened, and the role of conscience diminished, when persons act in groups. And he would learn that self-interest, and its intensifying in groups, would persist—it was not going to be wished or talked or argued away—and that groups, with their interest, seek to maintain and advance their power. Service in state legislatures seems to be a particularly potent teacher of these facts. He would have learned, as another great American leader who also served in legislatures, James Madison, had learned, that men are not angels, that enlightened statesmen will not always be at the helm, that where power is, there is the threat to liberty, that ambition must be made to counter ambition.

Nevertheless he affirmed also a contrasting reality. Standing there in the hall, at state fair time in Springfield, with the great senator listening and preparing to tear him apart, Lincoln said that "slavery is founded in the selfishness of man's nature—opposition to it in his love of justice." "These principles," said this lanky new eminence among the great senator's many opponents, "are an eternal antagonism." So there are *two* principles at least, not just one—selfishness, but also love of justice.

Lincoln was explaining the much-deplored recent turmoil in American politics. "[W]hen [these principles] are brought into collision so fiercely, as slavery extension brings them, shocks, and throes, and convulsions much ceaselessly follow." And the antagonism reaches deeper than recent events. "Repeal the Missouri compromise—repeal all compromises— repeal the declaration of independence—repeal all past history"—the speaker is being swept along by his thought—"you still cannot repeal human nature." And what has human nature to do with it? "It still will be the abundance of man's heart, that slavery extension is wrong; and out of the abundance of his heart, his mouth will continue to speak." ("Slavery extension is wrong"? Surely the abundance of the speaker's heart really meant that slavery *itself* is wrong.)

"Human nature" includes, along with selfishness, human sympathy and a natural sense of justice. In one of the most effective passages of the speech Lincoln argued that that was so by addressing rhetorical questions to "the South." To be sure, no one in "the South" was actually listening to this western Whig politician; he was using this device, as he would again at Cooper Union, to make points to his hearers in the North, in this first case in the hall in the Illinois State Capitol. He intended to show by his questions that these theoretical Southerners did not, really, think there was no difference between Negroes and hogs. They were not able—most of them—in their hearts, to deny the humanity of the Negro. "It is kindly provided," said Lincoln, "that of all those who come into the world, only a small percentage are natural tyrants." Repeating his insistence on the common elements in humanity across the sections, he said, the percentage of such tyrants is no larger in the slave states than in the free. He made a rather strong statement of a common element in the makeup, at least, of most human beings: "The great majority, South as well as North, have human sympathies of which they can no more divest themselves than they can their sensibility to physical pain."

Lincoln then embarked on the first great example of a rhetorical device he would use again on later occasions with a racist audience, a device we may call wounding from behind. That means, without assailing the racial prejudice head-on, going around behind it, as it were, to shake its foundations by exposing contradictions. He did it in this instance by addressing the Southerner who denied this human sympathy "a few plain questions."

First, why had they joined, almost unanimously, with the North in 1820 to declare the slave trade piracy and to punish it by *hanging*? "Why did you do this? If you did not feel that it was wrong, why did you join in providing that men should be hung for it?" And also, "You never thought of hanging men for catching and selling wild horses, wild buffaloes or wild bears." So there was something in you that led you to make a distinction between Negroes and hogs, horses, buffaloes, and bears.

Lincoln's second and most extended question to the South was almost a little literary piece, like those "characters" that writers long ago would produce describing stock figures. "You have amongst you," he said, "a sneaking individual, of the class of native tyrants, known as the slave-dealer." He described this "tyrant" and the ways his hearers shrink from, avoid, and despise him:

> He watches your necessities, and crawls up to buy your slave, at the speculating price. If you cannot help it, you sell to him; but if you can help it, you drive him from your door. You despise him utterly. You do not recognize him as a friend, or even as an honest man. Your children must not play with his; they may rollick freely with the little negroes, but not with the "slave-dealer" children. If you are obliged to deal with him, you try to get through the job without so much as touching him. It is common with you to join hands with the men you meet; but with the slave dealer you avoid the ceremony—instinctively shrinking from the snaky contact. If he grows rich and retires from business, you still remember him, and still keep up the ban of non-intercourse upon him and his family. Now why is this? You do not so treat the man who deals in corn, cattle or tobacco.

And then Lincoln had a third question: There are in the United States 433,643 free blacks.

> At $500 a head they are worth over two hundred millions of dollars. How comes this vast amount of property to be running around without owners? We do not see free horses or free cattle running at large . . . All these free blacks are descendants of slaves, or were slaves, and would be slaves now but for SOMETHING which operated on their white owners, inducing them, at vast pecuniary sacrifice, to liberate them. What is this something? Is there any mistaking it? In all these cases it is your sense of justice, and human sympathy, continually telling you that the poor negro has some natural right to himself, that those who deny it, and make mere merchandise of him, deserve kickings, contempt, and death.

The rather brutal specificity of this last little, un-Lincolnian, jaw-tightening phrase—"deserve kickings, contempt, and death"—reminds one of the moment when as president of the United States this generally forgiving man will turn aside all pleas and allow the execution of Nathaniel Gordon, the only man ever executed for slave-trading by the American government.

But his focus in the passages we have cited is not on his own grim condemnation of slave traders and slave dealers but on the unexpunged natural sympathy in his proposed Southern interlocutors: You have such feelings of condemnation, said Lincoln, whether you admit it or not, and you have a parallel "sense of justice and human sympathy" that will not let you deny a fellow human being's humanity.

At the same time there was much evidence in his address of Lincoln's realism about humankind—a concrete realism. Throughout his career he would think realistically about what would happen among actual human beings. Now that this Kansas-Nebraska Act had been passed and signed into law, he was thinking about what it would mean in practice:

> The people are to decide the question of slavery for themselves, but WHEN they are to decide; or HOW, they are to decide; or whether, when the question is once decided, it is to remain so, or is it to be subject to an indefinite succession of new trials, the law does not say. Is it to be decided by the first dozen settlers who arrive there? or is it to await the arrival of a hundred? Is it to be decided by a vote of the people? or a vote of the legislature? or, indeed by a vote of any sort? To these questions the law gives no answer.

That Lincoln had read the congressional debates carefully is evident in what he would say next: "There is a mystery about this; for when a member proposed to give the legislature express authority to exclude slavery, it was hooted down by the friends of the bill." The friends of the bill, this Illinois Whig has noted, do not want it made explicit that popular sovereignty can be exercised by a legislature to *exclude* slavery. "This fact is worth remembering," he will add, significantly. And then he will go on presciently to anticipate what the unclarified law will mean:

> Some Yankees, in the east, are sending emigrants to Nebraska, to exclude slavery from it; and, so far as I can judge, they expect the question to be decided by voting, in some way or other. But the Missourians are awake, too. They are within a stone's throw of the contested

ground. They hold meetings, and pass resolutions, in which not the slightest allusion to voting is made. They resolve that slavery already exists in the territory; that more shall go there; that they, remaining in Missouri, will protect it; and that abolitionists shall be hung, or driven away. Through all this, bowie knives and six-shooters are seen plainly enough; but never a glimpse of the ballot box.

Reading the debates and the law and the newspaper carefully, and thinking carefully, he had seen what it would mean: Bleeding Kansas.

5. THE SPIRIT OF '76

As this surprisingly potent critic of the great senator rounded into the peroration of his three-hour speech, he combined exhortation with dramatic historical summary—both in affirmation of what he said was the original moral premise of the nation. As is often the case, even with leaders more "revolutionary" or reformist than Lincoln was, he was *not* proposing some altogether new departure. On the contrary, he was calling for a *return* to what had been—to the Founders' own spirit and principles.* He was objecting to the *change* from the Founders' program now introduced by the Kansas-Nebraska Act (that is, largely by the Little Giant now listening to him). Lincoln set "the spirit of seventy-six" squarely over against "the spirit of Nebraska." They are "utter antagonisms."

> I particularly object to the NEW position which the avowed principle of this Nebraska law gives to slavery in the body politic. I object to it because it assumes that there CAN be MORAL RIGHT in the enslaving of one man by another. I object to it as . . . a sad evidence that . . . liberty, as a principle, we have ceased to revere. I object to it because the fathers of the republic eschewed, and rejected it.

Lincoln the historical researcher and summarizer went rapidly through those eschewings and rejectings.

> [The Founding Fathers] found the institution existing among us, which they could not help; and they cast blame upon the British King

---

* To be sure, he made "the fathers of the republic" a bit more consistently antislavery than they had been. We do tend, when we urge a return to that Golden Age, to do a little cleaning up.

for having permitted its introduction. BEFORE the constitution, they prohibited its introduction into the north-western Territory—the only country we owned, then free from it.

Lincoln reminded his listeners of those euphemistic circumlocutions the framers went through to avoid ever using the words "slave" or "slavery" in the Constitution, quoting each of the three awkward avoidances. "Thus, the thing is hid away, in the constitution," Lincoln said, "just as an afflicted man hides away a wen or a cancer, which he dares not cut out at once, lest he bleed to death; with the promise, nevertheless, that the cutting may begin at the end of a given time."

The earliest Congress "hedged and hemmed it in to the narrowest limits of necessity," prohibiting an outgoing slave trade in 1794; prohibiting the bringing of slaves from Africa into the Mississippi Territory in 1798, prohibiting American citizens from trading in slaves between foreign countries in 1800, restraining some state-to-state slave trade in 1803; and then in 1807, "in apparent hot haste," "nearly a year in advance," they passed the law to take effect on the first day of 1808—"the first day the constitution would permit"—prohibiting the African slave trade. And then in 1820 "they declared the trade piracy, and annexed to it, the extreme penalty of death . . . Thus we see that the plain unmistakable spirit of the age, towards slavery, was hostility to the PRINCIPLE, and toleration, ONLY BY NECESSITY."

But now it is to be transformed into a "sacred right." His concluding exhortation rang the bells of America's moral meaning:

Our republican robe is soiled, and trailed in the dust. Let us repurify it. Let us turn and wash it white, in the spirit, if not the blood, of the Revolution. Let us turn slavery from its claims of "moral right," back upon its existing legal rights, and its arguments of "necessity." Let us return it to the position our fathers gave it; and there let it rest in peace. Let us readopt the Declaration of Independence, and with it, the practices, and policy, which harmonize with it. Let north and south—let all Americans—let all lovers of liberty everywhere—join in the great and good work. If we do this, we shall not only have saved the Union; but we shall have so saved it, as to make, and to keep it, forever worthy of the saving. We shall have so saved it, that the succeeding millions of free happy people, the world over, shall rise up, and call us blessed, to the latest generations.

And Lincoln sat down.

The speech he had just given—his state fair speech—was better than any he would give in the famous debates four years later, and had in it many of the points he would argue throughout the six extraordinary years 1854–60; it was the introduction to the world (although the world didn't know it yet) of a new Lincoln.

6. WHAT WAS HE DOING?

Douglas then rose to answer. There is some suggestion that Douglas himself had been impressed by Lincoln's speech, although of course Democrats said that in his two-hour response he demolished Lincoln.

Among the reverberations of Lincoln's speech was a significant attempt by a cadre of abolitionists to add him to their roster. Northern Illinois now had, from eastern migration, some self-starting opponents of slavery, such as Ichabod Codding and Owen Lovejoy, both Protestant pastors and both originally from New England. The handful of Illinois abolitionists held a little organizing meeting in connection with the state fair, actually on the evening of the day Lincoln spoke. Presumably because they were moved by his speech (despite his differences with them), they added his name to the new organization's committee without his authorization.

Yet another such reverberation was that he was invited to speak elsewhere around the state. Twelve days after the state fair speech, in Peoria, on October 16, he had another exchange with Douglas. Lincoln was in the audience when Douglas gave his scheduled speech, and after the cheers there were calls for Lincoln to speak. Douglas had spoken for three hours, a whole afternoon, and it was five o'clock, so Lincoln said it was too late just then, but that if they would come back (with the enticement that Douglas would have a chance to "skin" him after he spoke) he would hold forth in the evening. Which he did, once again by candlelight.

The first four-fifths of this Peoria speech was a repetition of the state fair in Springfield. But in reading it as it is printed one comes to the obvious Lincolnian climax quoted above: "Our republican robe is soiled. . . . Let us readopt the Declaration of Independence. . . ." Then the next paragraph plainly begins the Peoria addition: "At Springfield, twelve days ago, where I had spoken substantially as I have here . . ." He then gave added material responding to what Douglas had said in the meantime, most of it quite particular debating points about the history of the slavery in the states and territories. But there is one further glimpse of the core issue. Lincoln said that Douglas's remarks show that

> the Judge [Douglas] has no very vivid impression that the negro is a human; and consequently has no idea that there can be any moral question in legislating about him. In his view, the question of whether a new country shall be slave or free, is a matter of as utter indifference, as it is whether his neighbor shall plant his farm with tobacco, or stock it with horned cattle.

Lincoln continued, then, with one of his affirmations of a fundamental and persistent sense of justice in the human heart, which slavery offends:

> Now, whether this view is right or wrong, it is very certain that the great mass of mankind take a totally different view. They consider slavery a great moral wrong; and their feeling against it, is not evanescent, but eternal. It lies at the very foundation of their sense of justice; and it cannot be trifled with. It is a great and durable element of popular action, and, I think, no statesman can safely disregard it.

We have noted that he had said at the state fair in Springfield about white racial prejudice that "a universal feeling, whether well or ill-founded, cannot be safely disregarded." Now he says, about that love of justice in the human heart that finds slavery a great moral wrong, that it is *eternal,* a "great and durable element of popular action" and—again—something no statesman can safely disregard.

Lincoln, now established as the leading anti-Douglas, anti-Nebraska speaker, then gave his speech without benefit of Douglas but reportedly to great effect in Urbana on October 24 and then in Chicago on October 27, where, the *Chicago Journal* said, "his eloquence greatly impressed all his hearers."

What was Lincoln doing in this autumnal rhetorical outburst? He certainly was doing something larger than just running himself for a Sangamon seat in the state legislature; he paid no attention to that at all, and mostly spoke outside his county. We have already suggested that he was doing something more than helping Yates's congressional candidacy; he repeatedly put himself forward as an opponent of Douglas outside Yates's district. In the main speech Yates's name was not mentioned (Yates would lose, by the way, perhaps because of suspicions about his alleged Know-Nothing sympathies, about which Lincoln had warned him). On November 1, Lincoln spoke in Quincy in behalf of "our old friend Archie Williams," who like Yates was an anti-Nebraska Whig candidate for Congress (and who also did not win), but even the electing of two anti-Nebraska congressmen could not have fulfilled Lincoln's purpose. An anti-Nebraska Congress was an objective, but not the center of his purpose; it was not mentioned in Lincoln's speech until he was two-thirds through, and then only in a single sentence in a three-hour speech: "We ought to elect a House of Representatives which will vote its [the Missouri Compromise's] restoration." But then Lincoln had to grant that because of the Senate the immediate restoration was quite unlikely: "[T]hough we elect every member of the lower House the Senate is still against us. It is quite true that of the Senators who passed the Nebraska bill, a majority of the whole Senate will retain their seats in spite of the elections of this and the next year." So however heroic his efforts, and those of other opponents of the Kansas-Nebraska Act, they would not see the Missouri Compromise restored any time soon. Nevertheless, those senators will pay attention if their constituencies now vote against Nebraska. And "even if we fail to technically restore the compromise, it is still a great point to carry a popular vote in favor of the restoration. The moral weight of such a vote can not be estimated too highly."

So what Lincoln sought in the first place was the moral weight of such a nationwide vote for anti-Nebraska candidates.

Was he thinking already that he himself might be chosen senator by the new legislature? Scholars differ as to when that entered his head, and in the nature of the case it is hard to know. I think it did not become a firm central purpose until after he saw the results of the election for the legislature in November, and in any case such an aspiration certainly does not fully explain his undertaking the state fair–Peoria speech.

If his *sole* purpose had been getting someone elected in the balloting that fall (Yates, Williams and others, Whigs generally), or getting someone defeated or diminished (Douglas, Shields, Democrats generally), or getting himself in a position to be chosen senator by the new legislature, his speech could have been quite different from what it was. If he had had his eye strictly on electing or defeating someone, there were issues he could have used—nativism, temperance, even some remnant of an old Whig issue like rivers and harbors—on which the Democrats were vulnerable.

And he could have tailored his attack on Douglas on topic A, the Kansas-Nebraska Act, more carefully to such an immediate practical purpose. He could have attacked the act without making large claims about slavery and the Negro and the nation's future that were susceptible in the overwhelmingly prejudiced white electorate to Douglas's hammering attack. If all that he wanted to do was to *win*—to win, that is, in the fall election, for Yates, Williams, Whigs, himself—he could have diversified his appeals. He could have honed his attack on the Nebraska Act, not carrying it all the way to first principles. He did not need to condemn slavery *everywhere;* he needed only to condemn it in Nebraska. He did not need to condemn it morally; he could have condemned it only *practically,* as a kind of society free white voters do not want to see established, for a variety of self-interested reasons, in the free territory to the west. And he did not need, for any immediate political purposes, to insist that the Declaration of Independence includes the equality of the Negro. In fact, Douglas was going to beat him over the head with that. He was in effect speaking not solely to audiences in Illinois (his speech has surprisingly little local reference) but to the whole nation, although the nation did not know it. His speech was more ambitious intellectually than can be explained by any immediate practical purpose. He focused sharply, excluding all subjects except slavery—a point we may miss, looking back, because that is our focus, too. But it need not have been his sole focus. And concentrating on Nebraska-slavery, he carried the issue, as he need not have done, all the way to the nation's original moral self-definition.

CHAPTER ELEVEN

Our Duty as We Understand It

1. IF SLAVERY IS NOT WRONG, NOTHING IS WRONG

Lincoln, mousing in the libraries, had clearly worked hard on the material he presented in his autumnal outburst in 1854. He had worked hard not only on the history and the debates in Congress but also on the underlying moral premises—and on how to express them.

How much of a thinker was he going to be? He could not be a formal philosopher, writing out his "system" in the calm seclusion of what James Madison, with a touch of disdain, would call the philosopher's "closet." He was not, as a Supreme Court justice in the next century would put it, also a little disdainfully, "composing for the anthologies." Until he debated the famous Douglas in 1858, and got the debates in print, he could not have thought his productions would be known beyond their moment or beyond the borders of Illinois. Until he was elected president, he had no idea that what he would write and speak would ever be remembered and read by anyone after his own time. Even in that august position he could on one famous occasion say, with spectacular and perhaps disingenuous inaccuracy, "The world will little note, nor long remember what we say here." Almost everything he wrote, except for a stray poem or two, was produced under the pressure of an immediate political situation.

When one reads interpretations linking the busy and practical politician and lawyer Abraham Lincoln to great thinkers and great traditions of thought, one is reminded of that amusing moment when John L. Scripps of the *Chicago Tribune* wrote in his campaign biography of Lincoln that Lincoln had read Plutarch, and then, on second thought, a little worried, suggested to the amiable Lincoln that he go get a copy and read it so that the report would *become* true. Lincoln, it is said, much amused, did as he was told—and loved to tell the story.

I suggest this interpretation: Lincoln was indeed a man of ideas, but he was a man of his *own* ideas. And these ideas were confined, almost of necessity, in the mature man, to a relatively narrow range that fit his purposes. Within that range he was a thinker indeed, but he was not one, like Thomas Jefferson, who wished (or said he wished) that he could get out of politics and get back to his books and his violin, and who ranged across the world of thought and set up shop as something of a philosopher himself.

As Lincoln's life settled into shape, he no longer read "everything he could get his hands on." Starting from scratch, he went into two demanding professions, politics and law. In a recent essay David Herbert Donald presents the picture of Lincoln writing out, by hand, the papers for the thousands of law cases in which he was involved—in one case a forty-three-page response at one sitting. He was not exactly a folksy country lawyer, without much to do, rambling on with his partner about big ideas. And we know how well he kept up with the issues and the cast of characters in Illinois and national politics. What he read in his mature years was mostly newspapers and journals. And he did research for a purpose—usually a speech. His intellectual work was highly directed after 1854 to the one huge argument about the moral foundations of this republic.

He did make some interesting notes to himself on that subject. It is not easy for a person in a later century, when slavery has long since been abolished and its essential evil universally taken for granted, to imagine a time when slavery was a big, actual, thriving institution in the United States, with vigorous defenders. Because it is so hard to recreate in our minds that situation, it may also be hard to take seriously Lincoln's arguments against that obviously evil institution. The inclination in a later time is to skip over his treatment of slavery, about which there is no longer any issue, and to move immediately to his treatment of race, about which there still are many issues.

But to do that is to falsify Lincoln's own situation. The primary *practical* issue for him in his time was not race but slavery—race only as it figured (as of course it did in a large way) in the argument about slavery. Although Lincoln and Douglas differed radically about race—and although Douglas, as Lincoln charged, systematically exploited what we today would call "racism" to make his argument—nevertheless the point of immediate decision between him and Senator Douglas (as he said many times) was that he (and the Republicans) believed slavery to be morally wrong, and Douglas (and many Democrats) did not.

Lincoln certainly did not need to persuade himself that slavery was a moral evil; he had believed that all of his life. In April of 1864, as president, he would say in a letter to a Kentucky newspaperman named Albert Hodges that is often quoted, "I am naturally anti-slavery. If slavery is not wrong, nothing is wrong. I cannot remember when I did not so think and feel." But although he had always been morally opposed to slavery, he had not until 1854 made that opposition central to his life or his politics.

The editors who have gathered together his "papers" assign to some of the notes to himself the date July 1, 1854, in the middle of this summer of reflection and preparation for his autumn outburst. These editors call these items "fragments," but I think this first one is a complete argument.

Picture Abraham Lincoln, forty-five years old, a minor politician now practicing law, enormously stimulated by that debate in Washington, sitting at a table in the state library in Springfield, scratching out this fundamental argument about the moral wrong of slavery. (The numbering is mine.)

[1] If A. can prove, however conclusively, that he may, of right, enslave B.—why may not B. snatch the same argument and prove equally that he may enslave A.?

[2] You say A. is white, and B. is black. It is color, then; the lighter, having the right to enslave the darker? Take care. By this rule, you are to be slave to the first man you meet, with a fairer skin than your own.

[3] You do not mean color exactly?—You mean the whites are intellectually the superiors of the blacks, and, therefore have the right to enslave them? Take care again. By this rule, you are to be slave to the first man you meet, with intellect superior to your own.

[4] But, say you, it is a question of interest; and, if you can make it your interest you have the right to enslave another. Very well. And if he can make it his interest, he has the right to enslave you.

What is most interesting about this little composition is what it does *not* say about race.

Paragraph 1 starts with two persons who are just letters, utterly undifferentiated ("behind a veil of ignorance"?). We do not know whether A or B is black or white. It is always significant in these fundamental reasonings how one *starts* one's argument, what one takes as a given. John C. Calhoun *started* his argument in behalf of slavery as a "positive good: under certain conditions," with two races. *Two* there are—different in racial essence. *Where* there are two races occupying the same society (as though Africans had just dropped onto the American continent out of the sky), *then* the best arrangement (for both!) was for the "superior" to hold the "inferior" as slaves. And of course it was not just defenders of slavery who thought that way about superiority and inferiority and twoness; much of the culture did. But Abraham Lincoln, thinking things out in private on this occasion, does *not*.

With that nonracial beginning, the first Lincolnian item can apply the challenge of reversibility that appears everywhere in moral thought and argument. It appears in the formal work of moral philosophers and the maxims of popular morality, like the Golden Rule and walking-a-mile-in-another's-shoes and there-but-for-the-grace-of-God-go-I. It appears instinctively in daily arguments about the equities of the office and the shop and the playground: Suppose the positions were reversed? Suppose you stood where he stands (or where *I* stand)? Put yourself in her place (my place). Children start making such comparative appeals almost before they can talk.

To be sure, this reversing (and the related generalization test: Suppose everybody did what *you* do?) implies a fundamental equivalence. It assumes that we are in the end reversible—that what can be asked of me can (for the purpose of moral reasoning, in theory) be asked of you, and vice versa, because there is at bottom no *radical distinction* between us that justifies categorically different moral expectations. Again, Lincoln simply assumes away any such radical distinction—assumes ultimate human equality.

Then in the next short paragraph (2) Lincoln does appear to take account of race, because he mentions "white" and "black" and "color"— but he still does not deal in racial terms. He promptly takes "color" *literally.* And he applies this literal color test to *individuals,* one by one.

We use phrases about "color" when discussing race—"colored people," "people of color," and "black" and "white." But there are millions of human beings of a wide variety of shades and hues who are called "white," but none of whom, not even the palest albino, is literally *white.* And there are millions of human beings, of a very broad spectrum of hues and shades, who are called (in the times and places in which this is the accepted terminology) "black," but none of them is literally *black.* But Lincoln immediately takes the designation by color *literally* and *individually*—which is really to cut through the racial categories altogether. Treating actual color literally and individually effectively jettisons taking "color," culturally defined, as the indicator of "race."

And in (3) he does the same with intellect. Although he hears in the voices around him a correlation of intellect with race, he promptly makes it an *individual* comparison. As you individually (whatever your "race") may be darker than another individual, so you individually may be less intelligent than another—and by that test properly subject to enslavement by that more intelligent person. Implicitly again he cuts through the sharp *collective* basis, the *racial* basis, of the actual attitude he is arguing against, and makes the issue turn not on the alleged differences between two radically different human groupings ("whites" and "blacks") but only on an unbroken gradation of individual intelligence. To do that—to put each human being, individually, on his or her point on a single unbroken continuum of color, or of intelligence, is implicitly to reject that categorical separation that "racism" affirms and American slavery rested upon.

I believe—although I have not found any scholar to confirm it—that Lincoln may have been reading, around the time that he produced this A.- and-B. "fragment" on slavery, Francis Wayland's *The Elements of Moral Science*. The first reason for this guess is that we know that he read Wayland's *Elements of Political Economy* as part of his self-education in economics, and it would not be much of a leap to think of his reading the much more widely available book by the same author as part of his self-education in moral philosophy. Wayland was one of those nineteenth-century university presidents—in his case at Brown—who gave a required course to seniors on moral philosophy and out of his lectures produced a textbook. His was one of the most widely read of college texts on that subject, first published in 1835 but reprinted many times, abridged for secondary schools, translated and sold all over the world. That is a second reason for guessing that Lincoln read it: it was very widely available, much more so than Wayland's *Elements of Political Economy*. (Like Adam Smith, Wayland was a moral philosopher who out of the innards of that discipline developed a political economy.) For all the mature Lincoln's lack of interest (Herndon tells us) in purely speculative subjects, he did tend to seek out books on topics he felt he needed to know about, and if he felt that about moral philosophy in 1854, Wayland's book would have been a likely choice.

Wayland's sections on slavery became—not surprisingly, given the times—the most controversial part of the book, and caused it to be rejected in the South. Although he made a strong and clean moral rejection of slavery, he then disappointed opponents of slavery by leaving the ending of this evil solely to the consciences of slaveholders. The public controversy over Wayland's views might be another reason to guess that Lincoln looked at the book, because he tended from this point on to get hold of books that caused a stir about slavery.

But the primary reason for this guess is the form and content of some of Wayland's arguing, matched with a few patches from Lincoln. Here, for example, is what Wayland wrote about the "equality of right," as distinct from an "equality of condition," as the essential standing of all men in relation to each other, and about the duties of "reciprocity" that equality of right entails. He is refuting any claim of superiority grounded in some unequal attribute or condition:

> For the principle asserted is that superiority of condition confers superiority of right. But if this be true, then every kind of superiority of condition must confer correspondent superiority of right. Superiority in muscular strength must confer it as much as superiority of intellect or of wealth; and must confer it in the ratio of that superiority. In that case, if A, on the ground of intellectual superiority, have a right to improve by his own means of happiness by diminishing those which the Creator has given to B, B would have the same right over A, on the superiority of muscular strength; while C would have a correspondent right over them both, on the ground of superiority of wealth; and so on indefinitely. . . .

To be sure, Lincoln could have read some other philosopher who used A and B in little cases and exercises, or he could have absorbed it from the atmosphere, or he could have made it up on his own. But I suggest that he had encountered something like Wayland. In his discussion of personal liberty Wayland wrote, "[A] man has an entire right to use his own body," and, again, "In other words, a man has a right to himself," which parallel statements by Lincoln about the Negro's right to the work of his hands. Perhaps the most clear-cut parallel to Lincoln appears in this sentence from Wayland's discussion of slavery: "Would the master be willing that another person should subject him to slavery, for the same reasons and on the same grounds that he holds his slave in bondage?" That would appear to be exactly the premise of Lincoln's "fragment."

Lincoln's condemnation of slavery, in a letter on April 6, 1859, because "this is a world of compensation and he would who would *be* no slave must consent to *have* no slave," might have been composed after looking into Wayland's passages on "reciprocity." In a famous short "definition of democracy" that he wrote on a scrap of paper kept by Mrs. Lincoln, to which the editors—just guessing—gave the date August 1, 1858, he would make the point in the first person: "As I would not be a slave, so I would not be a master." This recurring explanation of the wrongness of slavery on the basis of reciprocity and parallel among ultimate moral equals might have received at least a decent grade in President Wayland's class at Brown.

Once all moral justification founded on human differences vanishes, the structure rests simply on power and interest.

As we have seen, Lincoln, although like most politicians a realist about human nature, has nevertheless a little thread running through his thought that explicitly rejects the common cynicism that reduces politics *exclusively* to interest. In the first argumentative paragraph in the speech he is composing that summer and fall—his first great paragraph, as I called it, in his first great speech—he would say that he hated slavery not only for its monstrous injustice and for its undercutting of America's worldwide moral influence, but also for what it does to the thought of its American defenders. They are driven, he said, to "criticizing the Declaration of Independence, and insisting that there is no right principle of action but self-interest." In other words, the sorry task of defending slavery warps thought into cynicism.

Lincoln will say, more than once in the next six years, that slavery has no moral basis whatever and rests exclusively on power and on self-interest. We have seen that he will say at the state fair and in Peoria, "Slavery is founded in the selfishness of man's nature—opposition to it, in his love of justice. These principles are in eternal antagonism. . . ." He will link the moral evil that slavery represents, grounded in human selfishness, to other expressions of the same principle, notably the tyranny of kings and nobles the American Revolution opposed. He will say not just that slavery is wrong in itself, but—as John Quincy Adams observed in his diary—that it warps the moral sense in general.

Slavery is not only a violation of the founding ideals of the American nation; it violates the core of the human sense of right and wrong. We have already noted that he would write, "If slavery is not wrong, nothing is wrong." If you cannot condemn human slavery, what can you condemn?

Lincoln working away with his books and his papers in the middle of

the year 1854 made some notes also about that new and more extreme form
of the defense of slavery that had appeared in the middle 1830s, the blunt
assertion, in the teeth of abolitionist attack, that slavery was not just a sad
necessity, or a matter of indifference, but rather a *positive good:* good for
whites, good for blacks, good for the country, good for the elegant aristocratic culture it supported in the South. The sarcastic comment that Lincoln made on that idea is preserved in a piece that really is a "fragment,"
also given the date (though no one knows when he wrote it) July 1, 1854:

> [F]or although volume upon volume is written to prove slavery a very
> good thing, we never hear of the man who wishes to take the good of it
> by being a slave himself!

He would say that same thing again in what is headed "Fragment in
Pro-Slavery Theology," to which the date October 1, 1858, had been
assigned:

> As a *good* thing, slavery is strikingly peculiar, in this, that it is the only
> good thing which no man ever seeks the good of, *for himself.*

Again, Lincoln in making his little joke bypasses all racial categories,
and ironically treats all human beings as equally possible candidates for
this "good."

But of course the point is the invidious power relationship at the foundation of slavery: I, who benefit, say it is "good" for you, whom I enslave,
but I don't ask your opinion. The "good" for me is not for me to be a slave
myself, but for *you* to be my slave.

Lincoln the moral realist would note throughout his six-year argument
about slavery the immense warping effect of the great personal advantage
to those who defended slavery. Another of these notes to himself—this one
later, given the date October 1, 1858—has been called "Fragment on Pro-
Slavery Theology." In addition to reiterating his observations that no one
seeks this alleged "good thing" for himself, Lincoln comments on the argument that slavery is "good" for some but not for others. One may infer that
Lincoln wrote this document after looking at one of the widely read
defenses of slavery, *Slavery Ordained of God* (published in 1857) by the
Reverend Frederick A. Ross. Lincoln deals with the argument that slavery,
though not a universal good, like health, happiness, and wisdom, is nevertheless good "for some people!!!" (the three exclamation points are his).

He asks the realistic question, one might say the modern question: Just *who* is to decide which people it is good for and which not?

"The sum of proslavery theology seems to be this: 'Slavery is not universally *right,* nor yet universally *wrong;* it is better for *some* people to be slaves; and, in such cases, it is the Will of God that they be such.'" But Lincoln does not grant to clerics like Dr. Ross unquestioned authority to expound and apply the "Will of God":

> Certainly there is no contending against the Will of God; but still there is some difficulty in ascertaining, and applying it, to particular cases.

Lincoln does not have the foreknowledge that would prevent him from using the name "Sambo," but that should not detract from his point:

> For instance we will suppose the Rev. Dr. Ross has a slave named Sambo, and the question is, "Is it the Will of God that Sambo shall remain a slave, or be set free?" The Almighty gives no audable answer to the question, and his revelation—the Bible—gives none—or, at most, none but such as admits of a squabble, as to its meaning.

Having set aside any unequivocal authoritative answer from God or the Bible, Lincoln then indulges in a certain satire:

> No one thinks of asking Sambo's opinion on it. So, at last, it comes to this, that Dr. Ross is to decide the question. And while he consider[s] it, he sits in the shade, with gloves on his hands, and subsists on the bread that Sambo is earning in the burning sun. If he decides that God wills Sambo to continue a slave, he thereby retains his own comfortable position; but if he decides that God wills Sambo to be free, he thereby has to walk out of the shade, throw off his gloves, and delve for his own bread. Will Dr. Ross be actuated by that perfect impartiality, which has ever been considered most favorable to correct decisions?

Then Lincoln drops the satirical voice and bursts out at the end of this document with passionate condemnation of the idea that slavery is a good thing "for some people!!!":

> Nonsense! Wolves devouring lambs, not because it is good for their own greedy maws, but because it [is] good for the lambs!!!

In one little note—a preliminary to this criticism of Ross—he strikes a more distinctly Christian theme, only in this case dealing in racial categories:

> Suppose it is true, that the Negro is inferior to the white, in the gifts of nature; is it not the exact reverse of justice that the white should, for that reason, take from the Negro, any part of the little which has been given him? "Give to him that is needy" is the Christian rule of charity; but "Take from him that is needy" is the rule of slavery.

It is significant that Lincoln here abruptly segues—without noticing he is doing it—from "justice" in the first sentence to "charity" in the second, collapsing two huge moral terms that are distinguished from, and related to, each other in all sorts of ways, including conflict. For Lincoln, "charity" certainly did season justice.

But Lincoln's more usual form of argument in these notes to himself did not deal in racial categories (even, as here, in a sense sympathetically) and did not grant moral significances to any group characteristics—inferiorities, superiorities—but dealt with *individual* claims and comparisons, as we have seen.

Lincoln affirmed—took for granted, really—an original universalism, an egalitarianism, an individualism, that found no attribute or collective category that could justify radically different ultimate moral expectations from different individual human beings. And slavery as a radical violation of this ultimate equality was grounded simply in "selfishness." It was maintained, then, out of selfishness, to the advantage, of course, of the dominating group—wolves devouring lambs because it is good for their own greedy maws!!!

Lincoln's explicit condemnation of the evil of slavery certainly did not lead to the position of the "moral" wing of the abolitionist movement, which abjured all "politics" and dealt strictly in exhortation and appeals for a change of heart. His morality would certainly be expressed in the contest for power and the calculation of what is possible, of politics. It also, however, did not lead to the positions taken by the more radical antislavery politicians further east—Sumner, Chase, or Giddings, or abolitionists Owen Lovejoy and Ichabod Codding in Illinois. His reasons for declining to support the farthest-out antislavery political position, as we have seen in the case of fugitive slave laws, combined constitutional and legal scruple with an awareness of public opinion in Illinois. As a practical western politician, all that he proposed that the nation should now *do,* with respect to this manifest evil, slavery, was to draw the line against any *new* slave territory, specifically right now in Kansas/Nebraska. But if that was a minimal position, it was a minimal position that he held to with great firmness, persistence, and clarity straight through to his inauguration as president of the United States. And Lincoln combined that (as we may call it) minimum practical policy position with something else: a consistent and rigorous condemnation of slavery as an "unqualified evil," a moral wrong, stated and restated in many ways, constantly in his speeches from 1854 to 1860. He insisted that there should be no new slave territory and that there be no ambiguity about the nation's fundamental judgment that slavery is wrong.

To call him a "conservative" or a "moderate" opponent of slavery may be therefore a little misleading. These too-simple terms—these terms from our meager supply, or our single spectrum, left-right, conservative-moderate-progressive-radical—may be inadequate to capture complexities that require more than one axis. Lincoln insisted on a consistent "radical" moral condemnation of slavery (as we might say), for all his "moderation" on the immediate application. He would prove to be more resolute and clear-minded about the evil of slavery in the full playing-out of the events ahead than some of those who were ostensibly more "radical" on particular policies in the disputes of the 1850s.

And in his view, keeping the moral judgment clear, even while the application to immediate affairs necessarily can be only limited, was centrally important. In "pragmatic" America that point is sometimes missed or misunderstood. One sometimes hears it said or implied that Lincoln's opposition to slavery was not particularly strong because he "only" opposed slavery "morally," which doesn't mean much because in concrete practical policy all he did was to oppose its spread into territories where it wasn't going to go anyway—only two or three slaves out there in the dust and the uncongenial climate of Kansas. And it was therefore said or implied that there was not much real difference between Douglas and Lincoln so far as actual results are concerned. Douglas, who was indifferent to slavery and proposed that the people of each territory decide, thought it unlikely that slavery would take hold in the uncongenial climate of the Great Plains. Lincoln opposed slavery "morally," but practically proposed no more than a restoring of the Missouri Compromise, to stop slavery from going into that territory. The practical result, say some interpreters, was the same. Lincoln, his moral strictures notwithstanding, was not proposing to overturn this evil thing in the original slave states—nobody, not even the American Anti-Slavery Society, was proposing that.

But Lincoln's position was the very reverse of this dismissive attitude

toward the independent importance of the moral judgment. He did not see
moral clarity as mere fluff or window dressing. For Lincoln the moral issue
was the heart of the matter.

Or perhaps we should say that the heart of the matter for Lincoln was
the moral issue *as it was appropriated by the public*. Lincoln will have
another persistent theme about the central importance of the shaping and
the misshaping of the opinion of the public. When you alter public convictions, you alter the very foundations of the nation. Lincoln is convinced
that through the repeal of the Missouri Compromise, and the defense of it
in the language of "popular sovereignty," and the "don't care" position
about slavery, Douglas and company are mining and sapping the nation's
foundations. What is important about this act is the *principle* it embodies
(that slavery and freedom are on a moral par) and the impact of that principle on the public.

Lincoln would later say that this question (slavery) must be settled "on
some philosophical basis. No policy that does not rest on some philosophical public opinion can be permanently maintained." The phrase
"philosophical public opinion" is striking: not "philosophy" in the closet,
not the "public opinion" ephemera of the moment, but a lasting fundamental public conviction.

And he would go on then to contrast two policies with two contrasting
philosophical bases: the "property view" that slavery is right, which leads
to encouraging it, and the view that it is wrong, which leads to "doing
everything we ought to do if it is wrong." Lincoln then would be quick to
say that does not mean "to attack it where it exists," but it does mean reso-
lutely and firmly to oppose any move to take it outside those limits.

And it was here that Lincoln used his analogy of the venomous snake in
bed with the children: You could not kill it for fear of harming the children,
"but if there was a bed newly made up, to which the children were to be
taken," you certainly would not agree to a proposal to put "a batch of
young snakes in it." Lincoln's policy had an analogy in the "containment"
policy of American cold warriors: not to attack, not to roll back, but to
keep the moral condemnation clear, and strictly to prevent any expansion.

"Immediatists"—the abolitionists—could not understand this combination: If slavery is wrong, then one should act to end it everywhere immediately. Practical—"pragmatic" (antifoundational?)—politicians, on the
other hand, could not understand it, because why would one keep insisting on that (merely?) "philosophical" point that slavery is wrong if you are
not going to oppose the Fugitive Slave Laws, let alone attack slavery in

South Carolina? At a later point in these events, as we shall see, another version of the pragmatic politician would say: Since the practical implication of your position is to resist the admission of Kansas under a proslavery constitution, and Douglas for his own reasons strongly resists that admission, why let merely "philosophical" differences keep you from making an ally of Douglas? Why not support his return to the Senate? But Lincoln kept insisting that explicit public clarity about that philosophical ground—that slavery is a great moral evil—was essential to the permanent solution to the problem of slavery.

He would speak of "the profound central truth" that "slavery is wrong and ought to be dealt with as a wrong." He would say that "we have before us this whole matter of the right or wrong of slavery in this Union, though the immediate question is as to its spreading out into new territories and states." He would call slavery "a moral, social, and political wrong." He would call it "an unqualified evil to the Negro, to the white man, to the soil, and to the state."

At various times Lincoln referred to slavery as an "injustice" (March 3, 1837); as a "monstrous injustice" (October 4, 1854); as "a great moral wrong" (October 16, 1854); as a "wrong [that] ought to be dealt with as a wrong" (March 1, 1859); as wrong "morally and politically" (September 17, 1859); as a "moral, social, and political wrong" (March 1, 1859). He would say it was an "evil"; "an unqualified evil" (September 11, 1858—an *unqualified* evil, in this world of endless qualifications); a "vast moral evil" (July 10, 1858); and "the sum of all villainies" (c. late December 1857). He would describe it as an "odious institution" (August 27, 1856) and as a "tyrannical principle" (October 15, 1858). He compared it to a "deadly poison" (May 18, 1858); to a "cancer," a "wen"—an ugly growth that one hides (October 16, 1854); and to "wolves devouring lambs" (1858). He saw it as "the same old serpent" (July 10, 1858); a rattlesnake (March 5, 1860); a venomous snake (March 6, 1860). When Stephen Douglas tried to say that God gave Adam and Eve *choice,* as in choice between slavery and freedom, Lincoln responded by saying no—God commanded Adam and Eve *not* to eat that *evil* fruit (October 16, 1858). President Lincoln would say to black Americans, "Your race are suffering, in my judgement, the greatest wrong inflicted on any people" (August 14, 1864). And if you think about it, "If slavery is not wrong, nothing is wrong," is about as powerful a statement as one can make.

2. HOW TO MAKE A STRONG MORAL ARGUMENT
WITHOUT BEING MORALISTIC

Lincoln was doing more than writing notes to himself; he would be, for five and a half years after 1854, making his argument to public audiences in a political setting. The *substance* of what he said against the extension of slavery was mostly not distinctive; the *way* he presented it often was. Many of Lincoln's arguments had been made by other anti-Nebraska, antislavery speakers. In these later centuries we lift Lincoln, the famous one, out of all the surrounding symphony, or cacophony, of voices and listen to him alone, because he is the one we know and want to know. If, however, we listened at length to others, we would hear that Lincoln was not, on most points, exactly original. But his voice was nonetheless unusual: He managed to excoriate the Kansas-Nebraska Act, and resist the proposal to expand slavery, and condemn slavery itself, and vigorously to oppose Douglas and his supporting cast, without giving off that odor of haughty superiority and peremptory oversimplification that arose from other presentations.

It is difficult indeed to mount a sustained ethical criticism of some part of the existing world without oversimplifying that world and implying that you are superior to it. The moralizer is notoriously prone to the vices of distortion and self-righteousness. The new American nation, with its grounding in evangelical Protestantism and the Enlightenment, with its unusually heavy load of moral expectations, and its perhaps exaggerated picture of the range of human choice, was particularly prone to cast up examples of these vices—as well as of the earnest moral effort from which (along with human vanity) they spring.

We may deploy moral categories in an objectionable way, by too sharply separating the world into right/wrong along a single axis, and by heightening one set of considerations as "moral" while neglecting others that also have value. We may exaggerate the freedom of human action to alter that real world, and imply by our posture toward the ills of the world that we are above and apart from and superior to those others to whom we ascribe the entire blame for them.

At the same time, the solution to those difficulties cannot be to remain silent or inert in the face of the ills, evils, and injustices in the world. One cannot, as a moral being, be passive because one might fall into self-righteousness or moralism—or seem to. The defenders, perpetrators, and beneficiaries of these ills will charge any opponent, no matter how scrupulous, with those vices—as would be overwhelmingly the case with the decades-long American argument over slavery. One must find ways to combine one's moral responsibilities with a larger vision and with self-criticism.

Now, out in the American West in the middle of the nineteenth century, there arose this politician who dealt with this problem unusually well as he confronted the greatest evil in his society. Abraham Lincoln, after the autumn of 1854, was unequivocal, clear, and persistent in condemning American slavery as a monstrous injustice. His moral condemnation of slavery was not occasional but continual. It was not window dressing, in the way "moral" pretenses sometimes are, gestures without meaning, but the core of a political policy, with consequences. Lincoln's presentation of himself to the national political world from 1854 to 1860 was extraordinary in its concentration and insistence on affirming certain general moral ideas.

But—he managed to do it while avoiding the bane of moralistic distortion and self-righteousness of which Sumner, Chase, and leading abolitionists were, with some reason, accused.

Let us ask how he did it.

First, he did not indulge in epithetical condemnation of the South, and the residents of slave states, or of even the slaveholders. He did not isolate the blame for this great national evil on these particular individuals or on this section of the country or these states. From the speech at the state fair in Springfield on October 4, 1854, until his Second Inaugural on March 4, 1865, he treated the monstrous injustice of slavery, which would be "somehow" the cause of a terrible war, as the responsibility of the entire nation.

He began this pattern of nonblaming, of inclusiveness of responsibility, as we have seen, immediately after the I-hate-it paragraph in his 1854 speech in which he first stated his full moral condemnation of American slavery. He followed that paragraph by going out of his way carefully and explicitly to assert that "they [the Southern people] are just what we would be in their situation."

To glance forward: Even as an embattled president leading one side in a terrible war, he would insist on the both-sidedness of its origin, the diffusion of blame. He would be unequivocal about what caused the war: *Slavery* caused the war, not any of those unlikely other causes later proposed by apologists and revisionists—but slavery caused the war *somehow.* The usually exact Lincoln, the reader of Euclid, would be at some moments blessedly *in*exact: the *almost* chosen people; slavery *somehow* caused the war. I love the Lincoln of the "almost" and the "somehow."

The war was not caused by the secessionists (as he, above all persons, with his quite specific warning in his First Inaugural, could have claimed). Nor by the Slave Power. Nor by the South. The war came somehow because of *slavery*—in which the whole nation was implicated.

The further distinction of Lincoln's presentations lies not only in these themes but in their being combined with undiminished clarity about the moral evil of slavery. His granting that the people of the South are not, in essence, different from or worse than the people of the North, and that he himself is baffled by the complexities of the situation, do not have the effect of acquiescence, despair, or indifference. These admissions do not, in his case, lead to the cutting of the nerve, the relaxing of the will to act. Despite these admissions and concessions, he has quite clear moral and political conclusions, which he presents with force and persistence: Slavery is morally wrong; the Negro has ultimate human rights; no new territory for slavery; public opinion should be restored to the antislavery position of the Founders, who tolerated it only out of necessity.

Both the strictly practical politician and the moralizer have difficulty with this Lincolnian combination. So, we might say, does the ordinary human being—any of us. If we are to be roused to deal with the wrongs, evils, and injustices of the world, then we want *blame.* And simplicity. We prefer villains—the menace of the *slave power,* for example. If, on the other hand, we are to be told that responsibility is diffused, and we are included in it, and that the evils are complicated and hugely resistant, not soon to be overcome—then our will diminishes, our interest flags and turns elsewhere. The "pragmatist" (not a word yet in use in Lincoln's day, but a perennial type, particularly in America) says: Why keep announcing large moral ideas that cannot be fully applied to this current real world? Lincoln kept self-criticism, complexity, responsibility, clear on the one side, the vast evil of slavery clear on the other, and stubbornly held to the relevant applications: no new territory for slavery; no blurring of the national commitment to freedom—against slavery.

The way Lincoln kept the general moral ideas clear was not by the epithets and denunciations that marked the Senate debate and much of the slavery argument. He also did not pile up horror stories. The collection of gruesome facts about slavery put together by the abolitionists Theodore Weld and the Grimké sisters, called *American Slavery as It Is,* played its worthy role in the larger deliberation of society, and so did the powerful fiction of *Uncle Tom's Cabin* that was stimulated by it. But Lincoln was in a different line of work, with different responsibilities and a different audience, from these advocates and propagandists. And he differed from most abolitionists not only in his constituency and his tone, but also in his underlying rhetorical, moral, and social philosophy. Their faces were all toward Zion, but they had differing choices of the road.

Telling horror stories risked implicitly spilling the blame for these horrors on any white person in slave country while implicitly exculpating the describers of the horror. Lincoln insisted that the huge matter of American slavery had to be settled on the basis of principle, and principle grasped and held by public opinion. He did not ordinarily dramatize brutalities of the actual functioning of the institution—except for occasional little sharp eruptions in the service of an argument. He would describe those held in the slave pens of the District as being treated "exactly like droves of horses." In Columbus, Ohio, on September 16, 1859, arguing satirically against Douglas's notion that slavery is a minor matter, Lincoln said, "He [Douglas] is so put up by nature that a lash upon his back would hurt him, but a lash upon anybody else's back does not hurt him [laughter]. That is the build of the man, and consequently he looks upon the matter of slavery in this unimportant light." In New Haven on March 6, 1860, satirizing the inclination to blame all slave resistance on Northern agitators, he said: "So long as we call slavery wrong, whenever a slave runs away they will overlook the obvious fact that he ran because he was oppressed, and declare he was stolen off. Whenever a master cuts his slaves with the lash, and they cry out under it, he will overlook the obvious fact that the negroes cry out because they are hurt, and insist that they were *put to it by some rascally abolitionist* [great laughter]." Lincoln will drop into his speeches a few such swift references to the brutal human reality of slavery, but he will do so only in the course of, and for the purpose of, argument about the principle. The piling up of evidence, of horror stories, is someone else's work.

Writing carefully, conscious of, and respectful of an audience drawn from the great public, insisting that the matter had to be settled on the bases of principle, he developed a nonaccusatory way of conveying a strong moral conviction by *describing* it. By *reporting* it. By *analyzing* the moral differences between this party and that other one.

What he did in that "first great paragraph" in October of 1854 was to *testify* to his own conviction ("I hate it because of the monstrous injustice . . .") rather than flatly to assert, as though directly from God or nature or the moral order, an unequivocal certitude ("Slavery is a monstrous injustice"). The difference may seem slight, and subtle, but when it is extended to paragraphs and whole speeches, it becomes significant.

To be sure, Lincoln held as strongly as any abolitionist did that slavery is indeed a monstrous injustice. But putting it his way subtly implies to the hearer, "I hate it because of [what I perceive to be] the monstrous injustice." I am explaining to you what I believe, not in the first instance proclaiming what has come down from on high, what you must believe. The strong statement we have quoted several times now—if slavery is not wrong, nothing is wrong—appears, characteristically, in a private letter, in the context of personal testimony: "I am naturally anti-slavery . . . I cannot remember when I did not so think and feel."

As the Republican Party would develop and Lincoln in 1856 and after would become one of its interpreters, he would regularly *describe* the party's mission in sharply focused moral terms, and *analyze* and *report* the difference between the parties, also sharply focused on the moral difference. The Republicans regard slavery as a moral wrong and will treat it so; the Democrats don't and won't. One might say that what Lincoln was doing throughout was a work of moral *clarification*.

Even the "house divided" speech, which Lincoln will deliver on June 16, 1858, just after the state Republicans have acclaimed him as their "first and only" choice for senator, would not have exactly the flavor that interpreters past and present, focusing only on the initial "house divided" passage, have attributed to it. It has been thought to be, if not exactly moralistic, then an inflammatory call to arms. But Don Fehrenbacher's authoritative reinterpretation of the *whole* speech shows it to be, instead, an *analysis* (with political consequences). Setting aside many of the familiar notions about this speech, Fehrenbacher wrote that "nowhere in these sentences does he reproach the South or suggest a program of aggressive action against slavery. Like many of his countrymen, he sees another 'crisis' approaching, but there is no mention here of 'irrepressible conflict,' no apocalyptic vision of the bloody years ahead."

What Lincoln *would* do in that speech is to make an interpretation of the current scene (after the Dred Scott decision) that implies a grave warning, especially against that promoter of moral indifferentism, Stephen A. Douglas.

Lincoln certainly would employ *exhortation*—but characteristically addressed to his own side: Here is our moral conviction; let us stand firm in support of it. So it will be in his speech to the Republicans of Chicago in their victory celebration on March 1, 1859. First he would give a succinct statement of the Republican position:

> Never forget that we have before us this whole matter of the right or wrong of slavery in this Union, though the immediate question is as to its spreading out into new Territories and States.

Then he would rise to his concluding exhortation, which is not nearly as eloquent as the peroration of the Cooper Union Address, or the well-known passage from his speech in Alton in the 1858 debates, but in its more plodding way may reveal as clearly Lincoln's moral earnestness:

> All you have to do is to keep the faith, to remain steadfast to the right, to stand by your banner. Nothing should lead you to leave your guns. Stand together, ready, with match in hand. Allow nothing to turn you to the right or to the left. Remember how long you have been in setting out on the true course; how long you have been in getting your neighbors to understand and believe as you now do. Stand by your principles; stand by your guns; and victory complete and permanent is sure at the last.

He did not often exhort, berate, or condemn those on the other side, but he often gave fundamental moral clarification and a strong call to stand firm to his own side.

He developed a formula that he used both for mixed audiences and for private correspondence in which he would summarize the difference, again as though making a factual report: You think slavery right, we think it wrong; that's the whole story. Something like that, in a more complex formulation, flavors his correspondence with his old friend the Kentucky slaveholder Joshua Speed. He would use this formula quite explicitly in a private letter to his old congressional friend and the future vice president of the confederacy, Alexander Stephens, as president-elect in the face of the impeding hurricane of secession and war on December 22, 1860: "You think slavery is *right* and ought to be extended; while we think it is *wrong*

[Lincoln's emphasis, both times] and ought to be restricted. That I suppose is the rub."

In the sixth of the famous senatorial debates, in Quincy on October 13, 1858, Lincoln expanded on this descriptive analysis—we think right / you think wrong—for the last third, and most substantive part, of his opening speech: "I suggest that the difference of opinion, reduced to its lowest terms, is no other than the difference between the men who think slavery a wrong and those who do not think it a wrong." To be sure, Lincoln recognized that some Democrat might object to this description of the difference between the parties, and might protest that he is "as much opposed to slavery as anybody" (a phrase Lincoln will use satirically elsewhere). Lincoln answers this antislavery Democrat that "his leader [Douglas] don't talk as he does, for he never says it is a wrong." And his policies assume it not to be wrong. "He [Douglas] has the high distinction, so far as I know of never having said slavery is either right or wrong [laughter]." Lincoln makes a little argument, mildly flavored with satire, to try to bring this Democrat opposed to slavery to see the error of his ways—or other listeners to be strengthened in their attachment to the Republicans:

> You say it is wrong; but don't you constantly object to anybody else saying so? Do you not constantly argue that this is not the right place to oppose it? You say it must not be opposed in the free States, because slavery is not here; it must not be opposed in the slave States, because it is there; it must not be opposed in politics, because that will make a fuss; it must not be opposed in the pulpit, because it is not religion. [Loud cheers.] Then where is the place to oppose it? There is no suitable place to oppose it.

In the often-quoted passage in the 1858 debate in Alton, Lincoln grandly enlarges this one-side-thinks-wrong / the-other-right into a struggle persisting through all history:

> That is the real issue. That is the issue that will continue in this country when these poor tongues of Judge Douglas and myself shall be silent. It is the eternal struggle between these two principles—right and wrong—throughout the world. They are the two principles that have stood face to face from the beginning of time; and will ever continue to struggle. The one is the common right of humanity and the other the divine right of kings. It is the same principle in whatever

shape it develops itself. It is the same spirit that says, "You work and toil and earn bread, and I'll eat it." [Loud applause.] No matter in what shape it comes, whether from the mouth of a king who seeks to bestride the people of his own nation and live by the fruit of their labor, or from one race of men as an apology for enslaving another race, it is the same tyrannical principle.

To be sure, Douglas's supporters are not going to like or agree with *that* description of the contest, any more than—perhaps even less than—they do the more directly condemnatory utterances of Sumner, Chase, and leading abolitionists. Nevertheless, in the address to the whole Illinois public, and by extension the whole national public, filled with citizens with widely varying and often shifting and conflicted views, Lincoln's slightly less direct, less condemnatory, less proclamatory style may have both a rhetorical advantage and, running through his entire six-year argument, a worthier moral purchase on the issue and on the dispute.

In his address at Cooper Union in February of 1860, he not only ended with a famous exhortation to his Republican comrades but preceded it with the fullest exposition of the formula he had devised: They say it's right, we say it's wrong, that's the whole story. And when, to the astonishment of the American political world, he would stand before it as newly sworn president giving his inaugural address, he would say, "One section of our country believes slavery is *right,* and ought to be extended, while the other believes it is *wrong,* and ought not to be extended. That is the only substantial dispute."

The peroration at Cooper Union included another form of his deft stylistic sidesteppings of too proclamatory a style. He said, in capital letters, in the very last clause: "LET US, TO THE END, DARE TO DO OUR DUTY AS WE UNDERSTAND IT." He did not need to add "as we understand it" as his final words. A critic might say he weakened his ending by tacking it on. But from another point of view, it was a Lincolnian touch that fits. The same would apply to President Lincoln saying in the great last paragraph of his Second Inaugural Address, "with firmness in the right—as God gives us to see the right." He includes a little confessional reminder that the speaker is aware of the possible distortion of his own perception.

Lincoln employed another device, related to this method of clarifying moral summary, particularly on the racist underpinnings of slavery: a kind of wounding from behind, or approaching from the blind side, by means of questioning and probing analysis. We saw this in the state fair speech: Why did you join in prescribing *hanging* for slave traders? Why refuse to shake hands with slave dealers? Why are there free blacks whom someone manumitted? Instead of head-on "denunciation and crimination" (to quote Lincoln himself from his youthful Temperance Address) he finds a way to bring out to his audience their own contradictions.

It is important, if you are to make an effective ethical criticism of some part of the existing world to the broad public, that your moral judgment not be thrown at the heads of your hearers like a rock. There is often a problem in that regard with the religious ground of political argument—on which ground, of course, much of the American slavery controversy was fought. Lincoln did not make his moral affirmations by grand authoritative proclamation, as from on high, speaking on behalf of God.

In the "appeal" that Chase and Sumner and their colleagues issued at the start of the Nebraska fight there was an explicit call upon "Christians and Christian ministers" to intervene. And this fervent appeal told them why: "Their divine religion requires them to behold in every man a brother, and to labor for the advancement and regeneration of the human race." The document was published widely in religious journals. Chase and Sumner sent copies to the Congregational, Presbyterian, Methodist, and Baptist ministers in the Northern states. (Douglas would accuse them, with some justice, of deliberately using the clergy and the churches as the base of a new sectional antislavery movement.) There were sermons by clergymen high and low; editorials in the religious press; petitions and memorials signed by long lists of clergymen. Harriet Beecher Stowe used part of her royalties from *Uncle Tom's Cabin* (published in 1852) to help make that happen. The clergy of the North were active opponents of the Nebraska bill to an extent beyond even the opposition to the Fugitive Slave Law, and *perhaps beyond anything up to that point in American history*. Three thousand and fifty New England clergy protested against the Nebraska bill "in the name of Almighty God"; Chicago clergymen gathered signatures to protest to the chief sponsor, their own senator. Douglas assailed these ministerial productions: these ministers had been led "to desecrate the pulpit, and prostitute the sacred desk to the miserable and corrupting influence of party politics." He particularly objected to the memorialists protesting "in the name of Almighty God" and claiming to speak "in the name of the Almighty upon a political question." Ministers protested his protesting; he presented their protest, and objected to it; further ministers objected to his objecting.

Picture Lincoln reading the Chase-Sumner appeal to the clergy, and the petitions that poured out in response, and then Douglas's sizzling indignation. We may certainly infer that Lincoln was not one of those who admired Douglas's combative return fire, but also that he was not one who uncritically admired the appeal, or the clerical invocation of the will of Almighty God, either.

What was Lincoln's criterion for the condemnation of the moral evil of slavery, as he presented it to the broad public in a political context? Not *primarily* religious belief. He did make deft, tangential, illustrative use of the Bible, which he knew as well as, or better than, other participants in this fight. In condemning slavery, he would refer repeatedly to Adam being expelled from Eden to earn his bread by the sweat of *his* brow—*not* somebody else's brow. And he could refer to a just God and to the Golden Rule. When challenged on religious grounds, he certainly could respond.

But Lincoln on his own initiative would not be quick to make unqualified religious claims. He would be careful, thoughtful, not claiming too much about what God's judgment might be. His presentations would have a powerful religious undertone, but few blunt religious assertions.

One problem with introducing into the general ("secular," nonreligious) world of politics arguments based on religious belief is that there is often sharp disagreement about its application to particular issues. When the new abolitionists arose, largely out of the evangelical revivals in the 1830s, quoting biblical passages and references in their apodictic condemnation of slavery as a sin and slaveholders as sinners, much of the Protestant-churchly world of the very churchly South recoiled in anger and horror, and preachers like the Reverend Mr. Ross sprang to the barricades with biblical and theological artillery to defend slavery. As Lincoln says in that fragment about Dr. Ross, there is no authoritative resolution of these contending claims about the word of God. And as he might have said: The relentless insistence that other believers make the same ethical application of our shared belief that I do is a particularly unpersuasive, even infuriating argumentative attack. Eleven years later, in his Second Inaugural Address as president of the United States, Lincoln would observe that the two sides in the terrible war read the same Bible, prayed to the same God, and each invoked God's aid against the other. Then, almost as an aside, would he state his own position, not exactly as condemnation, but as wonderment: "It may seem strange that any man should dare to ask a just God's assistance in wringing their bread from the sweat of other men's faces." But then he would add the higher religious reservation: "[B]ut let us judge not that we be not judged." There would be a thread of profundity, distinguished from the noisy combatants, running through his presentations all the way to the greatness of that inaugural.

But in the argument over slavery in the 1850s, Lincoln did not ordinarily rest his argument on religious grounds. The further trouble with biblical or religious references presented as decisive moral criteria in this American debate about slavery (as indeed in other disputes) was not only that they could be, and were, deployed on all sides—and fervently—but also that they introduced putative supra-rational absolutes into the relativities of the common life, as Douglas and the preachers flailing at each other illustrated. It is as though one reached out for a transcendental club to beat one's opponent into submission, against his reason and his will.

The authoritative criterion that Lincoln *did* use was an earthbound one: the Declaration of Independence. This document out of America's own history had by Lincoln's time become an authority, a criterion for moral judgment, that citizens of this country could not easily evade or dismiss. When eminent Americans would try to do so, Lincoln would effectively mock the attempt.

Pauline Maier tells in *American Scripture* the story of the document, originally a statement of revolutionary purpose, that had then for two or three decades been neglected. It was then put back into play as a partisan document by the Jefferson party, and then by about the time of Lincoln's entry into public life had begun to acquire a normative status for Americans generally. In its original setting the Declaration was, more or less as Douglas would argue, a proclamatory explanation to England and the world of the colonies' reasons for now separating themselves from the mother country. The second paragraph ("We hold these truths . . ."), with its echoes of John Locke, was at the time a little summary of the commonplaces of political philosophy in the atmosphere of the American colonies, put down in this document as premises for the real argument which came later, in the pounding string of charges against the king ("He has . . . He has . . . He has . . ."). But as the years passed and the now independent people settled into nationhood, and looked back to the founding, and looked about for national self-definition, those early parts of the Declaration shifted slightly in their place in the nation's conversation with itself. Those phrases became not just the premises of a particular revolutionary argument but the continuing moral foundation of the new nation that emerged from it: all "men" with inalienable rights; life, liberty, and (Jefferson's change from the Lockean "property") the pursuit of happiness; governments deriving their just powers from the consent of the governed; and—above all—all men created equal.

Abolitionists and antislavery spokesmen in the 1830s made reference regularly to the Declaration. As we have seen, Senator Benjamin Wade of Ohio in the Senate debates over the Nebraska bill vigorously defended it as the "immortal instrument" bearing "great truths" for which our forefathers fought and which now furnished "a new principle of government" to the nation they founded. So Abraham Lincoln's use of the Declaration as the moral guide for the nation was by no means original. But Lincoln's use of it would be unusually persistent. He would both draw upon and feed the growing American treatment of this document as a statement of national moral premises.

Lincoln had another criterion, or a clutch of criteria, to which he appealed as the grounding of the condemnation of slavery: human reason; human sympathy; a natural sense of justice. Lincoln would appeal to them all, sometimes in tandem; sometimes implicitly, sometimes explicitly. By the way he stated his arguments, carefully, logically, cleanly, he showed a respect for his hearer's capacity to follow an argument, to reason. And sometimes he would appeal to a human sense of sympathy with the oppressed slave—his own sympathy, and the sympathy he was sure others felt as well. Or he would appeal to a "natural sense of justice." He was appealing to something in the makeup of human beings. Making that respectful appeal to our moral reasoning and/or our human sympathy and/or our natural sense of justice was the ultimate method of moral leadership without the bane of moralism.

CHAPTER TWELVE

The Worthy Work
of Party-Building

1. A POINT MERELY PERSONAL TO MYSELF

A climax of sorts to Lincoln's extraordinary efforts of the fall of 1854 came in the afternoon and evening of February 8, 1855, when he almost achieved his heart's desire: to be elected to the United States Senate.

The outcome of the elections of the fall of 1854 had been nearly all that Lincoln, with his anti-Nebraska campaigning, could have hoped to achieve. Among the results were apparent anti-Nebraska majorities in the two houses of the Illinois General Assembly. So why should they not choose as senator the leading anti-Nebraska orator? Lincoln wanted the post badly and tried hard to get it. In that nearly successful effort he displayed once more, as he had in his earlier effort to become congressman, both the little chugging engine of his ambition and his capacity in the pinch of moral necessity to curb that ambition. At least according to the older interpretation, Lincoln gave up his personal ambition by his own initiative and positive act in the service of a high purpose.

That was the reigning interpretation, both among his friends and supporters at the time and among many of the first scholars and writers looking back. Even though he had had at the outset more votes than any rival, almost enough to win, and even though he had had *far* more than anyone else on the anti-Nebraska side, when he saw that the vote might go to a Democrat, a supporter (or at least a nonopponent) of the noxious Kansas-Nebraska Act, Lincoln told his supporters to leave him and to vote for the anti-Nebraska Democrat Lyman Trumbull. Trumbull had had on the first ballot only five votes, to Lincoln's forty-five. Lincoln himself asked in a postmortem: How was it that forty-five yielded to the five? He yielded, in the older view, because it served the larger antislavery purpose.

Nicolay and Hay would write: "In this critical moment Lincoln exhibited a generosity and a sagacity above the range of the mere politician's vision." "It was a most magnanimous and generous act," wrote Isaac Arnold, "and exhibited such an unselfish devotion to principle as to call forth the admiration of all." "[B]y his quick wit and his devotion to the cause," wrote Ida Tarbell, "[he] secured an Anti-Nebraska Senator for the State." The anti-Nebraska "triumph," wrote Josiah Holland, "was due simply to the magnanimity of Mr. Lincoln and his devotion to principle." Herndon put it most grandly: "The student of history in after years will be taught to revere the name of Lincoln for his exceeding magnanimity in inducing his friends to abandon him at the critical period, and save Trumbull, while he himself disappeared beneath the waves of defeat."

But now we have to say that there has been at least one strong dissent from all this—that of Albert Beveridge—and that some twentieth-century Lincoln writers, looking at the evidence in the cool distance of later scholarship, modify and complicate the story and sometimes spare the encomiums.

The story begins well before the February day of its climax, with the first response to the Nebraska bill when Douglas introduced it a year earlier. It was a measure managed by the leading Democrat Stephen Douglas, signed into law and made a matter of party loyalty by Democratic President Franklin Pierce, supported (perforce) by most Democrats—but opposed, partly on some mixture of party and principle, by most Northern Whigs. But the geographical-ideological undertow cut across the parties, nationally and in Illinois. Southern Whigs helped Douglas pass it in Washington. Democrats in some Northern places had a hard time supporting it. In the bustling, rapidly growing northern section of Illinois, with Chicago swelling, with new residents from the Northern states, including New England, there were Democrats, despite Douglas and Pierce, who did not like the Nebraska bill and the repeal of the Missouri Compromise.

In the discussion on the floor of the Illinois Senate, a handful of Democratic senators not only persisted in their opposition but gave speeches against the resolution endorsing their party leader's bill. The leader of these dissident Democrats was Senator Norman Judd of Chicago; another was John Palmer—these are names that will appear again. They would form a little platoon of "anti-Nebraska Democrats" that would be pivotal in the choice of a United States senator the following February.

The elections of the following fall, as already noted, were a Democratic debacle, an anti-Nebraska success. The Douglas-led regular Democrats suffered major losses nationwide and in Illinois. The "fusion" of opponents trounced Douglas, Nebraska, and the regular Democrats in the elections for the two houses of the Illinois state legislature. The Democrats were reduced to a minority status they had never held during Lincoln's terms in the state legislature two decades earlier.

And the new Illinois General Assembly would have in its grasp the great gift of a United States Senate seat. They would be choosing a colleague for Senator Douglas. So the question arose in many alert and eager Illinoisan political minds as they looked at the astonishing election results: Who should this new Illinois legislature choose to be senator?

One place where the answer was clear was the parlor at Eighth and Jackson Streets in Springfield. Lincoln had made himself the leading spokesman for the anti-Nebraska forces in the state. So when anti-Nebraska forces carried the election, should he not be chosen senator?

It is significant that Lincoln had already been writing letters as well as making speeches in the anti-Nebraska cause well before the November elections, and that his correspondence was not confined to Whigs. One of the most interesting of his letters was written on September 7, 1854, to John Palmer, part of that little anti-Nebraska Democratic cohort in the Illinois Senate. Lincoln apologizes for "obtruding" his letter upon Palmer, "to whom I have even been opposed in politics." But, he says, the important thing is that Nebraska be "rebuked." He respectfully asks this oldtime party opponent to make "a few public speeches" stating his reasons for opposing his own party on the Nebraska matter. "You have had a severe struggle with yourself, and you have determined *not* to swallow the *wrong*," Lincoln wrote, sympathetically. Then Lincoln closes this private, confidential letter to a member of the party opposed to his own by saying that had Palmer been chosen to be his party's congressional nominee (as he should have been, had it not been for the Democrats making support of Nebraska mandatory), he, Lincoln, would still have voted for his Whig opponent, "but I should have made no speeches, written no letters, and you would have been elected by at least a thousand majority." If you were

the incumbent Whig congressman Richard Yates and if you discovered
this letter, you would surely have been miffed that this leading Whig had
already signaled that he would not *actively* support you against this particular opponent.* And you would have been further unsettled that the letter rather implies that Lincoln would not mind if this opponent of his
party's nominee won big, because he is an able anti-Nebraska man. Lincoln was already, to this degree, putting the anti-Nebraska cause in a higher
place than Whig victory. This letter also shows, if it needs any showing,
that Lincoln's political activity in that fall was by no means confined to
promoting either his own senatorial chances or those of the Whig Party. It
shows that anti-Nebraskaism in Lincoln's eyes now overrode everything
else. And there may be also something else implied, which will later come
round to cut down Lincoln himself: In the anti-Nebraska cause Democrats
(from Douglas's own party, the party that sponsored the obnoxious act)
are worth much more pound for pound than any Whig, because they are
crossovers.

Once the composition of the new legislature was known, Lincoln's letter writing did center on promoting his own chances to be elected senator.
Again, as in his quest for Congress in 1843–46, they are tactful and gracious, but at the same time not bashful in their request for support and for
help. These are a study in Lincoln's conduct as a quite ambitious politician who is nevertheless respectful of others and—in the end—promoting
something larger than his own advancement. He will say forthrightly on
November 11, "I really have some chance," and on November 27, "I want a
chance to be the man [the Whig chosen senator]." To merchant Charles
Hoyt, on November 10, he wrote: "You used to express a good deal of par-
tiality for me; and if you are still so, now is the time." Twice (to the editor of
the *Fulton County Republican* on November 29 and to his longtime friend
Joseph Gillespie on December 1) he will use the faintly self-mocking
phrase that "I have ['really' to Gillespie] got it into my head to try to be
U.S. Senator," adding to Gillespie, "and if I could have your support my
chances would be reasonably good."

He would be scrupulously deferential to the claims of others; to Gillespie he will go on to say, "I know, and acknowledge, that you have as just
claims to the place as I have; and therefore I do not ask you to yield to
me, if you are thinking of becoming a candidate yourself." But he would,

---

* In the newly numbered Sixth District, from the redrawn districts after the 1850
census.

characteristically, go on to say to Gillespie: "If, however, you are not, there I should like to be remembered affectionately by you; and also, to have you make a mark for me with the anti-Nebraska members, down your way."* To anti-Nebraska house member Thomas Henderson, who may have hinted in response to Lincoln's first letter that he might vote for Archibald Williams, Lincoln, with a characteristic mixture of candor and modesty, would write: "Of course I prefer myself to all others, yet it is neither in my heart nor my conscience to say I am any better than Mr. Williams." But by way of persuading Henderson, nevertheless, he did send him a copy of his Peoria speech, adding once again a self-deprecating touch: "You may have seen it before; or you may not think it worth seeing now."

He is scrupulous and tactful, but he is also persistent and energetic, calling in all his chips. To his friend Congressman Elihu Washburne on December 11, he was careful to say: "I have not ventured to write all the members in your district, lest some of them should be offended by the indelicacy of the thing—that is, coming from a total stranger." But then he made a straightforward request of Washburne: "Could you not drop some of them a line?"

These letters are just the small part of Lincoln's effort that reached the lasting visibility of ink. He *wanted* that job. He also *wanted* Douglas and Nebraska defeated. It was exactly in the discussion of his seeking this election to the Senate in 1855 that Herndon lofted into all subsequent writing about Lincoln his picture of Lincoln's ambition as a restless engine. It gains force from the sentences around it:

> The man who thinks Lincoln calmly sat down and gathered his robes about him, waiting for the people to call him, has a very erroneous knowledge of Lincoln. He was always calculating, and always planning ahead. His ambition was a little engine that knew no rest. The vicissitudes of a political campaign brought into play all his tact and management and developed to its fullest extent his latent industry.

---

* Stephen Logan, Lincoln's campaign manager in the senatorial election, would still remember eleven years later that on the first ballot Gillespie voted not for Lincoln but for Cyrus Edwards (*HI*, p. 467).

During the weeks between the election and the first meeting of the new legislature at the start of 1855, Lincoln slept, Herndon wrote, like Napoleon, with one eye open.

Lincoln bought some little notebooks and by one account, with Mary's help, made a useful list in them—not just one list for himself, but also several copies for use by his supporters, all written out in his own hand. Each list named all one hundred members of the two houses—twenty-five in the Senate, seventy-five in the House—with the county of each and a letter indicating member's affiliation: W for Whig, D for Democrat, and A.N.D. for anti-Nebraska Democrat, the crucial group. There was also one N.W.—a lonely Whig supporter of the act—and one Abn., for abolitionist, Owen Lovejoy.* Now add it up—could it be that Mary was there calculating this with him? The biographer of Mary Todd Lincoln, Jean Baker, suggests that it might have been so. Adding all the Whigs but one, plus the A.N.D.'s and the one Abn., did result in a "majority" in the combined houses of fifty-seven (shaky, volatile) presumed anti-Nebraska votes to forty-one rather solid Douglas Democratic votes. The anti-Nebraska forces surely ought to be able to obtain the fifty-one votes necessary to elect an anti-Nebraska senator.

Would it not have seemed to be so if one had sat in that parlor in the winter of 1854–55 and considered whether one might not soon become the wife of a United States senator?

But the composition of the legislature was not as tidily structured as the listing in the Lincolns' notebooks made it seem. Matthew Pinsker, in the leading article about this episode, sees the most important cross-cutting division to have been regional in this state with its long north-south stretch. In the north, ex-Whig and ex-Democratic and ex-Free-Soil anti-Nebraska folk were already working together and calling themselves "Republican"; in the south, although opponents of Nebraska were also working together, they were wary of the radical implications of that label.

Lincoln's political problem on the one side was to get the support of these "Republicans"—the most thoroughgoing and focused antislavery men. This he managed to do, with the help of a testimonial from a man with enormous prestige in that ideological wing, the longtime antislavery

---

* By Lincoln's count there were, in the Senate, eleven Democrats, nine Whigs, and five A.N.D.'s. In the House the Lincolns listed thirty Democrats, twenty-eight Whigs, fourteen A.N.D.'s. And there was the one vacancy.

warhorse in Congress, his old messmate Joshua Giddings, who told Elihu Washburne he would "walk all the way to Illinois" to elect Lincoln.

But then, meanwhile, he had to draw support from the diverse collection of other members who were wary about those "Republicans." One action he took was to resign from, or rather to decline to serve on, the state committee of this new "Republican" party that Owen Lovejoy and Ichabod Codding had formed the evening of the day that Lincoln gave his address at the state fair in Springfield—October 5. When in November he received a note from Codding asking him to attend a Republican State Central Committee meeting, Lincoln took the occasion, in a letter written November 27, 1854, to make clear his disengagement from them: "I was not consulted on the subject, nor was I apprised of the appointment, until I discovered it by accident . . ." He then stated the relationship between his views and those of these Republicans: "I suppose my opposition to slavery is as strong as that of any member of the Republican party; but I had also supposed that the extent to which I feel authorized to carry that opposition, practically, was not at all satisfactory to that party."

He had also to tender another, much more difficult resignation. The reader may remember that in early September, almost incidentally—one senses—as part of his vigorous new anti-Nebraska political activity, he had allowed his friends to put him up (along with Stephen Logan) for a seat from Sangamon in the state House of Representatives. And then he *won*, and with the largest vote, just like the old days. But the new six-year-old state constitution appeared to forbid the legislature from choosing one of its own members as senator—an awkward fact. And there was awkwardness in the opposite direction, too: the election of a United States senator in the General Assembly was surely going to be close, and every anti-Nebraska vote would be important. If he resigned, he opened his now safely anti-Nebraska seat to the prospect of being taken over in a special election by a pro-Nebraska Democrat. He did resign, and that is what happened.

How did he get himself into this pickle? He has come in for a deal of reproof from historians and biographers for not having checked out the constitutional restriction before allowing his name to be entered for the legislative seat. We may suggest, in his quasi-defense, that presumably at that time, in early September, he was engaged in a general anti-Nebraska political effort, and had not yet focused closely on the possibility that he himself might have a real chance to become a United States senator—a possibility that came clearly into view only after the results of the election were known in November. He himself explained, perhaps rather lamely, when he resigned that he had let his name be offered in the state legislative race only because he was told that it would help the Whig anti-Nebraska candidate for the U.S. House seat, Richard Yates. Pinsker offers the further defense that the state constitutional provision was new and untested, and later to be found unconstitutional because no state may alter requirements for federal office. The restriction was "dubious and open to challenge."

That Lincoln nevertheless chose to resign, to remove that shadow, was yet another indication of the strength of his ambition to be chosen senator.

Then the sin of his resigning a safe anti-Nebraska seat was compounded when in the special election two days before Christmas the Democrats won the seat. They did it by skillful organization, or trickery, depending upon your point of view. They pretended to run no candidate—but they silently organized their voters, and suddenly on the special election day featured the name of their candidate in their paper, got their people to the polls, and "favored by a rainy day" in a *much* reduced turnout, won the seat by eighty-two votes.

Lincoln seems to have taken no steps to ensure that the seat he had won and resigned be retained for the anti-Nebraska side. Overconfidence may have been one reason; a month earlier, in the congressional election, Richard Yates, though he would lose in the U.S. congressional district as a whole, carried Sangamon County with 2,166 votes. But "on the rainy day" of the special election, "our man" got only 984 votes. (On these rainy election days the rain, in contrast to the biblical assurance, seems to fall more on the just than on the unjust.)

Strong antislavery politicians were much annoyed with Lincoln in this episode, and said about him the exact reverse of the praise that supporters and biographers would shower upon him for his eventual role in the choice of a senator: By running for the state House seat, and then, after winning, resigning because he wanted to be senator (and perhaps they would say by then ignoring the special election so that a Democrat won), he put his personal advancement ahead of the cause.*

---

* There was a possibility, although just the possibility, of a yet more discreditable motive, beyond overconfidence or inertia, for Lincoln's neglect of the special election. A letter from Judge David Davis, his old friend and active political supporter in this and all future contests, indicated that the Whig candidate who was defeated (on a rainy day) by eighty-two votes, one Norman Broadwell, had already indicated that if elected he would vote in the choice of a senator for *Richard Yates.* (Yates, having lost his congressional seat, generated a brief boomlet for himself now to be senator.) It would indeed have damaged Lincoln's prospects, the ultra-realistic Davis wrote, to have his own home district representative vote for someone else. Had Lincoln been influenced by that Machiavellian twist? Without denying Lincoln's political realism and ambition, one may still be permitted to doubt it. He

On January 1, the two houses of the Illinois General Assembly gathered in Springfield. The loosely allied "anti-Nebraska" forces were able to control the organization of both houses, although the twenty-five-member senate was close. The two houses had to meet jointly to choose the senator; either house, by declining to meet, could cause the election to go over to another time—delay it. It was a victory and a good omen when the anti-Nebraska forces managed to get the two houses to vote to meet jointly. The maneuvering for the Senate seat intensified.

A lobbyist who watched him, one Elijah M. Haimes, described Lincoln at work in the hallways of the General Assembly. Lincoln "was not forward in pressing his case upon the attention of members, yet, before the interview would come to a close, some allusion to the senatorship would generally occur, when he would respond in some such way as this: 'Gentlemen, that is a rather delicate subject for me to talk upon, but I must confess that I would be glad of your support of the office, if you shall conclude that I am the proper person for it.'" These personal appeals would seem to have had the same tactful but persistent flavor as his letters. By the combination he gathered more "committals" than any rival on the anti-Nebraska side.

But the other side, the Democrats, had not been sleeping. They realized that it would be difficult to reelect the Democratic incumbent, James Shields, an active longtime Democrat whom Mary Todd and Lincoln had encountered in that episode of the near-duel in 1842. Douglas, back in Washington, insisted that the Democrats should stand by his colleague and support Shields all the way, never giving up, and that they should, if they couldn't reelect him, condemn the opposition for nativist bigotry because Shields was born in Ireland. The Nebraska issue, said Douglas, with spectacular overconfidence, was decided and over with, not an issue.

But Democrats on the ground in Illinois knew the situation better than Douglas did. Shields would be hard to reelect exactly because he had been a loyal Douglas supporter, and had actually cast his vote for the noxious Kansas-Nebraska Act. Democrats would have to give the sitting senator their courtesy votes for a time, but they needed another candidate to win.

That other candidate, quietly making his own calculations, was the Democratic governor of the state, Joel Matteson. Matteson, as a governor,

---

pursued his ambition, in general, within honorable limits. The hint that it might not have been so bad that this Broadwell was defeated comes only from Davis, and not from anything of Lincoln's; Davis, moreover, wrote not *before* but *after* the election, consolingly: At least there is this benefit. Lincoln's postelection attitude was just an embarrassed effort to discount the importance of the result of the special election. (King, *David Davis*, p. 106.)

not a senator or congressman, had not had to vote on the Kansas-Nebraska Act. He had not taken a public position on it, and could hint in the right circles that he could be persuaded or instructed to stand against it. He was a Joliet businessman who had been associated with the work on that Illinois and Michigan canal for which state representative A. Lincoln had long ago voted, and as governor Matteson had support for reasons that had nothing to do with the Kansas-Nebraska Act. He looked promisingly (or dangerously, depending upon your point of view) to be the sort of semi-compromise candidate who might bring enough of the anti-Nebraska Democrats back to the fold—they were, or had been, Democrats, after all—to join with the regular Democrats and win. The political logic of this was clear enough that even though it was not public at all, knowledgeable hostesses in political Springfield, quoted in the leading article by Matthew Pinsker, would write that Governor Matteson appeared to have it sewed up. But did he?*

The voting did not start on January 31, because a ferocious snowstorm—the worst since "the winter of the deep snow" in Lincoln's first year in Illinois—smothered Springfield.

At three o'clock in the afternoon of February 8, 1855, in the Hall of Representatives of the State Capitol in Springfield, where so many noteworthy events of Lincoln's life would take place, the Nineteenth General Assembly of Illinois met in joint session to choose a senator. The galleries were bursting. Among those who had climbed the stairs to watch the vote was Mary Todd Lincoln. Would she go to bed that night the wife of a senator?

Also in the gallery were the wife and daughter of Governor Matteson. Why were they there?

The anti-Nebraska members had held a caucus and had decided to support Lincoln. But Judd, Palmer, and the others in the little platoon of anti-Nebraska Democrats did not attend the caucus.

On the first ballot Lincoln received forty-five votes (forty-four, Lincoln would say in letters afterward, but the Speaker also voted for him);

* Pinsker wrote at one point that the usual accounts of this episode overlook the fact "that by the end of the campaign [the prevoting scramble] Lincoln fully expected to lose," but later made the point more gently: Just as the balloting began, after interruptions, "Lincoln had little hope of winning." David Herbert Donald puts it a little more softly still: "As January 31, the scheduled day for the election approached, he was still about three votes short of a majority, and he did not see where they could come from" (Donald, *Lincoln*, p. 183).

Shields, forty-one votes; Trumbull, five votes—the five anti-Nebraska Democrats—with eight votes scattered among others. Perhaps Mary in the gallery gave a gasp of rather great annoyance when her husband's old friend and political associate Joseph Gillespie voted not for Lincoln but for her relative-by-marriage Cyrus Edwards. Why do that? Cyrus Edwards wasn't going anywhere. Still, her husband was only six votes away from the needed majority of fifty-one, and in the gallery she might have thought he was almost there, because in the little notebook it would appear that there were many more possible accessions to him from anti-Nebraska members than there were for his chief rival, James Shields, who already had all that he might ever be expected to get. So it might have seemed to her, watching from the gallery, full of hope that the next ballot would bring that mere handful of needed votes to her husband.

As the names were called a second time Lincoln lost four of his first-ballot supporters—but, on the other hand, gained two new ones (including Gillespie, now voting as he should have the first time). In a letter summarizing the whole episode Lincoln would say that at one time or another he received votes from forty-seven (must it not have been forty-eight?) members—just four, or three, short—tantalizingly close. Shields got his forty-one once more, and he would keep on getting forty-one votes on almost every ballot.

On the third ballot Lincoln himself slipped to forty-one, so the two apparent chief contenders were momentarily in a dead heat.[*]

Lincoln lost three more votes on the fourth ballot and dropped to thirty-eight, with Shields still getting his forty-one. Trumbull now came up to eleven votes, five of them coming from members who had at first voted for Lincoln. On the fifth ballot Lincoln would drop further to thirty-four. One of the four departing votes would be Owen Lovejoy. One can imagine the anxiety and frustration in one section of the gallery with Lincoln's gentle trend downward on these repeated roll calls. On the sixth ballot he would recover two returnees, coming back up to thirty-six.

Nicolay and Hay, who knew many of the key participants, wrote that

[*] After this deadlocked third ballot Stephen Logan, Lincoln's floor manager, moved that the joint session adjourn—without having chosen a senator. The choice would then "go over" to another joint session, at which perhaps the anti-Nebraska forces, and specifically the Lincoln forces, might mobilize the necessary votes. But the joint session, by a vote of fifty-two to forty-six, declined to adjourn. The forty-six voting to adjourn were almost exactly Lincoln's original vote, plus only one. The fifty-two negative votes thus included not only all the regular Democrats, but also Judd, Palmer, and the other recalcitrant anti-Nebraska Democrats.

"the proceedings had wasted away a long afternoon of most tedious suspense. Evening had come; the gas was lighted in the hall, the galleries were filled with eager women, the lobbies were packed with restless and anxious men. All had forgotten the lapse of the hours, their fatigue, and their hunger, in the absorption of the fluctuating contest."

That absorption got a sudden jolt as the clerk began to call the roll for the seventh ballot. Up to that point the main patterns had held steady through the repeated roll calls, Shields and Lincoln locked in almost equal combat with a shifting scattering of votes for others and only small numbers of individual variations this way and that. The tension would have come from the arithmetic: would either Shields or Lincoln add, on this next ballot, significant votes to his previous total?

But now, as the roll call began on the seventh ballot, there came votes that must have sent a shiver through some sections of the gallery. Voices that had been saying "Shields" all afternoon now suddenly said "Matteson": one, and then another, and then another, and then another of the regular Democrats who had been voting for Shields voted instead for Governor Matteson. Matteson up to that point had had at most two votes, usually only one, and on two ballots none. Those who had not known it before—did Mary Lincoln?—now certainly were made aware that there was a concerted strategy to switch all of Shields's votes to Matteson.

The Lincoln forces tried to rally and were able to bring two wandering ones back into the fold to boost his vote back up to thirty-eight, but Matteson suddenly shot up to forty-four—Shields's forty-one and the three more—and was now abruptly a real threat.

The incumbent Shields, who himself in the Senate actually cast his vote for the hated Nebraska bill, and who was a faithful associate of Douglas throughout, was never going to make it: none of the A.N.D.'s would come over to him, as the repeated balloting showed. But Matteson might be another story.

It must have been with trepidation that the Lincoln forces, and the Lincoln partisans in the gallery, watched the voting on the next ballot, the eighth, and with the results their hearts must have sunk. Matteson gained two more votes to stand at forty-six; Lincoln lost nine votes, to fall to his lowest count thus far, twenty-seven votes, and nine of these went to Lyman Trumbull, who hitherto had fluctuated between five and eleven, far behind the leaders, but who now had eighteen votes.

· · ·

It is at this point, after the eighth ballot, Albert Beveridge said, that Lincoln should have thrown his support to Trumbull. Lincoln's vote, Beveridge wrote, had already "crumbled"—down to twenty-seven from forty-five—and Trumbull's had "shot up" to eighteen and Matteson stood at a dangerously high forty-six—so Lincoln should have seen the obvious, that he could not win, and that there was a grave and immediate danger that Matteson would get the few last votes he needed. Lincoln therefore should have done then, after the eighth ballot, what he belatedly would do after the ninth—to tell his supporters to shift to Trumbull. "In view of his skill as a politician," Beveridge wrote, "it is hard to understand why, under the circumstances, Lincoln risked another ballot, for the speedy election of the Democratic governor was more than probable." Beveridge even went so far as to venture explanations for this conduct—an expert politician "risking" another ballot—that he finds "hard to understand." "If eagerness had not dulled his judgment, the fact that Mrs. Lincoln was in the gallery is a possible explanation of the hazard he now took, for she was determined that her husband would win." There's a picture: Lincoln the astute but perhaps overly eager politician down on the house floor, now aware that he can't win, and that a Matteson victory is an imminent threat, and that he should throw his votes to Trumbull—but then looking up into the gallery, where he sees his wife's narrowed eyes and resolute chin and decides to "risk" another ballot. (I don't think it happened that way.)

There may be a kind of perverse perfectionism in this treatment by Beveridge, of a sort that appears elsewhere in Lincoln writing. Because this man has been elevated so high—turned into such a talismanic moral hero—any human complexity in his conduct as one actually examines the details, any deviation from the simple story line, comes as a shock and induces overreaction. Beveridge takes what Lincoln *did* do—which not many persons would have done—and then uses that as the criterion by which to judge that he should have done it one ballot earlier! Lincoln's having done it opens the possibility of a candidate in such a race doing such a rare thing. To chide Lincoln for not doing that one ballot earlier, while he was still standing at twenty-seven votes, in a volatile situation in which he and others had and would go up as well as down, when Trumbull had still only eighteen votes, is surely to impose an impossibly exacting standard. It is using Lincoln's eventual magnanimity against him, as the source of the model of conduct that then the critic now says he waited too long to do.

.   .   .

On the dangerous ninth ballot Matteson gained only one vote, to stand at forty-seven, but still more of Lincoln's supporters among anti-Nebraska Democrats fell away to Trumbull, bringing Trumbull all the way up to thirty-eight votes. Lincoln now had only fifteen votes—"humiliating," says Beveridge. All of these fifteen Lincoln loyalists were Whigs who had been with him from the start and—according to Lincoln and others—never would leave him. A contest that had begun as a struggle between Shields and Lincoln had now been transformed into a contest between Matteson and Trumbull—with Matteson the far more likely winner.

It was at this point that Lincoln made his famous decision. Joseph Gillespie came to Lincoln and asked what to do, and Lincoln "said unhesitatingly, 'You ought to drop me and go for Trumbull. That is the only way you can defeat Matteson.'"

According to Gillespie, Judge Logan came up about that time and insisted on running Lincoln still. But Lincoln "said if you do you will lose both Trumbull and myself and I think the cause in this case is to be preferred to men."

And so there came one of those dramatic moments by which such sessions are sometimes marked. "Amid an excitement that was becoming painful, in a silence where spectators barely breathed, Judge Stephen T. Logan . . . arose and announced the purpose of the remaining Whigs to decide the contest, whereupon the entire fifteen changed their votes to Trumbull. This gave him the necessary fifty-one votes and elected him a Senator of the United States."

Late in the evening of February 8, 1855, Mary Todd Lincoln learned that she would not be a senator's wife—not this time, anyway. She was, unlike her husband, a person who really knew how to hold a grudge. For the rest of her life she kept in place her resentment against Norman Judd, the leader of those pernicious five anti-Nebraska Democrats who held out against voting for her husband and thereby forced the outcome. Judd went on to become a close Republican associate of her husband, but when he badly wanted a cabinet appointment in the new Lincoln administration, Mary Lincoln with a long memory went out of her way to argue against it. She called on Lincoln's friend and political helper Judge David Davis, who also resented Judd's role, to help her prevent it. She and Davis actually developed a certain new rapport in their shared resentments.

Davis, who had worked to get Lincoln votes in the preliminaries but who had to be out of Springfield on the day of the voting, also proved to be a solid grudge-holder. He never after this day trusted Lyman Trumbull. Mary Lincoln also believed Trumbull himself to have been reprehensible and deceitful, to have taken the nomination (and the Senate seat) that in her view should have gone to her husband. But her most spectacular display of grudge-holding was against Trumbull's wife, who was her old friend Julia Jayne. Julia Jayne had been a collaborator in the partisan journalistic undertaking, the infamous "Rebecca letters" mocking Shields, that had precipitated the Shields/Lincoln near-duel, and she had been Mary's bridesmaid. But for the crime of her husband's victory on this February evening, Mary—to put it in the most dramatic of the forms it is put—never spoke to Julia Jayne again. She described her in disparaging terms in various letters. A year later, according to Mrs. Trumbull, when the two almost met outside church, Julia came over to speak to her old friend Mary, but "she turned her head the other way and pretended not to see me."

One can surely make a case, using the universal human language of resentment, for her position. Her husband had forty-five votes (or forty-seven, or forty-eight); his chief anti-Nebraska opponent had but five. They shared the common, overriding objective, to administer a "rebuke" to Nebraska. So then should not *they* have yielded to *him,* instead of the other way around? One of the clear reasons for their obstinacy—that despite their opposition to Douglas and Nebraska they had been elected as Democrats, and could never vote for a Whig—simply increased one's indignation. So men elected as Whigs should now vote for a Democrat? That Judd and company put it in those terms would increase the inclination on the other side to respond in kind: If they refuse, ballot after ballot, with their little total of five, to subordinate their partnership to the cause and give those last few votes for a victory, then how much less would we Whigs, with our original large majority, abandon *our* partisanship and turn around and vote for the candidate of folks who make an argument like that one! If you were elected as Democrats, there we were, just as much elected as Whigs. And if Lincoln is in your circles a notorious Whig, whom you have fought on the issues through the years, so Lyman Trumbull is in our circles just as much a notorious Democrat, whom we have fought on the issues through the years. If the resentful spirit of Mary Todd Lincoln, or David Davis, or of many—perhaps most—human beings, had prevailed, then the fragile fusion of anti-Nebraska politicians might have ground to a halt, in a reciprocity of mutual recrimination, and Matteson the Democrat elected.

Joseph Gillespie told Herndon that after Lincoln had lost and Trumbull won, "there was considerable bitterness displayed by some of the old Whigs who regarded it as an affront. . . ."

Her husband had no such talent for grudges. He did, however, in a letter to his supporter Congressman Washburne, make a comment for which both Matthew Pinsker and David Herbert Donald have chided him: "an uncharacteristic lack of generosity," wrote Donald; "uncharacteristic malice," wrote Pinsker. The sentence thus reproved is directed not at any of his wife's villains but at Joel Matteson. It goes like this: "I could have headed off every combination and been elected had it not been for Matteson's double game—and his defeat now gives me more pleasure than my own gives me pain."

It is not required of our project to defend Lincoln on every front and all the time. On the contrary, it is both a premise and a discovery of this book that Lincoln was human, that he was not born on Mount Rushmore, that he would be good but God knew when, that he acquired such moral distinction as he did achieve by deliberate effort over time, and that that moral excellence (of course) never was or would be anything like perfection. Still, I do not think we need to count this little postelection pout—written the day immediately after a quite painful defeat—very heavily against him. It appears that Lincoln really did believe that Joel Matteson played a double game—and that he may actually have done so. Obviously he did in the sense that he used Shields as a stalking horse for six ballots and then burst onto the scene. He may also have presented different faces to different constituencies with respect to the Kansas-Nebraska Act. And it is suggested that he may have been trying to buy the last few needed votes, using his powerful role with respect to the canal, with members from northern districts adjacent to the canal.

But in any case, as the episode receded and he reported to other friends, Lincoln would make clear that his satisfaction in the defeat of Matteson did not have primary reference to Matteson personally. Writing to William H. Henderson on February 21, he interpreted the event this way: "My larger number of friends had to surrender to Trumbull's smaller number, in order to prevent the election of Matteson which would have been a Douglas victory." Of course preventing a *Douglas* victory for Lincoln in these years was not simply personal, but a *cause* with moral substance—it would have been a Nebraska Act victory. In another sentence in the letter to Henderson Lincoln said: "I could not . . . let the whole political result go to ruin on a point merely personal to myself." That he would speak of the "whole political result" and use the word "ruin" to describe a Matteson victory (which he saw to be a Douglas victory) shows that he interpreted a possible Matteson victory in high policy terms: It would have been a Nebraska Act victory and a defeat for the anti-Nebraska side, particularly galling and significant after the anti-Nebraska forces had swept to a large victory in the election. I suggest it might require little if any generosity on our part to revise the offending passage thus: "The defeat of the Nebraska/Democratic/Douglas forces gives me more pleasure than my own merely personal defeat gives me pain."

Was there anything admirable, after all, now that we know more of the complicating details, in Lincoln's decision on the evening of that February day, to urge his supporters to go over, en masse, to Trumbull? Yes, we may say there was.

One can say that by the time of the later ballots at least, if not before, it was *almost* clear that Lincoln could not win. One can say that the race had *almost* come down to Matteson versus Trumbull. But one does not need to go on to say, as critics do, that Lincoln had no choice but to throw his support to Trumbull. Ethics is about choice; Beveridge and others imply that Lincoln did not have, in the end, any choice. One may answer: He certainly did have choices. Most human beings, in Lincoln's situation, would let the balloting go on—which is, after all, a choice. Most of us would not even have presented to ourselves the option of telling our voters to go for Trumbull. We would let the ballots roll on out of inertia and resignation, tinged perhaps with denial and wild hope. And taking the initiative that Lincoln took would be blocked, for most of us, by resentment. What he proposed, after all, was to hand the victory, by his own initiative, exactly to those who prevented his own victory—to Trumbull, Judd, Palmer, and the rest. Mary Todd Lincoln, David Davis, and—one infers—most of Lincoln's core supporters would not have done it.

To appreciate Lincoln's decision we should imagine his situation. He really did want to be senator; as he would put it in another connection later, the taste was in his mouth a little—in this case, more than a little. And, as he and Mary looked at the lists in the little notebooks, he could see that he nearly had it in his hand. The votes were there if the anti-Nebraska forces voted together. He was by all means the obvious, and the deserving, choice. Joseph Gillespie remembered it this way: "There was a majority for the first time in the history of Illinois against the Democratic party in the Legislature. This result was mainly attributed to his [Lincoln's] efforts and he was the first choice of all but five of the opposition members." So would you reward that recalcitrant five by handing them the victory?

Lincoln had to make a positive and definite choice, against the force in particular of the despairing inertia of most losing candidates in a race. He had to be "earnest and decided" to persuade his Whig supporters to vote for Trumbull, which they hated to do.

Looking back from the days of Lincoln's full life and vast fame, we can be complacent about this event because we know that history has mammoth future triumphs in store for him. But in February of 1855, that was not something that he or his wife or his supporters knew. Joseph Gillespie would say: "We (his friends) regarded this as perhaps his last chance for that high position."

That Lincoln's decision was not overwhelmingly obvious is indicated by the resistance of his supporters; by the grudges of Mary and of Davis and the lasting resentment of some Whigs; and by the gratitude of Trumbull, Judd, Palmer, and future Republicans generally. Lincoln's act in this case was an important impetus for the insistence of Republicans in county after county in 1858, the next race, that Lincoln was their "first and only" choice for senator. Lincoln himself would write, after it was done, that a "less good-natured man" than he would not have done what he did.

Lincoln did not hold a grudge against Lyman Trumbull, with whom he went on to collaborate in the Republican Party for the rest of his life. He would not nurse any resentments against John Palmer, who one year later would urge that Lincoln be nominated for vice president by the new Republican Party, and who at the state Republican convention in 1860 would introduce the resolution endorsing Lincoln as the candidate of Illinois Republicans for the presidency, and make the key motion that Illinois vote in the convention under the unit rule unanimously for Lincoln. And, perhaps most notably, Lincoln would hold no "malice" against Norman Judd, who would serve as state Republican chairman, arrange to have the 1860 convention in Chicago, and serve as a Lincoln manager.

While Lincoln held no grudge against Judd, Lincoln supporters were less forgiving. In a letter dated December 9, 1859, Lincoln explained to Judd that the lingering resentment others felt toward Judd on Lincoln's behalf was not shared by the candidate himself:

> You did vote for Trumbull against me; and, although I think, and have said a thousand times, that was no injustice to me, I cannot change the fact, nor compel people to cease speaking of it. Ever since that matter

occurred, I have constantly labored, as I believe you know, to have all
recollection of it dropped . . . I have, in no single instance, permitted a
charge against [you] such as above alluded to, to go uncontradicted,
when made in my presence.

Who would it be who would nominate Abraham Lincoln on the floor of
that convention to be president of the United States? Norman Judd.

Back in 1855, if one could put aside personal ambition and rise to the
level of high politics, there was a strong case for choosing Trumbull
instead of Lincoln as Illinois's anti-Nebraska senator: Trumbull was a
Democrat, or an ex-Democrat—a member of Douglas's own, the Nebraska
Act's own, side—so he represented a net accretion to the opposition. Lincoln as a Whig, on the other hand, had been an opponent of Douglas and
the Democrats all his life.

Perhaps Lincoln came to see it that way. Samuel Parks, a Whig, a friend
of Lincoln who supported him all the way in that balloting, gave to Herndon, eleven years later, a good summary of Lincoln's deed: "Mr. Lincoln
was very much disappointed, for I think that at that time it was the height
of his ambition to get into the U.S. Senate. He manifested however no bitterness towards Mr. Judd or the other Anti Nebraska Democrats by whom
practically he was beaten, but evidently thought that their motives were
right. He told me several times afterwards that the election of Trumbull
was the best thing that could have happened."

2. FOLLOWING HIS OWN ADVICE

The year 1855 had its setbacks, but 1856 would be a political year and an
important year in Lincoln's rise. He would be the key figure in shaping the
new Republican Party in Illinois.

Does skillful political organization have any moral substance? Maybe.
It might be affirmed already just as a worthy part of the civic process, but in
this particular case there was more: a *new* party was coming into being,
and the issues were both what its organizing principle would be and
whether it could be put together around that principle in such a way as to
win. And the contending principles, in the flux of the 1850s, had an unusually far-reaching moral significance. Lincoln had accepted the Whig Party
as he found it; but the Republican Party in Illinois he helped to shape.

Ending slavery in America required that there be an abolitionist movement. But it also required that there be a Republican Party—in fact, the formation of that party was the key.

But building a *major* party—a party seeking a majority—is always sausage making, however much one may try to flavor the sausage with moral conviction. Lincoln was a leader in fitting together different groups of voters and giving order to different principles.

On August 11, 1855 (just before he traveled to Cincinnati for the famous reaper case in September, of which more in a later chapter), we find him saying this in answer to a letter from Owen Lovejoy: The time is not quite ripe. It is one of the many Lincoln letters that reveal an able political operator at work. "Know-Nothingism has not yet entirely tumbled to pieces," and "Until we can get the elements of this organization, there is not sufficient materials to successfully combat the Nebraska democracy with." Seventeen months earlier Owen Lovejoy (brother of the martyred Elijah, with his four presses at the bottom of the Mississippi) had tried to form that radical "Republican" organization at the state fair, and Lincoln avoided affiliation with that premature and too narrow effort. Now Lincoln is advising Lovejoy that the anti-Nebraska movement needs the support of the nativists who are antislavery in order to defeat the Douglas Democrats. "We cannot get them so long as they cling to a hope of success under their own ["Know-Nothing," or American, Party] organization," Lincoln the political realist wrote, "and I fear an open push by us now, may offend them, and tend to prevent our ever getting them." Parson Lovejoy had not been the sort of person who would make such a calculation. But Lincoln was that sort of person.

He went on to say in the letter to Lovejoy that around Springfield "they [the Know-Nothings] are mostly my old political and personal friends; and I have hoped their organization would die out without the painful necessity of my taking an open stand against them." Lincoln went on to explain that he did indeed, in his private heart, reject nativism: "Of their principles I think little better than I do of those of the slavery extensionists. Indeed I do not perceive how any one professing to be sensitive to the wrongs of the negroes, can join in a league to degrade a class of white men." If Lincoln's strong but private negative opinions on Know-Nothingism had become a major part of his public identity and known to the Republican convention delegates in 1860, he might not have been nominated or elected.

When he wrote to Lovejoy in August of 1855, the party situation was in flux in Illinois, as in other states. Scholars in later years would debate when Lincoln stopped being a Whig, and it would not be an easy question to answer, because Lincoln himself did not know. In that same month he would write to Joshua Speed that "I think I am a Whig but others say there are no Whigs and I am an abolitionist. I do no more than oppose *extension* of slavery. I am not a Know-Nothing." Lincoln wrote to Lovejoy, in the August 11, 1855 letter we have already quoted: "I have no objection to 'fuse' with anybody provided I can fuse on ground I think is right; I believe the opponents of slavery extension could now do this if it were not for this K.N.ism [Know-Nothingism]. In many speeches last summer [he should have said last fall] I advised those who did me the honor of hearing to 'stand with anybody who stands in the right'—and I am still quite willing to follow my own advice."

There was a sorting and a shaping going on in the politics of 1855–56, and in Illinois Abraham Lincoln was a primary sorter and shaper. The trick was to make opposition to the extension of slavery instead of opposition to immigrants and Catholics, or "temperance," or any of the old Whig principles, the foundation of the major party that would challenge the Democrats—and then, while building around that principle, to draw enough support to win. One had to have the bulk of the old Whigs, most of whom would be at best only mildly antislavery, but who were opposed to Douglas and the Democrats and could oppose slavery's *extension*. One had to get the votes, simultaneously, of the nativists who were antislavery, about whom Lincoln was writing to Lovejoy, and at the same time of the immigrant German Protestants who were becoming an increasingly large part of the Illinois population, who were antislavery but regularly offended by nativists, and by moralistic temperance reformers who would take away their beer. It was particularly important to attract and to hold the sprinkling of anti-Nebraska Democrats like Trumbull, Judd, and Palmer, drawn off from Douglas's own ranks. That was why, in generous retrospect, Lincoln decided it was better that Trumbull had been chosen as senator in 1855, and why he would be careful to give attention to ex-Democrats in the Republican Party all the way up into his cabinet making as president-elect. Last but not least, one had to keep the support of the small but growing group of strongest opponents of slavery, who would be found particularly in the northern part of the state, abolitionists like Lovejoy. David Davis and other of Lincoln's friends detested Lovejoy and his ilk, but Lincoln was developing a friendly, businesslike collaborative relationship. At the start of this letter to Lovejoy he assures him that "not even *you* are more anxious to prevent the extension of slavery than I." Earlier, when he had written Lovejoy's abolitionist colleague Codding to decline membership in the premature "Republican" antislavery organization in 1854, he had said the same of slavery itself: I oppose *slavery* every bit as strongly as you do.

By the following February, of 1856, the time was ripe for a group of anti-Nebraska newspaper editors (key political operatives in those days) to hold a meeting in Decatur to call for a convention to organize a new free-soil party. Surely it is significant that only one non-editor was invited: Abraham Lincoln. Lincoln helped to make the policy fit the political realities and played a large role in the drafting of the document that this Decatur gathering issued.

The Decatur meeting in February was to the meeting that followed in Bloomington in May as the Annapolis gathering in 1786 had been to the Constitutional Convention: the smaller preliminary that issued the call for the larger and more official meeting. The May 1856 gathering in Bloomington was the founding meeting of the Illinois Republican Party. Lincoln would be proposed as the gubernatorial nominee of the new party, but he declined the honor and suggested the name of the ex-Democrat William Bissell instead. Bissell would be the Republican nominee and would be elected governor that fall—the first governor of Illinois elected by the party opposed to the Democrats. Thus Lincoln, although still a private citizen himself, had helped both men who would be senior Republican officials—Senator Lyman Trumbull and Governor William Bissell—to attain their posts. That is another reason the Republican organization in county after county would insist in 1858 that Lincoln was their "first and only" choice for senator, and perhaps also why the Illinois delegation to the 1860 Republican convention would put forward the name of private citizen Lincoln as their choice for presidential nominee rather than either of the state party's senior officeholders, Senator Trumbull or Governor Bissell.

Lincoln gave a closing address at the Decatur meeting that was described as so eloquent as to cause anyone there who might have reported it—even Herndon—to drop his pencil and listen in wonderment. And so it has passed into legend as his "lost speech."

"Lost" though the speech may be, we know from everything Lincoln was saying elsewhere that it would have insisted that Republicans oppose the extension of slavery because slavery was a moral wrong, and that that had been the original commitment of the Founders of this nation.

Lincoln's reputation had become such that the Illinois delegation to the first national Republican convention in Philadelphia in June of 1856 finagled to get his name placed in nomination for the vice-presidential slot, after John C. Frémont had been nominated for president. Lincoln got a respectable 110 votes to 253 for the nominee, William Dayton of New Jersey. Told of this vote, Lincoln amiably remarked, with not very convincing pseudo-modesty, that there was a famous Lincoln in Massachusetts and the delegates must have thought they were voting for that fellow.

His effort to form an anti-Nebraska opinion in 1854–1856, and a Republican Party in Illinois in 1856–1858, and to carry the message to other states in 1859–1860, and to obtain the nomination of the Republican Party in 1860, would be shaped on the one side by the "unqualified evil" of slavery—by the violation of the nation's core represented by the threatened expansion of slavery—and by the "debauching" of American opinion by the spreading of Douglas-style indifference to the institution of slavery. But it would be shaped on the other by a prudent recognition of the "average deficiencies of mankind," as specifically represented by the heavy racial prejudice of the white population of Illinois, and then of the whole nation.

Lincoln as the emerging leader of the Illinois Republicans was insisting on the concentration of the party on opposition to the expansion of slavery because it was a moral evil; at the same time, he was persuading Illinois Republicans to set aside these more advanced antislavery positions—like opposition to a Fugitive Slave Law, and ending slavery in the District without consulting the District population—that Republicans in less conservative states, and abolitionists like Lovejoy in Illinois, were strongly insisting upon. The responsible Illinois politician Abraham Lincoln would explain, with admirable clarity, why he would not oppose an "efficient" and "fair" Fugitive Slave Law—in a letter he would write five years later, in anticipation of the 1860 convention, to Salmon Chase over in Ohio:

Hon: S.P. Chase: Springfield, Ills.
Dear Sir
June 9, 1859
   Please pardon the liberty I take in addressing you, as I now do. It appears by the papers that the late Republican State convention of Ohio adopted a Platform, of which the following is one plank, "A repeal of the atrocious Fugitive Slave Law."
   This is already damaging us here. I have no doubt that if that plank be even *introduced* into the next Republican National convention, it will explode it. Once introduced, its supporters and it's opponents will quarrel irreconcilably. The latter believe the U.S. constitution declares that a fugitive slave *"shall be delivered up"*; and they look upon the above plank as dictated by the spirit which declares a fugitive slave *"shall not be delivered up."*
   I enter upon no argument one way or the other; but I assure you the cause of Republicanism is hopeless in Illinois, if it be in any way made

responsible for that plank. I hope you can, and will, contribute something to relieve us from it.

Your Obt. Servt.

Lincoln, the sensitive gauge of statewide opinion and calculating politician, says that a plank condemning "the atrocious Fugitive Slave Law" would kill us here in Illinois and so asks Chase and Ohio Republicans not to bring resolutions like that one to the floor of the Republican convention.

But then, in correspondence with this radical opponent of slavery, he significantly just steps aside from any argument on the merits. The politics are overwhelming—"hopeless"—so there is no need to enter upon the substantive argument one way or the other. This mature Lincoln is not going to go down with the ship of lost causes—or, as he would see it, worse-than-lost causes, perverse efforts at moral purity that do damage to the cause. This is not exactly the young man who had pictured himself standing "boldly and alone," never "faultering" in disaster, in chains, in torture, in death.

Lincoln the builder of a new party both outlined the issues and gathered needed constituencies. When an old Washington Whig proposed a foolish platform of nothing but opposition to the resumed slave trade and "eternal hostility to the rotten democracy [i.e., the Democratic Party]," Lincoln responded, on June 23, 1859, that such a platform might carry Maryland but could not carry any other state, north or south. And he explained the importance of ex-Democrats to the Republicans this way:

> [T]he republican party is utterly pow[er]less everywhere, if it will, by any means, drive from it all those who came to it from the democracy [i.e., the Democratic Party] for the sole object of preventing the spread, and nationalization of slavery. Whenever this object is waived by the organization, they will drop the organization; and the organization itself will dissolve into thin air.

By 1859 Lincoln would begin to do on the national scene the political arranging and shaping he had already been doing in Illinois. A letter to Indiana Republican leader Schuyler Colfax on July 6, 1859, shows Lincoln the political leader sifting issues and seeking unity on all sides:

> My main object in such conversation [meeting Colfax and talking politics] would be to hedge against divisions in the Republican ranks gen-

erally, and particularly for the contest of 1860. The point of danger is
the temptation in different localities to *"platform"* for something
which will be popular just there, but which, nevertheless, will be a
firebrand elsewhere, and especially in a National convention. As
instances, the movement against foreigners in Massachusetts; in New
Hampshire, to make obedience to the Fugitive Slave law, punishable as
a crime; in Ohio, to repeal the Fugitive Slave law; and squatter sovereignty in Kansas. In these things there is explosive matter enough to
blow up half a dozen national conventions . . . What is desirable . . . is
that in every local convocation of Republicans, a point should be made
to avoid everything which will distract republicans elsewhere. Massachusetts republicans should have looked beyond their noses; and then
they could not have failed to see that tilting against foreigners would
ruin us in the whole North-West. New-Hampshire and Ohio should
forbear tilting against the Fugitive Slave law in such way as [to] utterly
overwhelm us in Illinois with the charge of enmity to the constitution
itself. Kansas, in her confidence that she can be saved to freedom on
"squatter sovereignty"—ought not to forget that to prevent the spread
and nationalization of slavery is a national concern, and must be
attended to by the nation. In a word, in every locality we should look
beyond our noses; and at least say *nothing* on points where it is probable we shall disagree.

But we should not think that Lincoln was functioning simply as a
coalition-building political manager. He was at the same time keeping the
central moral principle clear. Muting distractions was one party-defining
task; accentuating the core principles was another. Lincoln kept clearly in
mind the new party's defining commitment: opposition to the extension of
slavery because slavery was a huge moral wrong. Set aside everything else;
keep your eye on that.

Many would support the party only for the first, practical position—
oppose slavery extension, for whatever reason. And of course we want
their votes. But Lincoln consistently emphasized the moral grounding as
fundamental.

In a characteristic statement at Edwardsville, Illinois, on September 11,
1858, in the middle of the Douglas/Lincoln debates, although not as a part
of them, Lincoln, asked to give a concise statement of the difference
between the Democratic and the Republican parties, responded that the
Republicans regard slavery as "a moral, social, and political wrong," while
the Democrats do *not* consider it such a wrong. The Republicans "will

oppose, in all its length and breadth, the modern Democratic idea [implication: this had not always been the Democrats' idea] that slavery is as good and right as freedom."

> The Republican party hold(s) . . . that slavery is an unqualified evil to the Negro, to the white man, to the soil, and to the state. Regarding it as an evil, they will not molest it in the states where it exists . . . but they will use every constitutional method to prevent the evil from becoming larger and involving more Negroes, more white men, more soil, and more states in its deplorable consequences.

June 16, 1858, would be an important day in the life of Abraham Lincoln, of the Republican Party of Illinois, of the United States of America, and of the world.

The convention of the Republicans of Illinois, meeting in Springfield on that day, did a quite unusual thing: They specified their candidate for the Senate seat then held by the Democrat Stephen A. Douglas. That would not seem unusual to a later age—that a party convention would name its candidate—so we need to remind ourselves about the different situation, when senators were still chosen by state legislators, not by popular vote. Parties played whatever role they played in the electing of the state legislators, who then in turn chose the senator; we have seen this working back in Lincoln's own first effort to become a senator in the General Assembly in 1855. The naming of a candidate that all Republicans in the legislature would be expected to support (and they all did) was quite extraordinary, and that action, combined with the eminence of his Democratic opponent, Douglas, would make this campaign distinct from all others at the time.

The Republicans of Illinois made Abraham Lincoln their choice for senator, and in the evening Lincoln gave his "house divided" speech, which had more to it than the famous opening passage. It described a powerful tendency in the land, in which Douglas so far had played a big role on the wrong side. His "squabble" with President Buchanan over the pro-slavery Lecompton constitution for Kansas dealt with "a *mere* question of FACT," whether that constitution was or was not made by the people of Kansas. On "the right of a people to make their own constitution," Douglas and the Republicans have never differed. But on the issue of slavery itself, Douglas declared that he cares not whether it be voted *down* or voted *up*.

But Republicans *do* care.

Lincoln kept insisting that explicit public clarity about that philosophical ground—that slavery is a great moral evil—was essential to the permanent solution to the problem of slavery.

On March 1, 1859, Lincoln said to Republicans in Chicago that "the Republican principle" was "the profound central truth that slavery is wrong and ought to be dealt with as a wrong." He was speaking at a Republican rally on the night of a Chicago municipal election. "Never forget," he urged his fellow Republicans, in the now fully organized party, "that we have before us this whole matter of the right or wrong of slavery in this Union, though the immediate question is as to its spreading out into new territories and states."

In the best book on this period in Lincoln's career, *Prelude to Greatness,* Don Fehrenbacher concludes that "in the actual construction of an effective organization from the raw materials of anti-Nebraskaism, and in the determination of its essential character, no citizen played a more important part than he." And Fehrenbacher again: "Never in his presidency did he surpass the political skill with which he shaped the Republican Party of Illinois, held it together, and made himself its leader."

And—we add—kept its concentration, through complexity, on its moral premise.

CHAPTER THIRTEEN

Not So Much Greater
Than the Rest of Us

The magnanimity that Lincoln exhibited, if we agree to call it that, after the election of Trumbull as senator, and the concentration on the principled core in shaping the party in Illinois, did not mean the little engine of strictly personal ambition had altogether stopped chugging. We may take note, once again and for a last time, of his desire that his name be writ large in the human story, now in the form of his feelings of competition with the great figure of Douglas.

The occasion for doing so is, first, the curious little note, mentioned before, that he jotted down at some time in 1855 or 1856 after his failure to be chosen senator, and after he was snubbed in Cincinnati in a great law case. This is the fragment in which he said that Douglas's name, unlike his own, "fills the nation, and is not unknown, even, in foreign lands." The other occasion for raising this matter is the sequence of events in 1857–58 that tempted some members of Lincoln's own party to support Douglas for the Senate seat that Lincoln wanted. And all this leads up to the great encounter of 1858–59.

Looking back, one may notice in the speeches of the not yet altogether successful Lincoln a certain edge where Douglas was concerned. As one among many examples we exhume a paragraph from Lincoln's bank speech of 1840. Whigs, including Lincoln, had made charges about the Van Buren administration's expenditures in 1838 being outrageously high. Douglas, who always seemed to be there, debating against Lincoln, had explained, with pointed general disdain for the uninformed and even more specific disdain for this merely local officeholder, Lincoln, that there had been extraordinary *reasons* for those extraordinary expenses. Lincoln now answered, point by point, with research and in detail: No, there were *not*. Our interest in this ancient, altogether extinct, and perhaps not even in its own time particularly interesting political controversy is not in its content but in its tone.

Douglas had made his argument, as noted, with explicit disdain, and Lincoln in his turn referred to Douglas's personal remarks and concluded:

> Those who heard Mr. Douglas, recollect that he indulged himself in a contemptuous expression of pity for me. "Now he's got me," thought I. But when he went on to say that five millions of the expenditure of 1838, were payments of the French indemnities, which I knew to be untrue; that five millions had been for the Post Office, which I not only knew to be untrue, but supremely ridiculous also; and when I saw that he was stupid enough to hope, that I would permit such groundless and audacious assertions to go unexposed, I readily consented, that on the score both of veracity and sagacity, the audience should judge whether he or I were the more deserving of the world's contempt.

That was back in 1840.

Then there was a curious episode in the 1852 presidential campaign, in which Lincoln was roused to speak to the Scott Club of Springfield (Winfield Scott was the Whig nominee for president in that year), not at the club's request, but at Lincoln's own request, and not in response to the issues of the campaign in general, but in response specifically to an attack on Scott by Stephen A. Douglas.

This was during the period in which Lincoln had somewhat withdrawn from politics, and it came in the midst of the campaign in which he played the smallest role of his mature political life. The Whig cause was widely regarded as doomed in Illinois, and indeed the Democratic candidate Franklin Pierce, and the Democrats generally, did go on to a sweeping victory both in Illinois and nationwide. But back in August, before that happened, when the young man who was to have spoken to the Scott Club was taken ill, Lincoln *asked* to speak instead: "I do not appear before you on a flattering invitation," he said, "or on any invitation at all, but, on the contrary I am about to address you, by your permission, given me at my own special request."

And why had Lincoln made that request? He gave his own answer:

Soon after the Democratic nomination for President and Vice-President in June last in Baltimore, it was announced, somewhat ostentatiously, as it seemed to me, that Judge Douglas would, previous to the election, make speeches in favor of these nominations, in twenty-eight of the thirty-one states. Since then, and as I suppose, in part in performance of this undertaking, he has actually made one speech in Richmond, Virginia . . . When I first saw [Douglas's speech], and read it, I was reminded of old times—of times when Judge Douglas was not so much greater man than all the rest of us, as he now is—of the Harrison campaign, twelve years ago, when I used to hear, and *try* to answer many of his speeches; and believing that the Richmond speech though marked with the same species of "shirks and quirks" as the old ones, was not marked by any greater ability, I was seized with a strong inclination to attempt to answer it, and this inclination it was that prompted me to seek the privilege of addressing you on this occasion.

So Lincoln was stimulated to drum up a speaking opportunity for himself from the sole motive of once more answering his longtime rival, who once "was not so much greater man than all the rest of us" and whose recent speech "was not marked by any greater ability" than the old ones. Lincoln then outlined "Judge" Douglas's speech (he *always* calls him "Judge," though Douglas was in fact only a short time a state judge, and was now of course a leading—perhaps *the* leading—United States senator, and almost a nominee for president). Lincoln answered "the Judge" in unremitting detail, not just for the one meeting of the club but spilling over into a second. These answers were filled with more little scornful and mocking pokes of the sort we have seen in the opening paragraph. After a relentless attack on Douglas's criticism of the (Whig) Fillmore administration, showing to Lincoln's satisfaction that it was full of mammoth errors, Lincoln concluded: "Judge Douglas is only mistaken about twenty millions of dollars—a mere trifle for a giant!" If you want to see Lincoln at his feeblest, this production for the Scott Club on August 14 and 26, 1852, will serve; that it was delivered not much more than two years before the state fair/Peoria speech reinforces the conclusion that the middle of 1854 saw in him a marked moral escalation.

In 1854, then, the Kansas-Nebraska Act had as its sponsor, legislative engineer, and public advocate none other than Lincoln's old rival, who held exactly the office that Lincoln most wanted and twice would try to attain: senator from Illinois.

And Douglas was now what Lincoln would have liked to be but wasn't: an eminent man, famous throughout the land. Lincoln had slain his thousands, but Douglas had slain his ten thousands.

If you were deliberately designing a relationship that would generate the ugly green vice of envy, you could not have done much better than the relationship between Stephen A. Douglas and Abraham Lincoln. They were in the same line of work, began in the same provincial place, had the same strivings. We may not be envious (or so envious) of those who achieve fame and glory in some realm utterly remote from ourselves; we are more likely envious of those whose claims on the world's praise are like our own, close to our own, but more successful, more honored, perhaps even (this is really unbearable) objectively superior.

Abraham Lincoln was a young man who by his own testimony and that of many others yearned and strove for distinction, for accomplishment and recognition—and specifically in politics, in legislative bodies, in the United States Senate. And here was Douglas, who, although he was younger than Lincoln and had started out at the same level in the same time and place, had sped past him at every stop along life's way. Douglas had come to the Illinois state legislature while Lincoln was a member, but had quickly risen out of there, to a presidential appointment in Springfield, to a statewide office, to the briefly held judgeship on the state supreme court, and then to the United States House of Representatives, four years before Lincoln arrived there. And then Douglas was reelected, as Lincoln would not be. As the unknown Lincoln came to the House for his one term in 1847, the widely known Douglas, already a considerable figure in Washington, moved up to the Senate, where he rapidly emerged, as we have said, as one of the most powerful senators—before long *the* most powerful. In 1852, at the age of just thirty-nine, he almost received his party's nomination for the presidency, and he certainly would be a prime contender for the nomination in the presidential years to come.

So we come to the item mentioned above, the little jotting Lincoln made at some point in the middle 1850s. The editor of his papers did not know what to call this extraordinary little paragraph except "Fragment on Stephen A. Douglas." But—as in some other cases—I do not think it is a fragment; it seems to me complete as it stands. Don Fehrenbacher, in the

Library of America volumes, called it simply "On Stephen Douglas." But I suggest that a title conveying the real subject might be: "On Stephen Douglas—and Me."

Here is this curious item in its entirety:

> Twenty two years ago Judge Douglas and I first became acquainted. We were both young then; he a trifle younger than I. Even then, we were both ambitious; I, perhaps, quite as much as he. With *me* the race of ambition has been a failure—a flat failure; with *him* it has been one of splendid success. His name fills the nation; and is not unknown, even, in foreign lands. I affect no contempt for the high eminence he has reached. So reached, that the oppressed of my species, might have shared with me in the elevation, I would rather stand on that eminence, than wear the richest crown that ever pressed a monarch's brow.

Every sentence in this remarkable document cries out for exegesis. "Twenty two years ago"—he remembers the starting date, with significant exactitude. "We were both young"—and he significantly remembers and acknowledges that Douglas was a little younger. Douglas was certainly an ambitious young man—but, says Lincoln, looking back across the years at his youthful self, so was I, maybe even (disturbing though it may be to admit it) as ambitious as he was. And then comes the stark contrast of the result: not just failure but "flat" failure for Lincoln; not just success but "splendid" success for Douglas. The measure of his success (the only measure Lincoln mentions) is that his name is known—even internationally. (And mine, by implied contrast, is scarcely known beyond Peoria.) Although most of us have jealous feelings like these, few of us admit it plainly to ourselves, or put it into words, or write it on paper. Moralists often observe that envy is the vice we are least likely to admit, and the vice that does not have any compensating "gain," as it were (as, for example, gluttony, lust, pride, perhaps even avarice, wrath, and sloth may have).

Lincoln was not, in fact, a "flat failure," or anything close to it. He was one of the ablest lawyers in Illinois, making money at his profession, and he was a public figure in the state as well. He had been a leading Whig, and by 1856 would become a leader—one might say *the* leader in Illinois—of the new Republican Party. But Lincoln's implicit standard of self-measurement was not confined to the boundaries of Illinois or of his profession.

I don't think you can dismiss Lincoln's little blip of pouting self-sympathy on the ground that he must *really* in his heart have known that he would go on the triumphs that would dwarf those of Stephen A. Douglas—that, indeed, would ironically by their reflected glory give Douglas a larger place in history than he would otherwise have had. (In the 1850s, Lincoln profited from Douglas's fame; in history, Douglas has profited from Lincoln's.) Lincoln could not have known whenever he wrote that little paragraph that that would be the outcome. The apotheosis of Lincoln has indeed gone too far if we attribute to him omniscience and foreknowledge.

In 1855, as we have seen, he worked very hard to become Douglas's colleague in the Senate, and almost did, but gave over his votes in the Illinois legislature to Trumbull to ensure the election of an anti-Nebraska senator and prevent the election of a Democrat. That near-miss must have been part of the backdrop when private citizen Lincoln wrote out his private musing on Stephen Douglas and himself.

To a remarkable degree, Lincoln's six-year argument of 1854–1860 would be an argument with, and about, Stephen A. Douglas. Douglas was never far from Lincoln's mind and pen and tongue. Lincoln grew in stature as the most effective spokesman for the disparate anti-Nebraska forces, as the Whig Party faded away and the anti-Nebraska elements drew together—and anti-Nebraska, particularly in Illinois, meant anti-Douglas.

Douglas's power in Washington and fame in the nation were already established when Lincoln made his full-throttle reentry into politics in 1854, and Lincoln borrowed from Douglas's eminence step by step to enhance his own. In Bloomington on September 26, 1854, the mighty but momentarily beleaguered Senator Douglas, home from Washington, turned down the proposal that he debate this local champion Lincoln (why give this rising local Whig that visibility, that equality?). Lincoln and his partisans then used the device they would use for four years: They borrowed Douglas's audience. They used the audience gathered by his drawing power to announce an answering speech by Lincoln. So it would be at the state fair in Springfield on October 3–4 and in Peoria on October 16. Surely a key to his rise to statewide eminence as an anti-Nebraska Whig was his direct argument, both statewide and nationally, with the arch-opponent Stephen A. Douglas.

Lincoln's borrowing of Douglas's drawing power was illustrated by a humorous (but serious) remark that Lincoln made when, at the end of Douglas's long speech in Peoria in 1854, at five in the afternoon, some in the crowd called for Lincoln now to give his answer. (Douglas had announced at the start of his remarks that they had agreed that Lincoln should give a response.) Lincoln said that if the crowd would come back at six-thirty or seven to hear him, they could take a break. And to be sure they would return, he reminded them that after he finished, Douglas, as had been announced, would have an hour to reply:

> The Judge has already informed you that he is to have an hour to reply to me. I doubt not but you have been a little surprised to learn that I have consented to give one of his high reputation and known ability, this advantage of me. Indeed, my consenting to it, though reluctant, was not wholly unselfish; for I suspected if it were understood, that the Judge was entirely done, you democrats would leave, and not hear me; but by giving him the close, I felt confident you would stay for the fun of hearing him skin me.

Then, in 1857, after the Republican Party had been formed and had run its first campaign, Lincoln's rivalry with Douglas would take a peculiar and exquisitely exasperating turn. The newly installed Democratic president, James Buchanan, would astonish the political world by supporting the admission of Kansas as the sixteenth slave state on the basis of the preposterously proslavery Lecompton constitution. Buchanan had promised beforehand that he would support admission only under a state constitution that had been submitted to the people in a referendum. But now Buchanan agreed that the Lecompton constitution, composed by a ridiculously proslavery convention, chosen in a rigged election in which the territory's antislavery majority declined to participate, was *not* to be submitted, in entirety, to the people.

Buchanan's disastrous decision nevertheless to support admission under that constitution caused outrage not only among Republicans but also among many of his own party in the North, and was not supported by everybody in the South. Douglas was coming up for reelection as senator by an Illinois legislature to be chosen in 1858; he would have had difficulty running as a supporter of Lecompton.

Buchanan and Douglas, leading Democrats, did not get along well in any case. Now Douglas broke with his party's president and opposed the admission of Kansas as a slave state under the Lecompton constitution. He said that constitution did not represent true "popular sovereignty," as, indeed, it certainly did not; free-state supporters clearly outnumbered the supporters of slavery in Kansas.

All of this meant that Douglas was suddenly on the same side as most of the Republicans—against an administration of his own party. And Douglas was never lukewarm or a mere follower; he was a *leader* in this fight. There he was in Washington in the spring of 1858, collaborating—actively, congenially collaborating—with Lincoln's fellow Republicans William Seward, Henry Wilson, Schuyler Colfax against the Democratic Party and the Democratic administration.

For some Republican and antislavery commentators in the East there was now a wonderful, apparently high-minded line to take: Let us welcome Douglas to the fold. Here is our able, honorable, eminent, erstwhile adversary, now come over to the antislavery side. A great catch. Let us embrace him. So said the *Atlantic Monthly,* the *New York Times,* the *Springfield Republican*—all key Republican and antislavery publications— and, especially important, Thurlow Weed's paper in Albany, especially important because of the relationship between Weed and Seward: Did this mean that Seward was endorsing this Republican bear hug for Douglas? One of the intriguing features of this event was the cordial collaboration between Senator Seward of New York, the nation's leading Republican, and Senator Stephen A. Douglas of Illinois, the nation's leading Democrat. There they were, the probable nominees of their respective parties for president in 1860, working together to defeat the Buchanan administration's Kansas bill.

That energetic vibraphone, the editor Horace Greeley, was particularly taken with the idea that the antislavery forces should now embrace this eminent accession to their side—to the point that Illinois Republicans should roll over cheerfully and hand Douglas his reelection to the Senate on a platter of unanimity.

Out in Illinois all this looked different than it did in the hothouse of Washington or the lofty detachment of editorial offices on the East Coast. And it must have been particularly galling to the prospective nominee of the Illinois Republicans to run against Douglas in 1858—Abraham Lincoln.

Lincoln ruefully wrote to Trumbull (December 28, 1857) asking what was going on: What does Greeley's *Tribune* mean by its "constant eulogizing, and admiring, and magnifying" of Douglas? "Have [the Republicans at Washington] concluded that the republican cause, generally, can be best promoted by sacrificing us here in Illinois? If so we would like to know it soon . . ."

But even under the considerable provocation of that constant eulogizing and that hint, Lincoln was honorably and characteristically careful not to charge Greeley with any duplicity:

> I have believed—do believe now—that Greeley, for instance, would be rather pleased to see Douglas re-elected over me or any other republican; and yet I do not believe it is so, because of any secret arrangement with Douglas. It is because he thinks Douglas's superior position, reputation, experience, and *ability,* if you please, would more than compensate for his lack of a pure republican position, and therefore, his re-election do the general cause of republicanism, more good, than would the election of any one of our better undistinguished pure republicans [like, Lincoln does not say, me]. I do not know how you estimate Greeley, but *I* consider him incapable of corruption, or falsehood.

Republicans opposed the admission of Kansas as a slave state; Douglas opposed the admission of Kansas as a slave state under the current proposal. So they are now on the same side, right? No, said Lincoln. Not really. When Douglas first broke with Buchanan, a startled Connecticut senator had said that Douglas might be "indulging in the luxury of conscience," but Lincoln would say: if so, not a Republican conscience.

Even against this great opponent Lincoln is scrupulous: Douglas may indeed have acted on principle, but his principle was not only at odds with Republican principle, it was the most insidious sort of opposition to it. It was "debauching" the public mind, playing its key part in all those other steps in sequence toward nationalizing slavery.

> Now, as ever, I wish not to misrepresent Judge Douglas's *position,* question his *motives,* or do ought that can be personally offensive to him. Whenever, *if ever,* he and we can come together on *principle* so that *our great cause* may have assistance from *his great ability,* I hope to have interposed no adventitious obstacle. But clearly, he is not *now* with us—he does not *pretend* to be—he does not *promise* to *ever* be. Our cause, then, must be entrusted to, and conducted by its own undoubted friends—those whose hands are free, whose hearts are in the work—who *do care* for the result.

What Lincoln could not know—lacking, as we have said, foreknowledge—was that this effort by Greeley and other meddling easterners to force Douglas on Illinois Republicans would in the end work to his—Lincoln's—advantage.

He was already the presumptive senatorial choice of the Republicans because he was by all odds the ablest speaker defining the Republican case in Illinois; because of his labors for, and leadership of, the emerging party; because he had been a Whig while the other two prime nominees of the Illinois Republicans—Trumbull in the Senate and Bissell as governor—had been Democrats; and because in 1855 he had yielded to Trumbull. But the meddling pressure of Greeley and the others caused the Illinois Republicans, in resentment and defiance, to solidify and make explicit their commitment, so that in county after county the Republican organization endorsed Lincoln as the "first and only" choice for senator, setting the stage for the state party to do the same.

On July 17, 1858, Douglas traveled south and spoke in Bloomington and Springfield. Lincoln, his trailer, and his designated Republican opponent, spoke in each of those places, too. Douglas spoke in Springfield in a grove near the edge of town, where a stand had been erected in the afternoon. Lincoln spoke at the state house in the evening, and started off discussing the peculiar disadvantages the Republicans faced in the coming choice of a senator by the Illinois legislature: the apportionment was out of date, so that the Democratic South had a disproportionately large representation in comparison to the Republican North, and there were Democratic holdovers who would still be there to vote in January on a new senator. Historians have sometimes said that these disadvantages did cost the Republicans—that is, Lincoln—the election in 1859, but Don Fehrenbacher demonstrated that the injustice was small: "[T]hough Lincoln did unquestionably labor under some disadvantage, the Illinois apportionment law, compared with other apportionments past and present, was actually somewhat better than average . . . The closeness of the race made a relatively minor injustice seem decisive."

But then Lincoln in Springfield named a disadvantage of a radically different kind:

> There is still another disadvantage under which we labor, and to which I will ask your attention. It arises out of the relative positions of the two persons who stand before the State as candidates for the Senate. Senator Douglas is of world wide renown. All the anxious politicians of his party, or who have been of his party for years past, have been looking upon him as certainly, at not distant day, to be the Presi-

dent of the United States. They have seen in his round, jolly, fruitful face, post offices, land offices, marshalships, and cabinet appointments, charge ships and foreign missions, bursting and sprouting out in wonderful exuberance ready to be laid hold of by their greedy hands. [Great laughter] And as they have been gazing upon this attractive picture so long, they cannot, in the little distraction that has taken place in the party, bring themselves to give up the charming hold; but with greedier anxiety they rush about him, sustain him, and give him marches, triumphal entries, and receptions beyond what even in the days of his highest prosperity they could have brought about in his favor.

So much for the world-renowned Douglas. And the unrenowned Lincoln?

On the contrary nobody has ever expected me to be President. In my poor, lean, lank, face, nobody has ever seen that any cabbages were sprouting out. [Tremendous cheering and laughter] . . . I am, in a certain sense, made the standard-bearer in behalf of the Republicans. I was made so merely because there had to be some one so placed—I being in no wise, preferable to any other one of the twenty-five— perhaps a hundred—we have in the Republican ranks.

One response of envy, the more usual one, is, of course, to slight, undercut, disdain, and deprecate its object—as one might sense, in a subtle form, perhaps in Lincoln's constant use of the word "Judge" to refer to Douglas, and more certainly in the way Lincoln would use, referring to Douglas, the word "Giant" with a flavoring of sarcasm: "The Giant himself has been here recently [laughter]" (Columbus, Ohio, September 16, 1859). Lincoln's picture of Douglas's "round, jolly, fruitful face" sprouting with offices, and of the greedy anxiety of his followers to "rush about him" and give him "marches, triumphal entries, and receptions" partakes of that, combined, as often happens, with its apparent opposite, an exaggerated picture of the envied one's (alleged) triumphs—contrasted with an exaggerated deprecation of one's own qualities (she's so beautiful; I am so ugly). Certainly Lincoln's picture of himself, in contrast to Douglas, exhibits this last—exaggerated self-deprecation in contrast to the envied other. Nobody has seen any cabbages of patronage sprouting in his "poor, lean, lank, face," and he just *happens* to be the Republican standard bearer, as though he were chosen by drawing straws, with twenty-five or a hundred equally good. Abraham Lincoln did *not* believe that.

In 1858, then, this time armed with the designation by the assembled state Republican as "the first and only choice" by the new party to oppose Douglas for his Senate seat, Lincoln again began piggybacking on advertised speeches by Douglas, from the balcony of the Tremont House in Chicago, once more in Springfield and Bloomington. He and his advisers even thought of continuing throughout, with a deliberate strategy of "trailing" Douglas. Douglas supporters, not surprisingly, found this annoying: Can't he gather a crowd on his own? In this context Lincoln proposed joint appearances, and Douglas reluctantly accepted a set of formal debates, not by any means everywhere he would speak, but in seven places in the congressional districts in which they had not appeared.

Because of Douglas's eminence, the formal debates had a national press coverage that state campaigns had not had before, and Lincoln, trading blow for blow with the Little Giant himself, was lifted to national visibility. Douglas had something of the problem that Vice President Richard Nixon, as the Republican presidential nominee, would have just over a hundred years later when challenged to debate on television by the Democratic nominee for president, the young senator from Massachusetts, John F. Kennedy. Douglas, like Nixon, was the already established figure, already holding the higher office and long nationally known, while his challenger was the lesser known, more recently arrived, perhaps rising figure: Should one give to such an opponent the advantage of equal standing on a debate platform? Is it not true that he has everything to gain while you can only lose, not gain anything? But then, turning down the challenge might present a bad appearance. And both Douglas and Nixon were accomplished, self-confident, usually victorious debaters. As it turned out, both challengers did benefit, in gaining national stature, from the debates.

When after the famous debates Lincoln was invited to speak in other states in 1859, as now a figure of more than statewide eminence, he made constant references to Douglas, sometimes with a touch of sarcasm. Douglas published in the September 1859 issue of *Harper's* magazine an article defending "popular sovereignty" to which Lincoln several times referred as "the copy-right essay." He also said, of Douglas's treatment of popular sovereignty, "His explanations explanatory of explanations explained are interminable" (Columbus, September 16, 1859). Indeed, he was talking about Douglas and his ideas almost all the time.

In fact, although it certainly could not have felt like it to Lincoln at the time, the presence of Douglas in Illinois, and his career, was an enormous advantage to Lincoln. It enabled him to be a direct, continual local opponent of the most powerful Democrat in the land.

What happened with the Douglas/Lincoln rivalry?

Douglas was a blatant racist, and a man who lived on the surface of life; but he was also an able man in his energetic way, and would acquit himself honorably at the climax of his career in 1860–61. When he became aware during the extraordinary four-sided and two-sectioned presidential campaign of 1860 that he could not, as Lincoln's only serious rival in the Northern states, win the election, he shifted his emphasis from trying to win to trying to defend the Union, and exhausted himself speaking not only in the North but in the South, doing what he could to hold the Union together. When Lincoln had been inaugurated, Douglas, as the leading Northern member of the opposition party and the new president's defeated rival, went out of his way to indicate his support on the overwhelming issues of secession, the Union, and war. For his part, Lincoln was, as would be expected, gracious in return, and the two lifelong rivals had a certain political and social rapport in the early months of the administration, before Douglas's death in June of 1861.

The competition between these two men did not end with their deaths: historians and biographers have continued to debate about the debaters. Although Lincoln has gone on to monumentalized greatness, Douglas has not lacked defenders.

Lincoln was not above feeling some twinges of jealousy toward Douglas, no doubt; but what he clearly felt more strongly, as he got into it, was deep moral disagreement. He was an adversary not only by party but in moral convictions. And so we may infer that the sense of personal rivalry came to be subordinated, even finally swept aside, by concentrating on the moral and intellectual battle.

Those who look back from another era at the two men's positions can, indeed, make quite a list of points on which Douglas and Lincoln seemed to agree, or appeared to be not far apart. But the core and foundation, and therefore the direction, of Lincoln's position was radically at odds with that of Douglas—as both men, we may suggest, and not just for debating purposes, would agree. And both men would agree that these core differences represented radically different readings of the essence of their country.

We may conclude, then, that the importance of these overriding issues drowned out, in Lincoln's inner ear, that little squeaking sound of his envy of Douglas. I did not comment yet on a phrase in that revealing paragraph Lincoln wrote about Douglas and himself. The last sentences, fully quoted, with the formerly unnoticed part now underlined, go like this: "I affect no contempt for the high eminence he has reached. *So reached, that the oppressed of my species, might have shared with me in the elevation,* I would rather stand on that eminence, than wear the richest crown that ever pressed a monarch's brow." In other words, Lincoln, in his rueful imagining, would want an eminence like Douglas's—*if (only* if? in *contrast* to Douglas?) it were attained in a way that benefited "the oppressed of my species." Actually, in the event, he did attain that.

More than once in their six-year argument, Lincoln, rising to some peroration, would insist that what happened either to him or to Douglas personally did not matter—what mattered instead was the triumph of a moral ideal. It is significant, surely, that formulations of this kind came so often to his pen and tongue, indicating that winning over Douglas was not the ultimate or sole objective.

An instance is in the seventh debate, in Alton, near the end, in an oratorical paragraph often quoted about the "real issue" in this contest being the "eternal struggle between these two principles—right and wrong—throughout the world"; two principles "that have stood face to face from the beginning of time," one "the common right of humanity" and the other "the divine right of kings." "One race of men" "enslaving another" is another example of the second, the "tyrannical principle." Introducing this strong paragraph, Lincoln said this eternal issue "will continue in this country when these poor tongues of Judge Douglas and myself shall be silent."

Another instance came in the peroration on the Declaration of Independence at the end of his speech in Lewistown, Illinois, on August 17, 1858, on his way to the first of the formal debates in Ottawa. Lincoln closed with two paragraphs of the most extraordinary insistence upon the importance of the egalitarian principle of the Declaration of Independence, the second and last of which, ending the speech, insists extravagantly on his own insignificance in comparison to that principle:

> Think nothing of me . . . but come back to the truths that are in the
> Declaration of Independence. You may do anything with me you

choose, if you will but heed these sacred principles. You may not only defeat me for the Senate, but you may take me and put me to death.

Why this extravagant rhetorical gesture? It is another little reminder of the Lincoln of his youthful speech endings.

While pretending no indifference to earthly honors, I *do claim* to be actuated in this contest by something higher than an anxiety for office.

That is a point that will recur: while he does not claim to be indifferent to political success, he does claim that he stands for something higher.

He had already slipped in an anonymous dismissal of Douglas back in an earlier passage: "Think nothing of me—take no thought for the political fate of any man whatsoever." Now he drops in a specific name. As he sweeps into insignificance the mere success, the merely personal career, of any individual (in comparison to the great principle he is affirming), he manages to sweep aside Judge Douglas along with himself:

It [any man's success] is nothing. I am nothing; Judge Douglas is nothing. But do not destroy that immortal emblem of Humanity—the Declaration of American Independence!

Now one more instance, in which he sweeps himself alone into insignificance, even if it means Douglas's triumph, if the principle prevails. This came in October 30, 1858, at the end of the campaign, in the last remarks he made before the vote, in Springfield:

Ambition has been ascribed to me. God knows how sincerely I prayed from the first that this field of ambition might not be opened. I claim no insensibility to political honors; but today could the Missouri restriction be restored, and the whole slavery question replaced on the old ground of "toleration by *necessity*" where it exists, with unyielding hostility to the spread of it on principle, I would, in consideration, gladly agree, that Judge Douglas should never be *out,* and I never *in,* office, so long as we both, or either, live.

Some things were more important even than his own personal victory over Judge Douglas.

CHAPTER FOURTEEN

Lincoln's Defense of Our Common Humanity

1. DOUGLAS'S ASSAULT ON LINCOLN'S EGALITARIANISM

A week after the renowned seven Lincoln/Douglas debates were over, on October 23, 1858, when Lincoln entered the little Illinois town of Dallas City on the Mississippi (one of his many other speaking engagements during that exhausting campaign), he found a huge banner greeting him, spread across the main street, apparently presenting the residents' summary of what they had understood his message in the debates to be. The banner displayed a large picture of an African-American (not the term then used) and the single word "Equality." It was not intended as an endorsement.

Twentieth-century historian Eric Foner would write: "At times during the 1850s it seemed that the only weapon in the Democrats' political arsenal was the charge that the Republicans were pro-Negro. . . . In the Lincoln-Douglas campaign of 1858, the organ of the Democratic Party urged readers to 'keep it before the people of Illinois that the Abolition-Republican party headed by Abraham Lincoln are in favor of Negro equality.'"[*]

And in a most fundamental sense, Lincoln was indeed arguing in favor of "Negro equality"—but in a sense so fundamental as to be invisible to a time less permeated by a deep racial caste division, grounded in slavery, than the United States in the middle of the nineteenth century.

---

[*] "In Indiana, a Democratic parade featured a group of young ladies carrying the banner, 'Father save us from nigger husbands'" (Foner, *Free Soil, Free Labor, Free Men*, p. 263).

The great issues between Lincoln and Douglas in the debates had to do with slavery: whether slavery could go into the territories; whether "the people" of the territory could decide that question, and if so, *when* they could decide; whether after the Dred Scott decision had seemed to preclude doing so, there was any way a territory could exclude slavery; whether the next step would bring slavery to the *states;* whether Lincoln's position would require a "uniformity" among the states. Douglas and Lincoln went at each other about those matters not only in the celebrated seven debates but in dozens of other speeches as well. Behind all these issues, giving them their bite, was the question whether American slavery was or was not what Lincoln said it was: a monstrous injustice, a huge moral wrong. And that matter in turn rested on the question of whether black persons had the moral right at the very least not to be treated as "property." Lincoln opposed slavery in the territories because he saw slavery as a great moral evil, and Douglas did not oppose it because he didn't. And Lincoln saw it to be an evil because he recognized the black person's right not to be enslaved, and Douglas did not see it to be an evil because he did not recognize that right.

Stephen A. Douglas, for all his eminence, had a political problem. He would never be elected president if he was not reelected to the Senate. The choice was to be made by a new session, chosen in 1858, of that same Illinois state legislature that had the last time refused to reelect his own man, James Shields, and had almost elected this fellow Lincoln. And it had then in fact elected the renegade Democrat Lyman Trumbull. And now these anti-Nebraska forces had made themselves into a new party, and had, in an unprecedented move, named already their choice to oppose him when the votes were taken in the new General Assembly. This already-named opponent was the tall, humorous, smarter-than-he-looks ex-Whig who had been dogging his trail and borrowing his audiences since 1854. And Douglas had split with a President of his own party over the Lecompton matter, and President Buchanan and his troops were fighting him.

So how could Douglas defeat Lincoln and get himself reelected? There was one surefire issue: race.

Whereas issues about *slavery* divided Democrats, issues about *race* united them, North and South, urban and rural, Irish immigrant and native, Buchanan supporter and Douglas supporter. And with a racist attack one could do terrible damage to Republicans in a state like Illinois.

The story of the Lincoln/Douglas debates has been amply told and retold, and the debates of course are much celebrated, but I believe the persistent and deliberate exploitation of racial prejudice by Douglas is not part of the general public awareness. Presenting the debates with that focus will help to summon the atmosphere in which the debates were conducted, and in which Lincoln had to make his case.

Douglas's attack on Lincoln's racial egalitarianism had begun back in 1854, at the start of their long dispute, and now was to be pursued implacably throughout this season of debate, with a Senate seat at stake.

CHICAGO, JULY 10, 1858.

Douglas just back from his Senate duties in Washington. A hero's welcome this time. An enormous crowd below the balcony of the Tremont House. Lincoln, since June 16 his official opponent, sitting on a chair on the balcony. Douglas is quite explicit about his understanding of the nation's foundation:

> I am free to say to you that in my opinion this government of ours is founded on the white basis. It was made by the white man, for the benefit of the white man, to be administered by white men, in such manner as they should determine.

Passages like that would appear continually. He also would make explicit, repeatedly, his conviction (in specific *contrast* to Lincoln's) of the inferiority of the Negro:

> [Lincoln] objects to the Dred Scott decision because it does not put the Negro in the possession of the rights of citizenship on an equality with the white man. I am opposed to Negro equality. I repeat that this nation is a white people ... and I am in favor of preserving not only the purity of the blood, but the purity of government from any mixture or amalgamation with inferior races.

The concept of "purity of the blood" had already had a dreadful history, and would have worse in the century that followed; Douglas was not the only American leader who made a link between "purity of the blood" and "purity of government." Lincoln did not do that.

This eminent world figure, "whose name is not unknown, even, in foreign lands," reinforced his energetic racism with personal observation from his vast world travels, which, to be sure, his provincial opponent could not match:

I have seen the effects of this mixture of superior and inferior races [said lofty world traveler Douglas]—this amalgamation of white men and Indians and Negroes; we have seen it in Mexico, in Central America, in South America, and in all the Spanish-American states, and its result has been degeneration, demoralization, and degradation below the capacity for self-government.

Douglas made quite explicit, in this first speech and in others, the thoroughgoing racial subordination that was his declared conviction and policy:

I am opposed to taking any step that recognizes the Negro man or the Indian as the equal of the white man. I am opposed to giving him a voice in the administration of the government . . . equality they never should have, either political or social, or in any other respect whatever. My friends, you see that the issues are distinctly drawn.

And they *were* distinctly drawn. Douglas said so, Lincoln thought so, the audiences of the time on both sides thought so—but some scholars and Lincoln writers looking back in later years have not thought so. Some have said instead that the differences between the two men were minor. Don Fehrenbacher, however, stated the matter accurately when he wrote, "[I]t was when they discussed fundamentals that the two men disagreed most sharply." The fundamentals were the ultimate human status, the ultimate human right, and the inclusion in the meaning of the Declaration of Independence, of black persons now held as slaves.

The distinctly drawn and major issue between them was whether slavery should be permitted to spread to the territories (to which Douglas said yes and Lincoln said no), which turned on whether slavery was morally wrong (to which Lincoln said yes and Douglas said no), which turned on whether the Negro was a fellow human being with the right not to be enslaved (to which Douglas said no and Lincoln said yes).

In this first 1858 exchange in Chicago, they were not yet embarked on the formal debates. Lincoln followed his older practice of trailing Douglas, speaking twenty-four hours later this time. It is in this Chicago speech that he tied equality to the biblical injunction "Be ye perfect" as an aspiration continually approached, persistently sought.

And as he rose to his impassioned conclusion, Lincoln made a sweeping appeal that would certainly seem to support racial equality:

My friends . . . I have only to say, let us discard all this quibbling about this man and the other man—this race and that race and the other race being inferior, and therefore they must be placed in an inferior position . . . Let us discard all these things and unite as one people throughout this land, until we shall once more stand up declaring that all men are created equal.

SPRINGFIELD, JULY 17, 1858.

A Douglas speech. A platform erected in a grove outside the city.

Douglas interprets what Lincoln had said in Chicago. What an opponent *claims* that one is saying is one important indication of the real significance of one's presentation in the context of a particular time and place, a particular audience. Surely it should be counted unto Lincoln for righteousness that Douglas repeatedly, disdainfully, unrelentingly attacked him for defending Negro equality. Douglas attacked him for doing so in Lincoln's criticism of the Dred Scott decision; in his interpretation of the Declaration of Independence; and in his reading of God's intention, as here:

> In his Chicago speech [Lincoln] says in so many words that [Negroes] were endowed by the Almighty with the right of equality with the white man, and therefore that that right is divine—a right under the higher law; that the law of God makes them equal to the white man, and, and therefore that the law of the white man cannot deprive them of that right. . . . I do not doubt that he in his conscience, believes that the Almighty made the negro equal to the white man. He thinks that the negro is his brother. [Laughter.] I do not think the negro is any kin of mine at all. [Laughter and cheers.] And here is the difference between us.

Once again, Douglas insisted, to laughter and cheers, that Lincoln did, and he, Douglas, did not, think the Negro was his brother, and that that was the difference between them.

The great issue between them has usually been seen as an argument over states' rights: Douglas saying let each state decide for itself on slavery, Lincoln insisting that slavery is of a different order from cranberry laws and oyster laws. But the argument over states' rights, as is usually the case, was the bearer of an argument over policy and morality: Lincoln claimed, and Douglas denied, that slavery violates the moral essence of the nation itself. Here is a sample of the calm callousness with which Douglas places human slavery as a state's right alongside others:

> [Lincoln's] principal objection to the [Dred Scott] decision is that it was intended to deprive the Negro of the right of citizenship in the different states of the Union. . . . Well, suppose it was? . . .
>
> In the state of Maine they have decided . . . that the negro shall exercise the elective franchise and hold office on an equality with the white man. Whilst I do not concur in the good sense or correct taste of that decision on the part of Maine, I have no disposition to quarrel with her. . . . If the people of Maine desire to be put on an equality with the negro [laughter], I do not know anybody in this state [who] will attempt to prevent it. If the white people of Maine think a negro is their equal, and that he has the right to come and kill their vote by a negro vote, they have a right to think so, I suppose. . . .
>
> [We] find that in [New York] they have provided that a negro may vote provided he holds $250 worth of property . . . they think a rich negro is equal to a white man. Well, that is a matter of taste with them. [Laughter.]

And now see how casually he accepts and would defend the decision of another state (that is, of its white male voters) to hold people in slavery:

> Kentucky has decided that it is not consistent with her safety and her prosperity to allow a negro to have either political rights or his freedom, and hence she makes him a slave. That is her business not mine. . . . I will maintain and defend her right against any assaults.

And on this matter Douglas said yet again: "I have a direct issue with Mr. Lincoln."

Lincoln and Douglas each made a great many other speeches. But then in Ottawa began the series of much-examined formal debates.

OTTAWA, AUGUST 21.

Eighty miles southwest of Chicago. Dust. Hubbub. Bands. Hot sun. The then Sixth Congressional District was represented on the platform by the abolitionist Owen Lovejoy, who was running for reelection. Douglas would sneer at Lincoln's friend "Parson Lovejoy."

The agreement for the seven debates: Douglas would speak first four times; Lincoln, three. In each case, the first speaker would speak for an hour, and be allowed a half-hour rebuttal after his opponent's hour and a half.

Douglas, first speaker in the first debate, immediately launched a fierce attack, charging Lincoln and Trumbull with trying to "abolitionize" the old parties under the Republican name, and firing a prosecutorial series of questions at Lincoln based on the pre-Lincoln, 1854 "Republican" platform. Then he reached a point that was, he said, "a far more important one to you" even than the question of slavery, "and that is, what is to be done with the free Negro?" He began a series of rhetorical questions with audience responses:

I ask you, are you in favor of conferring upon the Negro the rights and privileges of citizenship?
("No, no.")
Do you desire to strike out of our state constitution that clause which keeps slaves and free Negroes out of the state, and allow the free Negroes to flow in,
("Never.")
—and cover your prairies with black settlements? Do you desire to turn this beautiful state into a free Negro colony,
("No, no.")
—in order that when Missouri abolishes slavery she can send one hundred thousand emancipated slaves into Illinois, to become citizens and voters, on an equality with yourselves?
("Never," "no.")

Douglas is referring to the black-exclusion clause enacted in 1853 as part of a new state constitution. The clause forbidding blacks to enter the state at all was submitted to a popular vote and endorsed by a margin of well over two to one: 50,261 votes to 21,297. In Sangamon County the margin was higher: 1,483 votes to 418. A modern scholar calls this "undoubtedly the most severe anti-Negro measure passed by a free state."

Douglas continued: If you desire Negro citizenship, if you desire to allow them to come into the state and settle with the white man, if you desire them to vote on an equality with yourselves, and to make them eligible to office, to serve on juries, and to adjudge your rights, then support Mr. Lincoln and the Black Republican party, who are in favor of the citizenship of the Negro.

("Never, never.")

For one, I am opposed to Negro citizenship in any and every form. (Cheers.)

I believe this government was made on the white basis.

("Good.")

I believe it was made by white men, for the benefit of white men and their posterity for ever, and I am in favor of confining citizenship to white men, men of European birth and descent, instead of conferring it upon Negroes, Indians and other inferior races.

("Good for you." "Douglas forever.")

Douglas proceeded to describe Lincoln as being like all "Abolition orators, who go around and lecture in the basements of schools and churches" appealing to the equality that God and the Declaration awarded to Negroes. Douglas gave this account of the difference between them:

I do not question Mr. Lincoln's conscientious belief that the Negro was made his equal, and hence is his brother, (Laughter,) but for my own part, I do not regard the Negro as my equal, and positively deny that he is my brother or any kin to me whatever. ("Never." "Hit him again," and cheers.) . . .

He holds that the Negro was born his equal and yours, and that he was endowed with equality by the Almighty, and that no human law can deprive him of these rights which were guaranteed to him by the Supreme Ruler of the universe. Now I do not believe that the Almighty ever intended the Negro to be equal of the white man. ("Never, never.")

If he did, he has been a long time demonstrating the fact. (Cheers.) For thousands of years the Negro has been a race upon the earth, and during all that time, in all latitudes and climates, wherever he has wandered or been taken, he has been inferior to the race which he has there met. He belongs to an inferior race, and must always occupy an inferior position.

Douglas, David Potter would observe, "seemed to go out of his way to express a certain callous scorn for the blacks, as people with whom he did not recognize any affinity."

The cheers for Douglas's blunt, explicit, nasty, and thorough assertion of white supremacy and Negro inferiority were vociferous enough that it was hard for Lincoln to get started, in this first of the seven debates. On race, he did make some of the concessions and denials for which he was in later times censured—we will give a sample of these when we get to Charleston—but he regularly did so as a preliminary to the affirmations that were his own point and the issue in that time and place:

> I hold that notwithstanding all this [the current racial inequalities that he conceded], there is no reason in the world why the Negro is not entitled to all the natural rights enumerated in the Declaration of Independence, the right to life, liberty and the pursuit of happiness. (Loud cheers.) . . . [I]n the right to eat the bread, without leave of anybody else, which his own hand earns, *he is my equal and the equal of Judge Douglas, and the equal of every living man.* [Great applause.]

FREEPORT, AUGUST 27.

Speeches elsewhere independently. Lincoln, told by friends he did not do too well in Ottawa, regrouped and planned. Separate trains to Freeport, the farthest north of their seven debates, the first that Lincoln opened. Lincoln recovered a little from perhaps not having done as well as Douglas, in sheer debate terms, in the first debate.

Lincoln began by answering questions ("interrogatories") posed by Douglas, and then posed his famous set, the second of which—the "Freeport question"—was once thought to have caught Douglas in a political bind that hurt him in the South, when he tried to explain how "the people" could keep slavery out of a territory.

Lincoln made no discussion of race in his opening—he was ordinarily not the one to introduce the subject—but Douglas, in his turn, introduced a new piece of demagoguery, a picture of the black abolitionist Frederick Douglass riding in a carriage with a white woman, which he associated with Lincoln:

> I have reason to recollect that some people in this country think that Fred. Douglass is a very good man. The last time I came here to make a speech . . . I saw a carriage and a magnificent one it was, drive up and take a position on the outside of the crowd; a beautiful young lady was sitting on the box seat, whilst Fred. Douglass and her mother reclined

inside, and the owner of the carriage acted as driver. (Laughter, cheers, cries of "right, what have you to say against it" &c.)

I saw this in your own town. ("What of it.")

All I have to say of it is this, that if you, Black Republicans, think that the Negro ought to be on a social equality with your wives and daughters, and ride in a carriage with your wife, whilst you drive the team, you have a perfect right to do so. ("Good, good" and cheers, mingled with hooting and cries of "white, white.")

I am told that one of Fred. Douglass's kinsmen, another rich black Negro, is now traveling in this part of the state making speeches for his friend Lincoln as the champion of black men. ("White men, white men" and "What have you got to say against it." "That's right" &c.)

All I have to say on that subject is that those of you who believe that the Negro is your equal and ought to be on an equality with you socially, politically, and legally, have a right to entertain those opinions, and of course will vote for Mr. Lincoln. ("Down with the Negro," "No, no," &c.)

JONESBORO, SEPTEMBER 15.

The farthest *south* of the debates, in the hills above the confluence of the Ohio and Mississippi rivers. The fairgrounds. This was to be the smallest audience, twelve hundred to fifteen hundred, virtually all Democrats, in the heart of what was called "Egypt"—southern Illinois, populated by settlers from slave states. Country people, old-fashioned wagons, ox teams.

Douglas, opening, repeated in more succinct form his charge about Frederick Douglass in the carriage.

Why, they brought Fred Douglass to Freeport when I was addressing a meeting there in a carriage driven by the white owner, the Negro sitting inside with the white lady and her daughter. ("Shame.")

And he said again:

I do not believe that the Almighty made the Negro capable of self-government.

Douglas exploited the inclination to instant pouting in racial self-sympathy at the slightest advance, or hint of a suggestion of an advance, by black people, that one finds, now as then, in a white racist public. In New York, said Douglas, a platform was adopted "every plank of which was as black as night, each one relating to the Negro, and not one referring to the interests of the white man." In Chicago, he said, there was a group that "advocated Negro citizenship and Negro equality, putting the white man and the Negro on the same basis under the law."

Lincoln in Jonesboro did not make any ringing affirmation of racial equality.

CHARLESTON, SEPTEMBER 18.

A big crowd—twelve thousand perhaps. Democrats out in force. A large and garish banner: "This government was made for white men—Douglas for life."

It was Lincoln's turn to give the opening speech, and he delivered the longest and worst and most-often-quoted passage denying that he supported "a perfect equality between the Negroes and white people." He started right off with it. He claimed to have been asked by "an elderly gentleman" whether he supported such equality, and to have decided to spend five minutes on the topic. Thus the whole passage arose as an answer to fears about Lincoln that Douglas in particular had aroused, in the white racist public of the state in which Lincoln was trying to be elected senator. Lincoln then asserted that he was not in favor of "bringing about in any way" social and political equality; not in favor of Negroes being voters or jurors or intermarrying with white people. He said that there was a "physical difference" between blacks and whites that "I believe" will forever forbid the two races living together on terms of "social and political equality." And then there is a still worse note, that since they cannot live together as equals, there must be a superior and an inferior, and "I, as much as any other man, am in favor of having the superior position assigned to the white race." Here, if you are a racist looking for support from Lincoln, or a debunker seeking to discredit Lincoln, is the prime text for claiming that he was a "white supremacist." But even in this worst of his statements, he immediately makes the "nevertheless" addition that is not a concession to the other side and to the prejudices of the audience, but his own affirmation: "I do not perceive that because the white man is to have the superior position the Negro should be denied everything." There is *something* still he is not to be denied—his humanity, and his right *not* to be a slave to any other man.

Douglas mentioned once more FRED. DOUGLASS, THE NEGRO, as he repeatedly called him here (the sneering capitals are in the text), and another "distinguished colored friend" of Lincoln, and their attempt to "show how much interest the colored brethren felt in the success of their brother Abe. (Renewed laughter.)" In a radically different climate in the following century, scholars would use a phrase from Frederick Douglass to describe Lincoln as "only a stepbrother" to African-Americans; to Stephen Douglas before a jeering white audience in 1858, however, he was "their brother Abe." Douglas said that a speech made by Douglass in Poughkeepsie "conjures all the friends of Negro equality and negro citizenship to rally as one man around Abraham Lincoln, the perfect embodiment of their principles, and by all means to defeat Stephen A. Douglas."*

GALESBURG, OCTOBER 7.

Cold. A speaking stand on the east side of a Knox College building. The largest audience so far. More Republicans and more sympathy for Lincoln than in Jonesboro or Charleston.

Douglas, opening, attacked Lincoln for standing up for Negro equality in one part of the state, and in another discarding that doctrine. He charged that Lincoln's egalitarianism was a "monstrous heresy" and that Lincoln was in effect accusing the Founders of hypocrisy: "[N]o one [of the Founders] emancipated his slaves, much less put them on an equality with himself."

His standard passage affirming white supremacy now extended racial domination forever: This government was made "by white men for the benefit of white men and their posterity forever, and was intended to be administered by white men in all time to come."

Lincoln responded, as best he could, to the charge that he changed his tune in different parts of the state. He said that the speeches were in print, and he knew they would be in print, to be read in all parts of Illinois.

For all the concessions to current prejudice he made, Lincoln insisted continually not only that the "created equal" in the Declaration included Negroes, but that to hold otherwise, as Douglas did, and to impute such a view to the Founders, was to destroy that great document's meaning for all

---

* Lincoln, in a vastly different context, would say of Frederick Douglass that "considering the conditions from which Douglass rose, and the position to which he had attained, he was, in his [Lincoln's] judgement, one of the most meritorious men in America" (as quoted by John Eaton, cited in *VFA*, p. 77; note p. 86).

Americans and all time. At Galesburg he specifically said that thus to exclude the Negro was to prepare the public mind for the nationalizing of slavery, to muzzle the cannon that thunders the Fourth of July's annual joyous return; to blow out the moral lights around us (these phrases borrowed from his youthful hero Henry Clay); and to eradicate the light of reason and the love of liberty.

QUINCY, OCTOBER 12.

The public square in the afternoon. Farthest west, on the Mississippi, central Illinois.

Lincoln, speaking first, again tried to defend himself against the charge that he said different things in different parts of the state, and attacked Douglas again for his "don't care" attitude toward slavery. Douglas "has the high distinction, as far as I know, of never having said slavery is either right or wrong." He made one of his many clear statements of his (and the Republicans') view of it as wrong. Douglas, in response, said the nation could go on to greatness half slave and half free.

In his rebuttal, Lincoln seized immediately on Douglas's admission that he "contemplates that it [slavery] shall last forever," and insisted that the Founders had no such idea.

ALTON, OCTOBER 15.

The Mississippi River town where Elijah Lovejoy had been killed. The last formal debate. In front of the new city hall.

Douglas's opening statement included a summary of the issues throughout the great debates. There have been three points at issue, said Douglas, and we may note that two of the three turn on racial equality explicitly, a third implicitly.

The point that rested implicitly on race was whether the nation could survive half slave and half free. Another point was Lincoln's "crusade against the Supreme Court" because the Dred Scott decision deprived Negroes of constitutional rights, privileges, and immunities. And the third point at issue was introduced by Lincoln when he "adopted . . . the argument [of] Lovejoy and Codding, and other Abolition lecturers that the Declaration of Independence having declared all men free and equal, by Divine law, negro equality was an inalienable right, of which they could not be deprived . . .":

[T]he Abolition party [i.e., the Republican Party and Lincoln] really think that under the Declaration of Independence the Negro is equal to the white man, and that Negro equality is an inalienable right conferred by the Almighty, and hence, that all human laws in violation of it are null and void. With such men it is no use for me to argue. I hold that the signers of the Declaration of Independence had no reference to Negros at all when they declared all men to be created equal. They did not mean Negros, nor the savage Indians, nor the Fejee Islanders, nor any other barbarous race.

Douglas claimed that, whereas he had held to such a position without wavering a hair's breadth, Lincoln as the debates went on had begun to "crawfish" a little.

Lincoln in his response at Alton made one of his most eloquent statements describing the eternal battle between right and wrong—now in the form of freedom and slavery—which we quote elsewhere in these pages.

Douglas in his rejoinder would make a couple of statements that were, even for him, unusually blunt: "I care more for the great principle of self-government, the right of the people to rule, than I do for all the Negroes in Christendom," he said, and "I would not blot out the great inalienable rights of the white men for all the Negroes that ever existed."

2. THE MODERN ASSAULT ON LINCOLN'S "WHITE SUPREMACY": SOME CONSIDERATIONS

In response to this racist attack and the racist atmosphere he knew well, Lincoln had done—as we saw in his remarks at Charleston—what almost all Republicans, at least outside New England, did: he made defensive concessions to reassure the heavily Negrophobic white male Illinois electorate that he did not propose to upset the racial patterns in contemporary Illinois. These are the statements, often quoted, that are now embarrassments for his admirers and weapons for his critics. He made defensive concessions to racial prejudice on all points except the crucial minimum (the Negro's humanity and basic right to live his own life) and then used those introductory concessions as a preliminary to a ringing affirmation of that basic right which was the point at issue. But in a later time when that basic right is no longer in question, his preliminary concessions, not his affirmation, become the focus of attention.

He said that although he supported a state's right to grant Negro suffrage, he did not support Negro suffrage in Illinois; we may observe that no one seeking statewide office in that state in the 1850s could have survived politically supporting Negro suffrage. He worked up a sentence that he repeated, that because he did not want a woman to be a slave did not mean that he wanted her to be a wife; she could be neither. He repeated on several other occasions those denials that he supported "social and political equality" that we have reported from his Charleston remarks.

And, although it did not figure large in the Lincoln/Douglas debates, he had endorsed the movement that proposed the colonizing of freed slaves—originally in Liberia, later in the Caribbean or Central America. In the passage of reassurances that followed the "monstrous injustice" paragraph in his speech at the state fair in the fall of 1854, which he got out his specs and read at length in Ottawa, he had included a particularly egregious and foolish and objectionable version of it: "My first impulse would be to free all the slaves and send them to Liberia—to their own native land."

For these statements and positions, Lincoln has come under another assault, in the vastly different atmosphere since about the last third of the twentieth century, for the exact opposite charge from the one the citizens of Dallas City put upon their hostile banner and that Douglas relentlessly attacked him for throughout their debates. Now he has been attacked as an *opponent* of racial equality, as a white supremacist and even as a "racist."

It has been said, with all the authority of David Herbert Donald, that it would be a mistake to try to "palliate" Lincoln's racial views by saying that he grew up in a racist society and that his ideas were shared by many, because there were "numerous" Americans—notably, many of the abolitionists—who were committed to racial equality. (Not to quibble, but can one say "numerous"?) In any case, there were some—Angelina and Sarah Grimké, to take my favorite examples. Born in a prominent slave-holding South Carolina family, they became "tip-top" abolitionists (to use Lincoln's faintly, but perhaps amiably, satirical term). Not only that, they passed the test that racists, imputing to others their own bigotry, think they will flunk: They discovered black members of their own family, "brothers"—whom they wholeheartedly embraced. There were other white folk in Lincoln's time, although not many, who affirmed full racial equality in contemporary practice, as Lincoln did not do.

I want nevertheless to engage in a quasi-defense of Lincoln, or at the least an attempt to understand him, that begins with his setting. It is not simply that he was, in the cliché, a "man of his time"; he was a man of his *time,* his *place,* and his *role.* He was a *politician,* a mainstream politician, seeking to shape major party victories, and much of the time seeking office himself, in one of the most racially prejudiced—perhaps the most prejudiced—of Northern states.

The little sprinkling of white abolitionists over on the far edge of American politics in the 1830s–1850s did their worthy service, and mostly deserve our admiration; but we should not mistake their rare and advanced opinions for the big bow-wow of broad public attitudes, and the crunch of practical possibility, that a mainstream politician in a prejudiced province has to deal with. The enormous accomplishment of ending the huge and powerfully entrenched institution of slavery in this country would require not only the abolitionists raising consciousness but also Republican politicians gearing that consciousness into the central machinery of the society.

In that radically different time from our own, Lincoln lived and worked in a particular place. For all of us, there are fixed facts and circumstances about our lives, beyond all choosing, and one of those in Lincoln's case was that his father had moved the family, after the sojourn in Indiana, to the new state of Illinois. Making his political career in Illinois would be a great advantage to Lincoln in the politics of 1854–60, because it was a growing swing state and the home of Stephen A. Douglas. But it would be a great disadvantage in the cultural criticism of later centuries, when general racial understanding in the United States, whatever its continuing defects, would at least be a long way forward from what it was back then and there, when heavy racial stereotypes were a part of the common culture. If Lincoln's father had somehow taken him to Massachusetts or Vermont, we would probably never have heard of him; but if we *had* heard of him, we probably would not discover him to have made vulnerable comments about race.

The modern derogation of Lincoln on racial grounds is a perverse reflection, on the one side, of the progress we have made, which makes it extremely difficult and unsettling to think one's way back into the conditions of that time and place. And it is an ironic reflection on the other side of the formulaic celebration that has turned Lincoln into such a legendary figure of stipulated and absolute wonderfulness as to make any encounter with the failings of an actual life disillusioning.

If he had never been elected president and become a legend, if he were a little-known figure from 1850s Illinois named John Doe, he might be regarded by the handful of historical specialists who might know about him as somewhat better, or less bad, on race than most of those who sought statewide office in that time and place. But John Doe does not have a monument on the Mall.

In no domain is it as important as it is with respect to race to set aside our exalted expectations; to bring Lincoln back down from his pedestal, to forget the memorial and descend from Mount Rushmore and ignore the face on the penny and the huge name in American legend, and to think, instead, about an actual human being living a real life in a particular time in a particular setting. This was a white man born early in the nineteenth century in a state in which slavery itself was a visible daily reality, who was raised in two settings—southern Indiana and central Illinois—that were severely unenlightened with respect to race. Black persons—slaves, and a very rare free black, like Billy the Barber—were, we can assume, on the periphery of his consciousness. There were almost no black persons in Spencer County, Indiana, as he was growing up, from his eighth to his twenty-first year. There were scarcely more in his Illinois settings—none at all, apparently, among the fewer than three hundred citizens who made up New Salem. Lincoln would have had very few associations with black persons at all—slaves or free persons—before he came to Springfield, and not many there. He certainly would not have had what twentieth-century social scientists, in their jargon, would call "equal status contacts." Late-twentieth-century digging has, of course, brought out that he used the n-word; told jokes that turned on racial stereotypes; enjoyed minstrel shows. He would use, as we have seen, the name "Sambo" as a designation for a black man, even in a note to himself that is otherwise marked by a humane egalitarianism rare in his setting.* As Lincoln himself perceived, and indicated in that they-are-as-we-would-be paragraph in his Peoria manuscript, most human beings most of the time have their attitudes and practices shaped by their surroundings. Although we have seen the young Lincoln making perhaps surprising rejections of elements of his

---

* In the Illinois Historical Library there is a typed copy of an extraordinary statement by a man named Henry Samuels reporting an interview with President Lincoln in 1864 about making the pay for the labor of escaped slaves equal to that of whites. A six-man delegation, including young Samuels as functionary, was ushered into the president's office by Secretary of War Edwin Stanton. "The President was seated at his desk with his long legs on the top of it, his hands on his head and looking exactly like a huge katydid or grasshopper," Samuels remembered twenty-five years later. Lincoln "quietly listened" while the committee members made their case and then "turned his head and jocularly said, with one of those peculiar smiles of his, 'Well, gentlemen, you wish the pay of "Cuffie" raised.'

environment—fighting, shooting, drinking, farming and manual labor, Jacksonian politics, mistreating Indians, churchgoing, cruelty to animals—at the same time he was no rebel or radical who rejected his society fundamentally. On the contrary. In his personal life, his book reading and melancholic moments notwithstanding, he was in the main gregarious, amiable, joke-telling, markedly popular. In his life purposes he did not include overthrowing the society in which he lived, but rather attaining distinction by serving within it: to become truly esteemed of his fellow men, by rendering himself worthy of their esteem. His ambitions drew him not into some prophetic or revolutionary role outside his society, but into its central machinery. And the society in which he sought to be a worthy and esteemed leader had built into it a radically exploitative institution, and a radically demeaning cultural stereotype of the human beings exploited in that institution.

Early in his life—let us say when he was twenty-three—this young lad from the unenlightened boondocks set out to be a party politician, running for office with a chance to win. That meant that he had to pay attention to the attitudes of the broad public by which he was surrounded, not of a selected audience only. His role was different from that of an editorial writer, a Congregational minister, a professor at Jacksonville College, a lawyer in private practice, or a transcendentalist writer proclaiming eternal truths to an elite audience. And his place was different than it would have been in Massachusetts or in Maine; in the Western Reserve—the *Connecticut* Reserve—of Ohio; or even, as migration from New England and from Germany and other places somewhat changed the rapidly growing northern part of Illinois, in Chicago. He was presenting himself as an acceptable lawmaker to be voted upon by the white male citizens of Sangamon County; of the Seventh Congressional District in the middle of the state; and now, in 1858, indirectly, of the whole state of Illinois.

He had said at the state fair and in Peoria in the autumn of 1854, precisely with reference to white racial prejudice, that a "universal feeling,

---

"I was at that time about twenty-five years of age," Samuels noted. "I said, 'Excuse me, Mr. Lincoln, the term "Cuffie" is not in our vernacular. What we want is that the wages of the American Colored Laborer be equalized with those of the American White Laborer.'" The president's response, as Samuels remembered it, is striking. He then said, "I stand corrected, young man, but you know I am by birth a Southerner and in our section that term is applied without any idea of an offensive nature. I will, however, at the earliest possible moment do all in my power to accede to your request." The delegation was "surprised by my audacity," Samuels reported, "but Lincoln was impressed, I suppose, by my sledgehammer remarks." Stanton commended Samuels as they were leaving the room, and thirty days later wages were equalized.

whether well- or ill-founded, can not be safely disregarded." It cannot, that is, if you propose to become a representative and lawmaker for a body of men infested overwhelmingly with that ill-founded feeling. It is characteristic of Lincoln that he would hint (even to an audience soaked in those feelings) that it *is* ill founded; it is also characteristic that he would not altogether disregard it.

And now Lincoln had risen to the peak of his ambition: an opportunity to be chosen to be United States senator. He was already designated, even before the legislature that would make the choice had been elected, as the one for whom members of his new party would vote. And his opponent was the Giant himself. Imagine what it would mean to be the man who beat the great Stephen A. Douglas for his Senate seat!

Lincoln's political problem was the reverse of Douglas's: He wanted to keep the focus on the evil and menace of slavery, and fend off, deflect, dampen down appeals to racial prejudice.

Here are considerations before singling out the nineteenth-century provincial white politician Abraham Lincoln for the late-twentieth-century epithet "racist":

1. White racial prejudice was pervasive and deep in most of the North, especially in the West, and particularly in Illinois, probably the most racially prejudiced free state in the Union.*

2. The Democrats, nationwide and in Illinois, made a relentless, nasty attack on all Republicans as "amalgamationists," "mongrelizers," "race-mixers." James McPherson would make a remark about the high tide of Democratic Party racism in the campaign to dislodge President Lincoln in 1864: "The vulgarity of their [the Democrats'] tactics [on race] almost surpasses belief."

3. The key point: Slavery, not *race,* was the issue in the 1850s. One might say with blunt realism that the Republicans as a major party had to disassociate themselves from racial equalizing in order to gain power to restrain slavery.

4. Almost all Republicans in the West and lower North made statements disavowing practical racial equality, most of them worse than those made by Lincoln.

---

* llinois was the worst of the free states, or tied with Indiana for that distinction, for these reasons: slavery's preexistence in the region, early migration from slave states, distance from the enlightening influences of New England and the East, and the frontier's unsettling fluidity.

5. Many Republicans (not to mention Democrats) adopted pseudo-scientific and pseudo-biblical ideas about differences in racial essence and origins, and genetic racial inferiority, accompanied by demeaning racist comments; Lincoln, even under Douglas's assault, did not do that.*

6. Colonization was not a peculiar proposal by Lincoln but a movement with a history. It could boast some quite distinguished earlier supporters (Henry Clay, Thomas Jefferson, James Madison, Daniel Webster), some black support, and in the late 1850s, widespread Republican endorsement.†

7. Although the colonization movement could rest on a demeaning racist premise, it could include also or instead a humanitarian motive, and always regarded itself as antislavery; for Lincoln it was always voluntary, and closely tied to emancipation and the moral condemnation of slavery.‡

8. Part of the reason for putting forward colonizing ideas was political expediency, as an answer to racist fears about what would happen after slavery.

9. Lincoln chose to oppose slavery's extension on *moral* grounds, which he did not need to do; and which many antislavery politicians did *not* do, insisting that their opposition to slavery rested in some "white" ground. The moral grounds that Lincoln made primary meant affirming common humanity with the enslaved black persons.

In the middle of the twentieth century, scholars examining race in America described the "vicious circle" by which racial discrimination and

---

* If one reads some pages of the appalling material in James D. Bilotta's *Race and the Rise of the Republican Party, 1848–1865* (New York: Peter Lang Publishing, 1992), one finds that in contrast to other Republicans Lincoln was restrained.

† Among its endorsers were Senator Lyman Trumbull and Governor William Bissell of Illinois; Montgomery Blair and Edward Bates, who would be in Lincoln's cabinet, and Hannibal Hamlin, who would be his vice president; Benjamin Franklin Wade, the radical Republican from Ohio; and Congressman James Ashley, also of Ohio, who would introduce what became the Thirteenth Amendment.

‡President Lincoln would make some objectionable arguments to the five black leaders he invited to the Executive Mansion in August of 1862, but he would tie his colonization proposal to the radical injustice of slavery ("Your race are suffering, in my judgement, the greatest wrong inflicted on any people") and the reason for his proposal was the depth of white racism: "But even when you cease to be slaves, you are yet far removed from being placed on an equality with the white race. . . . The aspiration of men is to enjoy equality with the best when free, but on this broad continent, not a single man of your race is made the equal of a single man of ours. Go where you are treated best, and the ban is still upon you." The question is less whether Lincoln had deep-seated racial prejudices, and more whether he thought a biracial society possible in the United States. I believe at the end, just barely, with black men serving in the Union Army, he did.

racial prejudice, the line in society and the line in the mind, mutually reinforced each other. There were racially distinguished schools, water fountains, railroad cars, parts of theaters, Pullman porters, and sections of
town; Langston Hughes would write, in the voice of a little black girl,
"Where's the Jim Crow car on the merry-go-round?" James Baldwin could
come home from fighting for democracy in the American army abroad to
find in a Southern railroad station signs saying, on the one hand, "White
Ladies" and on the other, "Colored Women," and could find German prisoners (being "white") admitted through the front door of the restaurant
while American soldiers with black faces were sent around to the back
door. And those practices reflected and reinforced derogatory stereotypes,
jokes, and epithets. Suppose that the line in society is not just racial segregation by law and custom, but the vast economic and social institution of
human slavery, under which a racially identified segment of humankind is
reduced to the status of chattels, devoid of human rights. What kind of a
vicious circle of attitudes reinforcing conditions, in turn reinforcing attitudes, does *that* create, with powerful economic and social and political
incentives to maintain those attitudes.

An unattached philosopher or advocate may ask simply, What is right?
What is the good? An engaged politician must ask, What aspect of the
right and the good is possible under these circumstances? What, here and
now, is better? He (now she as well) may also ask—I believe Lincoln did—
How may I under these circumstances make what is right and good (or
righter and better) *become* possible *tomorrow,* as it is not today?

But he or she—this engaged politician—may also have to ask: How can
I *prevent* this *worse* situation from coming about? That preventing of retrogression is a moral task, too. Perhaps it is not enough observed that
much of what Lincoln was doing in the 1850s was attempting to counter
the retrogressions that Douglas was promoting—"debauching" public
opinion, blowing out the moral lights, "imbruting" African-Americans.
And on the central topic, slavery, Lincoln and Republicans generally were
trying to prevent Douglas and company from preparing the ground for
slavery to become national and perpetual. Lincoln really did fear that one
more Supreme Court decision in line with *Dred Scott* would prevent *any*
state from excluding slavery, and would invalidate the antislavery provisions of free-state constitutions. History—even American history—does
not necessarily move steadily upward, morally speaking; twentieth-
century history would certainly establish that it does not do so in world
terms. Lincoln and the Republicans were battling against the spread of an

evil, against the softening of the disapproval of an evil. When they won, and there was a terrible war, the circumstance was created in which slavery *could* be ended, and the first steps toward racial equality begun. That effort would be stalled with the ending of Reconstruction in 1877, and turned back with the institution of Jim Crow and lynch law and North-South white reconciliation. Racial equality would then require a renewed effort in the twentieth century—say, from 1948 to 1968—by a new set of advocates and politicians, creating and taking advantage of new possibilities to take further steps. In this view it was not a mistake for the Lincoln Memorial to be chosen for the site of the great gathering in August of 1963 at which Martin Luther King Jr. spoke.

To appraise Lincoln fairly one should compare him not to unattached abolitionists in Massachusetts or to anyone a century and a half later but to other engaged politicians in the Old Northwest in the 1850s. In stark contrast to Douglas (and the Democrats generally) and to many western Republicans, Lincoln was a steadfast and eloquent defender of the humanity of black persons—and their right not to be enslaved. He opposed the extension of slavery, not primarily to protect the territories for white labor, as did many antislavery politicians, but primarily because of the monstrous injustice to the enslaved and the threat to the nation's moral foundations. That was a choice. He could have done otherwise, as did many Republicans.

Eric Foner, in the leading study of ideology of 1850s Republicans, made this summary about Lincoln's stands on racial issues: "Many eastern Republicans would go further [than Lincoln would go]; many westerners, on the other hand, felt that Lincoln had gone too far; but Lincoln himself articulated a shaky consensus within the party."

Critics of Lincoln on race compare him unfavorably to a list of abolitionists and antislavery politicians, almost all of whom come from New England or from pockets of New England migration like the Western Reserve or the burnt-over district in upstate New York,* or from places of comparative enlightenment in the East. Would not the more relevant comparison be, if we have pulled Lincoln down from a pedestal and are looking at him as a human being making choices, first, the friends and associates of his own youth, and second, politicians seeking office in the same political environment?

---

* The district much evangelized—"burnt over"—by the multiple revivals of the Second Awakening in the first half of the nineteenth century, from which region came an impressive array of social and religious movements.

The fact that the Lincolns and the Hankses almost all supported Democrats, even after their great relative was a leader of the Republicans, had plain implications for their racial views. If Lincoln had any mentor and sponsor, it would be John T. Stuart, who spotted him in the militia, encouraged him to study law, loaned him books, took him in as a partner, encouraged him to run for office, and treated him as a protégé in their first session in the assembly. And what were Stuart's racial views? Such as to show "slight pro-slavery proclivities," according to Lincoln himself. Stephen Logan, Lincoln's second law partner, would already in the 1855 Senate fight be worrying about statements of Lincoln's that tended towards abolitionism. David Davis particularly abominated Lovejoy and abolitionists; and Ward Lamon as marshal of the District of Columbia during the war would enforce the Fugitive Slave Law with a ferocity that led to protests. Lincoln's brother-in-law Ninian W. Edwards in 1852 became a Democrat and Douglas supporter. Were there any friends and close associates of Lincoln's youth and young manhood whom we know to have transcended the white racism of the common culture? I do not think so.

To be sure, there were politicians as well as abolitionist leaders whose record on race, in what they did and said and did not say, was superior to Lincoln's: Charles Sumner and Salmon Chase are clear examples, and Joshua Giddings and a quite small sprinkling of congressmen. But none, I believe, came from as far out on the frontier, or with a constituency reaching as deep into the lower North, as Illinois. Owen Lovejoy was not running statewide but ran only for a congressional seat, from the most "abolitionized" northern Illinois district; and even he, as he moved from preaching to face a larger slice of his fellow citizens and seek their votes, drew away from his former abolitionist associates in his hometown of Princeton, Illinois, and said things that dismayed William Lloyd Garrison about Negro inferiority and the United States belonging to the white man.

The most relevant comparison for Lincoln, looking at his realistic choices, might be Lyman Trumbull, the man who with Lincoln's help had come to fill the office he, Lincoln, aspired to, senator from Illinois. Trumbull has rather surprisingly been made into something of a hero by Lincoln's critics in an effort to counter the argument that Lincoln's positions were necessitated by his role as a political leader in that state.* But the ele-

---

* Lerone Bennett Jr.'s *Forced into Glory: Abraham Lincoln's White Dream* (Chicago: Johnson Publishing, 2000), a passionate polemic against Lincoln on race, rather surprisingly includes Trumbull among the "Real Emancipators" (in contrast to Lincoln) on his

vation of Trumbull over Lincoln with regard to racial attitudes surely is bizarre. Trumbull, the ex-Democrat, certainly made statements and took positions on race that were far worse than Lincoln's. Eugene Berwanger, the scholar of racism on the frontier, squarely made it a general point: "No individual did more to assure the Negrophobes about the principles of the Republican Party than Lyman Trumbull." Berwanger puts Trumbull and Douglas right there together on race, as surely would not have been the case had Lincoln rather than Trumbull been chosen senator in 1855: "The Illinois senators, Lyman Trumbull and Stephen A. Douglas, were always in the front ranks when a defense of black laws was required . . . on this issue [Negro exclusion laws] both senators were in complete agreement." The books examining racial attitudes in the politics of the time swarm with quotations from Trumbull about the whiteness of the Republican Party and the inferiority of the Negro and the necessity of colonization, by force if necessary.

If in 1860 the Republican Party had chosen as its nominee for President not Lincoln but another Republican from the swing state of Illinois, Senator Lyman Trumbull, and if (as I think quite unlikely) Trumbull had gone on to become a national hero, then we may be sure that critics today would be denouncing Trumbull and perhaps setting in contrast to him that forgotten other Illinois Republican named Lincoln, who in a six-year contest with Douglas, although he made concessions on race, nevertheless had steadfastly defended as his primary position the humanity of black persons.

3. ON LINCOLN'S MORAL COMPOSITION

The distinguished historian David Potter saw in Lincoln this dynamism: "In the long-run conflict between deeply held convictions on one hand and habits of conformity to the cultural practices of a binary society on the other, the gravitational forces were all in the direction of equality. By a static analysis, Lincoln was a mild opponent of slavery and a moderate defender of racial discrimination. By a dynamic analysis, he held a concept of humanity which impelled him inexorably in the direction of freedom and equality."

I surmise that two parts of Lincoln's moral machinery, at two levels, personal and philosophical, independent of race, would move him forward on that matter as well as others. I infer that this dynamism would

---

page of dedication, and several passages in the body of his book praise Trumbull, again in pointed contrast to Lincoln.

have continued to work against his prejudices, in this continually self-improving man, had he lived. Some treatments have said (in contrast to Potter) that it was Lincoln's sharing in the pervasive racial prejudice of his environment that was "deep-seated," but I do not see the evidence for that deep-seatedness. I would have said that his racial prejudices were conventional, opportunistic—and changeable. He did not give voice to the worst anti-Negro stereotypes, as not only Democrats but many Republicans did. And the concessions to white prejudice he made regularly had a qualified, tentative cast; they were concessions made under polemical and political fire. And—this is a key disputed point—they did change in the changed conditions of the last years of his presidency.

I think the two parts of his makeup mentioned above were working against racial prejudice. Each in turn has two levels. First, in his personal life, the testimony is overwhelming that Lincoln, man and boy, had an unusually intense sympathy with the suffering of his fellow creatures: for lost cats, mired-down hogs, birds fallen out of the nest, turtles with hot coals on their backs. This sympathy extended also, as is not always the case with animal lovers, to his fellow human beings: to the old Indian who wandered into the camp; the woman whose drunken husband beat her; the farm boy who is going to be shot for falling asleep on sentry duty; the coffle of slaves on the boat in the Ohio, chained together like fish on a line. This natural human fellow-feeling he found in himself must have been part of the reason he discovered in human beings generally a natural sympathy for the slave—that is, for the human beings who are enslaved—that, he affirmed, would still be there even if the Declaration of Independence had not been written.

Secondly, still at the personal level, partly built on that natural sympathy but partly a development of a conscious mature discipline, Lincoln came to be unusually respectful in his personal conduct of the dignity and independence of the human beings with whom he dealt. That had not necessarily been true of the ambitious younger Lincoln, with his awareness that he was abler than those around him, and with his satirical inclination and self-confident polemical power—his "power to hurt." But as he matured, one can almost observe him curbing that inclination and becoming scrupulous and respectful.

To some extent that is already true of his dealing with his fellow Whigs seeking to go to Congress in 1843–46, but it became clearer after 1854. He was gracious to those who opposed him in Illinois in the senatorial battle in 1855, and again to those who opposed him outside Illinois in the contest in 1858. His letters seeking support, his dealings with editors, supporters, opponents, clients, have a distinct quality of tact, generosity, and civility. It is not rare to find theoretical democrats who are, in their personal lives, practical tyrants. Not Lincoln. Don Fehrenbacher, in *Prelude to Greatness,* concludes about these six years, 1854–1860: "One finds the same patience and respect for human dignity that characterize the wartime presidency." His respect for human dignity as president would extend to a wide range of human encounters—including those he now came to have with black persons.

Those personal attributes of Lincoln's—natural sympathy and cultivated respect—would, I suggest, reciprocally have reinforced, and been reinforced by, his convictions in the realm of ideas. There were his *American* ideas and there were his broader moral-philosophical-religious ideas. As to the latter, he often affirmed human equality as a fundamental principle. Despite his quiet rejection of the doctrinal core of the Christian religion, he grasped its moral meaning better than most believers. His universalistic philosophical presuppositions would appear not only (as we have seen) in those so-called "fragments" but occasionally in his letters, arguments, little glimpses in speeches: "No man is good enough to govern another man *without that other's consent*"; "Allow ALL the governed an equal voice in the government, and that, and that only is self-government."

And as to his American ideas, he had that romantic conception of the nation as founded in an egalitarian ideal that was not only a major theme in his speeches but surely also a defining conviction of his own. For all the disadvantages he faced in promoting what was functionally the more pro-Negro side in the debates in white racist Illinois in 1858, he did have that one great advantage on his side: that document out of the nation's founding moment, the Declaration of Independence, which had become, by that time, widely celebrated. Of course it was a rhetorical godsend. Lincoln would use the phrase "that all men are created equal" and the symbol of the Declaration from which it came as an authoritative argument for Americans—a kind of scripture—with a regularity, an insistence, and a forcefulness one may not quite appreciate from collections of the major speeches or from the biographies. This was a constant: The United States was founded upon the proposition that all men are created equal, as stated in the Declaration of Independence. That is what this country is all about.

He would use the Declaration to affirm equality to a racist public with a range of rhetorical devices, surrounding his audiences with the revered document on all sides:

- scorn for detractors of the Declaration—for those who would call it a "self-evident lie" full of "glittering generalities";
- regret for the falling off of the present generation, from the great days of the Declaration;
- disdain for the utterly implausible transfer of the ideal of equality from men to *states,* as President Buchanan and others had tried to do;
- satire, for Douglas's "dried-prune" restriction of the Declaration's reach to the white British colonists at the time;
- an appeal to memory—to an audience's recollection of what the Declaration had meant to them a short time ago, before Douglas and the others had attacked it;
- patriotism—drumrolls of celebration of the Spirit of '76;
- pride in the worldwide and historical significance it gave to the United States;
- original principle, equating the freedom fought for against King George with the freedom of today's slaves;
- personal testimony, to its meaning to him when he read about it as a boy.

The Declaration as a moral norm functioned:

- as a barrier against retrogression;
- and as a beacon and a promise, a transcendent ideal, not fully achieved, always to be approximated as closely as we can.

We have already noted an extraordinary invocation of the Declaration, in spontaneous remarks just before the beginning of the debates with Douglas in the senatorial campaign, at Lewistown, Illinois, on August 17, 1858. He quoted the "We hold these truths" paragraph and commented: "This was [the Founders'] majestic interpretation of the economy of the Universe. This was their lofty, and wise, and noble understanding of the justice of the Creator to His creatures [applause]." And then, as we noted before, he underlined the inclusiveness of this fundamental conception: "Yes, gentlemen, to *all* His creatures, to the whole great family of man . . . nothing stamped with the divine image and likeness was sent into the world to be trodden on, and degraded, and imbruted by its fellows." The now peculiar word "imbruted," which would appear also in abolitionist literature, reflected another Lincoln theme, to be noted in a moment.

In the debates themselves one of the ways he could sneak up on his racist audience from the blind side was to mock Douglas's conception of

the Declaration of Independence. The audiences, for all their racial prejudice, had come to have an attachment to the Declaration as a national icon
and had presumably accepted, without examining it closely, its grand universal sweep. So Douglas was vulnerable to Lincoln's satirical touch, his
formulation of the "mangled ruin" Douglas made of the Declaration: "We
hold these truths to be self-evident, that all British subjects who were on
this continent eighty-one years ago, were created equal to all British subjects born and *then* residing in Great Britain."

At Lewistown, Lincoln said that the "wise statesmen" who founded
this country set up a beacon so that "when in the distant future some man,
some faction, some interest, should set up the doctrine that none but rich
men, or none but white men, were entitled to life, liberty and the pursuit of
happiness," the Declaration of Independence would give "courage to
renew the battle." He slipped in the phrase "none but white men" to draw
a parallel to other tyrannies.

And in Springfield, Lincoln would challenge Douglas to amend the
Declaration of Independence, to "make it read that all men are created
equal except negroes."

I affirm that these passionate invocations of the Declaration were heartfelt; that the primary point of the invocation was that all men are created
equal with rights; that the primary meaning of *that* clause, in this context,
was that black persons were included; and that this affirmation was—as he
certainly testified that it was—a central belief for Lincoln. This belief,
in this view, meshed with broader ideas and personal characteristics to
make a racially inclusive egalitarianism the dynamic element in Lincoln's
makeup.

Lincoln himself, for all his upbringing in a state with a black code and
an atmosphere of common, taken-for-granted white prejudice, assumed
and affirmed the black man's humanity. When one reads the bookfuls of
racist statements from the time, it is then quite striking that this border-
state politician writing those fragments in the privacy of his own reflection
would deal with human beings one by one, without regard to race.

On other occasions he would deal with particular events in the same
way. When he wrote his long letter to Joshua Speed's sister Mary on September 27, 1841, after a visit to the Speed home in Kentucky, he mentioned
the scene of the twelve Negro slaves on shipboard, chained together "precisely like so many fish upon a trout line." Lincoln writers have noted the
difference between this passage and the reference he would make to this
same scene in a letter to Joshua Speed fourteen years later, on August 24,
1855. In that letter, he would use this scene as an example of his feelings

when he encounters slavery: the sight of the slaves "shackled together with irons" was "a continual torment to me." But there was nothing like that in his letter to Mary, filling her in on his and Joshua's doings after her gracious hospitality. What he does write to Mary—more interesting, perhaps—is a general observation about the human condition under humiliation and deprivation. Lincoln, writing a long, friendly semi-thank-you letter to his friend's sister and his recent hostess, presented the scene to Mary as an occasion for contemplating the effect of "condition" upon *human* happiness—it concerned, not some peculiarity of the black "race," but universal *human* responses.

Or, again, another example, now looking forward to his time as president: Lincoln, writing (on August 26, 1863) to heavily prejudiced Springfield Union supporters who did not like the Emancipation Proclamation, said that "negroes, like other people, act upon motives," and that risking their lives must be prompted by the strongest motive—the promise of freedom.

4. LINCOLN ATTACKS THE IMBRUTING OF BLACK AMERICA

Even in the atmosphere we have described, even with the purpose of getting himself and his party elected with the votes of racist majorities, Lincoln could still circumspectly appeal to the better angels of his audience's nature—to their sense, in spite of everything, of common humanity. Human beings are mixtures—even those who howled agreement with Douglas in the exchanges quoted above. There were other ways to wound their prejudice from behind.

Lincoln's questions in his state fair/Peoria speech of 1854, putatively to his Southern friends but effectively, of course, to his Illinois audience—about why they did not shake hands with the slave dealer, why they joined in enacting the penalty of *hanging* for Atlantic slave traders, why there were free blacks around, showing that "masters" in some past day had emancipated their "property"—were of this kind. He was appealing to a latent human sympathy and a sense of justice, of common humanity.

Although in general the Democrats were worse in the racial demagoguery than the Republicans, there was among the latter, in addition to whatever the members of that party shared of the pervasive racial prejudice of the environment, an additional politically defensive racism—to counter the attacks made on them. Some Republicans (certainly Lyman Trumbull) insisted that *their* party was really the white man's party, and volunteered matching versions of the racist stereotypes about physical repulsiveness, innate intellectual inferiority, laziness, and licentiousness with which the Democrats' propaganda material was loaded. Lincoln did not indulge in this sort of thing; many of his Republican colleagues did. A little exposure to quotations from fellow Republicans, including antislavery stalwarts, will persuade a reader that Lincoln was more restrained than even the Republican norm.

In the remarks added to his state fair speech, as he gave it again in Peoria after hearing Douglas respond to him back at the state fair, Lincoln remarked that Douglas "has no very vivid impression that the Negro is human, and consequently has no idea that there can be any moral question about him." That implied that, of course, the humanity of the Negro *does* raise moral questions about his mistreatment.

After Lincoln's failure back in 1855 to get himself elected to be Douglas's colleague in the Senate, and after the new Republican Party that Lincoln helped to build in Illinois did rather well in the presidential year 1856 (the Republican William Bissell was elected governor in Illinois), and after the inauguration of Buchanan in 1857, the Supreme Court issued the Dred Scott decision. Both men made speeches in Springfield dealing with the case, Douglas scrambling to defend his doctrine of unfriendly legislation— that the people of a territory could keep slavery out, despite *Dred Scott,* by not enacting the supporting legislation—and Lincoln scrambling to explain what one does with a Supreme Court decision that one strongly morally rejects.*

Lincoln did something else in that speech, something that he did not need to do. He vigorously rejected a statement by Chief Justice Roger Taney that "the public estimate of the black man is more favorable *now* than it was in the days of the Revolution." Lincoln was provoked by that sentence to write a long and spirited denial, complete with a literary effort at the end. I want to quote this passage at some length, because it is not as often quoted as other passages, and seems to me significant when we consider Lincoln, in his context, on race. It is also illuminating to us today, about the specific conditions then: again, he had done some research.

---

* Lincoln made close discriminations—affirming the authority of the Court decision on constitutional questions "when fully settled"—but then cited a series of criteria for "full settlement" that the Court's decision in this case did not meet (degree of unanimity, accordance with precedent and steady practice, accuracy of fact, absence of partisan bias, affirmation and reaffirmation when before the Court more than once). He sided with the dissenting opinions of Justices McLean and Curtis.

Here is Lincoln's rhetorical flight, rebutting Justice Taney, on the state of the Negro in 1857:

> In some trifling particulars, the condition of that race had been ameliorated; but, as a whole, in this country, the change between then and now is decidedly the other way; and their ultimate destiny has never appeared so hopeless as in the last three or four years. In two of the five States—New Jersey and North Carolina—that then gave the free Negro the right of voting, the right has since been taken away; and in a third—New York—it has been greatly abridged; while it has not been extended, so far as I know, to a single additional state, though the number of states has more than doubled.

Now here is a curiosity: Lincoln is here plainly *deploring* the failure to extend Negro suffrage, indeed to shrink it. Lincoln the politician would explicitly say he did not support Negro suffrage in Illinois. But he would say he supported the right of states in general, when they chose to do it, to extend that suffrage. And here he is plainly and passionately treating the shrinkage of Negro suffrage as a distressing development.

Now on manumission:

> In those days, as I understand, masters could, at their own pleasure, emancipate their slaves; but since then such legal restraints have been made upon emancipation, as to amount almost to prohibition. In those days, Legislatures held the unquestioned power to abolish slavery in their respective States; but now it is becoming quite fashionable for State Constitutions to withhold that power from the Legislatures. In those days, by common consent, the spread of the black man's bondage to new countries was prohibited; but now, Congress decides that it *will* not continue the prohibition, and the Supreme Court decides that it *could* not if it would. In those days, our Declaration of Independence was held sacred by all, and thought to include all; but now, to aid in making the bondage of the Negro universal and eternal, it is assailed, and sneered at, and construed, and hawked at, and torn, till, if its framers could rise from their graves, they could not at all recognize it. All the powers of the earth seem rapidly combining against him. Mammon is after him; ambition follows, and philosophy follows, and the Theology of the day is fast joining the cry.

Now Lincoln brought this passionate passage about the desperate condition of the American Negro to a climax with an extended metaphor:

> They have him in his prison house; they have searched his person, and left no prying instrument with him. One after another they have closed the heavy iron doors upon him, and now they have him, as it were, bolted in with a lock of a hundred keys, which can never be unlocked without the concurrence of every key; the keys in the hands of a hundred different men, and they scattered to a hundred different and distant places; and they stand musing as to what invention, in all the dominions of mind and matter, can be produced to make the impossibility of his escape more complete than it is. It is grossly incorrect to say or assume, that the public estimate of the Negro is more favorable now than it was at the origin of the government.

Why did he do that? What advantage could there be, given the racial attitudes of the relevant white constituency? If he is an ambitious politician seeking advancement in racially prejudiced Illinois, and if he is, as charged by critics in later centuries, a self-starting white supremacist—why take off on this long and rather passionate and perhaps even moving flight of sympathy for the *increasing* oppression of "the Negro"? There were many other ways to oppose the Dred Scott decision.

The next year, 1858, Lincoln and Douglas stood on the same platform in the famous debates. In Lincoln's speech in that last debate in Alton he used a word—one of those not-very-graceful modern words, literally speaking, that end in "ize," but morally important—a word that we might expect to appear in a discussion of such matters in a later century: "dehumanize."

> And when this new principle—this new proposition that no human being ever thought of three years ago [Douglas's new principle that "created equal" did not apply to the Negro]—is brought forward, I combat it as having an evil tendency to dehumanize the Negro. . . . I combat it as being one of the thousand things constantly done in these days to prepare the public mind to make property, and nothing but property of the Negro in all the states of this Union.

What Douglas is doing, said Lincoln, is carrying on a deliberate attempt to bring the white public to look at the Negro as something less than a human—to cut the ties that bind us as one human community; to degrade the Negro to the level of a brute.

In the Senate race, Douglas managed to pull out a victory in the state legislature, because of holdovers and some malapportionment. But Lincoln, in the aftermath of the well-publicized debates with the Little Giant, found that his stature was enhanced, locally and nationally, and began to be asked to speak in other states. I believe he moved a step further from the defense, fending off Douglas's attacks on his racial egalitarianism, over to the attack, now finding illustrations to explain more aggressively what was wrong with Douglas's demeaning treatment. His situation was now different, as he was invited to speak to audiences in Indiana, Wisconsin, Kansas, and, particularly, in Ohio. Now, he was not himself a candidate for office in any of these states, and except perhaps for Indiana (one speech in Indianapolis) none of them manifested such deep racial prejudices as did Illinois. A year had passed since his great encounter with the "Judge"; these speeches took place in the fall and early winter of 1859. He was not now in the constricted situation of seeking support for himself in Illinois, but was an emerging spokesman for the new Republican Party nationally.

Lincoln included in his speeches in Ohio and Indiana this argument that he had just started to make in the debates in Illinois: that until quite recently no one had thought to exclude the Negro from the "all men" referred to in the Declaration. But Douglas was now teaching his hearers to do that. Speaking in Indianapolis on September 19, 1859, Lincoln dramatized what he said Douglas was doing with his amending of the meaning of the Declaration:

> Five years ago no living man expressed the opinion that the Negro had no share in the Declaration of Independence. But within that space Douglas had got his entire party, almost without exception, to join in saying that the Negro has no share in the Declaration. The tendency of that change, that debauchery in public sentiment is to bring the public mind to the conclusion that when white men are spoken of, the Negro is not meant, and when Negroes are spoken of, brutes alone are contemplated. That change had already depressed the black man in the estimation of Douglas himself, and the Negro was thus being debased from the condition of a man to that of some sort of a brute.

On September 16, 1859, in Columbus, Ohio, Lincoln had made the point by a rhetorically effective challenge to the crowd:

Did you ever five years ago, hear of anybody in the world saying that the Negro had no share in the Declaration of National Independence; that it did not mean Negroes at all; and when "all men" were spoken of Negroes were not included? . . . I call upon one of them to say that he said it five years ago.

If you think that now, and did not think it then, the next thing that strikes me is to remark that there has been a change wrought in you (Laughter and applause); and a very significant change it is, being no less than changing the Negro, in your estimation, from the rank of a man to that of a brute. They are taking him down, and placing him, when spoken of, among reptiles and crocodiles, as Judge Douglas himself expresses it. . . .

Douglas and others are "debauching" public opinion. The report of the first of his two speeches in Leavenworth, Kansas, has him using the word "brutalize" to describe the effects of Douglas's advocacy: "to brutalize the Negro in the public mind."

Lincoln had meanwhile picked up a figure that Douglas kept using which, as Lincoln insisted, illustrated Douglas's relentless effort to dehumanize, to brutalize, the Negro. Lincoln got this from a speech Douglas gave in Memphis, but he said Douglas had made the remark a good many times in the campaign in Illinois, although it had not been reported. It goes like this: while in all contests between the Negro and the white man Douglas was for the white man, in all questions between the Negro and the crocodile, he was for the Negro (laughter from the audience). Lincoln emphasized that Douglas had used this line frequently, a great many times. "It is, then, a deliberate way of expressing himself upon that subject," said Lincoln in Cincinnati on September 17, 1859. "It is a matter of mature deliberation with him [Douglas] thus to express himself upon that point of his case. It therefore requires some deliberate attention."

So, giving it his deliberate attention, Lincoln made his analysis:

The first reference seems to be that if you do not enslave the Negro you are wronging the white man in some way. . . . Is that not a falsehood? . . . I say there is no such necessary conflict. I say there is room enough for us all to be free. . . .

I don't know that there is any struggle between the Negro and the crocodile, either (Laughter) . . . But what, at last, is this proposition? I believe it is a sort of proposition in proportion which may be stated thus: as the Negro is to the white man, so the crocodile is to the Negro, and as the Negro may rightfully treat the crocodile as a beast or reptile, so the white man may rightfully treat the Negro as a beast or reptile. This is really the "knip" of all that argument of his.

In remarks reported in the *Beloit* (Wisconsin) *Journal* of a speech given October 1, 1859, Lincoln fit together this condemnation of Douglas's demeaning crocodile passage with his condemnation of his shoulder-shrugging denial that there was any moral issue about slavery:

> Mr. Douglas takes it for granted that slavery is not a moral wrong. To him it is a matter of indifference whether it is "voted up or voted down." . . . It is right and necessary in the South, he says, and he sneers at the idea of an "irrepressible conflict" between Negro bondage and human freedom. "They are an inferior race." Between the white man and the Negro, he goes for the white man, but between the Negro and the crocodile he goes for the Negro. These are Douglas's sentiments. The man who expresses such sentiments can see no moral wrong in slavery.

Lincoln would appeal to the Declaration as his own, as well as the nation's, moral grounding in a moment not yet to be imagined in the fall of 1859: less than a year and a half later he will be president-elect, on his way to Washington. Speaking to the New Jersey Senate, he would recall—as we have noted before—his youthful reading of Weems's *Life of Washington* and his feeling that the men who fought in the battles at Trenton and elsewhere fought for "something even more than National Independence, . . . something that held out a great promise to all the people of the world to all time to come." Then in Philadelphia the next day, speaking in Independence Hall itself, on Washington's birthday, he made remarks, again extemporaneous and again starting off with personal testimony, that put the Declaration at the heart of his own worldview. "I have never had a feeling politically," he said, "that did not spring from the sentiments embodied in the Declaration of Independence." Those sentiments, he would say, "gave promise that in due time the weights should be lifted from the shoulders of all men, and that *all* should have an equal chance."

The weights should be lifted from the shoulders of black persons as well as others; "*all* should have an equal chance."

CHAPTER FIFTEEN

Such an Impression

1. MENTAL CULTURE IN NEW YORK

The year 1860 was to be a mammoth example of that Lincolnian surprise—that shock of recognition and wild surmise—that we have said recurred throughout Lincoln's life. At the beginning of the year he was a private citizen, a lawyer in a provincial western state, a politician never chosen by any electorate larger than that of the Seventh Congressional District of central Illinois and that only once, a one-term congressman out of office for eleven years. At the end of the year, he was president-elect of the United States.

How did that happen? Of course it was not the result exclusively of events within that one year—but those events brought a spectacular culmination to developments across the preceding six years.

The autumn of 1859, before that climactic year, had brought a sharp rise in Lincoln's standing, as Lincoln gave the speeches in Iowa, Wisconsin, Kansas, and particularly in Ohio, that we have already noted. His responses to Douglas in Ohio were given some credit for Republican victories in that state. Then, after that running start, the explosive Lincolnian rise in 1860 started with an invitation to speak in the famous Plymouth Church in Brooklyn with its even more famous preacher, Henry Ward Beecher. This was the most important of the invitations that came to him in his new national visibility after his debates with Douglas. Lincoln quickly accepted, with the reservation that they take "a political speech" if he did not have time to prepare another kind. But surely they had not wanted another address on "discoveries and inventions."

On Saturday, February 25, he arrived in New York City and learned that

375

the venue of the speech had been transferred to the Cooper Union in downtown Manhattan and the sponsorship to the Young Men's Central Republican Union of New York. This "Young Men's" committee included such youths as William Cullen Bryant, aged sixty-five; Horace Greeley, aged forty-nine; the fifty-one-year-old Hamilton Fish; and the fifty-four-year-old William Curtis Noyes. Most of the key figures making the invitation—Greeley most prominent among them—were opponents of William Seward in New York politics.

Lincoln retired to the Astor House to make changes in his speech; perhaps gawked a little at the big city sights; met the great historian George Bancroft at a photographer's; and attended the Reverend Mr. Beecher's church on Sunday.

On Monday evening he came forward in his wrinkled suit to speak to the most distinguished audience, by a wide margin, he had ever addressed. The revised invitation from the Young Men's Union had told him that "the audience . . . is not that of an ordinary political meeting. These lectures have been contrived to call out our better, but busier citizens, who never attend political meetings. A large part of the audience will consist of ladies." Reports of this event often list a couple of lines of the then famous names who attended. The *New York Tribune* of Horace Greeley (who was one of those famous attendees) said the next morning: "Since the days of Clay and Webster no man has spoken to a larger assemblage of the intellect and mental culture of our city." There were some fifteen hundred in the audience, and they paid twenty-five cents each to hear this new man.

The way he was introduced demonstrated two things: one, that it could be assumed that the audience had now heard this man's name; but also, two, that they did not yet know him personally. William Cullen Bryant, the poet and editor of the *New York Evening Post,* said: "It is a grateful office that I perform, in introducing to you an eminent citizen of the West, hitherto known to you only by reputation."

As he stepped to the podium and began to speak, the first New York impressions of this western man known only by reputation featured (of course) his height, his unhandsomeness, his ill-fitting suit, and his Hoosier accent. And then there came that surprised upgrading of first impressions that we have said would mark Lincoln's entire course through life. The way he won over this audience, as he worked his way through his manuscript, was not by oratorical elegance but by sheer preparation and relentless clarity. Lincoln in this stage of his life was not—as perhaps he had made a stab at being in his youthful addresses—an orotund Websterian orator, as was his friend Edward D. Baker, or Owen Lovejoy, with the great organ music of their orations. Lincoln's speeches were marked by clarity, logic, intelligence, and aptness. They were not dependent on the spontaneous excitement of the moment, as the orator's flights often are, but were carefully written out beforehand. This particular speech would begin with a factual argument so complete as to overwhelm a reader and probably a hearer. This first part of the Cooper Union Address is often omitted in collections of Lincoln's speeches, but it surely must have been an important part of the persuasive impact of the address as given. A reader today who wants to encounter a Lincoln different from the myth—a diligent assembler of facts presented with stunning clarity—should seek out the full text of this address. Once again one should emphasize the amount of work Lincoln put into the speech. As in 1854, so now even more in 1859–60: there had to have been long sessions in the state library. Once again there is a long, carefully stated historical section at the outset—nearly one-half of the speech.

Once yet again Stephen Douglas was his chief opponent, although this time only in providing a one-sentence text for Lincoln to refute. Lincoln may also be seen as responding indirectly to Chief Justice Roger Taney in the Dred Scott decision and to all the Democrats and supporters of slavery who had lined up behind him to claim that the Founding Fathers did *not* intend Congress to decide about slavery in the territories. With a mountain of evidence, Lincoln would claim that they did.

Douglas had said (rather loosely, one assumes) that "our fathers understood this question [the federal government's control of slavery in the territories] as well as, or better than, we do." All right then, Lincoln said, I quite agree—and let us see what the Founding Fathers actually *did* believe and do with respect to that question. He pursued the matter with utter thoroughness and scrupulous care, first giving a painstakingly precise definition of just whom we mean by the constantly invoked category the "Fathers." He took, not a vaguely inclusive term like the revolutionary generation, or just the familiar names of the greatest Founders, but rather precisely the thirty-nine signers of the Federal Constitution on September 17, 1787. (Not the sixty-five who were chosen to attend the Constitutional Convention, nor the fifty-five who were there at least part of the time, and excluding the sixteen who did not sign, six of whom gave their reasons—just the thirty-nine who first signed the United States Federal Constitution.) They were surely, unmistakably, "Fathers" of this country. He then went through, with ostentatious thoroughness and care, the votes of these thirty-nine on proposals having to do with slavery in the territories. Four of them, giving their names, had voted to exclude slavery in the Northwest Territory in 1784, and one had voted against exclusion. (Lincoln's scrupulosity of course includes carefully giving the votes on the other side and claiming absolutely no more than hard evidence supports.) In 1787, while the Constitution was being framed, the Northwest Ordinance excluding slavery in that territory was passed with two more of the thirty-nine, giving their names, voting for the prohibition. Lincoln acknowledged, scrupulously still, that the *precise* question at issue did not come before the Constitutional Convention itself, but it did come before the First Congress in the form of an act to enforce the ordinance of '87, introduced by one of the thirty-nine, with sixteen joining in the unanimous passage of the act—again, he gave the names of the sixteen—and one, George Washington, signing it. And Lincoln went on in the same manner through congressional acts on cessions of territory, on the congressional action on the Louisiana Purchase, and the "Missouri question" in 1819–1820, showing with names in each case some of the thirty-nine voting for, or acquiescing in, congressional action with respect to (not always prohibition of) slavery in the territories. He kept repeating in each instance the refrain that these named "fathers" saw no line prohibiting federal action with respect to slavery in the territories. Long before he reaches his summation, the reader—and probably the hearer in Cooper Union on the evening of February 27, 1860—is ready to concede the point. But the sheer thoroughness and scrupulosity of argument must have had its own rhetorical effect: How could Douglas after *this* display wave his hand in the direction of the Founding Fathers and claim their support for his position? Lincoln conscientiously tallied up the results, and conscientiously and specifically subtracted those counted twice or three times, again by name, and gave the result, the number of the thirty-nine who had voted for or acquiesced in federal action with respect to slavery in the territories: twenty-one, a clear majority. Two had voted against one of the measures he had considered, but it is characteristic of Lincoln's thoroughness in this effort that he does not leave them behind, but carefully explained that even these two may have voted as they did from expediency, not constitutional principle. And even then he did not stop, but went on to explain that the sixteen of the thirty-nine who were not counted in this majority could not necessarily be counted on the other side; they included some of the most clearly antislavery of the Founders—Alexander Hamilton, Benjamin Franklin, Gouverneur Morris.

And still he did not stop. He was apparently determined to overwhelm these city folk, these "mental culture" people. Lincoln had to have known what stereotype New Yorkers held of westerners and, insofar as they had heard of him, of himself. It is to be noted that there is no joke, nor any hint of a joke, anywhere in this speech, and in this first half no illustration or turn of phrase, either. He marches on through an analysis of the facts. He went on to consider the passage by the First Congress of the first ten amendments to the Constitution, which included the Fifth Amendment, upon which the Dred Scott decision was based, and the Tenth, which Douglas relied on for his claims of state sovereignty. He proceeded to show that the seventy-six members of that Congress simultaneously with their consideration of those amendments were considering and passing the act confirming the Northwest Ordinance's prohibition of slavery. So those men, who also could be considered as among the Fathers strictly defined, did not apparently see any inconsistency in these two actions—and is it not presumptuous of us in a later day to charge them with inconsistency? Lincoln pounded away at Douglas's assertion that the "fathers understood this question . . . better than we," and turned it to the support of his—the Republicans'—side of the issue. The understanding "the fathers" had is exactly what we Republicans seek—and *only* that.

It was primarily to this historical portion of the speech that this encomium, written by two members of the committee that invited him and included in the preface to the printed speech, would apply:

> No one who has not actually attempted to verify its details can under-stand the patient research and historical labor which it embodies. The history of our earlier politics is scattered through numerous journals, statutes, pamphlets, and letters; and these are defective in complete-ness and accuracy of statement, and in indices and tables of contents. Neither can any one who has not traveled over this precise ground appreciate the accuracy of every trivial detail, or the self-denying impartiality with which Mr. Lincoln has turned from the testimony of "the fathers" on the general question of slavery, to present the single question which he discusses.

But that was not the whole speech. With that foundation, Lincoln took up the issues of the day, addressing first "the Southern people" (although of course, as he said, the South wasn't listening) and then addressing remarks to his fellow Republicans.

To the southern people he said, as he had been doing consistently since his state fair speech: You are a "reasonable and a just people," and "in the general qualities of reason and justice you are not inferior to other peoples." So why then (he asked now) do you call us Republicans reptiles and refuse to hear us?

You say we are a sectional party; we deny it: "[T]hat we got no votes in your section, is a fact of your making, and not of ours." You Southerners flaunt in our faces George Washington's warning against sectional parties—but he approved the prohibition of slavery in the Northwest, and wrote to Lafayette that that prohibition was wise, and that he hoped all states would one day be free. You say you are the "conservatives," while we are "revolutionary," "destructive," or something of the sort. But what is conservatism? Is it not adherence to the old and tried? We stick to the old policy of the Fathers—while you reject and "scout and spit" upon it.

Slavery *is* more prominent than it was—but that is not our doing, but the doing of those who have discarded the old policy of the Fathers. Slave insurrections are *not* more frequent than in the past—Lincoln gave a careful and sophisticated explanation of their paucity.

And Harper's Ferry? John Brown's raid in October of 1859—just four months before Lincoln's address—and, even more, the acclaim for Brown in many circles in the North, had infuriated many in the South. Democrats and Southerners were inclined to blame the raid on Republicans and to point to it as an example of the slave insurrections they claimed that Republican speeches were encouraging. Distinguished literary and intellectual leaders, who ought to have known better, encouraged and supported Brown, and when he was hanged there were, in sections of the Northeast, astonishing sermons, articles, and celebrations picturing Brown as a noble martyr. If you were a Republican, you would be uneasy about all that celebration, and the Democrats' charge that your party was responsible for that sort of thing. You would be wondering how to respond. Lincoln supplied an answer at Cooper Union:

> John Brown was no Republican, and you have failed to implicate a single Republican in his Harper's Ferry enterprise. . . .
>
> John Brown's effort was peculiar. It was not a slave insurrection. It was an attempt by white men to get up a revolt among slaves, in which the slaves refused to participate. In fact, it was so absurd that the slaves, with all their ignorance, saw plainly enough it could not succeed.

Lincoln made an argument against breaking up the Union that anticipated the inaugural address that he must have had only the barest hint that he might conceivably be delivering just a year later. Your purpose, you Southerners, is, "plainly stated," to "destroy the government unless you be allowed to construe the Constitution as you please." But no constitutional right "plainly written down in the Constitution" has been denied to you. "An inspection of the Constitution will show" that the right of property in a slave is not, as the *Dred Scott* majority claimed, "*distinctly* and *expressly*" affirmed in it. Neither the word "slave" nor "slavery" is to be found in the Constitution, nor the word "property" even, in any connection with slavery. Lincoln had in other speeches noted in detail the circumlocutionary euphemisms the Founders had used in their specific references to slavery in the Constitution, in order to keep themselves from using those words. Now he reiterates, borrowing from without specifically quoting James Madison, why they went to that trouble: exactly to avoid giving constitutional sanction to the idea that there could be property in man.

Turning then in his remarks to Republicans, he asks what we can say or do to satisfy the Southern people. They "will not so much as listen to us," but let us nevertheless, just among Republicans, calmly consider our duty, and what we can do to preserve peace.

Will they be satisfied if the territories are unconstitutionally surrendered to them? No. Will they be satisfied if we swear off invasions and insurrections? No. We have never had anything to do with invasions and insurrections in the first place, but that total abstaining has not exempted us from being denounced. Will leaving them alone do it? No. We have left them alone and said we will leave them alone, but they have not believed us.

What will satisfy and convince them? This, and only this: that we cease to call slavery *wrong,* and join them in calling it *right.* Lincoln was here pressing back to that foundation in sheer moral conviction that, before the year was out, he would learn both from events and from the hand of his old friend Alexander Stephens was the final pivot of the terrible division: The expressed moral conviction that slavery was wrong *alone,* without any new act or policy, was enough to cause Southern condemnation of the Republicans, and then of the Union.

"The whole atmosphere must be disinfected from all taint of opposition to slavery, before they will cease to believe that all their troubles proceed from us." Lincoln made now, as he had on other occasions, an application of this point that may have dropped out of the collective memory: this "disinfecting" of the national atmosphere of all "taint" of opposition to slavery would mean that these strong states'-rights people

would be requiring of the free states that they disavow their own state constitutions, which declare the wrong of slavery with solemn emphasis.

As we have said, Lincoln had found the ways in these speeches, all the
way from the state fair in 1854 to this Cooper Union effort in 1860, to bring
off a difficult combination: to state the full moral condemnation of slavery,
in all its intellectual and emotional power, without being self-righteously
superior or moralistically simple. One of the ways he did that, as we have
seen, was constantly to reiterate that the Southerners are no worse than we,
that we are no better than they, that if we were in their situation we would
conduct ourselves as they do, and vice versa. That note, sounded at the
state fair, anticipated on another subject in his Temperance Address when
he was thirty-two, sounded steadily through all his speeches, and
appeared briefly in this speech.

And another rhetorical device to the same end appears here in full
force: a Niagara of scrupulously accurate and fairly stated facts. Still
another, which he used often before but now in this speech brings to its
fullest development, is simply to describe the moral disagreement—in all
its force, but as a pair of hypotheticals, not as a fierce assertion; as an
exhortation to his side, not a condemnation of the other. Here is the way he
did it in a key passage at the end:

> Holding, as they do, that slavery is morally right, and socially elevat-
> ing, they cannot cease to demand a full national recognition of it, as a
> legal right, and a social blessing.
>
> Nor can we justifiably withhold this, on any ground save our con-
> viction that slavery is wrong. If slavery is right, all words, acts, laws,
> and constitutions against it, are themselves wrong, and should be
> silenced, and swept away. If it is right, we cannot justly object to
> its nationality—its universality; if it is wrong, they cannot justly
> insist upon its extension—its enlargement. All they ask, we could
> readily grant, if we thought slavery right; all we ask, they could
> as readily grant, if they thought it wrong. Their thinking it right, and
> our thinking it wrong, is the precise fact upon which depends the
> whole controversy.

And each side then acts out of the logic of its moral position:

> Thinking it right, as they do, they are not to blame for desiring its full
> recognition, as being right; but, thinking it wrong, as we do, can we
> yield to them? Can we cast our votes with their view, and against our

own? In view of our moral, social, and political responsibilities, can we do this?

The answer to his own rhetorical question was no: In view of our "moral, social, and political responsibilities," we cannot yield—cannot cast our votes for their view, against our own. Before the year was up Lincoln will be called on to act upon this conviction.

In the last paragraph, his exhortation to his fellow Republicans, he explains now the "duty" upon which he himself will soon act. We will yield what we must yield: "[W]rong as we think slavery is, we can yet afford to let it alone where it is, because that much is due to the necessity arising from its actual presence . . ." But not more than that. "Can we, while our own votes will prevent it, allow it to spread into the National Territories, and to overrun us here in these Free States?" Lincoln closed by invoking our duty: "If our sense of duty forbids this, then let us stand by our duty, fearlessly and effectively." He then implicitly urged the rejection of the Douglas alternative by his plea that we not be "diverted" by "sophistical contrivances" like "groping for some middle ground between the right and the wrong" "such as a policy of 'don't care' on a question about which all true men do care." There was an anticipation of events to come in his exhortation to fellow Republicans to resist "Union appeals beseeching true Union men to yield to Disunionists . . . calling, not the sinners, but the righteous, to repentance. . . ." Given that slavery is a monstrous wrong, why is it that those who say so are called upon to "compromise," while those who defend the unjust institution are not?

After a penultimate invocation, a little like the extravagances of his youth, of some rather unlikely dungeons, he rose to dramatic capitals in his concluding appeal, quoted earlier, to his fellow Republicans:

Neither let us be slandered from our duty by false accusations against us, nor frightened from it by menaces of destruction to the Government nor of dungeons to ourselves. LET US HAVE FAITH THAT RIGHT MAKES MIGHT, AND IN THAT FAITH, LET US, TO THE END, DARE TO DO OUR DUTY AS WE UNDER-STAND IT.

His address was interrupted by "frequent applause," according to the *New York Tribune,* and at its conclusion many stopped to congratulate him. The committee introduction to the printed speech said:

From the first line to the last, from his premises to his conclusion, he travels with a swift, unerring directness which no logician ever excelled, an argument complete and full, without the affectation of learning, and without the stiffness which usually accompanies dates and details. A single, easy simple sentence of plain Anglo-Saxon words, contains a chapter of history that, in some instances, has taken days of labor to verify, and which must have cost the author months of investigation to acquire.

Four New York newspapers printed the entire text the next day, and the *Tribune* said in its report: "The vast assemblage frequently rang with cheers and shouts of applause, which were prolonged and intensified at the close." And then the *Tribune* writer, carried away, wrote this sentence: "No man ever before made such an impression on his first appeal to a New York audience."

And that was not to be the only audience for this address. It would be printed as a pamphlet by the Young Men's Central Republican Union, with exhaustive notes by two members that Lincoln himself thought "exceedingly valuable." It would be printed in pamphlet form more quickly also by the *New York Tribune,* the *Chicago Tribune,* and, at Lincoln's instigation, back home by the *Illinois State Journal.* Lincoln would write to an associate naming three places the pamphlet was available. If you were an active Republican, or for that matter an earnest citizen of any stripe, in 1860, you would have been quite likely to have obtained and read this astounding production by this emerging spokesman for the Republican position.

2. THE HUGENESS OF SLAVERY

On the day after his triumph at Cooper Union Lincoln took the train to Providence and gave the first of a series of speeches in New England. The next day he went to Exeter, New Hampshire, to visit his son Bob, who was a student at Phillips Exeter Academy. Bob went with him to Concord, where he spoke the next afternoon, and the senior Lincoln went on to Manchester where he spoke to an "immense gathering." The next day, March 2, he spoke in Dover, New Hampshire, where, according to the *Dover Journal,* he spoke nearly two hours and "we believe he would have held his audience had he spoken all night." Then came a weekend, which he spent largely with his son in Exeter, giving a speech there on the Saturday evening. He wrote letters—one to Mary—complaining a little about the "toil," and anticipating being "worn down" before he was through. He wrote to his wife that the "speech in New York" went off "passably well" and gave him "no trouble whatsoever" because it had been "within my calculation before I started." But this man who liked to prepare his speeches carefully was now swamped by a speech a day "before reading audiences who had already seen all my ideas in print."

Nevertheless, this speaking tour was clearly a large success; these "reading audiences" now knew about him, and turned out in impressive numbers. And I surmise that he spent some hours on that weekend in Exeter writing some new material.

He went on the next week to give six speeches in six days, one in Woonsocket, Rhode Island, and five in Connecticut—in Hartford, New Haven, Meriden, Norwich, and Bridgeport. Early biographer J. G. Holland wrote of the effect that Lincoln's speeches in that state would have on the elections of the fall: "Connecticut was that year carried by the republicans by about five hundred majority, against the most powerful efforts of the democrats—a fact which was due more to the speeches of Mr. Lincoln than to any other cause."

We may surmise also that the New England speeches, together with the circulation of the Cooper Union address, significantly influenced the Republican convention in Chicago in May. The New England states, in the geographical north-to-south, east-to-west way they called the roll then, would be the first states to vote. They would give a surprising little dividend of votes to this new candidate, Lincoln of Illinois.

Holland also quoted an item from a New York newspaper in September of 1864 about the appraisals of Lincoln's speeches by these folks back in the East. It seems that a Norwich minister named Gulliver who had heard Lincoln speak encountered him the next day on the train and told him it had been the most remarkable speech he had ever heard. Lincoln in gratified response told about a Yale professor of rhetoric who had not only heard him in New Haven but had followed him to Meriden to hear him again, and had lectured on him to his class. Lincoln found this extraordinary. Here is Holland again: "He had been sufficiently astonished by his success in the West, but he had no expectation of any marked success at the East, particularly among literary and learned men." Lincoln said: "Certainly I had a most wonderful success for a man of my limited education." He asked the Reverend Mr. Gulliver to tell him what he found so remarkable about his speeches. Gulliver replied: "The clearness of your statements, the unanswerable style of your reasoning, and, especially, your illustrations, which were romance and pathos and fun and logic all welded together."

Some of what Lincoln said in New England, notwithstanding his worrying about the "reading audiences," was a spillover from Cooper Union. But in the particularly good speech he gave in New Haven—and probably pretty much also repeated in Meriden, Woonsocket, Norwich, and Bridgeport—he explained the dynamism and size and the economic power of the institution of slavery more fully than he had done before.

I think he came to comprehend slavery's size and weight more concretely than did some of the more isolated and ideological abolitionists, and certainly more than we do in some later century, long after the institution has been abolished. Let us make an analogy to racial segregation. In these later years, young citizens have difficulty imagining that there ever was such a thing as racial segregation by *law*—Jim Crow—with water fountains, lunch counters, and seats on buses separated by race. They blink their eyes in disbelief: Did that ever really happen? How much more difficult is it then for any later generation to comprehend the actual existence on American soil of human slavery—human beings as property, bought and sold. Collective memory develops a quick amnesia, aided by retrospective guilt. In the slaveowning regions the war itself is made over into a war strictly for states' rights, with slavery shrouded. But it was not so in 1861 when the war started, and the result hung in the balance: for the rebels in the first blush of the newness of their "nation," slavery was explicitly its foundation.

And when Lincoln was speaking in New England in the late winter of 1859–60, American slavery, although perhaps a rather distant reality for many of his listeners in that region, was a huge and potent reality in the United States as a whole. Lincoln comprehended it, in particular, as a functioning social and economic reality.

These institutions, once planted in the soil of a social order, grow in organic interconnection with the rest of the society and are therefore much more difficult to uproot than moralists at a remote distance understand. Lincoln was rather good, as a mainstream politician in the North, at comprehending and expressing both the actual social reality of American slavery, and at the same time the depth of its fundamental wrongness.

Here is a sample from the earlier debate about the Kansas-Nebraska Act of his realism about the way things will actually work out in the planting of slavery in a territory:

While I am speaking of Kansas, how will that operate? Can men vote truly? We will suppose that there are ten men who go into Kansas to settle. Nine of these are opposed to slavery. One has ten slaves. The slaveholder is a good man in other respects; he is a good neighbor, and being a wealthy man, he is enabled to do the others many neighborly kindnesses. They like the man, though they don't like the system by which he holds his fellow-men in bondage. And here let me say, that in intellectual and physical structure, our Southern brethren do not differ from us. They are, like us, subject to passions, and it is only their odious institution of slavery, that makes the breach between us. These ten men of whom I was speaking, live together three or four years; they intermarry; their family ties are strengthened. And who wonders that in time, the people learn to look upon slavery with complacency? This is the way in which slavery is planted, and gains so firm a foothold. I think this is a strong card that the Nebraska party have played, and won upon, in this game.

Lincoln comprehended slavery, in particular, as an economic reality. Imagine today some enormous industry, already present and functioning in the economy, with careers and fortunes and lives and whole communities and a way of life of an entire section of the nation invested in it—which then is discerned to be morally objectionable. Suppose there was an industry already established and in business, with stockholders and workers and fortunes made, actually doing what Jonathan Swift proposed with heavy satire in his modest proposal, buying and boiling Irish children for consumption as a delicacy by the English aristocracy. That's far too extreme, to be sure; but buying and selling human beings as "property" was rather extreme also, and it did happen.

Think of the rationalizations, the resistance, the difficulty of winning even small victories over the tobacco industry, at the time of this writing. And tobacco is a much less egregious evil, and is a much smaller industry, than was slavery. And its harmful effects are differently distributed across the population.

In one of his first passages on the economics of the matter, a speech-preparation document given the date of July 23, 1856, Lincoln had written: "[T]he people of the South have an immediate palpable and immensely great pecuniary interest; while, with the people of the North, it is merely an abstract question of moral right, with only *slight,* and *remote* pecuniary interest added." Lincoln would go on, in that document—probably used in

speeches in Galena and elsewhere—to an estimate of the value of American
slaves and to a dynamic picture of the economic institution, in which value
could be, by new measures, enhanced: "The slaves of the South, at a moderate estimate, are worth a thousand millions of dollars. Let it be permanently settled that this property may extend to new territory, without
restraint, and it greatly *enhances,* perhaps quite *doubles,* its value at once."

In New Haven, with that Yale professor listening and taking notes for
his rhetoric class, Lincoln argued that solutions so far proposed are too
small for the immense problem—"plasters too small to cover the wound."
"Look at the magnitude of the subject!" he said:

> One sixth of our population, in round numbers—not quite one sixth,
> and yet more than seventh,—about one sixth of the whole population
> of the United States are slaves! The owners of these slaves consider
> them property. The effect upon the minds of the owners is that of
> property, and nothing else—it induces them to insist upon all that will
> favorably affect its value as property, to demand laws and institutions
> and a public policy that shall increase and secure its value, and make it
> durable, lasting and universal.

Lincoln's analysis proceeded to say that this interest impelled owners not
just to try to increase their "property's" value, but also to find moral justification for it. He would make explicit the impact that the slaveowner's
economic interest had on his ideas. One hears a hint of what James Madison had said; one hears a hint of those ideas of "ideology" and "super-
structure" that were just then boiling up from the intellectual underground
of the nineteenth century in Europe, to have their huge impact on the
twentieth.

> The effect on the minds of the owners is to persuade them that there is
> no wrong in it. The slaveholder does not like to be considered a mean
> fellow, for holding that species of property, and hence he has to strug-
> gle within himself and sets about arguing himself into the belief that
> Slavery is right. The property influences his mind.

He told a joke to illustrate how property influences how one may see, or
not see, the world:

> The dissenting minister, who argued some theological point with one
> of the established church, was always met by the reply, "I can't see it

so." Then he showed him a single word—"Can you see that?" "Yes, I see it," was the reply. The dissenter laid a guinea over the word and asked, "Do you see it now?" (Great laughter) So here. Whether the owners of this species of property really do see it as it is, it is not for me to say, but if they do, they see it as it is through 2,000,000,000 of dollars, and that is a pretty thick coating. (Laughter) Certain it is, that they do not see it as we see it. Certain it is, that this two thousand million of dollars, invested in this species of property, all so concentrated that the mind can grasp it at once—this immense pecuniary interest, has its influence upon their minds.

If you ask what Lincoln's "solution" was—whether he himself had a plaster big enough to cover the wound—you would receive what might seem, especially to later generations, when it is all over and therefore seems easy, not a very satisfactory answer. But what would you *then* have proposed? Early abolitionists, with the model of evangelical revivals, proposed converting slaveholders so that they would manumit their slaves, a radically unrealistic expectation even before slave states enacted laws prohibiting such emancipation. Abolitionists and antislavery politicians were careful to avoid any hint of a call to revolt on the part of the slaves; it was quite clear from the experience of Denmark Vesey, Nat Turner, and John Brown, as well as from the atmosphere and numbers, that any effort at revolutionary violence would lead to murderous repression and dead slaves. All of Lincoln's concrete proposals—as congressman for the District, and as president for the border states—involved graduated, voluntary, compensated emancipation, and proved unrealistic, too.

But what *was* realistic, in the setting of the 1850s? Lincoln was firm and clear and consistent about two ways to contain American slavery, toward its ultimate extinction—both of these firmnesses, he insisted, vindicated by the Founders' original intention. One was practical: no *new* territory. No expansion. Containment, physically. The other, as we have already said, was moral and philosophical. It was in New Haven that he made that clearest statement of the importance of philosophical clarity and persistence:

Whenever this question shall be settled, it must be settled on some philosophical basis. No policy that does not rest upon some philosophical public opinion can be permanently maintained. And hence, there are but two policies in regard to slavery that can be at all maintained. The first, based on the property view that slavery is right,

conforms to that idea throughout, and demands that we shall do everything for it that we ought to do if it were right. We must sweep away all
opposition, for opposition to the right is wrong; we must agree that
slavery is right, and we must adopt the idea that property has persuaded the owner to believe—that slavery is morally right and socially
elevating. This gives a philosophical basis for a permanent policy of
encouragement.

The other policy is one that squares with the idea that slavery is
wrong, and it consists in doing everything that we ought to do if it
is wrong.

Treating it as a wrong does not mean attacking it where it exists. The
snake is in bed with the children. But it does mean excluding it everywhere
one can, and firmly opposing its spread. Keep the moral condemnation
clear and contain it—long-term measures dictated exactly by its huge
present reality.

A war would come, and the speaker in New Haven would himself be president. A new possibility would present itself: the war power. President Lincoln's use of the war power to issue the Emancipation Proclamation was
impressive to those who knew what it meant because they were living at
the time, or not long afterward. The Emancipation Proclamation would be
altogether his initiative. He would then take the initiative in 1864 to bring
the Republican convention to endorse a constitutional amendment ending
slavery, and then followed with the initiative he took in the following winter
to secure the needed two-thirds vote in the House.

And in his last great utterance, the Second Inaugural Address, there
would be a paragraph, not always noticed in this connection, that would
surely testify to the intensity of the writer's conviction that American slavery was an immense evil. It is the passage just preceding the famous last
paragraph, with its call for malice toward none and charity for all, and by
its dark power it sets off and strengthens the noble ending paragraph. We
have mentioned this paragraph before for the style; now let us attend more
closely to what he is saying, to the terrible cost that might justly be paid for
the *national* offense of slavery:

Fondly do we hope—fervently do we pray—that this mighty scourge of
war may speedily pass away. Yet, if God wills that it continue, until all

the wealth piled by the bond-man's two hundred and fifty years of toil shall be sunk, and until every drop of blood drawn with the lash, shall be paid by another with the sword, as was said three thousand years ago, so still it must be said, "the judgments of the Lord, are true and righteous altogether."

That second, long sentence would contain an excruciating picture of the justice of God, and, like the address as a whole, would make stunningly clear that in Lincoln's view this would be a war about slavery, and that the whole nation was responsible, and must pay a terrible price.

3. HOW DID THIS MAN EVER BECOME PRESIDENT?

Still no one knew, when Lincoln returned on the Great Western Railroad to Springfield from his speaking tour in the East on March 14, 1860, successful though it had been, that he would ever be giving First and Second Inaugural Addresses. It was by then just barely possible, though, that he might be a contender for the nomination. If your list of possibilities was long enough, his name might appear upon it.

How would it ever be that this middle-aged private citizen would be abruptly elevated to the nation's highest office?

Abraham Lincoln is unusual, perhaps unique, in that while being nominated entirely out of a political background, he had no national experience except that now ancient one term in Congress, no statewide victories at all, no executive experience at all, no appointments to high-level positions at all. Alongside the political resumes of his immediate predecessor, James Buchanan, his longtime adversary Stephen Douglas, or his chief rival for the nomination in 1860, William Seward, Abraham Lincoln's list of posts and accomplishments would look ridiculously puny. His credentials were markedly less impressive, on paper, than those of any of the men being mentioned for the Republican nomination in addition to Seward: Salmon Chase, Edward Bates, Simon Cameron, William Dayton, Jacob Collamer, John McLean, perhaps even John C. Frémont. Lincoln had not been governor of a big state, a senator, or a celebrated general in a war; he had not been a Supreme Court justice (as McLean was); he had not been the visible head of any great national undertaking. I believe it can be said that by the formal test of offices held and great deeds accomplished, he was the least qualified man ever elected, perhaps ever nominated by a major party.

Moreover, this was a valuable nomination; Seward and Chase had not tried for the Republican nomination in 1856 because they thought, correctly, that this first-time party was not going to win. In 1860, on the other hand, the indications were strong that the Republican nominee would win. The Republicans had, actually, done quite well in 1856, for a new party making its first run. They carried all of the (then) sixteen free states except for Pennsylvania, Illinois, Indiana, New Jersey, and the new state of California.

The Democratic administration elected in 1856, that of James Buchanan, had proceeded to suffer one heavy blow after another. President Buchanan seems to have had some foreknowledge of, perhaps even some implicit collaboration in, the Dred Scott decision, which was handed down immediately after he took office—a decision that was intensely unpopular in the North. In the autumn of 1857 there came the most severe economic panic since 1837—not a healthy development for the Democrats in power in the White House and in Congress. But the most severe blow to what was then called "the democracy"—meaning the Democratic Party— had to do with Bleeding Kansas, which under the invitation to battle implied in the repeal of the Missouri Compromise and the doctrine of "popular sovereignty" threatened to bleed again. As we have noted in an earlier chapter, Buchanan, after solemn assurances that he would insist that any proposed constitution for the new state be submitted to the people for ratification, nevertheless supported the admission of Kansas under the outrageous Lecompton constitution proposed by the proslavery forces, without its being fully submitted to the people. The congressional elections of 1858 were another defeat for the Democrats. And just to round out the Democrats' troubles, the Buchanan administration proved to be the most corrupt in American history to that point.

Except for John Brown's raid in 1859, which Democrats tried to associate with the Republicans, every major event and public theme from Buchanan's inauguration until the election of 1860 hurt the Democrats, and favored this new party that was opposing them.

And now in 1860, by the time the Republicans would hold their convention in May the Democrats would already have had, or tried to have, their convention in Charleston, in late April, and had fallen apart. Stephen Douglas, although supported by a majority of the delegates, had been blocked by the South from the required two-thirds. Southern delegates walked out when defeated on platform planks on slavery. The rest of the democracy would later reconvene in Baltimore, and *did* nominate Douglas, but as candidate of a shattered party. The Southern wing nominated Buchanan's vice president, John Breckinridge. And in between these two Democratic conventions a rump group mostly of old Whigs formed a "Constitutional Union" party and nominated John Bell. The Republicans' chances against this battered and divided opposition looked good indeed. So with this great chance to win, and all that was at stake, and all the experienced men available, why then would the Republican convention nominate, and the electoral system elect, the comparatively unknown, comparatively untried fellow from the Western Plains?

The answer to the narrow question of how he was *elected*—to anticipate the result in order to sort out our point—would not have much to do with anything distinctive to the actual human being Abraham Lincoln. He would be elected president because he would receive the Republican nomination in the convention in Chicago in May of 1860, and because his public identity was such that it maximized the Republican vote.

In retrospect we can see that there were probably only two possible results of the 1860 presidential election: Either the Republican candidate would be chosen by the electoral college, or no candidate would receive a majority of electoral votes, and the election would be thrown into the House. It is hard to see how Douglas or Breckinridge could have assembled a majority of the electoral votes, and Bell certainly could not have done so. The reduction of the possible outcomes to the two named would become clear enough to play a role in the campaign itself. After a strong Republican showing in the state elections in Ohio, Pennsylvania, and Indiana in mid-October it was indisputable, as had appeared probable before that, that only the Republican nominee could win an electoral college majority. Thurlow Weed charged, in fact, that only the Republicans were trying to *elect* a president; the other three parties were trying to *prevent* the election of a president—to pitch the election into the House.

The results of the pivotal 1860 election were foreshadowed in the changing populations, and hence changing electoral votes, of the North and the South. Immigration and migration, swelling the population of the North, were changing the shape of the nation, and therefore of House delegations and electoral votes. Slave states had dominated presidential elections for all of the early decades of the nation's life, but by 1860 the free states had 183 electoral votes, the slave states only 120.

The slave states would not vote against Lincoln himself, whom they did not know at all, but against a Black Republican—any Black Republican. All members of that outrageous new party looked alike to slave-state voters, and any other Republican—certainly Seward—would have provoked the same total wipeout. In the Deep South it was not even possible to vote for the Republican, whoever he was.

Lincoln would win because he was the Republican nominee. The question is pushed back a stage: How did Lincoln come to be nominated by the Republicans? The answer to that question still does not have much to do with distinctive personal qualities of Abraham Lincoln. He received that valuable nomination because enough delegates were convinced that William Seward, the presumptive nominee, could not win enough electoral votes from the key states the Republicans had lost in their first run in 1856 and had to have some of this time—Pennsylvania, Illinois, Indiana, New Jersey—and because Lincoln emerged at the convention itself as the best alternative to Seward and the best candidate to win those swing states.

Seward was by all odds the leading Republican, as he had been a leading Whig; he had been governor of the nation's largest state, and was now senator from that state. He had a long and distinguished record. But long records, even including distinguished records, have their drawbacks. Seward had openly attacked the nativists, openly dealt with immigrant voters, including Catholics; and Lincoln was not publicly identified on the issue. Seward had personal enemies like Horace Greeley and ideological opponents who knew him for his references to a "higher law" and to an "irrepressible conflict."* He was thought to be more radical on slavery than he really was, while Lincoln was conveniently thought to be more conservative than he really was.

Seward came into the convention the clear front-runner, almost the presumptive nominee; his forces came from New York and the East by the trainload. Were Thurlow Weed—Seward's manager—and the marching bands of Seward supporters too cocky? Already there was a certain western resistance to eastern presumption.

If you had been a Lincoln delegate in Chicago in May of 1860, your first argument to persuade your fellow delegates would have been that the Republican candidates for governor in Indiana (Henry Lane) and in Pennsylvania (Andrew Curtin) were saying that Seward could not carry their states—even saying that in the event of his nomination they would resign their candidacies because Seward at the head of the ticket would be sure to bring defeat.

And why could the new man Lincoln carry those lower Northern

---

* Lincoln in a telegram to his managers at the convention would scribble that he agreed with Seward on the irrepressible conflict but not on the higher law.

states? Because he came from one of them. Because he had been born in a border slave state, moved to a contested lower North state (Indiana), and had spent his career in a contested, newly populous lower North state in the West. Because he was a westerner—we need a westerner to beat Douglas. Because he was a common man, born in a log cabin, self-educated, recently discovered to have been a railsplitter. Because he was an ex-Whig, rather than an ex-Free-Soiler or ex-Democrat; more of the Republicans had come out of the Whig Party than from any of the other party sources, and most of the votes you needed to win over were ex-Whigs. Because on the key issue of slavery he was neither too radical (as Seward and Chase were perceived to be) nor too conservative (as Bates was perceived to be). In addition, Lincoln was neither so opposed to tariffs as to lose Pennsylvania, nor so prominently protectionist as to offend ex-Democrat free-traders; neither too old (as perhaps Justice McLean had come now to be), nor too young (as perhaps Frémont had been in 1856); from a spot neither too far north (as was favorite son Collamer of Vermont) nor too far south (as was Bates, from slave state Missouri).

And then there was the quite important matter of the nativist vote and the foreign-born vote.

The antiforeigner Know-Nothings had become strong in the 1850s, and had run the Whig ex-President Millard Fillmore as their candidate for president in 1856. Politicians like Lincoln of Illinois pointed out that if the Fillmore votes had been combined with the Republican Frémont votes, they would have defeated the Democratic nominee, James Buchanan. So this time let us combine them. Which candidate can do that?

Not Seward. As governor of New York he had been antinativist and cooperative with new immigrants, including Irish Catholics. Bates, perhaps a nativist himself, could win the nativist vote; but he would lose the Republicans all foreign votes, including the German Protestants they had to have.

And who could win both nativist votes and German votes? Abraham Lincoln. Why? Because he had established good relationships with immigrant voters, but had expressed his antinativist sentiments only in private.

Lincoln had the advantage, as well as the disadvantage, of being less well-known than others: he had not acquired their enemies. So—you would argue—Lincoln, not Seward, can carry the needed votes and needed states.

Those are the large realistic reasons that Lincoln was nominated. They are not unlike the reasons for other major party nominations in American history—calculations about who can carry which states, which segments of the population. There is nothing in them particularly distinctive to Lincoln.

There were also more immediate reasons at the level of political skill and tactics, which had to do with Lincoln distinctively only in that he and his supporters were good at this sort of thing:

1. Lincoln had shrewd, energetic managers and operatives, led by David Davis.

2. They secured the location of the convention in Chicago—ironically, back before there was thought to be any contender from Illinois (Lincoln had encouraged Norman Judd, the Illinois national committeeman, to push for the selection of Chicago).

3. Having Illinois cast *all* its votes, under the unit rule (the entire delegation for the majority's candidate), was symbolically and actually a big help; it hurt Salmon Chase of Ohio and Simon Cameron of Pennsylvania that they could not command all the votes even of their own states.

4. His managers, though told not to make promises, said, "Lincoln ain't here"—and made promises. The most important were to Cameron (who would be named secretary of war) and (it has sometimes been said) to Caleb Smith, of Indiana (who would be named secretary of the interior). The gain of Indiana's twenty-two votes already on the first ballot was an important broadening of Lincoln's vote beyond Illinois; the coming over to Lincoln of forty-eight Pennsylvania votes on the second ballot was important in providing momentum.

5. The plan, in proposing which Lincoln himself played a role, of gently persuading delegates otherwise pledged to make Lincoln their second choice did work well in helping to produce the momentum-increasing accretions on the second and third ballots.

6. When the convention postponed voting from Thursday until Friday, the Lincoln managers printed a large supply of extra tickets, forged official signatures, spent the night rousing Lincoln supporters, packed the hall—a trick, a Lincoln supporter said with local pride, "known only in wicked Chicago." When the confident Seward supporters with their marching band arrived the next morning to take the seats they had occupied on other days, they found them already taken by Lincoln people and had to wait, furious, outside.

Lincoln's nomination by the convention was the result, as are most such nominations, of geography, skill, luck, and acceptable ideological placement, and did not reflect anything extraordinary about the candidate.

But now, when we push the analysis back one more step, to ask how this private citizen could even have come to be competitive with these more prominent and experienced men, and even to have been considered by the Republicans for this valuable nomination, we find something that is more distinctive to Lincoln himself.

4. THE CANDIDATE OF MORAL ARGUMENT

How did Lincoln even get above the threshold of consideration? One part of the answer once again has nothing to do with Abraham Lincoln's personal characteristics, but is a double dose of sheer luck: He had the good fortune to live in a swing state that the Republicans needed to win in 1860, and, furthermore, the same state as the leading Democrat, Stephen Douglas. He would not have risen to national visibility—and even if he had done so would not have been nominated by the Republicans—if he had lived in a small state like Vermont, with no Douglas to argue with and only a handful of electoral votes, certain to be Republican in the election.

But coming from a swing state and having Douglas to debate yields only part of the explanation of Lincoln's remarkable rise to visibility. Pennsylvania was an even more important swing state, so why not nominate Simon Cameron? And Lincoln was not the only prominent Republican from Douglas's state; he did not hold, and had never held, a statewide office, while Lyman Trumbull was there in the Senate itself as Douglas's colleague, debating him every day. Why not nominate Lyman Trumbull?

Douglas's presence in Illinois gave Lincoln an enormous *possible* advantage over candidates from other states, but it was an advantage only if he responded effectively to that opportunity; only if the presentations he made were particularly strong and convincing.

So now we come to the element that is distinctive to Lincoln: the quality of his public argument. His presentation first of the anti-Nebraska case, and then of the Republican case, in debates and speeches over six years, made him stand out as a leader, even without holding any office. His speeches, or rather the moral-political argument presented in his speeches and the clarity and force with which it was presented, was the essential ingredient in Lincoln's rise.

We have seen this effect at work: Lincoln speaking in answer to Douglas at the state fair and in Peoria and elsewhere in the fall of 1854, and powerfully formulating the anti-Nebraska case; Lincoln inspiring the new Illinois "Republicans" with his "lost speech" at the founding meeting in Bloomington in 1856 ("When he concluded, the audience sprang to their feet, and cheer after cheer told how deeply their hearts had been touched"); Lincoln giving the Illinois Republican response to the Dred Scott decision, and to Douglas's defense of the decision, in 1857; Lincoln, named the "first and only" choice for senator in 1858, delivering the "house divided" speech, which offered a sophisticated argument for opposing Douglas.

And then there were the debates of the 1858 senatorial contest, including the seven famous appearances on the same platform with Douglas. Those debates were enormously important to Lincoln's crossing the threshold of eligibility for the presidential nomination for these reasons:

1. The national stature of Stephen Douglas, as we have already said.
2. The press covered them. This was unique: senatorial candidates, already named, debating. Two Chicago newspapers brought into being a new institution: press coverage. There were reporters taking notes and writing out the speeches, as had not been the case with other such contests. The resulting reporting was not confined to Illinois, but was carried by some papers elsewhere as well.
3. And that meant that the verbatim reports could make a book, which would have a wide *national* circulation.

The brighter glow generated by the debates around Lincoln's name outside Illinois led to his being invited to speak in 1859 in Ohio, to answer Douglas, in speeches that are often said to be a continuation of the 1858 Illinois debates. The executive committee of the Republicans of Ohio, attributing their success in the elections of that year in considerable part to Lincoln's speeches, proposed to publish the Illinois joint debates and the Ohio speeches as a book; Lincoln pasted together the newspaper accounts, and they were published and widely circulated.

As a pro-Lincoln delegate to the Republican convention in 1860, you would argue that Lincoln had already made the case against the likely Democratic nominee, Stephen Douglas, more fully and better than anyone else.

His rise in Illinois had been a compound of intellectual-rhetorical excellence with shrewd and devoted organizational work: asking his delegates to support Trumbull to advance the anti-Nebraska cause in the Senate race in 1855; giving the new party shape in the Decatur meeting in 1856; carrying on political correspondence; giving the speeches that defined and inspired the party.

Looking back, one can see that Lincoln's first step toward the Republican nomination for president would be winning strong support in his home state: When the time came, he would have the united support—and in most cases also the enthusiastic and constant support—of the entire Illinois delegation in Chicago. There would be some Seward sentiment in the northern part of the state, but the delegation under the leadership of Lincoln's managers would decide to vote by the unit rule, which meant Lincoln got every Illinois vote in the convention, and energetic home-state enthusiasm as well.

The glow around Lincoln's name was already bright enough for his name to have been put forward for the vice-presidential nomination at the *first* national convention of the Republican Party in Philadelphia in June of 1856. An Illinois supporter of Lincoln persuaded a Pennsylvania delegate to place Lincoln's name in nomination, and of the 110 votes he received, only 33 came from Illinois. He received 26 votes from Indiana, 12 each from Pennsylvania and California, and a scattering of votes from seven other states. In other words, his candidacy even at this early date was not that solely of a favorite son of his home state. The vote for Lincoln at this first convention in the very young life of the Republican Party—just forming as a national party—both shows that he was acquiring a reputation beyond Illinois and itself increased that embryonic reputation.

Beyond the borders of Illinois Lincoln's reputation would rest entirely on his speechmaking: on the 1858 Illinois debates and 1859 Ohio speeches as published; on his speeches in Kansas, Wisconsin, and Indiana; and especially then—of prime importance—the speech at Cooper Union and those in New England that we have just described. This body of argument had been heard or read by some significant portion of the public, particularly by Republicans.

The delegates to the Republican convention in Chicago in May of 1860 could not have known many of the qualities of the man they would nominate for president of the United States—qualities that would make him a great president. They could not have known that he would have the "executive force" to make the necessary decisions, stay the course through a terrible war, keep his eye on the prize, plan military strategy, sift through generals until he found Grant. They could not have known that he would prove to have a rare generosity of spirit. What they did know, however—a significant body of Republicans by then did know—was that he had a superb moral-political mind and tongue. They knew that he could give clear and intelligent expression to the Republican cause.

Lincoln's rise to political prominence by speechmaking almost alone was not like that of the other rare cases in American history of which that might be said—William Jennings Bryan at the end of the nineteenth century, for example. Lincoln would not be described exactly as a "spellbinder," making presentations in which pathos—the emotional content—is the largest ingredient, and the effect fades when the compelling power of the speaker's presence and the crowd and the fervor of the immediate occasion is gone. Lincoln's presentations were powerfully persuasive on paper as well as in the halls in which they were given. They had, as we have seen spectacularly in the Cooper Union case but in the state fair speech and others as well, a prominent element of historical fact drawn out of research and clearly summarized. They had as their primary element *logos*—rational argument, logic, again clearly stated. Many of the lesser speeches—although not the mightiest ones, the State Fair speech, the "house divided," the Cooper Union—had Lincoln's humor in them, in stories that with remarkable aptness illustrated his points.

I have in shorthand described him as a candidate of moral argument, but he was certainly not presenting, as a pamphleteer or moral philosopher might do, a pure moral argument isolated from the limited possibilities of a particular historical situation. On the contrary: it was exactly the prudent adaptation to the political possibilities, on the one side, that made the moral argument effective on the other. He managed, while responsibly attending to the political complexities and while dealing respectfully with those who disagreed, to state with great force, clarity, and persistence the moral argument at the foundation of the new majority-seeking political party.

The impact of these expressions of Lincoln's mind on—as it must have been—many delegates to the Republican convention in May of 1860 is the intangible element in the background, making him an acceptable possibility for the nomination. Interpreters looking at the whole event would emphasize the tangible realistic political elements. One may suggest this prior element had to be there, too, for that realistic process to begin.

In a letter written to Herndon many, many years afterwards—in 1889—a man named Edward Pierce, an associate not of Lincoln but of Salmon Chase, a delegate not from Illinois or the Midwest but from Massachusetts, said that "too much weight" had been given to the alleged convention bargains as an explanation of Lincoln's nomination. "Our delegation and all I met were governed by no such considerations. Lincoln was nominated because his debates with Douglas and his Cooper Institute speech showed him to be sound . . ."

To an unusual degree, Abraham Lincoln rose to political visibility by moral *argument*. I am not saying his role as a speaker-thinker caused him to be nominated and elected; I am saying that that was the way he crossed the threshold to become one who could be seriously considered and voted for at the convention—at which point the machinery of realistic politics I have described carried him on to victory.

5. LINCOLN FOR PRESIDENT

These old-time conventions were wonderful in their way. The decision-making was *real*.

The new Republican Party in convention in the newly built building the Wigwam in the new city of Chicago in May of 1860. Assembling; hoopla; the dramatic restoration of the Declaration of Independence to the platform; now, on Friday, May 18, nominations.

Immediately after William M. Evarts of New York nominated Seward, to immense cheering, Norman Judd abruptly placed Lincoln's name in nomination, to even more immense cheering. Before the first round of nominations was complete, the delegates were surprised when Caleb Smith of Indiana, on behalf of his delegation, seconded the nomination of Lincoln—a stroke planned by his managers—and set off another in the rounds of competitive cheering. Before the nominations were complete, there was another planned Lincoln stroke: an unexpected seconding speech from Ohio.

Salmon Chase would surely have regarded that as the unkindest cut. Going into the election year, he would have been next after Seward the leading Republican possibility; in his own view, to be sure, he would have been the leading possibility bar none. Chase never would stop believing that he more than any other person should be president of the United States; but at this early decisive moment his managers could find only a scattering of delegates outside Ohio who agreed—and this seconding speech showed that not everyone in Ohio agreed, either. Chase would receive on the first ballot only 49 of the total of 465 votes, and in his home state of Ohio seven delegates would vote for old Justice McLean. And worse than that from Chase's point of view—when the roll was called, Ohio, where Lincoln had made those speeches in 1859, would cast eight of its votes for the Illinois lawyer with nothing but speeches to his credit!

Simon Cameron of Pennsylvania did not quite receive all the votes of his large delegation, either—four voted for Lincoln (cheers again). In the prenomination maneuvering you might have placed in contrast to Boss Cameron's reputation your man's sobriquet Honest Abe. Cameron was not known as Honest Simon.

Edward Bates of Missouri got not only his state's entire vote (eighteen) but a scattering of other votes, but they were mostly from border states the Republicans had little hope of carrying; he was not going to be the nominee. Favorite sons in New Jersey and Vermont held their votes on the first ballot.

And finally: the call of the roll of the states.

They called the roll of states (as we have noted before) not alphabetically but, as they did in the House of Representatives, geographically, starting with the Northeast.

Seward had expected to hold *all* of New England—he had to, really, if he was going to win, because the territory the farthest north and the most firmly Republican (and an old Whig territory too) had to be his base.

The clerk called the state of MAINE—

Maine casts ten votes for Senator Seward, six votes for Lincoln of Illinois (a big cheer from the Lincoln crowd).

NEW HAMPSHIRE—

New Hampshire casts Seward one vote, Chase one vote, Frémont one vote, Lincoln seven votes (another big cheer).

VERMONT—

Ten votes for favorite son Jacob Collamer—which meant Seward did not get them.

Lincoln even got four votes of Massachusetts's twenty-five.

Seward, in other words, did not sweep New England, and Lincoln did better there than might have been expected.

Of course, when New York was called, it gave the Seward supporters a chance to cheer:

"The state of New York casts her seventy votes for William H. Seward!"

The first thing that was clear was that Seward would not win on the first ballot.

First ballot results: Needed to nominate, 233. Seward: 173½ votes.

And the second thing that was clear was that Lincoln was Seward's only real rival.

Lincoln: 102.

No other candidate got half of Lincoln's total, three coming in the fifty-vote range (Bates, Cameron, Chase), with no realistic hope of increases. The alternative to Seward was—Lincoln.

One could not *quite* know, although one suspected, how the second ballot would go.

The biggest cheer by Lincoln supporters came when the vote of Pennsylvania was announced:

Lincoln votes from Pennsylvania on the first ballot: four.

Lincoln votes from Pennsylvania on the second ballot—forty-eight.

Seward's manager, Thurlow Weed, must have known in that moment that his cause was lost.

As the favorite sons withdrew and the delegates who had voted for other candidates did their shifting, Seward gained eleven votes but Lincoln gained seventy-nine votes and drew almost even.

Second ballot results: Seward: 184½ votes. Lincoln: 181.

And so, in the sudden portentous silence in which the third ballot began, the Seward supporters in grim apprehension, the Lincoln delegates in suspended glee, must have guessed what would happen. As the roll was called, the Seward vote in state after state was no more than it had been—with a single vote gain here and there, and the *loss* of four votes to Lincoln from Massachusetts (cheers, from one section, again). Lincoln in one state and another made gains, with most of the New Jersey favorite-son votes, Maryland's Bates votes, a big jump in Chase votes from Ohio.

Third ballot results: Needed to nominate, 233. Seward—down slightly—180 votes. Lincoln—if you had a pencil and had calculated you knew how breathtakingly close it was: 231½ votes.

The tellers silently counting, the chair making no announcement, the atmosphere pregnant . . .

Who would do it?

An Ohio delegate sprang upon a chair and changed four Ohio votes from Chase to Lincoln.

A deep silent moment while the throng comprehends what that means; then cheers, dancing, shouting, the firing of a cannon, delegation after delegation changing votes to Lincoln, the chairman to the New York delegation after gracious custom moving to make it unanimous—Abraham Lincoln of Illinois was the Republican nominee.

They had done far better than they knew.

But that doesn't get him elected. Why then was he elected in the fall, in the most significant election in American history? Because the claims made by Lincoln supporters proved true. He did carry Illinois, Indiana, and Pennsylvania—indeed, every one of the now eighteen free states except for a split in New Jersey. He did make big gains in the formerly Know-Nothing, Fillmore vote—and at the same time increased the Republican share of the foreign vote, mostly from German Protestants. In addition, the Republicans as the new party on the scene did unusually well with new voters and young voters.

It is not true that Lincoln won because the opposition was split. If the votes of all three of his opponents had been combined in a fusion ticket—as was attempted in some part in five states—that would still have subtracted only three states (New Jersey, California, and Oregon) with eleven electoral votes from his total.* He would still have had 169 electoral votes, a majority of 35—and won.

It is not true that Lincoln won because the Democrats were split. Don Fehrenbacher wrote that "the Democrats divided were in some ways more formidable than if they had been united, because a Douglas untainted with the support of the slave holders probably had a better chance of winning enough electoral votes in the North to prevent Lincoln's election." He continues: "It is therefore reasonable to argue that Lincoln became president in spite of the split in the Democratic Party, not because of it."

Did he win only a minority of the popular vote, and did he win because of the Electoral College, and was that a disgrace to the American Republic? Yes, he won with a tad less than 40 percent of the popular vote; yes, he won because of the Electoral College—and no, that was not a disgrace to the Republic.

The 1860 election was peculiar—two elections, really: Lincoln vs. Douglas in the North, and Breckinridge (the Southern Democrat) vs. Bell (the old Whig Constitutional Union Party) in the South.

Lincoln as the candidate of the Black Republicans was wiped out in the slave states. Breckinridge and Bell each received more than half a million votes in the slave states, and Douglas another 160,000. And Lincoln? Only 26,000 in all fifteen slave states, 17,000 of them in Missouri alone. Lincoln's popular-vote percentage was thus drastically reduced by a large pile-up of "wasted" votes in states in which he was effectively excluded from the competition. In the Deep South states it was difficult or impossible to vote for him. It does indeed damage your popular vote if in a long string of states you get zero.

* See Appendix 2.

William Gienapp, the political historian, says in a footnote: "Historians who lament the undemocratic features of the electoral college usually silently pass over the use of intimidation and coercion to prevent the Republican party from running candidates in the South . . ." ("surely a more direct denial of the basic principles of the American political system," he goes on to say).

One can present the popular vote in various ways. One can say that Lincoln received a popular vote (39.9 percent) almost as feeble as Herbert Hoover, who was swamped and discredited in 1932 (39.6 percent). Or one can point out that even in the states that remained in the Union Lincoln still ran behind the combined vote of his three rivals (because in Maryland, Kentucky, Delaware, and Missouri—slave states that were kept in the Union—there was that near-wipeout for the Republican Party that marked all the slave states). But if we now ask about the *free* states—the states in which, we might put it argumentatively, the Republican Party was allowed to be competitive—then Lincoln's vote looks quite respectable. In the free states Lincoln won almost 55 percent of the popular vote, a margin that in other elections looks like a landslide. It was an election distorted already by what was coming.

In any case, we do not elect presidents by popular vote. The Founders arranged that we elect our presidents through the Electoral College. Lincoln received 180 electoral votes from eighteen states; the aggregate of electors opposed to Lincoln was 123.* So he won rather handily.

Although there were fears that there might be some disruption on February 13, 1861, while the president-elect-to-be, as it were, was making his way across the country to Washington, the Congress of the United States in joint session took the official count, and declared the president of the United States for four years, beginning March 4, 1861, to be Abraham Lincoln.

---

* Breckinridge, 72 electoral votes, from eleven slave states (including Delaware); Bell, 39, from Virginia, Tennessee, and Kentucky; Douglas, 12: 9 from Missouri and 3 from the split of the votes of the free state of New Jersey.

CHAPTER SIXTEEN

The Man with the Blue Umbrella

1. A VERY POOR HATER

So there was this Illinois lawyer—from the point of view of official Washington, an inexperienced man from the provinces whom no one knew—suddenly and rather astonishingly elevated to the highest post in the land. And his election would precipitate the nation's worst crisis.

What qualities would this man bring to the high post in this time of peril? He would begin to exhibit his magnanimity, as well as his shrewdness, already now in the choosing of his cabinet—particularly when that choosing was really completed, after ten tumultuous months of his presidency.

Lincoln's suppression of any resentment toward Judd, Trumbull, and Palmer was an early sample of a mode of conduct that was becoming characteristic; his praise of General Taylor for not seizing an opportunity for revenge showed that this was a matter of reflection on his part. In the years to come he would make explicit reference to avoiding malice and to not seeking revenge and to not planting thorns often enough both in public speeches and in private letters, both in informal comment and in formal orders, to indicate that it was a settled conviction. He had thought or was thinking about the matter sufficiently often, and sufficiently deeply, for the words and ideas to come to his pen and his lips repeatedly and to be reflected in his deeds repeatedly.

Leonard Swett would say it well, in an interview with Herndon in 1866, after the whole story of Lincoln's presidency had been told:

He [Lincoln] was certainly a very poor hater. He never judged men by his like, or dislike for them. If any given act was to be performed, he could understand that his enemy could do it just as well as any one. If a man had maligned him, or been guilty of personal ill-treatment and abuse, and was the fittest man for the place, he would put him in his Cabinet just as soon as he would his friend. I do not think he ever removed a man because he was his enemy, or because he disliked him.

This virtue would be particularly notable in an active and aspiring person seeking both to rise himself and to accomplish great and controversial objects in an arena of nation-shaking conflict over power, policy, and philosophy, in which the process itself necessarily casts up both personal and factional adversaries—to most of us, enemies.

Lincoln's generosity of spirit would be joined, in a combination difficult to put together, to great resolution, strength of will, "executive force," as William Seward himself would one day call it. That virtue too would begin to be evident to the nation in the months after his election, as we will see. Charitable persons are not always strong-willed or resolute; forcefully resolute persons are often not particularly generous, charitable, magnanimous. This new man who would become president of the United States would, to the astonishment someday of the world, be both. How? First of all, by a clarity of mind that sorted matters wisely. We know that he had a good mind—a good *political* mind. But that is not enough: His "ego," as we call it now, did not distort his good mind's working. His considerable self-confidence notwithstanding, he would achieve a detached and proportionate sense of himself in relation to an unflinching measure of the scope and meaning of the enormous human drama that confronted him. His self did not get in the way.

Generous, charitable people who pardon simple soldier boys who fall asleep on sentry duty and forgive enemies may just be dodging difficult decisions, indulging a softness in themselves. These resolute politicians, on the other hand, with their self-sympathizing insistence on how *hard* their decisions are, how *tough* they have to be, may just be giving rein to proud self-assertion. One does not perceive in Lincoln that either his generosity or his resolution was self-indulgent—or was an occasion for self-congratulation. One of his great statements as president—which adds something even to the Second Inaugural Address—was his saying in passing in a letter to a Louisiana Unionist on July 28, 1862, "I shall do nothing in malice. What I deal with is too vast for malicious dealing." Too vast for anything merely personal, we might also say.

We observed about that youngster reading his books and discovering that his abilities were greater than those of anyone else in Pigeon Creek, and writing his name and imagining his future distinction, that the combination of his life story with the great power of the wartime presidency might create a moral monster, a tyrant indeed. But that did not happen. His ego would not be stoked and enlarged by his rise from nowhere all the way to the supreme position, or inflated by the immense power that he held when he got there.

On the contrary. The higher he went and the greater his power, the worthier his conduct would become—something like the opposite of Lord Acton's dictum. More notable even than young Lincoln's rise to eminence from unpromising beginnings would be the fact that that rise would not corrupt him, but something like the reverse.

Lincoln began to exhibit in the selection of his cabinet, along with the virtues we have named, political shrewdness. He rather promptly wrote to his chief Republican rival, William Seward, courteously offering him the post of secretary of state, assuring him that the offer was not made (as rumor had it) in the expectation that it would be turned down. Seward, after a brief interval, graciously accepted. On the eve of the inauguration, when it was clear that his ideological enemy Salmon Chase would also be in the cabinet, Seward tried to withdraw; but Lincoln, as he remarked, could not let him take the first trick, and skillfully dissuaded him.

Lincoln also soon offered the post of attorney general to Edward Bates of Missouri, and after complicated dealings, the Treasury to Chase and the War Department to Simon Cameron. That meant that Lincoln gave four of the seven cabinet posts—and the four most important ones—to his four most prominent defeated rivals from the Wigwam, as not everybody would do. He made unsuccessful efforts to find a Southerner who could serve in his cabinet without compromise of principle on either side, but this proved impossible. He appointed Gideon Wells of Connecticut to the Navy Department and Montgomery Blair of Maryland postmaster general, both of them ex-Democrats. When the lineup was complete, Lincoln had four ex-Democrats to only three ex-Whigs; when this was pointed out, he answered that he himself was an ex-Whig, making it even.

The cabinet he put together had those balances that cabinets need:

radical/conservative/moderate; ex-Whig/ex-Democrat; all sections of the country except for the Deep South. Two of the seven—Blair and Bates—came from slave states. Four or five of Lincoln's appointees were able people, making the result a much stronger cabinet than Buchanan's, and a stronger and more complex group—Seward and Chase at odds in particular—than one might have thought a new man on the national scene would think he could handle.

The two weakest members—Caleb Smith of Indiana at Interior and Simon Cameron at the War Department—were appointed in some measure as a result of promises made or expectations aroused at the convention, and partly by the logic of state power. Indiana's support on the first ballot, and Pennsylvania's on the second, had been of pivotal importance, and they were both states that cried out for representation. Smith had made an important early seconding speech for Lincoln. Cameron—a powerful political boss in Pennsylvania but with a somewhat unsavory reputation and strong opposition in the state—was the most problematic appointee. It has been said that by assigning Cameron to the War Department (he had wanted Treasury) Lincoln showed that he did not expect the war.

In explaining to a disappointed alternative choice for the Indiana slot, Lincoln put into words what would *not* guide him in his administration. There was another Hoosier, other than Caleb Smith, who might have been appointed: the rising Republican Congressman Schuyler Colfax. Colfax had at first not supported Lincoln in the convention in Chicago. Lincoln wrote to him shortly thereafter—on May 26, 1860—"You distinguish between yourself and my *original* friends—a distinction which, by your leave, I propose to forget." But Colfax had earlier committed the much more heinous sin, if Lincoln had been a grudge-holder, of having, as a Republican officeholder from the Midwest in those strange days after Douglas broke with Buchanan over the Lecompton matter, of supporting Douglas for the Illinois Senate seat in 1858. But Lincoln, four days into his presidency, on March 8, 1861, went out of his way to assure Colfax that that had nothing to do with the matter ("indeed, I should have decided as I did, easier than I did, had that matter never existed"). He concluded with a characteristic Lincolnian plea: "I now have to beg that you will not do me the injustice to suppose, for a moment, that I remembered anything against you in malice."

The most extraordinary evidence that Lincoln was not going to remember anything in "malice" in shaping his cabinet was still to come when he completed the original appointments and took office on March 4, 1861. One enormously important appointment—as it promptly proved to be— that of secretary of war, turned out to be a particular problem. To tell the story of Lincoln's solution to the problem properly, we must go back to 1855, to the perhaps rather low point in Lincoln's life after he had failed to be chosen senator that February. And then to complete the story we must look forward to January of 1862 after he has served as president through the first months of the war.

2. THE GREAT REAPER CASE

The story begins with a lawsuit. In 1854 Cyrus McCormick sued John H. Manny of Rockford, Illinois, who McCormick thought had infringed on one of his patents for his reaper. It was a hugely important case, in every way—certainly in financial impact. Other competitors with McCormick joined with Manny; they had a stake in opening up the reaper business too, as McCormick had a stake in stopping them. There was plenty of money for lawyers, and each side retained attorneys of national stature. McCormick retained Edward M. Dickerson of New York, who had been the junior counsel in the last great case of Daniel Webster, and was one of the great men of the bar himself. Alongside him stood the renowned Reverdy Johnson of Baltimore, who had been, and would be again, a senator from Maryland. Johnson, who had been attorney general under President Taylor and would be minister to Great Britain after the war, was famous for his courtroom oratory and had probably argued more cases before the Supreme Court than any other attorney of the day.

The John H. Manny side, not to be outdone, retained two of the ablest and most experienced patent attorneys in the nation. Peter H. Watson of Washington, who had secured Manny's patent in the first place, was given the overall management of the defense. He engaged a particular star in the patent-law world, George Harding of Philadelphia. A lawyer who knew about these matters spoke about the "air of expectancy" that would come over a court, including the Supreme Court, whenever Harding or Dickerson arose to address them.

The case was to be tried in the United States District Court for northern Illinois, in Chicago. It was decided by the defense, in keeping with a not uncommon practice, to retain some local lawyer who was known in the circles of that court and would be known to the judge to whom the case was assigned, a man named Thomas Drummond. George Harding, whose remarkable reminiscences years later are a chief source of information about these events, confessed that he had reservations about this tactic. He doubted, in his elevated Philadelphia wisdom, that this raw frontier boomtown of Chicago could supply any lawyer "who would be of real assistance in the case." (So a certain anticipatory disdain was already in place even before this local lawyer was selected.) Harding did want another, junior attorney on the complicated case, but he had a candidate of his own in mind, a lawyer who had won distinction in the more developed eastern world. But the Illinois clients pressed their suggestion that a local man be retained, so an invitation was issued to a lawyer with what passed for legal talent in 1850s Chicago, named Isaac Arnold. But Arnold had conflicting commitments that compelled him to turn the offer down; so the man eventually chosen would be the second choice for a position that his associates had not wanted to fill in the first place.

Someone in the Illinois contingent suggested the name of one "A. Lincoln" or "Abe Lincoln" from Springfield. Harding was even less enthusiastic about this proposal—reaching still deeper into the darkest hinterland. But the Illinois clients persisted, so Peter Watson made the trip to Springfield to check out this fellow Lincoln and, if he would do at all, to offer him a retainer.

When he arrived in Springfield, Watson was surprised to find, in the afternoon of a business day, that Mr. Lincoln's law office was closed, so he made his way through the poorly laid-out streets of Springfield to Lincoln's house, at Eighth and Jackson, and was again surprised, by how small it was—not the dwelling of a lawyer suitable for a major national patent case—and further surprised that it offered neither a knocker nor a doorbell. He was surprised yet again that Lincoln's wife (as she proved to be) answered his resort to knocking with his knuckles on the door by calling down from an upper window, and that, standing there at the door, he had to tell her whether he wanted Mr. Lincoln for "business or politics." He was surprised yet again that, when she summoned her husband, that worthy came to the door in his shirtsleeves, without a coat or a vest, and that this attorney proposed as counsel in a major national case explained that, on this afternoon of a business day, he had just been putting up a bed. Watson was still further surprised, finally, by the "small, plainly furnished room" into which this lawyer then ushered him. Watson's multiple surprises had by this point convinced him that this man just would not do— indeed, to wonder just what this "local lawyer" idea had got them into. But some conversation with Lincoln gave him pause; maybe, after all, this fellow could be somewhat effective "in that community." Moreover, Watson, making a quick calculation, decided that, having made the trip and had the meeting, it was probably better not to generate local hostility to the defense by leaving this man flat. So he offered Lincoln a retainer and the promise of a fee at the end of the case.

One can imagine from the tone of Harding's reconstruction what the conversation must have been when Peter H. Watson, later to be president of the Erie Railroad, reported to George Harding of Philadelphia, one of the most eminent patent lawyers in the country, about his venture into downstate Illinois. (There will be two clues coming soon to the flavor of Watson's report to Harding about this A. Lincoln.) Watson explained what he had done and why—it was better to "keep Lincoln in line"—but his description of Lincoln was such (this is the first of the clues just mentioned) that it did not change but rather confirmed Harding's original opinion that "it would be quite out of the question to have him take part in the argument." Watson proposed that, "without disabusing" Lincoln, they quietly go ahead and employ the attorney Harding really wanted and then look for a way later "for sidetracking Lincoln."

And that is what they did. They left Lincoln undisabused, but quietly employed the other lawyer.

And then came yet another undercutting of any role for a local lawyer from Illinois. Because this was such a weighty case, it was assigned to Supreme Court Justice John McLean (in the nineteenth century Supreme Court justices sat on the circuit courts), with Judge Drummond as associate. And because Justice McLean lived in a suburb of Cincinnati, the parties agreed to move the case from Chicago to Cincinnati, breaking the last thin thread of a reason for employing any Illinois person.

Meanwhile, back in Springfield, our hero thinks he has been employed to make the argument in a very big case—the biggest he had ever been in, working with and against some of the grandest lawyers in the land. He had a retainer and the promise of a fee. He went to work with greater thoroughness than ever before, the sort of thoroughness he would have occasion to display again and again in the years just ahead. Up to this point Lincoln had no knowledge of the condescension and affronts-in-absentia toward himself (or anyone like himself) that had already prepared the ground for affronts to come in the offices of George Harding, Esq., counsel for the defense in the great case of *McCormick v. Manny*.

But perhaps now he got his first inkling: from Philadelphia and from Washington there was total silence. There is in the collected papers of Lincoln a little letter Lincoln wrote on July 25, 1855, revealing (and perhaps a little touching) if you know this context. It was addressed to Peter H. Watson, Esq., in Washington:

> My dear Sir:
> At our interview here in June, I understood you to say you would send me copies of the Bill and Answer in the case of McCormick vs. Manny and Co. and also of depositions, as fast as they could be taken and printed. I have had nothing from you since.

They had not bothered even to send him the papers with which to do his work! But the industrious Westerner had carried on on his own initiative. His letter to Watson continued:

> However, I attended the U.S. Circuit Court at Chicago, and while there, got copies of the Bill and Answer. I write this particularly to urge you to forward on to me the additional evidence as fast as you can. During August, and the remainder of this month, I can devote some time to the case; and, of course, I want all the material that can be had.

This fellow had not taken the hint that he was not wanted and needn't bother with this effort. He even took the further initiative of doing some research:

> During my stay at Chicago, I went out to Rockford, and spent half a day, examining and studying Manny's machine.

And so he is doing research—on his own initiative! He is so far under illusions about his role as to offer advice:

> I think you ought to be sworn before the evidence closes; of this however I leave you and the others to judge.
>
> *Very truly yours,*
> *A. Lincoln*

Leave others to judge! Ha! This fellow thinks he is right in there in the planning for the defense.

Then came another hint that he was not: there was no answer whatever to his letter to Watson. On September 1, 1855, we find him writing to the Illinois clients:

Messrs. Manny and Co.

Rockford, Ill.

Since I left Chicago about the 18th of July, I have heard nothing concerning the Reaper suit. I addressed a letter to Mr. Watson at Washington, requesting him to forward me the evidence, from time to time, but I have received no answer from him.

Is it still the understanding that the case is to be heard at Cincinnati on the 20th instit.?

He is reduced to asking the client to confirm the time and place. Reassured (one infers) by the Illinois clients, he made his way the then long miles from Springfield, Illinois, to Cincinnati, Ohio, and was greeted there by his putative colleagues in a manner that surely gave another hint, or more than a hint, of their idea of him and of his role.

These colleagues now included the new man, the Pittsburgh lawyer Harding had wanted all along instead of some hick from Illinois. This lawyer's name was Edwin M. Stanton; Harding and Watson had gone ahead and engaged him for their 1850s legal dream team.

Stanton was five years younger than Lincoln, but he would seem to have been Lincoln's superior as a lawyer in every way. He had been to college, for one thing—Kenyon College—which Lincoln had certainly not. Stanton had grown up in a solid middle-class family; his father was a doctor, his mother the daughter of a wealthy Virginia mill owner. He had lived his whole youth in one settled community, Steubenville, Ohio, which was bigger and more developed than any of the frontier places of Lincoln's youth. He had studied law in a more systematic way than Lincoln, with a group of lawyers who undertook orderly instruction. Although he was an active Jackson Democrat, he had forged ahead in the law without any lengthy interruptions by politics. After his young wife died, he moved the seat of his practice to Pittsburgh, a burgeoning industrial metropolis, and rose in the urban Eastern ranks of his profession. Stanton had been admitted to practice before the United States Supreme Court. On one of the occasions on which he appeared before the high court, the opposing counsel was Reverdy Johnson, the great advocate who now would be on the other side in the reaper case. Lincoln had certainly not, in 1855, and perhaps not later, either, argued in such a setting against an attorney of such national caliber.

Stanton could be brusque, peremptory, and disdainful, as Lincoln was to learn. When Frederick Douglass would later come to know Stanton, he would make this wonderful observation: "Politeness was not one of his weaknesses." But Stanton was also highly intelligent, extremely energetic, and capable of mastering and marshaling great bodies of complicated facts—as he had demonstrated in a famous, long-drawn-out case involving a bridge over the Ohio River. This bridge, Stanton argued for his clients, would block big-river traffic from access to Pittsburgh, and effectively make Wheeling, instead of Pittsburgh, the regional hub of transportation and therefore of commerce. For the forty-one-year-old Stanton to win (eventually) the "Wheeling Bridge" case, he had to master and deploy a wide range of complicated data—about commerce on the river, the height of smokestacks on various vessels, the comparative value of rail and river transport, and a host of other technical matters—just the sort of thing you might want your lawyer to be able to manage if you were involved in a complicated patent suit about reaping machines. If you had been George Harding or Peter Watson, you very well might have preferred this rising Pittsburgh lawyer, who had proved himself in the bridge case, and in the big leagues in other cases, to some circuit-riding lawyer from the middle of the frontier state of Illinois.

Harding had asked Stanton to join the defense, and Stanton arrived in Cincinnati before Lincoln got there. Harding and Stanton had already "determined that [Lincoln] should be altogether dispensed with," as Harding's reminiscence was to put it, and that resolve was strengthened by Harding's first glimpse of Lincoln in Cincinnati. Harding was to claim (this is the second clue mentioned above, to the character of Watson's report about the Springfield lawyer) that he recognized Lincoln instantly from Watson's description. There he was, standing on a platform in Cincinnati, "a tall, rawly boned, ungainly backwoodsman, with coarse ill-fitting clothing, his trousers hardly reaching his ankles, holding in his hands a blue cotton umbrella with a ball at the end of it. I can still see distinctly that umbrella with Lincoln standing there with it."

When Lincoln introduced himself, Harding and Stanton barely mumbled their salutations, and then Harding proposed to Stanton that the two of them—obviously not including Lincoln—go to the court. At this point Harding's report reproduced some actual dialogue, with a certain pathos.

"Let's go up in a gang," said Lincoln.

"Let that fellow go up with his gang," said Stanton, aside to Harding, on this occasion of his first meeting with his future chief. "We [meaning Stanton and Harding] will walk together." Which they did, leaving Lincoln, with his blue umbrella, to make his way as he might.

The three men stayed at the same Cincinnati hotel, the Burnet House, but neither Stanton nor Harding was ever to confer with Lincoln, or to ask him to dine with the two of them at their table, or to ask him to their rooms, or to walk to court with him.

The slights, snubs, and affronts continued in the court itself. Although his colleagues showed no respect for him, there were those, certainly among the Illinois clients and possibly among the opposing counsel for McCormick, who knew Lincoln and did have respect for him. Whether for that reason or, as Harding and Stanton instantly concluded, for reasons of strategy, the plaintiff's counsel, seeing three attorneys at the opposing table, amiably volunteered to waive any objection to there being more than two arguments on that side, if their own chief counsel could speak twice if he wished to. Harding and Stanton instantly interpreted this as a trap, to give their opponents the advantage of speaking both before and after Harding. Stanton stood and stated belligerently that there was no intention on their side of making more than two arguments, and that he himself would forgo making an argument rather than so violate the usage of the court.

To be sure, he didn't mean it. He had someone else in mind for the sacrifice. The hint, now, was unmistakable, and perhaps Stanton reinforced it. In any case, the uncouth westerner finally got the point and offered to withdraw. His offer was instantly accepted, and Harding and Stanton treated Lincoln thereafter as though he had nothing to do with the case.

So there he was in Cincinnati, an arduous trip away from home, with a thorough written-out argument he had spent part of July and August, and a half-day trip to Rockford, preparing, with no part at all in the big case. He (rather touchingly, we may feel) sent, through Watson as the intermediary—he had no further direct contact whatever with Harding—the carefully written-out manuscript of the argument he had intended to make, thinking there might be something in it Harding could use. Harding's memory of his response to this offer reflects once again the attitude that had already been made abundantly manifest: "I was so sure that it would be only trash on which I must not waste my time that I never glanced at it or even opened it." Lincoln—a bit of pathos again—asked Watson whether the great lawyer had read his manuscript. Watson had to answer candidly, no. Lincoln asked for the manuscript back so that he could destroy it, and it was brought back to him unopened. (If somehow it has survived and, poking around in Rockford or Cincinnati or Springfield, you should find it, this "trash" would be worth many times more than all the arguments George Harding, Esq., ever made in his entire career.)

There are two more slights, and then we are done. The judge in the case, Justice John McLean of the United States Supreme Court, invited counsel from both sides to dinner at his home, in Clifton, a Cincinnati suburb. Lincoln, alone in the hotel, was not invited. And when it was all over, although Lincoln had stayed on in Cincinnati and attended the case, both Harding and Stanton left the city without any farewell or other word whatever to him. Thus concluded the first encounter of the great future president and the also rather great future secretary of war.

Watson sent Lincoln, when he got home, the agreed-upon—and quite substantial—fee of $1,000. Lincoln returned it, saying he had made no argument and did not deserve any fee beyond the original retainer. Watson sent the check back again, insisting that because he had prepared an argument he was entitled to it, and this time Lincoln kept it.

William Herndon, in his biography of his longtime law partner, describes a (surely altogether understandably) rather wounded Lincoln on his return from his trip to try the great case in Cincinnati. Herndon reports that Lincoln was (again altogether understandably) rather uncharacteristically shut-mouthed about what happened in the great case. Usually Lincoln would return bubbling with entertaining stories. But not this time. Herndon remembered Lincoln telling him not only that he had been rather "roughly handled by that man Stanton," but also that he—Lincoln—actually overheard through a slightly open door Stanton saying of Lincoln (can this really have happened?), "Where did that long-armed creature come from, and what can he expect to do in this case?"

Herndon also quotes Lincoln expressing a lasting dislike of the city of Cincinnati because of what happened to him there, but that is a little hard to believe. Lincoln certainly could have directed legitimate anger in several directions, but one would not think the city itself would be one of them.

Moreover, after being bumped from the case he did not shake the sand of the city from his feet and leave, but stayed on. Denied participation himself in the proceedings, he nevertheless went to the court and listened closely to the arguments these great lawyers gave. And—here we are in danger of sounding like that book of moral lessons for the young from the life of Abraham Lincoln, or the one that shows how he illustrates Kipling's "If"—he not only overcame his hurt enough to stay on in Cincinnati and go each day to the case—he *learned* from doing so. He became a better lawyer by listening to these great lawyers make their arguments. And whom did he learn most from? Harding and Stanton!

So, at least, goes the story, as told by a man named Ralph Emmerson and passed on by Lincoln biographer Albert Beveridge. Emmerson, a young associate of John H. Manny, knew Lincoln from Illinois and claimed to have been the one who proposed that he be added to the defense team. He was present—watching Lincoln among the spectators—throughout the case in the courtroom. He claimed, many years later, that Lincoln said to him as they talked there in Cincinnati one evening that "these college-trained men who have devoted their whole lives to study are coming west . . . They study on a single case perhaps for months, as we never do. We are apt to catch up the thing as it goes to the jury and trust to the inspiration of the moment. They [college-trained lawyers] have got as far as Ohio now. They will soon be in Illinois . . . I'm going home and study law . . . when they get to Illinois I will be ready for them." Emmerson went on to say that he heard Lincoln in many later law cases, and that, indeed, the inspiration of hearing those highly trained lawyers in Cincinnati did cause him to improve his own performance.

3. THE PRESIDENT APPOINTS A SECRETARY OF WAR

And so now our flashback is complete. Incredible as it must have been to Harding and Stanton, just five years after the serial snubbings in Cincinnati, this A. Lincoln or Abe Lincoln, the ill-dressed, long-armed fellow from downstate Illinois, turned out to be the nominee of a major party for the highest office in the land. That must have presented everyone who had been there in Cincinnati with something of a problem.

George Harding was a devoted Republican, but he had not changed his opinion of that Lincoln with his blue umbrella. Therefore he had a certain difficulty about his vote for president. Because of the great events on the national stage, he finally did hold his nose and vote for his party's nominee, but it cannot have been easy for him to do so. (New president Lincoln, remembering how impressed he had been with the technical knowledge and skill displayed by patent attorney George Harding in the celebrated case of *McCormick* v. *Manny et al.*—Harding and Stanton won the case, by the way—would nominate Harding to the office of commissioner of patents: "an office which, of course, I declined at once.")

Edwin Stanton, on the other hand, was a fierce and partisan Democrat—and not only a Democrat, but a *Buchanan* Democrat, a *Breckinridge* Democrat. He had moved to Washington, partly on the strength of his share of the success, and his connections and visibility, in the reaper case, and in Washington he had cases sent his way by the Democratic administration of James Buchanan. Stanton's particular friend was the attorney general in the Buchanan administration, Jeremiah Black, an able lawyer who had become Stanton's friend when Black had served as chief justice of the Pennsylvania Supreme Court. When, early in the Buchanan administration, Senator Douglas broke with the president of his own party over the dubious proslavery Lecompton constitution, cabinet member Black of course supported his president. Stanton, Black's friend and beneficiary, supported Black, and therefore President Buchanan. With the approach of the 1860 election the Democrats split apart, the Northern faction nominating Stephen A. Douglas, the Southern faction nominating John Breckinridge of Kentucky, who was vice president under Buchanan. President Buchanan supported Breckinridge, and so did his cabinet member Jeremiah Black. And so Stanton supported Breckinridge as well. As the 1860 election approached, Stanton was already a supporter of the candidate in furthest opposition to Lincoln and the Republicans: the Democratic nominee supported by the secessionists and fire-eaters, John Breckinridge.

Meanwhile the Republicans had done this incredible thing. They had nominated that fellow from downstate Illinois whom Stanton remembered from the reaper case. Most of the high-level Washington figures and Eastern lawyers with whom Stanton consorted were completely unfamiliar with this Lincoln—a virtual unknown, particularly in Buchanan's Washington—but Stanton did know him, and his opinion had not changed from five years earlier. Jeremiah Black would later remember that in their circles Stanton, uniquely, "knew Mr. Lincoln personally and the account he gave of him was anything but favorable." Stanton in 1860 and 1861 stood about as far as could be from Lincoln, by party, by ideology, and—especially important—in his personal appraisal and personal relationship.

But Stanton was after all close to Lincoln in one regard: in devotion to the Union. Stanton had supported Breckinridge in the belief (quite naive in the view of many then and later) that in spite of (or because of) his being the secessionists' candidate, Breckinridge was the only choice among the candidates who might keep the Union from splitting.

We do not know (we can surmise) exactly what Edwin M. Stanton thought when, on a family visit to Steubenville, he learned—as he had by that time come gloomily to expect—that this A. Lincoln fellow, whom he had treated so disdainfully in Cincinnati just five years earlier, was now to be president of the United States. But the focus of his anxiety had by that time come to be not who would be president of the Union but whether there would *be* a Union for anyone to be president of. A little later he would worry that Washington itself might fall to the secessionists, and Jefferson Davis become the new president. Jeremiah Black called on him to help in the message-drafting and memo-writing intended to stiffen the spine of the timorous and vacillating President Buchanan—to show him his duty to defend the Union and its remaining outposts, such as the garrison under Major Robert Anderson that had moved to Fort Sumter in Charleston harbor.

When the cabinet shufflings of this anxious time caused the president to move Black from the Justice Department to the Department of State, Black proposed that Stanton be named his successor as attorney general, and Buchanan made the appointment: Stanton became a member of Buchanan's cabinet on December 20, 1860, the same day that South Carolina passed its ordinance of secession. Stanton found that although the Union-supporting contingent in Buchanan's cabinet had been strengthened, the secessionist component was still very strong, and Buchanan weak. As attorney general of the United States, Stanton had now to tell the president that he must not negotiate with the "commissioners" from South Carolina, which would implicitly validate their claim to represent a sovereign, independent power; they were *traitors,* and as the chief legal officer of the United States, Stanton must not even know that the president might imply recognition of them.

Along with Black, Stanton stiffened Buchanan's resistance to South Carolina's demand that Major Anderson's forces at Sumter be removed. He wrote to friends and colleagues urging that they put public pressure on Buchanan to support Anderson; one of these correspondents was, in Philadelphia, his colleague in the reaper case George Harding. Philadelphia held a mass meeting of seven thousand praising Anderson and urging the president to give him all support.

Stanton found the secessionist influence within Buchanan's cabinet so strong, and Buchanan in the face of it so weak, and in his view the Union so much in danger, that within the first ten days of his attorney-generalship he made a momentous decision, which could furnish a case for study in seminars in ethics in calmer times: He decided to inform Republican leaders in Congress, secretly, what was happening within the top levels of the Buchanan administration. He established what later generations would call a back channel of secret communication with some Republican leaders in Congress, chief among them William Seward. He rarely met with Seward personally, but he sent messages almost daily to him through an intermediary. And who was this intermediary? Another colleague from the reaper case, Peter H. Watson. (Later, after Stanton became secretary of war, he would appoint Watson as one of two assistant secretaries—therefore another member of the Lincoln administration. Thus, if Harding had accepted the offered post, the entire defense team in the reaper case would have been serving in that administration, now in rather a different configuration of power.)

Stanton's secret reports on the doings of the president and the cabinet, carried by Watson to Seward, were then in a few cases passed on by Seward, without his revealing the source, to the president-elect out in Springfield, who was composing his inaugural address and dodging office-seekers and writing private letters to Republican leaders telling them not to compromise on points respecting the integrity of the Union or the expansion of slavery.

To look forward briefly: Stanton was the only member of Buchanan's cabinet to stay in Washington after the inauguration of Lincoln, of whom he continued to have the opinion he had held before. As the early events of the war and the Lincoln administration unfolded, he twice (at least twice) used the word "imbecility" to describe Lincoln and his performance as president: to his friend General John Dix in New York on June 11 ("no one can imagine the deplorable condition of this city . . . who did not witness the weakness and the panic of the administration and the painful imbecility of Lincoln") and to ex-president Buchanan, who was watching events from his retirement in Pennsylvania, after the Battle of Bull Run in July ("the imbecility of the administration culminated in that catastrophe [Bull Run]; an irretrievable misfortune and national disgrace never to be forgotten are added to the ruin . . . as the result of Lincoln's 'running the machine' for five months"). There is an anonymous document called "The Diary of a Public Man," written by some important person in early Civil War Washington whose identity has never been discovered, which quotes Stanton as having said things as malignant and bitter as could be about the new president, launching into a "tirade" against him, and saying that he "had met him [Lincoln] at the bar, and found him a low, cunning clown."

When the new commander of the Army of the Potomac, General George McClellan, asked a Democratic friend who could give a legal opinion about the *Trent* affair (Southern emissaries to England and France taken by force off a British mail packet), that Democrat suggested Stanton, and when Stanton and McClellan met, they discovered they had much in common, including contempt for the president. They are the two men we know from the written record to have called Lincoln a "gorilla"—in Stanton's case, "the original gorilla," at this meeting with McClellan.

Lincoln's appointee as secretary of war, the dubious Pennsylvania politician Simon Cameron, turned to Stanton as an able, Union-supporting Washington lawyer with cabinet-level government experience to advise him on technical legal matters arising from the unprecedented and rapid expansion of the War Department. So, in spite of belonging to the party out of power, Stanton thus had close connections with two key people in early wartime Washington, General McClellan and Secretary of War Cameron.

Cameron, who had been appointed to his post, as noted earlier, only for reasons of political necessity, was not up to the job. It was under his administration of the War Department that the word "shoddy" came into wide use, to describe the material used in uniforms that fell apart. In January of 1862 Lincoln found the occasion to remove Cameron by appointing him minister to Russia. But the president handled this removal, and later dealings with Cameron, with such grace as to retain Cameron's strong support.

And so the key post of secretary of war was vacant. Whom would Lincoln appoint?

George Harding, calling on the president (that must have been some meeting), was told: "You know the War Department has demonstrated the great necessity for a Secretary of Mr. Stanton's great ability, and I have made up my mind to sit down on all my pride, it may be a portion of my self-respect, and appoint him to the place."

In any case, shortly before Cameron's removal, the president did send word (apparently by way of Harding) to Stanton that he would like to see him. George Harding came as well. So there they were—the team from Cincinnati, reunited ("Let's go up in a gang"). Harding, of course remembering the reaper trial, understandably thought that the meeting might be a little strained. Stanton and Lincoln had not met since the day five years earlier when Lincoln had been sent away from the defense counsel's table. But, Harding reported, he was himself the most embarrassed of the three. Apparently there was no reminiscing about old times; but one would surely like to have been a witness to this encounter. "The meeting was brief but friendly, and Lincoln and Stanton shook hands cordially at parting both thanking him [Harding] for the trouble he had taken in bringing them together."

Not many days later, immediately after Cameron resigned to take the post in Russia, President Lincoln named as head of the War Department, surely the most powerful and significant position in his cabinet: Edwin M. Stanton.

Was there anything remarkable in this? No, you might answer. Persons who have been at odds, rivals, even enemies, are repeatedly brought into common effort by larger historical forces and political necessities; the political making of strange bedfellows is a cliché.

Moreover, one can make a good case in politics and in policy for Lincoln's appointing Stanton—as one can for other acts of putative magnanimity that mark his career. It made sense, as it has to other wartime presidents (Roosevelt in World War II appointing Republicans Stimson and Knox to the War and Navy Departments), to appoint a member of the opposing political party to key military departments, to help to bind the whole nation together. Still better: Stanton was a Buchanan-Breckinridge Democrat, not just a Douglas supporter.

It could be argued, further, that Stanton came from Pennsylvania (although his home now was Washington), as Cameron had done, so that geographical balance was retained.

In the turbulent year of 1861 Stanton managed to have the sympathetic support, simultaneously, among Republicans, of Seward (with whom he had established the secret back channel) and Seward's great rival in Lincoln's cabinet, Salmon Chase (whom Stanton had known well in his earlier days in Ohio). In addition and at the same time, Stanton had a good relationship with the former leading Democrat, ex-president Buchanan, in retirement, with whom he carried on a friendly correspondence, and the leading rising Democrat, General George McClellan. Impressive.

Although because of this political dexterity (as we may call it), no one was tempted to give Stanton the nickname "Honest Edwin," he was known to be in another sense incorruptibly honest—with respect to money, contracts, favors, bribes. And that was of enormous importance, following Simon Cameron, of whom that could not be said, and heading a War Department now rapidly expanding to unprecedented proportions.

Probably none of this was as important in determining Lincoln's choice as Stanton's ability. That had been conveyed to Lincoln by many around him, and by Stanton's recent Washington reputation. But Lincoln knew of Stanton's ability already himself—from sitting, listening to Stanton make arguments in a Cincinnati courtroom in September of 1855, in a case from which he had himself been rudely excluded. Possibly Lincoln even counted in his favor for *this* job Stanton's peremptory brusqueness, which he knew about firsthand.

So it is not noteworthy that Lincoln appointed Stanton? Surely there is another thread of politics, and human life, that would suggest a different outcome. There are, more than the general public realizes, threads of compelled cooperation, and even of largeness of spirit encouraged by the largeness of events, that run through high politics. But of course there is also a less appealing thread, of the sort the broad public would be more likely to expect: vindictiveness, resentment, rivalry, and revenge, given opportunity by accessions of power. Is not politics an arena in which the widespread human inclination to pay back those who (we allege) have used us ill is both magnified and given heightened opportunity?

Think of other American presidents. Franklin Roosevelt was said, not just by his enemies but by his admirers, to have a vindictive streak. In the circles around John F. Kennedy and his brother Robert there was a common saying, "Don't get mad, get even." President Kennedy's successor, Lyndon Baines Johnson, from San Marcos State Teachers College, resented the Harvard men and Kennedy loyalists he inherited even as he had to work with them. One major twentieth-century American politician, Richard M. Nixon, was almost defined by the deep well of his endlessly proliferating, festering resentments. A thousand powerful political leaders have been said, in some combination of admiration and fear, to have long memories. Machiavelli has taught a thousand princes that it is well to be loved and feared, but that if one has to choose, it is better to be feared (which means, among other things, to retaliate against any lack of respect).

Lincoln need not have appointed Stanton. Even if he had independently determined to make a link with Buchanan Democrats, there was another who would serve: Joseph Holt of Kentucky, another late addition to Buchanan's cabinet, who had joined with Stanton and Black to make the Union contingent. Holt had supporters, and one could certainly have argued that a link with the crucial border state of Kentucky was more important than Stanton's dubious tie to Pennsylvania. But there would have been other political advantages, and other valuable qualities, to be discovered in other candidates had the president wanted to discover them, and to avoid appointing Stanton. At the personal level it was certainly an arrangement that offered the now powerful Lincoln the opportunity to get his own back, as the saying goes, against that Stanton fellow, who had been so contemptuous of him in Cincinnati, and for that matter, as Lincoln probably knew, still was contemptuous of him.

George Harding would give this summary:

Stanton's attack on him and ridicule of him during the campaign must have further exasperated him, and there was probably no man in the country towards whom he had reason to feel so much personal resentment. When convinced that the interest of the nation would be best served by bringing Stanton into his cabinet, he suppressed his personal resentment, as not many men could have done, and made the appointment.

Lincoln offered, and Stanton accepted, the most powerful civilian post within his gift, and the rest is Civil War history. The two men established the closest daily working relationship that Lincoln had with any of his cabinet members—the two men, back and forth to each other, conducting this great war.

The president would cross the street to the War Department almost every day to check the telegraph room's report from the battlefields, and often to confer with his war secretary. The continual stream of notes that went back and forth between them came to include that implicit reciprocity about punishment and leniency for soldierly derelictions that most of the biographies comment on and illustrate: Lincoln letting Stanton deny what Lincoln could not deny, Stanton sending to Lincoln for the permissions that Stanton should not permit—a tacit arrangement that bespeaks an unusual degree of mutual understanding. In argument on policy Stanton could dispute his president as an equal, up to the point of clear decision, which then rested with Lincoln. In the conduct of this giant civil war, almost wholly unprecedented in its proportions and in its form, Lincoln, at the decision center, had many problems with the military arm, choosing that sequence of generals, one after another, trying this one, trying that one, sprinkling the pages of Civil War histories with all those names of generals until he arrived at Grant. On the civilian side, though, on which there might also have been a complicated search for the right leadership, once he dismissed Cameron and appointed Stanton his search was ended.

Harding told of an encounter he had with Stanton after he had been in Lincoln's cabinet for some months. He and others had noticed "remarkable passages in certain state papers," which they thought to be "quite beyond anything that could be expected of Lincoln." Admirers of Seward and of Chase had each attributed these passages to their champion. Harding, however, thought that Stanton was abler than either Seward or Chase.

When he met Stanton he referred to a state paper that had recently appeared and said to him, "I know who is the author of that."

Stanton asked, "Who do you suppose?"

Harding replied, "You."

"Not a word of it, not a word of it," Stanton said. "Lincoln wrote it— every word of it. And he is capable of more than that. Harding, no men were ever so deceived as we at Cincinnati."

And then, according to Harding, Stanton launched into so fervent a paean of praise for Lincoln that he could hardly credit it. "Never afterwards," Harding said, "would any disparagement of Lincoln be tolerated by Stanton or members of his family."

How shall we end this story? Mark Neely offers us the testimony of Robert Todd Lincoln that for more than ten days after his father's death Stanton called on the son in his room every morning "and spent the first few minutes of his visits weeping without saying a word."

Donald accepts the more familiar legend. A week after the war was over, on the morning of April 14, 1865, in a boardinghouse across from Ford's Theater, it would fall to his fierce onetime critic Edwin Stanton to utter, over the dead body of his fallen chief, one of those lines in the Lincoln story that might have been composed by a dramatist: "Now he belongs to the ages."

CHAPTER SEVENTEEN

Let Grass Grow Where It May

1. ONCE A FRIEND AND STILL NOT AN ENEMY

No one suspected on November 6, 1860, as the election returns began to "tap in" to the telegraph office in Springfield, Illinois, that this raw newcomer would ever belong to the ages. But in truth "the moon and the stars and all the planets" (as a later president, Harry Truman, would put it) fell upon him that evening.

While he waited the four long months from November 6, 1860, to March 4, 1861, the nation of which he was to become president appeared to be coming apart. President-elect Lincoln did not at first take the full measure of his situation. He dismissed the possibility of civil war, sometimes almost flippantly. He underestimated the relentless determination of the disunionists of the Deep South. He overestimated the strength of Southern Unionism. He made these misreadings throughout November, at least.

He was not alone. Much of the North and most Republicans made the same mistakes. The first reason Lincoln and all these others misread the signs was the long record of slave-state threats to withdraw. Given a history of so many wolf-cryings, it seemed safe to assume that there wouldn't be any wolf this time either. A second reason for these errors on the part of Republicans generally, I surmise, was the hangover of the campaign: One surely did not want to acknowledge those ominous rumblings to the South while one sought votes in the North, as though to say, "Vote for our party and the country will be pulled apart and there will be a terrible civil war." Thirdly, there were many evidences of strong Unionist feeling in the South, and for Lincoln personally there was the further influence of the friends he had, particularly those Southern Whigs he had come to know in Congress, who were certainly strong supporters of the Union.

One of the most important of these was Alexander Stephens of Georgia, Lincoln's friend from their days together in Congress, who gave a speech upholding the Union on November 14, which Lincoln read "in the newspapers." When the South came to its senses, would not these able and honorable Union supporters win out?

And finally, out in Springfield, Lincoln was rather isolated from the bluntest expressions of Southern fire-eating, and a long way as well from the pressure cooker of Buchanan's Washington. Swamped by visitors, almost all of them from the North, every other minute filled with complicated negotiations over his cabinet, Lincoln may not have had the depth of the crisis brought home to him.

The most egregious misstep—in hindsight—was a statement that he wrote for insertion in a speech by Senator Trumbull. Lincoln had decided to remain silent throughout these tumultuous months of secession winter, but he made this one rather odd and indirect exception. When Trumbull gave his speech at the Springfield celebration of Republican victory on November 20, everyone knew that statement came from Lincoln. The first part of the statement might have been rather a deft argument, had the situation been as Lincoln thought it was: it is fortunate for the whole country, said Lincoln through Trumbull, that Republicans are now about to demonstrate that they will leave the states and their "property" alone. That will undercut the arguments of the "disunionists" who are now in "hot haste" to get *out* of the Union, exactly because once a Republican administration does come to power, all of those alarms about the threats to "their homes, and firesides, and lives" by the federal government will be proved false. So it is now or never for the disunionists.

Lincoln then made a more dubious short addition, which Trumbull wisely declined to use. This was a sentence, which seems radically insensitive in retrospect, about the gathering of arms in Southern states: "I am rather glad of this military preparation in the South. It will enable the people the more easily to suppress any uprisings there, which their misrepresentation of [Republican] purposes may have encouraged."

That would be the last time Abraham Lincoln would speak favorably about the assembling of weapons and of armies in the Southern states.

On November 30, 1860, Lincoln wrote to Alexander Stephens requesting a copy of his pro-Union speech. Lincoln admired Stephens. While they had been in Congress together, Stephens had delivered a speech denouncing the Mexican War that had evoked superlatives and tears from Congressman Lincoln. "I just take up my pen to say," Lincoln had written to Herndon on February 2, 1848, "that Mr. Stephens of Georgia, a little slim, pale-faced consumptive man . . . has just concluded the very best speech, of an hour's length, I ever heard. My old, withered dry eyes are full of tears yet." (Lincoln was then thirty-nine; his eyes must have withered rapidly.)

Now, twelve and a half years later, Stephens responded with businesslike courtesy to Lincoln's request, telling him that he had not revised the speech and that the report of it in the newspapers was essentially accurate. Then Stephens ended his letter, on December 16, 1860, to the president-elect of the United States, with this earnest observation: "The country is certainly in great peril and no man ever had heavier . . . responsibilities resting upon him than you have . . ." Lincoln in his answer on December 22 responded to this last observation: "I fully appreciate the present peril the country is in, and the weight of responsibility on me." By that time, with the rush of events in December, perhaps he did. The exchange with Stephens itself must have been sobering.

Each man tried to assure the other of his continuing friendship. In his December 22 letter Lincoln wrote, "I wish to assure you, as once a friend, and still, I hope not an enemy," that there was no cause for the South's fears. Stephens then, on his part, in a long, candid letter on December 30, responded, "Personally I am not your enemy—far from it. . . . I would have you understand me as being not a personal enemy, but as one who would have you do what you can to save our common country."

And something of this friend-not-enemy relationship would still be there—to look far ahead, and to follow this Stephens/Lincoln thread to its end—when they would finally, a little over four wartorn years later, meet again. They would in the meantime have played their respective roles in a vast civil war. They would come together in the cabin of the *River Queen* at Fortress Monroe, actually meeting for the first time in sixteen years—their exchange in 1860 having been correspondence only—since that quite different time when they had served together in Congress, and Stephens had been much the more prestigious figure. Now Abraham Lincoln, president of the United States, greeted Alexander Stephens, vice president of the Confederate States but to Lincoln just one of the "three gentlemen from Richmond," with a warm smile and a handshake and a soon-to-be-celebrated joke. Stephens was still "little" and "slim"—ninety pounds—and was wrapped in layers of coats and shawls. As he unwrapped himself

Lincoln laughed: "Never have I seen so small a nubbin come out of so much husk." Lincoln and Stephens found time around the edges to reminisce.

But the conference itself—the Fortress Monroe (Hampton Roads) Conference of February 1865—led nowhere. Jefferson Davis, proposing a conference, had declared as its purpose "to secure peace to the two countries." Lincoln responding had welcomed informal emissaries for peace in "our one common country." So it would be in the address Lincoln wrote in 1861; so it would be at Hampton Roads in 1865. But as the delegates to the conference rose to leave, Lincoln would ask Stephens if there was anything he could do for him. Stephens, after a moment's thought, mentioned his young nephew, John A. Stephens, held prisoner on Johnson Island. Lincoln wrote down the name. Almost immediately on his return to Washington, Lincoln ordered that Lieutenant Stephens be "paroled" and sent to him in Washington. Upon their meeting, the president gave young Stephens three things: a five-day pass to visit friends in Washington; a note to his uncle asking that the senior Stephens arrange the release of a Union soldier held as prisoner, of equal rank, "whose physical condition most requires his release"; and a startling souvenir for this Confederate officer: an autographed picture of the president himself, across which Lincoln wrote—surely accurately about Georgia in February of 1865—"Don't have many of these where you're from."

But all of this—a human connection preserved in the midst of the giant chaos and destructive oppositions of war—did not mean, back in 1860–61, any mitigation of Lincoln's firmness. On the contrary: Stephens's speeches and letters may have clarified the necessity to be more explicitly firm. Those speeches and letters from the man whom Lincoln most respected among the leaders of the Confederacy would show how deep the chasm went, and how necessary it would be, as Lincoln himself wrote, to hold to inflexible core principles with a "chain of steel."

In the speech that occasioned Lincoln's initial letter Stephens had argued against secession—but his full argument cannot have been reassuring to Lincoln. The speech had been delivered before the Georgia legislature and had, indeed, opposed secession: "[S]hall the people of the South secede from the Union in consequence of the election of Mr. Lincoln to the Presidency of the United States? My countrymen, I tell you frankly, cordially, and earnestly, that I do not think that they ought." But Stephens's reasons for not seceding hung by a very thin thread. He did express the arguments that President Buchanan in his last Annual Message on December 3, and Lincoln himself in his First Inaugural, would in their different words and tones of voice also make: Lincoln had been constitutionally elected, with no force or fraud; he was the head of one branch of government only, checked by Congress and the courts; his term was a short four years; as yet, no "Southern rights" had been violated—don't act until there is sufficient reason. But Stephens then qualified these arguments with a consideration that not even the Southern-leaning Buchanan would accept, let alone Lincoln: It would constitute an "aggressive act" "to exclude us, by an act of Congress, from the territories with our slave property"; if that policy of Lincoln "and his Republican associates" should be carried out, or even attempted, "no man in Georgia would be more willing or ready than myself to defend our rights, interests, and honor, at every hazard and to the last extremity." What Stephens was describing as an aggressive act, to be resisted to "the last extremity," had been the essence of the Republican Party's, and Lincoln's, program for six years.

And there was no doubt, in a clash between Georgia and the United States, which side Stephens would choose. Reporters, "who very often make me say things which I never did," made me say, in Savannah (said Stephens), that I "was first for the glory of the whole country, and next for that of Georgia. I said the exact reverse of this." "Next to the honor and glory of Georgia, the land of my birth, I hold the honor and glory of our common country."

But it would not require even that "aggressive act" (continuing to try to exclude slavery from the territories) to provoke, and in Stephens's view justify, revolt. In his letter to Lincoln on December 30—a fuller and sharper reply to Lincoln's note than Lincoln might have expected—Stephens explained that the fears of the slave states were *not* founded on the expectation that a Lincoln administration would attack slavery in the slave states themselves, even indirectly. That "disquietude" arose, instead, from the fact that the "central idea" of the "triumphant [Republican] party ... seems to be simply, and wantonly, if you please, to put the institutions of nearly half the states under the bar of public opinion and national condemnation." That alone is enough "to arouse a spirit not only of general indignation but of revolt ..." So imagine Lincoln reading this letter from his old and respected friend saying that the insistence that slavery was morally wrong was *itself* sufficient to cause, and to justify, revolt. There could not be a more direct conflict with all that Lincoln believed and had come to stand for.

Speeches that this most respected of Southern leaders had given, and would soon give, further revealed the moral chasm. Unlike other defenders of American slavery, Stephens would accept the "Higher Law" invoked in an uncharacteristic moment by Seward and in more characteristic moments by many opponents of slavery. Yes, there is a Higher Law, said Stephens in his speech on retiring from Congress on July 2, 1859, but Seward and company have it wrong: the Almighty has decreed, in the Divine Law upon which all constitutions must rest, the subordination of the African race to the White. "African slavery rests with us upon principles that can never be successfully assailed by reason or argument."

After South Carolina, Mississippi, and Florida passed ordinances of secession, Georgia followed on January 19, 1861, while Stephens's friend Lincoln was still out in Springfield, starting to work on his inaugural address. Stephens spoke and voted against Georgia's secession, but was nevertheless chosen to go as a delegate to the gathering of the six seceded states (not yet including Texas) in Montgomery, and was there chosen unanimously as the provisional vice president of the new Confederacy. In that role he would make a celebrated speech in Savannah on March 21, 1861, with an eager, cheering crowd, more than the hall could hold, surging outside, so that the frail new vice president would have to stop and sit down and appeal for order. The "great truth" he expressed in this speech he had stated before, but now it had a new context: It was the foundation—the "cornerstone"—of a new nation. In this speech, widely reviewed and well received in the new Confederacy—greeted by the audience that heard it, according to the collection of his speeches, with "rapturous applause"—Stephens would issue a clear message on what slavery meant in the debate over secession. Slavery, he said, was the "immediate cause of the late rupture and revolution."

Stephens did not dispute the claim of Lincoln that the American Founders had regarded slavery as unjust; on the contrary, he joined in that summary of the Founders. But—he says—the Founders were wrong. Now this new nation, the Confederate States of America, would build on a sounder foundation. Stephens was bold and direct, answering some of his old friend President Lincoln's foundational, moral, and historical arguments.

Mr. Jefferson was right in many ways, said Stephens, but he was *wrong* when it came to all men being endowed equally and inalienably by their creator. There was simply no moral (or political) right—in 1776 or 1861—in "attempting to make things equal which the Creator had made unequal." Here is an extended passage from this remarkable speech:

The prevailing ideas entertained by him [Jefferson] and most of the leading statesmen at the time of the formation of the old constitution, were that the enslavement of the African was in violation of the laws of nature; that it was wrong in principle, socially, morally, and politically. It was an evil they knew not well how to deal with; but the general opinion of that day was, that somehow or other, in the order of Providence the institution would be evanescent and pass away. This idea, though not incorporated in the Constitution, was the prevailing idea at the time. The Constitution it is true, secured every essential guarantee to the institution while it should last, and hence no argument can be justly urged against the constitutional guarantees thus secured, because of the common sentiment of the day. Those ideas, however, were fundamentally wrong. They rested upon the assumption of equality of races. This was an error. It was a sandy foundation, and the government built upon it fell when the storm came and the wind blew. Our new government is founded upon exactly the opposite idea; its foundations are laid; its corner-stone rests, upon the great truth that the negro is not equal to the white man; that slavery, subordination to the superior race, is his natural and normal condition.

This, our new government, is the first in the history of the world, based upon this great physical, philosophical, and moral truth.

Three months earlier, in his letter of December 22, 1860, Lincoln had written: "The South would be in no more danger in this respect [federal interference with slavery in the slave states] than it was in the days of Washington." But then he recognized that this reassurance was not enough: "I suppose, however, this does not meet the case." And he stated again the core difference, now in this letter to an old friend on the other side: "You think slavery is *right* and ought to be extended; we think slavery is *wrong* and ought to be restricted. That I suppose is the rub. It is certainly the only substantial difference between us."

2. HERE I STAND

How important an actor Lincoln would be in this intricate and dangerous panorama depended in large part on himself. At the moment he held no office. The office to which he would succeed on March 4 had not had a strong occupant since Andrew Jackson. Lincoln was the least known, least experienced, and on paper least qualified of men elected to that high office, something of a surprise nominee and therefore a surprise president-elect. Although strongly pressed to issue statements, especially to reassure the South, after the paragraphs in the Trumbull speech he remained silent.

Starting in early December of 1860, Lincoln made the two clear and fateful moral decisions that would guide his conduct in the tumultuous months ahead, up to and into the presidency, up to and into the war. Perhaps we should not say he "made" these decisions; rather, they represented the political manifestations of convictions he had long since held. The two issues were intertwined. The first was that no new territory should be yielded to slavery, which in turn rested on the deep conviction, given expression now repeatedly for six years, that American slavery was a monstrous injustice. The second was that the Union is perpetual and unbreakable, and may not be broken by the unilateral decision of an individual state.

Although he was still—certainly—a calculator of consequences, and although he would compromise on much, his own role, and the march of events, brought him to bedrock principles on which he could not compromise.

The first of these bedrock principles appeared in a letter he wrote on December 10 to Senator Trumbull in Washington. Without preliminaries, he came right to the point in the first sentence. We might regard this sentence as Abraham Lincoln's first intervention in high policy as a national leader: "My dear Sir: Let there be no compromise on the question of *extending* slavery."

On the next day, December 11, he wrote almost the same thing to Congressman William Kellogg, who had been appointed as the Illinois member of the House Committee that was attempting to mold a sectional accommodation, the Committee of 33 (one from each of the 33 states). Again he came right to the point: "Entertain no proposition for a compromise in regard to the *extension* of slavery."

Two days later, Lincoln reaffirmed his stance yet again in response to a letter from his friend Congressman Elihu Washburne, who had written about the imminent peril of secession and the distraction represented by the Committee of 33. Again Lincoln was quick and blunt: "Prevent, as far as possible, any of our friends from demoralizing themselves, and our cause, by entertaining propositions for compromise of any sort, on '*slavery extension*.'"

Although letters to Illinois colleagues were short, each contained a swift summary of his reason and ended with forthright admonitions: "Have none of it. Stand firm . . . Hold firm as with a chain of steel."

.   .   .

He wrote the same thing to be conveyed to a much wider audience, in a letter to Thurlow Weed on December 17, using the word "inflexible." He would employ that word again to his most important Republican correspondent, William Seward, whom he would later persuade to be secretary of state, and whom many regarded as the real center of power in the incoming Republican administration:

> I say now, however, as I have all the while said, that on the territorial question—that is, the question of extending slavery under the national auspices,—I am inflexible. I am for no compromise which *assists* or *permits* the extension of the institution on soil owned by the nation. And any trick by which the nation is to acquire territory, and then allow some local authority to spread slavery over it, is as obnoxious as any other.
>
> I take it that to effect some such result as this, and to put us again on the high-road to a slave empire is the object of all these proposed compromises. I am against it.

Lincoln has been criticized for not lending his support to the leading possibility for compromise, the plan presented by Senator John J. Crittenden of Kentucky. In particular, what has been called "the wisest book covering the fateful five months between Lincoln's election and the start of the Civil War" contains a strong suggestion that Lincoln in these months should have backed the Crittenden Plan.* The book is *Lincoln and His Party in the Secession Crisis,* by one of the most eminent historians of his time, David Potter. The book was published as long ago as 1942, but

---

* The Crittenden Plan consisted of a battery of six proposed constitutional amendments, the last of which would have made the other five "permanent" and themselves unamendable—a status of debatable legality which nevertheless reflected the sponsors' eager effort to placate the slaveholding interest. The amendments provided that (1) slavery would be protected south of the Missouri Compromise borderline in all existing American territory and "all acquired hereafter"; (2) Congress should have no power to abolish slavery in territory otherwise under its jurisdiction, such as forts or arsenals, when slavery existed in the surrounding state; (3) amendment 2 applied with equal force to the District of Columbia; (4) Congress should have no power—under the interstate commerce clause of the Constitution, article 1, section 8—or any other instrument—to regulate or "interfere" with the interstate slave trade; (5) the federal government should be responsible for compensating slaveowners whose attempts to recover a fugitive slave were prevented by violence; (6) the five amendments above should be made unalterable by any future congressional action, nor should Congress have the power to abolish slavery in any state where it existed.

republished in 1962 and again as recently as 1995, with the praise I have quoted, written by Daniel Crofts, in the new introduction. Potter himself wrote a Rip Van Winkle introduction in 1962, which on the whole reaffirmed—after twenty years—the book's argument and added important observations about the value even of a "stopgap" peace, on the analogy of the Cold War. He had argued in the book itself not only that Lincoln should have supported the Crittenden Plan but also that had he done so, that compromise would have had a strong chance of success, preserving for a time the peace, although without resolving the underlying issues.

Other scholars have disputed the assertion that the Crittenden Plan had any chance of success. But our own interest is, independent of that, whether Lincoln *ought* to have supported it instead of doing what he actually did, which was to intervene actively *against* any such compromise. His opposition clearly did not rest upon a merely practical assessment of its possibility of success. In other circumstances, the decision of this prudent and responsible politician did turn on practical assessments of the possibilities (at which, his recent misjudgment of the strength of Southern Unionism notwithstanding, he was generally discerning); but on this question in this circumstance he was driven back to fundamental principles. He opposed the plan because it had a radical moral defect at its core: It not only permitted the expansion of slavery but preserved the institution forever. Lincoln did not want the Crittenden Plan, or anything like it, to be enacted.

Does that mean that Lincoln in the winter of 1860–61 did not give sufficient weight to the immense human good of peace? That he did not measure the enormous destruction, death, pain, and suffering of a fratricidal war? Potter's careful, thoughtful book, and his 1962 preface, do not quite join these dots, but the implication seems to be there: A peace, even though only a stopgap, would have been an immense good; the Crittenden Plan would have established such a (temporary) peace, and could have been achieved had Lincoln thrown the whole weight of his influence behind it. Lincoln's influence, it was said, was of great importance, probably decisive: "These forces [squelching 'conciliation' among Republicans] may have been multiple, but certainly none was more potent than the intervention of Lincoln." So Lincoln bore a heavy responsibility (I am inferring a conclusion Potter does not quite state) for the coming of—at least for the nonpostponement of—the terrible scourge of war, for this particular war, coming at the time it did.

And the war that actually "came" (as Lincoln memorably said, in the

Second Inaugural Address) was disproportionately bloody and destructive. Potter in his 1962 preface used a striking retrospective utilitarianism to indicate the disproportionate destructiveness of the war: "[I]t can hardly be said that these immense values [saving the Union and freeing 4,000,000 slaves] were gained at a bargain. For every six slaves who were freed, approximately one soldier was killed; for every ten white Southerners who were held in the Union, one Yank or one Reb died. A person is entitled to wonder whether the Southerners could not have been held and the slaves freed at a smaller per capita cost." Potter was perceptive about the easy complacency with which some of us may now tolerate the war's destruction: "Since all of these individuals would be dead by now even if the Rebs or the Yanks had not killed them, we can afford to be very bland about how right it was that the issue was met in 1861, and not put off." But Potter then used the then-current Cold War to argue that "historians" who believe in facing up to issues in the past ought not to believe in the expedients of peace in the present. "If an interval of peace is worth something today, it was worth something in 1861 . . . If [a stopgap peace] has any merit, it is only the merit of being better than war, and that is the merit which peace in 1861 might have had."

Without accepting the analogy of the Cold War, which seems to me to include radically different elements that vitiate the comparison, we may grant the general point, that many times "peace" in human history, although only temporary, with underlying issues not settled but postponed, may be valuable nonetheless. But does that apply in this case? Is Lincoln to be criticized for not throwing all his considerable influence on the side of a stopgap peace that might have been achieved through the Crittenden proposals? I think not.

As I read him, Lincoln would see a compromise on that basis as a total moral capitulation. It would have made slavery the permanent moral equal of freedom, thus transforming the ethical meaning of "our one common country." Of the three great moral motifs—slavery/freedom; union/secession; peace/war—Lincoln as president-elect affirmed his fundamental principles on the first two. What happened with respect to the third, as he said at the climax of the draft of his inaugural address, was for others to decide.

About Potter's per capita assessment of the costs and benefits of the war as it played out, we might say that Lincoln did not bear the primary responsibility for the costs, and that this ethical method—"retrospective utilitarianism," I called it above, this numbering of heads on each side and using the number to weigh costs and benefits—is not an adequate way to measure the "benefits," or the moral meaning of the huge event of the war. It is not just that that day's four million slaves were freed; their progeny, otherwise destined to be slaves themselves, were freed. And it is not just that the slaves current and future were freed; their white masters were freed from the incubus of slavery. The rest of the American population was freed from it. An institution which was radically unjust in its very essence was overcome. It is not only that a certain number of living Southerners were "held" in the Union; the principle of the American Union was defended, and not only defended but given a deep redefinition, now with equality at the center alongside freedom.

Weighing goods and evils against each other is an appropriate method in a wide range of social and political questions—more so than a popular moralism with its premature absolutes and "principles" may grant. In a giant social collaboration like national life, compromise is necessary and usually worthy. But then there do come these occasions on which those methods are no longer appropriate—when there is, indeed, a sharp turning point and unambiguous choice. Ending slavery was not in this decisive moment just a "benefit" to be weighed alongside other harms and benefits. This intrinsic evil came now to a sharp national decision point. In one direction was the huge backward step of acquiescence in its legitimacy and moral acceptability, its permanence, and its spread. In the other direction lay disapproval, resistance, and the possibility of a new birth of freedom.

Looking at his presidency before the Emancipation Proclamation and at the strict limitations of that instrument itself, and at a notable Lincoln letter to Horace Greeley seeming to say that he would save the Union, with or without slavery, recent critics have tended to regard Lincoln as at best a late and reluctant emancipator. Looking at this decisive moment during his months as president-elect tells a different story. And that gives meaning both to the war that followed and to the reborn Union that came out of it.

Max Weber, in the peculiarly affecting ending of the essay from which we have taken the concept of an ethic of responsibility, describes the moment when a mature politician confronts that boundary situation of intrinsic goods and evils, calculates no longer, and says in the words of Martin Luther well known to his German audience: "Here I stand: I can do no other."* Lincoln, the prudent and responsible calculator, reached a

---

* The passage from Weber reads:

[I]t is immensely moving when a *mature* man—no matter whether old or young in years—is aware of a responsibility for the consequences of his conduct and really feels such responsibility with heart and soul. He then acts by following an ethic of responsibility and-somewhere he reaches the point where he says: "Here I stand; I can do no other." That is

moment like that more than once in the years 1860–65. In 1864 he would write of the promise of freedom to black Union soldiers, "and the promise being made, must be kept." In his last Annual Message he would insist that he would return no one to slavery, and that "if the people should make it an Executive duty to reenslave such persons, another, and not I, must be the instrument to perform it." Now here before he is president there is this comparable moment: On the extension of slavery I am inflexible. Have none of it. Stand firm. As with a chain of steel.

The several reasons that Lincoln gives for his chain-of-steel inflexibility on the territorial question are not independent of each other but deeply interwoven:

• **The core moral reason:** "[The compromise] acknowledges that slavery has equal rights with liberty" (to John D. Defrees, the chairman of the Indiana Republican Party, December 18). "Pop. Sov." in all its forms made slavery a legitimate choice for those who want it in American territory. The Crittenden compromise would have gone still further: it would not only have permitted but would explicitly have recognized and protected slavery in all territories south of the Missouri Compromise line extended to the Pacific, not only in all territory now held but in all territory *"hereafter acquired,"* and these guarantees to slavery were not only to be embodied in a constitutional amendment, but that amendment was to have been made unamendable. Slavery was not only to have been elevated to a plane of total moral acceptance in the land of liberty, but fastened onto it permanently.

• **The loss-of-all-we-have-gained reason:** "[A]ll our labor is lost, and ere long must be done again" (to Trumbull, December 10); "The instant you do [compromise on territory] they have us under again; all our labor is lost, and sooner or later must be done over" (to Kellogg, December 11); "There is no possible compromise upon it [slavery extension], but which puts us under again, and leaves all our work to do over again" (to Washburne, December 15), "and surrenders all we have contended for" (to Defrees, December 18). In the letter to Weed he put the point this way: "[E]ither [compromise] would lose us everything we gained by the election." Lincoln had a dynamic and a realistic understanding of the immense

---

something genuinely human and moving. And every one of us who is not spiritually dead must realize the possibility of finding himself at some time in that position. Insofar as this is true, an ethic of ultimate ends and an ethic of responsibility are not absolute contrasts but rather supplements, which only in unison constitute a genuine man—a man who can have the "calling for politics" (H. H. Gerth and C. Wright Mills, eds., *From Max Weber,* p. 127).

and consequential battle then going on—a battle, one may say without exaggeration, for America's soul. The moment had to be seized, or there would be a tremendous loss and retrogression.

• **The expansion-of-slavery reason:** "Let either [compromise] be done, and immediately filibustering and extension of slavery recommences" (to Washburne, December 13); "Once fastened on us as a settled policy, filibustering all south of us, and making slave states of it, follows in spite of us, with an early Supreme Court decision, holding our free state constitutions to be unconstitutional" (to Defrees, December 18). Lincoln had an awareness not only of the dynamism of the historical process but in particular of the aggressive intensity of the slavery interest—of its eagerness and its need to expand. Once fully legitimated in the American political system, the slave interest would push and shove and drive and thrust for more. "A year will not pass," he wrote to Defrees, "till we shall have to take Cuba as a condition upon which they[the slave states] will stay in the Union."

• **The integrity-of-government reason:** Collapsing, under threat, the central principle upon which the Republicans have been elected would have been a disaster not only for the Republican Party but for the American government. When a Pennsylvania congressman named James T. Hale wrote him a letter including an elaborate set of compromising amendments proposed by border-state congressmen, Lincoln on January 11, 1861, made this point bluntly:

> What is our present condition? We have just carried an election on principles fairly stated to the people. Now we are told in advance, the government shall be broken up, unless we surrender to those we have beaten, before we take the offices. In this they are either attempting to play upon us, or they are in dead earnest. Either way, if we surrender, it is the end of us, and of the government. They will repeat the experiment upon us *ad libitum.*

Perhaps one should underscore in this letter of Lincoln's the phrase "or they are in dead earnest." There has been a scholarly view that Lincoln underestimated the strength of Southern secessionism all the way down to Fort Sumter and beyond. I suggest an alternative view: that he began to recognize in midwinter that they might indeed be "in dead earnest," but that he held to his fundamentals, whether they were or whether they were not.

Their seriousness was strongly indicated on the afternoon of December 20, when the news reached Springfield that South Carolina had actually passed the long-threatened ordinance of secession. Of course there was a tremendous public sensation. Lincoln, who was on that day conferring with Thurlow Weed, did not appear to a reporter to be at all shaken by the news. Henry Villard of the *New York Herald* wrote that "the President elect did not experience any extraordinary shock. . . . It certainly does not make him any more willing to listen to compromises. Timidity is evidently no element in his composition."

On December 22 when Lincoln arrived at his office, his newly appointed secretary John Nicolay told him that the *Times* was reporting that Buchanan had instructed Major Anderson to surrender if attacked. A Nicolay memorandum has Lincoln responding: "If that is true they ought to hang him!"

During these first days after a state had actually voted to secede, in the days just before Christmas of 1860, the president-elect was exchanging messages with Winfield Scott, commanding general of the army, about *retaking* the nation's forts, if any should be yielded before his inauguration: "According to my present view, if the forts shall be given up before the inauguration, the General must retake them afterwards" (to Francis Blair Sr., who had sent a report of an interview with Scott, December 21); "I shall be obliged to him [General Scott] to be as well prepared as he can to either *hold,* or *retake* the forts, as the case may be" (to Elihu Washburne, December 21); "If the forts fall, my judgment is that they are to be retaken" (to Major David Hunter, December 22). To Senator Lyman Trumbull on December 24 he proposed making this intent public:

> Despatches have come here two days in succession, that the Forts in South Carolina, will be surrendered by the order, or consent at least, of the President.
>
> I can scarcely believe this; but if it prove true, I will, if our friends at Washington concur, announce publicly at once that they are to be retaken after the inauguration. This will give the Union a rallying cry . . .

As South Carolina proceeded to occupy most federal facilities, Lincoln in a letter to a New York editor named James Webb on December 29 did some sorting: "I think we should hold the forts, or retake them, as the case may be, and collect the revenue. *We* shall have to forego the use of the federal courts, and *they* that of the mails, for a while."

Back on December 21, immediately after the news of South Carolina's action had arrived in Springfield, Henry Villard had said in his dispatch to the *New York Herald:*

> I cannot resist the conviction that the passage of the secession ordinance by the South Carolina Convention has, instead of intimidating the President elect, only made him firmer and more decided in his views on the reckless and unjustifiable attempt to break up the Union. He will not swerve from the conscientious and rigorous fulfillment of what he considers his constitutional obligations. . . .

And Villard proceeded to make an invidious comparison to Buchanan: "He [Lincoln] will not, like his predecessor, give way to unmanly terror and childish despair should events demand prompt and vigorous action."

3. THE UNION IS UNBROKEN

Lincoln's other unequivocal commitment was to the unbroken Union. He never said, "Let the erring sisters go." In late January, he began to put on paper his argument and his plea. Herndon wrote many years later that "he locked himself in a room upstairs over a store across the street from the State House and there, cut off from all communication and intrusion, he prepared the address." In the "unromantic surroundings" of a "dingy, dusty, and neglected back room," Lincoln wrote out the first words he would speak to the whole people as one who would be their president.

When (we may assume) he started thinking about his address, in November after his election and in early December, the Union of which he would become president was still intact; when he finished his draft, in early February, seven states, one after another in rapid succession, had held conventions and passed ordinances declaring that they were no longer a part of the Union. It all happened with astonishing rapidity; on February 4—just three months after his election, and even before the electoral votes had been counted by the House—a new "nation" (in its own eyes) had been declared in Montgomery.

But not a nation in Lincoln's eyes. Throughout the weeks of January there was a kind of a counterpoint (known only to Lincoln) between these actions by conventions in the states that claimed to be seceding and the sentences the president-elect of the Union they claimed to be leaving was composing in the backroom in Springfield.

"I hold," wrote Lincoln, "that in contemplation of universal law and of the Constitution, the Union of these states is perpetual." He gave reasons. He *argued.* He engaged in careful moral reasoning, legal reasoning, political reasoning, of a high order. The remarks he would one day make at the dedication of a cemetery in Gettysburg, and the much briefer address he would give on his second inauguration, would be stripped-down, deeply felt concentrations of eloquence, wisdom, and charity that would in years to come justly attain much greater worldwide popularity than this address. But still, in a sense, this was to be the speech of his life. This was, as in a full-fledged sense the shorter two were not, an *address.* This address included a full argument for the core of his understanding, the underpinning of his policy and his action.

"In contemplation of universal law": From the very nature of the institution of government everywhere, of governments as such, this unilateral seceding is impermissible. "Perpetuity is implied," he wrote, "in the fundamental law of all national governments." He also implied—he *assumed*—that this is a *national* government like all others. "It is safe to assert," he wrote, "that no government proper, ever had a provision in its organic law for its own termination."

Lincoln himself certainly held that the American Union was a "government proper." But even, for the sake of argument, suppose that the United States was "an association of states in the nature of contract merely"; even then, "one party to a contract may violate it—break it, so to speak, but does it not require all to rescind it?" When editing what he had written, Lincoln inserted the word "lawfully"—"to lawfully rescind it." Although that meant that he split an infinitive, it made his meaning clear: even if this were "an association of states" merely, "with only a contractual engagement," South Carolina and the others could not *lawfully* rescind that contract by their own unilateral action. Even were that the situation, that the United States was just a contractual association of independent states, what these seven states were doing even as he wrote these words would be *breaking* their contract—"an unlawful act."

But the United States was much more than such an association; it was a government proper, a national government, and what these states were doing was (he would later say) insurrectionary at least, or, depending on the circumstances, *treasonable.*

Later in his draft Lincoln would give argument and illustrations suggesting the reduction to absurdity—the fissiparous principle that would be set in motion—if each dissatisfied part—each changing minority—could drop out of the Union at its own choice.

"Descending from these general principles" (as Lincoln put it) about the essential nature of government everywhere, Lincoln appealed to the particular history of *this* government, as confirming that the Union is perpetual. "The Union is much older than the Constitution," Lincoln affirmed, and traced American history from that first gathering in Philadelphia in the autumn of 1774, through the maturing and continuing by the Declaration of Independence in 1776, through the express plighting of faith and express engagement that the Union should be perpetual in the Articles of Confederation in 1778 (the full formal name was "The Articles of Confederation and Perpetual Union") to the preamble to the Constitution itself, which declares one of the purposes to be "to form a more perfect union." A union would be less than perfect if it lacked the vital element of perpetuity.

"The Union is perpetual"; "the Union is unbroken"; "the Union is older than the Constitution." The Declaration of Independence transformed the "United Colonies" into the United States, Lincoln held. Without this Union there would never have been any "free and independent states." President Lincoln would keep refining the statement of his thought and would say in his message to the first session of Congress in July: "The Union is older than any of the states, and, in fact, created them as states." It would be startling indeed to hear, one hundred and twenty years later, a new president of Lincoln's own party, in *his* inaugural address, declare, in direct although presumably unconscious contradiction to Abraham Lincoln: "All of us need to be reminded that the Federal Government did not create the States; the States created the Federal Government." Maybe in Ronald Reagan's view; not in Abraham Lincoln's.

Lincoln had written out his reasons why this Union is perpetual—from the nature of government everywhere and from the particular history of this nation; now he stated, in a ringing paragraph, the conclusion, applicable to the events that were taking place as he wrote: "It follows from these views that no state, upon its own motion, can lawfully get out of the Union—that *resolves* and *ordinances* to that effect are legally nothing and that acts of violence within any state or states [later, to make clear which acts of violence he had in mind, he would write in the phrase "against the authority of the United States"] are insurrectionary or treasonable...."

When South Carolina at the convention called by the state's legislature had met in Charleston and unanimously passed an ordinance severing the state's ties with the Union, and declaring South Carolina an independent republic, that ordinance, for all the fireworks, marching bands, flags, rallies, unanimity, and defiant speechmaking, was *legally nothing*.

When, after Christmas, Mississippi (on January 9), Florida (on January 11), Georgia (on January 19), Louisiana (on January 26), and Texas (on February 1) passed "ordinances" to the same effect, they too were legally nothing. When six of the seven states (Texas coming soon) that had acted in this way joined in Montgomery on February 4 to declare a new nation, the Confederate States of America, that entity did not, in the counterdeclaration of the president-elect of the United States of America, have any legal existence; it, too, was legally nothing.

And the acts of violence taken in the name of these legally nonexistent entities—against the installations and activities of the United States—the taking-over of forts, mints, and armories, the interference with the mail, the firing on the *Star of the West,* the threats to Forts Sumter and Pickins—this violence was ("according to circumstances," Lincoln would write) either *insurrectionary* or *treasonable*.

When the president-elect arrived in Washington in the middle of February, and showed the draft of his address to a few advisers, his secretary-of-state-to-be William Seward would propose a number of softening changes, including a couple of important changes of wording in this key paragraph. Change "nothing" to "void," making the characterization of all those ordinances and resolves now read "legally void." Lincoln accepted the change, which made a marked *rhetorical* difference—"nothing" may have a dismissive, perhaps even contemptuous, flavor that the lawyer's word "void" does not possess—though of course the meaning is the same. Seward also proposed to remove the word "treasonable" in the description of those acts of violence against the United States and to substitute a word much more acceptable to the American ear, "revolutionary." Lincoln accepted that change, too, so his description of those Confederate acts in the address as he delivered it on March 4, 1861, was that they were "insurrectionary or revolutionary, according to circumstances." Again, there was not, to Lincoln, any change in meaning, but there was a quite considerable change in rhetorical effect. Many secessionists did not at all mind being called, and indeed called themselves, "revolutionary."

Lincoln included in this draft a touch of his own philosophy of revolution: Yes, it could on rare occasions be a moral right—but only when exercised in a morally justifiable cause, which, he made plain, he did not believe the seceding states represented in the present case. "Revolution" in a cause *not* morally justifiable is "simply a wicked exercise of power."

Lincoln's argument led him to discuss, twice, in the later parts of his draft, the moral standing of majorities, and he stated it (we may say) about right. On the one hand, despite that very impressive deference throughout his political life to the "people" and public opinion, he does not regard the voice of the people as the voice of God, or the principle of majority rule as an absolute, either practically (that the majority should always rule in fact) or morally (that what a majority decides is necessarily morally right). He was aware that a majority has moral dignity only if assembled under conditions of freedom, with freedom to overturn it maintained. He used the phrase "the mere force of numbers," reflecting an awareness that a majority assembled and maintained under unfree conditions could lack moral standing, and represent oppressive, sheer power. "If, by the mere force of numbers," he wrote, "a majority should deprive a minority of any clearly written constitutional right, it might, in a moral point of view"—it is notable that this practical politician so often writes from a moral point of view—"justify revolution—certainly would, if such a right were a vital one."

But no such denial has occurred in the present case. What right, vital to republican government, has been denied to the citizens of the seceding states? Even their "rights" (not regarded as such by many) of holding slaves, and taking them into free states and territories as "property," have been conceded and protected; Lincoln had begun his address with that elaborate recognition of his obligation to enforce the Fugitive Slave provision, as much a part of the Constitution as every other provision, and he expressed his willingness to see a constitutional amendment making explicit the "rights" (not his quotation marks) of slaveholders in the slave states.

And which of the great rights of humankind, or of republican government, had been denied to the seceding population? They voted in the election just past. They retained the freedom to speak, argue, organize, and oppose this administration. And in four years there would be the opportunity to vote again, to oppose, and perhaps to overturn, this president. In a paragraph Lincoln cut out in his editing of the draft he wrote: "I do not deny the possibility that the people may err in an election"—thus, again, showing that he did not hold that the people, or majorities, can do no wrong—"but, if they do, the true cure is in the next election. . . ."

And then he made the argument—mildly amusing, perhaps, if the occasion were not so serious—that, after all, this government is so constrained, and four years is so short a time, that no president can do too much damage:

By the frame of government under which we live, [the people] have wisely given their public servants but little power for mischief; and have, with equal wisdom, provided for the return of that letter to their own hands at very short intervals.

Why should there not be a patient confidence in the ultimate justice of the people? [Notice that he said the ultimate justice.] Is there any better or equal hope, in the world?

So there was an incoming president making the peculiar plea: Don't worry. I won't be here long. I am so constrained, and the time is so short, that even my folly and wickedness cannot hurt the government too badly. (Stephens had said something like this in his speech against secession.)

But if Lincoln knew and specifically granted the limitations and constraints on majorities (and on majority-chosen short-term officeholders), he also knew and defended the necessity and the right of majorities, within those limitations and constraints, to rule.

He did not hold that any man more right than his neighbors is a Majority of One already—Thoreau's ringing phrase. Many of the intelligentsia and literati, and the reformers, contemplating the assertively common-mannish muddy-booted democracy of the Jacksonians, saw that they were on the wrong side on most of the reforms and deeply prejudiced over race. So they made disparaging remarks about this "people." Reading abolitionists, one can find much disengagement from the broad generality of the people, the majority. To quote Thoreau again: "When were the good and brave ever in the majority?" Or Wendell Phillips: "In God's world there are no majorities, no minorities; one, on God's side, is a majority."

Would it be unfair to observe that Phillips was quite sure he was that one? Like Thoreau in his similar claim, Phillips implied great assurance that he was himself unequivocally on God's side. Lincoln, on the other hand, in his references to God's role in this contest, usually did, in his manner of expressing the point, keep a certain distance between himself and his "side" and God and his righteousness and justice.

In the draft that he was writing in the dusty, dingy backroom in Springfield, he characteristically worked out a more complex relationship between God's righteousness, the contending sides in politics, and the ultimate judgment of the people. In an anticipation, in this draft for a first inaugural, of what he would four years later say in a second, he wrote: "In our present differences, is either party without faith ["in being" added later] in the right? If the Almighty ruler of Nations, with his eternal truth and justice, be on our side, or on yours, that truth will surely prevail, by the judgment of their great tribunal, the American people."

That's not quite the same as saying the voice of the people is the voice of God. But it is also certainly not saying, "When were the good and brave ever in the majority?" as Thoreau asked, disdainfully.

In January of 1861, though, Lincoln was arguing about majorities not with the moralistic abolitionists but with Southern secessionists. He was arguing about their practical role in republican government: that one must make a (perhaps temporary, perhaps provisional) acquiescence in the result of a popular vote for the government to work: "If the minority will not submit—" Seward would propose "acquiesce" for "submit," and Lincoln would accept the change—"If the minority will not acquiesce, the majority must, or the government will cease. There is no other alternative...."

Again: "Whoever rejects [a constitutional majority] does, of necessity, fly to anarchy or despotism. Unanimity is impossible; the rule of a minority, as a permanent arrangement, is wholly inadmissible, so that, rejecting the majority principle, anarchy or despotism is all that is left."

Lincoln as a thoroughgoing rhetor, a trial lawyer, and a reader of Euclid pushed the logic of the argument to the future life of a recalcitrant minority: "If a minority, in such a case, will secede rather than submit [make it "acquiesce"], they make a precedent which, in turn, will divide and ruin them; for a minority of their own number [strike "number"] will secede from them whenever a majority refuses to be controlled by such minority [strike "such minority" and substitute "them"]. For instance, why may not South Carolina, a year or two hence, arbitrarily, secede from a new Southern Confederacy just as she now claims to secede from the present Union?" Jefferson Davis and other Southern leaders would have experiences during the war to come that would bear out Lincoln's warning.

Seward's cautious editing would propose cutting "South Carolina" in the sentence quoted above and substituting "Alabama or Florida." Why keep picking on South Carolina? Lincoln, considering this, would drop all specific state names and substitute just "any portion of the new confederacy."

But those editorial wrinkles would come later. Writing away in Springfield in late January and early February, he followed his indication of the logical absurdity of a unilateral defection from the Union with realistic sentences about its practical menace as well. After asking why South Carolina, having seceded from the present Union, might not a year or two hence secede yet again from a Southern confederacy, he observed: "Her people, and all secession people, are now being educated to the precise temper of doing this." Lincoln throughout his career, as we have observed, had this powerful sense of a dynamic, opinion-changing public continually being educated and miseducated—misled, for example, by the deceptive notion of "popular sovereignty" presented by Senator Douglas, or now by the example of South Carolina's unilateral secession. That teaches us something: Ahha! We can, when we have a grievance, do the same.

"Is there such perfect identity of interests among the states to compose a Southern Union," he asked, "as to produce harmony only, and prevent a renewed secession?" He added a specific illustration that he would later strike out: "Will South Carolina be found lacking in either the restlessness or the ingenuity to pick a quarrel with Kentucky?" One is reminded again of James Madison's ruminations seventy-four years earlier, which also called up examples of potential, or in his case actual, conflicts of interest among states: "See the law of Virginia restricting foreign vessels to certain ports—of Maryland in favor of vessels belonging to her own citizens—of N. York in favor of the same."

The conclusion? One of Lincoln's strong sentences, which lasted through all the editing: "Plainly, the central idea of secession is the essence of anarchy."

The central idea of majority rule cannot be quite so simply stated. Lincoln first wrote: "A constitutional majority is the only true sovereign of a free people." Then (as a president chosen by a popular plurality only) he slightly improved his description of the majority by calling it "a constitutionally expressed majority." But then, in late February, Seward, who would cover six pages with suggested editorial changes, would draw back and rewrite this sentence with a fuller, more complex formulation: "A majority, held in restraint by constitutional checks and limitations, and always changing easily, with deliberate changes of popular opinions and sentiments, is the only true sovereign of a free people." Lincoln adopted that proposal as it stood, and it became his sentence, in the inaugural.

Having made the case for the integrity and perpetuity of the Union as a genuine government, he declared, borrowing constitutional language, his obligation and purpose: "The Union is unbroken; and, to the extent of my ability, I shall take care, as the Constitution itself expressly enjoins upon me, that the laws of the Union be faithfully executed in all the States." This last was a matter of important emphasis: It was his duty to take care that the laws be faithfully executed not in some but in *all* of the states.

He said this "not as menace" but as the "declared purpose" of the

Union. As he wrote the draft in Springfield, he continued: "All the power at my disposal will be used to reclaim the public property and places which have fallen"—the clause that on February 17 in the Willard Hotel his friend Senator Orville Browning would persuade Lincoln to strike out: no need to speak explicitly of "reclaiming." Nevertheless, "All the power at my disposal [!] will be used . . . to hold, occupy, and possess" government property, and to collect duties. "[B]ut beyond these [objects]," Lincoln at first wrote, in mild reassurance, "there will be no invasion of any State." When he edited his draft (obviously he was thinking out his position as he wrote and revised), he realized, apparently, that "invasion of any State" was the language being used by others, which did not accord strictly with his views, that the United States was one country and could not "invade" itself. But instead of striking the word "invasion," as perhaps he should have done, he struck the word "State" and left the politically charged word "invasion" (he was denying there would be any, after all); he then added the elaborating phrase "no use of force against any part of the country."

Lincoln finished his draft of the address, had twenty copies printed at the office of the *Illinois State Journal,* showed a copy to a few friends, and took the copies with him when, after making his famous farewell remarks to the citizens of Springfield, he left by train on February 11 with Robert, Tad, and Willie, and his trunks marked A. LINCOLN, THE WHITE HOUSE, WASHINGTON, D.C. (Mary, shopping in Saint Louis, would join them in Indianapolis.) Lincoln took with him also, we may infer, a head full of the arguments he had been writing about the Union and the states. Although his speeches and remarks along the way were for the most part guarded and noncontroversial, he did, in Indianapolis, reveal something of the thought more formally expressed in the draft, now set in type, of the inaugural address he had written and now carried with him. What he had been writing for the last month, and had now in print and formal language in his trunk, boiled up now in informal language to a cheering and laughing crowd.

I am not going to make any long speech, he said, but what do these constantly used words "coercion" and "invasion" mean? "[I]f the Government . . . simply insists on holding its own forts, or retaking those forts which belong to it [cheers] or the collection of duties . . . [renewed cheers] or even the withdrawal of the mails for those portions of the country where the mails themselves are habitually violated, would any or all of these things be coercion?" (At this stage he includes the retaking of forts already taken.)

About these secessionists' attitude toward the Union as a mere association, to be broken when they want to, he has now a colorful analogy: "In their view, the Union, as a family relation, would not be anything like a regular marriage at all, but only as a sort of free love arrangement [laughter] to be maintained on what that sect calls passionate attraction [continued laughter]."

Then he suddenly burst out with a question that stood in stark contrast to Alexander Stephens's piety toward Georgia: "What is the particular sacredness of a state?"

Lincoln did not mean to deny the "sacredness"—the word he had got started using—that is given to a state "in and by the Constitution of the United States," but he did question whether "a state can carry with it out of the Union that which it holds in sacredness by virtue of its connection with the Union." And he challenged the "assumed right of a state" to "rule all that is less than a state and ruin all that is bigger than itself [laughter]." He asked—twice he would say he was asking questions, posing issues, not deciding anything—why a *state* is any better than a *county*. Suppose a county were a state's equal in size and population—what is the difference, just a *name*? "Can a change of name [from "county" to "state"] change the right? By what principle of original right is it that one-fiftieth or one-nineteenth of a great nation, by calling themselves a State, have the right to break up and ruin that nation . . . ? Now—I ask the question—I am not deciding anything [laughter]."

From Indianapolis Lincoln, now accompanied by Mary as well as the boys, was carried by the Wabash Railroad to Cincinnati. His fifty-second birthday. Columbus: speech to the state legislature. Back in Washington that day the House counted the electoral votes and officially declared him president-elect. Pittsburgh. Back into Ohio to Cleveland. Mayors, governors, cheering crowds, short speeches, apologies for not making speeches. Westfield, New York: meeting the little girl who had proposed he grow a beard. Buffalo. Rochester, Syracuse. Utica. February 18: news that Jefferson Davis took his oath in Montgomery. Albany. Down the Hudson River to New York City. A procession. A silent crowd. Speech at City Hall. Wrong gloves at the opera. The New Jersey Assembly at Trenton. Philadelphia: the news about the threat in Baltimore. The arrangement for the secret trip through Baltimore: not, symbolically, a good way to enter the nation's capital. A considerable embarrassment, in fact: the new president sneaking, disguised, through Baltimore at night. The Willard Hotel. Finishing the selection of the cabinet, finishing the editing of the address, which, on March 4, he will deliver in front of the Capitol and take the oath as the sixteenth president of the unbroken and perpetual Union.

Abraham Lincoln, after his election in November of 1860, was a man about to undertake a most demanding duty, heavy with obligations, to which he would be committed by the most solemn oath.

Henry Villard, who saw Lincoln more than did other newsmen during the interregnum, wrote in his regular report "Springfield Correspondence" that "the most distinctive element in Mr. Lincoln's moral composition is his keen sense and comprehensive consciousness of duty. . . . That he will endeavor to fulfill the obligations [of his oath of office] faithfully and fearlessly may be expected with the utmost certainty." His solemn awareness of a duty (and also a right) extended to the government of which he was about to become the head; he wrote privately not only that the *government* had "the legal power, *right,* and *duty* of maintaining its own integrity" (my italics) but also that "it was the *duty of the president* to execute the laws and maintain the existing government" (my italics again). He wrote doubly interesting advice (which I italicize below) to the Republican governor-elect of Pennsylvania, Andrew Curtin, about what Curtin should say about union and secession in his own address: "I think you would do well to express, *without passion, threat, or appearance of boasting,* but nevertheless with firmness, the purpose of yourself, and your state, to maintain the Union *at all hazzards.*" It is significant that Lincoln would write "without passion, threat, or appearance of boasting," which advice would apply to himself and to his firmness on slavery extension as well as, now, on the maintenance of the Union. But even though there was to be no threat or boast (no swagger, let us say, no implied self-congratulation), the position objectively stated was to be defended with firmness, the Union maintained "at all hazzards."

Lincoln's friend Orville Browning heard him say, in Springfield, that the duty that was devolving upon him was "to maintain the Constitution and the Union," a purpose in which he was "firm and decided."

But there was more in this than ordinary everyday firmness: there was to be an *oath.* Lincoln had that oath in mind, and took it very seriously as the day of his inauguration approached. We know he did from much evidence. One striking instance came after he had reached Washington, in the remarks of his recorded by the secretary of the so-called old man's conference, chaired by ex-president John Tyler. This gathering had met in Washington since February to attempt to bring, or maintain, peace. The members of that conference, Northerners and Southerners, including Northern capitalists, many of whom had ties to the South, were much disturbed by the effects the sectional crisis was already having on business. The delegates to the conference paid a courtesy visit to the president-elect at the Willard Hotel a few days before the inauguration. One New York businessman implored Lincoln to prevent national bankruptcy and said that it was up to Lincoln to determine "whether grass shall grow in the streets of our commercial cities."

Lincoln's first, mollifying response was that "if it depends upon me, the grass will not grow anywhere except in the fields and meadows." But when the New York businessman pushed further, asking whether that reply meant that the new president would yield to the "just demands" of the South, Lincoln gave a quite different reply, beginning with a reference to the oath he would take, and quoting it ("preserve, protect, and defend the Constitution") in words I will reproduce in a moment, and then finished off the grass-growing issue as follows: "The Constitution will not be preserved and defended unless it is enforced and obeyed in every part of every one of the United States. It must be so respected, obeyed, enforced and defended, let grass grow where it may."

"Let grass grow where it may," "at all hazzards," "cost what it may," "though the heavens fall": not ignoring consequences, but *because* of the perceived consequences, refusing to yield.

This was not only a statement of end-of-the-line firmness; it would be an *oath*. Lincoln began his response to the pressing second question from the commercial New Yorker, before he came to the growing of the green grass, with an anticipation of the solemn promise he would, in a few days, make:

> If I shall ever come to the great office of President of the United States, I shall take an oath. I shall swear that I shall faithfully execute the office of President of the United States, of all the United States [he added significantly] and that I will, to the best of my ability, preserve, protect, and defend the Constitution of the United States. This is a great and solemn duty. With the support and the assistance of Almighty God I shall undertake to perform it.

Then followed the words already quoted, affirming that the Constitution would not be so protected and defended unless it was enforced and obeyed "in every part of every one" of the United States, and that it would be so enforced and obeyed, whatever happened to the grass.

The oath he would take, and the words of the oath, were evidently in his mind, and he had already made powerful reference to that oath in the inaugural address he had written in Springfield and was now showing to a select few in the nation's capital. In his original draft he *ended* with a rhetorically powerful reference to the oath—the oath he would take to pre-serve the Union. Seward suggested a softer, more conciliatory ending, and offered some phrases, which Lincoln then transformed. Editing in Wash-ington, Lincoln fashioned one of the loveliest passages in the corpus of American political speech, ending the address as it was given, and as it is printed in collections and as we know it: the appeal to "mystic chords of memory" and, at the very end, to "the better angels of our nature."

But before that graceful new conclusion there was a remnant of the end-ing that Lincoln had originally written, with its reference to the oath he would take. Here is the concluding paragraph of the address as Lincoln originally wrote it, with the important phrase and closing two sentences that would be omitted in the final address in brackets. The italics are Lin-coln's own, running the sharp contrast between *your* situation and *mine* down through the whole paragraph.

> In *your* hands, my dissatisfied countrymen, and not in *mine,* is the momentous issue of civil war. The government will not assail *you* [unless you *first* assail it]. You can have no conflict, without yourselves being the aggressors. *You* have no oath registered in Heaven to destroy the government, while I shall have the most solemn one to "preserve, protect, and defend it." [*You* can forbear the *assault* upon it; *I* can *not* shrink from the *defense* of it. With *you,* and not with *me,* is the solemn question of "Shall it be peace, or a sword?"]

That's it. That is where he, at first, proposed to end the address, the first words he would speak to the whole people as the man who would soon be their president. It would have sharply dramatized the con-trast between *your* situation (as "dissatisfied" countrymen) and *mine* (as a sworn, oath-bound, Union-defending public servant). In a moment our situations will be radically—morally—different. *I* will have sworn an oath—a "most solemn one," "registered in Heaven." You, on the other hand, will remain on the lower, more fungible plane of calculation, of less and more, better and worse, courses of action—you have no sworn oath registered in heaven. *You* can forbear the assault upon the government—Lincoln continued the sharp contrast of moral situations in sentences that would be stricken—while I "can *not* shrink" (I am morally bound, I have no choice) from the defense of it. So it is up to you. The ball is in your court. Only you have a choice; I am bound.

The beautiful, conciliatory new ending, appealing to common memories North and South, that the alchemy of Lincoln's rewriting fashioned out of Seward's pedestrian words, was surely a moral and political improvement, as well as a literary one, over Lincoln's original last paragraph. The ending as Lincoln had written it probably carried the sharp you/me contrast a step too far, a note too long, and, particularly coming at the very end of his very first speech, may in its repetition and its final question posed to *you* (not me) have tipped in the direction of prospective exculpation of himself, and blame of the other as the emerging emphasis: War is going to be *your* fault, not mine.

But Lincoln, at Seward's urging, fixed it. Cutting, at Seward's suggestion, "unless you first assail it" (which could be taken as an explicit threat), and the last sentences, with the ending question, began the change of tone. But then the new ending—we are not enemies but friends; passion must not break "our bonds of affection"; the beautiful, long last sentence—makes the final effect much different than it was, much more conciliatory.

But, still, what mellifluous sound is it that the "mystic chords of memory," which stretch this way and that across this broad land, will make when they are touched again by "the better angels of our nature"? Those vibrating mystic chords will "yet swell the chorus [not of secession but] of the *Union*"—my emphasis, but, in underlying meaning, Lincoln's also.

And the reference to his solemn oath to preserve, protect, and defend the government—and your *not* having any such oath to "destroy" it—is still there, as he delivered the address on March 4, 1861, though shortened and by its now penultimate placement slightly subordinated.

Lincoln's way of referring to this—shall we say—transcendent dimension of a sworn oath is, typically, indirect, a step away: the oath is "registered in Heaven."

Throughout the long and terrible war that followed, filling his whole presidency—far longer and more destructive than he, or anyone else, expected—he never wavered on these Union-affirming points: There is no legitimate "secession"; there is no legitimate independent nation called the

Confederate States of America. What happened after the firing on Fort Sumter was a *rebellion,* an *insurrection,* not an international war between two sovereign states. From the sheer size of the rebellion he had to modify that view in practice, to treat captured Southern soldiers as prisoners of war, not as criminals, and to impose a naval blockade on Southern ports, expecting other nations to abide by it, which on his theory that the Union was unbroken meant that the United States was blockading itself. But these were practical accommodations to the unique situations that did not cause him to modify his theory: the Union was unbroken. He did, indeed, do (in his view) what he said beforehand his duty would be: to hand on to his successor the unbroken Union. And so we today count the presidents from George Washington to the present incumbent, and Congresses from the first to the present Congress, and celebrate our nation's bicentennial and beyond, because the sixteenth president insisted that the Union was, and should remain, unbroken.

Lincoln finished his half-hour address on the portico of the Capitol in the early afternoon of March 4, 1861, with his appeal to the "mystic chords of memory" and "the better angels of our nature." He took the solemn oath, administered by the aged and stooped Chief Justice Roger Taney and "registered in Heaven," to the best of his ability to preserve, protect, and defend the Constitution of the United States. As president of the United States he had bid farewell to the departing president, Buchanan; with his wife, Mary, had seventeen guests at their first White House dinner; arrived at the inaugural ball at 11:00 p.m.; left at 1:00 a.m. He was later to recall that Joseph Holt, "the then faithful and vigilant Secretary of War" (left over, of course, from Buchanan's term), handed him a letter and documents from Major Robert Anderson at Fort Sumter, saying that their provisions would be exhausted before any expedition could be sent to their relief. Holt's accompanying letter carried an endorsement by General Winfield Scott saying that, because of the shortage of men, he saw "no alternative but surrender."

But the new president did not surrender.

APPENDIX 1

REFLECTIONS ON TWO WAR PRESIDENTS

The conspicuous differences between war president James K. Polk and, fourteen years later, war president Abraham Lincoln would epitomize the great moral distinction to which Lincoln would one day rise.

The two wars, and the situations more broadly, were no doubt vastly dissimilar. Polk's conflict was the first foreign war of a young, muscle-flexing nation against a feeble and aggravating neighbor, an external force, looked upon with disdain, with the vast prize of California and Pacific ports and huge additional territory dangling there as bait. Lincoln's war was the terrible scourge of an immense civil conflict, a rebellion, Americans fighting Americans, with the president necessarily aware that he would be reuniting with the people he was fighting. Nonetheless, at a quite general level, certain common questions arise: How do you portray the moral stance of the nation you are leading in battle? How do you vindicate the righteousness of your cause? How generous are you to the foe? How do you relate what your nation is doing to ultimate affirmations—to God and his purposes?

The Union side in the American Civil War, in the hands of another president, could in its different way have been at least as blatant an exercise in national self-righteousness as was Polk's Mexican War. (There have been Southerners, and perhaps still are a few, who argue that in fact it did become so—that the North by its victory for the Union and, eventually, over slavery stored up a Treasury of Self-Claimed Virtue upon which it would draw for decades. I would insist, however, that that was not true of President Lincoln himself.)

To be sure, no chief of state in wartime (nor in peacetime either, really) can disengage altogether from the collective egotism of the nation he leads. But he can qualify it, he can give it a sense of proportion, he can shape and direct it, and he can appeal to the better angels of his country's nature. (Or—when this day comes—*she* can do all these things.)

457

Both the glory and the peril of the nation of which Polk and Lincoln were president was its original moral self-definition. It thought of itself not simply as one nation among other nations but as a new kind of nation, sharply distinguished from and morally superior to the quarreling old monarchies and despotisms of Europe, with their power politics and hereditary rule and imperialisms. As President Polk declared in an annual message listened to by Congressman Lincoln:

> The success of our own admirable system is a conclusive refutation of the theories of those in other countries who maintain that a "favored few" are born to rule and that the mass of mankind [should] be governed by force.

This, said President Polk, is "the country whose dominion belongs alone to the people." And other presidents, including Lincoln, and American leaders in general would repeatedly say something like that. Would such claims state or imply that the United States was unique in its realization of that governmental ideal? And further, that the ideal ought to be applied in its American form everywhere? That because the original governmental form and social ideal were worthy, whatever the nation did would therefore be worthy too? Therein would lie the perils of national presumption. The American expansionism of the 1840s, carried out under the banner of "Manifest Destiny," exhibited these moral hazards to the full.

All moral ideals can turn from being critically applied to the self as well as others, to being applied defensively for the protection of the self, and aggressively for the elevation of the self, against and over others. No moral ideal, no matter what its content, is immune to this human inclination. One is almost tempted to say that more important than the content of a moral ideal is whether it is applied critically or defensively.

What I am talking about is more than the ubiquitous phenomenon of hypocrisy, that tribute that vice pays to virtue, that familiar distance between what is professed and what is actually done. I mean something further, that the moral ideal itself becomes a justification for, even an impetus to, unworthy deeds, including at the extreme its own Orwellian contradiction.

This human inclination to self-deception and self-exculpation, plain enough in the lives of individuals, is magnified in collective life—in the behavior, in particular, of nations. Every nation (including this new one, the United States of America) has a magnified ego and a minimized conscience. The national egotism is a compound of the egotism and the idealism of the individuals who compose it. The American had read in his penny press the story of the siege of the Alamo, in which, as he read it, a small brave band of 188 Texans, including Davy Crockett, was given no quarter by the 2,400 Mexicans who stormed the old monastery. Then they read about the still more blatant episode of Mexicans killing Texans at Goliad—and then about the splendid Texan victory at San Jacinto. The American press presented a story of a continuing, impertinent unwillingness on the part of successive Mexican governments to recognize the independence of Texas and its subsequent entrance into the Union; then in the years leading up to Polk, stories of Mexican failure to pay American claims; and in the Polk years the rejection of American minister John Slidell—among other irritations and outrages. The presentation of these matters in the penny press was not subtle or complex, let alone marked by self-criticism. Finally there came the climactic report of the killing of nineteen American soldiers under Colonel Thornton between the Nueces River and the Rio Grande, and the president's war message saying that war had come by action of Mexico.

Most of the country, including for the moment most of Polk's Whig opponents, rallied to the national cause as the president defined it. In this "rally around the flag" the egotism and the idealism of individual citizens would be inextricably combined. Supporting the nation in righteous battle is a giant extension of one's own ego, as are—to use a much lower-level analogy—the cheering and booing of fans at a football game, chanting "We're number one," booing referees, exulting in touchdowns and victories, cast down by intercepted passes and defeats, all of it happening to a kind of expanded self. So it is, vastly multiplied and more compelling, in national life, and particularly in war. The Mexican War furnished unusually quick gratification to American self-esteem, with General Taylor's forces winning two thrilling victories on the Rio Grande at Palo Alto and Resaca de la Palma before the first month was over. Although it was then a long time before further victories, and the war would last (as wars tend to do) much longer than Americans had expected, and the public support would diminish (as the public support for long wars tends to do), the long twenty months would be punctuated by an unbroken sequence of American victories that intermittently renewed national enthusiasm.

But along with the accumulation of individual egotisms into a giant national cheering section, there was also the contribution to the national egotism of the idealism of individual citizens—volunteering, risking their lives, dying. The idealism of individuals, selflessly serving the nation, becomes then a reinforcement to the egotism of the nation. We have noted that among Lincoln's associates, Hardin would be killed at Buena Vista and Edward Baker and James Shields would be wounded in battle. John S. D. Eisenhower notes that the Mexican War "had the highest death rate of any war in our history," 13,768 men dying out of 104,556 who served.*

Behind the mixture of idealism and egotism in the war itself there was the same compound in the 1840s American enthusiasm for expansion of the nation's territory. The phrase "Manifest Destiny" was coined, or at least given popular currency, in 1845, the first year of Polk's presidency, by an editor on the magazine

---

* John S. D. Eisenhower, *So Far from God: The U.S. War with Mexico 1846–1848*. (New York: Random House, 1989), p. xviii. The deaths from disease far outnumbered those from gunfire.

of Polk's party named John L. O'Sullivan. In the mixture of reasons for American expansionism—the popular hunger for land, the desire of commercial interests for a Pacific harbor, the fear of European powers who might seek to control parts of the continent—the most distinctive were the moral and religious ingredients. The universalism of the creed in which the new nation had been born not only could become an element in a nation's egotism, but itself could become a justification for it. Because the United States regarded itself as a bearer and a distinctive, even unique, embodiment of Liberty, popular government, and human rights, it could allow itself not to be unduly scrupulous about the rights of Indians, or of Mexicans, or of the residents of lands along the eastern bank of the Rio Grande who fled at the approach of the American army. (If their true allegiance was to Texas, and therefore the United States, Whig orators would ask, why did they flee from these their liberators?)

Not to mention African slaves. Liberty tended to come with a white face. One of the slogans justifying American expansion in these years was: Expand the Area of Freedom. But that slogan carried unintentional ironies with respect to the population of Mexico, and was paradoxical in the extreme with respect to slavery. Mexico had abolished slavery, on paper at least, in 1829; therefore when Texas, with many American slaveholding residents, declared its independence in 1836, and again when the United States annexed it as a slave state in 1845, what happened was that the area of *slavery* was expanded, under the aegis of the very nation that presented itself as, in Jefferson's fine phrase, the "Empire of Liberty" (a fine phrase, that is, if one does not explore it too closely).

These ironic controversions of national moral ideals were then given supernatural reinforcement. Already in the Puritan background there were ideas of a "special" Providence, and the idea that God had extended *particular* favors to the United States was by no means missing from the founding period. Now such ideas exploded, and the final critical edge they had had (that God *required* something difficult from a nation he favored) faded; almost all that remained was a heavenly endorsement of American national egotism. God had shown his intentions for his chosen people through Nature itself, by a kind of geographical fiat: He intended this nation to extend, not to the Appalachians merely, but to the great natural barrier (and essential commercial route), the Mississippi River. Obviously God meant for the United States to have Florida, as he made manifest by attaching Florida to the mainland. The vast reaches of the Louisiana Purchase came into our hands, clearly also by providential design, and now we discovered that Nature had plainly shown that our favored nation should extend not just to the Mississippi but all the way to that great natural frontier, the impenetrable barrier of the Rocky Mountains. But wait: there is the Puget Sound. Oregon. And San Francisco Bay. California! God and Nature, it now became apparent, did not intend for the nation to be bounded even by the Rockies, but rather to extend all the way to the Pacific Ocean, which now constituted the true and ultimate boundary marked out by God for his America. There were those at the height of expansionist fervor, and frustration with Mexico—including perhaps President Polk—who pictured "All Mexico" taken over by the United States. And some went on to include all of Central America, too, to the Isthmus of Panama. And there were those who hinted at our taking over Canada as well. A tidy all-continental package, God's manifest intention for his chosen people.

To this point, territorial contiguity was the major argument: God had made manifest America's destiny in that geographical way, and the oceans—"from sea to shining sea"—were the new defining boundaries. But then . . . there arose repeated American proposals to annex Cuba. Was there not some water separating Cuba from the U.S.? Well, yes, but not, after all, that much water. It was discovered that God and Nature intended Cuba to become a part of the United States because it was so *close* (a mere ninety miles from Florida, as was to be emphasized in a twentieth-century crisis). But then—to look ahead to another outbreak of expansionist fervor—when with victory in the Spanish-American War in 1898 there came the desire for the Philippines, separated from the U.S. by three thousand miles of ocean, surely, one would think, the argument from contiguity must now break down. But no. Albert Beveridge, the eventual Lincoln biographer who was then an expansionist senator from Indiana, had the answer: "Our navy will make them contiguous!"

Although the situation in the Civil War would be in many respects vastly different from Polk's war, it offered in full measure the temptation to bloated claims to be righteous warriors on the side of God. It is part of Lincoln's great moral distinction that he put that strong and understandable impulse into a larger context that admitted a substantial degree of national self-criticism.

Lincoln would certainly not neglect or disavow the large original claims about the moral role of this nation in world history. He would not avoid the problem of national presumption in the way Old World diplomatic wisdom might have recommended, by deflating those universalistic assertions back down to the boundaries of the national interest, and presenting this nation as just one more nation alongside other nations, representing no more than herself and doing no more and no less than defending her own national interest. On the contrary: President Lincoln would give incomparable expression to the new nation's affirmation of its historic and universal moral significance. This nation, "conceived" and "dedicated" by "our fathers," had at birth the universal values of Liberty and Equality, and was, in the war fought in Lincoln's time, determining whether "any nation so conceived and so dedicated" could long endure," or whether government of, by, and for the people would "perish from the earth." A skeptical Old World realist might ask: You mean the whole history of Liberty in the world turns on what happens in this one bumptious new country? If the Union should fail, Liberty will not endure on the whole planet? Democracy will perish from the earth?

Lincoln would even refer to the United States—in the last paragraph of his second annual message—as "the last, best hope of earth," a presumption that might easily have invited a snort from some grumpy anti-American abroad.

But I suggest, snorts or no, that President Lincoln's way of presenting America's role as the bearer of universal values would furnish something of a corrective to the unabashed national egotism of, for example, Manifest Destiny.

He would insist, with rare pertinacity, that the principle of universal human equality, enunciated in the Declaration of Independence, joined Liberty in the core ideals of this nation. That disallowed any claim of a racial or tribal basis for the institutions of the United States—not Anglo-Saxon or "Teutonic" or English-speaking, and certainly not "white." And it also disallowed, one would assume, disdainful stereotypes of "savage" and servile peoples. I have not emphasized as much as I might have how loaded with a sense of racial superiority were the justifications of Manifest Destiny and the Mexican War. Lincoln, with all the limitations of his background in a totally white and racially prejudiced environment (as Frederick Douglass noted, from a state with a black code), was a lifelong moral learner, and in the midst of the Civil War he rapidly expanded his own identification with black Americans, especially as they came to fight in the Union army. President Lincoln would, moreover—in line with what I have said above about the problem of moral ideals, particularly among nations—apply this high universal principle of Equality not simply in praise for this nation but also critically *against* this nation for falling short of it.

President Lincoln had far more justification than had President Polk for blaming the other side for starting the war. But once the war had begun, he did not deal in blame.

Lincoln in his First Inaugural would make a most powerful plea against what his "dissatisfied countrymen" were doing. He argued from political philosophy (the principle of secession is the essence of anarchy); and from history (the states did not antedate the Union but acquired their being only through the Union). He bent over backwards to give explicit reassurances to the South. At Seward's suggestion, he closed his Inaugural Address with a touching appeal to the shared experience of common memories as a people, North and South. And at the end of his draft in Springfield—the next-to-last paragraph as he would deliver it in Washington—he dramatized his own moral situation in contrast to theirs: You have no oath registered in heaven to destroy the Union, whereas I shall have taken the most solemn oath to protect and preserve it. He posed the issue in words that could not have been plainer: "In *your* hands, my dissatisfied countrymen, and not in mine, is the momentous issue of civil war. The government will not assail *you*. You can have no conflict, without being yourselves the aggressor."

And then, as his momentous first days as president unfolded, he carefully sent to the beleaguered American fort in Charleston harbor only supplies not arms, and he carefully notified the rebel governor of South Carolina that that was what he was doing—and the rebels nevertheless fired the first shot, captured the American fort, lowered the American flag, and raised their own flag.

Now imagine what President Polk would then have said, as the secessionists defied all his arguments, took over the arsenals and mints and forts and other installations, fired on and took over Fort Sumter, launched aggressive attacks on the nation's capital, and persisted in rebellion. Imagine what his themes would have been throughout the long war, what his attitude would have been toward leaders of the other side, what triumphalism he would have shown in the moment of victory.

But Lincoln—in stark contrast to what we may guess might have been—did not cast the war in absolutes, never referred again to his argument in the First Inaugural, except to say in his Second that he had on that "first appearing" described a course to be followed (a benign inaccuracy). Once the war had begun, he did not go back and underline the guilt of the rebels for beginning it. When the war was over, he would say that neither side had wanted war, which with reference to Southern fire-eaters would be perhaps another benign inaccuracy. And at its end, looking back, he would describe the war's beginning in an astonishingly impersonal and unblaming way: "And the war came."

He would resist the strong impulse to turn the battle against rebellion and slavery into a contest of moral absolutes and a holy war; He (God) may have loosed his fateful lightning and his terrible swift sword, and his truth might be marching on, but the notes the president would strike would not be exactly those of the "Battle Hymn of the Republic." *He* would not be trampling out the vineyard where the grapes of wrath are stored, or crushing any serpent with his heel. Even before becoming president, as he was giving voice with rare persistence to the moral case of the Republicans, Lincoln would say, at Cooper Union, let us do our duty *as we understand it,* and in his Second Inaugural he would say "with firmness in the right *as God gives us to see the right.*" Both sides, he would say, pray to the same God; he would remark that it may seem strange that one should dare to pray for a just God's assistance in wringing bread from the sweat of other men's faces—but then he would quickly add, let us judge not that we be not judged. He would show that one could be resolute, tenacious, persistent, undaunted, without being self-righteous, simplistic, or absolutist. And despite the appeals of many and the strong reasons for doing so, he would not claim the unambiguous endorsement of God; on the contrary, he would say, in the end: "the Almighty has His purposes."

Those phrases in which Abraham Lincoln might seem to be endorsing the national egotism are seen to be, when examined in context, doing something rather different. Although he would—once—use the phrase "chosen people" in reference to Americans, he would do so in a radically different way than Beveridge and many others. The occasion was his appearance before the New Jersey Senate in Trenton on February 21, 1861, while on his way to Washington. He spoke spontaneously, as he did not like to do; he recalled his youthful reading of Parson Weems's *Life of Washington,* and his youthful belief that there was an "original idea" beyond national independence, and he said that he himself would be most happy indeed if he could be "the humble instrument in the hands of the Almighty and of this, his *almost* chosen people." The context, and his addition of the modifier *"almost,"* changes the phrase fundamentally.

I have already mentioned the snort-worthy and apparently extravagant phrase describing the United States as "the last, best hope of earth." In one of the final writings of the great American religious-political thinker Reinhold Niebuhr, he lined up before his rhetorical firing squad statements by American presidents that would seem to be thanking God that we are not as other nations, and included this phrase of Lincoln's, declaring that Lincoln was thereby "repeat[ing] the obtuseness of our founding fathers to the continued growth of free societies in Western Europe, in the form of parliamentary democracy under the aegis of constitutional monarchy." One might argue, on Lincoln's behalf and against Niebuhr, about what the European situation really was, with respect to democracy in 1862, but leaving that aside, let us look at the allegedly objectionable phrase in context. It appears in the remarkable ending to Lincoln's second annual message to Congress in December 1862, in between the preliminary and the final Emancipation Proclamation, in which annual message he would argue for his plan for gradual emancipation. The whole passage in which the phrase occurs, the graceful three-paragraph ending of this message, is a sober appeal to change our thinking and ourselves and to alter our national condition—to "disenthrall" ourselves, to put aside the "dogmas of the quiet past" because they are "inadequate to the stormy present"; to "rise with the occasion" because "our case is new." This appeal to think and to change is addressed, in a most direct, grave, and portentous manner, to his fellow national leaders who, with him, cannot escape history, who, with him, must pass through this fiery trial, and who, with him, will be remembered in spite of themselves. "We know how to save the Union," Lincoln said, and the world knows we know. We have—Lincoln interjected for emphasis, "even we *here*" have—the power and the responsibility. It is then that the phrase "the last best hope of earth" occurs, as the profound description of that which *we here now* may by our actions "nobly save, or meanly lose." The context for the phrase, in short, is Lincoln's appeal, and his warning, to the American leaders of the day not so to act as to "meanly lose" this precious human hope entrusted to them.

And *how* might the leaders of the day nobly save, instead of meanly losing, this best hope for the world? By a radical change in the nation's current institutions. By giving freedom to the slave, which will also assure freedom to the free, "noble alike in what we give and what we save"—noble, that is, *if* we do it, something as yet not done.

The phrase has the effect, in context, not of encouraging an egotistical national complacency or sense of superiority, but of adding weight and sober meaning to the serious choice American leaders had then to make.

APPENDIX 2

THE ELECTION OF 1860 "THROWN INTO THE HOUSE"

John Breckinridge, the candidate of the slave-state rebellion within the Democratic Party, could not win the election of 1860, because even if he had won all fifteen slave states—which he did not do, losing four border states—he would have had only 120 electoral votes, 32 votes short of the 152 needed for a majority of the total of 303 electoral votes. It is quite unlikely that Breckinridge would win any free state, and in fact he finished well behind both Lincoln and Douglas in every free state except sparsely populated, three-vote Oregon, whose popular senator Joseph Lane was Breckinridge's running mate. Breckinridge was not, however, completely wiped out in the North, as was Lincoln in the South; he was vice president and the candidate of the sitting president, after all, and of his administration minions, and Breckinridge had pockets of support in the Northern states. (It is a little startling to realize that Edwin M. Stanton voted for Breckinridge.) But still—he was not going to carry any Northern state.

How could Douglas have won? He was not going to carry any state of New England or of the upper North, or any Deep South state against Breckinridge. He did carry one slave state—Missouri, which was the only state to have something like a four-party contest, the Republicans doing well among Germans in St. Louis.

The results of the pivotal 1860 election were foreshadowed in the changing populations, and hence changing electoral votes, of the North and the South. Northerners, particularly opponents of slavery, including Abraham Lincoln, had for years complained about the unfair advantage the Constitution's three-fifths clause gave the South not only in the House but also—because House numbers were used to make the count—in the Electoral College. The usual estimate in the decades before the war was that that clause gave the South an "extra" twenty seats—hence, twenty electoral votes. The Adamses, father and son, believed they would have won reelection in, respectively, 1800 and 1828 had it not been for that boost to the slave states. Up to 1860, the United States had elected slaveholders as president in thirteen of the eighteen presidential elections, and Democrats acceptable to the South in three others; if Van Buren as Jackson's protégé be put in the latter category, then only the two Adamses were nonslaveholders not supported by the South, and John Quincy was not chosen by the electoral college but by the House.

But immigration and migration were changing the shape of the nation's population, and hence House delegations and electoral votes. As noted in the text, in 1860 free states had 183 electoral votes, the slave states 120.

When it was apparent that Lincoln was headed for victory in the free states, the other three parties mounted a desperate effort at a fusion in New York State, which was one state with enough electoral votes—thirty-five—that if they were subtracted, Lincoln would be left short of an electoral college majority, and the choice would have been, as the phrase has it, "thrown into the House"; the creaking constitutional machinery would have been called into play for only the third time in American history.

And what might have happened then?

Two important points about the election being thrown into the House.

First, during the framing of the Constitution, Roger Sherman of Connecticut and other small-state delegates shrewdly arranged that in the election in the House the vote should be by *states*—one state, one vote: New York, one vote: Rhode Island, one vote. The brand-new states of Oregon and Florida, and the old state of Delaware, with only one representative, cast as many votes as New York, with thirty-three representatives, and Pennsylvania, with twenty-five. Under these conditions, that one representative suddenly becomes a very important fellow, as was demonstrated in 1825.

Does that not nevertheless mean that Lincoln, having won seventeen and a half of the states, would therefore receive their votes and a bare majority in the House? Not necessarily. The key is not the election result but the composition of the House delegations. The Republicans did have a majority in fifteen state delegations, but they would have needed two more to make the majority of seventeen. On the last occasion in American history on which such a vote actually took place, the election of John Quincy Adams in 1825, there was pressure, surprise, allegedly a corrupt bargain—and a winner who had not been either the popular or the electoral leader.

How would this have played out in the circumstances of 1861? Could Oregon and California, Democratic states with considerable Buchanan support, conceivably have cast their votes for Breckinridge?

The second key fact—sometimes overlooked—is that the Twelfth Amendment, redoing the original constitutional arrangement after the awkward tie between Jefferson and Burr in 1800, provided that the choice be made from the top *three* finishers in the Electoral College—which would have meant that Douglas would have been eliminated (Lincoln, 180; Breckinridge, 72; Bell, 39; Douglas, 12). That presumably would have meant that Lincoln would have received at least the votes of the 18 free states, and won. On the other hand, it would have been necessary only to deny Lincoln the votes of two free states to have blocked him, and if Breckinridge had received the votes of the four slave states he lost—the three Bell states plus Missouri, which Douglas took—he would have had seventeen, and won. Seventeen states would have constituted the majority of the thirty-three states.

If the House had voted and voted and not managed a majority by the beginning of the term, March 4, 1861, the new vice president would have become president. But who in this situation would have been the new vice president? The Twelfth Amendment provides that this choice, in the absence of an electoral college majority, is made by the *Senate,* from the top two candidates—who would have been Hamlin on the Republican ticket and Lane on the Breckinridge Democratic ticket. The Democrats had control of the Senate—so, presumably, Joseph Lane could have been chosen president in 1861. This possibility was mentioned during the campaign.

But the American machinery, on this occasion, provided a better result.

NOTES AND SOURCES

It is not the purpose of this book to try to add to the vast storehouse of factual information about Abraham Lincoln but rather to make an interpretation. The most important source, therefore, has been Lincoln's own writing, in his speeches, letters, and other papers. I have tried to make this an encounter with Lincoln himself, although I have relied on many scholars. I have in fact taken his words, usually, from Roy P. Basler and others' edition of *The Collected Works of Abraham Lincoln* (eight volumes, plus index; New Brunswick: Rutgers University Press, 1953), and everything quoted from Lincoln in this book can be found there. I have, however, almost always included in the text itself the date of the speech, letter, or other production, which not only allows consultation in any of the other collections of his work, but also gives a little piece of added information instead of sprinkling the pages with initials, volume numbers, and page numbers. There are endnotes to quotations from Lincoln only when the date is not included in the text. I have sometimes, in fact, taken Lincoln quotations from the Library of America two-volume set, edited by Don Fehrenbacher, *Abraham Lincoln: Speeches and Writings 1832–58* and *Abraham Lincoln: Speeches and Writings 1859–65*, as well as from the one-volume version (New York: Vintage, 1965). Almost all of the items in those volumes are taken from Basler; none of the handful of exceptions figures in this book. In only one case, in chapter 13, is there any significance to the source of Lincoln's words, and that has to do with the editor's heading.

The next-most-important source has been the enormously valuable gathering-together by Douglas L. Wilson and Rodney O. Davis of the materials that Lincoln's partner and biographer, William Herndon, collected after his death from persons who knew him: *Herndon's Informants: Letters, Interviews, and Statements About Abraham Lincoln* (Urbana and Chicago: University of Illinois

Press, 1998), hereafter referred to as *HI*. My debt to this enormously important resource will be evident. The thorough index is in itself a major contribution.

The question arises, for a project like this one, what sources to use from the truly immense library of books about him. Of course one must select carefully. I have relied, more than the text or the notes indicate, on David Herbert Donald's most recent one-volume biography, *Lincoln* (New York: Simon & Schuster, 1995), usually taking it as the norm for contemporary Lincoln scholarship. I have found Mark E. Neely Jr.'s *The Last Best Hope of Earth: Abraham Lincoln and the Promise of America* (Cambridge: Harvard University Press, 1993—hereafter referred to as *LBH*), with its great virtues of selectivity and compression, particularly useful. I have also taken much from an older biography of Lincoln, Albert J. Beveridge's four-volume *Abraham Lincoln* (Boston: Houghton Mifflin, 1928). Beveridge reached only 1858, but covers in satisfying detail most of the territory of this book. For my purpose it was useful to read and to draw from the grand old multivolume biography by Lincoln's secretaries, John G. Nicolay and John Hay, *Abraham Lincoln: A History* (New York: The Century Co., 1917), hereafter referred to as Nicolay and Hay, and also sometimes from Herndon himself (with Jesse W. Weik): *Life of Lincoln* (New York: Da Capo Press, 1983). I made some use of other recent biographies—Thomas's and Oates's—and of some from an older time, Tarbell's in particular and Barton's and Arnold's and Holland's, all cited below. The first book I ever read about Lincoln was not Sandberg's but Lord Charnwood's, cited below, in a now ancient paperback that fell apart during this project.

I want to single out two books from the recent scholarship that have been particularly important to this undertaking: Don E. Fehrenbacher's *Prelude to Greatness: Lincoln in the 1850s* (Stanford: Stanford University Press, 1962) and Douglas L. Wilson's *Honor's Voice: The Transformation of Abraham Lincoln* (New York: Alfred A. Knopf, 1998), hereafter referred to as *HV*.

PREFACE

PAGE

xii **"Here is one of the few speeches ever delivered by a great man at the crisis of his fate"**: Godfrey R. B. Charnwood, *Abraham Lincoln* (New York: Henry Holt, 1917), p. 438.

xiv **"It is a matter of historical record"**: Benjamin Quarles, *Lincoln and the Negro* (New York: Da Capo, 1990; originally New York: Oxford University Press, 1962), foreword.

CHAPTER ONE

3 **"The Great Methodist . . . was equally astonished"**: Nicolay and Hay, vol. 1, pp. 101–102. This happening led a modern scholar, Robert Bray, to see the analogy of Jesus with the elders ("The Power to Hurt," pp. 40, 45). And I

too hear a voice saying: "They were astonished, for he spoke as one with authority."

4 **"Abe was a long tall raw boned boy"**: All quotations about Lincoln's appearance are from *HI:* p. 201 (Robert Wilson); p. 113 (Nathaniel Grigsby); p. 170 (Abner Y. Ellis); p. 254 (Coleman Smoot); p. 728 (Jonathan Birch).

6 **"He often . . . commented or talked to me"**: This and preceding quotations on Lincoln's intellectual abilities are from *HI,* pp. 94, 112 (Nathaniel Grigsby); p. 121 (David Turnham); p. 132 (Anna Gentry).

7 **"talked too much with his mouth"**: Nicolay and Hay, vol. 1, p. 79. Richard Luthin (*The Real Abraham Lincoln,* p. 24) informs us that Denton Offutt, perhaps still talking too much with his mouth, allowed his store, with Lincoln as clerk, to fail while he pursued another of his projects—importing Tennessee seed corn. Offutt the talker then passed off the stage of the Lincoln story, not to be heard from again until his former clerk was president-elect of the United States, at which point Offutt wrote to him asking for a job—which President-elect Lincoln did not grant.

7 **"He was a very tall, gawky"**: Nicolay and Hay, vol. 1, p. 108. I guess we have to define "gawky" as looking like young Lincoln.

8 **"He was, on the stump"**: *HI,* pp. 204–205 (Robert L. Wilson).

10 **"When Lincoln rose to speak"**: All of the quotations about the Cooper Union speech come from Nicolay and Hay, vol. 2, p. 224, except for the quotation from the member of the audience, which appears in the introduction to this speech in Abraham Lincoln Online, <http://showcase.netins.net/web/creative/lincoln/speeches/cooper.htm>, downloaded March 15, 2001.

10 **"Why, sir, they told me he was a rough diamond"**: Ida Tarbell, *The Life of Abraham Lincoln* (two volumes; New York: McClure, Philips, 1895), vol. 1, p. 360. (Hereafter cited as Tarbell.)

11 **"I went directly from the depot"**: A. K. McClure, *Abraham Lincoln and Men of War Times* (Lincoln, NE: University of Nebraska Press, 1996), pp. 48–49 (originally Philadelphia: Times Publishing, 1892).

12 **"He was arrayed"**: *Illinois Journal,* October 9, 1879, quoting the *St. Louis Republican.* From *Lincoln Lore,* March 3, 1930.

12 **". . . as I heard his closing paragraph"**: *Boston Evening Transcript,* February 26, 1897. From *Lincoln Lore,* March 3, 1930.

12 **"He is the best of us"**: John M. Taylor, *William Henry Seward: Lincoln's Right Hand* (New York: Harper Collins, 1991), p. 181.

12 **"no one but Abraham Lincoln could have made that address"**: Taylor, *William Henry Seward,* p. 224.

13 **"I once remarked to him that his mind"**: *HI,* p. 498 (Joshua Speed). In six pages of concluding analysis of Lincoln's mental qualities, the colorful and volatile Herndon wrote about his rather different partner, among other things, that "Mr. Lincoln's perceptions were slow, cold, clear, and exact. Everything came to him in its precise shape and color . . . He saw all

things through a perfect mental lens. There was not diffraction or refraction there . . . He threw his whole mental light around the object, and, after a time, substance and quality stood apart, form and color took their appropriate places, and all was clear and exact in his mind . . ." (Herndon and Weik, *Life of Lincoln,* pp. 475–476).

14 **"Mr. Douglass, I do not think the charge":** Christopher N. Breiseth, "Lincoln and Frederick Douglass: Another Debate," in Thomas F. Schwartz, ed., *For a Great Future Also: Essays from the Journal of the Abraham Lincoln Association* (New York: Fordham University Press, 1999), p. 75 (hereafter *GFA*).

15 **"His peculiar distinction does not consist":** Herbert Croly, *The Promise of American Life* (New York: E. P. Dutton, 1963), p. 94 (originally New York: Macmillan, 1909).

16 **"The amorphous and coarse-meshed Sandburg":** Wilson, *Patriotic Gore,* p. 117.

19 *Lincoln on the Coming of the Caterpillar Tractor:* David Herbert Donald, *Lincoln Rediscovered* (New York: Vintage, 1961), p. 3. All of the other titles of the various Lincoln books come from Jay Monaghan, ed., *Lincoln Bibliography 1839–1939,* 2 vols. (Springfield: Illinois State Historical Library, 1943).

CHAPTER TWO

26 **"Like most Pioneers [Thomas Lincoln] delighted":** *HI,* p. 27 (Dennis Hanks).

27 **"Kelso loved Shakespear and fishing":** *HV,* p. 72, quoting Thomas Reep and Caleb Carman. "Strangely enough Abraham did not care for fishing or hunting," Beveridge wrote: vol. 1, p. 69.

27 a youthful sermon defending the right-to-life of ants: *HI,* p. 109 (Matilda Johnston Moore). His stepsister said of his youthful pretend sermons on the stump: "Abe preached against Cruelty to animals, Contending that an ants life was to it, as sweet as ours to us."

28 two little birds the wind had blown from their nest: This came about when he was an adult, a lawyer, traveling with a pack of lawyers. According to Joshua Speed (*HI,* p. 590), Lincoln turned back on the road so he could restore them to their nest. "He finally found the nest, and placed the birds, to use his own words, 'in the home provided for them by their mother.'" Significantly, when he rejoined the traveling lawyers they laughed at him, but he responded, earnestly, "I could not have slept tonight if I had not given those two little birds to their mother."

28 a little squealing pig who was being eaten by its mother: According to J. D. Wickizer (*HI,* p. 423), a colleague on the Eighth Judicial Circuit—this, too, is from Lincoln as an adult—"Mr Lincoln and myself were traveling by buggy

from Woodford Co. court to Bloomington Ills.—and in passing through a little grove, we suddenly heard this terrific squealing of a little pig near by us. Quick as thought Mr L. leaped out of the buggy, seized a club, and pounced upon an old sow, and beat her lustily, that was in the act of eating one of her young ones and thus he saved the pig and then remarked 'By jings! the unnatural old brute shall not devour her own progeny.' "

28 "crossing a prairie one day": *HI*, p. 262 (Mary Owens Vineyard).

28 hot coals on the backs of turtles: Nathaniel Grigsby (*HI*, p. 128) reported that while attending Andrew Crawford's school in Indiana "we were in the habit of catching Turrains—a Kind of turtle and put fire on their back and Lincoln would Chide us—tell us it was wrong—would write against it." Grigsby also remembered, in the same interview, a scene in which Lincoln got up in the dark of night to attend to a mewing kitty.

28 Louis Warren found decorative mantels: Warren, *Lincoln's Youth: Indiana Years, Seven to Twenty-One, 1816–1830* (Chicago: Donnelly, 1959), pp. 139–141. Nathaniel Grigsby said that "he sometime worked at the cabinet business his father being a carpenter and cabinet maker" (*HI*, p. 94).

30 "I suppose it is not expected of me": From earlier in this address: "I presume I am not expected to employ the time assigned me, in the mere flattery of the farmers, as a class. My opinion of them is that, in proportion to numbers, they are neither better nor worse than other people. In the nature of things they are more numerous than any other class; and I believe there really are more attempts at flattering them than any other; the reason of which I cannot perceive, unless it be that they can cast more votes than any other. On reflection, I am not quite sure that there is not cause of suspicion against you, in selecting me, in some sort a politician, and in no sort a farmer, to address you."

30 "Lincoln fought his entire political life": *LBH*, p. 10.

31 "was lazy—a very lazy man": This and the following quotations on Lincoln's work habits are from Beveridge, vol. 1, p. 68, citing interviews in the Weik MS.

31 "Attaining manhood entailed more": *HV*, p. 295.

31 bet five dollars that Lincoln could defeat Armstrong: This according to one version of the fight. Chapter 1 of *HV* presents a full discussion of the sources of information about this fight.

32 All of the quoted incidents about Lincoln's fighting come from *HI*, p. 450 (Russell Godbey); p. 440 (Isaac Cogdal); pp. 7, 92 (J. Rowan Herndon).

32 "No difference if grain was scarce or dear": notes in Beveridge, vol. 1, p. 51.

32 "I never knew him to drink": *HI*, p. 15 (Henry McHenry); "He never drank whiskey or other strong drink": *HI*, p. 108 (Sarah Bush Lincoln); "He never drank liquor of any kind": *HI*, p. 90 (N. W. Branson).

32 "One could with safety wager any sum": Dr. William Jayne, in typed, undated manuscript in the Illinois Historical Society.

33 **"Never used Bad Langag"**: And also that "he Nor seldom if ever Drank any sperits": *HI*, p. 7 (J. Rowan Herndon).

33 **"During all this time—during all these years"**: *HI*, p. 15 (Henry McHenry).

33 All of the quoted incidents about gambling come from *HI*, p. 15 (Henry McHenry); p. 73 (James Short); p. 142 (William Greene); p. 374 (Caleb Carman).

34 **"[William Pitt] Fessenden, enraged over an issue of patronage"**: William J. Wolf, *Lincoln's Religion* (Philadelphia: Pilgrim's Press, 1970), pp. 138–139. There is another version of this story featuring a coachman as the initial swearer.

35 **"the only other passenger in the stage"**: Don E. Fehrenbacher and Virginia Fehrenbacher, eds., in *Recollected Words of Abraham Lincoln* (Stanford: Stanford University Press, 1996), p. 139, attribute a version to Edward Dicey, an English journalist, and note variants told by Herndon and two others. Another version is to be discovered in an article by William E. Barton in the *Dearborn Independent,* November 27, 1926, in the files at the Illinois Historical Society.

37 **"If any man thinks I am a coward"**: William Dean Howells told this story about the old Indian in his campaign biography of Lincoln, which Lincoln read and corrected—and let the story stand. The chief further source in *HI* is William G. Greene, Lincoln's helper in Denton Offutt's store and a fellow volunteer in the militia (pp. 19, 390), with further details from Royal Clary (pp. 372–373).

38 **"all the Lincolns continued to be Democrats"**: Beveridge, vol. 1, pp. 96, 99. Beveridge gives as his evidence the interview that Jesse Weik, William Herndon's associate, had with Dennis Hanks in Charleston. Nathaniel Grigsby, regarded by some as a more reliable witness than Hanks, told Weik that "we were all Jackson boys and men at that time in Indiana." Douglas Wilson, close student of the Herndon interviews, observes that if Thomas Lincoln had been a Whig back in those Indiana years, he would have stood out among his associates, and some of the interviewees from Pigeon Creek would surely have noted that distinguishing fact. It is possible that Thomas became a Whig later, in Illinois.

40 On Billy the Barber: Quarles, *Lincoln and the Negro,* pp. 28, 211; John E. Washington, *They Knew Lincoln* (New York: E.P. Dutton & Co., Inc., 1942), part 4 passim.

41 **"I was never more quickly or more completely put at ease"**: Henry Louis Gates Jr., ed. *Frederick Douglass: Autobiographies* (New York: Library of America, 1994), p. 785; Richard Current, *The Lincoln Nobody Knows* (New York: McGraw-Hill, 1958), p. 235.

47 The 1820 census for Spencer County: Earl Schenck Miers, ed., *Lincoln Day by Day* (Dayton: Morningside, 1991), p. 8.

47 **"Farming, grubbing, hoeing, making fences"**: All of the quoted incidents

about Lincoln's labors come from *HI,* p. 94 (Nathaniel Grigsby); pp. 129–130 (Green Taylor); p. 335 (Elizabeth Crawford).

48 **"I found him ... cocked on a haystack":** With the exception of the haystack from Lord Charnwood, all of Lincoln's reading postures quoted here come from *HI,* p. 430 (Caleb Carman); pp. 407, 512 (Harriet Chapman); p. 142 (William Greene); p. 41 (Dennis Hanks).

50 **"Lincoln's knowledge of the Bible far exceeded":** Wolf, *Lincoln's Religion,* p. 39. This book was first called *An Almost Chosen People,* and then *The Religion of Abraham Lincoln.* It is now on its third title.

50 William Scott's *Lessons in Elocution:* subtitled *A Selection of Pieces in Prose and Verse for the Improvement of Youth in Reading and Speaking* (Ezra Collier, 1825; stereotype by T. H. Carter and Co., Plymouth, MA).

51 **"the Declaration, the Constitution":** Beveridge, vol. 1, p. 74. Beveridge in his text and accompanying notes deals thoroughly with young Lincoln's reading.

52 **"In Washington Mr. Lincoln had been a puzzle":** Douglas L. Wilson, *Lincoln Before Washington: New Perspectives on the Illinois Years* (Chicago: University of Illinois Press, 1997), p. 4. Notice that it is said that Congressman Lincoln did not "bet."

53 **"He studied first Kirkhams Grammar":** *HI,* p. 426 (Robert R. Rutledge).

CHAPTER THREE

54 **"in the midst of the most unpromising circumstances":** Nicolay and Hay, p. 25.

57 Lincoln wrote three autobiographical statements. The first was just six lines for a dictionary of Congress, given the date June [15?] 1858 by Basler. Then there were two lengthier sketches: a summary for Jesse Fell, December 20, 1859, from which this quotation comes; and a longer statement written for John Locke Scripps and other editors, circa June 1860.

58 All quotations about Nancy Hanks, and about Lincoln's intelligence and character, are from *HI.* Those who knew Nancy Lincoln and were interviewed by Lincoln's law partner William Herndon after her death said that she was "of good intelligence" (Dennis Hanks, p. 598); "shrewd" (John Hanks, p. 615); "beyond all doubt an intellectual woman" (John Hanks again, p. 454); one with "Remarkable Keen perseption" (Dennis Hanks again, p. 149); "a lady of intiligence" (Nathaniel Grigsby, p. 94); one who "had a clear intiletual mind" (Hanks once more, p. 5), "a woman known for the Extraordinary Strength of her mind ... a brilliant woman—a woman of great good sense" (Grigsby again, p. 113) and, significantly, "superior to her husband in Every way" (Grigsby once more, p. 113).

58 **"No one in all the vast Lincoln literature":** *LBH,* p. 5.

60 Beveridge's disparagement of Thomas Lincoln (in chapters 1 and 2 of vol-

ume 1) includes the following: "pallid mind"; held in "low esteem" by his brother; "felt no . . . impulse for intellectual improvement"; "the peak of his sluggish energy"; "so ended Thomas Lincoln's only period of sustained and constructive effort"; "perhaps the intellectual foment . . . bewildered him"; "winning a livelihood with the least possible effort"; "reluctant shoulders"; "even Thomas Lincoln could stand it no longer." Beveridge presents Thomas Lincoln as not having sense enough to locate his Indiana cabin near water.

61 "Lincoln did not immediately answer two letters": John Y. Simon, "House Divided: Lincoln and His Father," lecture delivered May 21, 1987 (Fort Wayne: Louis Warren Lincoln Library and Museum, 1987), p. 15.

62 "I can say what scarcely one woman": *HI*, p. 107 (Sarah Bush Johnston Lincoln).

63 "his power of analysis": William H. Herndon and Jesse W. Weik, *Life of Lincoln*, pp. 2–3.

64 "Bill, if that is what they call a science": *HV*, p. 67.

64 "[Lincoln's] intellectual self-confidence was galling": John Hay, letter to Herndon, September 5, 1866, in Michael Burlingame, ed., *At Lincoln's Side: John Hay's Civil War Correspondence and Selected Writings* (Carbondale, IL: Southern Illinois University Press, 2000), p. 110.

66 "Out of [the] local Indiana context": Robert Bray, "The Power to Hurt," in the *Journal of the Abraham Lincoln Association*, vol. 16, no. 1 (Winter 1995). Bray here assembles examples of Lincoln's "satire and invective." He examines these youthful and not-so-youthful woundings as a phase in Lincoln's *literary* development. But surely they are at least as pertinent to his *moral* development. See also Michael Burlingame, *The Inner World of Lincoln* (Urbana and Chicago: University of Illinois Press, 1994), chapter 7, "Lincoln's Anger and Cruelty." Comments on "The Chronicles of Reuben" come from David Herbert Donald's *Lincoln*, p. 35; Herndon and Weik, *Life of Lincoln*, p. 48; Reinhard H. Luthin, *The Real Abraham Lincoln* (Englewood Cliffs, NJ: Prentice-Hall, 1960), p. 14.

69 "to connect his name with the events transpiring": *HI*, p. 197 (Joshua Speed).

70 Edgar Lee Masters . . . creating his Spoon River characters: from *Spoon River Anthology* (Urbana: University of Illinois Press, 1992), "John Hancock Otis," p. 205:

> As to democracy, fellow citizens,
> Are you not prepared to admit
> That I, who inherited the riches and was to the manor born,
> Was second to none in Spoon River
> In my devotion to the cause of Liberty?
> While my contemporary, Anthony Findlay,

Born in a shanty and beginning life
As a water carrier to the section hands . . .
Was a veritable slave driver,
Grinding the faces of labor,
And I say to you, Spoon River,
And to you, O republic,
Beware of the man who rises to power
From one suspender.

CHAPTER FOUR

71 **"square built"** . . . **"the genial Captain"**: descriptions of Thomas and Abraham Lincoln's physical strength from *HI*, p. 28 (Dennis Hanks); p. 96 (A. H. Chapman); p. 454 (John Hanks); also Beveridge, vol. 1, pp. 122, 363.

72 **"Thomas Lincoln the father of Abraham"**: testimony to Thomas Lincoln's and Abraham Lincoln's storytelling from *HI*, pp. 37, 105 (Dennis Hanks); p. 91 (N. W. Branson); p. 114 (Nathaniel Grigsby). As to "at no man's expense," see also p. 180 (Joseph Gillespie); p. 500 (Abner Y. Ellis); p. 539 (Jason Duncan).

72 **"It cannot be too often stated"**: Beveridge, vol. 1, p. 67.

73 **"When he first came among us his wit"**: *HI*, p. 432 (James Matheny); p. 541 (Jason Duncan).

73 **"His world-wide reputation for telling anecdotes"**: *HI*, p. 499 (Joshua Speed).

74 **"many were the laconic remarks"**: *HI*, p. 541 (Jason Duncan).

74 **"Salem in those days was a hard place"**: *HI*, p. 170 (Abner Y. Ellis).

74 **"All the men in the Company"**: this and following testimonials in *HI*, p. 15 (Henry McHenry); p. 12 (William Greene); p. 353 (Benjamin Irwin).

76 **"not very fond of girls"**: Comments on Lincoln's relations with women from *HI*, p. 108 (Sarah Bush Lincoln); p. 105 (Dennis Hanks); p. 131 (Anna Gentry); p. 15 (Henry McHenry); p. 142 (William Greene); p. 91 (N.W. Branson); p. 350 (David Davis); p. 455 (John Hanks).

76 **"making the best of circumstances"**: John Y. Simon, "House Divided: Lincoln and His Father," p. 9.

77 **"Lincoln had terribly strong passions for women"**: Quoted in Richard Current, *The Lincoln Nobody Knows*, p. 32. Douglas Wilson gives some credence to a report from the ubiquitous Herndon, indignantly rejected by other scholars, that Lincoln was afraid he had contracted syphilis in a "connection" in Beardstown in 1836–37. Herndon is also the source of a tale—not, I think, believed by anybody—that Current calls "more comic than pornographic" and Charles Strozier labels "preposterous." Strozier tells this tale (which Herndon reported to Weitz in a letter in 1889 as coming from Joshua Speed) which has Lincoln "undressed and in bed with the woman before he

asks how much she charged. On learning the fee was five dollars, whereas he had only three, Lincoln got up and dressed but offered her the three dollars for her trouble. 'Mr. Lincoln,' she replied, 'you are the most conscientious man I ever saw.'" Strozier's comment is perfect: "Somehow one senses a Lincoln joke that got lost in translation" (Strozier, *Lincoln's Quest for Union,* p. 48).

79 **"If your own endeavors are deficient"**: This and the following quotations from Lincoln's readings are from Scott's *Lessons in Elocution,* pp. 53, 52, 73, 84.

80 **"A careful examination of the books"**: quoted in Wilson, *Patriotic Gore,* pp. 120–121.

82 **"Let us not only declare by words"**: quoted in Beveridge, vol. 1, p. 74.

85 **this poem of Burns's "was Lincoln's religion"**: *HV,* p. 75.

87 **"Though Lincoln was increasingly unwilling"**: *HV,* p. 80.

CHAPTER FIVE

David Herbert Donald's essay "A. Lincoln, Politician," in his *Lincoln Reconsidered* (New York: Vintage, 1956), argued with detailed evidence that Lincoln as president was not successful in "selling himself" to the press, to his fellow politicians, or to the broad public, but that he was nevertheless a successful "politician" because he was "an astute and dextrous operator of the political machine" (p. 65). Although by "politician" we often mean just that, in these pages we mean considerably more than that. Lincoln joined in the organized contest for governmental power, with the object not only of achieving eminence himself but of realizing large social purposes—of having an effect on the polity.

93 **"adjustable buoyant chambers"**: Donald, *Lincoln,* p. 156.

97 **She too could count and calculate votes**: Jean Baker, *Mary Todd Lincoln: A Biography* (New York: W. W. Norton, 1987), p. 149.

99 **the younger Lincoln's use of his "power to hurt"**: Bray, "The Power to Hurt," passim.

99 **"Suborning votes by private detectives"**: *LBH,* p. 5.

100 **"every man who is eligible for the office of president"**: *LBH,* pp. 20–21.

100 **"should any longer be against conventions"**: Paul Simon, *Lincoln's Preparation for Greatness: The Illinois Legislative Years* (Norman, OK: University of Oklahoma Press, 1965), p. 275.

101 **"Lincoln initiated the most sweeping removal"**: Mark E. Neely Jr., *The Abraham Lincoln Encyclopedia* (New York: Da Capo, 1982), p. 234.

101 **"political merry-go-round"**: All the quotations in this paragraph come from Randall, *Lincoln the President,* vol. 1, p. 15.

102 **"Though it cramped his soul to operate"**: The quotations in this paragraph come from Randall, vol. 1, pp. 29–30.

103 **"Lincoln was using the word 'politician'"**: Randall, vol. 1, p. 25.

107 There was a fear on the part of the dominant Democrats: *HV,* p. 148.

111 **"not an alliance of convenience"**: *LBH,* p. 10.

112 See generally Daniel Walker Howe, *The Political Culture of the American Whigs* (Chicago: University of Chicago Press, 1979). Of added interest is Howe's more recent article "Was Abraham Lincoln a Whig?" in the *Journal of the Abraham Lincoln Association,* vol. 16, no. 1.

CHAPTER SIX

116 Vandalia: The story of the vote in the Illinois General Assembly on January 20, 1837, is taken from *House Journal of the Illinois Legislature,* 11th Session, 1836–37, pp. 134; 241–243; 309–311. On the morning at the time of the vote there were eighty-three present and voting. The Tenth General Assembly of Illinois (1836–38) had, formally, ninety-one representatives, as would the Eleventh and Twelfth. The Ninth, the first of which Lincoln was a member, had had only fifty-five representatives. (See Charles Thompson, *The Illinois Whigs Before 1846* [published under the auspices of the Graduate School of the University of Illinois, 1915], p. 132.) The story of Lincoln's service in the Illinois legislature is fully told in Paul Simon, *Lincoln's Preparation for Greatness: The Illinois Legislative Years* (Norman, OK: University of Oklahoma Press, 1965). Chapter 6 tells of several encounters by the young Lincoln with the issue of slavery, including the vote on the resolution reported here, and the Lincoln/Stone protest.

118 I have taken many of the identifications of legislators from Senator Simon's book. For biographical information on Dan Stone, see John Carroll Power, *History of the Early Settlers of Sangamon County, Illinois* (Springfield: Edwin A. Wilson & Co., 1876), p. 690.

123 So what is the difference from what the assembly said?: The *House Journal,* after reproducing the entire joint committee report, does not carry the resolutions in their final form as revised by the McClernand house committee, and they cannot be found in the Illinois archives. But on the basis of the rather minimal floor action that is reported in the *Journal,* one can conclude that the final form could not have differed much from the form first proposed by the Ralston joint committee. And so we use that for comparison. *House Journal of the Illinois Legislature,* 11th Session, 1836–37, pp. 309–311.

124 **"The only real difference between his [Lincoln's] views"**: Beveridge, vol. 1, p. 195.

125 **"as to Abolitionists, no member disapproved"**: Beveridge, vol. 1, p. 195.

127 the timing of the Lincoln/Stone "protest": David Herbert Donald suggests that the initiative *may* have had a link to the fight over the location of the capital, with Usher Linder and other opponents of Springfield pushing the resolutions to expose Sangamon/Springfield as less sympathetic to the slave

states' complaints than Alton or Vandalia, and thus damage Springfield's chances. If Donald's speculation is correct and that was indeed the strategy, it had at best only limited success: Three of the Long Nine voted no, but four voted aye. (Donald, *Lincoln,* pp. 63–64. For Douglas Wilson's view, see *HV,* pp. 164–167.)

130 An older lyceum sometimes heard nonpolitical addresses: Thomas Schwartz, *Illinois Historical Journal,* spring 1990. Schwartz also indicates that this was a *repeat* session on Lincoln's topic of the day; it had been discussed also in November of 1836: apparently "the signs of the present time," in 1835–38, provoked worries about the downfall of government, the perpetuation of institutions.

131 What Lincoln did or did not do about the Lovejoy killing: See Simon, *Lincoln's Preparation for Greatness,* pp. 129–137.

132 **"died as the fool dieth":** Beveridge, vol. 1, p. 225.

140 **"that Lincoln has projected himself into the role":** Edmund Wilson, *Patriotic Gore,* p. 108. Harry Jaffa, *The Crisis of the House Divided: An Interpretation of the Issues in the Lincoln-Douglas Debates* (Chicago: University of Chicago Press, 1982), pp. 214–221 (originally Garden City, NY: Doubleday, 1969).

141 **an embarrassingly grandiloquent reference to George Washington:** The ending of the Lyceum Address, even in the garbled form that has come down to us, leaves no doubt that Lincoln was extolling Washington: "[T]hat we revered his name to the last; that, during his long sleep, we permitted no hostile foot to pass over or desecrate his resting place shall be that which to learn the last trump shall awaken our WASHINGTON."

141 **"Lincoln's exaggerated style, in the most rhetorical parts":** Jaffa, *The Crisis of the House Divided,* p. 250.

144 **"Bishop Simpson quoted Lincoln accurately":** G. S. Boritt, *Lincoln and the Economics of the American Dream,* p. vii.

145 **"in the unlikely context of defending the national bank":** Donald, *Lincoln,* p. 83.

146 **"there is a quality of deep feeling":** Carl Becker, *The Declaration of Independence* (New York: Vintage, 1970; originally 1922), pp. 215–216.

147 He mentioned the subject to Herndon only once: The scene: the last meeting between the partners in the law firm of Lincoln and Herndon before the former leaves for Washington to become president. Near sunset. Reminiscences. Sentimental reassurance that the firm will stay open, will resume after the presidential interlude.

"Billy, there is one thing I have, for some time, wanted you to tell me, but I reckon I ought to apologize for my nerve and curiosity in asking it even now."

"What is it?"

"I want you to tell me how many times you have been drunk."

Jesse Weik, Herndon's collaborator, reports Herndon as saying that he answered this rather blunt inquiry as promptly and as definitely as he could, preparing himself for the "lecture or moral admonition: that would follow." But none *did* follow. Lincoln relieved the tension by telling Herndon of efforts to induce him to drop Herndon and take other partners (whom he named), but that he believed in Herndon and would not desert him. Other than that one reference, said Herndon, Lincoln never joined in the "popular denunciation" of his drinking. (Herndon and Weik, *Life of Lincoln*, pp. 391–393.)

(This incident comes not exactly from Herndon himself but initially from Weik. Herndon did not include this story in the original edition of his own biography, but told it to Weik during their collaboration, and confirmed it to Weik when they later worked on Weik's Lincoln book, and later editions of *Herndon's* book picked it up from there.)

153 "the society was composed mainly of the roughs": Herndon and Weik, *Life of Lincoln,* pp. 206–207.

154 "If there are any Whigs in Tazwell [County]" and "Do not suppose, Esq.": both from AL correspondence, February 14, 1843, to Alden Hull.

155 "I wish you as a personal friend of mine": to Richard Thomas, February 14, 1843.

155 "With all these things Baker, of course": Lincoln's discussion of his loss to Baker is in a letter to Martin S. Morris, March 26, 1843.

156 "a fellow who is made a groomsman": to Speed, March 24, 1843.

156 "bound not to hinder [Baker]": to Morris, March 26, 1843.

156 "Surely Baker would not do the like": to Morris, April 14, 1843.

156 "that he would rather Cut his arm off": *HI*, pp. 472–473 (George U. Miles).

157 Hardin had been one of those who intervened: Donald, *Lincoln*, pp. 90–93.

158 "Let nothing be said against Hardin": to Benjamin James, December 6, 1845.

158 "That Hardin is talented, energetic": to Robert Boal, January 7, 1846.

159 "I am sorry to hear that any of the whigs": to John Bennet, March 7, 1843.

161 "few congressional districts in the republic": Issac N. Arnold, *The Life of Abraham Lincoln* (Lincoln, NE: University of Nebraska Press, 1994), pp. 72–73 (originally Chicago: A. C. McClurg and Co., 1884).

CHAPTER SEVEN

164 For more on popular reactions to the Mexican War, see Robert W. Johanssen, *To the Halls of the Montezumas: The Mexican War and American Imagination* (New York: Oxford University Press, 1985). On opposition to it, see John H. Schroeder, *Mr. Polk's War: American Opposition and Dissent, 1846–1848* (Madison: University of Wisconsin Press, 1973).

164 Polk's address quoted in this chapter is his Third Annual Message, Wash-

ington, December 7, 1847, as cited in *Messages and Papers of the Presidents: James K. Polk* (Washington, DC: Government Printing Office, 1903).

165 "I expected to be greatly embarrassed and to have my voice tremble": cited in W. L. Miller, *Arguing About Slavery* (New York: Alfred A. Knopf, 1996, p. 338).

165 "As you are all so anxious for me to distinguish myself": to Herndon, December 13, 1847.

168 On Polk not mentioning Lincoln, see Allan Nevins, ed., *Polk: The Diary of a President 1845–49* (New York: Capricorn Books, 1968).

168 "There is no doubt now": Glenn W. Price, *Origins of the War with Mexico: The Polk-Stockton Intrigue* (Austin: University of Texas Press, 1967), p. 158. Price's position has not been held, at least in its stark form, by many other American historians who dealt with the Mexican War, since Justin H. Smith, in *The War with Mexico* (New York: Macmillan, 1919), at the time of the First World War, took a more favorable view of the American role in the Mexican War than had been usual before him. As to *Mexican* scholars' views on the Mexican-American War, on the other hand, see the remarks by Don Fehrenbacher, *Lincoln in Text and Context,* chapter 1, "The War with Mexico."

171 "Literal-minded and unimaginative, he had so little feeling": Charles Sellars, *James K. Polk: Continentalist* (Princeton: Princeton University Press, 1966), p. 214. See Paul Bergeron, *The Presidency of James K. Polk* (Lawrence: University Press of Kansas, 1987).

173 "Without conscientious principle": Donald W. Riddle, *Congressman Abraham Lincoln* (Urbana: University of Illinois Press, 1957), p. 69.

173 "It must be repeated that if Lincoln had based": Riddle, *Congressman Abraham Lincoln,* p. 55.

174 "under the influence of the Eastern . . . national scope . . . lost contact with the situation in Illinois": Riddle, *Congressman Abraham Lincoln,* p. 53.

177 Lincoln did not commit political suicide: For the argument against the political-suicide view I am drawing on G. S. Boritt, "Lincoln's Opposition to the Mexican War," in the *Journal of the Illinois State Historical Society,* vol. 67, no. 1 (February 1974), pp. 79–100; Mark Neely Jr., "Lincoln and the Mexican War: An Argument by Analogy," in *Civil War History,* vol. 24, no. 1 (March 1978); and on Neely again in his *Abraham Lincoln Encyclopedia,* pp. 209–210.

177 "Whig newspapers defended him": Neely, "Lincoln and the Mexican War," p. 7.

178 "was a notoriously poor campaigner": Neely, "Lincoln and the Mexican War," p. 7.

179 "If Lincoln had opposed the administration's war policy": Riddle, *Congressman Abraham Lincoln,* p. 41.

179 "This work has asserted that Lincoln, in his Spot Resolutions": Riddle, *Congressman Abraham Lincoln,* p. 59.

180 **"nor should a just estimate scorn"**: Riddle, *Congressman Abraham Lincoln,* p. 57.

182 **"[I]n the 1840s . . . [Lincoln] was as thoroughly principled"**: Paul Findley, *Abraham Lincoln: The Crucible of Congress* (New York: Crown Publishers, Inc., 1979), p. 158. I assume he means the 1850s—after 1854—as well as the presidential years.

182 **"economics took a back seat"**: Boritt, *Lincoln and the Economics of the American Dream,* p. 100.

184 The treaty of peace was signed in Mexico: David Potter, *The Impending Crisis 1848–1861,* completed and edited by Don E. Fehrenbacher (New York: Harper and Row, 1976), chapter 1 passim. When the treaty with Mexico was finally signed, the United States gained an enormous spread of 619,000 square miles, an area bigger than the territory of the original thirteen colonies, and almost as large as the Louisiana Purchase. When his four years in the president's office were completed, James K. Polk would have added to the United States the huge state of Texas, including the disputed area between the Nueces and the Rio Grande rivers; the American piece of "Oregon," which included today's states of Oregon and Washington; the territory that is now the states of California, Nevada, and Utah, most of New Mexico and Arizona, and parts of what have become Wyoming and Colorado. If the test of presidential greatness should be sheer *acreage,* then James K. Polk would rank very high indeed.

CHAPTER EIGHT

195 The citations of Max Weber throughout this chapter are taken from his essay "Politics as a Vocation," in H. H. Gerth and C. Wright Mills, eds., *From Max Weber: Essays in Sociology* (New York: Oxford University Press, 1958), pp. 77–156; the section dealing with ethics and politics begins on page 117.

200 **"Mr. Clay's chance for an election"**: to Archibald Williams, April 30, 1848.

202 This was the period of the greatest prominence: Michael Holt, *The Political Culture of the 1850s* (New York: John Wiley and Sons, 1978), chapter 5 and passim.

204 **"I hear the old saw"** . . . **"Fail! Did the martyrs fail"**: Sumner's speech in Worcester is quoted from *Charles Sumner: His Complete Works,* 15 vols. (Boston: Lee and Shepard, 1870–1883), vol. 2, pp. 233–235.

213 The discussion of Lincoln's cooperation with Giddings draws on Paul H. Verduin, "Partners for Emancipation: New Light on Lincoln, Joshua Giddings, and the Push to End Slavery in the District of Columbia, 1848–49," an article in preparation generously made available by Mr. Verduin.

215 **"strange fortune"**; **"The same hatred of slavery"**: Nicolay and Hay, vol. 1, p. 288.

216 **"Not one man recommended by me"**: to George W. Rives, May 7, 1849.

218 **"the very worst that can be said"**: Beveridge, vol. 2, p. 491 (footnote).

CHAPTER NINE

231 "Tremendous in length, vigor, and ill-temper": Allan Nevins, *Ordeal of the Union* (New York: Charles Scribner's Sons, 1947), vol. 2, p. 143.

231 "The reports of his speech which will reach you": *New York Tribune,* March 7, 1854. The *Tribune* on that day carried two reports of that remarkable night in the Senate, Friday–Saturday, March 3–4. The one headed "A Night in the Senate" was written in the first person by "W." and included a number of remarks on the vulgarity of Douglas's presentation; it closed with the observation, "I believe such a scene as was enacted in the Senate last night is almost unprecedented, and every person who has the least respect for his country will pray that such scenes may never occur again." A longer report, by "K.," included further colorful deploring of Douglas's "torrents of vehement vituperation," and praise for Sumner, Seward, Chase, Fessenden, and others for maintaining dignity under Douglas's assault.

233 "mousing about the libraries in the State House": Nicolay and Hay, vol. 1, p. 376.

233 "nosing for weeks in the State Library": Donald, *Lincoln,* p. 173, quoting George Fort Milton quoting the *Illinois State Register.*

241 "the storm of agitation ... dwarfed": Nicolay and Hay, vol. 1, p. 350.

241 "a struggle of unprecedented intensity": David M. Potter, *The Impending Crisis,* completed and edited by Don E. Fehrenbacher (New York: Harper, 1976). So it is held that no congressional battle matched this fight up into the 1970s. The last night's debate on the Nebraska bill in the Senate is printed as an appendix to the *Congressional Globe,* Thirty-third Congress, 1st session, pp. 323–342.

242 "Abolitionists . . . would allow territorial governments": *Congressional Globe,* Thirty-third Congress, 1st session, January 30, p. 280.

244 "Did you ever see a joke in one of my speeches?": David Herbert Donald, *Charles Sumner* (New York: Da Capo, 1996), p. 218.

244 The Sumner-Chase "Appeal of the Independent Democrats in Congress to The people of the United States: Shall Slavery be Permitted in Nebraska?" appears in *Congressional Globe,* Thirty-third Congress, 1st session, January 30, pp. 281–282.

247 The Democratic war hero Thomas Harris had defeated Stephen Logan in the election after Lincoln retired, but then Yates had defeated Harris in the following election, in 1852.

249 "[H]e had taken the measure of each": George Fort Milton, *The Eve of Conflict: Stephen A. Douglas and the Needless War* (Boston: Houghton Mifflin, 1934), p. 141.

249 "was doubtless the most formidable legislative pugilist": Allan Nevins, *Ordeal of the Union* (two volumes; New York: Charles Scribner's Sons, 1947), vol. 1, p. 142.

CHAPTER TEN

252 **"I do not propose to question"**: The quotations come from the printed version of the speech in Peoria, October 16, 1854, in the *Collected Works;* I am assuming, as I believe would be generally assumed, that the speech in Springfield, up to the break point, was virtually identical—written out, in fact.

252 **"Mr. Lincoln spoke of Judge Douglas"**: Miers, *Lincoln Day by Day,* p. 128.

CHAPTER ELEVEN

278 **"For the principle asserted is that superiority of condition"**: Francis Wayland, *The Elements of Moral Science* (Cambridge, MA: Belknap Press of Harvard University Press, 1963; originally 1837), p. 175.

278 **"Would the master be willing that another person"**: Wayland, *The Elements of Moral Science,* p. 192.

290 **"nowhere in these sentences does he reproach"**: Don E. Fehrenbacher, *Prelude to Greatness: Lincoln in the 1850s* (Stanford: Stanford University Press, 1962), p. 74.

296 On the Declaration, see Pauline Maier, *American Scripture: Making the Declaration of Independence* (New York: Alfred A. Knopf, 1997).

CHAPTER TWELVE

299 **"In this critical moment Lincoln exhibited"**: Nicolay and Hay, vol. 1, pp. 388–389.

299 **"It was a most magnanimous and generous act"**: Arnold, *The Life of Abraham Lincoln,* p. 123.

299 **"[B]y his quick wit and his devotion"**: Tarbell, vol. 1, p. 287.

299 The anti-Nebraska **"triumph"**: J. G. Holland, *Holland's Life of Abraham Lincoln* (Lincoln, NE: University of Nebraska Press, 1998; originally Springfield, MA: Gurdon Bill, 1866), p. 143.

299 **"The student of history in after years"**: Herndon, *Life of Lincoln,* p. 305.

302 **"Of course I prefer myself to all others"**: Lincoln to Henderson, December 15, 1854.

302 **"The man who thinks Lincoln calmly sat down"**: Herndon, *Life of Lincoln,* p. 304.

303 Lincoln bought some little notebooks: Baker, *Mary Todd Lincoln: A Biography,* p. 149.

305 **"dubious and open to challenge"**: Matthew Pinsker, "Senator Abraham Lincoln," in *Journal of the Abraham Lincoln Association,* vol. 14, no. 2 (1993), p. 5.

306 "was not forward in pressing his case": Pinsker, "Senator Abraham Lincoln," p. 11.

309 "the proceedings had wasted away a long afternoon": Nicolay and Hay, vol. 1, p. 389.

309 Trumbull . . . now had eighteen votes: One of those switching on the eighth ballot to Trumbull (in his case from Ogden, to whom he had switched from Lincoln four ballots back) was Owen Lovejoy.

310 "In view of his skill as a politician": Beveridge, vol. 1, p. 386.

311 "Amid an excitement that was becoming painful": Nicolay and Hay, vol. 1, pp. 389–90.

312 "she turned her head the other way": Concerning this and Mary Todd Lincoln's other grudges, see Baker, *Mary Todd Lincoln: A Biography*, pp. 149–151, 162.

313 "there was considerable bitterness displayed": *HI*, p. 344 (Joseph Gillespie).

313 "an uncharacteristic lack of generosity": Donald, *Lincoln*, p. 184.

313 "uncharacteristic malice": Pinsker, "Senator Abraham Lincoln," p. 17.

315 "We (his friends) regarded this as perhaps his last chance": *HI*, p. 182 (Joseph Gillespie).

316 "Mr. Lincoln was very much disappointed": *HI*, p. 538.

324 "in the actual construction of an effective organization"; "Never in his presidency did he surpass": Fehrenbacher, *Prelude to Greatness*, pp. 47, 161.

CHAPTER THIRTEEN

325 a certain edge where Douglas was concerned: Joseph Gillespie twice said Lincoln had no envy, and specifies Douglas as one he did not envy. *HI*, pp. 186, 507.

329 "Twenty two years ago Judge Douglas and I": The editors of the *Collected Works* guess the date of this item to be December 1856, because Lincoln says "twenty two years ago" and elsewhere says that he first met Douglas at the Illinois General Assembly in December 1834. But that may be too precise a calculation from Lincoln's two remarks. One would think Lincoln to have been more likely to write it in 1855, a down year in which he was defeated in his bid for the Senate and treated with contempt in Cincinnati by Stanton and others; in 1856, with his central role in forming the Illinois Republican Party, his 110 votes for the vice-presidential nomination, and his emerging role as the leading Republican in the state, his fortunes improved. But our secret personal emotions do not always correlate perfectly with objective conditions. We do not know exactly when he wrote it.

334 "[T]hough Lincoln did unquestionably labor": Fehrenbacher, *Prelude to Greatness*, pp. 118–120. Among the historians who seem to make the differ-

ence between Douglas and Lincoln less than it is are the eminent figures of Beveridge and J. G. Randall. George Fort Milton, in *The Eve of Conflict* (1934), seems to see a marked difference and to interpret it in Douglas's favor.

CHAPTER FOURTEEN

The greater depth of racial prejudice in the West, very much including Illinois, in the period of Lincoln's rise, is made quite clear indeed by the material in Eugene H. Berwanger's *The Frontier Against Slavery: Western Anti-Negro Prejudice and the Slavery Extension Controversy* (Urbana: University of Illinois Press, 1967) and in Leon F. Litwack's *North of Slavery: The Negro in the Free States, 1790–1860* (Chicago: University of Chicago Press, 1961).

The persistence of deep white prejudice in the war and after is shown in J. Jacques Voegli, *Free But Not Equal: The Midwest and the Negro During the Civil War* (Chicago: University of Chicago Press, 1967); and Forrest G. Wood, *Black Scare: The Racist Response to Emancipation and Reconstruction* (Berkeley: University of California, 1968). Chapter 4 of the latter book shows the origins of the word "miscegenation" in the work of Democratic Party operatives in 1864.

As to the Republican Party, James D. Bilotta, *Race and the Rise of the Republican Party, 1848–1865* (New York: Peter Lang Publishing, 1992), certainly does establish that there was "racism" in the Republican Party, and in the Free-Soil Party that fed into it. This book shows "racism" indeed—"scientific" theories promulgated by intellectuals, scientists, learned writers, that claimed that "race" was the determining essence of human beings.

340 the banner at Dallas City: Fehrenbacher, *Prelude to Greatness,* p. 103.
340 **"At times during the 1850s it seemed":** Foner, *Free Soil, Free Labor, Free Men,* p. 263. Chapter 8 of this book, "Republicans and Race," is still the best, most balanced summary and interpretation I have found.
342 I have taken the quotations from the debates from Paul Angle, ed., *Created Equal? The Complete Lincoln-Douglas Debates of 1858* (Chicago: University of Chicago Press, 1958).
343 **"[I]t was when they discussed fundamentals":** Fehrenbacher, *Prelude to Greatness,* p. 111.
346 **"undoubtedly the most severe anti-Negro measure":** Berwanger, *The Frontier Against Slavery,* p. 49.
347 **"seemed to go out of his way to express":** Potter, *The Impending Crisis,* p. 329.
350 **"This government was made for white men":** Angle, *Created Equal?,* p. 233.
358 **"The vulgarity of their [the Democrats'] tactics":** James M. McPherson, *Battle Cry of Freedom: The Civil War Era* (New York: Oxford University Press, 1988), p. 789.

361 "Many eastern Republicans": Foner, *Free Soil, Free Labor, Free Men*, pp. 294–295.

362 "slight pro-slavery proclivities": Neely, *Encyclopedia*, p. 292.

362 and said things that dismayed William Lloyd Garrison: Berwanger, *The Frontier Against Slavery*, p. 133.

363 "No individual did more": Berwanger, *The Frontier Against Slavery*, p. 133.

363 "The Illinois senators, Lyman Trumbull and Stephen A. Douglas": Berwanger, *The Frontier Against Slavery*, pp. 124–125.

363 "In the long-run conflict between deeply held convictions": Potter, *The Impending Crisis*, p. 354.

364 On the alleged "deep-seatedness" of Lincoln's racial views, Fehrenbacher, in "Only His Stepchildren," in *Lincoln in Text and Context*, p. 103, quotes two scholars: George Sinkler, *The Racial Attitudes of American Presidents from Abraham Lincoln to Theodore Roosevelt* (Garden City, NY: Doubleday, 1971), p. 75; and George Fredrickson, "A Man but Not a Brother: Abraham Lincoln and Racial Equality," *Journal of Southern History*, vol. 41 (1975). Neither of these scholars insists very strongly on the deep-seatedness. Sinkler writes, almost as a concession in passing, that "there is no reason to doubt that his racial beliefs were matters of deep conviction." I suggest that there *is* reason to doubt it. Fredrickson's excellent article, one of the leading essays on this topic, does accept, as scholars generally no longer do, the report of Benjamin Butler that Lincoln was still considering colonization in the last months of his life. He does show how much Lincoln owed to Henry Clay. He says in his concluding paragraph, "[T]he deeply rooted attitudes and ideas of a lifetime do not change easily." But again—*were* they deeply rooted?

369 A little exposure to quotations from fellow Republicans: See generally Bilotta, *Race and the Rise of the Republican Party, 1848–1865*.

372 On Lincoln's speeches in Ohio, Harry V. Jaffa and Robert W. Johannsen, eds., *In the Name of the People: Speeches and Writings of Lincoln and Douglas in the Ohio Campaign of 1859* (Columbus: Ohio State University Press, 1959).

CHAPTER FIFTEEN

376 On members of the Young Men's Central Republican Union, see Randall, vol. 1, p. 135.

376 "the audience . . . is not that of an ordinary political meeting": Nicolay and Hay, vol. 2, p. 217.

379 "No one who has not actually attempted": Preface to the pamphlet edition of Lincoln's speech by Charles C. Nott and Cephas Brainerd of the committee, quoted in Nicolay and Hay, vol. 2, p. 225. J. G. Holland reported: "Gentlemen who afterward engaged in preparing the speech for circulation

as a campaign document were much surprised by the amount of research that it required to be able to make the speech, and were very much wearied with the work of verifying its historical statements in detail. They were weeks in finding the works consulted by him." Holland, *Holland's Life of Abraham Lincoln,* p. 207.

380 "[T]hat we got no votes in your section": David Potter in *The Impending Crisis* distinguishes between a *sectionalized* party—which the Republicans certainly were—and a "sectional" party, which Lincoln and Republicans insisted they were not, for the reason Lincoln stated. They were concentrated in one section not from their own intent but by the decision of others, and by the process.

384 "No man ever before made such an impression": Nicolay and Hay, vol. 2, p. 224.

384 "we believe he would have held his audience": quoted in *CW,* vol. 3, p. 552.

385 "Connecticut was that year carried": Holland, *Holland's Life of Abraham Lincoln,* p. 213.

385 On the encounter with the Reverend Mr. Gulliver see Holland, *Holland's Life of Abraham Lincoln,* pp. 213–214.

387 "While I am speaking of Kansas": This speech was given in Kalamazoo, Michigan, on August 27, 1856.

397 "When he concluded, the audience sprang": *Illinois State Journal,* June 4; quoted in Miers, ed., *Lincoln Day by Day,* p. 170.

400 "Our delegation and all I met": *HI,* p. 677 (Edward L. Pierce).

401 Section 5, "Lincoln for President," draws upon William Baringer, *Lincoln's Rise to Power* (Boston: Little, Brown, 1937); Richard Luthin, *The First Lincoln Campaign* (Gloucester, MA: Peter Smith, 1964; originally Cambridge: Harvard University Press, 1944); Willard King, *Lincoln's Manager David Davis* (Cambridge: Harvard University Press, 1960).

404 "the Democrats divided were in some ways more formidable": Fehrenbacher, *Prelude to Greatness,* p. 160.

405 "Historians who lament": William E. Gienapp, "Who Voted for Lincoln?" in John L. Thomas, ed., *Abraham Lincoln and the American Political Tradition* (Amherst: University of Massachusetts Press, 1986), p. 92.

CHAPTER SIXTEEN

407 "He [Lincoln] was certainly a very poor hater": *HI,* p. 166 (Leonard Swett). On the matter of Lincoln combining charity with resolution, we might quote another paragraph, featuring in particular Lincoln's pardons of Union soldiers, from the same page:

He had very great kindness of heart. His mind was full of tender sensibilities; he was extremely humane, yet while these attributes were fully developed in his character and unless intercepted by his judgment controlled him, they never did control him contrary to his judgments. He would strain a point to be kind, but he never strained to breaking. Most of the men of much kindly feeling are controlled by this sentiment against their judgment, or rather that sentiment beclouds their Judgment. It was never so with him. He would be just as kind and generous as his judgment would let him be—no more. If he ever deviated from this rule, it was to save life. He would sometimes I think, do things he knew to be impolitic and wrong to save some poor fellow's neck. I remember one day being in his room when he was sitting at his table with a large pile of papers before him. After a pleasant talk, he turned quite abruptly and said, "Get out of the way, Swett; to morrow is butcher-day, and I must go through these papers and see if I cannot find some excuse to let these poor fellows off."

410 the renowned Reverdy Johnson: The time would come, on July 26, 1862, when the roles of the two lawyers would be radically reversed and the president of the United States would have occasion to write a letter responding to a complaint from Senator Johnson of Maryland about the complicated politics of Maryland in the early years of the Civil War. Lincoln's response to the complaining senator would be resolute, yet also patient and charitable: "I am a patient man—always willing to forgive on the Christian terms of repentance; and also to give ample *time* for repentance. Still I must save this government if possible. What I *cannot* do, of course I *will* not do; but it may as well be understood, once for all, that I shall not surrender this game leaving any available card unplayed."

410 A reader can get key points of the episode of the reaper case in the expertly compressed page-and-a-half in Donald's biography (pp. 185–187). There are only quick tastes of it in passing in Benjamin P. Thomas's *Abraham Lincoln: A Biography* (New York: Modern Library, 1968, pp. 158–159) and Stephen B. Oates's *With Malice Toward None: The Life of Abraham Lincoln* (New York: New American Library, 1977, p. 112). Reinhard Luthin's one-volume biography *The Real Abraham Lincoln* (1960) gives the story two and a half pages.

I have drawn primarily upon the account in Albert Beveridge's big old biography, whose multivolume spread gave him the space to give detail and the full effect (vol. 2, pp. 278–286). The way Beveridge got his material is a little complicated. He drew largely on a statement George Harding, the chief snubber of Lincoln, gave to a young lawyer named Robert H. Parkinson, who, having heard that Harding somehow helped make Lincoln president, seized the opportunity to ask him when Harding was in an unusually expressive mood after a successful law case in Nashville in 1876, and got the story. Parkinson wrote it out, whether right away or only when asked to do so by Beveridge many years later—1923—is not clear. Parkinson also got a statement from Ralph Emmerson (two *m*'s), an official of the Manny Company who was present at the trial. There is a copy of a typescript of Parkinson's account, headed "The Patent Case that Lifted Lincoln into a Presidential Candidate," in the Illinois Historical Society. Beveridge trusted the accuracy of this full, frank, self-critical account because of its self-criticism and detail and because it accorded with the reminiscence of others. I trust Beveridge trusting Harding, at least for the retelling of the story for our purposes here; I include some points from Harding's statement that Beveridge did not.

Ida Tarbell got another statement from Harding in the 1890s, by then the last survivor of the Reaper trial, and she got it directly from his own hand and printed it in her biography (vol. 1, pp. 260–264). This recollection by Harding differs somewhat from the one Beveridge uses; in his old age, Harding was clearly trying to counter the folklore that had grown around the case, picturing Stanton himself being the chief agent of Lincoln's dismissal. Harding explains in the Tarbell account that the Manny Company gave Peter H. Watson the overall management of their case, and that it was he who determined that Lincoln should be dismissed.

On the larger points, the sources agree: Lincoln was dismissed; there was a certain rudeness and brusqueness involved; Stanton took an important part in the rudeness.

Sources for the material about Stanton are Benjamin P. Thomas and Harold M. Hyman, *Stanton: The Life and Times of Lincoln's Secretary of War* (New York: Alfred A. Knopf, 1962); and Fletcher Pratt, *Stanton: Lincoln's Secretary of War* (New York: W. W. Norton, 1953).

The quotation about Lincoln and the college-trained lawyers comes from Emmerson, writing his recollections in 1909; he put it all in direct quotes, as from Lincoln. Don Fehrenbacher, and his wife, Virginia, in their authoritative collection and appraisal of such remembered words of Lincoln, give the credibility of this direct quotation a very low grade, a D.

426 **"and spent the first few minutes of his visits weeping":** the entry on Stanton in Neely's *Abraham Lincoln Encyclopedia,* p. 289.

426 **"Now he belongs to the ages":** Donald regarded the phrase to be authenticated sufficiently to use it as the ending of his biography. But he notes the variants: "He belongs to the ages now" and "He is a man for the ages" (Donald, *Lincoln,* p. 686).

CHAPTER SEVENTEEN

429 **"The country is certainly in great peril":** A facsimile of this letter of December 16, 1860, from Stephens to Lincoln (and of the two Lincoln letters) appears after page 150 in Henry Cleveland, *Alexander H. Stephens, In Public and Private* (Philadelphia: National Publishing, 1866).

429 On Lincoln's meeting and photographic gift to John A. Stephens, see Thomas E. Schott, *Alexander H. Stephens of Georgia: A Biography* (Baton Rouge: Louisiana State University Press, 1988), p. 447.

430 "[S]hall the people of the South secede": Cleveland, *Alexander H. Stephens,* p. 705.

431 "who very often make me say things": Cleveland, *Alexander H. Stephens,* p. 712.

431 That "disquietude" arose, instead, from the fact: Cleveland, *Alexander H. Stephens,* pp. 151–152.

432 "African slavery rests with us upon principles": Cleveland, *Alexander H. Stephens,* p. 647.

433 The Cornerstone Speech is given in full in Cleveland, *Alexander H. Stephens,* pp. 717–729; the quotation here is from p. 721. "Rapturous applause" on p. 720.

435 "the wisest book covering the fateful five months": Daniel Crofts, introduction to the 1995 reprint edition of David M. Potter's *Lincoln and His Party in the Secession Crisis* (Baton Rouge: University of Louisiana Press, 1995), p. xxvi.

436 "These forces [squelching 'conciliation' among Republicans]": Potter, *Lincoln and His Party in the Secession Crisis,* p. 186.

437 "[I]t can hardly be said that these immense values": Potter, *Lincoln and His Party in the Secession Crisis,* 1962 preface, p. xli.

441 "the President elect did not experience": *New York Herald,* December 25, 1860, as quoted in William E. Barringer, *A House Dividing: Lincoln as President Elect* (Springfield, IL: The Abraham Lincoln Association, 1945), p. 204.

442 "I cannot resist the conviction" . . . "He [Lincoln] will not, like his predecessor": dispatch of December 21, *New York Herald,* December 27, 1860, quoted in Barringer, *A House Dividing,* p. 208.

442 "he locked himself in a room": Herndon, *Life,* p. 386.

442 My examination of the First Inaugural Address is drawn from Basler et al., *Collected Works,* vol. 4, "First Inaugural Address—First Edition and Revisions," pp. 249–262, and then the final text, pp. 262–271. These texts have full and excellent notes on which I have relied.

452 "the most distinctive element in Mr. Lincoln's moral composition": dispatch of January 27, 1861, *New York Herald,* published on Feb. 1, 1861, quoted in Barringer, p. 231.

453 "whether grass shall grow in the streets": L. E. Chittenden, *Personal Reminiscences* (New York, 1893), pp. 74–75. I know about this episode through the courtesy of Michael Burlingame.

ACKNOWLEDGMENTS

I wrote this book in the Miller Center of Public Affairs at the University of Virginia, in the amiable surroundings of young researchers with headphones listening to tapes from presidents a good deal more recent than the one I was concerned with. I am deeply grateful to the Miller Center, and to its director, Philip Zelikow, and its staff, for supporting me in what was perhaps to them a slightly anachronistic undertaking. I did not conduct any oral history of the Lincoln presidency, or find any recordings of his conversations with Seward or Stanton. The Miller Center generously provided an office, an assistant, a computer-link, attentive audiences at Miller Center forums, and lunches with assembled scholars. I thank the participants in those events, and also the able students in the seminars of the interdisciplinary honors program Political and Social Thought, for many helpful comments.

Among the graciously supportive Miller Center staff, I would like to thank in particular Margaret Edwards, Rachel Kelley, and Kimberly Girard. Robin Kuzen, the chief of staff, with a picture of Lincoln on her own wall, not only assisted this project in various practical ways but found time to give a helpful reading to four chapters.

The two primary readers of the entire manuscript, both of them taking time from their own books to give this effort of mine their detailed attention, were Lou Cannon, the eminent political journalist and biographer, and Edward Ayers, the distinguished American historian. Both read the whole thing chapter by chapter, and not only caught particular errors but supplied broader critical appraisals that improved the work overall. Of course, neither of them nor any of the others I name is responsible for whatever defects remain.

Michael Smith—my colleague and successor as the director of the Political and Social Thought program, and a leading scholar of ethics and politics—gave me strong encouragement and valuable appraisals both inside and outside the PST seminars.

When I was first considering this undertaking, I described my idea of a serious "ethical biography" to my friend Merrill Peterson, who had recently traversed the whole territory for his *Lincoln in American Memory,* and asked whether in all the thousands of Lincoln books such a thing had been done, and after reflection he said, no, not really. He introduced me to Douglas Wilson, the author of the distinguished book on Lincoln *Honor's Voice,* and Doug Wilson became an early friend of this work, and has remained a friend giving strong encouragement on the last lap and a generous reading of four chapters in their penultimate form.

The Miller Center has enabled me to have successively three superlatively able assistants: Ashley McDonald, whom I knew as an extraordinarily capable undergraduate in Political and Social Thought, and who is now a student in Yale Law School, was "present at the creation" and with great intelligence and conscientiousness helped to mold the book from the start; Jason Baker, to whom she handed the baton, then a University of Virginia undergraduate and now a reporter for the *Providence Journal,* dug out essential material in the library and energetically carried the work through the middle chapters; and finally, Jonathan Riehl, a rising third-year University of Virginia law student, a commentator on and participant in public affairs in his own right, performed every service in bringing the project to closure, with the most excellent and devoted attention.

Working on Lincoln proves to be unlike working on another figure, another topic; there is—to use a Lincoln word—a "vast" world out there, going far beyond the usual clutch of professors or journalists or policy specialists who gather around any given subject. I found it to be a most welcoming world, instantly willing to take some trouble to help a newcomer. Thomas Schwartz, the Illinois state historian, and leading figure at one center of the Lincoln world, Springfield, Illinois, went out of his way to help me with this project, as did his able associate Kim Bauer; they were as well personally gracious to Linda Miller and me on our visits.

In the East Coast branch of the Lincoln world, I have had help from more persons than I can name. I would mention in particular Michael Burlingame who, although deep into his own comprehensive Lincoln project, repeatedly, and immediately, answered questions both by e-mail and in person, and gave every assistance with an unusual willingness to help.

At the University of Virginia, my colleague Sid Milkis of the Government Department and the Miller Center, the expert on presidential greatness, not only read several chapters but gave me much encouragement. Gary Gallagher, the eminent Civil War historian, offered appraisals of various chapters at Miller Center lunches and then read and evaluated two further chapters, all to my great benefit. Clifton McCleskey brought his expert knowledge of American politics to bear on Chapter Fifteen. Michael Holt, the leading authority on the American Whigs, who helped me in a large way on a previous book, carefully read and criticized and improved Chapter Five in this one.

I am privileged to have as my editor at Knopf the most distinguished of editors of American history, Jane Garrett, who supported this book from the start and gave it the benefit of her incisive criticism at key points. Linda Miller, who might in another life herself have been a distinguished editor, gave all the chapters her critical attention more than once, and really did help in all those ways that authors say in their acknowledgments that their spouses helped and supported and comforted and aided and encouraged them. She really did.

INDEX

abolition movement, 235
  "evil committed in order to do good"
    issue, 192–7
  horror stories about slavery, use of,
    289
  Illinois General Assembly's
    condemnation of abolitionism and
    Lincoln's subsequent protest,
    116–20, 121–9, 139, 479–80
  Lincoln's disapproval of, 122, 124, 129
  Lincoln's recruitment, efforts toward,
    269
  mob attacks on abolitionists,
    Lincoln's condemnation of, 129–39
  religious authority claimed by, 294–5
Adams, Abigail, 57
Adams, Charles Francis, 259
Adams, John, 174, 465–6
Adams, John Quincy, 57, 99, 106, 109,
    174, 175, 176, 180, 207, 259, 279,
    465–6
  Lincoln and, 175*n*
African-Americans, xiv
  Douglas's racist views, 341–53, 371–4
  wage equalization for, 356–7*n*
  see also Lincoln, Abraham, racial
    attitudes of; slavery
Age of Reason (Paine), 84

"A. Lincoln, Politician" (Donald), 478
American Party, *see* nativism
American Scripture (Maier), 296
American Slavery as It Is (Weld), 289
Anderson, Maj. Robert, 420, 441, 456
Armstrong, Jack, 7, 31
Arnold, Isaac, 161, 299, 411
Ashley, James, 359*n*
Ashmun, George, 10, 167, 175, 176

Baker, Edward D., 154, 155, 156, 157–8,
    161, 176–7, 183, 217–18, 377, 459
Baker, Jean, 303
Baldwin, James, 360
Bancroft, George, 376
banking, 142–6, 325–6
Basler, Roy, 80–1
Bates, Edward, 359*n*, 391, 395, 402, 408,
    409
"Battle Hymn of the Republic," 463
Becker, Carl, 146
Beecher, Henry Ward, 375, 376
Beecher, Lyman, 112
Bell, John, 393, 404, 405*n*, 466–7
Bennett, Lerone, Jr., 362–3*n*
Berry, William, 92

Berwanger, Eugene, 363

Beveridge, Albert, 32, 38, 60, 72, 124, 125, 173, 217–18, 299, 310, 311, 314, 417, 461, 490–1

Bible, 49–50, 83–4

Birch, Jonathan, 5

Birney, James G., 193

Bissell, William, 319, 334, 359*n*, 369

Black, Jeremiah, 419, 420

Black Hawk War, 7, 24, 31, 36–7

blacks, *see* African-Americans

Blair, Francis, Sr., 441

Blair, Hugh, 80

Blair, Montgomery, 359*n*, 408, 409

Boritt, G. S., 109*n*, 144

Bray, Robert, 66

Breckinridge, John, 393, 404, 405*n*, 419, 465, 466–7

Broadwell, Norman, 305–6*n*

Brown, John, 10, 228, 389
Lincoln's views on, 380

Browning, Orville, 450, 452

Bryan, William Jennings, 400

Bryant, William Cullen, 9, 376

Buchanan, James, 91, 200, 236, 249, 323, 331, 341, 366, 391, 418, 419, 420, 421, 423, 431, 441, 456
problems of his presidency, 392

Burns, Anthony, 234–5

Burns, Robert, 43, 85

Burr, Aaron, 141

Butler, Benjamin, 488

Butler, William, 25

Butterfield, Justin, 217, 218–19, 220–1

Byron, Lord, 82

Calhoun, John, 24

Calhoun, John C., 113, 126, 211, 246, 275–6

Cameron, Simon, 10, 391, 396, 397, 401–2, 408, 409, 422

Carman, Caleb, 6–7, 34

Cartwright, Peter, 3, 86, 107, 153, 162

Cass, Lewis, 8, 200, 202, 203, 240

Charnwood, Lord, xi–xii, 48

Chase, Salmon P., 64, 210, 249, 294, 362, 391, 392, 395, 423
Kansas-Nebraska Act, 242, 243–5
in Lincoln's cabinet, 408, 409
Lincoln's letters to, 320–1
Republican presidential nomination of 1860, 401, 402

Christianity, 23, 83–90

civil liberties, Lincoln's defense of, 135–7

Civil War, 456
cost/benefit analyses regarding, 437–8
Fortress Monroe conference, 429–30
Fort Sumter assault, 420, 441, 456, 462–3
Lincoln's assessment of cause of, 287–8
Lincoln's conduct during Civil War compared with Polk's during Mexican War, 191, 457–64
Lincoln's pre-war indications of willingness to fight, 441–2, 452
Lincoln/Stanton collaboration during, 425
slavery as cause of, 287–8, 431, 432
stopgap peace through Crittenden Plan, Lincoln's rejection of, 435–40

Clary Grove Boys, 5, 7, 24, 31, 37

classless culture, Lincoln as beneficiary of, 16–25

Clay, Henry, 6, 38, 96, 97, 99, 106, 109, 114, 157, 217, 219, 229, 352, 359
antislavery position, 193
Compromise of 1850, 210–11
Lincoln's admiration for, 83, 107, 199–200

Lincoln's eulogy for, 103, 114, 227–8, 246

Mexican War, denunciation of, 162–3

presidential election of 1844, 193

Whig presidential nomination of 1848 denied to, 199–201

Clemens, Samuel, 92

Clinton, DeWitt, 109

Codding, Ichabod, 269, 304, 318

Cogdal, Isaac, 32, 87

Cold War, 437

Colfax, Schuyler, 332

Lincoln's letters to, 321–2, 409

collaboration in politics, 224–5

Collamer, Jacob, 391, 395, 402

colonization movement, Lincoln's endorsement of, 354, 359, 488

Compromise of 1850, 210–12, 230, 238, 239, 241

Congress, U.S.

Kansas-Nebraska debate in Senate, 231–2, 242–7, 484

slavery in the territories, right to decide about, 377–9

see also House of Representatives, U.S.; Mexican War debate

Constitution, U.S.

Thirteenth Amendment, 237

three-fifths clause regarding slaves, 258–61

"Union is perpetual" perspective and, 444

convention system, 100, 158–60

Crawford, Andrew, 67

Crawford, Elizabeth, 48

Crawford, Joseph, 28

Crittenden, John J., 435

Crittenden Plan, 435–40

Crockett, Davy, 458

Crofts, Daniel, 436

Croly, Herbert, 15–16

Curtin, Andrew, 394, 452

Curtis, Benjamin R., 369*n*

Davis, David, 76, 217, 222, 305–6*n*, 311–12, 318, 362, 396

Davis, Jefferson, 420, 430, 448, 451

Davis, Rodney, 58*n*

Dawson, John, 118

Dayton, William, 319, 391

Declaration of Independence, 88, 338 9

Kansas-Nebraska Act and, 245–7

Lincoln's antislavery position and, 296–7

Lincoln's use of Declaration to affirm racial equality, 351–3, 365–7, 372–3

Lincoln's worldview, central position in, 374

as moral norm for all times, 246

"Union is perpetual" perspective and, 444

Declaration of Independence, The (Becker), 146

Defrees, John D., 439, 440

demagogue threat to America, Lincoln's warning about, 131, 140–1

Democratic Party

antislavery minority, 204

campaigning methods, 100–1

convention system, 100

fracturing in 1860, 392–3, 404

Lincoln's independent judgment regarding, 38

patronage by, 101

racism of, 358

Dickerson, Edward, 410

District of Columbia abolition of slavery issue

House's consideration of, 126, 127, 212–15

District of Columbia abolition of slavery
    issue *(continued)*
    Illinois General Assembly's
        consideration of, 122, 125–7
Dix, Gen. John, 421
Donald, David Herbert, 19, 41, 61–2, 66,
    144–5, 178, 274, 307n, 313, 354, 426,
    478, 479–80
Douglas, Stephen A., 69, 97, 100n, 118,
    141, 142, 229, 283, 285, 289, 291,
    294, 323, 363, 366, 377, 379, 383,
    409, 419, 449
    alliance with Republicans in 1857
        regarding Kansas admission issue,
        331–4
    Compromise of 1850, 212, 239
    debating skills, 249–50
    on Declaration of Independence, 296
    as Democrat of convenience, 108
    honorable actions of 1860–61, 337
    "Judge" title used by Lincoln in
        referring to, 327, 335
    Kansas-Nebraska Act, 231–2, 239,
        240–3, 245, 299
    Lincoln's document about Douglas
        and himself, 328–30, 338, 486
    Lincoln's envious feelings toward,
        327–30, 335, 338
    Lincoln's moral disagreement with,
        337–9
    Lincoln's scornful remarks about,
        325–7, 335, 336
    Lincoln's use of Douglas's eminence
        to enhance his own, 330–1
    on Missouri Compromise, 253
    political career's trajectory, 328
    political stature, 248–9
    presidential election of 1860, 391,
        392–3, 404, 405n, 465, 466–7
    racist views, 341–53, 371–4
    religious critics, response to, 294–5
    senatorial election of 1855, 306

see also Lincoln/Douglas debates;
    senatorial election of 1858
Douglass, Frederick, 14, 40, 41, 236, 462
    Douglas's racist references to, 348–9,
        351
    Lincoln's attitude toward, 351n
    on Stanton, 414–15
Dred Scott decision, 236, 342, 345, 352,
    360–1, 369, 379, 381, 392
Drummond, Thomas, 410, 412
Dubois, Jesse, 118, 126
Duncan, Jason, 73, 74
Durante, Jimmy, 223
Durley, Williamson, 228
    Lincoln's letters to, 192, 193–6

Edwards, Cyrus, 217–18, 302n, 308
Edwards, Matilda, 77
Edwards, Ninian W., 25, 118, 126, 127n,
    217, 362
Edwards family, 77n
Eisenhower, John S. D., 459
electoral college, 193, 393, 465–7
"Elegy Written in a Country
    Churchyard" (Gray), 17–18, 20–1,
    25
Elements of Moral Science (Wayland),
    277–9
Elements of Political Economy
    (Wayland), 277
Elkin, W. F., 118
Ellis, Abner Y., 4, 33, 74
Emancipation Proclamation, 69, 237,
    390
Emmerson, Ralph, 417–18, 490, 491
Enloe, Benjamin, 118
Evarts, William M., 401
"evil committed in order to do good"
    issue, 192–9, 202–4, 206–9
Ewing, Thomas, 220, 221

expansionism, 458, 459–61, 462
Lincoln's position on, 185
Polk's achievements, 184, 483

Fehrenbacher, Don, 290, 324, 328–9, 334, 343, 365, 404, 491
Fell, Jesse, 29, 44
Fessenden, William Pitt, 34
Fillmore, Millard, 39, 211, 395
Fish, Hamilton, 376
Fleurville, William de (Billy the Barber), 40–1
Foner, Eric, 340, 361
Forced into Glory (Bennett), 362–3n
Ford, Thomas, 107, 161
Forquer, George, 107
Founding Fathers, 267–8, 432–3
on Congress's right to decide about slavery in the territories, 377–9
as politicians, 104
Francis, Simeon, 25
Franklin, Benjamin, 51, 81, 378
Fredrickson, George, 488
freedom to make choices, 55–6
Free-Soil Party, 203–10
Frémont, John C., 39, 96, 319, 391, 395, 402
Fugitive Slave Law, 211, 212, 230
Lincoln's position on, 234–7, 239, 320–1

Garrison, William Lloyd, 237, 362
Gentry, Allan, 6
Gentry, Anna, 4, 6, 74, 76
Gentry, James, 22, 28
Giddings, Joshua R., 112, 163, 165, 175, 176, 180, 193, 210, 244, 304, 362

District of Columbia abolition of slavery issue, 212, 213–15
Gienapp, William, 405
Gillespie, Joseph, 308, 311, 312–13, 314–15
Lincoln's letters to, 301–2
Godbey, Russell, 32
Gordon, Nathaniel, 266
Graham, Mentor, 24
Gray, Thomas, 17–18, 20–1, 25
Greeley, Horace, 201, 332–3, 334, 376, 394, 438
Green, Bowling, 24, 74
Greene, William, 33–4, 64, 74, 76
Grigsby, Nathaniel, 4, 6, 48, 74, 473, 474
Grigsby, William, 31
Grimké, Angelina and Sarah, 289, 354
Grimshaw, William, 51, 82
Gulliver, Reverend Mr., 385–6

Haimes, Elijah M., 306
Hale, James T., 440
Hamilton, Alexander, 102, 378
Hamlin, Hannibal, 359n
Hammond, James Henry, 126
Hanks, Dennis, 26, 29, 31, 37, 47, 49, 58, 72, 76, 107
Hanks, John, 12, 29, 47, 60
Hanks, Thomas, 58
Hardin, John J., 118, 154, 156–7, 158, 161, 176, 459
Lincoln's letters to, 159–60
Harding, George, 410–11, 412, 414, 415–16, 417, 418, 420, 422, 425–6, 490–1
Harris, Thomas, 178
Harrison, William Henry, 96, 146, 193
Hay, John, 7, 64, 215, 241, 299, 308–9
Hayne, Robert, 83, 113
Henderson, Thomas, 302

Henderson, William H., 313

Henry, A. G., 41, 178

Herndon, John Rowan "Row," 32, 33

Herndon, William H., xiii, 6, 19, 28, 33, 35, 45, 48, 58–9, 63, 64–5, 66, 73, 76–7, 79, 85, 87, 89, 152, 153, 167, 245, 277, 299, 319, 400, 406, 417

    drinking habit, 147, 480–1

    on Lincoln's ambition, 302–3

    Lincoln's letters to, 183–4, 186, 187–9, 200, 429

    on Lincoln's mental qualities, 471–2

    on Lincoln's role in Mexican War debate, 173, 183–4

Herrera, José Joaquín, 188

Hill, Samuel, 93

History of the United States (Grimshaw), 51, 82

Hodges, Albert, 39, 275

Hofstadter, Richard, 237

Hogan, John, 118

Holiday, Billie, 135*n*

Holland, J. G., 299, 385, 488–9

Holmes, Oliver Wendell, 180

Holt, Joseph, 424, 456

"Holy Willie's Prayer" (Burns), 85, 88

Honor's Voice (Wilson), 77

Hoover, Herbert, 405

House of Representatives, U.S.

    District of Columbia abolition of slavery issue, 126, 127, 212–15

    Free-Soilers' impact on, 209–10

    internal improvements issue, 197–9

    Kansas-Nebraska Act, 232, 242

    Lincoln's decision against reelection try, 178

    Lincoln's desire for leading role, 165

    Lincoln's election in 1846, 86, 95, 153, 162

    Lincoln's nomination for House seat by Whig Party, 153–60

    Lincoln's oratory, 8

    Lincoln's swearing in, 163

    presidential election of 1860 "thrown into the House" scenarios, 393, 465–7

    see also Mexican War debate

Howe, Daniel Walker, 112

Howells, William Dean, 474

Hoyt, Charles, 301

Hughes, Langston, 360

human nature, Lincoln's conception of, 263–7

Hunter, Maj. David, 441

Illinois black code, 117, 346

Illinois General Assembly

    abolitionism, condemnation of, 116–20, 121–9, 139, 479–80

    District of Columbia abolition of slavery issue, 122, 125–7

    internal improvements issue, 120–1

    Lincoln's election in 1834, 111

    Lincoln's election in 1854 and subsequent resignation, 247–8, 304–5

    Lincoln's oratory, 7–8

    Lincoln's tenure in, 95

    see also senatorial election of 1855

Indians, Lincoln's attitude toward, 36–7

Interior Department, U.S., 220*n*

internal improvements

    House consideration of, 197–9

    Illinois General Assembly's consideration of, 120–1

    Lincoln's advocacy of, 96–7, 109–11, 121, 198–9

Irish immigrants, 38–9

Irwin, Benjamin, 74

Jackson, Andrew, 36, 106, 107, 112, 114, 141
  Lincoln's independent judgment regarding, 37–8
Jaffa, Harry, 140–1
James, William, 200
Jayne, Julia, 119*n*, 312
Jefferson, Thomas, xi, 13, 38, 55, 84, 88, 104, 274, 297, 359, 432–3, 460
  Lincoln's estimation of, 102–3
  writing style's missing element, 146
"John Hancock Otis" (Masters), 476–7
Johnson, Andrew, 91
Johnson, Lyndon Baines, 424
Johnson, Reverdy, 410, 414, 490
Johnson, Samuel, 13, 84
Johnston, Elizabeth, 47
Johnston, John D., 31, 47, 58, 61, 76, 80
Jones, "Colonel" William, 6, 106–7
Judd, Norman, 99, 300, 307, 308*n*, 311, 318, 396, 401
  Lincoln's letters to, 315–16

Kansas admission controversy, 331–4, 392
Kansas-Nebraska Act, 230, 283
  alteration of nation's moral premise regarding slavery, 238–9, 267–9
  Declaration of Independence and, 245–7
  Douglas's motivations regarding, 240–2
  Lincoln/Douglas debates on, 248, 250–1, 252–70
  Lincoln's abandonment of party loyalty in favor of anti-Nebraskaism, 300–1
  Lincoln's opposition on moral grounds, 232–4, 238–9, 243, 253–5, 267–9

Lincoln's strategy in speaking against, 244–5
  Missouri Compromise repeal resulting from, 240–2
  opposition by antislavery senators, 243–5, 246
  opposition in Illinois, 239–40, 299–300
  passage into law, 232
  "popular sovereignty" approach to deciding legality of slavery in new states, 240, 241, 256–63, 266–7
  relative power of free and slave states, impact on, 258–61
  Senate debate, 231–2, 242–7, 484
  violence resulting from, 266–7, 392
Kant, Immanuel, 211*n*
Keats, John, 6, 68
Kellogg, William, 434, 439
Kelso, Jack, 27, 51
Kennedy, John F., 174, 336, 424
Kennedy, Robert F., 424
King, Martin Luther, Jr., 361
Know-Nothings, *see* nativism

Lamon, Ward, 5, 222, 362
Lane, Henry, 394
Lane, Joseph, 465, 467
Last Best Hope of Earth, The (Neely), 30
Lessons in Elocution (Scott), 50–1, 79–80
Liberty Party, 193, 194–5
Life on the Mississippi (Clemens), 92
Lincoln, Abraham
  abstentions by, 26–34, 43
  ambition of, 21, 64–70, 302–3, 325
  animals, kindness toward, 27–8, 472–3
  assassination of, 17
  autobiographical sketches, 27, 29, 41, 44–5, 52, 57, 61, 68, 178, 186–7, 232, 475

Lincoln, Abraham *(continued)*
  charity of, 90, 489–90
  childhood years, 6, 54–5
  civil liberties, defense of, 135–7
  classless culture, beneficiary of, 16–25
  collaboration in politics, 224–5
  commercial ventures, 92–3
  commonness as appealing
    characteristic, 11–12
  demagogue threat to America,
    warning about, 131, 140–1
  dress of, 4–5, 11
  educational self-deprecation, 44–5
  ego of, 407–8
  emotional apprehension of
    experience, 146–7
  eternal punishment concept, rejection
    of, 87–8
  "evil committed in order to do good"
    issue, 192–9, 202–4, 206–9
  expansionism, position on, 185
  family life, 221–2
  farming and manual labor,
    disinclination to, 29–31
  fighting and wrestling, 31–2, 71–2
  freedom to make choices, 55–6
  Free-Soil challenge in 1848, response
    to, 206–9
  funeral of, 144
  grammatical shortcomings, 5
  historians' obsession with, 18–20
  honesty of, 218
  human equality, defense of, 88–9
  human nature, conception of, 263–7
  humor of, 5, 12, 72–4
  idealism of, 82–3, 112
  imperatives of, 225–6
  independent judgment by, 34–44,
    74–5
  Indians, attitude toward, 36–7
  influences that shaped his character,
    57–9

  initial impression made by, 3–13
  intellectual abilities, 3–16, 63–4, 471–2
  internal improvements, advocacy of,
    96–7, 109–11, 121, 198–9
  as inventor, 93
  journey to Washington in 1861, 450–2
  "last, best hope of earth" description
    of United States, 464
  legal career, 52–3, 94, 130, 222, 226,
    410–18
  magnanimity of, 227, 406–7, 409,
    423–5
  majority rule, views on, 104–5, 446–9
  manual labor by, 47–8
  McCormick v. Manny (reaper case),
    410–18, 490–1
  military service, 7, 22, 24, 31, 36–7, 74
  mob violence, condemnation of,
    129–39
  moral realism, 147–53, 181, 228–30
  moral self-development, 57–9, 79–82
  mythic picture of, xii–xiii, 13
  nativism, attitude toward, 317
  oath to preserve the Union,
    importance placed on, 452–5
  Oregon governorship offered to, 221
  patronage, philosophy of, 101, 216–21
  physical appearance, 4–5, 76
  physical strength and athletic ability,
    71–2
  poetry, liking for, 17, 146
  political career, decision on, 92–5
  political career's significance for
    appraisal of Lincoln's life, xiv–xv,
    105, 115
  political partisanship, 95–7, 98–104
  politicians, joking criticism of, 103
  the poor of Gray's poem, contrast
    with, 17–24, 25
  popularity among personal
    acquaintances, 24–5, 72–4
  prudence of, 222–4, 228–30

raft trips on Mississippi, 92

"Rail-splitter" image, 12

reading by, 46–53, 59, 64–5*n,* 79–83, 274, 277

religious opposition to, 155

religious views, 42–3, 49, 83–90, 295–6, 365

reputation for greatness, xi–xii

resolution of (gem of his character), 56, 77–9, 407, 489–90

respectful conduct toward everyone he dealt with, 364–5

responsibility, ethic of, 192, 195–7, 202–3, 204, 219, 225–6, 228–30

romantic dealings, 76–9, 130, 477–8

school experiences, 6, 41–2

self-confidence, 46–7, 53, 63–4

self-education, 20–1, 44–53, 59, 64, 79–83

as self-improver, 90–1

self-interest in politics, views on, 254–5, 260, 263

signature writing, 67–8

social criticism, personal method of, 74–5

storytelling by, 72–4

suffrage and political participation, views on, 261–3, 370

surveying work, 52

Taylor's presidential candidacy, support for, 199–203, 206–9

temperance movement, views on, 147–50, 152–3

"Union is perpetual" perspective, 113–14, 380–1, 434, 442–56

vice-presidential candidacy in 1856, 399

vices of others, liberal attitude toward, 34–5

wounding articles and speeches, 66

see also Civil War; House of Representatives, U.S.; Illinois General Assembly; Kansas-Nebraska Act; Lincoln, Abraham *headings;* Lincoln/Douglas debates; Lincoln presidency; Mexican War debate; presidential election of 1860; Republican Party; Republican presidential nomination of 1860; senatorial election of 1855; senatorial election of 1858; Whig Party; *specific persons*

Lincoln, Abraham, antislavery position of brutal reality of slavery, references to, 289

compromise on extension, refusal regarding, 434–40

conflict between "right" and "wrong" perspectives on slavery, analysis of, 381–3

Congress's right to decide about slavery in the territories and, 377–9

constitutional framework, 236–7

"containment" approach to slavery, 284

Declaration of Independence and, 296–7

description and analysis of slavery to convey moral conviction (moral clarification), 284–5, 289–94

diffusion of responsibility for slavery, 287–9

District of Columbia abolition of slavery issue, 122, 125–7, 212–15

Emancipation Proclamation, 69, 237, 390

eternal love of justice and, 270

first principles regarding slavery, development of, 233–4, 250, 273–85

Fugitive Slave Law and, 234–7, 239, 320–1

humanity of the Negro, recognition of, 243, 263–6

Lincoln, Abraham, antislavery position
of brutal reality of slavery,
references to *(continued)*
Illinois General Assembly's
condemnation of abolitionism,
protest of, 119–20, 121–9, 139,
479–80
lifelong opposition, 39–40, 215
Lincoln's racial attitudes and, 276–7,
282
magnitude of slavery problem,
recognition of, 386–91
manumission issue, 370
Mexican War opposition, comparison
with, 182–3
"moderate" charge against Lincoln's
position, 282–4
"monstrous injustice" charge against
slavery, 253–5, 290
moralistic distortion and self-
righteousness, avoidance of, 150–1,
286–97
religious arguments against slavery,
muted use of, 294–6
retrogressions promoted by
proslavery forces, prevention of,
360–1
social and institutional context of
slavery, recognition of, 255–6,
386–9
solution of slavery problem, proposals
for, 389–90
see also Kansas-Nebraska Act
Lincoln, Abraham, oratory of
bank speech (1840), 142–6, 325–6
Bible's influence on, 50
Chicago speech (1858), 343–4
Chicago speech (1859), 291, 324
clarity and thoroughness in, 376–7,
400
Clay eulogy, 103, 114, 227–8,
246

Cooper Union Address, 9–10, 293,
385, 463, 488–9; analysis of, 375–84
"Discoveries and Inventions" lecture,
45–7
Easterners' appreciation of, 385–6
exhortation in, 291
extemporaneous speaking, dislike of,
14
first effort at political self-
presentation (1832), 94–5, 109–10
First Inaugural Address, 12, 113–14,
236, 293, 462; analysis of, 442–50,
454–5
Gettysburg Address, 12, 443
"house divided" speech, 290, 323
House speech on Cass, 8
in Illinois General Assembly, 7–8
impression made on listeners, 10
Indianapolis speech (1861), 450–1
Lewistown speech (1858), 338–9, 367
"lost speech" of 1856, 319
Lyceum Address, 125, 142, 246, 480;
analysis of, 130–41
Mexican War debate, 90, 165–7,
168–71, 187, 189–90
Milwaukee speech (1859), 30, 473
New England speaking tour (1860),
384–6
New Haven speech (1860), 388,
389–90
New Jersey Senate speech (1861),
463–4
Peoria speech (1854), 269–70
personal attacks in, 169–71
Republican Party spokesman in 1859,
372–4
quality of public argument as key to
Lincoln's nomination in 1860,
397–401
satire and caricature in, 141–2, 257–8,
260, 261, 289
Scott Club speech, 326

Second Inaugural Address, xi–xii, 50, 90, 146, 191, 293, 295, 390–1, 443, 463

speaking style, 8

Springfield speech (1858), 334–6, 339

state fair speech, 151, 235–6, 247, 250–1, 290, 294; analysis of, 252–72

sweeping extravagance (rodomontade) in, 139, 140–7

Taylor campaign speeches, 201–3

Taylor eulogy, 226–7

Temperance Address, 79, 90, 140, 141–2; analysis of, 147–53

Worcester speech (1848), 185, 206–9

"wounding from behind" device, 264–6, 293–4, 366–7

see also Lincoln/Douglas debates

Lincoln, Abraham, racial attitudes of

colonization movement, endorsement of, 354, 359, 488

contemporary politicians' attitudes, comparison with, 361–3, 368–9

cordial and welcoming treatment of African-Americans, 40–1

dehumanization of the Negro, fight against, 371–4

equality of races, belief in, 340, 343–4, 348, 351–2, 365–8, 372–3

humanity of the Negro, recognition of, 243, 263–6

Lincoln's antislavery position and, 276–7, 282

moral inclination away from racial prejudice, 363–8

racial stereotypes and jokes, use of, 356, 356–7n

social context of Lincoln's life and, 256, 354–60

suffrage issue, 261–3, 370

white supremacist attitudes imputed to Lincoln, xiii–xiv, 350, 353–5

worsening condition of African-Americans, lamentation regarding, 369–71

Lincoln, Abraham (grandfather), 36

Lincoln, Eddie (son), 154, 222

Lincoln, Mary Todd (wife), 14, 19, 25, 38–9, 61, 87, 119n, 127n, 130, 147, 154, 155, 163, 213, 221, 222, 411, 450, 451, 456

grudge-holding by, 311–12

Lincoln's decision to marry, 77–9

Lincoln's letters to, 385

political interests, 97–8

senatorial election of 1855, 303, 307, 308, 310, 311–12

Lincoln, Mordecai (uncle), 36

Lincoln, Nancy Hanks (mother), 49, 68

Lincoln's debt to, 63

personal qualities, 58

Lincoln, Robert Todd (son), 81, 154, 222, 384, 426, 450

Lincoln, Sarah (sister), 42, 47, 55, 58, 66n

Lincoln, Sarah Bush Johnston (stepmother), 32, 33, 42, 46, 47, 48, 55, 62, 68, 76

Lincoln's relationship with, 58–9

Lincoln, Tad (son), 222, 450

Lincoln, Thomas (father), 5, 6, 19, 42, 47, 54, 58

carpentry skills, 28–9

farming life, 29

hunting by, 26

Lincoln's relationship with, 60–2, 68

personal qualities, 59–60, 71, 72, 476

politics of, 474

poverty of, 36

"yeoman" designation, 21–2

Lincoln, Willie (son), 222, 450

Lincoln and His Party in the Secession Crisis (Potter), 435–8

Lincoln and the Negro (Quarles), xiv

Lincoln/Douglas debates, 9, 88–9, 93, 95
  agreement to debate, 336
  Alton, 292–3, 338, 352–3, 371
  analysis of 1858 debates, 340–53
  Charleston, 350–1
  courage required of Lincoln to debate
    Douglas, 248–50
  eminence disparity as problem for
    Douglas, 336
  Freeport, 348–9
  Galesburg, 351–2
  Jonesboro, 349–50
  Kansas-Nebraska Act debates of 1854,
    248, 250–1, 252–70
  Lincoln's ambition and, 66–7
  Mexican War debate, Douglas's
    criticism of Lincoln's role in, 172–3
  national stature for Lincoln resulting
    from, 336–7, 398
  Ottawa, 172, 345–8
  Quincy, 292, 352
  rules for, 346
  slavery as central issue, 341
  states' rights issue, 344–5
Lincoln presidency, 12, 95
  cabinet selection in 1861, 408–10
  inauguration of 1861, 456
  Lincoln's inflexibility on slavery
    extension issue, 434–40
  Lincoln's personal conduct during,
    406–8
  Lincoln/Stanton relationship in,
    425
  patronage in, 101
  Sioux executions, 36
  Stanton's appointment as secretary of
    war, 422–6
  see also Civil War
Lincoln's Religion (Wolf), 50
Linder, Usher, 125, 132
Lippmann, Walter, 174
Locke, John, 296

Logan, Stephen T., 7, 155, 178, 302*n*,
  304, 308*n*, 311, 362
Lovejoy, Elijah, 125, 131, 132–3, 134
Lovejoy, Owen, 269, 303, 304, 308, 345,
  362, 377
  Lincoln's letters to, 317, 318
Luther, Martin, 225, 438
Luthin, Richard, 66
lyceums, 130

Machiavelli, Niccolò, 424
Madison, James, 41, 104, 263, 273, 359,
  381, 388, 449
Maier, Pauline, 296
majority rule, Lincoln's views on, 104–5,
  446–9
"Manifest Destiny" concept, 458,
  459–61, 462
Mann, Horace, 112
Manny, John H., 410
Marx, Karl, 75, 237
Masters, Edgar Lee, 70, 476–7
Matheny, James, 73, 85
Matteson, Joel, 306–7, 309, 310, 311,
  313
McClellan, Gen. George, 421–2,
  423
McClernand, John, 119
McClure, A. K., 10–11
McCormick, Andrew, 119
McCormick, Cyrus, 410
McCormick v. Manny (reaper case),
  410–18, 490–1
McHenry, Henry, 33, 74, 76
McIntosh, Frank, 134, 136–7
McLean, John, 369*n*, 391, 395, 401, 412,
  417
McPherson, James, 358
Mexican War, 161, 162
  Lincoln's conduct during Civil War

compared with Polk's during
Mexican War, 191, 457–64
treaty of peace, 184, 483
Mexican War debate
absolute opponents of war (Immortal
Fourteen), 176, 180
Ashmun amendment, 167–8, 177, 183,
189
Clay's denunciation of war, 162–3
criticism of Lincoln's role in, 171–82
Lincoln's ambition and, 66
Lincoln's letters defending his
actions, 183–5
Lincoln's national perspective,
174–5
Lincoln's position on war compared
with his antislavery position, 182–3
Lincoln's silence during war's
progress, 161–2
Lincoln's sincerity in criticizing Polk,
175–7
Lincoln's speeches critical of Polk's
actions, 90, 165–7, 168–71, 187,
189–90
morality of Lincoln's actions, 179–82
notes toward the speech that Lincoln
might have given on the American
role in the war, 185–91
"political suicide" perspective on
Lincoln's position, 173, 177–9
Polk's defense of U.S. actions, 164–5
Spot Resolutions, 166–7, 169, 179, 181,
187
Miller, William, 74
Milton, George Fort, 249
Missouri Compromise, 238
Douglas's assessment of, 253
repeal through Kansas-Nebraska Act,
240–2
Mitchum (slave), 234
mob violence, Lincoln's condemnation
of, 129–39

Moore, Matilda Johnston, 27, 42–3, 47,
74, 472
Morris, Gouverneur, 378

nativism, 202, 317–18, 395
Lincoln's attitude toward, 317
in Whig Party, 38–9
Nebraska Bill, *see* Kansas-Nebraska Act
Neely, Mark E., Jr., 30, 58, 99, 111, 177,
178, 426
Nevins, Allan, 231, 249
Nicolay, John G., 7, 215, 241, 299, 308–9,
441
Niebuhr, Reinhold, 180, 464
Nixon, Richard, 336, 424
Norris, George W., 174
Noyes, William Curtis, 376
nullification issue, 113–14

Offutt, Denton, 7, 24, 31, 93, 471
old man's conference (1861), 453
O'Sullivan, John L., 460
Owens [Vineyard], Mary, 28, 77, 130

Paine, Tom, 43, 84, 85, 87
Paley, William, 86
Palfrey, John, 175
Palmer, John, 300, 307, 308n, 315, 318
Lincoln's letters to, 300–1
Paredes y Arrillaga, Mariano, 188
Parker, Theodore, 234
Parkinson, Robert H., 490
Parks, Samuel, 316
Patriotic Gore (Wilson), 16
patronage, Lincoln's philosophy of, 101,
216–21

Peck, John M., 185, 186, 188, 190–1
Pettit, John, 246, 247
Phillips, Wendell, 447
Pierce, Edward, 400
Pierce, Franklin, 231, 232, 234, 241–2, 248, 249, 299, 326
Pinsker, Matthew, 303, 305, 307, 313
Poe, Edgar Allan, 18
Political Culture of the American Whigs, The (Howe), 112
"Politics as a Vocation" (Weber), 195, 438
Polk, James K., 157, 161, 163, 200, 229
    expansionist achievements, 184, 483
    internal improvements policy, 197–8
    Lincoln's conduct during Civil War compared with Polk's during Mexican War, 191, 457–64
    Lincoln's personal attacks on, 169–71
    Mexican War policy, defense of, 164–5
    obliviousness to Lincoln's criticisms, 168
    on opponents of his Mexican War policy, 181
    presidential election of 1844, 193
Pope, Nathaniel, 220–1
"popular sovereignty" approach to deciding legality of slavery in new states, 240, 241, 256–63, 266–7
Potter, David, 241, 347, 363, 435–8
pragmatism, 222–3
Prelude to Greatness (Fehrenbacher), 324, 365
presidential election of 1840, 142, 145–6, 193
presidential election of 1844, 157, 193, 194–7
presidential election of 1848, 182, 184
    Free-Soil challenge, 203–9
    results of, 209–12
    Taylor's candidacy for Whig Party, 199–204

presidential election of 1852, 326
presidential election of 1856, 399
presidential election of 1860
    Lincoln's speaking tour of New England and, 385
    Lincoln's unusual circumstances, 391
    Lincoln's victory, 403–5
    population changes and, 393
    Republicans' favorable situation, 392–3
    "thrown into the House" scenarios, 393, 465–7
    see also Republican presidential nomination of 1860
"principle," politics of, 179–82
Promise of American Life, The (Croly), 15–16
prudence, virtue of, 222–4, 228–30

Quarles, Benjamin, xiv

railroads, 110, 240, 249
Ralston, James, 119
Ramsay, David, 51
Randall, James G., 45, 93–4n
    on Lincoln as party politician, 101–3
Reagan, Ronald, 444
reaper case, 410–18, 490–1
Republican Party
    coalition-building for, 317–18
    favorable situation in presidential election of 1860, 392–3
    Illinois party, organization of, 304, 316–24
    Lincoln's switch to, 317–18
    national convention of 1856, 319–20, 399
    opposition to extension of slavery as

defining commitment, Lincoln's focus on, 290, 320–3, 324

origins of, 206, 210*n*

politically defensive racism within, 368–9

senatorial election of 1855 and, 303–4

senatorial election of 1858 and, 323, 334

Republican presidential nomination of 1860, 319

Lincoln/Douglas debates and, 398

Lincoln's notification of his nomination, 10

Lincoln's speaking tour of New England and, 385

quality of Lincoln's public argument as key to his victory, 397–401

realistic reasons for Lincoln's nomination, 394–7, 400, 401

voting for, 401–3

responsibility, ethic of, 192, 195–7, 202–3, 204, 219, 225–6, 228–30

Revised Statutes of Indiana (book), 51

rhetoric, 81

Riddle, Donald, 173, 174, 179–80, 181

Robinson, Donald, 41

Roosevelt, Franklin D., 423, 424

Roosevelt, Theodore, 15

Ross, Edward, 174

Ross, Frederick A., 280–2, 295

Rutledge, Ann, 19, 130

Rutledge, Robert, 53

Samuels, Henry, 356–7*n*

Sandburg, Carl, 16

Scott, William, 50–1, 79

Scott, Gen. Winfield, 96, 162, 201, 326, 441, 456

Scripps, John L., 17, 27, 44, 273

Seaton, William, 214–15

secession by Southern states

Buchanan's response, 420

exclusion of slavery from the territories cited by Southerners as justification for secession, 431

Lincoln's argument against legality of secession, 442–50, 455–6

Lincoln's underestimation of South's determination, 427–8, 440

logical absurdity of unilateral defection, 448–9

ordinances of secession, 432, 441, 442, 444–5

Stephens's speeches on, 428, 430–2, 447

Second Great Awakening, 42

self-interest in politics, Lincoln's views on, 254–5, 260, 263

Senate debate on Kansas-Nebraska Act, 231–2, 242–7, 484

senatorial election of 1855, 95, 298–316

Lincoln's promotion of his own candidacy, 300–3, 306

Lincoln's resentment toward Matteson, 313–14

Lincoln's resignation from Illinois General Assembly, 304–5

Lincoln's vote counting, 303

Lincoln's yielding to Trumbull, 298–9, 310, 311–16

majority status of anti-Nebraska forces in Illinois General Assembly, 299–300, 306

Republican Party of Illinois and, 303–4

voting by legislators, 307–11

senatorial election of 1858, 95, 319

disadvantages faced by Lincoln, 334–6

Douglas's reelection supported by Eastern Republicans, 331–4

senatorial election of 1858 *(continued)*
  Lincoln's endorsement by
    Republicans, 323, 334
  Lincoln's loss in 1855 and, 315
  Lincoln's piggybacking on Douglas's
    speeches, 336
  racist orientation of Douglas's
    campaign, 341–53, 371–4
  results of, 372
  see also Lincoln/Douglas debates
Seward, William, 105, 201, 210, 236–7,
    249, 332, 376, 391, 392, 407, 420,
    421, 423, 432
  Kansas-Nebraska Act, 231, 245
  in Lincoln's cabinet, 408, 409
  Lincoln's First Inaugural Address,
    445, 448, 449, 454, 455
  Lincoln's letters to, 235, 435
  Lincoln's relationship with, 12, 245
  Republican presidential nomination
    of 1860, 394, 395, 396, 401, 402, 403
Shakespeare, William, 27, 50–1, 81–2
Sherman, Roger, 466
Shields, James, 119, 177, 306, 308, 309,
    459
Short, James, 33
Simon, John Y., 61, 76
Simon, Paul, 131
Simpson, Matthew, 144
Sinkler, George, 488
slave insurrections, 380, 389
slavery
  as cause of Civil War, 287–8, 431, 432
  collective amnesia regarding, 386
  Compromise of 1850, 210–12, 230,
    238, 239, 241
  Congress's right to decide about
    slavery in the territories, 377–9
  Constitution's three-fifths clause
    regarding slaves, 258–61
  District of Columbia abolition of
    slavery issue, 122, 125–7, 212–15

Dred Scott decision, 236, 342, 345,
    352, 360–1, 369, 379, 381, 392
  economics of, 387–9
  ending of, 237
  expansionism and, 460
  Fugitive Slave Law, 211, 212, 230;
    Lincoln's position on, 234–7, 239,
    320–1
  as Lincoln/Douglas debates' central
    issue, 341
  morality of slavery, Stephens's
    assertion of, 432–3
  "positive good" argument regarding,
    280–2
  Republican Party's defining
    commitment regarding, 290,
    320–3, 324
  slaveholders' desire for slavery to be
    perceived as moral because of their
    economic interest in it, 388–9
  Taylor's policy regarding, 210–11
  warping effect of defending slavery on
    one's moral sense, 279, 280
  Wilmot Proviso on extension into
    new territories, 202, 203, 230, 238
  see also abolition movement; Kansas-
    Nebraska Act; Lincoln, Abraham,
    antislavery position of
Slavery Ordained by God (Ross), 280–2
slave trade, 264–5, 266, 268
Slidell, John, 459
Smith, Adam, 277
Smith, Caleb B., 163*n*, 396, 401, 409
Smith, James, 86
Smith, Lillian, 135*n*
Smoot, Colman, 4
Sorensen, Theodore, 174
Spanish-American War, 461
Speed, Joshua, 4, 13–14, 24–5, 73, 217,
    291, 472
  Lincoln's letters to, 29–30, 39, 68–9,
    78, 83, 156, 317

Speed, Mary, 367–8

Spot Resolutions, 166–7, 169, 179, 181, 187

Sprigg, Anna, 163 and *n*

Stanton, Edwin M., 11, 13, 356*n*, 357*n*, 465

    as attorney general in Buchanan administration, 420–1

    background of, 414

    criticisms of Lincoln as president, 421–2

    Democratic credentials, 418–19

    Lincoln's relationship with, 419, 425–6

    McCormick v. Manny (reaper case), 414–16, 417, 418

    personal qualities, 414–15

    secretary of war appointment by Lincoln, 422–6

    as Union supporter, 419–21

states' rights, 344–5

Stephens, Alexander, 175, 201, 229, 381

    Fortress Monroe conference, 429–30

    Kansas-Nebraska Act, 232

    Lincoln's correspondence with, 291–2, 428–9, 431, 433

    morality of slavery, assertion of, 432–3

    on secession by Southern states, 428, 430–2, 447

Stephens, John A., 430

Stimson, Henry, 423

Stone, Dan, 119, 121–9

Storey, Joseph, 97

Stowe, Harriet Beecher, 235, 294

"Strange Fruit" (song), 135*n*

Strozier, Charles, 477–8

Stuart, John T., 7, 24, 25, 52, 107, 120, 130, 154, 161, 362

suffrage and political participation, Lincoln's views on, 261–3, 370

Sumner, Charles, 64, 98, 249, 294, 362

    Free-Soil Party, 203–5, 206, 208, 209, 210

    Kansas-Nebraska Act, 242, 243–5

Supreme Court, U.S., 369

Swett, Leonard, 222, 406–7, 489–90

Swift, Jonathan, 387

Taney, Roger, 369, 377, 456

Tarbell, Ida, 299, 491

Taylor, Green, 48

Taylor, James, 48

Taylor, Zachary, 96, 99, 101

    death of, 211

    Lincoln's eulogy for, 226–7

    Mexican War, 161, 163, 167, 187, 188, 459

    patronage policy, 216, 220–1

    presidential election of 1848, 182, 184, 199–204, 209

    slavery policy, 210–11

temperance movement, 34–5, 202

    Lincoln's views on, 147–53

Texas, annexation of, 194–5, 196, 197, 460

Thayer, E. R., 33

Thompson, Waddy, 126

Thoreau, Henry David, 228, 447, 448

Tocqueville, Alexis de, 23

Todd, Robert, 25

Trist, Nicholas, 184

Truman, Harry, 427

Trumbull, Lyman, 95, 251, 318, 319, 334, 359*n*, 368, 397, 428

    Lincoln's letters to, 332–3, 434, 439, 441

    racial attitudes, 362–3

    senatorial election of 1855, 298–9, 308, 309, 310, 311–13, 315, 316

Turner, Nat, 389
Turnham, David, 4, 51
Tyler, John, 453

Uncle Tom's Cabin (Stowe), 235, 289, 294
"Union is perpetual" perspective, 113–14, 380–1, 434, 442–56

Van Buren, Martin, 100, 142, 145–6, 193, 204, 205, 466
Vesey, Denmark, 389
Villard, Henry, 441, 442, 452
Volney, Constantin de, 43
Voltaire, 137

Wade, Benjamin Franklin, 246, 297, 359*n*
Ward, Artemus, 141–2
Warren, Louis, 28–9, 41, 64–5*n*
Washburne, Elihu, 304
    Lincoln's letters to, 302, 313, 434, 439, 440, 441
Washington, George, xi, 13, 51, 82, 378, 380
    Lincoln's grandiloquent praise of, 141, 480
Watson, Peter H., 410, 411–12, 414, 416, 417, 421, 491
    Lincoln's letters to, 413
Wayland, Francis, 277–9
Webb, James, 441
Weber, Max, 195, 207, 219, 225–6, 438
Webster, Daniel, 83, 97, 99, 140, 201, 210–11, 217, 229, 359, 410

nullification issue, 113–14
Weed, Thurlow, 201, 210, 332, 393, 394, 403, 435, 439, 441
Weems, Parson, 51, 82
Weik, Jesse, 5
Weld, Theodore, 289
Wells, Gideon, 408
Whig Party
    antislavery minority, 192–3
    campaigning methods, 100–1
    convention system, 100, 158–60
    economic development policy, 96–7, 109
    executive power, distrust of, 112–13
    improvement theme, 112
    Lincoln's congressional nomination, 153–60
    Lincoln's partisan attachment to, 106–14, 182
    minority status in Illinois, 108
    nationalism and the Union, support for, 113–14
    nativism in, 38–9
    patronage jobs for Illinois Whigs, Lincoln's promotion of, 101, 216–21
    positions on issues, 96–7
    Taylor's presidential candidacy in 1848, 199–204
White, Hugh L., 96
Wickizer, J. D., 472–3
Wilder, Thornton, 62
Williams, Archibald, 271, 302
Williams, Roger, 70
Wills, Garry, xiii
Wilmot, David, 202
Wilmot Proviso, 202, 203, 230, 238
Wilson, Douglas, 6, 31, 52, 58*n*, 77, 85, 87, 128, 474
Wilson, Edmund, 15, 16, 18, 140
Wilson, Henry, 332
Wilson, Robert, 4, 7–8

Wise, Henry, 126
Wolf, William I., 50

Young Men's Central Republican Union
of New York, 376, 384

Yates, Richard, 41, 233, 247, 270–1, 305
and *n*

Ziegler, Ron, 242

A Note about the Author

William Lee Miller, now Scholar in Ethics and Institutions at the Miller Center of Public Affairs at the University of Virginia, retired from the university faculty in 1999 as Commonwealth Professor, and the Thomas C. Sorensen Professor, of Political and Social Thought. Before his service at the University of Virginia, he had taught at Yale, Smith College, and Indiana University, and at Indiana he was founding director of The Poynter Center on American Institutions. He is the author of a number of books, including *Arguing About Slavery: John Quincy Adams and the Great Battle in the United States Congress,* which won the D. B. Haldeman Award for the best book on Congress in 1996. He has written numerous articles and essays on public affairs; his articles from his days as a writer and editor at *The Reporter* magazine were collected in *Piety Along the Potomac* (1964). His memoir of his service on the New Haven Board of Aldermen was published as *The Fifteenth Ward and the Great Society* (1966). He has made several forays into political campaigns, served on the Fund for the Republic's Commission on Religion and a Free Society, and repeatedly been a moderator of humanities seminars at the Aspen Institute. He received his Ph.D. in social ethics in 1958 from Yale.

A Note on the Type

This book was set in a typeface called Bulmer. This distinguished letter is a replica of a type long famous in the history of English printing which was designed and cut by William Martin about 1790 for William Bulmer of the Shakespeare Press. In design, it is all but a modern face, with vertical stress, sharp differentiation between the thick and thin strokes, and nearly flat serifs. The decorative italic shows the influence of Baskerville, as Martin was a pupil of John Baskerville's.

Composed by Creative Graphics, Allentown, Pennsylvania
Printed and bound by Berryville Graphics, Berryville, Virginia
Designed by Robert C. Olsson